Fodor's

SWITZERLAND

47th Edition

Fodor's Travel Publications New York, Toronto, London, Sydney, Auckland
www.fodors.com

FODOR'S SWITZERLAND

Writers: Kati Clinton Robson, Kelly DiNardo, Adam Graham, Katrin Gygax, Alexis Munier, Rachel Marusak Hermann, Susan Vogel-Misicka

Editors: Luke Epplin, Amanda Sadlowski, Mark Sullivan

Editorial Contributors: Linda Cabasin, Jess Moss

Production Editor: Evangelos Vasilakis
Maps & Illustrations: Mark Stroud, Moon Street Cartography, David Lindroth, *cartographers;* Rebecca Baer, *map editor;* William Wu, *information graphics*
Design: Fabrizio La Rocca, *creative director;* Tina Malaney, Chie Ushio, Jessica Ramirez, *designers;* Melanie Marin, *associate director of photography;* Jennifer Romains, *photo research*
Cover Photo: Front cover: SIME/eStock Photo [Castle of Chillon, near Montreux, Lake Geneva]. Back cover (left to right): Schweiz Tourismus/swiss-image.ch/ Christof Sonderegger; Valais Tourism/swiss-image/Thomas Andenmatten; S.Borisov/ Shutterstock. Spine: Vaclav Volrab/Shutterstock.
Production Manager: Angela L. McLean

COPYRIGHT

47th Edition

ISBN 978-0-89141-951-8

ISSN 0071-6553

SPECIAL SALES

This book is available at special discounts for bulk purchases for sales promotions or premiums. Special editions, including personalized covers, excerpts of existing books, and corporate imprints, can be created in large quantities for special needs. For more information, write to Special Markets/Premium Sales, 1745 Broadway, MD 3-1, New York, NY 10019, or e-mail specialmarkets@randomhouse.com.

AN IMPORTANT TIP & AN INVITATION

Although all prices, opening times, and other details in this book are based on information supplied to us at press time, changes occur all the time in the travel world, and Fodor's cannot accept responsibility for facts that become outdated or for inadvertent errors or omissions. So **always confirm information when it matters,** especially if you're making a detour to visit a specific place. Your experiences—positive and negative— matter to us. If we have missed or misstated something, **please write to us.** Share your opinion instantly through our online feedback center at fodors.com/contact-us.

PRINTED IN CHINA

10 9 8 7 6 5 4 3 2 1

CONTENTS

ABOUT
THIS GUIDE

Fodor's Ratings

Everything in this guide is worth doing—we don't cover what isn't—but exceptional sights, hotels, and restaurants are recognized with additional accolades. **Fodor's Choice★** indicates our top recommendations; ★ highlights places we deem **Highly Recommended**; and **Best Bets** call attention to notable hotels and restaurants in various categories. Care to nominate a new place? Visit Fodors.com/contact-us.

Trip Costs

We list prices wherever possible to help you budget well. Hotel and restaurant price categories from **$** to **$$$$** are noted alongside each recommendation. For hotels, we include the lowest cost of a standard double room in high season. For restaurants, we cite the average price of a main course at dinner or, if dinner isn't served, at lunch. For attractions, we always list adult admission fees; discounts are usually available for children, students, and senior citizens.

Hotels

Our local writers vet every hotel to recommend the best overnights in each price category, from budget to expensive. Unless otherwise specified, you can expect private bath, phone, and TV in your room. For expanded hotel reviews, facilities, and deals visit Fodors.com.

Our expert hotel picks are reinforced by high ratings on TripAdvisor. Look for representative quotes in this guide, and the latest TripAdvisor ratings and feedback at Fodors.com.

Restaurants

Unless we state otherwise, restaurants are open for lunch and dinner daily. We mention dress code only when there's a specific requirement and reservations only when they're essential or not accepted. To make restaurant reservations, visit Fodors.com.

Credit Cards

The hotels and restaurants in this guide typically accept credit cards. If not, we'll say so.

Ratings	Hotels & Restaurants
★ Fodor's Choice	Hotel
★ Highly recommended	Number of rooms
☺ Family-friendly	Meal plans
Listings	✕ Restaurant
✉ Address	Reservations
✉ Branch address	Dress code
☎ Telephone	No credit cards
🖷 Fax	$ Price
⊕ Website	**Other**
✉ E-mail	⇨ See also
🏷 Admission fee	☞ Take note
⊙ Open/closed times	Golf facilities
Ⓜ Subway	
⊹ Directions or Map coordinates	

Experience
Switzerland

WHAT'S WHERE

The following numbers refer to chapters.

2 Zürich. Zürich is surprisingly small, but its wealth of cultural riches more than makes up for its size. Tour the luxuriously gentrified **Altstadt** (Old Town), then take in the hulking **Grossmünster** cathedral, great modern art at the **Bührle** Museum, and top Old Masters at Winterthur's **Oskar Reinhart Collection.**

3 Eastern Switzerland. East of Zürich the Rhine snakes through some of the most untouched regions of Switzerland; in tiny towns and small cities, amid woodshingle farmhouses and grand Baroque churches, discover the old Rhine city of **Schaffhausen,** known for its medieval frescoes; **St. Gallen,** a busy textile center with an active Old Town; and princely **Liechtenstein.**

4 Graubünden. The mountains of what used to be called Rhaetia once made the region of Graubünden difficult to rule. Today emperors and kings have been replaced by new conquerors: tourists, who take the gorgeous train ride to **Arosa,** visit "Heidi country" in **Maienfeld,** hang out with writers in **Klosters** and billionaires in **Davos,** and ski and be seen in glitzy **St. Moritz.**

5 **Ticino.** With its intoxicating *italianità* (Italian flair), Ticino is an irresistible combination of Mediterranean pleasures and Swiss efficiency. The region's sinuous lakes, perhaps its greatest attraction, beckon with strolls along fashionable waterfront promenades. Concentrate on beauteous **Lugano**, serene **Locarno**, and elegant **Ascona**, set on the shore of Lago Maggiore.

6 **Luzern and Central Switzerland.** Central Switzerland is the most-visited region in the country. No wonder: you can take a paddleboat steamer on the **Vierwaldstättersee** (Lake Luzern) past some of the most beautiful lakeside vistas to the **Rütli Meadow**—"birthplace" of Switzerland—and the fabled Wilhelm Tell chapel. **Luzern** itself has an Old Town so cleanly refurbished it could be mistaken for a museum exhibit.

7 **Basel.** Set where Switzerland meets Germany and France, Basel's lovely Old Town, a Rhine River walk, and great modern art—including **Museum Tinguely** and **Fondation Beyeler**—make it a best bet. In the 15th century, the city won the right to hold an unlimited number of fairs, which today range from the famous Fasnacht carnival to the chic ArtBasel.

WHAT'S WHERE

8 Fribourg and Neuchâtel. Largely undiscovered, these two cantons (states) are favorite western Switzerland getaways. Fribourg, part German and part French, is divided into a checkerboard of fields with a neatness only the Swiss can achieve—the highlight is the stunningly picturesque castle at **Gruyères.** Other treasures: lakeside **Neuchâtel** and Gothic-era **Fribourg.**

9 Bern. A city of broad medieval streets, Switzerland's federal capital sits in the country's largest canton, whose size and influence mirror the pride of its citizens. The famed sandstone arcades, painted fountains, performing mechanical clock of the **Zytglogge,** Gothic **Münster,** and art-filled **Zentrum Paul Klee** are as ardently protected as the country's neutrality.

10 Berner Oberland. Kiss the sky in this hypermagical province—a "summit of summits" that includes the peaks of the **Eiger, Mönch, and Jungfrau.** From the hub of **Interlaken,** journey up to gorgeous eagle's-nest towns like **Mürren** and **Wengen** and down to the "Shangri-la" valley that is **Lauterbrunnen.** A taste of the high life awaits in glam **Gstaad.**

GERMANY

Rhine

Basel
Schaffhausen
Winterthur
Frauenfeld
Brugg
Baden
Aarau
Olten
Zürich
Küsnacht
lothurn
Zug
Langnau
Luzern
BERN
Schwyz
Sarnen
Altdorf
Thun
Meiringen
Interlaken
10
Grindelwald
Wassen
Wengen
Andermatt
BERNER ALPS
Jungfraujoch
LEPONTINE ALPS
Biasca
Rhône Rhône
Brig
Sierre
Visp
Simplon Pass
Locarno
Ascona
11
ENNINE ALPS
Zermatt
Lugano
atterhorn

ITALY

11 **Valais.** This is the Switzerland of raclette eaters, winemakers, yodelers—and, oh, yes, the **Matterhorn.** From the Rhône Valley explore the citadel of **Sion** and take resort luxury to new heights in **Saas-Fee, Verbier,** and **Crans-Montana.** Of course, you'll feel unsated if you miss Switzerland's most photographed icon, the Matterhorn, so stop by its lovely home, **Zermatt.**

12 **Vaud.** Centered around **Lac Léman** (Lake Geneva), this French-speaking canton harbors Alpine villages, glamorous lake resorts, and verdant vineyards. But be sure to visit the Old Town and hyperactive waterfront of **Lausanne,** harbor-front **Vevey,** Riviera-like **Montreux,** and lakeside **Château de Chillon**—Switzerland's most fabled castle.

13 **Geneva.** As the birthplace of Calvinism and the International Red Cross, home to the European headquarters of the United Nations, and a stronghold of private banks and exclusive boutiques, Geneva is, in many ways, a paradox. To get into its international vibe, begin by exploring the **Palais des Nations,** then after the **Vieille Ville** (Old City), head to the downtown waterfront and the feathery **Jet d'Eau.**

SWITZERLAND PLANNER

Getting Here	Getting Around

Getting Here

The two main airports—Geneva's Cointrin Airport (⊕ *www. gva.ch*) and Zürich Airport (⊕ *www.zurich-airport.com*)—will get you here from anywhere in the world, nonstop from New York, Miami, Los Angeles, Montreal, and London, for example.

The Basel/Mulhouse Airport (⊕ *www.euroairport.com*) offers flights from European locations and is less crowded. The smaller airports at Bern (⊕ *www.alpar.ch*) and Lugano (⊕ *www.lugano-airport.ch*) host local and short-haul flights as well as private-jet traffic.

Public transportation to and from all the airports is excellent (as it is throughout the country) and generally much faster and cheaper than taxis.

Think twice about domestic flights within Switzerland—if you calculate getting from your hotel to the airport, the flight time including delays, and getting to your next hotel, taking the train is often faster and more comfortable, as trains and buses will take you almost anywhere in Switzerland.

Getting Around

There's a reason the Swiss travel more miles by train each year than any other people in the world—the public transit network will whisk you away where you want, when you want, for a reasonable sum. Switzerland's excellent public transit network means you can even get to Corippo, Ticino (pop. 17), at least once an hour.

In general, trains are your best bet for all travel; even the direct intercity connections cut through the lush countryside, while the scenic mountain railways offer incomparable views.

The Swiss Federal Railways offers several discount cards to visitors, but the best deals must be purchased before entering Switzerland. The **Swiss Pass** allows unlimited travel on a specific number of days; the **Swiss Card** provides free round-trip transport between the airport and any location in Switzerland as well as a 50% reduction in fare; and the **Swiss Half-Fare Card** is valid for a 50% reduction in fare only. Often, the Half-Fare Card will give you the most for your money in the long run, but it all depends on the frequency and distance of your travel. Remember that most mountain railways are privately owned and operated, and as a result some discount cards are not accepted.

While cars are more convenient for visiting out-of-the-way villages, many Alpine roads wind precariously, with no barriers between you and the sheer drops. Novices or drivers without nerves of steel may want to avoid them altogether. As tempting as it is—having your own vehicle, taking off whenever you want, listening to Radiohead (or Wagner) full blast—driving in Switzerland is usually more work than enjoyment.

⇨ *For more information on getting around, see Travel Smart Switzerland.*

Gear: Essential Items to Pack

Even in July and August the evening air grows chilly in the mountains, so bring a warm sweater. And bring along a hat or sunscreen, as the atmosphere is thinner at high altitudes. You should wear sunscreen all through the year; many different brands are available at ski shops near the slopes. Glaciers can be blinding in the sun, so be sure to bring sunglasses, which should have side shields especially for high-altitude hiking or skiing. Good walking shoes or hiking boots are a must, whether you're tackling medieval cobblestones or mountain trails.

If you're heading up into the peaks, remember that the higher you go, the greater the chance that you'll suffer from altitude sickness—symptoms include numbness, tingling, nausea, drowsiness, vision problems, but most often headaches. Always have some aspirin on hand, just in case. If you plan to spend extended periods in rural areas and natural preserves, take precautions against ticks, especially in spring and summer. Wear long sleeves, long pants, and boots, and apply insect repellent containing the powerful repellent DEET. Two vaccines against tick-borne infections are available in Europe: TicoVac (also known as FSME Immun) and Encepur, but neither has been approved in the United States.

The one thing that seems to be the budgetary breaking point for practically every hotel manager in all categories: the washcloth. They are seldom seen, so bring your own. If you're planning on shopping and cooking, a tote bag will come in handy: most grocers do not provide bags, but sturdy, reusable plastic totes can be bought at checkout. Coin laundries are rare, so be prepared to wash your clothes by hand.

Visitor Information

The Switzerland Tourism website has trip ideas and transportation information. You can plan a vacation in Switzerland and even book it through an interactive travel planner.
Contact Switzerland Tourism ⊕ *www.myswitzerland.com*.

Speaking the Language(s)

The Swiss are champions of multilingualism: at least one foreign language is mandatory in most schools from the primary level. And lucky you: these days, the foreign language of choice is English.

A large percentage of the population speaks at least a little English, especially in cities and large towns or tourist regions. Don't forget to be polite, however: ask first before launching into English. That small bit of consideration will get you a lot further, especially with natives suffering from tourist overload.

Local languages are German, French, and Italian.

Although the homegrown variants of German and Italian are difficult to understand by those who speak the standard versions, Swiss Germans and Swiss Italians also speak High German or Standard Italian, which are the official written languages in those parts of the country.

Swiss French differs only slightly from Standard French and won't pose a problem.

Switzerland's fourth official language is Romansh, but is very rarely an individual's only language.

UNDERSTANDING THE SWISS

Though they're proud, sober, self-contained, independent culturally and politically, disdainful of the shabby and the slipshod, painfully neat, rigorously prompt—the Swiss have a weakness for cuteness, and they indulge in incongruously coy diminutives: a German *Bierstube* (pub) becomes a *Stübli*, *Kuchen* (cake) becomes *Küchli*, Wurst becomes *Würstli*, and a *coupe* (glass) of champagne becomes a *Cüpli*.

It is lucky for travelers, this dichotomy of the folksy and the functional.

It means your trains get you to your fire-lit lodge on time. It means the cable car that sweeps you to a mountaintop has been subjected to grueling inspections. It means the handwoven curtains are boiled and starched, and the high-thread-count bed linens are turned back with a chocolate at night.

There is an earthiness about the Swiss, and they're as at ease with the soil as they are appalled by dirt.

A banker in Zürich may rent a postage-stamp parcel of land in a crowded patchwork outside town, sowing tight rows of cabbages and strawberries, weeding bright borders of marigolds, and on Sunday he may visit his miniature estate, pull a chair out from the tidy toolshed, and simply sit and smoke, like Heidi's Alm-Uncle surveying his Alpine realm.

An elderly woman may don knickers and loden hat, board a postbus to the mountains, and climb steep, rocky trails at a brisk clip, cheeks glowing, eyes as icy bright as the glaciers above her.

There's a 21st-century counterpoint to this: the high-tech, jet-set glamour that splashes vivid colors across the slopes at St. Moritz, Gstaad, Zermatt, and Verbier.

Step out of a bulbous steel-and-glass cable car onto a concrete platform at 6,560 feet and see Switzerland transformed. Wholesome, healthy faces disappear behind mirrored goggles and war-paint sunblock, and gaudy skis and poles bristle militarily, like the pikes and halberds in the Battle of Sempach.

The contradictions mount: while fur-clad socialites raise jeweled fingers to bid at Sotheby's on Geneva's Quai du Mont-Blanc, the women of Appenzell stand beside the men on the Landsgemeinde-platz and raise their hands to vote in local elections—a right not won until 1991.

While digital screens tick off beef futures in Zürich, the crude harmony of cowbells echoes in mountain pastures.

While a Mercedes roars down an expressway expertly blasted through solid rock, a horse-drawn plow peels back thin topsoil in an Alpine garden plot, impossibly steep, improbably high.

And on August 1, the Swiss national holiday, while spectacular displays of fireworks explode in sizzling colors over the cities and towns, the mountain folk build the bonfires that glow quietly, splendidly, on every hillside of every Alp, uniting Swiss citizens as they celebrate their proud independence, their cultural wealth, and above all their diversity. It's that diversity and those quirky contradictions that make Switzerland a tourist capital—the folksy, fiercely efficient innkeeper to the world.

Cantons of Switzerland

SWITZERLAND
TOP ATTRACTIONS

The Matterhorn

(A) Of course. Alternatively called Il Cervino (Italian) or Le Cervin (French), this is Switzerland's trademark, drawing crowds every year. The pedestrian-only town of Zermatt offers a fairy-tale version of the typical Alpine village, with carriage rides, chalet restaurants and hotels, and shops galore, all under the shadow of the world's most recognizable peak. For a grand vista, head to the summit station of Gornergat, where nature's snaggletoothed masterpiece steals the thunder from all other surrounding mountains.

Mürren

(B) A town that perches on a cliff face over the southern end of the Lauterbrunnen Valley, this half-earthly, half-heavenly village is pasted like a wasp's nest 3,200 feet up a mountain. Dine on a nearly levitating terrace and it seems you can practically reach out and touch the Eiger and Jungfrau peaks. Continue on up the

mountain via cable car to reach the spectacular Schilthorn peak, crowned by the Piz Gloria viewing station and restaurant (you might recognize its starring role as Ernst Blofeld's hideout in the James Bond film *On Her Majesty's Secret Service*).

Luzern

(C) The town that's on everyone's list. A mere 9 square miles in size, Luzern is many of Switzerland's cities in a nutshell: a well-preserved medieval Old Town, a magnificent lakefront, and a wide variety of shops stuffed with souvenirs. As you stroll along the lakeshore promenade, many Alpine views will look familiar, as this is where all those travel poster photos originate.

The Jungfraujoch

(D) With an altitude of 11,400 feet, and an almost alien landscape slathered in whipped-cream snow all year round, this is the most accessible high-altitude peak in Europe. Don't try to attempt it all in

one day—add an overnight or at least a very long lunch midway, in Grindelwald, say—because the difference in altitude from valley floor to the "Top of Europe" literally will make your head spin.

Lake Geneva's Wine Country

(E) From Nyon to Aigle, the slopes of Lake Geneva are carpeted with vineyards that produce some of Switzerland's best wines. While a few varieties—mainly Chasselas or Pinot Noir—are exported to stores abroad, this is the only place to taste the rest. Say "santé" to your new best friends: Arvine, Gamaret, or Humagne Rouge, for example.

Lauterbrunnen Valley

(F) The "high" point of any trip to the mountainous Berner Oberland region may turn out to be Europe's most "viewtiful" valley. Sheltered from the world by picture-perfect mountains and threaded by more than 72 cascading waterfalls, Lauterbrunnen makes you feel as if you stumbled upon a film set for *Lost Horizon*'s Shangri-la.

St. Moritz

(G) Take New York luxury, Paris fashion, a bit of London and Milan, a drop of Munich, a handful of Rome, large swaths of premium ski slopes, add the bubbling "champagne climate" of dry air and sun, mix well, and pour onto a few acres in a gorgeous high-altitude valley. How can anything compare with this überchic resort?

The Tellskapelle, Lake Luzern

(H) Set on one of the most glorious stretches of the Urnersee—the southern leg of Lake Luzern—this High Victorian lakefront chapel honoring the legendary Wilhelm Tell is so magnificently picturesque it will practically click your camera for you.

SWITZERLAND TOP EXPERIENCES

Soak Up Soulful Sounds at the Montreux Jazz Festival

(A) From Miles Davis to Prince and everyone in between, this world-renowned festival hosts both jazz fixtures as well as up-and-coming pop acts. With numerous free concerts and a waterfront brimming with food and drink stalls, this is a must-do on every music fan's list.

Take a Hike

(B) Some of the world's loveliest trails await you in Switzerland. You'll see it all here: herds of grazing cattle, Swiss grannies with gams of steel, and a vast range of glaciers and wildflowers. With 30,000 miles of trails, there are options for slowpokes and the fleet-footed alike.

Ride the Rails of the Bernina Express

(C) With its 55 tunnels and 196 bridges, this spectacular train ride is not for the faint of heart. The section linking Thusis and Tirano is exceptional; UNESCO recently classified it a World Heritage Site.

Forget the first-class reservation and take in the pristine Alpine air in one of the rear open wagons.

Better than Brazil: Basler Fasnacht

(D) After a year of moderation, the Swiss try to make up for lost time in three days of wild revelry at Basler Fasnacht. Watch expertly costumed cliques wander through the city's Old Town in a (usually politically motivated) theme voted upon by the residents. One highlight of the carnival is the 4 am "darkening." All lights are extinguished except for the eerie glow of lanterns, while the haunting echo of piccolos draws you further into this strange, alcohol-soaked world.

Summer Ski in Saas-Fee

(E) Even when the mercury rises, you can descend this foreboding glacier above the resort village of Saas-Fee. Here the ice never melts, leaving you a wide range of year-round skiing at every level. No

1

wonder Olympic greats train here in the summer months.

Eat Fondue in Canton Fribourg

(F) Known for being the home of the best fondue, here this specialty is made with deliciously creamy—and piquant—Vacherin cheese. Washed down with a traditional glass of slightly sparkling Chasselas or Fendant, count on tripling your day's calorie intake and enjoying every bite.

Study Chagall's Stained-Glass Windows at Zürich's Fraumünster

(G) The year 1970 was good one for pet rocks, platform heels, and even stained glass. High in the choir of Zürich's Minster of our Lady, Marc Chagall's five magnificent stained-glass windows add sparkle to this stately gem. Many tourists choose to stay for an unforgettably beautiful mass.

Go for the Green at Golf Club Crans-sur-Sierre

(H) Frequently described as one of the world's most beautiful, this 18-hole golf course is set on a high Alpine plateau in Crans-Montana. The European Masters is hosted here, as well as a series of other competitions; with the sublime backdrop of sky-high summits like the Matterhorn and Mont Blanc, concentrating on the hole may prove challenging.

The Biggest Little Film Festival

(I) Every August, the Ticinese town of Locarno rolls out the red carpet for some of the world's best and brightest filmmakers. You can join 8,000 movie lovers in the lovely little town's Piazza Grande and feast your eye and ears on provocative, moving, and eclectic films from a wide range of countries.

QUINTESSENTIAL SWITZERLAND

Cheese: The Swiss Cure

It was Swiss cheese that put the apples in the cheeks of the hardy little mountain girl named Heidi, the storybook heroine who inspired Victorians to leave dark city streets for clear Alpine air. For Heidi and Clara—for whom daily meals of cheese and goat's milk worked a mountain miracle—butterfat was a virtue, and cholesterol a concept unborn. Today cheese, and fondue in particular, is still a way of life in Switzerland. Once the cheese is melted with a soupçon of garlic, a pinch of flour, and white wine, guests armed with long forks spear squares of bread and dip them into the bubbling pot. But the eating of fondue is a fine art: each guest who fails to withdraw his morsel is called upon to offer a bottle of wine to the company—a lady, they say, pays with a kiss to whomever she chooses.

What Makes Them Tick?

It lies on the beveled-glass countertop of Vacheron Constantin's Geneva store: centuries of technology compressed into a miniature of gold and glass, its second hand sweeping with unwavering accuracy. Vacheron is the world's oldest manufacturer of watches (it sold its first sober design in 1755) and these mechanical gems are a part of Swiss history. During the Reformation, Calvin banned gilded crucifixes and chalices, leaving scores of brilliantly skilled goldsmiths with idle hands. Before long, an industry was launched, which, to this day, makes you believe in national stereotypes: the Swiss are precise and persevering.

Yes, Swiss watchmaking is a science, but visit Geneva's Patek Philippe Museum of watches to be wowed by fantastical creations, brilliant colors, and awe-inspiring detail. Clearly, Swiss watchmaking is about much more than time.

If you want to get a sense of contemporary Swiss culture and indulge in some of its pleasures, start by familiarizing yourself with the rituals of daily life. These are a few highlights—things you can savor with relative ease.

How Now, Brown Cow?

Many images leap to mind when you think of Switzerland, but surely only one sound: cowbells tinkling in happy indiscipline. This is a sound many travelers often later hear in their dreams, one that many wish could be "photographed." Even city slickers fall under the spell of Switzerland's cows. Get up close to these pretty brown-and-white livestock and you can smell their sweet breath—testament to all the succulent grasses (which also go in many of the world's top perfumes) they've munched. Newspapers have reported that Switzerland's cows are "stressed," so these days many of them get to go on "vacations" from factories to spend summers up in the hills. After all, without the milk of these cash cows, Swiss cheese and chocolate wouldn't be half as famous. Now if they could only create a breed that produces *chocolate* milk!

Chock-full of the good stuff

The Aztecs may have invented chocolate, but the Swiss perfected it. From sugar-dusted white chocolate champagne truffles to plain old bars of solid milk chocolate, Switzerland magically transforms cacao to please every palate. But chocolate wouldn't be the same without the Swiss chocolatier Daniel Peter, who invented milk chocolate in 1887 using condensed Alpine milk. Pride, or perhaps just a genetic sweet tooth, inspires the Swiss to lead the world in chocolate consumption, devouring more than 25 pounds per person every year. Boutique chocolate shops are found in every town, where you can sample the freshest chocolates and truffles made in small, careful batches. Even chain grocery stores feature aisle upon aisle of well-known brands like Lindt, Cailler, Suchard, and Nestlé featuring everything from green tea flakes to bits of sea-salted caramel.

IF YOU LIKE

Great Food

La Cuisine? Die Kochkunst? La Cucina?
Like the patchwork that is Switzerland, fine Swiss food is a culinary trifecta drawn from three countries: France, Germany, and Italy. French areas like Vaud and Neuchâtel still seduce with *cuisine bourgeoise* and such delights as beef entrecôte and *truite meunière* (trout in a brown butter sauce). Over in German cantons such as Schwyz and Luzern, Teutonic nature conquers Gaul with servings of sausage and schnitzel in nearly Wagnerian proportions. Heading south, Italian risotto and gnocchi appear virtually unscathed in the Ticino. Today, however, a bevy of superstar chefs has begun to strike a diplomatic balance between French, German, and Italian styles.

Restaurant de l'Hôtel de Ville—Benoît Violier, Crissier, Vaud. Violier spent nearly 20 years with legendary chef Phillippe Rochat, who recently handed him the reins. This is your chance to taste an up-and-comer who is already winning rave reviews for his fresh twist on classic gourmand favorites.

Stucki, Basel. This landmark restaurant remains one of the trendiest spots in Basel, thanks to chef Tanja Grandits, a rising star on Switzerland's culinary scene. Her artistic dishes add exotic flavors to classic regional plates; pair them with a bottle from the 600-label wine list.

Restaurant-Vinothek Fletschhorn, Waldhotel Fletschhorn, Saas-Fee, Valais. Renowned Markus Neff wows foodies with his lobster dim sum and bison tournedos. To learn how he mix-masters Alpine foods with exotic styles, sign up for one of the cooking classes given by this red-haired wunderkind.

"Peak" Experiences

"Mountains are the beginning and end of all scenery," the great 19th-century writer John Ruskin once observed. And if mountains have a "home" it is truly Switzerland—a summit of summits. View collectors flock to that big schlock candy mountain, the Matterhorn. Adventurers are seduced by the "sheer" excitement of the Jungfrau. "Social climbers" head to the chic villages of Wengen and Mürren, which seem to levitate at either end of the Lauterbrunnen Valley, while daredevils worship at the foot of the Eiger's notorious north face. No matter where you head, you'll find hillside footpaths can be almost as crowded as supermarket checkout lines (remember: the higher the trail, the less "conversation"—you need to concentrate!). Here are some places that will leave you with that top-of-the-world feeling.

Matterhorn, Valais. From the summit station of Gornergrat, this jagged mountain steals the thunder from all surrounding peaks.

Jungfraujoch, the Berner Oberland. From the top of the 11,333-foot-high Jungfraujoch, the Aletsch Glacier looks like a vast sea of ice.

Neuhausen am Rheinfall, Eastern Switzerland. With its mists, roaring water, jutting rocks, and bushy crags, the Rheinfall, from the Neuhausen side, appears truly Wagnerian.

Lauterbrunnen Valley, the Berner Oberland. Looking more like a painting than real life, the jaw-dropping vista of this valley is spectacularly threaded by 72 waterfalls that plummet from sky-high cliffs.

Traveling Through Time

Wander the slopes of Klewenalp above the Vierwaldstättersee on a still spring day, gaze across the placid waters beneath, and it is easy to identify Switzerland as a land of peace. Continue on a mile or so and you are reminded that for much of its time Switzerland has been nothing of the kind. Here is the Rütli, the meadow where legend avers that the men of the three forest cantons, Uri, Schwyz, and Unterwalden, met in 1291 to plot the overthrow of their Habsburg landlords (thereby creating the world's first democracy). But move beyond this spot—hallowed by Wilhelm Tell—and you'll find Switzerland is practically crawling with history from border to border.

Old Town, Basel. When the sound of fife-and-drum music drifts from the upstairs windows of guild houses in Basel's Old Town, you'll think the Middle Ages have dawned again.

Tellfreilichtspiele, Interlaken, Berner Oberland. For a festive evening, rent a lap blanket and settle in to watch a grand retelling of the life of Wilhelm Tell, performed under the stars.

Monument de la Réformation, Geneva. The complex history of the Protestant Reformation as it unfolded across Europe is boldly rendered in granite.

Stiftsbibliothek and Kathedrale, St. Gallen. For Rococo splendor and opulence, nothing beats this complex of Abbey Library and Cathedral, adorned with spectacular excesses of 18th-century wedding-cake trim.

The Most Beautiful Villages

Whatever town or valley you pick, you'll have a battle on your hands insisting that your favorite spot in Switzerland is *the* top place in the country. The *whole* of Switzerland is undeniably beautiful. But there are certain places where the needle would fly right off the scale if they were rated on a beauty-measuring gauge. Oozing half-timbered houses and chapels, these storybook places have a sense of tranquillity not even tour buses can ruin. Here are some candidates for Perfect Swiss Village.

Guarda, Graubünden. This federally protected hamlet in the Lower Engandine is full of architectural photo ops, with cobblestone streets and flower boxes filled with red geraniums.

Stein-am-Rhein, Eastern Switzerland. A nearly perfectly preserved medieval village, Stein is replete with shingled, half-timber town houses boasting ornate oriels and flamboyant frescoes.

Gandria, the Ticino. Clinging vertiginously to a hillside, its flower-filled balconies overlooking Lake Lugano, the tiny town of Gandria retains the ambience of an ancient fishing village.

Mürren, Berner Oberland. Closer to the sky than the earth, this jewel presides over the majestic Lauterbrunnen Valley and offers a so-close-you-can-touch-it vista of the Eiger.

Gruyères, Fribourg. Right out of a fairy tale, this village is crowned with one of the most picture-perfect castles in Switzerland.

FLAVORS OF SWITZERLAND

Although fast food has made definite inroads in Switzerland, it's still a country deeply rooted in seasonality and fresh produce—it's been locavore all along. Wherever that has wavered, it's coming back as farmers and environmentalists encourage a move away from mass-food production. Other trends? Revived interest in Swiss recipes and regional cuisines: Swiss-German, Swiss-French, and Swiss-Italian, as well as the cuisine specific to Graubünden. In addition, Swiss wines are coming into their own as never before.

Natural Bounty

The countryside is a patchwork of farms, vineyards, and fields of cereals and plants used for cooking oil like sunflower and rapeseed. Various "belts" include Vully (Vaud, Fribourg), known for its rhubarb; Bern's Guerbetal for cabbage (and sauerkraut); and Geneva, which grows its own specific type of cardoon. Apples and pears are also common, as are natural or cultivated walnuts, chestnuts, and berries. Wild mushrooming is a national pastime during summer and fall, and honeybee keeping is popular: those houselike boxes, often painted in primary colors, that you see along forest edges are hives. Saffron crocuses grown in Mund (Valais) produce the highly prized spice. Alpine herbs flavor teas and bitters.

The country's lakes and rivers provide a bounty—some 50 delicacies, including crayfish. And the Swiss like their (fall) hunting season fare: hare, deer, wild boar, and game birds.

Cheese

More than 450 types of cheese are produced in Switzerland; some 11, including the quintessential "Swiss cheese," Emmentaler, are labeled AOC, which means production is controlled and protected. The term "Alp cheese" designates cheese produced from summer milk when cows graze in high-altitude meadows. But there aren't only semihard cow's milk wheels—there are hard cheeses, too, like Sbrinz AOC (made in central Switzerland), and soft patties like tomme (made in Vaud). An October-through-March must-try is spoonable Vacherin Mont d'Or AOC. Unusual regional items include Schabziger from Glarus: small, green, cone-shaped, and redolent with the smell of blue fenugreek. Favorite cheese dishes include fondue and raclette.

Wine

October is harvest season in Switzerland's six main wine regions: Valais, Vaud, Geneva, Ticino, the Swiss-German area including Graubünden, and the Three-Lakes area around Neuchâtel. Following a trend to diversify grape varieties, there are now hundreds, but top players include red Pinot Noir and Gamay, Merlot in Ticino, and Chasselas white. Fall wine festivals abound—participants revel in freshly pressed grape juice called *Most* or *moût*. Slightly fermented, lightly effervescent wine called *Sauser* is a favorite with hunt-season meals in German-speaking parts. In May, some areas feature "Open House Days" when wineries open for tastings to launch wines made from the previous year's harvest. You can get more information from the Swiss Wine Exporters' Association (⊕ *www.swisswine.ch*).

LODGING PRIMER

From luxurious palace-hotels that are home to well-off internationals to comfortable bed-and-breakfasts with eager hosts ready to meet your every need, Switzerland has a range of accommodation options. However, prices across the board can be lofty: you will pay more for minimal comforts here than in any other European country. And compared to the two double beds and bath-shower combos found in American motels, spaces can be small, bathtubs cost extra, and single rooms may only be big enough for a single bed. What you're paying for is service, reliability, and cleanliness.

Hotels

No matter how many stars they have, there are essentially two types of hotels in Switzerland: the old-style chintz-and-velvet venues, and the airy, parquet-flooring-and-modular-furniture boutique hotels of more recent years.

Hotel rooms generally have a television, telephone, and private bath, but if you're set on having a bathtub rather than a shower be sure to ask. One Swiss peculiarity is that the standard double room has two prim beds built together, with separate linens and, sometimes, sheets tucked firmly down the middle. If you prefer more sociable arrangements, ask for a "French bed," or *lit matrimonial*—that will get you a double mattress. Some hotels may offer extra beds—for example, to expand a double room to a triple.

Bring your own toiletries, as only the nicer hotels offer anything more than a tiny square of white soap. Same goes for an alarm clock—the watch-wearing, cell phone-carrying Swiss don't need them, but you might.

Bed-and-Breakfasts

Whether you're staying in a lavish chambre d'hôtes on the shores of Lac Léman or a rural mountain lodge high in the Alps, bed-and-breakfasts give you a taste of authentic Swiss hospitality without the hotel vibe. Rates can vary, but most often are calculated per person rather than per room. Many of the country's best rooms are found just above celebrated gastronomic restaurants; when you've finished your savory seven-course meal and bottle of local wine you can climb up the stairs to find a down-filled pillow topped with two tasty chocolates waiting for you.

Farmstays

Also known as agrotourism, staying on a working farm or vineyard can be a delightful way to soak up rural culture. Families may appreciate child-friendly activities like feeding and milking cows, while upscale singles might enjoy participating in the autumn grape harvest and winemaking duties. Options range from simply furnished but comfortable farmhouses to modern, ecologically minded agricultural co-ops.

⇨ *For more information and recommendations, see "Accommodations" in Travel Smart Switzerland.*

SWITZERLAND TODAY

People

After centuries of poverty, with fathers sending sons abroad as mercenaries (resulting in Swiss Guards at the Vatican, for example) and citizens emigrating in hopes of a better life, today's prosperity has led to a decrease in population growth and a marked increase in immigration.

These days, a large international population (about a fifth of the populace) lives alongside the Meiers, the Favres, and the Bernasconis.

They have arrived on Swiss shores brought here by unrest around the world (especially in the former Yugoslavia), the need for workers, and that old familiar search for a better life.

The resulting cultural mix has unnerved some, but it also works world-flattening magic—in the traditional town of Brütten there is a "Stars and Stripes" American-style restaurant in an old Swiss farmhouse run by a family from Sri Lanka.

Politics

Quick: can you name the president of Switzerland? Don't feel bad if you can't—the position is refilled once a year.

Every December the Swiss parliament elects or reconfirms seven of its members to make up the executive Federal Council. These seven are each the heads of an administrative department (Foreign Affairs, Home Affairs, Justice, etc.). They rotate annually to act as a "first among equals" president who has no individual power of his or her own.

Simply said, the president gets to represent the country in international and domestic matters but still has a day job.

Switzerland is also one of the most democratic countries in the world as far as citizen participation is concerned. Within this "direct democracy" any citizen can try to change a law—or propose a new one—by collecting at least 50,000 signatures within 100 days and presenting them to the local, regional, or federal government (depending on which level presides over the issue). The result is referendums and initiatives voted on by the population as many as six times a year.

Economics

With an economy that is stable, thanks mainly to its banking and taxation system (even in these volatile times), Switzerland enjoys a rare prosperity.

It is home to multinational corporations (often drawn here by low and flat-rate taxes) and local companies active in pharmaceuticals, chemicals, precision instruments, insurance, real estate, and, of course, banking.

With a decidedly business-friendly government, one area stands out in this capitalist utopia: agriculture.

Given that there is only so much space in roughly 16,000 square miles of country—much of which is made up of steep mountains that are hard to develop—and that green Alps are an essential draw for the tourism industry, great efforts are made to ensure that what Mark Twain once called "a large, humpy, solid rock, with a thin skin of grass stretched over it" doesn't all get paved over.

Culture

The rural traditions you'd expect—alphorns, yodeling, cows festooned with flowers—are alive and well, and not just a show put on for the tourists (although that's not unheard of either).

Almost every town has some kind of festival at least once a season, where you can sample the local food and do the local

dance, with an added Italian, German, or French flavor. Thanks to full government coffers and charitable businesses, you'll also find a wide variety of art, dance, and musical offerings. These happily range from the cutting edge to the traditional highbrow.

And not just in the expected urban settings, either, as evidenced by the gallery of surrealist artist H.R. Giger (the designer of the monster in Ridley Scott's 1979 movie *Alien*) in the tiny and quintessentially Swiss town of Gruyères.

The Sexes

Switzerland still tends to lag behind in terms of equality of the sexes. Granted, in most cities and large towns the issue is disappearing, but there is still a surprising number of companies where the corporate culture feels like an episode of *Mad Men*.

There are plenty of villages where an unmarried woman is considered an unnecessary waste.

And mothers sending their children to (extremely hard to find) day care are treated as if they were letting them be brought up by wolves. Welcome to the 19th century?

Sports

Switzerland is an extremely active country. Hiking, biking, windsurfing, kayaking, hang-gliding, and golf are just some of the amusements practiced by young and old. Traditional Swiss sports are played by only small fraction of the population, but beloved nonetheless as an important part of the culture. Schwingen or Hosenlupf wrestling competitions feature scantily clad opponents who grip, trip, and throw their opponents to the ground. These odd competitions are held throughout Switzerland.

Luckily, there is also this great thing called *Hornussen*: a puck is placed on a ramp and shot into the air with a whip-like staff. As it comes down, the opposing team members try to swat it with boards on posts that look like giant picket signs. While not technically a sport, Trotti bikes—scooters with large, fat tires—are a popular family-friendly way to descend the Alpine heights on a sunny summer day. Rentals and dedicated trails can be found in the many of the country's resort areas.

And then there's skiing. It's a sport enjoyed by Swiss of all ages, from preschoolers to hardy mountain folk in their nineties. Slopes are rated by level of difficulty, and there are areas reserved for everyone from newbies to experts. Snowboarding has made inroads as well, and is especially popular with the younger crowd. If you'd rather watch, catch one of the ski jumping competitions featuring world champion and local hero Simon Amman as he reaches death-defying heights.

As far as spectator sports go, in summer it's soccer; in winter, hockey. Both come with fan clubs and, unfortunately, hooligans eager for a fight.

BEST HIKES

Hiking is practically a religion for the Swiss, and it's easy to see why: more than 37,000 miles of marked and maintained trails braid across a landscape bursting with Alpine farms, flower-filled meadows, and towering peaks—not bad for a country slightly smaller than Massachusetts and New Hampshire combined. Here are a few of the best routes that can be done in a day or less.

Vaud

The Lavaux Vineyard Terraces (Lutry–St. Saphorin). This 11-km (6.8-mile) stretch perched above Lac Léman (Lake Geneva) offers the beauty trifecta: massive mountains, a deep blue lake, and lush green vineyards. One look and you'll see why it's a UNESCO World Heritage Site. You can always pop down to Lake Geneva below to catch a boat (or train), rather than walk the entire way. *Easy to Moderate.*

Berner Oberland

Eiger Trail (Alpiglen–Eigergletscher). If you think the brooding north face of the Eiger is impressive from afar, try walking right below it. The entire 6-km (3.75-mile) trail (built in 1997 in just 39 days with hand tools) bathes in breathtaking views of Grindelwald and the surrounding peaks. Hike it in reverse if your knees can handle the pounding descent on an uneven trail. *Strenuous.*

Graubünden

Muottas Muragl to Alp Languard. The ruggedness of Switzerland's most uninhabited canton is on full display on this 9-km (5.6-mile) trail. The craggy mountain views of the entire Engadine valley make the effort worth it, as does a plate of yummy smoked meats at the rustic Unterer Scharberg hut at the halfway point. *Moderate.*

HIKING TIPS

■ Remember to wear practical shoes with good soles and ankle support and to always bring water, a few snacks, and extra clothing.

■ Always check your transport connections before setting out—you don't want to miss the last bus.

■ Bring cash, as huts rarely take credit cards, and you never know when you'll run across a farm selling cheese or locally made wine.

■ Have an iPhone? Switzerland Tourism (⊕ www.myswitzerland.com) has a superb (and free) app offering descriptions, maps, and practical information on dozens of the country's top hikes.

Valais

Zermatt Lake Trail. With the iconic Matterhorn as a backdrop, just about any hike over Zermatt will be worth the toil. Particularly special is a 9-km (5.6-mile) route from Blauherd to Riffelalp; the path is relatively easy (no major ups or downs) but you'll still climb 800 vertical feet and lose almost 2,000. Numerous huts dot the route, offering plenty of chances to soak up refreshments with some of the region's most spectacular views. *Easy to Moderate.*

Ticino

Valle Verzasca (Sonogno–Lavertezzo). It's not hard to imagine life here centuries ago as you stroll over Roman bridges and past stone houses in this narrow valley, nestled in Switzerland's Italian-speaking canton. *Easy.*

MONEY-SAVING TIPS

Switzerland ranks as one of the most expensive countries in the world, but that doesn't mean you have to mortgage your home or sell a kidney to visit. Deals may not abound, but occasional discounts do exist, especially during low season. Don't be afraid to ask for one—the answer might surprise you.

Transportation

Prices for rental cars in Switzerland can be nearly double the rate you'd find at home. If you decide on a car after you've arrived, it is worth the time and hassle to head to an Internet café to book. You'll save roughly the equivalent of a night at a four-star hotel by avoiding the rental counter.

One secret to staying solvent while riding Swiss trains is the Swiss Half-Fare Card. Available monthly, it allows you to pay only 50% of the regular ticket price on nearly every train, boat, bus, and tram in the country. This deal is not available in Switzerland, so buy this pass online or at a travel agency before you arrive.

Willing to travel on a specific train at a specific time? Surf the Swiss Federal Railways website (⊕ *www.rail.ch*), which is loaded with money-saving goodies like the SuperSaver ticket. Simply click on your starting location to view destination and schedule options. There are even first-class tickets to choose from. Note: you must print the tickets yourself or have them sent directly to your mobile phones with the free app.

Sightseeing and Activities

Culture buffs on a budget can plan their visits around the free nights offered by local museums. These nights differ by museum and frequently by region, but most often occur on the first Saturday, Sunday, or Monday of each month.

In exchange for your passport and a small deposit, many Swiss cities offer free bikes from May to October. Whether you cruise up the Rhône River, stopping into vineyards and quaint chalet-strewn villages, or carefully navigate traffic in the trendy Zürich West district, you'll work off that heavy fondue without lightening your wallet.

Summer brings free festivals, concerts, and events to much of Switzerland. Dance into the wee hours of the morning at Zürich's famous Street Parade or bask in the glow of the biggest fireworks display in Switzerland at the Fêtes de Genève, both in August and absolutely free.

Food and Drink

For less than 20 SF, you can dine like a king at lunchtime by ordering a *Tagesmenu, plat du jour,* or *piatto del giorno.* These specials are cooked up fresh each day for less than half the price of a similar main dish in the evening.

Shop for snacks after 5 pm, when most grocery stores knock 25% to 50% off certain perishable items. If you're determined not to raid your hotel's extravagantly priced minibar, you can find chips, soda, pastries, and even prepared to-go dishes like fruit salad, sliced veggies, and pasta salad at bargain rates.

Every city, town, and village has a fountain where you can fill up a bottle with clean, fresh drinking water. Don't mind the pigeons—even Zürich's more than one thousand fountains are frequently tested to meet strict quality standards.

GREAT ITINERARIES

SWITZERLAND SAMPLER: A FIRST-TIMER'S TOUR

10 Days. This route offers a taste of this tiny country's various cultures and landscapes. From cosmopolitan Zürich and Geneva to the quaint charms of Luzern and Zermatt to sleepy Lauterbrunnen, this tour gives you a good sense of what's to be seen here.

Zürich

2 nights. Switzerland's commercial heart and largest city offers something for everyone. Visit the Grossmünster church, updated in a Gothic style in the 1700s. Then make your way through the maze of tiny cobblestone streets toward Bahnhofstrasse, where designer boutiques cater to the city's elite. ⇨ *Chapter 2.*

Luzern

2 nights. Cross this lovely city's Wooden Bridge, the oldest in Europe, before ascending the heights of nearby Mount Pilatus for a view over classic "Wilhelm Tell country." Hungry? Don't forget to try a *Lözarner Chögelipastete*, a meat-filled pastry that you can't find anywhere else. ⇨ *Chapter 6.*

Lauterbrunnen

2 nights. Lauterbrunnen is a gorgeous base from which to explore the Berner Oberland. Trek from Interlaken to St. Beatus-Höhlen's natural caverns and hillside pavilion. When your feet can't take you any farther, take the funicular from Grindelwald up to picturesque Mürren, a tiny tourist's delight of a town perched on a rocky cliff 5,361 feet up. ⇨ *Chapter 10.*

Zermatt

1 night. This picturesque car-free village sits in the shadow of the iconic Matterhorn . . . need we say more? ⇨ *Chapter 11.*

BY PUBLIC TRANSPORTATION

All points on this tour are easily, and comfortably, reached by train. Note that the villages of Zermatt and Mürren are off-limits to private cars—you'll have to park outside town and take a shuttle, train, or funicular into town.

Geneva

2 nights. After learning all about the Protestant Reformation that began here, stand in the spray of Geneva's Jet d'Eau, the tallest fountain in Europe. Take a cruise on Lac Léman for breathtaking views of Mont Blanc while enjoying a glass of Chasselas, grown next door in the celebrated vineyards of Canton Vaud. ⇨ *Chapter 13.*

SWISS GASTRONOMY

9 Days. This food-intensive itinerary offers aficionados an opportunity to travel from one great dining experience to another, sampling the very finest *haute gastronomie* at one stop, the most authentic regional classics—even the earthiest peasant cuisines—at another. Incidental pleasures—wandering in the Alps, for example, or strolling through medieval town centers in Switzerland's greatest cities—can be squeezed in between meals. Remember that reservations must be made well in advance.

Geneva

2 nights. Your first night, indulge in a hearty Lyonnaise meal at the Bistrot du Bœuf Rouge. For lunch the next day, head out to the vineyards for exquisite seasonal cuisine at the Domaine de Châteauvieux. Back in Geneva, have a relatively light Ticinese supper at La Favola. Fill the time

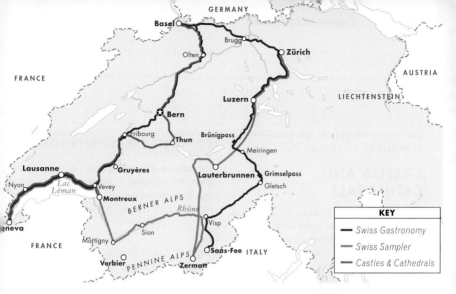

Basel
Brugg
Zürich
Olten
FRANCE
AUSTRIA
LIECHTENSTEIN
Luzern
Bern
Brünigpass
Fribourg
Thun
Meiringen
Gruyères
Lauterbrunnen
Grimselpass
Lausanne
Vevey
Gletsch
Nyon
Lac
Léman
Montreux
BERNER ALPS
Rhône
Visp
eneva
Sion
Saas-Fee
ITALY
FRANCE
Martigny
Verbier
PENNINE ALPS
Zermatt

KEY
— Swiss Gastronomy
— Swiss Sampler
— Castles & Cathedrals

between meals with a brisk stroll along the quais or a visit to one of the city's many museums. ⇨ *Chapter 13.*

Lausanne

1 night. Philippe Rochat has finally retired from Restaurant de l'Hôtel de Ville, but Chef Benoit Violier is already winning hearts—and stomachs—with his fresh twist on haute cuisine. This may be the triumph of the trip, but reserve judgment for after Basel and Zürich. At night, head down to the waterfront at Ouchy and have a chic, light supper at the Café Beau-Rivage. ⇨ *Chapter 12.*

Basel

1 night. Two hours north, lunch at Bruderholz, which gives Philippe Rochat a run for his money. Then, after visiting, say, the Münster and the history museum, relax in the downstairs bistro at the Teufelhof: the light specialties are prepared by Michael Baader, who is chef for the top-notch restaurant upstairs as well. ⇨ *Chapter 7.*

Zürich

2 nights. Step back in time for a meal at Zunfthaus zur Zimmerleuten, a medieval guildhall dating back to 1708. Then, after a thorough walking tour of Zürich's Old Town, you can settle in for an atmospheric, old-world evening at the

BY PUBLIC TRANSPORTATION

Each of the stopovers is accessible by train, though some of the restaurants may require cabs or tram rides; a rental car will give you more flexibility for reaching country inns.

Picasso- and Matisse-lined Kronenhalle. ⇨ *Chapter 2.*

Luzern

1 night. For a total contrast and perhaps the most authentically *Swiss* meal of your tour, head for Galliker and a lunch of real farm food. Having absorbed the Lion Monument, crossed the Kapellbrücke, and toured the history museum, you can think about the evening meal: a light, sophisticated river-fish entrée at Rotes Gatter, in the Hotel Des Balances, affords waterfront views. ⇨ *Chapter 6.*

Saas-Fee

1 night. From Luzern allow for a full day's scenic mountain drive south over the Brünigpass, then on over the Grimselpass and down the Rhône Valley to Brig and the spectacular little resort of Saas-Fee. Once there, retreat to the isolated Waldhotel Fletschhorn for a sophisticated dinner by star chef Markus Neff and a bare minimum of one night to take in the mountain air. ⇨ *Chapter 11.*

CASTLES AND CATHEDRALS

8 Days. Romantics, history buffs, and architecture fans can circle western Switzerland to take in some of the country's best medieval and Gothic landmarks.

Geneva
1 night. The excavations below the 12th-century Cathédrale St-Pierre, open to the public as the *site archéologique,* have yielded two 4th-century sanctuaries, Roman mosaics, and an 11th-century crypt. ⇨ *Chapter 13.*

Montreux
1 night. The Château de Chillon, partially surrounded by the waters of Lake Geneva, may be the most completely and authentically furnished in Switzerland. Lord Byron signed the pillar where his "Prisoner of Chillon" was manacled. ⇨ *Chapter 12.*

Gruyères
1 night. This magnificently beautiful castle-village draws crowds to its central street, souvenir shops, quaint inns, and frescoed castle, complete with dungeon and spectacular views. ⇨ *Chapter 8.*

Fribourg
1 night. This bilingual city is the last Catholic stronghold of western Switzerland, rooted in its single-tower Cathédrale St-Nicolas. The cathedral's Last Judgment tympanum and Art Nouveau stained-glass windows deserve attention—but leave time to explore the Old Town, with its multilevel fortifications constructed for the ubiquitous Zähringens. ⇨ *Chapter 8.*

BY PUBLIC TRANSPORTATION

The complete itinerary works by rail, with most sites accessible on foot from the station; Gruyères has bus connections to the elevated castle and the Old Town.

Thun
1 night. If you're driving, cut across Fribourg toward Thun (by train, connect through Bern), where you'll see the Bernese Alps in all their splendor. Schloss Thun, which dates from 1191, features a knights' hall, tapestries, local ceramics, and an intimidating collection of weapons. ⇨ *Chapter 10.*

Bern
1 night. The Zähringens fortified this gooseneck in the River Aare; its 15th-century Münster features a restored (full-color, painted) main portal. ⇨ *Chapter 9.*

Basel
1 night. In this historic, cosmopolitan city is a Münster with a lovely Romanesque portal and the tomb of the great humanist Erasmus. ⇨ *Chapter 7.*

1

WHEN TO GO

In July, Switzerland's best weather coincides with the heaviest crowds. August often sees high temperatures but also can be rainy. June and September are pleasant, and hotel prices can be slightly lower, especially in resorts. In May and June, the mountains are at their loveliest, with Alpine flowers blooming and the peaks capped with snow; however, as ski season is over and high summer hasn't begun, this is often considered low season, and many resort hotels close down. Those that remain open reduce their prices considerably. Another low-season disadvantage: some cable car and cogwheel train operations take a break between the midwinter and midsummer rushes; some must wait for snow to clear before reopening. The most prestigious ski resorts charge top prices during the Christmas–New Year holidays but reduce them slightly in early January. February through Easter is prime time again. Late autumn—from mid-October through early December—is the least appealing season for visiting the Alps because there's usually little snow, no foliage, and a tendency toward dampness and fog. If you stick to the cities to shop and tour museums, you won't notice the doldrums that take over the resorts.

The only exception to the rules of thumb above: the Ticino, which lies south of the Alps, boasts a Mediterranean climate and declares high season from April through October. Many of its hotels close down altogether from November through March.

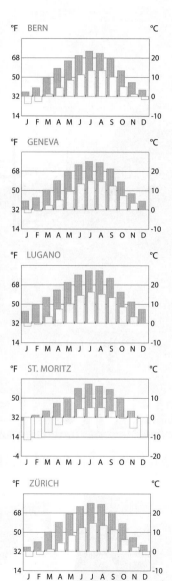

SCENIC JOURNEYS

GREAT TRAIN RIDES AND DRIVES

By Kati Clinton Robson

Switzerland's scenic beauty has drawn visitors to its peaks for more than 150 years—and traders were crossing the mountains long before that. The result is an extensive road and rail network enabling you to discover each corner of the country, from glistening, mineral-rich rivers to the glaciers that feed them.

The efficient rail system provides speedy transport options, but the real treat is to slow down and turn your journey into an experience. Most scenic routes link big cities, making them easy to incorporate into your travels. Or take to the road yourself, and explore sites off the beaten path. We've scoured the countryside to find the best scenic routes, whether you are the driver or merely a passenger.

CLASSIC SWISS ROUTES

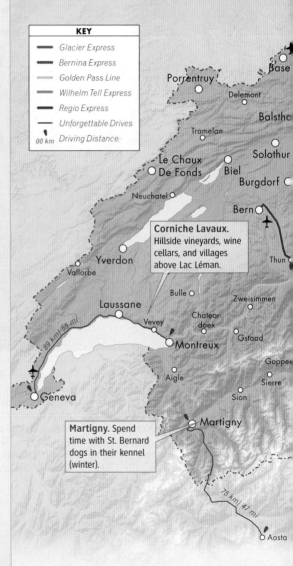

Vineyards in the Lavaux region

Whether you're riding the rails or behind the wheel, check out our favorite scenic routes in Switzerland. These rides and drives connect many popular Swiss destinations, and offer some unforgettable sights to see along the way. For more details on these routes, see the following pages.

SWISS PASS

If you'll be spending a week or more in Switzerland, and want to see as much of the country as possible, the Swiss Pass or Swiss Flexi Pass could be the perfect ticket. Both allow unlimited travel on trains, buses, and boats nationwide, including scenic routes and local trams in 75 towns, as well as free entry to more than 470 museums. They also offer a 50% discount on most mountaintop trains and cable cars. The Swiss Pass must be used on consecutive days and starts at 266 SF for a 4-day second-class ticket. The Swiss Flexi Pass lets you choose your travel dates over the period of one month, starting at 3 days (254 SF). The more days you buy, the better the deal becomes. ⊕ www. swisstravelsystem.ch

KEY

- Glacier Express
- Bernina Express
- Golden Pass Line
- Wilhelm Tell Express
- Regio Express
- Unforgettable Drives
- *00 km* Driving Distance

Porrentruy

Base

Delemont

Balsthc

Tramelan

Solothur

Le Chaux De Fonds

Biel

Burgdorf

Neuchatel

Bern

Corniche Lavaux. Hillside vineyards, wine cellars, and villages above Lac Léman.

Yverdon

Vallorbe

Thun

Bulle

Zweisimmen

Laussane

Vevey

Chateardoex

Gstaad

89 km/55 mi

Montreux

Goppe

Aigle

Sierre

Geneva

Sion

Martigny. Spend time with St. Bernard dogs in their kennel (winter).

Martigny

75 km/47 mi

Aosta

St. Bernard kennel in Martigny

Open-air museum in Brienz

Schaffhausen

Konstanz

Roamanshorn

Frauenfeld

Switzerland
Switzerland

Amriswil

Rorschach

Liestal
Baden

Winterthur

Wil

Sankt Gallen

Olten
Aarau

Zürich

Dubendorf

Gossau

Rankweil

Zofingen
Menziken

Ruti

Nesslau

Brienz. Visit one of Europe's best open-air museums, the Freilichtmuseum Ballenberg.

Zug

Chur. Switzerland's oldest town.

Luzern

Schwyz

Schwanden

Landquart

angnau

Giswil
Sarnen

190 km | 118 mi

Flüelen

Reichenau

Chur

Davos

Brienz
Brünig
Meiringen

Disentis/
Mustér

Thusis

Filisur

Interlaken

Göschenen

241 km | 150 mi

129 km | 80.2 mi

Sankt Moritz
(St. Moritz)

Pontresina

Spiez

Oberwald

Airolo

Bellinzona. Explore three UNESCO World Heritage castles.

Maloggia

Kandersteg

Bignasco

Poschiavo

Brig

Locarno

Bellinzona

Tirano

Visp

Zermatt

Domodossoi

Lugano

Menaggio

Val Verzasca. Sample local wines and cured meats at a *grotto* in this serene, untouched valley.

0   20 miles

0   20 km

TOP 5 SCENIC TRAIN RIDES

Glacier Express on the Landwasser Viaduct

GLACIER EXPRESS
Zermatt to St. Moritz

The queen of all scenic routes, the Glacier Express (also christened the world's slowest express train), begins and ends in two of Switzerland's most-frequented and fashionable resorts. But in between, it's the mountain landscape that people flock to see. Glaciated valleys, steep gorges, high meadows, and ancient townships are all viewed through panoramic cars, while the train passes over 291 bridges and through 91 tunnels.

Best For: Those who want to see the Alps, but aren't up for a lot of walking; food fanatics.

☎ 081/2886565 ⊕ www.glacierexpress. ch/en ✉ 136 SF (plus 33 SF for seat reservation in summer; 13 SF in winter) ◷ 7 hours, 30 min

WILHELM TELL EXPRESS
Luzern to Locarno or Lugano (includes steamer ride)

Connecting Central Switzerland with the swaying palms of Ticino, this route takes you down the length of Lake Luzern, through the precipitous inner Alps, and on to the Swiss-Italian hubs of Locarno and Lugano. A historic paddle steamer carries you past the Rütli meadow (the birthplace of the Swiss Confederation). At the end of the lake, you'll step aboard an SBB panorama train to continue your journey south.

Best For: Lake enthusiasts; history buffs; families.

☎ 041/3676767 ⊕ www.wilhelmtellexpress.ch ✉ 169 SF for boat and train (including seat reservation) ◷ 5 hours Luzern–Locarno; Lugano is an additional 15 min

GOLDENPASS/PANORAMIC EXPRESS
Montreux to Luzern

Travel in style in either a Belle Époque–inspired Orient Express train or a panoramic train from Lac Léman's "Swiss Riviera" into the cow-studded pastures and meadows of Central Switzerland. This journey squeezes through Vaud's vineyards to emerge in a higher valley strewn with chalets and farmsteads; later it scales the 1,000-meter-high Brünig Pass, before reaching Luzern. You must change trains twice, and with at least 10 trains plying this route per day, it's possible to hop on and off at any point along the itinerary.

Best For: Families (especially in the Orient Express cars); cow spotters; lake enthusiasts.

☎ 0900/245245 ⊕ www.goldenpass.ch ✉ 69 SF (plus 17 SF seat reservation) ◷ 5 hours, 20 min

BERNINA EXPRESS
Chur to Tirano (Italy)

The highest Alpine railway crosses some of Graubünden's most famous bridges and viaducts. The leg from Chur to St. Moritz is part of the Glacier Express route, but as the little red train continues southeast towards Italy, it also passes

Bernina Express

Europe's highest concentration of hilltop castles, as well as imposing glaciers and icy blue lakes. Once at the Italian town of Tirano, travelers can continue on to Lugano, via a Bernina Express bus across northern Italy. Don't forget your passport.

Best For: Those who want a taste of both Switzerland and Italy; food fanatics

☏ *081/2886565* ⊕ *www.rhb.ch* ✉ *Chur –Tirano 58 SF (plus 12 SF seat reservation); Chur–Lugano via Tirano 82 SF (plus 24 SF for seat reservation)* ⊙ *4 hours Chur–Tirano; 9 hours Chur–Lugano, via Tirano*

REGIOEXPRESS LÖTSCHBERGER
Bern to Brig

Jump aboard this scenic line to experience the beauty of the mountains between Bern and Brig. Rugged and romantic, the trip passes two picture-perfect spots for exploration: Kandersteg, with its cable car up to Oeschinensee, an otherworldly lake at the bottom of a sheer cliff face; and Goppenstein, the gateway to the Lötschen Valley, where you'll get a taste of classic Valaisan scenery. It's easy to hop on and off this train along the route.

Best For: Hikers and mountain enthusiasts; families; travelers en route to Zermatt

☏ *058/3272727* ⊕ *www.bls.ch/loetschberger* ✉ *48 SF (no seat reservations)* ⊙ *1 hour, 50 mins*

OTHER SCENIC TRAIN JOURNEYS

Generally speaking, most Swiss rail lines pass something scenic, even if it's only lower-lying "hills," ferry-filled lakes, vineyards, or distinct local architecture. Trains through the vibrant, rolling hills in Eastern Switzerland, the journey between Bern and Interlaken, and the train line running above Lac Léman are very picturesque ways of getting from place to place. And, the GoldenPass' chocolate train from Montreux to Broc (May–Oct.) is a delicious way to combine chocolate tasting at Nestlé's Cailler factory with a visit to a cheese-making dairy in Gruyères.

UNFORGETTABLE DRIVES

PALM EXPRESS: ST. MORITZ TO LUGANO VIA ITALY

129 km/80.2 miles; 4 hours

This trip on the famed yellow Post Bus begins among the frozen glaciers of the Engadine, winding over the Maloja Pass into the picturesque Bregaglia Valley. From here, you travel to Menaggio, situated on Italy's villa-fringed Lake Como, then on to Lugano. The scenery is as varied as the views are spellbinding. ☎ 058/4483535 ⊕ www.postbus.ch

GENEVA TO MONTREUX, ALONG THE LAKESIDE ROAD

89 km/55 miles; about 2 hours

Lac Léman's shoreline road links the hubs of Geneva, Lausanne, and Montreux. With the French Alps towering above you from across the lake, and local vineyards tempting you to travel higher, it's easy to forget you are driving parallel to one of Switzerland's busiest highways, and in between some of its most frequented cities.

ZURICH TO LUGANO, OR ANY TWO DESTINATIONS IN BETWEEN

241 km/150 miles from Zurich to Lugano (3 hours, 15 mins)

When traveling from Germanic Switzerland to Ticino, you can avoid some of the holiday traffic jams at the Gotthard tunnel entrance by scaling the pass instead. The landscape is a bit bleak, but the hairpin turns and fresh mountain air make up for the time saved in the 16-km-long Gotthard Tunnel.

INTERLAKEN TO CHUR VIA THE GRIMSEL, FURKA, AND OBERALP PASSES

190 km/118 miles; 3 hours, 30 mins

This epic drive from the chalet-dotted Berner Oberland to the country's oldest town takes drivers over three winding mountain passes and past snow-capped peaks, glaciers, and gorges.

A Swiss Post Bus

MARTIGNY TO AOSTA, ITALY VIA THE GREAT ST. BERNARD PASS

75 km/47 miles; 1 hour, 30 mins

Switzerland's oldest and most famous pass, the Great St. Bernard, has served travelers (including Julius Caesar, Hannibal, and Napoleon) since Roman times. It links the country's forbidding, mountainous southwest region with historic Aosta and bustling Milan in Italy, including a photo-op with some St. Bernard dogs at the drive's summit.

PRACTICAL DRIVING TIPS

■ Be sure to check when these routes are open, as most high passes close during winter.

■ Include satellite navigation in your rental package to reduce stress during the journey.

■ Control your speed: Switzerland is the land of speed cameras just waiting to catch—and heavily fine—unsuspecting speed racers.

For more driving tips and helpful hints, see Travel Smart Switzerland.

2

Zürich

WORD OF MOUTH

"Zürich has a compact medieval old town in pristine condition, a beautiful river and lake you can actually swim in, an amazing number of hip restaurants and bars, museums, and gorgeous views of the Alps."

—Sesi

WELCOME TO ZÜRICH

TOP REASONS TO GO

★ **A dip into the Middle Ages:** Museum-perfect in their leaded-glass and Gothic-wood details, a dozen medieval guildhalls have been transformed into time-burnished restaurants.

★ **Extreme shopping:** Luxury-encrusted with noted shops, Bahnhofstrasse is also lined with banks to refill your empty wallets—the nearby Altstadt has other "Ring bell to enter" boutiques, one of which may have that $10,000 belt you've been looking for.

★ **Amazing architecture:** The Old Town and the Left Bank's Oberdorf and Niederdorf have barely changed since the 18th century—savor their pedestrians-only cobblestone streets, medieval churches, and see-and-be-seen outdoor cafés.

★ **The "Great Church":** The Grossmünster lords over the city, both architecturally and psychologically, for here Ulrich Zwingli taught the city to buckle down, fear the Lord, and hail the Protestant work ethic in the 15th century.

1 **Kreis 1: The Historic Core.** Zürich's Altstadt (Old Town) is the main reason you're here, thanks to Gothic treasures like the Fraumünster, shopping galore, and an amazing collection of restaurants, and it's all right on the lake. Less dignified and livelier, Zürich's east bank Niederdorf and Oberdorf neighborhoods are noted for both their cultural goodies, including the star-studded opera house and the Kunsthaus (Museum of Art), and their lively bars and restaurants.

2 **Kreis 2.** This splendid neighborhood of leafy streets and 150-year-old villas is home to the Museum Rietberg, which includes the Villa Wesendonck, where Richard Wagner wrote his famed Wesendonck Songs.

3 **Kreis 5: Zürich West.** For something completely different, head here to check out the latest modern architecture—since the 1990s the area has undergone an extreme makeover, and old factories have made room for trendy lofts and hip clubs.

4 **Kreis 7.** Upscale houses crawl up the Zürichberg hill, which is topped with an elaborate zoo and the cemetery where James Joyce was interred in 1941—and still draws many fans to the Irish writer's grave.

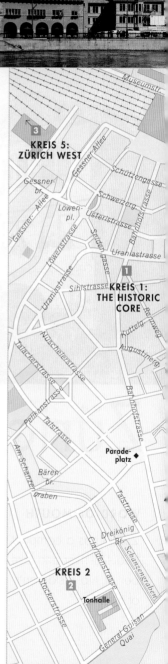

5 Kreis 8. With its long shoreline promenade and varied opportunities for swimming in the lake, this is especially a draw between May and September, when the city's residents flock outdoors during their leisure hours.

6 Winterthur. Roughly 20 minutes from Zürich, this museum-rich town is famed for its art collections.

GETTING ORIENTED

Visitors are often surprised by the beauty of Zürich, perhaps imagining it as one vast high-tech banking hall, all chrome and computers. But the city's location—straddling the Limmat River and flanked by two tiny mountains, the Zürichberg and the Üetliberg—would tempt any landscape painter. Zürich may be small—it can be crossed in a mere 20 minutes on foot—but it has international cachet.

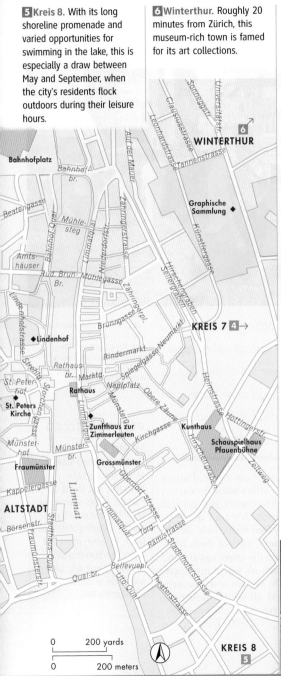

KREIS 1 SHOPPING

In the Altstadt, Zürich's Bahnhofstrasse is a worldwide phenomenon, attracting shoppers with gold cards from all over the globe. Across the river in the Niederdorf, smaller stores and vintage shops offer some debt relief and many items you won't find anywhere else.

Zürich's most luxurious shops line Bahnhofstrasse and its side streets (above). The sweets at Sprüngli (below, right) are a perfect way to end a day of retail therapy.

It's telling that Bahnhofstrasse starts out as a pedestrian zone near the train station and offers access to cars at the exclusive end near the lake—there's still no real parking, but there is enough room for your driver to hover while you shop. The busy foot-traffic-only section has four major department stores, two of them high-end, and chain boutiques. Down the street toward and beyond the exclusive Paradeplatz, it's worth investigating the side streets, especially In Gassen and Storchengasse, where smaller shops host all the big designers. In the Niederdorf, the main arteries are all pedestrian-only: Limmatquai, Marktgasse, Niederdorfstrasse, and Rindermarkt/Neumarkt.

–Katrin Gygax

BEST TIME TO GO

Saturday is the busiest; stores are closed Sunday, as are some smaller boutiques and shops on Monday. Locals stream out of offices and onto the nearby shopping streets at lunch, between noon and 2 pm. The biannual sales, in January and July, offer some real discounts and are worth a look.

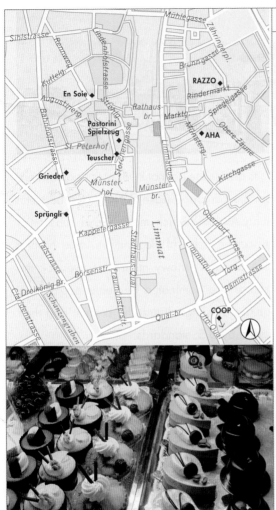

ZÜRICH'S FINEST

AHA: if there's someone on your list who already has everything—except their very own mirage box.

En Soie: for that silk Doris Day ball gown you've been looking for, only in lime green with pink accents.

Grieder: the chicest collections for men and women looking for under-stated elegance.

Pastorini Spielzeug: devoted to old-style playing: wooden toys, detailed dollhouse miniatures, and kids' tools for making handicrafts.

RAZZO: get last year's suit or vintage dresses at prices that won't shock you.

CHOCOLATE

Sprüngli: exquisite examples of what can be done with a cocoa bean.

Teuscher: fabulous chocolate; beautiful wrapping. For very special gifts.

COOP: avoid hokey, yodely packaging and go for the yummy flat bars for the best price/quality ratio.

REFUELING

Recharge with a chocolate truffle or an elegant sandwich at **Sprüngli,** Zürich's top café at the corner of banking and luxury shopping. You'll find your money goes a little further at **Odéon,** where a younger and hipper crowd nibbles on steak with herb butter or salads; the lunch special is always a good deal. At both these places, grab an outdoor table in warm weather and watch the chic crowds stroll by.

Updated by
Katrin Gygax

Zürich, which sits astride the Limmat River at the point where it emerges from the Zürichsee (Lake Zürich), is a beautiful city. Its charming Altstadt, which makes up a substantial part of the city center, is full of elegantly restored historic buildings. In the distance, snowy mountains overlook the lake, whose shores are dominated by centuries-old mansions. Few high-rise buildings disturb the skyline, and their heights are modest by U.S. standards.

Zürich was renowned as a center for commerce as early as the 12th century; many of its diligent merchants had made fortunes dealing in silk, wool, linen, and leather goods. By 1336 this privileged class had become too powerful in the view of the newly emerging band of tradesmen and laborers who, allied with a charismatic aristocrat named Rudolf Brun, overthrew the merchants' town council and established Zürich's famous trade guilds. Those 13 original guilds didn't lose power until the French Revolution—and even today they maintain their prestige. Every year Zürich's leading businessmen dress up in medieval costumes for the guilds' traditional march through the streets, heading for the magnificent guildhalls.

If the guilds defined Zürich's commerce, the Reformation defined its soul. From his pulpit in the Grossmünster, Ulrich Zwingli galvanized the region, and he ingrained in Zürichers a devotion to thrift and industriousness so successfully that it ultimately led them into temptation: the temptation to achieve global influence and tremendous wealth. Today the Zürich stock exchange is the fourth largest in the world, after those of New York, London, and Tokyo.

Nevertheless, Zürich is not your typical cold-hearted business center. In 1916 a group of artists and writers rebelling against the restraints of traditional artistic expression—among them Tristan Tzara, Jean Arp, and Hugo Ball—founded the avant-garde Dadaist movement here. The fertile atmosphere also attracted Irish author James Joyce, who spent years here while re-creating his native Dublin in *Ulysses* and *A Portrait*

Ulrich Zwingli, Freedom Fighter

Visitors to Zürich soon hear about Ulrich Zwingli, the no-nonsense (and, one suspects, humorless) religious reformer who taught the city to buckle down, work hard, and fear the Lord. But who was this much-revered man of the cloth, and why is he depicted holding a huge sword in the statue that stands in front of the Wasserkirche?

In 1484 Zwingli was born in the tiny village of Wildhaus in the canton of St. Gallen. He entered the priesthood, eventually rising to the head position at the Grossmünster in the city of Zürich. He had no problem declaring publicly where he differed with the teachings of the Catholic Church. His first quarrel, around 1512, was over the evils of the Swiss mercenary service propagated by the pope. A few years later, around 1519, he joined the fight against the church's growing practice of exacting payment for the forgiveness of sins.

Taking a closer look at the New Testament, Zwingli came up with his own very simple theology: if it's not in the Bible, it doesn't apply. This focus on both the Old and New Testaments soon spread throughout the Christian world, affecting Protestant congregations all the way to the English colonies in America. While Martin Luther's form of protest was largely peaceful, Zwingli was not above getting into the fray. As people took up arms over their right to worship as they saw fit, Zwingli suited up and went to battle. He died in 1531, along with 500 of his compatriots, clutching that very big sword at the Battle of Kappel am Albis in the canton of Zürich.

of the Artist as a Young Man. Today the city's extraordinary museums and galleries and luxurious shops along Bahnhofstrasse, Zürich's Fifth Avenue, attest to its position as Switzerland's cultural—if not political—capital.

ZÜRICH PLANNER

WHEN TO GO

The temperate climate has four distinct seasons. Spring can be a maddening mix of brilliant sun and rain, which means colorful blossoms abound. Summers are humid and have been quite hot in the last several years, rivaling some Asian nations; evening thunderstorms are frequent.

Fall becomes crisp around the end of October, and winter brings a low fog ceiling (this is when locals head for any nearby peak over 5,000 feet) or light-to-slushy snow that tends to melt after a week or so.

FESTIVALS

If you see an elephant wandering around the streets of Zürich, don't worry: it just means the circus is in town. In the winter months a series of circuses—with acrobats, fire-eaters, and lion tamers—travel throughout the country in red-and-white caravans, each stopping along the way in Zürich. In addition to the usual opera, theater, and concert seasons, the city holds a variety of events throughout the year.

One of Zürich's most important festivals is **Sächsilüüte,** a kind of Groundhog Day in which descendants of medieval guild members circle a burning snowman until its head blows off (how long this takes determines whether spring will come early or late).

When spring springs, so does **Jazznojazz,** with jazz musicians playing at venues all over town.

Summer is the time for the **Zurich Pride Festival,** a huge celebration of gay pride.

Even if you don't speak German, you should still attend the **Theater Spektakel,** a two-week outdoor theater festival, for the excellent food. Sensuous dancing marks the nine days in July of **Tangowoche,** while techno music is the sound track for August's three-day lovefest called **Street Parade.**

Fall arrives with the **Lange Nacht der Museen,** when museums leave their doors open all night. **Knabenschiessen,** a country fair held on the outskirts of the city, lets youngsters test their aim at shooting competitions. Toward the end of the year is **Expovina,** a wine exhibition, held on boats moored at Bürkliplatz.

PLANNING YOUR TIME

Despite its international stature, Zürich is a small city (some may argue "town"), which makes it ideal for a visit on foot. The historic center can easily be visited in a day, factoring in a nice lunch and a relaxing dinner or night at the opera. Add half a day for each museum you want to visit—and there are many—and one more for lakeside relaxation or hiking in the nearby hills.

GETTING HERE AND AROUND

AIR TRAVEL

Zürich Airport, 11 km (7 mi) north of the city, is Switzerland's most important airport and the 10th-busiest in the world. It's easy to take a Swiss Federal Railways feeder train directly from the airport to Zürich's Hauptbahnhof (main station), a 10-minute trip. A taxi into the center costs 50 SF to 60 SF and takes around 20 minutes. Most larger hotels have their own shuttles to and from the airport.

BOAT TRAVEL

Whether you feel like rowing out onto Lake Zürich, taking a cruise past waterfront villas, or zipping to one of the lakeside restaurants in a water taxi, there are all kinds of boats for rent in and around Zürich. Lago has a variety of boats for rent and operates a water taxi service, and Zürichsee Schifffahrtsgesellschaft runs passenger ships between communities on the lake.

Boat Contacts Lago ⊠ *Utoquai 6, Kreis 8* ☎ *044/2622220* ⊕ *www.lago-zuerich. ch.* **Zürichsee Schifffahrtsgesellschaft** ⊠ *Bürkliplatz, Kreis 1* ☎ *044/4871333* ⊕ *www.zsg.ch.*

CAR TRAVEL

The A2 expressway from Basel to Zürich leads directly into the city. The A1 continues east to St. Gallen. Approaching from the south and the St. Gotthard route, take the A14 from Luzern (Lucerne). It feeds into the A3, which takes you through the Üetliberg Tunnel and into the city at its southwestern edge.

If Swiss drivers have a reputation throughout Europe for being unnecessarily impolite in their lead-footedness, Zürich must be where they're all hatched and trained. With a good number of streets in town marked "one-way" or "pedestrian-only" or with a speed limit of only 30 kph (18 mph), many drivers take out their frustrations on their fellow man. The rate of road rage is unnervingly high in Zürich, although it's still not L.A.

TAXI TRAVEL

Taxis are very expensive, with an 8-SF minimum but no charge for additional passengers. An available taxi is indicated by an illuminated rooftop light. You can order a cab by calling Alpha Taxi or Züri Taxi.

Taxi Companies Alpha Taxi ☎ *044/7777777*. **Züri Taxi** ☎ *044/2222222.*

TRAIN TRAVEL

There are straightforward connections and several express routes leading directly into Zürich from Basel, Geneva, Bern, and Lugano. All take you to the Zürich Hauptbahnhof in the city center.

TRAM TRAVEL

ZVV, the tram service in Zürich, is swift and punctual. It runs from 5:30 am to midnight, every 6 minutes at peak hours and every 12 minutes at other times. All-day passes cost 8.60 SF and can be purchased from the same vending machines at the stops that post maps and sell one-ride tickets; you must buy your ticket before you board. Free route plans are available from VBZ Züri-Linie (Zürich Public Transport) offices, located at major crossroads (Paradeplatz, Bellevue, Central, Limmatplatz). Stops are clearly signposted.

Tram Contacts ZVV. ☎ *0848/988988* ⊕ *www.zvv.ch.*

⇨ *For more information on getting here and around, see Travel Smart Switzerland.*

TOURS

Bus Tours. The Zürich Tourist office's daily Cityrama tour covers the main city sights; the trip lasts three hours, leaving at 11 am; it costs 49 SF. The Zürich Trolley Experience (34 SF) gives a good general idea of the city in two hours; it leaves at 9:45 am, noon, and 2 pm. The Combo Tour goes farther and includes a train trip to the top of the nearby Üetliberg. This is also a daily tour, given at 9:45 am, noon, and 2 pm; it takes four hours and costs 42 SF. All tours start from the Hauptbahnhof. The tourist office also offers a weekend Segway City Tour for 109 SF from April through October, at 2 pm.

Walking Tours. Throughout the year the tourist office offers daily two-hour walking tours (25 SF) that start at the Hauptbahnhof. You can join a group with English-language commentary, but the times vary, so call ahead.

Bicycle Tours. From May to September, Friday through Sunday at 10:30 am, you can take a three-hour bike tour from the Hauptbahnhof for 50 SF (rates go up if you're fewer than three people). Tours are available in English; bikes are supplied. Reservations are necessary only for four or more people.

Top Trek ☎ *077/4546590* ⊕ *www.toptrek.ch.*

VISITOR INFORMATION

The **Zürich Card** (20 SF) gets you 24 hours of travel in the greater Zürich area on all trams, buses, trains, boats, cable cars and cogwheel trains, plus free entry into over 40 museums. It's available from the tourist information center.

Zürich Tourist Service ✉ *Hauptbahnhof, Bahnhofplatz, Kreis 1* ☎ *044/ 2154000* ⊕ *www.zuerich.com.*

EXPLORING ZÜRICH

From the northern tip of the Zürichsee, the Limmat River starts its brief journey to the Aare and, ultimately, to the Rhine—and it neatly bisects Zürich at the starting gate. The city is crisscrossed by lovely, low bridges. On the left bank are the Altstadt, the grander, genteel pedestrian zone of the old medieval center; the Zürich Hauptbahnhof, the main train station; and Bahnhofplatz, a major urban crossroads and the beginning of the world-famous luxury shopping street, Bahnhofstrasse. The right bank constitutes the livelier old section, divided into the Oberdorf (Upper Village) toward Bellevue, and the Niederdorf (Lower Village), from Marktgasse to Central and along Niederdorfstrasse, which buzzes on weekends. Most streets between Central and Bellevue are pedestrian-only zones, as is the Limmatquai from the Rudolf-Brun-Brücke to the Münsterbrücke.

Similar to the arrondissement system in Paris, Zürich is officially divided into a dozen numbered *Kreises* (districts), which spiral out clockwise from the center of the city. Kreis 1, covering the historic core, includes the Altstadt, Oberdorf, and Niederdorf. Zürich West is part of Kreis 5. Most areas in the city are commonly known by their Kreis, and a Kreis number is generally the most helpful in giving directions.

KREIS 1: THE HISTORIC CORE

LEFT BANK: THE ALTSTADT

The Altstadt is home to several of Zürich's most important landmarks—the Lindenhof, St. Peter's, the Fraumünster, and the Stadthaus—as well as the shop-lined Bahnhofstrasse.

TOP ATTRACTIONS

Bahnhofstrasse. Reputedly "the most expensive street in the world"—thanks to all of its extravagantly priced jewelry shops—Zürich's principal boulevard offers luxury shopping and hulking department stores, whereas much shifting and hoarding of the world's wealth takes place discreetly within the banks' walls. You can enjoy your window shopping here in relative peace: the only vehicles allowed are the municipal trams. ✉ *Begins south of the Haupbahnhof, Kreis 1.*

QUICK BITES

Sprüngli. Zürich's top confiserie, this landmark chocolatier and café for wealthy Bahnhofstrasse habitués concocts heavenly truffles and *Luxemburgerli*, small cream-filled cookies that require immediate eating. Good, plain hot lunches and salads are also served. There are also branches at the Hauptbahnhof and on Löwenplatz. ✉ *Paradeplatz, Kreis 1* ☎ *044/2244711* ⊕ *www.spruengli.com.*

★ **Fraumünster** (*Church of Our Lady*). Of the church spires that are Zürich's signature, the Fraumünster's is the most delicate, a graceful sweep to a narrow spire. It was added to the Gothic structure in 1732; the remains of Louis the German's original 9th-century abbey are below. Its Romanesque choir is a perfect spot for meditation beneath the ocher, sapphire, and ruby glow of the 1970 stained-glass windows by the Russian-born Marc Chagall, who loved Zürich. The Graubünden sculptor Alberto Giacometti's cousin, Augusto Giacometti, executed the fine painted window, made in 1930, in the north transept. ✉ *Stadthausquai, Kreis 1* ☉ *Nov.–Mar., daily 10–4; Apr.–Oct., daily 10–6.*

★ **Kirche St. Peter** (*Church of St. Peter*). Dating from the early 13th century, Zürich's oldest parish church has one of the largest clock faces in Europe. A church has been on this site since the 9th century. The existing building has been considerably expanded over the years: styles range from a Romanesque choir to a Baroque nave. The tower, for example, was extended in 1534, when the clock was added. Keep an eye out for inexpensive or even free classical concerts. ✉ *St. Peterhofstatt, Kreis 1* ☎ *044/2116057* ☉ *Weekdays 8–6, Sat. 10–4, Sun. 11–5.*

Paradeplatz (*Parade Square*). The hub of Bahnhofstrasse and a tram junction, this square is a great place to observe a microcosm of the local upper crust—furrowed-brow bankers striding to work while their fur-trimmed wives struggle with half a dozen bags and the dilemma of where to shop next. While you're at it, spoil your taste buds with incredible chocolate from the Sprüngli café. ✉ *Intersection of Bahnhofstr. and Poststr., Kreis 1.*

Zunfthaus zur Meisen. Set on the bank of the Limmat across the river from the towering Fraumünster is Zürich's most beautiful guildhall, comprising a magnificent suite of reception salons, several of which are topped by extravagant Baroque stucco ceilings. Erected for the city's wine merchants in the 18th century, the Zunfthaus today is a fitting showplace for the Swiss National Museum's ceramics collection. The Kilchberg-Schooren porcelain works flourished in Zürich from 1763 to 1790 and their masterwork—a 300-piece dining service created for the monastery Einsiedeln in 1775—takes center stage, along with exquisite figurines and table decor. Also on view are Nyon porcelains, Swiss pottery, and faience. Enter on the Fraumünster side. ✉ *Münsterhof 20, Kreis 1* ☎ *044/2212807* ⊕ *www.musee-suisse.ch* ⬚ *3 SF* ☉ *Thurs.–Sun. 11–4.*

WORTH NOTING

Alfred Escher. Leave it to Zürich to have a statue that honors not a saint, not a poet or artist, but rather the financial wizard who single-handedly dragged Zürich into the modern age back in the mid-19th century. Escher (1819–82) established the city as a major banking center,

A GOOD WALK

Begin at the **Hauptbahnhof**, a massive 19th-century edifice. Directly behind the Hauptbahnhof is the **Schweizerisches Landesmuseum**, housed in an enormous 19th-century neo-Gothic mansion; behind that is a shady green park. Walk northward to the tip of the park, cross on the left-hand side of the bridge, turn north a bit along Sihlquai, and head up Ausstellungsstrasse to the **Museum für Gestaltung**, which holds an impressive collection of 20th-century graphic art. Back at the train station, look across Bahnhofplatz and you'll see traffic careening around a statue of Alfred Escher, the man who brought Zürich into the modern age.

Cross the square to Bahnhofstrasse, Zürich's principal business and shopping boulevard. A quarter of the way up the street—about five blocks—veer left into Rennweg and left again on Fortunagasse, an atmospheric medieval street well removed from the contemporary elegance of Bahnhofstrasse. Climb up to the **Lindenhof**, a quiet, gravel square with a view across the river to the Niederdorf. From here a maze of medieval alleys leads off to your right. Nestled among them is **Kirche St. Peter**, whose tower has one of the largest clock faces in Europe.

From Kirche St. Peter, bear right on Schlüsselgasse and duck into a narrow alley, Thermengasse, which leads left; you'll walk directly over excavated ruins of Roman baths. At Weinplatz, turn right on Storchengasse, where some of the most elite boutiques are concentrated, and head toward the delicate spires of the **Fraumünster**. In the same square you'll see two of Zürich's finest guildhalls, the Zunfthaus zur Waag and **Zunfthaus zur Meisen**.

Wind left up Waaggasse past the Hotel Savoy to **Paradeplatz**. From here you can take a quick side trip to the art collection at **Haus Konstruktiv** by going up Talackerstrasse to Sihlstrasse, turning left onto Selnaustrasse. Back at Paradeplatz, continue south on Bahnhofstrasse, which, as it nears the lake, opens onto a vista of boats, wide waters, and (on a clear day) distant peaks.

At Bürkliplatz, look to your right: those manicured parks are the front lawn of the Hotel Baur au Lac, the aristocrat of Swiss hotels. Beyond, you'll see the modern structure of the Kongresshaus and the Tonhalle, where the Zürich Tonhalle Orchestra resides. Across General-Guisan-Quai is one of the local swans' favorite hangouts: the boat dock, which is the base for trips around the Zürichsee.

Here you can take General-Guisan-Quai west to Seestrasse to the **Museum Rietberg** (about a 25-minute walk) or turn left and cross the Quaibrücke (Quay Bridge) for one of the finest views in town, especially at night, when the floodlit spires are mirrored in the inky river, whose surface is disturbed only by drifting, sleeping swans.

TIMING

The area is surprisingly compact; half a day is enough time for a cursory visit. If you plan on museum hopping, the Schweizerisches Landesmuseum and Museum Rietberg merit at least two hours apiece.

championed the development of the federal railways and the city's university, and pushed through the construction of the tunnel under the St. Gotthard Pass. ⊠ *In the middle of Bahnhofpl., Kreis 1.*

Hauptbahnhof (*Main Railway Station*). From the bustling main concourse of this immaculate 19th-century edifice you can watch crowds rushing to their famously on-time trains. Beneath lies a shopping mall, open daily from 8 to 8 (an exception to the closed-on-Sunday rule), with everything from grocery stores to clothing boutiques and bookshops. ⊠ *Between Museumstr. and Bahnhofpl., Kreis 1.*

Haus Konstruktiv (*Museum of Constructivist Art*). Housed in a former electrical substation set by the River Sihl—an impressive 1930s Modernist architectural statement in its own right—this collection traces the history of Constructivist Art, which became one of the vogues of the '30s and '40s and had a big following in Switzerland (especially among its trailblazing graphic-art designers). The showpiece is the Rockefeller Dining Room, a 1963 salon designed by Swiss artist Fritz Glarner and looking very much like a pop-up Mondrian painting. Over the years the collection has broadened to include minimal art, concept art, and neo geo work (a style based on Japanese animation). Featured artists include Sophie Taeuber-Arp, Paul Klee, and Max Bill. During the year there are several temporary shows. ⊠ *Selnaustr. 25, Kreis 1* ☎ *044/2177080* ⊕ *www.hauskonstruktiv.ch* ☞ *14 SF* ☉ *Tues., Thurs., and Fri. noon–6, Wed. noon–8, weekends 11–6.*

Lindenhof (*Linden Court*). On the site of this quiet square, overlooking both sides of the river, a Roman customhouse and fortress and a Carolingian palace once stood. The fountain was erected in 1912, commemorating the day in 1292 when Zürich's women saved the city from the Habsburgs. As the story goes, the town was on the brink of defeat as the Habsburg aggressors moved in. Determined to avoid this humiliation, the town's women donned armor and marched to the Lindenhof. On seeing them, the enemy thought they were faced with another army and promptly beat a strategic retreat. Today, the scene could hardly be less martial, as locals play boccie and chess under the trees. ⊠ *Bordered by Fortunag. to the west and intersected by Lindenhofstr., Kreis 1.*

RIGHT BANK: NIEDERDORF AND OBERDORF

As soon as you step off the Quai Bridge on the right bank of the Limmat River, you'll notice a difference: the atmosphere is more casual. The area is also the center of Zürich's nightlife—both upscale and down, with the city's opera house and its historic theater, as well as plenty of bars and clubs. As you explore the area along Münstergasse to Marktgasse, parallel to the river, you'll notice a less Calvinistic bent. Each of the narrow streets and alleys that shoot east off Marktgasse (which quickly becomes Niederdorfstrasse) offers its own brand of entertainment. Niederdorfstrasse eventually empties onto the Central tram intersection, across the river from the main train station; from there it's easy to catch a tram along Bahnhofstrasse or the Limmatquai.

2

TOP ATTRACTIONS

Graphische Sammlung (*Graphics Collection*). The impressive collection of the Federal Institute of Technology includes a vast library of woodcuts, etchings, and engravings by such European masters as Dürer, Rembrandt, Goya, and Picasso. Pieces from the permanent collection are often arranged in thematic exhibitions. Take Tram 6 or 10 from the Bahnhofplatz or Central stops or Tram 9 from Bellevue to the ETH/Universitätsspital stop. ⊠ *Rämistr. 101, Kreis 1* ☎ *044/6324046* ⊕ *www. gs.ethz.ch* ☞ *Free* ☉ *Mon., Tues., Thurs., and Fri. 10–5, Wed. 10–7.*

Fodor's Choice ★ **Grossmünster** (*Great Church*). This impressive cathedral is affectionately known to English speakers as the "Gross Monster." Executed on the plump twin towers (circa 1781) are classical caricatures of Gothic forms bordering on the comical. The core of the structure was built in the 12th century on the site of a Carolingian church dedicated to the memory of martyrs Felix and Regula, who allegedly carried their severed heads to the spot. Charlemagne is said to have founded the church after his horse stumbled over their burial site. On the side of the south tower an enormous stone Charlemagne sits enthroned; the original statue, carved in the late-15th century, is protected in the crypt. In keeping with what the 16th-century reformer Zwingli preached from the Grossmünster's pulpit, the interior is spare, even forbidding, with all luxurious ornamentation long since stripped away. The only artistic touches are modern: stained-glass windows in the choir by Augusto Giacometti, in the western nave by Sigmar Polke, and ornate bronze doors in the north and south portals dating from the late 1940s. ⊠ *Zwinglipl., Kreis 1* ☎ *044/2513860* ⊕ *www.grossmuenster.ch* ☉ *Mar.–Oct., daily 10–6; Nov.–Feb., daily 10–5; cloister weekdays 9–6.*

Fodor's Choice ★ **Kunsthaus** (*Museum of Art*). With a varied and high-quality permanent collection of paintings—medieval, Dutch and Italian Baroque, and Impressionist—the Kunsthaus is Zürich's best art museum. The collection includes some fascinating Swiss works; others might be an acquired taste. Besides works by Ferdinand Hodler, with their mix of realism and stylization, there's a superb room full of Johann Heinrich Füssli paintings, which hover between the darkly ethereal and the grotesque. And then there's Picasso, Klee, Degas, Matisse, Kandinsky, Chagall, and Munch, all satisfyingly represented. There are plans to expand the museum by adding a modern building across the street, with an underground tunnel in between; it should be finished in 2017. ⊠ *Heimpl. 1, Kreis 1* ☎ *044/2538484* ⊕ *www.kunsthaus.ch* ☞ *Varies with exhibition* ☉ *Wed.–Fri. 10–8, Sat., Sun., and Tues. 10–6.*

WORTH NOTING

Haus zum Rüden. Now housing one of Zürich's finest restaurants, this 13th-century structure was the noblemen's society tavern. Peek inside at the barrel-vaulted ceiling and 30-foot beams; or better yet, stop for a meal. ⊠ *Limmatquai 42, Kreis 1.*

Helmhaus. The open court of this museum once served as a linen market. Inside there are changing exhibitions of contemporary, often experimental, art by Zürich-based artists. In spring the museum hosts an exhibition of works from the city's annual competition for young art-

You can get a good view of the Niederdorf from the Lindenhof

ists. ✉ *Limmatquai 31, Kreis 1* 🖾 *044/2516177* ⊕ *www.helmhaus.org* 🎟 *Free* 🕙 *Tues., Wed., and Fri.–Sun. 10–6, Thurs. 10–8.*

Kirchgasse. Antiques, art, and book enthusiasts will delight in the shops on this street. No. 13 was Zwingli's last home before he was killed in battle (1531) while defending the Reformation.

Rindermarkt. Fans of Gottfried Keller, commonly considered Switzerland's national poet and novelist, will want to visit this street. The 19th-century writer's former home, at No. 9, became famous thanks to his novel *Der Grüne Heinrich* (*Green Henry*). Opposite is the restaurant, Zur Oepfelchammer, where Keller ate regularly. ✉ *Between Marktg. and Neumarkt, Kreis 1.*

Schauspielhaus Pfauenbühne (*Peacock Theater*). During World War II this was the only German-language theater in Europe that wasn't muzzled by the Nazis, and it attracted some of the continent's bravest and best artists. It has been presenting plays ever since it was built in 1884; today its productions aren't always so risky, but they are stunningly mounted and performed, in German of course. There are no tours, so to see the interior you must see a show. ✉ *Rämistr. 34, Kreis 1* 🖾 *044/2587777* ⊕ *www.schauspielhaus.ch.*

Wasserkirche (*Water Church*). One of Switzerland's most delicate late-Gothic structures, this church displays stained glass by Augusto Giacometti. Both the church and the Helmhaus stand on what was once an island where martyrs Felix and Regula supposedly lost their heads. ✉ *Limmatquai 31, Kreis 1* 🕙 *Tues.–Fri. 9–noon, Sat. noon–5, closed during services.*

Overlooking the Limmat River, the Grossmünster is one of Zürich's most impressive churches.

Zoologisches Museum. Engaging and high-tech, the Zoological Museum allows you a close look at its accessible displays on Swiss insects, birds, and amphibians. You can examine butterflies and living water creatures through microscopes and listen to birdcalls as you compare avian markings. ⊠ *Karl Schmid-Str. 4, Kreis 1* ☎ *044/6343838* ⊕ *www.zm.uzh.ch* 🖃 *Free* ⊘ *Tues.–Fri. 9–5, weekends 10–5.*

Zunfthaus zur Saffran. Portions of this guildhall for haberdashers date from as early as 1389. The modern restaurant downstairs has outdoor seating underneath medieval arches facing the river. ⊠ *Limmatquai 54, Kreis 1* ⊕ *www.saffran.ch.*

KREIS 2

When Zürich's center got too cramped for 19th-century industrialists, they built themselves lakeside and hillside villas that still lend this neighborhood its quiet elegance.

Museum Rietberg. Dancing Indian Shivas, contemplative Tibetan thangkas, late-18th-century literary paintings from China, and royal Benin bronzes from Nigeria: these are just a few of the treasures in the prodigious gathering of non-European art on view. This is the only museum of its kind in Switzerland, with the main focus on Asia, Africa, and Ancient America. The main collection is on view in the huge underground Smaragd Building. The Villa Wesendonck, the famous Neoclassical jewel that was once a fabled home to Richard Wagner (it was for the lady of the house that he wrote his *Wesendonck Songs*) houses objects from India, the pre-Columbian Americas, Australia, and the Pacific Islands; there's more Indian, Islamic, and Oriental art in an adjacent museum, the Park-Villa Rieter. From the city center, follow Seestrasse south about 1¾ km (1 mile) until you see signs for the museum; or take Tram 7 to the Rietberg Museum stop. ⊠ *Gablerstr. 15, Kreis 2* ☎ *044/2063131* ⊕ *www.rietberg.ch* 🖃 *16 SF* ☉ *Tues.–Sun. 10–5, Wed. and Thurs. 10–8.*

KREIS 5: ZÜRICH WEST

Zürich West is one of the city's most happening districts. Empty warehouses from the city's machine industry days have been renovated, while others were torn down to make room for new glass-and-steel creations. The area is now chock-full of lofts, galleries, bars, restaurants, and dance clubs. The result is a swinging cultural center with a throbbing nightlife. The area is loosely bordered by Hardstrasse, Hardturmstrasse, and Pfingstweidstrasse; to get there by public transportation, take Tram 4, 13, or 17 to Escher Wyss Platz, or Tram 4 farther on to Schiffbau or Technopark. It's roughly a 10-minute trip from the Hauptbahnhof.

Kunsthalle (*Center of Contemporary Art*). Set in West Zürich, this is one of two major modern art venues on the top floors of a former brewery. Works are always cutting-edge: you can say you saw it here first. ⊠ *Limmatstr. 270, Kreis 5* ☎ *044/2721515* ⊕ *www.kunsthallezurich.ch* 🖃 *8 SF* ☉ *Tues., Wed., and Fri. noon–6, Thurs. noon–8, weekends 11–5.*

Migros Museum für Gegenwartskunst (*Migros Museum of Contemporary Art*). One floor below the Kunsthalle, this airy, white loft has the same focus—up-and-coming contemporary artists—but is privately funded by Switzerland's largest department store chain, Migros. Shows of recent work are interspersed with exhibitions from the extensive Migros collection, which includes works by Andy Warhol. The museum sponsors regular discussions with the artists, often in English. ⊠ *Limmatstr. 270, Kreis 5* ☎ *044/2772050* ⊕ *www.migrosmuseum.ch* 🖃 *8 SF* ☉ *Tues., Wed., and Fri. noon–6, Thurs. noon–8, weekends 11–5.*

Museum für Gestaltung (*Design Museum*). Envisioned as an academy devoted to design and applied arts, this imposing structure—designed by Adolf Steger and Karl Egender as a Functionalist manifesto—is today the main repository for Switzerland's important legacy in graphic design, posters, and applied arts. Innovative temporary exhibitions focus on architecture, poster art, graphic design, and photography, and recent shows included "The Plastic Garbage Project," "Formless Furniture," and "100 Years of Swiss Graphic Design." ⊠ *Ausstellungstr. 60, Kreis 5* ☎ *044/4466767* ⊕ *www.museum-gestaltung.ch* 🖃 *7 SF* ☉ *Thurs.–Tues. 10–5, Wed. 10–8.*

★ **Schweizerisches Landesmuseum** (*Swiss National Museum*). Housed in a gargantuan neo-Gothic building dating from 1889, the Swiss National Museum owns an enormous collection of objects dating from the Stone Age to modern times. There are costumes, furniture, early watches, and a great deal of military history, including thousands of toy soldiers reenacting famous battles. In the hall of arms there's a splendid mural, painted by the late-19th-century Bernese artist Ferdinand Hodler, called *The Retreat of the Swiss Confederates at Marignano.*

The Kunsthaus houses a fascinating collection of art.

The work depicts a defeat in 1515 by the French. ⊠ *Museumstr. 2, Kreis 5* ☎ *044/2186511* ⊕ *www.musee-suisse.ch* ✉ *7 SF* ⊗ *Fri.–Wed. 10–5, Thurs. 10–7.*

KREIS 7

Zürich's most luxurious residential neighborhood also is home to the zoo, wood-side walking paths with spectacular views of the Alps, and a cemetery that draws literary fans to James Joyce's grave.

James Joyce's Grave. The inimitable Irish author not only lived and wrote in Zürich, but died here as well. The city's most famous literary resident is buried in the Friedhof Fluntern (Fluntern Cemetery), not far from the Zürich Zoo. Atop his grave sits a contemplative statue of the writer, complete with cigar. A few steps away is the grave of another renowned author, Nobel Prize–winner Elias Canetti. The cemetery is adjacent to the Tram 6 terminus. ⊠ *Zürichbergstr. 189* ⊗ *Mar., Apr., Sept., and Oct., daily 7–7; May–Aug., daily 7 am–8 pm; Nov.–Feb., daily 8–5.*

Zürich Zoo. This is one of Europe's outstanding zoos, with more than 1,500 animals, including Asian elephants, black rhinos, seals, and big cats. One of the more unusual attractions is a huge dome stocked with flora and small free-range fauna you might encounter in a jungle in Madagascar, including frogs, lemurs, and the endangered Bernier's teal. Set in a tree-filled park, the zoo is just east of the city center and easily reached by Trams 5 and 6. ⊠ *Zürichbergstr. 221, Kreis 7* ☎ *044/2542505* ⊕ *www.zoo.ch* ✉ *22 SF* ⊗ *Mar.–Oct., daily 9–6; Nov.– Feb., daily 9–5.*

KREIS 8

This mainly residential area starts out as a long lakeside promenade dotted with swimming spots, rising up through several small parks to the Stiftung Sammlung E.G. Bührle, one of Zürich's most impressive private collections of Impressionist art.

Fodor's Choice ★ **Stiftung Sammlung E.G. Bührle.** A stunning array of Cézannes, Manets, Monets, and Degas make this eye-knocking collection one of the best art museums in Europe—unfortunately, since a spectacular robbery in 2008, visits are possible only on the first Sunday of each month. There are plans, however, to move the entire collection to Zürich's Kunsthaus by 2017. This fabled collection was put together in the space of a single decade. During the 1950s, Zürich industrialist E.G. Bührle purchased the finest offerings from the world's most prestigious art dealers, winding up with a collection studded with legendary Impressionist and Postimpressionist works, including Cézanne's *Self Portrait with Palette*, Renoir's *Little Irene*, and Degas's *Little Dancer*. Take Tram 11 from Bellevue, then Bus 77 from Hegibachplatz to the Altenhofstrasse stop. ⊠ *Zollikerstr. 172, Kreis 8* ☎ *044/4220086* ⊕ *www.buehrle.ch* 🖰 *25 SF* ⊗ *1st Sun. of each month.*

ZÜRICHSEE (LAKE ZÜRICH)

It's a bit too busy for waterskiing, but every other activity is on offer on this end of the beautiful lake, from swimming to walking along the promenade and people-watching.

This may be the only major city in the world where you can actually swim in the heart of downtown—as hundreds do on hot summer days at its four beaches (called "Badeanstalte," or "Badis" for short—literally bathing installations—and subject to 7 SF admission). Expect to find changing rooms, lockers, restaurants, and either soft green grass or wooden docks to lie on.

WINTERTHUR

Located 20 km (12 miles) northeast of Zürich, Winterthur made its fortune through the textile industry and blossomed thanks to prosperous merchants who developed a love of art. They bequeathed the town some notable art museums, including the sublime **Sammlung Oskar Reinhart Am Römerholz**; the **Villa Flora/Sammlung Hahnloser** (⊕ *www.villaflora. ch*), a Sezession-style villa with works by Van Gogh, Redon, Vuillard, and Matisse; and the **Museum Oskart Reinhart am Stadtgarten** (⊕ *www. museumoskarreinhart.ch*), which focuses on lesser-known painters that Reinhart hunted down, such as Caspar David Friedrich and Arnold Böcklin. To get here, take any one of the trains leaving from the Hauptbahnhof or the Bahnhof Stadelhofen in Zürich every hour. Once you arrive in Winterthur, take the "Museumsbus" (5 SF) from the train station's Sektor M; it runs daily except Monday and takes 15 minutes (the last return bus leaves the museum at 5 pm). By car, follow the autobahn signs for Winterthur–St. Gallen. Take the Winterthur-Ohringen exit onto Schaffhauserstrasse into town, then left on Rychenbergstrasse to Haldenstrasse.

Fodor'sChoice **Sammlung Oskar Reinhart "Am Römerholz"** (*Oskar Reinhart Collection*).
★ Lucas Cranach's *Portrait of Johannes Cuspinian,* Pieter Breughel the Elder's *Adoration of the Magi in the Snow,* Peter Paul Rubens's *Decius Mus,* Edouard Manet's *Au Café,* Toulouse-Lautrec's *Clownesse Cha-U-Kao*—you get the picture. This is one of the greatest private art collections in Switzerland, perhaps only rivaled by the Sammlung E.G. Bührle in Zürich. The jewel in the crown of Winterthur's art museums, Am Römerholz is virtually wallpapered with legendary paintings. Private collector Oskar Reinhart's most magnificent treasures are housed in his former villa "Am Römerholz," built in 1915 on the hill overlooking town. The collection ranges across five centuries, with pride of place going to 16th-century German and Early Dutch paintings, 17th-century French and Flemish paintings, and Impressionist masterworks. Works by Gerard David, Poussin, Daumier, Van Gogh, and nearly 200 other artists stagger the eye. ⊠ *Haldenstr. 95, Winterthur* ☎ *052/2692740* ⊕ *www. roemerholz.ch* 🗐 *12 SF* ☉ *Tues.–Sun. 10–5, open until 8 on Wed.*

WHERE TO EAT

Since the mid-1990s, Zürich's restaurant trade has boomed. The new establishments, both Swiss and international, tend to favor lighter, leaner meals served in bright spaces that often open out to the street. The traditional cuisine, no longer ubiquitous but still easily found, is called *nach Zürcher Art,* meaning "cooked in the Zürich style." Think meat, mushrooms, potatoes, butter, cream—an extremely rich cuisine, perfectly suited to the leaded-glass and burnished-oak guildhalls.

In exploring Zürich's core, you will want to enter at least one of these famous medieval "union clubhouses" scattered along the riverfront neighborhoods; the best way is to dine in one, as all but the Zunfthaus zur Meisen, the Zunfthaus zur Saffran, and the Zunfthaus zur Schmide have restaurants open to the public. On your way to the restroom, sneak a peek into their other dining rooms—they are, for the most part, museum-perfect in their leaded-glass and Gothic-wood detail.

Zürich's signature dish, which you'll encounter throughout both French and German Switzerland, is *Geschnetzeltes Kalbfleisch,* or in French *émincé de veau:* bite-size slices of milky veal (and sometimes veal kidneys) sautéed in butter and swimming in a rich brown sauce thick with cream, white wine, shallots, and mushrooms. Its closest cousin is *Geschnetzeltes Kalbsleber* (calves' liver), served much the same way. You may also find *Rösti,* a kind of hash-brown potatoes, and *Spätzli,* egg noodles that are either pressed through a sieve or snipped, gnocchi-style, and served in butter.

Another culinary must is Zürich's favorite portable food, sausage and *Bürli* (a crunchy roll), eaten separately, two-fisted style. The best are to be had at Bellevue at the Sterne-Grill; *Kalbsbratwurst* (veal) is mild, the smaller *Cervelat* (pork) saltier. Join the locals and munch away while waiting for a tram.

BEST BETS FOR ZÜRICH DINING

Fodor's Choice ★

Kaiser's Reblaube, p. 66
Kronenhalle, p. 68
Zum Kropf, p. 67
Zunfthaus zur Zimmer-
leuten, p. 69

Best by Price

$

Ah-Hua II, p. 70
Les Halles, p. 72
Odéon, p. 68
Rheinfelder Bierhaus,
p. 68

$$

Hiltl, p. 66

La Salle, p. 71

$$$

Caduff's Wine Loft, p. 71
Haus zum Rüden, p. 68
Kaiser's Reblaube, p. 66
Kindli, p. 66
Kronenhalle, p. 68

$$$$

Casa Ferlin, p. 68

Best by Cuisine

SWISS

Alpenrose, p. 71
Zum Kropf, p. 67
Zur Oepfelchammer, p. 69

MEDITERRANEAN

Casa Ferlin, p. 68

Best by Experience

ROMANTIC

Baur au Lac Rive
Gauche, p. 65
Kindli, p. 66
Zunfthaus zur Zimmer-
leuten, p. 69

KID-FRIENDLY

Swiss Chuchi, p. 69
Zeughauskeller, p. 66

Zürichers also have a definite sweet tooth: refined cafés draw crowds for afternoon pastries, and chocolate shops vie for the unofficial honor of making the best chocolate truffles in town.

Restaurants in Zürich have been smoke free by law since 2010—some offer smokers lounges, otherwise expect smoking at outdoor tables, where it is still allowed.

Prices in the reviews are the average cost of a main course or equivalent combination of smaller dishes at dinner or, if dinner is not served, at lunch. Use the coordinate (✛ B2) at the end of each listing to locate a site on the Where to Eat and Stay in Zürich map.

KREIS 1

LEFT BANK: THE ALTSTADT

$$$
ECLECTIC
✗ **Baur au Lac Rive Gauche.** Its nondescript entrance off a noisy street corner belies the light beige cubist decor inside, which attracts crowds of hip young business executives and expense-account padders open to the concept of dining to thumping chill-out music. Part and parcel of the noted Hotel Baur au Lac, this spot offers specialties that are light, trendy, and off-the-grill with names like "Dixie Chick"—grilled chicken breast—and "Found Nemo"—wild salmon with lime butter. "D for Two" offers minisamples of the dessert menu. The wine list taps Hotel Baur au Lac's impressive wine cellar. $ *Average main: 50*

SF ⊠ *Hotel Baur au Lac, Talstr. 1, Kreis 1* ☎ *044/2205060* ⊕ *www. agauche.ch* ⚐ *Reservations essential* ✛ *D6.*

$$ ✕ **Hiltl.** Founded in 1898, when vegetarians were regarded as "grass
VEGETARIAN   eaters," this restaurant has more than proved its staying power. It was
taken over in 1904 by Bavarian Ambrosius Hiltl, who married the
cook; the current patron, Rolf Hiltl, is their great-grandson. The enor-
mous buffet offers everything from curried chickpeas to stuffed jalape-
ños, from breaded cheese dumplings to peas with butter and mint. The
young business crowd stuffs the place full at lunch; DJs provide the
ambience on weekend evenings. $ *Average main: 27 SF* ⊠ *Sihlstr. 28,
Kreis 1* ☎ *044/2277000* ⊕ *www.hiltl.ch* ⚐ *Reservations essential* ✛ *C3.*

$$$ ✕ **Kaiser's Reblaube.** Get the most out of the Altstadt experience by eat-
SWISS   ing in one of its most beautiful medieval buildings, which dates back
Fodor'sChoice   to 1260. Goethe slept here, in a room named after him now used as
★   an extra dining room, the "Goethe Stübli." For the full effect, come
for the economical four-course Business Lunch (usually around 35 SF),
which may include cold apricot-tomato soup, duck liver mousse with
steamed mushrooms, lamb fillet with lentils, and—if you have room
left—crème brûlée. $ *Average main: 50 SF* ⊠ *Glockengasse 7, Kreis 1*
☎ *044/2212120* ⊕ *www.kaisers-reblaube.ch* ⚐ *Reservations essential*
🕓 *Closed Sun.* ✛ *E4*

$$$ ✕ **Kindli.** The meals served at this warm, inviting restaurant are prepared
SWISS   with seasonal ingredients. The results are such innovative dishes as rock
lobster with roasted pasta or sirloin of beef with mustard-onion butter
and roasted potatoes. Rich, colorful paintings, dark-wood paneling,
elegant bistro furnishings, and linen table settings add to the upscale,
warm comfort of the restaurant. $ *Average main: 50 SF* ⊠ *Pfalzg. 1,
Kreis 1* ☎ *043/8887678* ⊕ *www.kindli.ch* 🕓 *Closed Sun.* ✛ *E3*

$$ ✕ **Reithalle.** In a downtown theater complex behind Bahnhofstrasse, this
ECLECTIC   old military riding stable now does its duty as a noisy and popular res-
taurant. Its past is plain to see, as candles are perched on the mangers
and beams. Young locals share long tables arranged mess-hall-style to
sample international specialties—from curry to ostrich tenderloin—
many of them vegetarian, as well as an excellent list of open wines from
all over the world listed on the blackboard. In summer the courtyard
is lined with communal tables. $ *Average main: 30 SF* ⊠ *Gessnerallee
8, Kreis 1* ☎ *044/2120766* ✛ *C2.*

$$$ ✕ **Veltliner Keller.** Though its rich, carved-wood decor borrows from
SWISS   Graubündner Alpine culture, this dining spot is no tourist trap. The
house, built in 1325 and functioning as a restaurant since 1551, has
always stored Italian-Swiss Valtellina wines, which were carried over
the Alps to Zürich. There is a definite emphasis on the heavy and
the meaty, but the kitchen is flexible and reasonably deft with more
modern favorites as well: seafood in saffron sauce, chopped veal with
mixed mushrooms, and delicious fruit sorbets. $ *Average main: 50
SF* ⊠ *Schlüsselg. 8, Kreis 1* ☎ *044/2254040* ⊕ *www.veltlinerkeller.ch*
⚐ *Reservations essential* 🕓 *Closed weekends* ✛ *E4.*

$$ ✕ **Zeughauskeller.** Built as an arsenal in 1487, this enormous stone-and-
SWISS   beam hall offers hearty meat platters and a variety of beers and wines
in comfortable Germanic chaos. The waitstaff is harried and brisk,

When the weather's nice, try one of Zürich's casual Right Bank cafés.

especially at lunchtime, when crowds are thick. Unlike the shabbier beer halls in Niederdorf, this one is clean and bourgeois, reflecting its Paradeplatz location. They're not unaccustomed to tourists—menus are posted in English, Japanese, and at least 10 other languages—but locals consider this their home away from home. $ *Average main: 30 SF* ⊠ *Bahnhofstr. 28, at Paradepl., Kreis 1* ☎ *044/2201515* ⊕ *www. zeughauskeller.ch* ✛ *D5.*

$$
SWISS
Fodor's Choice
★

✕ **Zum Kropf.** Under the mounted boar's head and restored century-old murals depicting gallivanting cherubs, businesspeople, workers, and shoppers share crowded tables to feast on generous hot dishes and a great selection of sausages. The *Leberknödl* (liver dumplings) are tasty, and the perch, a local specialty, is breaded and baked and comes with tartar sauce and steamed potatoes. The *Apfelküchli* (fried apple slices) are tender and sweet. The bustle and clatter provide a lively, sociable experience, and you'll more than likely get to know your neighbor. $ *Average main: 35 SF* ⊠ *In Gassen 16, Kreis 1* ☎ *044/2211805* ⊕ *www.zumkropf.ch* ☾ *Closed Sun.* ✛ *E4*

$$$
SWISS

✕ **Zunfthaus zur Waag.** With its magnificent Renaissance-inspired facade, this airy guildhall, with whitewashed woodwork and leaded-glass windows looking out to the Fraumünster, remains a lovely dining spot. The Zunft-Saal (guildhall) is a pinewood showpiece, which greatly outshines the main restaurant—a rather dull Biedermeier room. The kitchen offers seasonal dishes such as fillet of perch in almond butter with spinach, or veal stuffed with local smoked bacon and served with potato mousse and seasonal vegetables. To drink in the impressive architecture, opt for outside tables on the edge of the cobblestone square in warm weather. $ *Average main: 50 SF* ⊠ *Münsterhof 8, Kreis 1* ☎ *044/2169966* ⊕ *www.zunfthaus-zur-waag.ch* ✣ *G6.*

RIGHT BANK: NIEDERDORF AND OBERDORF

$$$$
ITALIAN

✕**Casa Ferlin.** Crimson velvet wall hangings, a baronial fireplace, and 19th-century brocade banquettes add up to one of Zürich's most sumptuous interiors. Happily, the food is even more impressive, and the quality of what may be Zürich's best homemade pasta keeps regulars coming back. This family-run establishment, in business for almost a century, offers excellent traditional Italian dishes such as beef ravioli and beef fillet in green-pepper sauce. The lunch crowd is mostly financial bigwigs, while evenings attract local families. $ *Average main: 70 SF* ⊠ *Stampfenbachstr. 38, Kreis 6* ☎ *044/3623509* ⊕ *www.casaferlin.ch* ⌕ *Reservations essential* ⊘ *Closed weekends and mid-July–mid-Aug.* ✣ *F1*

$$$
SWISS

✕**Haus zum Rüden.** The most ambitious of the city's many Zunfthaus dining places, this fine restaurant is also the most spectacular, combining a wooden barrel-vaulted ceiling and 30-foot beams. Slick modern improvements—including a glassed-in elevator—manage to blend intelligently with the ancient decor and old-world chandeliers. Innovative entrées might include lobster-coconut bisque with dried prawns and mangos, or sautéed goose liver on balsamico grapes. The river views are especially impressive at night; ask for a window table. $ *Average main: 65 SF* ⊠ *Limmatquai 42, Kreis 1* ☎ *044/2619566* ⊕ *www. hauszumrueden.ch* ⊘ *Closed weekends and mid-July–mid-Aug.* ✣ *F4*

$$$
SWISS
Fodor'sChoice
★

✕**Kronenhalle.** From Stravinsky, Brecht, and Joyce to Nureyev, Deneuve, and Saint-Laurent, this beloved landmark has always drawn a stellar crowd. Every panel of gleaming wood wainscoting frames works by Picasso, Braque, Miró, Chagall, or Matisse, collected by patroness-hostess Hulda Zumsteg, who owned the restaurant from 1921 until her death in 1985. The tradition is carried on by the family trust, and robust cooking is still served in hefty portions: veal steak in morel sauce, duck *à l'orange* with red cabbage, and Spätzli. Unless you're a recognizable celebrity, make sure to insist on a table in the main dining room; ordinary mortals are otherwise seated in a less exciting room upstairs. $ *Average main: 65 SF* ⊠ *Rämistr. 4, Kreis 1* ☎ *044/2629900* ⊕ *www. kronenhalle.com* ⌕ *Reservations essential* ✣ *G6.*

$
CAFÉ

✕**Odéon.** This historic café–restaurant was once frequented by the pre-revolutionary Vladimir Lenin, who nursed a coffee while he read the daily papers. These days you can nurse a coffee in the morning or afternoon, or choose from a menu of burgers, sandwiches, and pasta at lunch or dinner. Afterwards it becomes a champagne bar that draws an increasingly gay clientele as the night wears on. $ *Average main: 23 SF* ⊠ *Limmatquai 2, Kreis 1* ☎ *044/2511650* ⊕ *www.odeon.ch* ✣ *G6.*

$
SWISS

✕**Rheinfelder Bierhaus.** Locals know this Niederdorf institution by its unsettling nickname: Bluetig Tuume, or the "Bloody Thumb." The venue is nonetheless often packed with happy patrons. It is famous locally for its *entrecôte café de Paris* (steak with herb butter), sausage standbys, and the pride of the Spanish/Romansch owners, a homemade paella that must be ordered in advance. Snag one of the few tables lined up outside in warm weather—a steady stream of passersby in this pedestrian zone makes for good entertainment. $ *Average main: 23 SF* ⊠ *Marktg.*

19, Kreis 1 ☎ 044/2512991 ▭ No credit cards ✛ F4.

$$ ✕ **Swiss Chuchi.** Right on the Nieder-
SWISS dorf's main square, Hirschenplatz, this squeaky-clean Swiss-kitsch restaurant has an airy, modern decor, with Alpine-rustic chairs. It serves good home-cooked national specialties: Geschnetzeltes, Rösti, Leberli, bratwurst, schnitzel, and battered fish with french fries and tartar sauce—the gang's all here. An added attraction if you're visiting in summer: fondue and raclette, usually winter dishes, are served year-round. Excellent lunch menus are rock-bottom cheap and served double quick. There's outdoor seating on the cobblestone pedestrian square in warm weather. $ Average main: 35 SF ✉ Roseng. 10, Kreis 1 ☎ 044/2669696 ⊕ www.hotel-adler.ch✛ F3.

$$ ✕ **Zum Grünen Glas.** This French-inclined international restaurant in a
FRENCH quiet corner of the Niederdorf is part of the trend toward lighter food and portions that don't overflow your plate. You might try beef tartare with wasabi and mango chutney, or lamb curry in yogurt mint sauce, then finish with a creamy slice of Napoléon. Wainscoting, parquet floors, and crisp white tablecloths make for a comfortable dining room; an outside courtyard is open in summer. $ Average main: 40 SF ✉ Untere Zäune 15, Kreis 1 ☎ 044/2516504 ⊕ www.gruenesglas.ch ⊘ Closed Sun. ✛ G4

$$$ ✕ **Zunfthaus zur Zimmerleuten.** Dating from 1708 and containing elements
SWISS that go back 850 years, this was the carpenters', masons' and coopers'
Fodor'sChoice guild. After a fire destroyed its top two floors in 2007, the building was
★ painstakingly restored by specialists, who uncovered a rare fresco dating back to the 14th century in one of the small dining halls. Its main restaurant is again drawing locals and tourists alike to its fabulous dark-wood halls, now polished to an amazingly high gloss, where the focus is on traditional dishes prepared for today's lighter tastes, such as chicken breast with lime risotto and seasonal vegetables. $ Average main: 50 SF ✉ Marktg. 20, Kreis 1 ☎ 044/2505363 ⊕ www.zunfthaus-zimmerleuten.ch ✛ F4.

$$ ✕ **Zur Oepfelchammer.** Dating from 1801, this was once the haunt of
SWISS Zürich's beloved writer Gottfried Keller. One section is a dark and heavily graffitied bar, with sagging timbers and slanting floors; there are also two welcoming little dining rooms with coffered ceilings and plenty of carved oak and damask—opt for the cozy, charming Gaststube (not the more staid Stübli). Traditional meat dishes—calves' liver, Geschnetzeltes Kalbfleisch—are lightened up with fresh seasonal veggies. The place is

Don't miss Zunfthaus zur Zimmerleuten, one of the city's medieval guildhalls-turned restaurant

always packed, and service can be slow, so stake out a table and plan to spend the evening. ■TIP→ Guest who succeed in swinging around the room's famous wooden rafters three times wins free wine for their table. You'd be amazed at the number of diners who make the attempt. $ *Average main: 40 SF* ⊠ *Rindermarkt 12, Kreis 1* ☎ *044/2512336* ⊕ *www. oepfelchammer.ch* ⊘ *Closed Sun. and Mon.* ✛ *F4*

KREIS 2

$$$ ✕ **Seerose.** As soon as it even vaguely looks like it'll be warm enough, the
SWISS hip deck-shoe crowd drives, runs, cycles, or even sails to one of the best places on the lake. It not only has its own dock, it *is* its own dock, jutting far out and offering fabulous views. The food isn't bad either: seasonal ingredients make the difference for dishes such as beef tournedos with matchstick-thin french fries, or spaghetti with lobster. Sunglasses required. $ *Average main: 50 SF* ⊠ *Seestr. 493, Kreis 2* ☎ *044/4816383* ⊕ *www.dinning.ch* ✛ *D6.*

KREIS 4

$ ✕ **Ah-Hua II.** Since opening their first tiny restaurant in 1998, the Te
THAI family has given locals an education in authentic Thai food. So many flocked to those premises that a second larger venue was opened in 2006, which has a clean café feel and is usually packed during lunch and dinner with young hipsters jonesing for rice noodle soup with octopus and vegetables, or beef with Thai basil, Kaffir lime leaves, and green

beans. $ *Average main: 20 SF* ⊠ *Ankerstr. 110, Kreis 4* ☎ *043/3668535* ⊕ *www.ah-hua.ch* ☉ *Closed Mon.* ✛ *A3*

$$$ ✕ **Caduff's Wine Loft.** In a 19th-century whitewashed former warehouse,
EUROPEAN industrial lighting, parquet floors, and the occasional strategically
placed cactus set the minimalist tone for the kitchen's delicious, simple
cuisine. The market determines the menu, which could be anything
from veal shoulder with spring potatoes to entrecôte with tomato-basil
gnocchi and seasonal vegetables. If you can't decide on a wine, you're
welcome to browse downstairs in the candlelit cellar—there are about
1,000 bottles to choose from. $ *Average main: 50 SF* ⊠ *Kanzleistr.
126, Kreis 4* ☎ *044/2402255* ⊕ *www.wineloft.ch* ☉ *Closed Sun.* ✛ *A3*

KREIS 5

$$ ✕ **Alpenrose.** It doesn't get more Swiss than this: the ingredients, the reci-
SWISS pes, the wines, and the decor are all Helvetian. The interior is elegantly
casual, with wainscoting and etched-glass windows, linen tablecloths,
a mounted chamois head, and paintings of the Matterhorn and other
well-known landmarks. Enjoy seasonal dishes such as *Engadiner pizo-
kel* (flour dumplings) with ham, or duck breast with dried plum sauce
and mashed potatoes. The owners' devotion to local ingredients means
the menu often changes. $ *Average main: 35 SF* ⊠ *Fabrikstr. 12, Kreis
5* ☎ *044/2713919* ☉ *Closed Mon. and mid-July–mid-Aug.* ✛ *E1*

$$ ✕ **Angkor.** A bit of Siem Reap in the middle of Zürich West: the lavish
ASIAN interior is full of stone carvings and wood latticework that seem right
out of Ta Prohm, minus the jungle. The menu is huge and includes gen-
erous amounts of green curry, oyster sauce, and ginger, covering India,
Thailand, Vietnam, and Japan. The lunch specials are a good deal for
those on a budget, while multicourse meals satisfy bigger appetites.
Tables double in number with outside summer seating on the square.
$ *Average main: 38 SF* ⊠ *Giessereistr. 18, Kreis 5* ☎ *043/2052888*
⊕ *www.restaurant-angkor.ch* ✛ *E1.*

$$$ ✕ **Clouds.** Boasting fabulous views over the entire city, the lake, and the
EUROPEAN distant mountains thanks to floor-to-ceiling windows (you'll see more
during the daylight hours than after dark), this 35th-floor eatery is cur-
rently on everyone's list. Start with a simple, elegant dish like ravioli
with egg yolk and ricotta, then fill up completely on pork medallions
with crispy sausage rings and baby onions in sherry vinegar. $ *Aver-
age main: 46 SF* ⊠ *Prime Tower, Maagplatz 5, Kreis 5* ☎ *044/4043000*
⊕ *www.clouds.ch* ⌕ *Reservations essential* ✛ *E1.*

$$ ✕ **La Salle.** This is a favorite haunt of theatergoers heading for the
EUROPEAN Schauspielhaus Schiffbauhalle—it conveniently shares the same build-
ing. The glass, steel, and concrete interior mixes well with the brick
elements left from the original factory building. Beneath an enormous
Murano-glass chandelier, elegantly dressed patrons enjoy delicate dishes
such as tagliatelle with black tiger prawns, langoustine in a lemon, chili
and olive sauce, or beef fillet in green pepper cream sauce. The hefty
wine list can be sampled at the apricot-color bar, where a smaller ver-
sion of the menu is available. $ *Average main: 35 SF* ⊠ *Schiffbaustr. 4,
Kreis 5* ☎ *044/2587071* ⊕ *www.lasalle-restaurant.ch* ✛ *E1.*

$ MEDITERRANEAN 🍴 **Les Halles.** This old warehouse space in Zürich West has not so much been renovated as cleaned up and then highlighted with an eclectic mix of antiques and '50s collectibles, all of which are for sale. The fare is health-conscious—made from organic ingredients sold in the attached health food store—and includes couscous with vegetables, tomatoes, and eggplant, or mussels with french fries. In summer, snag a table on the multitiered veranda out front. [$] *Average main: 20 SF* ✉ *Pfingstweidstr. 6, Kreis 5* ☎ *044/2731125* 🌐 *www.les-halles.ch* ⊕ *E1.*

WHERE TO STAY

For expanded hotel reviews, visit Fodors.com.

A string of small boutique hotels has popped up in the last decade, all with a strong focus on design, sleeping comfort, and generous bathrooms—think large bed covered with a fluffy down comforter and soft pillows, looking onto an outsized flat-screen TV that invariably includes video games and a selection of movies, and a white-tiled bathroom with black slate floors and lots of mirrors. On our list we've included the Seefeld, Widder, and Zürichberg.

Another passion taking over the city—in fact the country—is the trend toward so-called "wellness" vacations. Putting a new spin on the 19th- and early-20th-century tradition of the Swiss sanatorium—where convalescent patients from all over the world came to Switzerland to cleanse their lungs with Alpine air—hotels here are adding pools, saunas, steam rooms, and special areas for such ministrations as hot stone massages or body wraps.

Smaller venues like the Hotel Seefeld have simply added a cosmetics studio to cover their customers' skin-care needs. Upmarket houses cover everything from full-body peels, sports massages, and ice wraps (Park Hyatt) all the way through to the comprehensive spa services of the Dolder Grand Hotel, which also includes kotatsu footbaths, an aroma pool, and indoor and outdoor whirlpools. If you're still not feeling like a whole new you, there's even a clinic complete with a team of doctors for cosmetic surgery.

Prices in the reviews are the lowest cost of a standard double room in high season, including taxes. Use the coordinate (⊕ B2) at the end of each listing to locate a site on the Where to Eat and Stay in Zürich map.

KREIS 1

LEFT BANK: THE ALTSTADT

$$$ HOTEL 🏨 **Alden Splügenschloss.** Constructed at the turn of the 20th century as luxury apartments, this property consists entirely of suites, all done in beige with chocolate leather accents and filled with such amenities as flat-screen televisions. **Pros:** a very quiet neighborhood; so luxurious even Midas would feel at home. **Cons:** the location—in a spare banking district—is a little out of the way for sightseeing; very few restaurants or shopping opportunities nearby. [$] *Rooms from: 400 SF*

⊠ *Splügenstr. 2, Kreis 1* ☎ *044/2899999* ⊕ *www.alden.ch* ↩ *22 suites* |◯| *Breakfast* ✛ *B6*.

$$$$ 🏨 **Baur au Lac.** Austria's Empress Elisabeth was the first prominent figure
HOTEL   to stay at this hotel, whose signature classic room decor gleams with
rich fabrics and Empire mirrors. **Pros:** old-world style plus ultramodern
comforts. **Cons:** service can be a little stuffy. $ *Rooms from: 870 SF*
⊠ *Talstr. 1, Kreis 1* ☎ *044/2205020* ⊕ *www.bauraulac.ch* ↩ *84 rooms,*
42 suites |◯| *No meals* ✛ *D6*.

$$$ 🏨 **Haus zum Kindli.** This charming little bijou hotel is as artfully styled as
HOTEL   a magazine ad, with subtle grays and beiges underscoring the inviting
white bed linens and original bath fixtures refurbished to match modern
needs. **Pros:** just steps from where the town was founded; run home to
the bathroom while you're shopping—it's that close. **Cons:** no parking;
a little dark during winter. $ *Rooms from: 400 SF* ⊠ *Pfalzg. 1, Kreis*
1 ☎ *043/8887676* ⊕ *www.kindli.ch* ↩ *20 rooms* |◯| *Breakfast* ✛ *E3*.

$$$$ 🏨 **Park Hyatt.** A few blocks from the lake, the wide-open spaces of the
HOTEL   city's first American-style luxury hotel are accented in black marble,
rich maple, and lots of gleaming glass. **Pros:** more space than normally
found in a Swiss hotel; extremely friendly service; excellent restaurant.
Cons: neighborhood is business-oriented rather than tourist-oriented;
the glass-and-steel style lacks an "old world" experience. $ *Rooms*
from: 850 SF ⊠ *Beethovenstr. 21, Kreis 1* ☎ *043/8831234* ⊕ *zurich.*
park.hyatt.ch ↩ *142 rooms, 12 suites* |◯| *No meals* ✛ *C6*.

$$$$ 🏨 **Savoy Baur en Ville.** Directly on Paradeplatz, at the hub of the banking,
HOTEL   shopping, and sightseeing districts, this is one of Zürich's 19th-century
landmarks. **Pros:** you can't get more downtown than this; Sprüngli, a
must for chocolate lovers, is across the street. **Cons:** conservative to
the point of stuffiness; a business-minded atmosphere. $ *Rooms from:*
690 SF ⊠ *Am Paradepl., Poststr. 12, Kreis 1* ☎ *044/2152525* ⊕ *www.*
savoy-zuerich.ch ↩ *112 rooms, 8 suites* |◯| *Breakfast* ✛ *E5*.

$$$$ 🏨 **Sheraton Neues Schloss.** Managed by the Sheraton chain, this intimate
HOTEL   hotel in the business district, a few minutes from Paradeplatz and a
block from the Tonhalle, offers a warm welcome, good service, and
classic decor in earth tones, modernized by flat-screen TVs. **Pros:** one
block from the lake; excellent service. **Cons:** kids are free, but only if
they sleep with you in your bed. $ *Rooms from: 520 SF* ⊠ *Stockerstr.*
17, Kreis 1 ☎ *044/2869400* ⊕ *www.sheratonneuesschloss.com* ↩ *58*
rooms |◯| *No meals* ✛ *C6*.

$$$$ 🏨 **Widder.** Zürich's most captivating hotel was created when 10 adja-
HOTEL   cent medieval houses were gutted and combined—now steel fuses with
Fodor's Choice   ancient stone and timeworn wood. **Pros:** the spectacular Room 210; the
★   more modern Room 509. **Cons:** there are no "cons," since this place is
perfect. $ *Rooms from: 755 SF* ⊠ *Rennweg 7, Kreis 1* ☎ *044/2242526*
⊕ *www.widderhotel.ch* ↩ *42 rooms, 7 suites* |◯| *No meals* ✛ *E4*.

$$$$ 🏨 **Zum Storchen.** The central location of this airy 600-year-old struc-
HOTEL   ture—tucked between the Fraumünster and Kirche St. Peter on the
Fodor's Choice   gull-studded bank of the Limmat River—is stunning. **Pros:** expert and
★   friendly service; charming Old Town location; the views. **Cons:** mosqui-
toes in summer (don't sleep with the window open); can be noisy during
local festivals—and there are many. $ *Rooms from: 760 SF* ⊠ *Weinpl.*

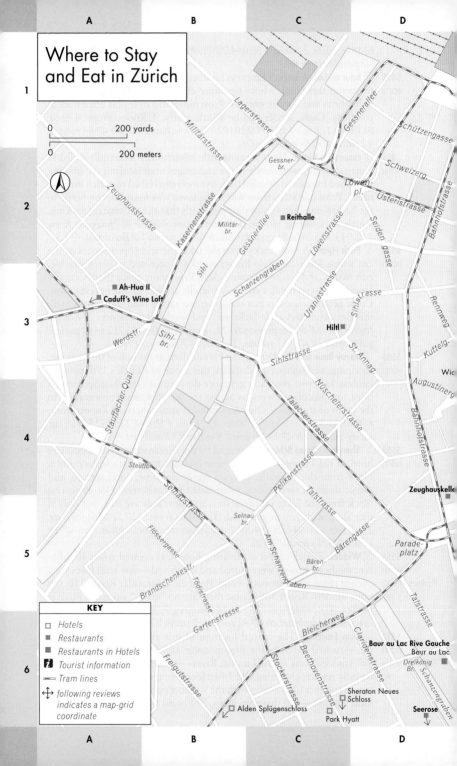

Where to Stay and Eat in Zürich

A B C D

1

0   200 yards
0   200 meters

2

Lagerstrasse
Militärstrasse
Gessner-br.
Gessnerallee
Gessnerallee
Reithalle
Löwen-pl.
Schützengasse
Schweizerg.
Üsteristrasse
Bahnhofstrasse
Löwenstrasse
Seiden gasse
Kasernenstrasse
Militär-br.
Sihl
Zeughausstrasse
Uraniastrasse
Schanzengraben

Ah-Hua II
Caduff's Wine Loft

3

Werdstr.
Sihl-br.
Sihlstrasse
Hiltl
Sihlstrasse
St. Annag.
Rennweg
Kuttelg.
Wic
Augustinerg
Bahnhofstrasse
Nüschelerstrasse
Talackerstrasse

4

Stauffacher-Quai
Stauffbr.
Pelikanstrasse
Talstrasse
Zeughauskelle

5

Selnaustrasse
Selnau-br.
Flössergasse
Todtstrasse
Am Schanzengraben
Bären-br.
Parade-platz
Talstrasse

6

Brandschenkestr.
Gartenstrasse
Freigutstrasse
Stockerstrasse
Beethovenstrasse
Bleicherweg
Claridenstrasse
Baur au Lac Rive Gauche
Baur au Lac
Dreikönig-Br.
Schanzengraben
Sheraton Neues Schloss
Alden Splügenschloss
Park Hyatt
Seerose

KEY

☐ Hotels
■ Restaurants
■ Restaurants in Hotels
🛈 Tourist information
— Tram lines
⊕ following reviews indicates a map-grid coordinate

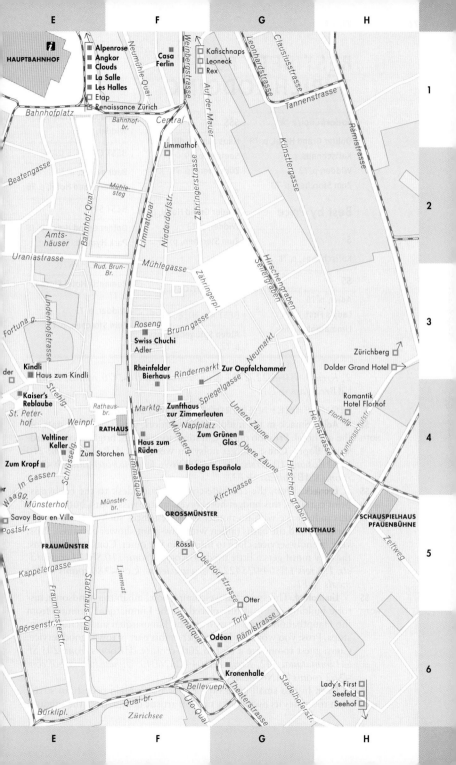

E

HAUPTBAHNHOF

Neumühle-Quai

Bahnhofplatz

Beatengasse

Mühle-steg

Amts-häuser

Uraniastrasse

Bahnhof-Quai

Rud. Brun-Br.

Fortuna g.

Lindenhofstrasse

Kindli
Haus zum Kindli

der

Kaiser's Reblaube

St. Peter-hof

Stehlg.

Veltliner Keller

Zum Kropf

Waagg.

In Gassen

Münsterhof

Savoy Baur en Ville

Poststr.

FRAUMÜNSTER

Kappelergasse

Fraumünsterstr.

Börsenstr.

Bürklipl.

Zürichsee

F

Casa Ferlin

Weinbergstrasse

Central

Limmathof

Bahnhof-br.

Zähringerstrasse

Mühlegasse

Niederdorfstr.

Limmatquai

Roseng.

Swiss Chuchi
Adler

Brunngasse

Rheinfelder Bierhaus

Zähringerpl.

Rindermarkt

Spiegelgasse

Zunfthaus zur Zimmerleuten

Marktg.

Rathaus-br.

RATHAUS

Haus zum Rüden

Münsterg.

Napfplatz

Zum Grünen Glas

Bodega Española

Schlüsselg.

Zum Storchen

Weinpl.

Münster-br.

GROSSMÜNSTER

Rössli

Oberdorfstrasse

Stadthaus-Quai

Limmat

Limmatquai

Otter

Torg.

Odéon

Kronenhalle

Bellevuepl.

Quai-br.

Ulo-Quai

Stadthaus-Quai

Theaterstrasse

G

Kafischnaps
Leoneck
Rex

Auf der Mauer

Künstlergasse

Hirschengraben

Seilergraben

Neumarkt

Zur Oepfelchammer

Untere Zäune

Obere Zäune

Kirchgasse

Hirschengraben

Heimstrasse

KUNSTHAUS

Rämistrasse

H

Leonhardstrasse

Clausiusstrasse

Tannenstrasse

Rämistrasse

Zürichberg

Dolder Grand Hotel

Romantik Hotel Florhof

Florhofg.

Kantonsschulstr.

SCHAUSPIELHAUS PFAUENBÜHNE

Zeltweg

Stadelhoferstr.

Lady's First
Seefeld
Seehof

Alpenrose
Angkor
Clouds
La Salle
Les Halles
Etap
Renaissance Zürich

1

2

3

4

5

6

BEST BETS FOR ZÜRICH LODGING

Fodor's Choice ★

Dolder Grand Hotel, p. 78
Kafischnaps, p. 78
Widder, p. 73
Zum Storchen, p. 73

Best by Price

$

Kafischnaps, p. 78

$$

Adler, p. 76
Lady's First, p. 79
Limmathof, p. 76

$$$

Haus zum Kindli, p. 73
Seefeld, p. 79
Zürichberg, p. 79

$$$$

Dolder Grand Hotel, p. 78
Widder, p. 73
Zum Storchen, p. 73

Best by Experience

BEST ARCHITECTURE

Alden Splügenschloss, p. 72
Dolder Grand Hotel, p. 78
Widder, p. 73

BEST GRANDE DAME

Baur au Lac, p. 73
Dolder Grand Hotel, p. 78

BEST SPA

Dolder Grand Hotel, p. 78
Park Hyatt, p. 73

MOST ROMANTIC

Romantik Hotel Florhof, p. 77
Widder, p. 73
Zum Storchen, p. 73

2, Kreis 1 ☎ 044/2272727 🌐 www.storchen.ch 🛏 70 rooms, 5 suites 🍴 Breakfast ✥ E4.

RIGHT BANK: NIEDERDORF AND OBERDORF

$$ HOTEL **Adler.** Smack in the middle of Niederdorf, this is a smart, state-of-the-art hotel. **Pros:** no phone call surcharges; clean, bright rooms; hardwood floors. **Cons:** can get noisy on weekends. [$] *Rooms from: 210 SF ✉ Roseng. 10, Kreis 1 ☎ 044/2669696 🌐 www.hotel-adler.ch 🛏 52 rooms 🍴 Breakfast ✥ F3.*

$$ HOTEL **Leoneck.** From the cowhide-covered front desk to the edelweiss-print curtains, this budget hotel revels in its Swiss roots, but balances this indulgence with no-nonsense conveniences such as built-in pine furniture and tile baths (albeit with cow-print shower curtains). **Pros:** very friendly service; close to the action but quiet. **Cons:** small rooms; the cow motif gets a little tired. [$] *Rooms from: 210 SF ✉ Leonhardstr. 1, Kreis 1 ☎ 044/2542222 🌐 www.leoneck.ch 🛏 80 rooms 🍴 No meals ✥ F1.*

$$ HOTEL **Limmathof.** This spare but welcoming hotel inhabits a handsome, historic building and is ideally placed on the Limmatquai, minutes from the Hauptbahnhof and steps from the Limmatquai and Central tram stops. **Pros:** you won't find it cheaper in this part of town; good service. **Cons:** guest rooms are a bit too 20th century. [$] *Rooms from: 205 SF ✉ Limmatquai 142, Kreis 1 ☎ 044/2676040 🌐 www.limmathof.com 🛏 62 rooms 🍴 No meals ✥ F1.*

$ HOTEL **Otter.** In this small hotel on the Oberdorf's main pedestrian street, each room has its own kooky take on artistic design, from the subdued

WHERE SHOULD I STAY?

	Neighborhood Vibe	Pros	Cons
The Altstadt	This is where half of everything in Kreis 1 is: churches, museums, restaurants, and the lake.	Everything's within walking distance (and often in the pedestrian zone); home to many elegant restaurants and hotels.	Not car-friendly; some parts are noisy; expensive.
Niederdorf and Oberdorf	This is where the other half of everything in Kreis 1 is: more churches, museums, restaurants, and the lake.	Almost exclusively car-free; very lively nightlife for every budget; a well-preserved architectural example of Medieval "Mitteleuropa."	Not a good spot if you have a car; can get very noisy due to revelers on summer nights.
Kreis 5	If you squint, it's a teeny-tiny bit like New York's East Village. Home to one of the cheapest hotels, cutting-edge galleries, and a warehouse-style nightlife.	Very lively entertainment district; draws local hipsters; a great place for the budget-conscious interested in a more modern experience.	Nightlife gets raucous well into the morning on weekends; although ridiculously clean by most urban standards, still the seediest part of town.
Kreis 6	This quiet area is a 10-minute walk to Bahnhofstrasse. Perfect for families and those who like to sleep with the window open.	Very little noise; residential neighborhood atmosphere.	Main sights are in the other Kreises; little-to-no nightlife.
Kreis 7	This hillside neighborhood is home to many of the city's most affluent residents and arguably its most luxurious hotel.	Lush and quiet, often with fabulous views of the city, the lake, and the mountains beyond.	Restaurants are few and far between; the nightlife almost nonexistent; if you don't have a car, you'll be depending on public transit or expensive taxis.
Kreis 8	Depending on the season, Zürich's "seashore" draws people in bathing suits or their smartest "promenading" clothes on their way past street musicians to swim or sample the variety of eateries.	The perfect place to decompress after "too much" culture; offering a wide selection of restaurants.	Can get overcrowded in summer, when street parking is next to impossible; basically a straight line: the farther out you go, the longer it will take to get back.

gray-and-violet decor of the Lila Room to the boudoir feel of the Purpur Room. **Pros:** very central; good service; fun styling. **Cons:** some noise from the downstairs bar; sharing a bath may be too personal for some. $ *Rooms from: 155 SF* ✉ *Oberdorfstr. 7, Kreis 1* ☎ *044/2512207* ⊕ *www.hotelotter.ch* 🛏 *16 rooms, 15 with shared bath* ℹ️ *Breakfast* ✚ *G6.*

$$$ 🏨 **Romantik Hotel Florhof.** Replete with an away-from-it-all atmosphere,
HOTEL this is a pretty-as-a-picture 17th-century merchant's mansion. **Pros:** close to everything, yet in a quiet oasis; the terrace with its Neptune fountain alone is worth the trip. **Cons:** terraced restaurant is closed on

Sunday. $\boxed{\$}$ *Rooms from: 430 SF* ⊠ *Florhofg. 4, Kreis 1* 🕾 *044/2502626* ⊕ *www.florhof.ch* ⮌ *33 rooms, 2 suites* ✎ *Breakfast* ✥ *H4.*

$$$ 🔲 **Rössli.** Ultrasmall but friendly, this hotel is in the heart of the Ober-
HOTEL   dorf. **Pros:** family-style service; nicely detailed styling. **Cons:** small rooms; can get noisy during local festivals. $\boxed{\$}$ *Rooms from: 330 SF* ⊠ *Rösslig. 7, Kreis 1* 🕾 *044/2567050* ⊕ *www.hotelroessli.ch* ⮌ *16 rooms, 1 suite* ✎ *Breakfast* ✥ *F5.*

$$$ 🔲 **Seehof.** Offering the best of both worlds, this lodging is in a quiet
HOTEL   neighborhood, yet is conveniently close to the opera, theaters, and the lake. **Pros:** small but very nice bathrooms; a good in-house sushi restaurant. **Cons:** on a narrow and charmless side street. $\boxed{\$}$ *Rooms from: 330 SF* ⊠ *Seehofstr. 11, Kreis 1* 🕾 *044/2545757* ⊕ *www.hotelseehof.ch* ⮌ *19 rooms* ✎ *Breakfast* ✥ *H6.*

KREIS 5

$ 🔲 **Etap.** Working on the principle that cheap should only mean inex-
HOTEL   pensive, this chain hotel is a dependable pick. **Pros:** deep in the heart of Zürich West; great value. **Cons:** charmless; one side looks out onto an industrial park. $\boxed{\$}$ *Rooms from: 110 SF* ⊠ *Technoparkstr. 2, Kreis 5* 🕾 *044/2762000* ⊕ *www.etaphotel.com* ⮌ *160 rooms* ✎ *No meals* ✥ *E1.*

$$$ 🔲 **Renaissance Zurich Tower Hotel.** Towering above the nightclubs and
HOTEL   galleries that surround it, this hip hotel offers a cutting-edge alternative to Zurich's historic gilded lodgings. **Pros:** cool spot for design buffs and hipsters; everything is brand-new. **Cons:** neighborhood may be too industrial for some; not walking distance most attractions. $\boxed{\$}$ *Rooms from: 340 SF* ⊠ *Turbinenstrasse 20, Kreis 5* 🕾 *044/6303030* ⊕ *www.renaissancezurichtower.com* ⮌ *252 rooms, 48 suites* ✎ *No meals* ✥ *E1.*

KREIS 6

$ 🔲 **Kafischnaps.** Away from the throb of downtown but only a 15-minute
B&B/INN   walk back, this is the best deal in town for anyone on a budget. **Pros:**
Fodor's Choice   beautifully designed rooms; very hip café; great value. **Cons:** far from
★   the madding crowd; check-in can be slow if the café is busy. $\boxed{\$}$ *Rooms from: 118 SF* ⊠ *Kornhausstr. 57, Kreis 6* 🕾 *043/5388116* ⊕ *www.kafischnaps.ch* ⮌ *5 rooms* ✎ *No meals* ✥ *F1.*

KREIS 7

$$$$ 🔲 **Dolder Grand Hotel.** Zürich has a new pinnacle of hotel luxury—or
HOTEL   should we say a new old pinnacle: this 1899 building, resplendent with
Fodor's Choice   towering turrets and timbered balconies, has been completely refur-
★   bished and is now flanked by two glass-and-steel wings that mirror the natural surroundings. **Pros:** gorgeous views; high-end service; very good restaurants. **Cons:** off the beaten track; a bit pricey; standard rooms are small, considering the cost. $\boxed{\$}$ *Rooms from: 970 SF* ⊠ *Kurhausstr. 65, Kreis 7* 🕾 *044/4566000* ⊕ *www.thedoldergrand.com* ⮌ *114 rooms, 59 suites* ✎ *No meals* ✥ *H3.*

The Widder's historic location and room decor offer a glimpse into the city's past.

$$$
HOTEL **Zürichberg.** Starkly and colorfully modern, the lobby of the Schneck-enhaus (Snail House) annex here includes a mini version of the white ramp of the Guggenheim Museum in New York. **Pros:** good restaurant; marvelous view of the city and the Alps from the terrace. **Cons:** a 100-yard schlep from the tram stop to the hotel. $ *Rooms from: 470 SF* ✉ *Orellustr. 21, Kreis 7* ☎ *044/2683535* ⊕ *www.zuerichberg.ch* 🛏 *66 rooms* ⭐ *Breakfast* ✛ *H3.*

KREIS 8

$$
HOTEL **Lady's First.** Once a rooming house for country girls attending school in the big city, this boutique hotel has two floors that cater exclusively to women—a first in Switzerland. **Pros:** very pro-female, but also respect-ful of the "modern man." **Cons:** bathrooms were added as niches into each room, so there's less noise insulation. $ *Rooms from: 290 SF* ✉ *Mainaustr. 24, Kreis 8* ☎ *044/3808010* ⊕ *www.ladysfirst.ch* 🛏 *28 rooms* ⭐ *Breakfast* ✛ *H6.*

$$$
HOTEL **Seefeld.** In the heart of the lakeside district—close to restaurants, the opera, and movie theaters—this friendly, no-nonsense hotel is a real find. **Pros:** the in-house restaurant is a local attraction; the roof terrace offers amazing views. **Cons:** on a busy street; directly between tram stops—you'll be doing a lot of walking. $ *Rooms from: 360 SF* ✉ *Seefeldstr. 63, Kreis 8* ☎ *044/3874141* ⊕ *www.hotel-seefeld.ch* 🛏 *64 rooms* ⭐ *Breakfast* ✛ *H6.*

The views don't get much better than from the riverfront Zum Storchen hotel

NIGHTLIFE AND THE ARTS

NIGHTLIFE

Of all the Swiss cities, Zürich has the liveliest nightlife. The Niederdorf is Zürich's nightlife district, with cut-rate hotels, strip joints, and bars crowding along Marktgasse, which becomes Niederdorfstrasse. On Thursday and weekend nights the streets flow with a rowdy crowd of club- and bar-hoppers. In Zürich West, the locales are all a shade hipper. In winter things wind down between midnight and 2 am, but come summer most places stay open until 4 am.

KREIS 1
BARS
Almodobar. A welcoming bar that tips a wink to Spain's most famous film director, Almodobar is an oasis for the young hipster crowd, set in a quiet neighborhood. ⊠ *Bleicherweg 68, Kreis 1* ☎ *043/8444488* ⊕ *www.almodobar.ch*.

Barfüsser. Established in 1956, Barfüsser claims to be one of the oldest gay bars in Europe. It has comfortable lounge chairs and space to mix and mingle. There's also excellent sushi. ⊠ *Spitalg. 14, Kreis 1* ☎ *044/2514064* ⊕ *www.barfuesser.ch*.

Café Central Bar. In the Hotel Central, Café Central Bar is a popular neo-Art Deco café by day and a piano bar by night. ⊠ *Central 1, Kreis 1* ☎ *044/2515555* ⊕ *www.central.ch*.

Cranberry. This popular place stocks a broad selection of rums and ports. It also has an upstairs cigar room. ⊠ *Metzgerg. 3, Kreis 1* ☎ *044/2612772* ⊕ *www.cranberry.ch.*

James Joyce Pub. The James Joyce Pub is a beautifully paneled Irish pub where the wood is as dark as the Guinness. ⊠ *Pelikanstr. 8, off Bahnhofstr., Kreis 1* ☎ *044/2211828* ⊕ *www.jamesjoyce.ch.*

Jules Verne Panorama Bar. This wine bar boasts a wraparound view of downtown. ⊠ *Uraniastr. 9, Kreis 1* ☎ *043/8886666* ⊕ *www.jules-verne.ch.*

Kronenhalle. The narrow bar at the Kronenhalle draws mobs of well-heeled locals and internationals for its prize-winning cocktails. ⊠ *Rämistr. 4, Kreis 1* ☎ *044/2511597* ⊕ *www.kronenhalle.ch.*

Metropol. Sit in the covered arcade at Metropol and select something from the extensive drinks list, which includes absinthe, elaborate cocktails, and a wide variety of whiskeys and whiskies. ⊠ *Fraumünsterstr. 12, Kreis 1* ☎ *044/2005900* ⊕ *www.metropole-restaurant.ch.*

Odéon. Serving a young, arty crowd until 4 am, Odéon is a cultural icon: a place where Mata Hari danced, Lenin and Trotsky plotted the revolution, and James Joyce scrounged drinks. It gets gayer as the evening wears on, but everyone goes because the place is so chic. ⊠ *Limmatquai 2, Kreis 1* ☎ *044/2511650* ⊕ *www.odeon.ch.*

DANCING

Adagio. The medieval-theme Adagio books classic rock, jazz, and tango musicians for well-dressed thirtysomethings. ⊠ *Gotthardstr. 5, Kreis 1* ☎ *044/2063666* ⊕ *www.adagio.ch.*

Kaufleuten. This local landmark draws a well-dressed, upwardly mobile crowd. It's a popular performance space for established artists, such as Suzanne Vega and Nina Hagen, looking for an intimate venue. The Rolling Stones once showed up unannounced for an impromptu concert. ⊠ *Pelikanstr. 18, Kreis 1* ☎ *044/2253333* ⊕ *www.kaufleuten.ch.*

Mascotte. Blasting everything from funk and soul to house and techno, Mascotte is popular with all ages. ⊠ *Theaterstr. 10, Kreis 1* ☎ *044/2524481* ⊕ *www.mascotte.ch.*

KREIS 5
BARS

Basilica. At Basilica, hipsters lounge in an Italianate setting of red velvet and marble statues. ⊠ *Heinrichstr. 237, Kreis 5* ☎ *043/3669383.*

Hard One. Once you get past the name, you'll find that Hard One has great views of Zürich West and a good choice of champagnes. ⊠ *Heinrichstr. 269, Kreis 5* ☎ *044/4441000* ⊕ *www.hardone.ch.*

Hotel Rivington and Sons. Decorated with vintage hotel and bar fixtures dating back to the 1930s, Hotel Rivington and Sons is one of the hippest bars of the moment. ⊠ *Prime Tower, Hardstr. 201, Kreis 5* ☎ *043/3669082* ⊕ *www.hotelrivingtonandsons.ch.*

I.Q. Not just for intellectuals, I.Q. has a fully stocked whiskey bar. ⊠ *Hardstr. 316, Kreis 5* ☎ *044/4407440* ⊕ *www.iqbar.ch.*

Zürich's Old Town is charming under a coat of snow in winter.

Spheres. This bar and bookstore stocks a great selection of international magazines. ☒ *Hardturmstr. 66, Kreis 5* ☎ *044/4406622* ⊕ *www. spheres.cc.*

DANCING

Indochine. Zürich's exclusive set meets at Indochine, whose gorgeous interior evokes Southeast Asia. The music floats between pop, disco, house, and techno. ☒ *Limmatstr. 275, Kreis 5* ☎ *044/4481111* ⊕ *www. club-indochine.com.*

KREIS 8

BARS

Purpur. At this Moroccan-style lounge you can enjoy your drinks lying down on a heap of throw pillows while DJs mix ambient sounds. ☒ *Seefeldstr. 9, Kreis 8* ☎ *044/4192066* ⊕ *www.purpurzurich.ch.*

KREIS 11

DANCING

Oxa Dance Hall. A legendary techno club, Oxa Dance Hall draws thousands of casual young Swiss who dance all night (and often well into the next day). Take Tram 11 from the Hauptbahnhof to the Messe/Hallenstadion station in Oerlikon. ☒ *Andreastr. 70, Kreis 11* ☎ *044/3116033* ⊕ *www.oxa.com.*

THE ARTS

Despite its small population, Zürich is a big city when it comes to the arts; it supports a top-rank orchestra, an opera company, and a theater. Check *Zürich News*, published weekly in English and German, or

"Züri-tipp," a German-language supplement to the Thursday edition of the daily newspaper *Tages Anzeiger.*

Züricher Festspiele. The city's annual Züricher Festspiele—a celebration of opera, ballet, music, theater, and art—runs from late June through mid-July. ☎ *044/2699090* ⊕ *www.zuercher-festspiele.ch.*

Ticketcorner. Tickets for almost any event can be purchased in advance from Ticketcorner. ☎ *0900/800800* ⊕ *www.ticketcorner.ch.*

Musik Hug. Depending on the event, Musik Hug makes reservations. ✉ *Limmatquai 28–30, Kreis 1* ☎ *044/2694100* ⊕ *www.musikhug.ch.*

Jecklin. The music store Jecklin sells tickets for various music events. ✉ *Rämistr. 30, Kreis 1* ☎ *044/2537676* ⊕ *www.jecklin.ch.*

KREIS 1

FILM

Zürich Film Festival. The Zürich Film Festival takes place every year from late September to early October. ☎ *044/2866000* ⊕ *www.zff.com.*

MUSIC

Tonhalle. The Zürich Tonhalle Orchestra, named for the concert hall that was inaugurated by Brahms in 1895, enjoys international acclaim. There are also solo recitals and chamber music programs. The season runs from September through July, and tickets sell out quickly. ✉ *Claridenstr. 7, Kreis 1* ☎ *044/2063434* ⊕ *www.tonhalle.ch.*

OPERA

Opernhaus. The permanent company at the Opernhaus is widely recognized and difficult to drop in on if you haven't booked well ahead, but single seats sometimes can be secured at the last minute. Performances are held from September through July. ✉ *Theaterpl., Kreis 1* ☎ *044/2686666* ⊕ *www.opernhaus.ch.*

THEATER

Schauspielhaus. The venerable Schauspielhaus has a long history of cutting-edge performances—during World War II it was the only German-language theater in Europe that remained independent. Nowadays its main stage presents finely tuned productions, while experimental works are presented in the Keller (cellar). ✉ *Rämistr. 34, Kreis 1* ☎ *044/2587777* ⊕ *www.schauspielhaus.ch.*

Theaterspektakel. During late August and early September the Theaterspektakel takes place, with circus tents housing avant-garde theater and experimental performances on the lawns by the lake. ✉ *Mythenquai* ☎ *044/4123030* ⊕ *www.theaterspektakel.ch.*

KREIS 4

FILM

Movies in Zürich are serious business, with many films presented in the original language. Check newspapers and the ubiquitous posters, and watch for the initials *E/d/f,* which means an English-language version with German (Deutsch) and French subtitles.

Metropol. The Metropol has a great sound system and the largest screen in Zürich. ✉ *Badenerstr. 16, Kreis 4* ☎ *0900/556789* ⊕ *www.kitag.com.*

Set in a quiet hillside neighborhood, the elegant Dolder Grand Hotel resembles a fairy-tale castle.

KREIS 5
THEATER
Schauspielhaus Schiffbauhalle. The sister stage of Schauspielhaus Pfauen-bühne, the Schauspielhaus Schiffbauhalle is home to large-scale productions in German. ✉ *Schiffbaustr. 4, Kreis 5* ☎ *044/2587777* ⊕ *www. schauspielhaus.ch.*

SHOPPING

Many of Zürich's designer boutiques lie hidden along the narrow streets between Bahnhofstrasse and the Limmat River. Quirky bookstores and antiques shops lurk in the sloping cobblestone alleyways leading off Niedorfstrasse and Oberdorfstrasse. The fabled Bahnhofstrasse—famous because it's reputedly the most expensive street in the world—is dominated by large department stores and extravagantly priced jewelry shops.

Bahnhofstrasse. The store-lined Bahnhofstrasse concentrates much of Zürich's most expensive (from elegant to gaudy) goods at the Paradeplatz end.

Löwenstrasse. There's a pocket of good stores around Löwenstrasse, southwest of the Hauptbahnhof.

Niederdorf. The Niederdorf offers inexpensive fashions that appeal to young people, as well as antiques and antiquarian bookshops.

Storchengasse. The west bank's Altstadt, along Storchengasse near the Münsterhof, is a focal point for high-end designer stores.

Many city-center stores are open weekdays 9–8, Saturday 8–5. Most close on Sunday, with the exception of the shops at the Hauptbahnhof, the Stadelhofen train station, and the airport. Many smaller shops, particularly in the Niederdorf area, open later in the morning or the early afternoon and are closed entirely on Monday.

KREIS 1

BOOKS

Biblion. The antiquarian bookshops in the upper streets of the Niederdorf area are rich with discoveries—and most have selections of books in English. Biblion specializes in antique books and bindings. ⊠ *Kirchg. 40, Kreis 1* ☎ *044/2613830* ⊕ *www.biblion.ch*.

EOS Buchantiquariat Benz. The EOS Buchantiquariat Benz is a superb general bookshop spread over two storefronts. Both sell secondhand books as well as antiquarian tomes. ⊠ *Kirchg. 17 and 22, Kreis 1* ☎ *044/2615750* ⊕ *www.eosbooks.ch*.

Medieval. This eclectic shop sells books, music, and replicas of medieval artifacts, including reproduction medieval shoes, jewelry, and water bottles. ⊠ *Spiegelg. 29, Kreis 1* ☎ *044/2524720* ⊕ *www.lemaroc.ch*.

CHOCOLATE

Teuscher. Teuscher is as famous for its extravagantly wrapped packages as for its amazing chocolates and sweets. There are two other locations on Bahnhofstrasse in Kreis 1. ⊠ *Storcheng. 9, Kreis 1* ☎ *044/2115153* ⊕ *www.teuscher.com*.

COLLECTIBLES

In the center of town virtually every street has some kind of antiques or collectibles shop. Especially intriguing are "modern antiques" shops, which carry odds and ends from recent decades.

1000-Objekte. This shop has modern and antique glass and collectibles. ⊠ *Schoffelg. 3, Kreis 1* ☎ *043/2110300* ⊕ *www.1000-objekte.ch*.

Eselstein. Look for items from the 1950s through the 1970s ranging from lamp shades to standing ashtrays, plus such finds as Russian samovars. ⊠ *Stadelhoferstr. 42, Kreis 1* ☎ *044/2611056* ⊕ *www.eselstein.com*.

DEPARTMENT STORES

COOP. Popular with locals, COOP is cheap and cheerful. ⊠ *Theaterstr. 18, Kreis 1* ☎ *043/2688700* ⊕ *www.coop.ch*.

CHOCOLATE SOUVENIRS

It's hard to fight constant cravings for decadent chocolates when you're walking around Zürich, thanks to the many chocolate confiseries (candy stores), especially the branches of **Teuscher** (⊠ *Storcheng. 9* ☎ *044/2115153* ⊠ *Bahnhofstr. 46* ☎ *044/2111390* ⊠ *Jelmoli, Bahnhofstr. at Seidengasse* ☎ *044/2204387* ⊠ *Felix Café am Bellevue, Bellevueplatz 5y* ☎ *044/2518060*). The shops blaze with boxes of pralines and champagne truffles all wrapped up in stunning fabrics, silk roses, and troll figurines. The beautiful packaging makes fine keepsakes.

Grieder is one of the top shops on the ultra-ritzy Bahnhofstrasse.

Globus. There is a pricey but irresistible delicatessen in the basement of Globus, which sells men's and women's designer clothes and housewares. ✉ *Bahnhofstr. and Löwenpl., Kreis 1* ☎ *044/2266060* ⊕ *www. globus.ch.*

Jelmoli. Switzerland's biggest department store, Jelmoli has top-notch brand-name merchandise and swarms of staffers. ✉ *Bahnhofstr. and Seideng., Kreis 1* ☎ *044/2204411* ⊕ *www.jelmoli.ch.*

Manor. Dependable and affordable, Manor is on the Bahnhofstrasse. ✉ *Bahnhofstr. 75, Kreis 1* ☎ *044/2295699* ⊕ *www.manor.ch.*

MARKETS

Bürkliplatz. There's a flea market from 6 am to 3:30 pm every Saturday from May to October on the Bürkliplatz. ✉ *Lake end of Bahnhofstr., Kreis 1* ⊕ *www.zuerich.com.*

Christmas market. A Christmas market is held in the main train station and along Niederdorfstrasse starting in early December.

Rosenhof. There's a curio market on the Rosenhof every Thursday from 10 to 9 and Saturday from 10 to 4 between April and Christmas. ✉ *Niederdorfstr. and Marktg., Kreis 1* ⊕ *www.zuerich.com.*

MEN'S CLOTHES

Grieder. Zürich's most elegant department store, Grieder carries designs by Armani and Zegna, among others. ✉ *Bahnhofstr. 30, Kreis 1* ☎ *044/2243636* ⊕ *www.bongenie-grieder.ch.*

Trois Pommes. Trois Pommes is the central boutique of a series of designer shops scattered through the Storchengasse area. The racks are heavily stacked with such high-profile international designers as Jil Sander,

Versace, Donna Karan, and Dolce & Gabbana. ⊠ *Weggeng. 1, Kreis 1* ☎ *044/2124710* ⊕ *www.troispommes.ch.*

TOYS

AHA. AHA sells hypnotic optical-illusion gifts in styles and sizes to suit all ages. ⊠ *Spiegelg. 14, Kreis 1* ☎ *044/2510560* ⊕ *www.aha-zurich.ch.*

Pastorini Spielzeug. This shop is a four-story mother lode of original and creative playthings, many hand-carved. ⊠ *Weinpl. 3, Kreis 1* ☎ *044/2287070* ⊕ *www.pastorini.ch.*

WOMEN'S CLOTHES

En Soie. This boutique stocks sometimes gleaming, sometimes raw-textured silks. Although the fabrics are sophisticated, there's still an element of whimsy. ⊠ *Strehlg. 26, Kreis 1* ☎ *044/2115902* ⊕ *www. ensoie.ch.*

Miu Miu. See what designs Miuccia Prada's gotten into her head at Miu Miu. ⊠ *Storcheng. 16, Kreis 1* ☎ *044/2128318* ⊕ *www.miumiu.com.*

RAZZO. For quality vintage clothing, go to RAZZO, where Zürich's well-heeled ladies sell their "old" things. ⊠ *Rindermarkt 23, Kreis 1* ☎ *044/2622859* ⊕ *www.razzo2ndhand.ch.*

Sonja Rieser. At Sonja Rieser the selection of gorgeous handmade hats runs from elegant to wild. ⊠ *Neumarkt 1, Kreis 1* ☎ *044/2513847* ⊕ *www.sonjarieser.ch.*

SPAS

Zürich's spas are known as "wellness centers" and focus more on baths, saunas, and massages than on beauty treatments. Mostly attached to hotels, wellness centers can include everything from outdoor pools with views of the city to private treatments rooms where you can order a relaxing rubdown. Some also offer medical procedures, including plastic surgery.

Dolder Grand Spa. Zürich's most extravagant spa does everything from manicures to cosmetic surgery. Part of the Dolder Grand Hotel, the 13,000-square-foot spa has a classic look with plenty of with Japanese touches. It uses products by Kerstin Florian, La Prairie, Amala, and Horst Kirchberger to pamper guests in private suites equipped with treatment couches, soaking tubs, and fireplaces. Personal trainers are on hand get you into shape. A "medical wellness" team can assess your health and develop a regimen to balance your physical and mental well-being. Doctors offer advice and treatment for "fine-tuning your physical features" in a medical facility attached to the hotel. ⊠ *Kurhausstr. 65, Kreis 7* ☎ *044/4566000* ⊕ *www.thedoldergrand.com* ☞ *Hair salon, hot tubs, sauna, steam room. Gym with: cardiovascular machines, free weights, weight-training equipment. Services: aromatherapy, body wraps, cosmetic surgery, facials, manicures, massage, pedicures, scrubs, tinting, waxing. Classes and programs: aerobics, body sculpting, cycling, fitness analysis, meditation. $190 60-min massage, $450 150-min packages.*

Fitnesspark Hamam Münstergasse. The highlight of this wellness center in the middle of the Niederdorf is a luxurious underground Turkish-style hammam. The treatment includes a warm herbal steam bath, a body scrub with a traditional *kese* glove, a hot herbal steam bath, a hot-stone relaxation space, and finally a relaxation room with herbal drinks and snacks. There are women-only rooms for the more intimate stops on the circuit, while the rest of the areas are mixed. A massage treatment using rhassoul clay from the Atlas Mountains in Morocco is a specialty. ⊠ *Blaufahnenstr. 3, Kreis 1* ☎ *058/5688182* ⊕ *www.fitnesspark. ch* ☞ *Hot tub, sauna, steam room. Gym with: cardiovascular machines, free weights, weight-training equipment. Services: massage. $43 admission to hammam, $63 including massage.*

Labo. One of Zürich's classic day spas offers the full package of face, skin, and body treatments for her and him. Centrally located for quick pit stops, the ambience is quiet and relaxing. Asian accents in the minimalist space enhance the experience. With friendly, professional therapists, the spa does everything from the usual mani-pedis and facials to special treatments for expecting mothers to sybaritic rituals like the "Cocoon," which includes an aroma bath, leg and foot peeling, and a full-body massage. The massage menu boasts 15 different techniques from all over the world. ⊠ *Talacker 41, Kreis 1* ☎ *043/4973440* ⊕ *www. labospa.ch* ☞ *Services: aromatherapy, body wraps, facials, manicures, massage, pedicures, scrubs, tinting, waxing. $150 60-min massage, $300 2-hr packages.*

Thermalbad & Spa Zurich. Off the beaten track but already a big draw with hiptsters and locals since its opening in January 2011, these extensive Irish-Roman thermal baths include a rooftop pool. Benefitting from the same natural spring as the brewery that used to operate on this site, the spa focuses on bathing, with the offering of massages, scrubs, and body wraps. The rooftop pool has a great view over the city and is therefore very popular—expect crowds on sunny days and evenings. Tuesdays are reserved for women. ⊠ *Brandschenkestr. 150, Kreis 2* ☎ *044/205 9650* ⊕ *www.thermalbad-zuerich.ch* ☞ *Hot tub, sauna, steam room. Services: body wraps, massage, scrubs. $32 admission.*

Eastern Switzerland and Liechtenstein

APPENZELL, SCHAFFHAUSEN, ST. GALLEN

WORD OF MOUTH

"Check out the 'Barfussweg,' the barefoot hiking path. We did this several years ago. Gently rolling hills (no mountainous paths) through meadows and cow pastures (love that permeating scent) and past brooks."

—Mokka4

WELCOME TO EASTERN SWITZERLAND AND LIECHTENSTEIN

TOP REASONS TO GO

★ **A bibliophile's paradise:** Admire the UNESCO-inscribed library at the Abbey of St. Gallen, which features an Egyptian mummy and 100,000 ancient books.

★ **The cows finally come home:** Take part in an Appenzell Alpfahrt festival, when cows are herded up into the nearby mountain slopes (in spring) and back down (in fall).

★ **Colorful medieval architecture:** St. Gallen, Schaffhausen, and Stein-am-Rhein are teeming with colorful frescoes, half-timber buildings, dragon-clad steeples, and ornate bay windows.

★ **The Rhine maidens:** See Europe's third-largest river as it snakes its way to Germany. Take a lunch-boat ride, swim in the pristine river, or cycle along the river's grassy banks, lorded over by storybook castles.

★ **Swiss cheese:** Pungent Appenzeller is beloved by the Swiss. Using a 700-year-old recipe, this cow's milk cheese is aged and washed with a secret herbal brine.

1 Schaffhausen and the Rhine. A trip from the Rhine Falls through Schaffhausen and upriver to the more tranquil village of Stein-am-Rhein transports you back to medieval and Renaissance times. The house facades, alive with colorful frescoes and bay windows, attract tourists by the busload.

2 Bodensee to Wallensee. Vast and windy, the Bodensee—also known as Lake Constance—is a favorite of visiting Swiss and Germans who come for its mellow vibe. Creative and hardworking St. Gallen's biggest draw is its manuscript-stuffed Abbey Library (as well as a picturesque Old Town full of great public arts, tasty restaurants, and a thriving theater scene). Wallensee's gorgeous, tranquil, cobalt blue lake is backed by the dramatically steep Churfirsten range.

3 Liechtenstein. The last remnant of the Holy Roman Empire, this tiny castle-topped principality offers an excellent contemporary art museum and breathtaking hikes.

GETTING ORIENTED

Quiet cousins to fast-paced, international Zürich, the eastern cantons often play the wallflower to more spectacular Alpine landscapes. Lush and hilly, with orchards, farms, and gardens, their northern edges are bordered by the romantic Rhine, now a swimming, biking, and kayaking paradise. Mt. Säntis (8,200 feet), beloved by hikers and skiers, stands guard at the east. The landscape is dotted with wildflower-strewn meadows, forest-capped hills, and hidden lakes that range from deep turquoise to icy blue. All are dwarfed by enormous Bodensee, also known as Lake Constance.

GERMANY

Untersee

Stein-am-Rhein

Konstanz

Gottlieben

Kreuzlingen

GERMANY

Bodensee

Romanshorn

A7 Frauenfeld

Amriswil

Wil

Rorschach

Gossau

A1

St. Gallen
2

Oberriet

Appenzell

Wattwil

Rhein river

AUSTRIA

ALPSTEIN

Nesslau

Haag

CHURFIRSTEN

Buchs

i LIECHTENSTEIN
3

A3

Walensee

Sargans

Vaduz

Näfels

Murg

Triesenberg

FLUMSER BERGE

A3

A13

Malbun

Sargans

Landquart

A3

0 ——— 10 mi

0 ——— 10 km

EATING WELL IN EASTERN SWITZERLAND

Eastern Switzerland's cuisine is the country's least cosmopolitan, but includes some of its heartiest and tastiest dishes. Specialties from Appenzell, St. Gallen, Thurgau, and Schaffhausen bear names that defy pronunciation, like Chäs Tschoope (fried bread cubes with cheese and cream) and *Chäshappech* (cheese-and-beer batter funneled into snail-shell shapes, then deep-fried). *St. Galler Kalbsbratwurst* is a popular sausage made from veal, milk, and bacon, and *Mostbröckli* is a gamey air-dried beef worth sampling.

Regional wines from Thurgau and Schaffhausen are notable, but so is Appenzeller beer, which is found across Switzerland. For once vegetarians have something to celebrate in otherwise meat-loving Switzerland. Appenzeller cheese has a robust flavor that comes from a secret herbal brine that reportedly includes roots, leaves, flowers, seeds, and bark. Chääsflade (cheese pie) and silky cheese soup are a few other must-try dishes, whether or not you're a vegetarian.

Don't leave without trying a regional sausage variety (above). Treat yourself to some of the country's most popular traditional dishes, from Spätzle (above, right) to Rösti (below, right).

SPECIAL TREATS

Head to **Böhli** (✉ 9 *Engelgasse, Appenzell* ☎ *071/7881570* ⊕ *www. boehli-appenzell.ch*) for *biber*, molded honey, spice, and almond-paste bakes, and for *chrempfli*, turnovers with hazelnut filling. *St. Galler Klostertorte*, with jam peeking through a lattice crust, is available in the tearoom and shop at **Chocolaterie am Klosterplatz** (✉ *20 Gallustrasse, St. Gallen* ☎ *071/2225770* ⊕ *www. chocolateriesg.ch*).

CHEESES

The earthy and pungent Appenzeller cheese dates back more than 700 years and is known as the "spiciest" cheese in Switzerland, but really it's just herbal. It adds a nice addition to the local fondue. If you're in the mood for something milder and creamier, Tilsit is your best bet. Unique to Thurgau, the cheese takes its name from the town of Tilsit, Russia, where an immigrant Swiss cheese maker helped develop the recipe before coming home to set up shop.

SAUSAGES

In St. Gallen, specialty sausages abound. Try the St. Galler Bratwurst, also known as the St. Galler Kalbsbratwurst, a white, unsmoked variety that custom dictates must be made with pork, at least 50% veal, and milk or milk powder. When ordered in St. Gallen, the legendary Olma-Bratwurst must be eaten with a hard piece of bread known as a *Bürli,* and never with mustard.

RÖSTI

These aren't your average hash browns. Deemed the national dish of Switzerland, *Rösti* is a dinner or lunch dish that is essentially grated, fried potatoes, covered with a variety of deliciously greasy toppings—bacon, bits of lard, ham, eggs, and cheese, or served alongside favorite regional main dishes. While Rösti can be found all over Switzerland, it is especially loved by Swiss-Germans,

so much so that the border between the French and German-speaking areas of Switzerland is known as the Röstigraben, which literally means Rösti ditch.

DUMPLINGS

Popular throughout Central and Eastern Europe, dumplings have been elevated to an art form in Switzerland. These tender egg noodles come in many forms and are known as *Spätzle,* or if in a smaller, rounded form as *Chnöpfli* (literally, little sparrows or little buttons, respectively). Eat them boiled then fried in butter until golden brown and crispy, or oozing with melted cheese, a preparation known as *Chäschnöpfli.*

SWEETS

Don't let all the cheese and sausages fool you: eastern Switzerland has sweet treats to finish off any meal. Fruit and nuts reign supreme in Switzerland, and you'll be hard-pressed to find a dessert without either. Thurgau is famous for its apple orchards, and there's no better way to enjoy a healthy dessert than to snack on the region's lightly dried apple rings. Those who yearn for a buttery treat can delight in *Hüppen*—these long, crisp waffle cookies are sometimes filled with chocolate and are thought to take their name from the Greek *hopyes,* meaning wafer.

Updated by
Adam H.
Graham

Despite its proximity to Zürich, this Germanic region, with Germany to the north and Austria to the east, maintains a personality apart—a personality that often plays the wallflower when upstaged by more spectacular touristy regions. Happily, the truth is that the region does not lack for a satisfying variety: its north is dominated by the romantic Rhine; the region is lush with orchards and gardens, a generous share of mountains (including Mt. Säntis, at roughly 8,200 feet), and swimmable lakes and rivers, as well as the enormous Bodensee (Lake Constance).

Because the east draws fewer crowds, those who do venture here find a pleasant surprise: this is Switzerland sans kitsch, sans the hard sell, where the people live out a natural, graceful combination of past and present. And although it's a prosperous region, with its famous history of textile manufacturing and agriculture, its inns and restaurants cost noticeably less than those in adjoining areas. They can also lack the amenities found in more cosmopolitan parts of the country.

The cantons of Glarus, Schaffhausen, Thurgau, St. Gallen, and Appenzell harbor some of Switzerland's oldest traditions. In the northern part of the region are the old Rhine city of Schaffhausen, the dramatic Rheinfall, and the preserved medieval village of Stein-am-Rhein. The Bodensee occupies the northeastern corner of Switzerland, just below Germany. Farther south is the textile center of St. Gallen, where lace is created for high-profile designers like Karl Lagerfeld. A magnificent Baroque cathedral lords over the valley. The hilly Appenzell region and the resort area of the Toggenburg Valley are lower-key destinations. The tiny principality of Liechtenstein lies just across the eastern border, within easy driving distance.

Although the cities have plenty of energy, the countryside in these parts has changed little over the years. In the plateau valley of Appenzell, women were prohibited from voting in cantonal elections until the federal court intervened on their behalf in 1991 (federal law had granted women the national vote in 1971). On the last Sunday in April in Appenzell, you still can witness the *Landsgemeinde,* an open-air election on cantonal issues counted by a show of hands.

Architecture along the Rhine resembles that of Old Germany and Austria, frequent features being half-timbers and rippling red-tile roofs. In cities like Schaffhausen, masterpieces of medieval frescoes decorate town houses, many of which have ornately carved bay windows called oriels. In the country, farmhouses are often covered with fine, feathery wooden shingles as narrow as Popsicle sticks, which weathering has turned to chinchilla gray. Appenzell has its own famous architecture: tidy, narrow boxes painted cream, with repeated rows of windows and matching wood panels. The very countryside itself—conical green hills, fruit trees, belled cows, neat yellow cottages—resembles the naive art it inspires.

EASTERN SWITZERLAND AND LIECHTENSTEIN PLANNER

WHEN TO GO

The four seasons are clearly defined here: nicely balanced periods of sun and rain bring springtime blossoms and flowers with a vengeance, thanks to the many orchards and fields; summer temperatures zoom upward to between 21°Celsius (70°F) and 32°C (90°F), depending on whether it's a dry or wet one; the abundance of deciduous trees in this region means splashes of color in a crisp-aired, windy fall; and winter dumps lots of snow and brings temperatures hovering around –5°C (23°F) in town, down to –25°C (–13°F) on some mountaintops.

Summers in eastern Switzerland provide the best weather and activities; spring and fall are good alternatives. Although most places in this region are not too terribly crowded even in summer, Schaufassen can become thick with tour buses and Stein-am-Rhein chocked with spandex-clad cyclists looping around the Bodensee. Go earlier in the day or on a weekday when crowds are a bit thinner.

PLANNING YOUR TIME

This is the more tranquil slice of Switzerland; a great place to enjoy the scenery while tooling down back roads or gazing out the train window at the cow-dotted meadows on the way to the next quaint town. Take along a stack of books to read on the hotel balcony or a picnic lunch for your stop in a field en route. In winter, pick a ski resort or a large town such as Schaffhausen or St. Gallen as your home base—unless you're looking for complete, peaceful seclusion. In summer, swimming, kayaking, hiking, and cycling opportunities abound near the Rhine and the Bodensee, so pack a bathing suit, your cycling shorts, and take a leisurely lunch-boat ride.

GETTING HERE AND AROUND

As in all parts of Switzerland, the trains are superb—punctual, afford-able, and comfortable— and offer stunning mountain views you won't see from behind the wheel of a rental car. Another great way to see the region is by the boats that ply the Rhine and the Bodensee.

AIR TRAVEL

Zürich Airport, just north of Zürich, is about 48 km (30 miles) south of Schaffhausen, about 75 km (46 miles) west of St. Gallen, and 130 km (81 miles) northwest of Liechtenstein.

BOAT AND FERRY TRAVEL

There's regular year-round service on the Bodensee through Schweizer Bodensee Schiffahrtsgesellschaft, though fewer boats run in winter. The Schweizerisches Schiffahrtgesellschaft Untersee und Rhein ship com-pany offers a boat ride on the Rhine with romantic views of story-book castles, citadels, and monasteries. Boats run regularly up- and downstream, docking at Schaffhausen, Stein-am-Rhein, Gottlieben, Konstanz, and Kreuzlingen. Prices vary according to the distance trav-eled. A one-way trip from Schaffhausen to Kreuzlingen takes about 4½ hours. On both boat lines, you'll travel free if you have a Swiss Pass.

Boat and Ferry Contacts Schweizer Bodensee Schiffahrtsgesellschaft ☎ 071/4667888 ⊕ www.sbsag.ch. **Schweizerisches Schiffahrtgesellschaft Unter-see und Rhein** ✉ Freierpl. 8, Schaffhausen ☎ 052/6340888 ⊕ www.urh.ch.

BUS TRAVEL

The famous yellow postbuses travel to every single town and village in Switzerland. The ride is comfortable, and the trip is free with your Swiss Pass. Bus schedules are usually posted outside town post offices, but you can also obtain information from any train station. The small-est towns have one bus in the morning and one in the evening, while larger towns are served several times a day.

CAR TRAVEL

Driving in eastern Switzerland doesn't give you the same amazing views as the trains, which chug over the meadows so close to cows you can practically hear them munching grass. If you do decide to drive, High-way 13 goes along the south shores of the Untersee and Bodensee and continues up through the hills to Appenzell. In cities, such as St. Gallen and Schaffhausen, you'll find it easiest to head directly for the center and abandon the car for the duration of your visit. Try to get into a parking lot, as finding a spot on the street can be difficult.

TRAIN TRAVEL

The narrow-gauge trains in Appenzell set it apart. The picture windows can be opened so you can lean out as you careen over green hills and sniff wildflowers and fresh cut grass. At St. Gallen, the main hub for regional trains, you can transfer to the Gossau–Appenzell–Wasserauen line. To see more of the territory, you may return to St. Gallen by way of Herisau. The Swiss Pass includes St. Gallen and Schaffhausen city transit, as well as overall rail privileges throughout Switzerland.

⇨ *For more information on getting here and around, see Travel Smart Switzerland.*

RESTAURANTS

Restaurants in this region are often in centuries-old structures that have been home to some kind of eatery (in a few occasions under the same name) for 200 or even 300 years. This is especially true of Schaffhausen's Wirtschaft zum Frieden, which dates back to 1789, or St. Gallen's Schlössli, located inside a small castle built in 1586. But architecture doesn't determine the style; you'll find everything from formal linen-tablecloth service to a laid-back country kitchen atmosphere in eastern Switzerland's restaurants. The same dress code applies as in the rest of the country: jeans and a tucked-in shirt are preferable to a jacket and tie.

Restaurants typically fill up around 7 pm, slightly earlier than most of Switzerland. The Swiss have impeccable table manners and the same is expected from visitors. Point your silverware away from you on the plate when finished, always look dinner companions in the eye when clinking glasses to saying *prostli!,* and always, always add *en guete!,* the Swiss-German equivalent of *bon appétite.* Don't be surprised if you're charged for tap water, as this custom is tolerated throughout Switzerland.

Prices in the reviews are the average cost of a main course or equivalent combination of small dishes at dinner or, if dinner is not served, at lunch.

HOTELS

During the summer high season, Stein-am-Rhein and Gottlieben swell with tourists because there's no town around to catch the overflow. St. Gallen has a large convention center, so you should make your reservation in advance. Other destinations will usually still have a room or two on short notice. For romantic getaways, consider the castellated Drachenburg und Waaghaus in Gottlieben, a teeny-tiny village on the misty bank of the Rhine, or something along the shore of Stein am Rhein, which quiets down in the evening when many of the bikers depart. For an adventurous getaway, try the Berggastaus Aescher-Wildkirchli, nestled high above Appenzell on the rocky face on Ebenalp. More and more hotels in this region are throwing away their Formica and commissioning hand-painted furniture to complement the beams they've so carefully exposed. The prices are somewhat lower on average here, with only slight variations from high to low season. Half board is rarely included, but hearty cheese and meat-laden breakfast buffets almost always are. Warm, good service is a given.

Prices in the reviews are the lowest cost of a standard double room in high season, including taxes.

VISITOR INFORMATION

The tourist office for all of eastern Switzerland is based in St. Gallen. There are small regional visitor information offices throughout eastern Switzerland. Liechtenstein's office is in its capital.

Tourismusverband Ostschweiz (*Tourist Association of Eastern Switzerland*). ✉ *Bahnhofpl. 1a, St. Gallen* ☎ *071/2273737* ⊕ *www.ostschweiz.ch.*

SCHAFFHAUSEN AND THE RHINE

Known to many Swiss as Rheinfallstadt (Rhine Falls City), Schaffhausen is the seat of the country's northernmost canton, which also shares its name. To gaze upon the grand mist-sprayed Rheinfal is to look straight into the romantic past of Switzerland. Goethe and Wordsworth were just two of the world's best-known wordsmiths to immortalize the falls' powerful grandeur.

SCHAFFHAUSEN

★ *48 km (29 miles) northeast of Zürich, 20 km (12 miles) west of Stein-am-Rhein.*

A city of about 34,000, Schaffhausen was from the early Middle Ages on an important depot for river cargoes, which—because of the rapids and waterfall farther along—had to be unloaded there. The name *Schaffhausen* is probably derived from the skiff houses along the riverbank. The city has a small but beautiful Altstadt (Old Town), whose charm lies in its extraordinary preservation; examples of late Gothic, Baroque, and Rococo architecture line the streets. Though the town can sometimes feel like a museum, these buildings are very much in use, often as shops or restaurants, and lively crowds of shoppers and strollers throng the streets. Many streets (including Vorstadt, Fronwagplatz, Vordergasse, and Unterstadt) are pedestrian-only.

GETTING HERE AND AROUND

The fastest connection from Zürich is the commuter train, which takes about an hour. There are also trains to and from St. Gallen that connect through Winterthur (travel time 86 minutes).

To reach Schaffhausen by car from Zürich, take A1 to Winterthur, then head north on the cantonal highway E41/15. You also can leave Zürich by way of the A4 expressway past Zürich Airport, crossing through Germany briefly and entering Schaffhausen through Neuhausen am Rheinfall. In Schaffhausen, there's underground parking at the Stadttheater underneath Herrenacker.

ESSENTIALS

Visitor Information Schaffhauserland ⊠ *Herrenacker 15* ☎ *052/6324020* ⊕ *www.schaffhauserland.ch.*

EXPLORING

TOP ATTRACTIONS

Fronwagplatz. Lined with shops and cafés, this square is a favorite place for young people to stroll, especially in the evening. A large 16th-century fountain-statue of a prosperous burgher, the Metzgerbrunnen, watches over the marketplace. The clock tower's astronomical clock (1564) records not only the time but also solar eclipses, seasons, and the course of the moon through the zodiac. Across the square, a reproduction of the 1535 Mohrenbrunnen (Moor's Fountain) represents Kaspar of the Three Kings. The original fountain is stored in the Museum zu Allerheiligen.

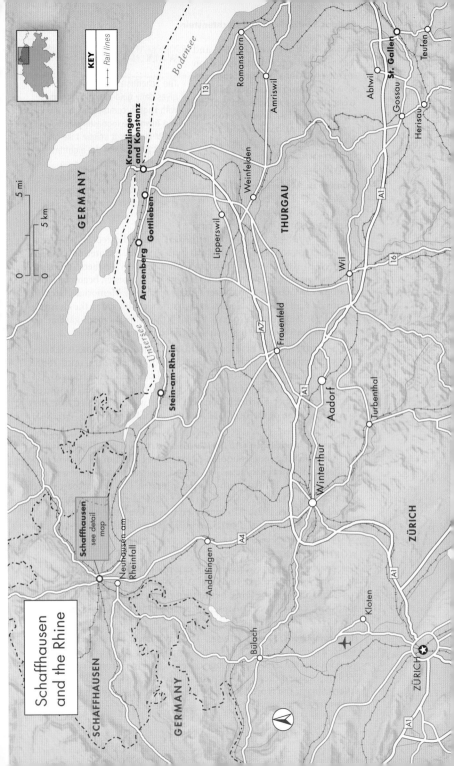

Schaffhausen and the Rhine

KEY

····· Rail lines

GERMANY

Bodensee

Kreuzlingen
and Konstanz

Gottlieben

Arenenberg

Untersee

Stein-am-Rhein

Romanshorn

Amriswil

Weinfelden

Lipperswil

THURGAU

Wil

Frauenfeld

Abtwil

Gossau

St. Gallen

Teufen

Herisau

Aadorf

Turbenthal

Winterthur

Schaffhausen
see detail
map

Neuhausen-am-
Rheinfall

Andelfingen

Bülach

Kloten

ZÜRICH

ZÜRICH

SCHAFFHAUSEN

GERMANY

13

A1

16

A7

A1

A1

A4

A1

5 mi

5 km

0

Munot. Built between 1564 and 1585 in full circle form based on an idea by Albrecht Dürer, the massive stone ramparts served as a fortress allowing for the defense of the city on all sides. From its top are splendid Schaffhausen and Rhine Valley views. ⊠ *Munotstieg* ☜ *Free* ⊙ *May–Sept., daily 8–8; Oct.–Apr., daily 9–5.*

Münster zu Allerheiligen (*All Saints Cathedral*). This beautiful cathedral, along with its cloister and grounds, dominates the lower city.

WALKING TOURS

The Schaffhausen tourist office gives daily guided walking tours with English commentary on the Old Town, the monastery, and the Munot. For a unique take on the city, try one of the nighttime guided walks, which focus on murders, pestilence, public hangings, and other dark events, available in English on request.

Founded in 1049, the original cathedral was dedicated in 1064, and the larger one that stands today was built in 1103. Its interior has been restored to Romanesque austerity with a modern aesthetic (hanging architect's lamps, Scandinavian-style pews). The cloister, begun in 1050, combines Romanesque and later Gothic elements. Memorial plates on the inside wall honor noblemen and civic leaders buried in the cloister's central garden. You'll also pass through the aromatic herb garden, so beautiful that you may feel you've stepped into a tapestry.

The centerpiece of the main courtyard, the cathedral's enormous Schiller Bell was cast in 1486; it hung in the tower of the cathedral until 1895. Its inscription, "vivos—voco/mortuos—plango/fulgura—frango" ("I call the living, mourn the dead, stop the lightning"), allegedly inspired the German poet Friedrich von Schiller to write his "Lied von der Glocke" ("Song of the Bell"). ⊠ *Klosterpl. 1* ☜ *Free* ⊙ *Tues.–Fri. 8–5, weekends 8–8.*

Museum zu Allerheiligen (*All Saints Museum*). This excellent museum on the cathedral grounds houses an extensive collection of ancient and medieval historical artifacts. The period rooms are definitely worth a look; they cover 15th- to 19th-century interiors. The best of these is the 15th-century refectory, which was rented out and all but forgotten until its rediscovery in 1924. Museum literature is available only in French or German. ⊠ *Klosterpl. 1* ☏ *052/6330777* ⊕ *www.allerheiligen.ch* ☜ *9 SF* ⊙ *Tues.–Sun. 11–5.*

WORTH NOTING

Gerberstube (*Tanners' Guildhall*). A pair of lions frames the doorway of the remarkable Baroque building. A two-handled tanner's knife used to stretch between the lions, but unfortunately the vibrations of nearby roadwork caused it to collapse. A restaurant now occupies the building. ⊠ *Bachstr. 8.*

Haus zum Ritter (*Knight's House*). The city's finest mansion dates from 1492. Its fresco facade was commissioned by the resident knight, Hans von Waldkirch. Tobias Stimmer covered all three stories with paintings on classical themes, which are now displayed in the Museum zu Allerheiligen; the reproduction of the original was made in the 1930s. ⊠ *Vorderg. 65.*

The best way to reach the dramatic Rhine Falls is to follow the Rhine Bank Trail from Schaffhausen.

Rheinfall. The Rheinfall is 492 feet wide, drops some 82 feet in a series of three dramatic leaps, and is split at the center by a bushy crag straight out of a 19th-century landscape painting. The effect—mist, roaring water, jutting rocks—is positively Wagnerian. Goethe saw in the falls the "ocean's source," although today's jaded globetrotters have been known to find them "cute." A visitor's center at the nearby Schloss Laufen includes a souvenir shop, restaurant, playground, and new bridge walkway that lets you see, hear, and get sprayed by the falls. ⊠ *Neuhausen am Rheinfall.*

Schmiedstube (*Smiths' Guildhall*). With its spectacular Renaissance portico and oriel dating from 1653, this building is an embodiment of Schaffhausen's state of suspended animation. Framed over the door are the symbols of the tongs and hammer for the smiths, and that of a snake for doctors, who depended on the smiths for their tools and thus belonged to the guild. ⊠ *Vorderg. 61.*

Schwabentorturm (*Swabian Gate Tower*). Once a part of the city wall, the tower dates from 1370. Inside the arch on the keystone is a relief from 1933 that bears a wise caution for anyone crossing the street: "lappi tue d'auge uf" ("Open your eyes, you idiot!"). The tower's counterpart, the Obertorturm, lies just off the Fronwagplatz.

Zum Goldenen Ochsen (*At the Golden Ox*). This late-Gothic building had a Renaissance-style portico and oriel window added to it in 1609. Flanking the windows are three floors of exterior frescoes depicting historic and mythological figures, most from the Trojan War. ⊠ *Vorstadt 17.*

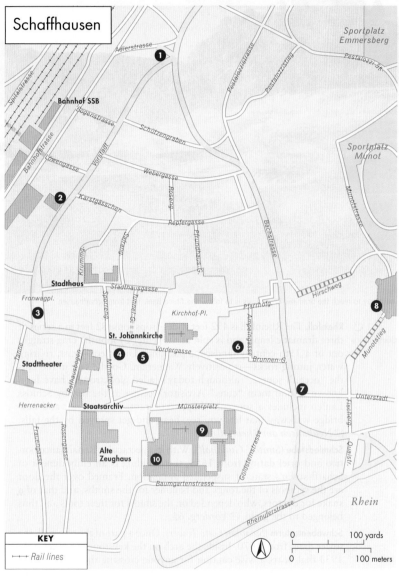

Schaffhausen

Zur Wasserquelle and Zur Zieglerburg (*At the Spring and At the Brick Castle*). This Rococo duplex dates from 1738; since they are now private residences, you can see them only from the outside. Across the street are the Tellenbrunnen, a fountain-statue of Wilhelm Tell copied from the 1522 original, and the St. Johannkirche (St. John's Church), whose Gothic exterior dates from 1248. ⊠ *Vorderg. 26/28.*

WHERE TO EAT

$$
MEDITERRANEAN

✕ **Beckenburg.** Well-heeled locals flock here to sample innovative twists on Mediterranean staples, such as pike perch saltimbocca with lemon risotto. The tables are set far enough apart to give you lots of privacy, and the staff is attentive without being intrusive. Beechwood and metal tables and chairs complement the 300-year-old wood accents and the imposing Venetian chandelier that hangs over the room. The leafy outdoor graveled terrace is a nice place to decompress in summer. $ *Average main: 29 SF* ⊠ *Neustadt 1* ☎ *052/6252820* ⊕ *www.beckenburg.ch* ⊗ *Closed Sun.*

$$
SWISS
⟳

✕ **Restaurant Falken.** This busy restaurant caters to crowds with a palate for simple local fare—*Rösti* (a kind of hash brown potatoes), *Geschnetzeltes* (sliced veal in cream sauce), and breaded fish. The *Tagesteller* (daily special) is an especially good deal at lunchtime. Though plain and cafeteria-like, it's an excellent choice for families; it even houses a small bowling alley. $ *Average main: 26 SF* ⊠ *Vorstadt 5* ☎ *052/6253221* ⊕ *www.falken-schaffhausen.ch.*

$$
EUROPEAN

✕ **Wirtschaft zum Frieden.** Dating back to 1789, this local favorite offers three delightful settings: a small *Stübli* (Swiss pub) full of waxed and weathered wood, a graceful tile-stove dining room with antiques, and a private garden thick with wisteria and luxuriant trees. Specialties include hearty dishes such as veal medallions in mustard sauce, and buttered Rösti with goat cheese. $ *Average main: 29 SF* ⊠ *Herrenacker 11* ☎ *052/6254767* ⊕ *www.wirtschaft-frieden.ch* ⊗ *Closed Sun. and Mon.*

WHERE TO STAY

For expanded hotel reviews, visit Fodors.com.

$
HOTEL

⊞ **Kronenhof.** This fine, quiet city hotel in the heart of Schaffhausen's Old Town has a traditional shutter- and flower-trimmed facade. **Pros:** central location; cobblestone terrace café. **Cons:** the variation in style is a bit incoherent; service sometimes hurried. $ *Rooms from: 125 SF* ⊠ *Kirchhofpl. 7* ☎ *052/6357575* ⊕ *www.kronenhof.ch* ⇆ *38 rooms, 2 suites* ⊗ *Breakfast.*

$
HOTEL

⊞ **Park Villa.** Except for the no-nonsense elevator tacked onto the exterior, this Belle-Époque mansion has been transformed into a small hotel with little disruption to its grand but familial style. **Pros:** you can pretend you live in an old mansion; tennis courts at this rate are rare. **Cons:** little refurbishment of late; somewhat musty. $ *Rooms from: 78 SF* ⊠ *Parkstr. 18* ☎ *052/6356060* ⊕ *www.parkvilla.ch* ⇆ *21 rooms, 4 suites* ⊗ *Breakfast.*

$$
HOTEL
★

⊞ **Rheinhotel Fischerzunft.** A Relais & Châteaux property, this lodging has a modern sheen that's welcoming but, to some, may seem a bit out of place in this medieval city on the Rhine. **Pros:** exquisite restaurant; rooms on the river; excellent service. **Cons:** occasional mosquito attacks

Stein-am-Rhein celebrates Christmas by decking its streets with festive flair.

in summer (remember that river); public salons that are so quiet you don't dare speak. $ *Rooms from: 210 SF* ✉ *Rheinquai 8* ☎ *052/6320505* ⊕ *www.fischerzunft.ch* ⇥ *6 rooms, 4 suites* ⚭ *Breakfast.*

SPORTS AND THE OUTDOORS

Bahnhof Schaffhausen. Bicycles are a popular mode of transportation. They can be rented at the train station in Schaffhausen. ✉ *Bahnhofst.* ☎ *051/2234217.*

STEIN-AM-RHEIN

Fodor's Choice
★

20 km (13 miles) east of Schaffhausen.

The riverside Stein-am-Rhein is one of Switzerland's loveliest (and wealthiest) communities. It lies at a pivotal point where the Rhine leaves the Bodensee, marked by three small leafy islands, one of which is still inhabited by monks. Crossing the bridge over the river, you see the village spread along the waterfront, its foundations and docks rising directly out of the water. Restaurants, hotels, and shops occupy 16th- and 17th-century buildings covered with ancient frescoes. Hovering over the walled town is a medieval castle surrounded by vineyards, home to an excellent restaurant with views.

GETTING HERE AND AROUND

The least complicated route from Schaffhausen is via train; the trip takes 25 minutes.

ESSENTIALS

Visitor Information Tourismus Stein-am-Rhein ✉ *Oberstadt 3* ☎ *052/7422090* ⊕ *www.stein-am-rhein.ch.*

EXPLORING

Hohenklingen. Directly above the town stands the 12th-century hilltop castle of Hohenklingen, which offers broad views of the Rhine Valley and the lake beyond. If you need sustenance after your trip up the hill, the castle houses an excellent restaurant. The tranquil vineyard trails up to the castle are a worthwhile diversion. ⊠ *Hohenklingenstrasse 1* ☎ *052/7412137* ⊕ *www.burghohenklingen.ch* 🎫 *Free* ☉ *Tues.–Sat. 10 am–11 pm, Sun. 10–4.*

Kloster St. Georgen (*Monastery of St. George*). The Benedictine Kloster St. Georgen, a half-timber structure built in 1007, houses a cloister and a small museum devoted to examples of woodwork and local paintings. ⊠ *Chirchhofplatz 7* ☎ *052/7412142* 🎫 *5 SF* ☉ *Museum: Apr.–Oct., Tues.–Sun. 10–5.*

KrippenWelt Stein-am-Rhein. Monika Amrein and Alfred Hartl's private collection of *krippen* (Nativity scenes) from around the world are tastefully displayed on two floors in their 14th-century home. There are more than 500 pieces in the collection, many made from paper, wood, metal, or even mushrooms. ⊠ *Oberstadt 5* ☎ *052/7210005* ⊕ *www. krippenwelt-ag.ch* 🎫 *10 SF* ☉ *Closed Mon.*

Rathaus (*Town Hall Square*). Stein-am-Rhein's Rathaus (Town Hall) is flanked by tight rows of shingled, half-timber town houses, each rivaling the next for the ornateness of its oriels, the flamboyance of its frescoes. The elaborate decor usually illustrates the name of the house: Sonne (Sun), Ochsen (Ox), Weisser Adler (White Eagle), and so on. Most of the artwork dates from the 16th century. The Rathaus itself was built between 1539 and 1542, with the half-timber upper floors added in 1745; look for its fantastical dragon waterspouts, typical of the region. ⊠ *Rathausplatz.*

WHERE TO EAT

$

BAKERY

✕ **Café Späth zur Hoffnung.** Small bakeries abound in Switzerland, but this one features such local specialties as *Steiner Scherben*, a chocolate-covered toffee that is said to bring luck to those who eat it. Also check out the homemade pralines, fruit tortes, and other butter-laden confections, or do as locals do and nab a light snack (the muesli is tasty) or lunch (open-faced shrimp sandwiches are the way to go). $ *Average main: 6 SF* ⊠ *Rathausplatz 21* ☎ *052/7412182* ⊕ *www.cafe-spaeth.ch*.

$$

SWISS

Fodor's Choice

★

✕ **Le Bateau.** Bypass the wacky Butterfly Bar in the lobby of the Hotel Chlosterhof and head directly to Le Bateau, on the terrace in overlooking the Rhein's three leafy islands, one of which is still inhabited by monks. Italian chef Antonino Messina whisks some bright Mediterranean flavors into the cosmopolitan menu. Panfried scallops bathe in a rich lemon sauce, sliced veal is amped up with ruby-red chunks of seared tuna, and lobster tail is cooked to perfection in a buttery tarragon sauce so delicious that the waiter doesn't think twice before giving you a spoon. With so much wood that it resembles a cruise ship's dining room, this is one of eastern Switzerland's best restaurants. $ *Average main: 39 SF* ⊠ *Hotel Chlosterhof, Oehningerstrasse 2* ☎ *052/7424242* ⊕ *www.chlosterhof.ch*.

$$ ✕**Restaurant Schiff.** Perched on a gentle bend in the Rhine at the end of
SWISS a colorful string of half-timbered buildings, this cozy restaurant is man-
aged by the warm and friendly husband-and-wife team of Stephan and
Bianco Roth. The couple has lured locals to its riverside terrace with a
fresh seasonal menu featuring dishes like *vitello tonatto* (thin veal slices
in a creamy tuna sauce), new takes on pike, perch, and whitefish, freshly
caught from the Bodensee, and heaping salads easily washed down with
local Rieslings and Pinot Noirs. $ *Average main: 26 SF* ✉ *Hotel Schiff,
Schiffländi 10* ☎ *052/741 22 73* ⊕ *www.hotel-restaurant-schiff.ch.*

WHERE TO STAY
For expanded hotel reviews, visit Fodors.com.

$ 🏨 **Adler.** With one of the most elaborately frescoed 15th-century facades
HOTEL on the Rathausplatz, this hotel has a split personality: flamboyant on the
★ outside, no-nonsense on the inside. **Pros:** top-notch restaurant; excel-
lent service. **Cons:** decor is in serious need of attention, with noticeably
absent frills. $ *Rooms from: 125 SF* ✉ *Rathauspl. 15* ☎ *052/7426161*
⊕ *www.adlersteinamrhein.ch* ⬅25 *rooms* ⊗ *Closed Jan. and Feb.*
🍴*Breakfast.*

$ 🏨 **Rheinfels.** Every room has a Rhine view in this waterfront landmark,
HOTEL which was built between 1508 and 1517. **Pros:** medieval atmosphere is
Fodor's Choice a thrill; locals come from miles away for the fish dishes. **Cons:** slightly
★ musty room decor; proximity to a busy thoroughfare. $ *Rooms from:
139 SF* ✉ *Rhig. 8* ☎ *052/7412144* ⊕ *www.rheinfels.ch* ⬅16 *rooms, 1
suite* ⊗ *Closed Jan. and Feb.* 🍴*Breakfast.*

$ 🏨 **Zur Rheingerbe.** Right on the busy waterfront promenade, this small
B&B/INN inn a delightful half-timbered facade with green shutters and some
lovely views of the Rhine, including from some of the rooms. **Pros:**
centrally located; café for hours of people-watching; excellent rates.
Cons: rooms are a bit sparse and lacking in style. $ *Rooms from: 90
SF* ✉ *Schifflände 5* ☎ *052/7412991* ⊕ *www.rheingerbe.ch* ⬅7 *rooms,
1 apartment* 🍴*Breakfast.*

ARENENBERG

*40 km (25 miles) east of Schaffhausen, 20 km (12 miles) east of
Stein-am-Rhein.*

East of Stein-am-Rhein the Rhine opens up into the Untersee, the
lower branch of the Bodensee. In its center lies the German island of
Reichenau. Charles the Fat, great-grandson of Charlemagne, is buried
here. Castles dominate the villages on either side of the Untersee.

EXPLORING
Fodor's Choice **Arenenberg Napoleonmuseum.** In the village of Salenstein, the Arenen-
★ berg Napoleonmuseum is housed in a magnificent villa given to the
municipality by Empress Eugnie of France in homage to her husband,
Napoléon III, who grew up here with his mother, Hortense, sister-in-
law of Napoléon I. Today the Schloss Arenenberg serves as a museum,
and lovers of decorative arts will prize its ravishing period rooms dat-
ing from the Second Empire. Outside is a glorious park studded with
ancestral statues as well as a separate seminar center with a small café.

✉ Schloss Arenenberg, off Arenenbergst, Salenstein ☎ 071/6633260 🌐 www.napoleonmuseum.tg.ch 🎟 12 SF ⏲ Mid-Apr.–mid-Oct., Tues.–Sun. 10–5, Mon. 1–5; mid-Oct.–mid-Apr., Tues.–Sun. 10–5.

GOTTLIEBEN

5 km (3 miles) east of Arenenberg, 45 km (28 miles) east of Schaffhausen.

The village of Gottlieben has a Dominican monastery-castle, where the Protestant reformers Jan Hus and Jerome of Prague were imprisoned in the 15th century by order of Emperor Sigismund and Antipope John XXIII, who was himself confined in the same castle a few years later. Although the castle can be viewed only from the outside, Gottlieben offers a romantic half-timber waterfront promenade—and two fine old hotels—before you reach the urban complex of Kreuzlingen and Germany's Konstanz.

WHERE TO STAY

For expanded hotel reviews, visit Fodors.com.

$ HOTEL Fodor's Choice ★ 🏨 **Drachenburg und Waaghaus.** On the Rhine between the Bodensee and the Zellersee, these two half-timbered apparitions of onion domes, shutters, and gargoyles were first built in 1702 and retain their historic air despite modern expansions. **Pros:** extremely quiet; tons of character; right on the Rhine. **Cons:** in an isolated town; overtly theme-parkish. [$] *Rooms from: 89 SF ✉ Am Schlosspark 7 and 10 ☎ 071/6667474 🌐 www.drachenburg.ch 🛏 58 rooms, 2 suites ⏲ Closed wk of Christmas 🍴 Breakfast.*

BODENSEE TO WALENSEE

Along the shores of the Bodensee orchards stripe rolling hills that slowly rise to meet the foothills of the Alps around St. Gallen. About 2,000 years ago this region lay on the northeastern border of the Roman Empire, Arbon (Arbor Felix) being the first stop on the trade route for goods coming into the empire from points east. Today the region is mostly rural, with clusters of farmhouses dotting the grassy slopes. In summer the lake teems with vacationers, but in other seasons it remains a distinctly tranquil area.

BODENSEE

Known in English as Lake Constance, the Bodensee is about 65 km (40 miles) long and 15 km (9 miles) wide, making it second in size in Switzerland only to Lac Léman (Lake Geneva). The strong German flavor of the towns on its Swiss edge is seasoned with a resort-village mellowness; palm trees fringe the waterfront. This isn't the Mediterranean, though; as the lake is not protected by mountains, it can be windy in spring and fall and quite humid in summer. European vacationers come here during the warmer months for swimming, windsurfing, and fishing. Small vacation homes alternate with opulent villas along the lakefront.

SPORTS AND THE OUTDOORS

BIKING

There's a great cycling path that starts outside of Sargans, runs along the Rhine down to the Bodensee, and goes all the way to Schaffhausen, with views of the water on one side and some of Switzerland's most beautiful agricultural land on the other. Rent bikes at the train station in Sargans, St. Margrethen, Romanshorn, Kreuzlingen, Stein-am-Rhein, or Schaffhausen. One-way rentals are possible for a surcharge. For detailed route information, see ⊕ *www.veloland.ch*.

HIKING

As a summer resort destination, the area around the Bodensee is usually thronged with hikers. For timed hiking itineraries, topographical maps, and suggestions on the areas best suited to your style of wandering, consult the Tourismusverband Ostschweiz at ⊕ *www.ostschweiz-i.ch*.

SWIMMING

The Bodensee is the region's local swimming hole; there are several public beaches, usually more grass than sand. Most have changing rooms and concession stands.

Arbon. With a gravel beach, Arbon makes getting into the water a little rough on tender feet. ⊠ *Hauptstr. 12, Arbon* ☎ *071/4461333.*

Kreuzlingen. This beach has some sand at the water's edge, though you'll be spreading your towel on the grass. ⊠ *Promenadenstr. 40, Kreuzlingen* ☎ *071/6881858.*

Romanshorn. The lakeside beach in Romanshorn includes a pool and a waterslide, as well as wide swaths of grass to lie on. ⊠ *Bahnhofstra. 19, Romanshorn* ☎ *071/4631147.*

> ## FLEA MARKET FINDS
>
> Some of the least developed land is in eastern Switzerland, which means there are still old houses stuffed with plenty of old furnishings, art pieces, and trinkets. This being Switzerland, commerce has responded: outdoor/indoor flea markets abound, as do secondhand thrift shops called *Bröckenhäuser* (Brockenhaus in the singular)—every town has at least one. Antiques dealers regularly troll the area, but it's still possible to find a bargain here and there, especially in out-of-the way villages. Let the hunt begin!

KREUZLINGEN AND KONSTANZ

7 km (4 miles) east of Gottlieben, 46 km (28 miles) east of Schaffhausen.

The German city of Konstanz, with its Swiss-side twin of Kreuzlingen, dominates the straits that open into the Bodensee. Though Kreuzlingen itself offers little of interest to travelers, Konstanz has a lovely, concentrated Altstadt (Old Town). It's easily accessible from the Swiss side, though your passport may be checked even if you pass on foot. Konstanz belonged to Switzerland until 1805; today the two border towns share the dominant German influence.

EN ROUTE

Arbon. Between Romanshorn and Rorschach on Highway 13, Arbon sits on a little promontory jutting out into the Bodensee, surrounded by lovely meadows and orchards. It was a Celtic town before the Romans

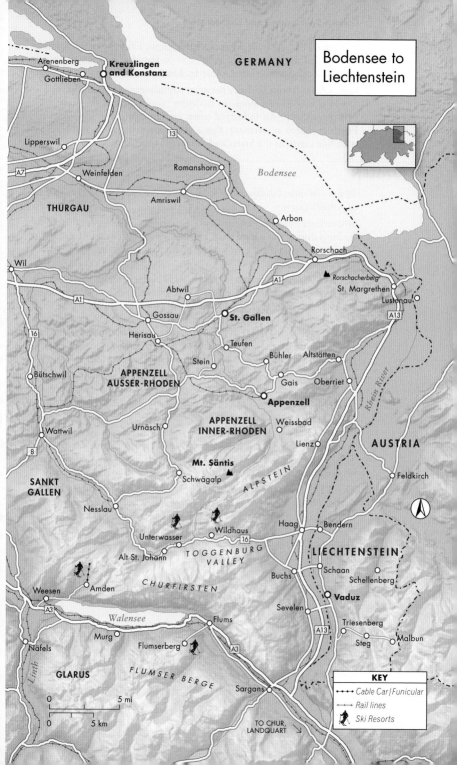

came in 60 BC and built military fortifications. Evidence of the Romans (who called the place Arbor Felix) can be found in an interesting collection of relics in the late-Gothic St. Martinskirche.

Romanshorn. About halfway between Kreuzlingen and Rorschach (follow Highway 13 east along the Bodensee) you'll come to the small town of Romanshorn. An industrial town and an important ferry port for Friedrichshafen in Germany, this is also a surprisingly enjoyable resort with fine views of the Swiss and Austrian mountains.

ST. GALLEN

38 km (24 miles) southeast of Kreuzlingen, 94 km (59 miles) southeast of Schaffhausen.

Switzerland's largest eastern city, bustling St. Gallen is dominated by students during the school year. The narrow streets of the Altstadt (Old Town) are flanked by a wonderful variety of boutiques and antiques shops.

St. Gallen has been known for centuries as both an intellectual center as well as the source of some of the world's finest needlework, including the embroidery that embellished the gown work by Michelle Obama at President Barack Obama's inauguration ceremony in 2008. But today its commitment to the latest trends in art, design, and architecture marks a new direction for the city, which seems to be competing against Zürich, Basel, and Winterthur as a contemporary art destination.

St. Gallus, an Irish monk, came to the region in 612 to live in a hermit's cell in the Steinach Valley. In 719 an abbey was founded on the site where he died. Soon a major cultural focus in medieval Europe, the abbey built a library of awesome proportions.

GETTING HERE AND AROUND

Trains run to St. Gallen from Zürich, clocking in at just over an hour. The S3 commuter does a scenic run up the Rhine to the Bodensee and St. Gallen every hour, stopping at almost every town along the way.

The A1 expressway from Zürich heads for St. Gallen through Winterthur. From the south, the A13 expressway leads from Chur along Liechtenstein to the east end of the Bodensee; from there, take A1 into St. Gallen. The Altstadt is surrounded by underground parking lots. You'll find entrances on Burggraben, Oberergraben, and, most conveniently, on St. Georgenstrasse, right by the abbey.

ESSENTIALS

Visitor Information St.Gallen-Bodensee Tourismus ✉ *Bahnhofpl. 1a*
☎ *071/2273737* ⊕ *www.st.gallen-bodensee.ch.*

EXPLORING

Altstadt. The grounds of the abbey and the cathedral border the Altstadt, which demonstrates a healthy symbiosis between scrupulously preserved Renaissance and Baroque architecture and a thriving modern shopping scene. The best examples of oriel windows, half-timbering, and frescoes can be seen along Gallusstrasse, Schmiedgasse, Marktgasse, and Spisergasse, all pedestrian streets.

The decadent Abbey Library in St. Gallen holds more than 100,000 books; you can also see an ancient Egyptian mummy here.

Drei Weieren. Atop Freudenberg Hill you'll find Drei Weieren, a quaint park and swimming area with several refreshing lily pad–topped ponds. Each is surrounded by grassy fields and have lifeguard stations and handsome striped changing cabins built in the 1920s. This lofty perch offers a fantastic lookout over the quaint steeples, tiled rooftops, and cow-grazed valleys below. ⊠ *Bitzistr. 65.*

★ **Kathedrale.** The cathedral is an impressive sight. Begun in 1755 and completed in 1766, it is the antithesis of the library, although the nave and rotunda are the work of the same architect, Peter Thumb. The scale is outsize and the decor light, bright, and open, despite spectacular excesses of wedding-cake trim. ⊠ *Klosterhof* ☎ *071/2273381* ☉ *Daily 9–6, except during services.*

QUICK BITES

Café Vivendi. Healthy and delicious fare is served at Café Vivendi, a bistro in the pedestrian zone of the Old Town. Light meals, salads, and pastries from the restaurant's own bakery are local favorites. The outside seating area is a must in summer. ⊠ *Bankg. 2* ☎ *071/2221806.*

Mühleggbahn. Just a few steps from the abbey, at the end of the Old Town, is the Mühleggbahn, a self-service funicular that runs up the hillside, offering lovely views of St. Gallen and the Bodensee. Once at the top, take two immediate right turns to the wooden stairs leading to a paved path with park benches. ⊠ *Steinachstr. 42* ☎ *071/2439595* ⊕ *www.muehleggbahn.ch* ⤳ *3 SF* ☉ *Daily 5:40 am–12:50 am.*

Mülenenschlucht. A 30-minute walk up the steep Mülenenschlucht takes you past the mossy Steinach Gorge, where St. Gallus allegedly befriended a bear in 612. To commemorate St. Gallus' 1,400th birthday in 2012, the city installed a public art exhibit here that includes a self-opening time capsule embedded in a river rock (by German artist Maria Eichhorn) and a haunting neon sign atop the gorge's railroad viaduct (by Welsh artist Bethen Hews). ⊠ *Gallusplatz* ⊕ *www. gallusjubilaeum.ch/en.*

Stadt Lounge. Native-born artist Pipilotti Rist's *Stadt Lounge,* created with artist Carlos Martinez, is a public art work project that has bathed an entire chunk of the city center under a coat of red paint, creating what they call a "red carpet effect." It has transformed the neighborhood into a sultry "public living room." ⊠ *Sömmerliwaldstr. 7* ⊕ *www.raiffeisen.ch/web/ stadtlounge.*

> ## TEXTILE TRADITIONS
>
> **Textilmuseum** (*Textile Museum*). St. Gallen's history as a textile capital dates from the Middle Ages, when convent workers wove linen toile of such exceptional quality that it was exported throughout Europe. The industry expanded into cotton and embroidery before collapsing in 1918. Today St. Gallen dominates the small luxury market for fine handmade textiles, and magnificently historic finery is on view at the Textilmuseum . ⊠ *Vadianstrasse. 2* ☎ *071/2221744* ⊕ *www. textilmuseum.ch* ☞ *10 SF* ⊙ *Daily 10–5.*

Fodor's Choice ★ Stiftsbibliothek (*Abbey Library*). Although the abbey was largely destroyed in the Reformation and closed down altogether in 1805, its library, built between 1758 and 1767, still holds a collection of more than 100,000 books and manuscripts. To visit the library hall, one of Switzerland's treasures, you are given gray felt slippers to protect the magnificently inlaid wood flooring. The hall is a gorgeous explosion of gilt, frescoes, undulating balconies, and luminously burnished woodwork, mostly walnut and cherry. Its contents, including 1,200-year-old illuminated manuscripts, constitute one of the world's oldest and finest scholarly collections. Also on display, incongruously, is an Egyptian mummy dating from 700 BC. Not to be missed is the giant globe representing the world in 1571, with grossly misproportioned continents. The original was stolen by Zürich about 300 years ago, and in 2009 this reproduction was given to St. Gallen in lieu of the original. ⊠ *Klosterhof 6c* ☎ *071/2273416* ⊕ *www.stiftsbibliothek.ch* ☞ *10 SF* ⊙ *Mon.–Sat. 10–5, Sun. 10–4. Closed mid-Nov.–early Dec.*

WHERE TO EAT

$ ✕ Am Gallusplatz. Rubbing shoulders with the town's cathedral, this culiSWISS nary landmark entices with a castellated exterior, turreted and hued in pink. Inside, things get more stolid, with most of the action taking place in the main Rôtisserie room—a large chamber replete with cross-vaulted ceilings and heavy chandeliers. The menu is based on market-fresh ingredients and may include such ample fare as a triumvirate of fillets (beef, veal, lamb) with fresh vegetables and potatoes but can also get nouvelle, as witness the veal Provençal. There's also an enormous wine list. ⑂ *Average main: 25 SF* ⊠ *Gallusstr. 24* ☎ *071/2233330* ⊕ *www. gallusplatz.ch* ⊙ *Closed Mon.*

$$ ✕ Engelis. *Engeli* are angels, and they make up the accents throughSWISS out this small but well-appointed bistro with a soft white interior that makes you think of Christmas, with stiff linens on the tables, candlesticks, and gold trim here and there. The kitchen staff adds a Mediterranean flavor to traditional dishes, such as pork tenderloin wrapped in bacon with tomato-arugula salad, or trout with ratatouille and lemon rice. The Old Town location adds that little bit of Old Europe charm, as does the outside seating in the cobblestone pedestrian street in warm weather. $ *Average main: 29 SF* ⊠ *Brühlg. 30* ☏ *071/2233332* ⊕ *www. engelis-restaurant.ch*.

$$
SWISS
★

✕ **Jägerhof.** This light and airy room in a 19th-century town house is St. Gallen's top address for organic ingredients, light, innovative cuisine, and heartfelt service. Chef Vreni Giger is a local institution and is committed to providing a gourmet experience without the snooty attitude that often accompanies it elsewhere. Local foodies and hipsters alike enjoy creations including rabbit stuffed with truffles, chicken liver with brioche and quince compote, or pike perch with risotto and celery. $ *Average main: 31 SF* ⊠ *Brühlbleichestr. 11* ☏ *071/2455022* ⊕ *www. jaegerhof.ch* ⊘ *Closed weekends.*

$$
MODERN
EUROPEAN

✕ **Lagerhaus.** Prosecco-boiled risotto, octopus salad, tender pork steak—the Swiss-Italian fusion dishes make Lagerhaus well worth a visit. The spacious and elegant eatery attracts a stylish and chatty crowd that appreciates the giant outdoor terrace and the epic list of local and international wines. $ *Average main: 28 SF* ⊠ *Davidstr. 40* ☏ *071/2237007* ⊕ *www.restaurantlagerhaus.ch* ⌂ *Reservations essential* ⊘ *Closed Sun. and Mon.*

$
SWISS
Fodor'sChoice
★

✕ **Lokal.** Part of a former industrial complex that houses a contemporary art museum, cinema, and theater, the Lokal is a spacious and uber-hip restaurant inside a former locomotive hall. It's surrounded by a spacious terrace strewn with tables full of St. Gallen's Dior- and Swarvoski-clad set. The service comes across as arrogant, but the food—savory carrot ginger soup, cordon bleu heaped with pomme frites, coq au vin, and mounds of fresh green salads—is surprisingly affordable and always excellent. Sunday brunch shouldn't be missed. $ *Average main: 25 SF* ⊠ *Lokremise, Grünbergstr. 7* ☏ *071/2722570* ⊕ *www.lokremise.ch* ⌂ *Reservations essential.*

$$
SWISS
★

✕ **Schlössli.** Tidy, bright, and modern, this second-floor restaurant may lack the historic feel of some of it neighbors but features remarkable cooking from an award-winning chef. Look for inventive dishes such as local *Bloderchäs* (sour cheese) fried in sage butter, or local lamb shanks with chanterelle mushrooms, seasonal vegetables, and bread dumplings. The café draws local families at lunch; business executives choose the slightly more formal dining room. $ *Average main: 26 SF* ⊠ *Am Spisertor, Zeughausg. 17* ☏ *071/2221256* ⊘ *Closed weekends.*

$
SWISS

✕ **Zeughaus.** The town's former armory houses a small, no-frills bistro serving tasty examples of the local fare, such as bratwurst in onion sauce with french fries. Local business executives come for the lunch specials, which include soup or salad and are a steal in comparison to more swanky places nearby. The location next to the cathedral makes it a perfect pit stop during a day of sightseeing. $ *Average main: 22 SF* ⊠ *Zeughausstr. 2* ☏ *071/2224468* ⊘ *Closed Sun. No lunch Sat.*

$$ SWISS 🍴 **Zum Goldenen Schäfli.** Of the second-story restaurants that are St. Gallen's trademark, this is the most popular, and its slanting floors groan under crowds of locals and tourists. The low ceiling and walls are all aged wood, and it's easy to imagine coach-and-four passengers lifting pewter steins in centuries gone by. The menu offers regional standards lightened up for modern tastes. Sirloin steak with peppercorn sauce, Spätzli, and seasonal vegetables is a favorite. [$] *Average main: 27 SF* ✉ *Metzgerg. 5* ☎ *071/2233737* ⏲ *Closed Sun. No lunch Sat.*

WHERE TO STAY

For expanded hotel reviews, visit Fodors.com.

$$ HOTEL ★ 🏨 **Einstein.** On the edge of the Old Town, this former embroidery factory is now an upscale hotel with sleek interiors (polished cabinetry, subdued floral fabrics), a uniformed staff, and a five-star attitude. **Pros:** St. Gallen's grand hotel; wonderful view from the top-floor restaurant; great service. **Cons:** focus on business clients makes for a hectic pace. [$] *Rooms from: 225 SF* ✉ *Berneggstr. 2* ☎ *071/2275555* 🌐 *www.einstein.ch* 🛏 *99 rooms, 14 suites* 🍽 *Breakfast.*

$ HOTEL 🏨 **Hotel Dom.** An excellent location in the heart of the Klosterviertel district puts you just steps from the Abbey Library at this warm, modern-design hotel. **Pros:** central location; friendly service. **Cons:** some rooms are small and cramped; street-facing rooms have a bit of street noise. [$] *Rooms from: 90 SF* ✉ *Webbergasse 22* ☎ *071/2277171* 🌐 *www.hoteldom.ch* 🛏 *31 rooms* 🍽 *Breakfast.*

$ HOTEL 🏨 **Vadian.** A narrow town house tucked behind half-timber landmarks in the Old Town, this is a discreet and tidy little place. **Pros:** quality personal service; very central and yet still quiet. **Cons:** no-alcohol policy in rooms; no service after 10 pm. [$] *Rooms from: 120 SF* ✉ *Gallusstr. 36* ☎ *071/2281878* 🌐 *www.hotel-vadian.com* 🛏 *20 rooms* 🍽 *Breakfast.*

SPORTS AND THE OUTDOORS

👶 **Säntispark.** This water park and wellness center just outside St. Gallen has added a tranquil spa to its already sprawling complex, making it an ideal place for both families and couples who want peace and quiet. There's something to please (and exhaust) everyone, including bowling, billiards, and miniature golf. Young people love diving into the wave pool and zipping down a slide that corkscrews around the entire facility. Adults enjoy half a dozen varieties of saunas and steam rooms where they can relax au naturel in a kid-free environment. ✉ *Wiesenbachstr. 5, Abtwil* ☎ *071/3131515* 🌐 *www.saentispark.ch* 🎟 *23 SF for 2 hrs,1.50 SF each additional hr* ⏲ *Daily 9 am–10 pm.*

SHOPPING

Akris. This local couture house has gained international acclaim by selling its own line of luxury clothing, all of it manufactured in Switzerland. Designer Albert Kriemler has dressed many lumanaries, including Michelle Obama, Nicole Kidman, and Princess Charlene of Monaco. ✉ *Felsenstr. 40* ☎ *071/2277722* 🌐 *www.akris.ch.*

Fodor's Choice ★ **Farmers' Market.** St. Gallen's Saturday Farmers' Market—full of farmers hawking tubes of local rapeseed mayonnaise, regional cheeses, fruit preserves, cured meats, and wine—ends promptly at noon, so be sure to get there early. A Wednesday produce market in the same square

is equally busy, but the food doesn't come directly from the farmers. ⊠ *Marktplatz.*

Stich-Galerie Osvald. An outstanding assortment of antique prints of Swiss landscapes and costumes is sold at a broad range of prices at Stich-Galerie Osvald. The pictures are cataloged alphabetically by canton for easy browsing. ⊠ *Marktg. 26* ☎ *071/2235016.*

APPENZELL

20 km (12 miles) south of St. Gallen, 98 km (60 miles) southeast of Schaffhausen.

Isolated from St. Gallen by a ridge of green hills, Appenzell is divided into two sub-cantons, Appenzell Ausserrhoden and Appenzell Innerrhoden. Both make up one of Switzerland's least-explored regions. The Appenzellers are known for their quirky senses of humor, old-fashioned costumes (including hoop earrings for most men), and their good-natured anstand, which loosely translates as "decorum" or "decency." But more than anything, Appenzell is cheese and beer country, and you would be remiss to leave without a taste of either.

Named Appenzell after the Latin *abbatis cella* (abbey cell), the region served as a sort of colony to the St. Gallen abbey, and its tradition of fine embroidery dates from those early days. The perfect chance to see this embroidery is during a local festival, such as the Alpfahrten, when cows are herded up or down the mountains. Women's hair is coiffed in tulle, and their dresses have intricate embroidery and lace, often with an edelweiss motif; men wear embroidered red vests and suspenders decorated with edelweiss or cow figures. These traditional costumes are taken very seriously; they can cost thousands of francs, but in this case, pride supersedes economy.

To get your bearings in Appenzell, head to the Landsgemeindeplatz, the town square where the famous open-air elections (men-only until 1991) take place the last Sunday in April. The streets are lined with bright-painted homes, bakeries full of *Birnebrot* (pear bread) and souvenir *Biber* (almond and honey cakes). Embroidery is big business, but it's rare to find handmade examples of the local art; though women still do fine work at home, it's generally reserved for gifts or heirlooms. Instead, large factories have sprung up in Appenzell country, and famous fine-cotton handkerchiefs sold in specialty shops around the world are made by machine here at the Dörig, Alba, and Lehner plants.

GETTING HERE AND AROUND
The direct train from/to St. Gallen takes 48 minutes, or if you want a change of scenery, an alternate route goes via Herisau. A small highway (No. 3) leads into the hills through Teufen; the quaint Appenzell–Teufen–Gais rail line also serves the region.

ESSENTIALS
Visitor Information Appenzellerland ⊠ *Hauptg. 4* ☎ *071/7889641* ⊕ *www. appenzell.ch.*

DISCOUNTS AND DEALS

Available free to travelers staying for three or more nights in a local hotel, the Appenzell Gold Card gives you complimentary admission to five museums and two wellness centers, transport on three cable car lifts, a complimentary bike rental, and a self-guided tour of the factory where Appenzeller cheese is made, along with several other perks. It could save you hundreds of dollars.

EXPLORING

Appenzeller Volkskunde Museum (*Folklore Museum*). The Appenzeller Volkskunde Museum displays local arts and crafts, regional costumes, and hand-painted furniture. ⊠ *Dorf, Stein* ☎ *071/3685056* ⊕ *www. appenzeller-museum-stein.ch* ⊠ *7 SF* ⊗ *Tues.–Sun. 10–5.*

Brauquöll Appenzell. The locally brewed Appenzeller Quöllfrisch—just one of the high-quality beers made by Appenzell's family-owned Brauerei Locher—is an iconic drink in an old-fashioned flip-top bottle and found everywhere across Switzerland. The brewery's excellent new shop and visitor's center on the Sitter River let you sample local beers, including sweet dunkels, hoppy pilsners, malty chestnut and hemp beers, and even a special beer brewed under a full moon. An interactive English tour offers insight into the unique brewing processes. The company also makes fantastic whiskeys with peat from a bog just outside Appenzell. The staff is exceptionally friendly and will gladly arrange a flight of beers or whiskeys for you. ⊠ *Brauereiplatz 1* ☎ *71/7880176* ⊕ *www. appenzellerbier.ch.*

Ebenalp. The northernmost peak of the Appenzeller Alps, the 5,380-foot Ebenalp is accessible via cable car from Wasserrauen, 7 km (4 miles) south of Appenzell. At the top is an easy hike that connects to others trails that lead to a mountain lake or loop back to the cable car. Also here is the Wildkirchli, a cave that was home to humans in the Paleolithic era and today houses a large bear skeleton that dates back 90,000 years. Five minutes farther along the trail is the Berggastaus Aescher-Wildkirchli, a mountainside hotel and restaurant with eye-popping views of the valley below. ⊠ *Schwendetalstrasse 82, Wasserauen* ☎ *071/7991212* ⊕ *www.ebenalp.ch* ⊠ *27 SF round-trip.*

Museum Appenzell. Showcasing handicrafts and local traditions, regional history, and an international embroidery collection, the Museum Appenzell provides a good general overview of the area's history and culture. The building itself dates from 1560. An English-language guide is available. ⊠ *Hauptg. 4* ☎ *071/7889631* ⊕ *www.museum.ai.ch* ⊠ *7 SF* ⊗ *Apr.–Oct., daily 10–noon and 2–5; Nov.–Mar., Tues.–Sun. 2–5.*

Museum für Appenzeller Brauchtum (*Museum of Appenzeller Tradition*). Costumes, cowbells, and a cheese wagon are on display at the Museum für Appenzeller Brauchtum, along with examples of farmhouse living quarters. ⊠ *Dorfplatz, Urnäsch* ☎ *071/3642322* ⊕ *www.museum-urnaesch.ch* ⊠ *6 SF* ⊗ *Apr.–Oct., Mon.–Sat. 9–11:30 and 1:30–5, Sun. 1:30–5; Nov.–Mar., Mon.–Sat. 9 am–11:30.*

Schaukäserei. Modern cheese-making methods are demonstrated at the Schaukäserei, a combination of a factory and a museum. Cheese is made 9–2, so it's worth coming early in the day. A self-guided tour (free with the Appenzell Gold Card) reveals the history of the local cheese, and a movie about the region is a surefire way to whet your appetite. The attached restaurant is one of the best places to sample some traditional dishes made with Appenzeller cheese, including a silky cheese soup, gooey fondues and raclettes, and a savory *chääsflade* (cheese pie). ⊠ *Dorf 711, Stein* ☎ *071/3685070* ⊕ *www. showcheese.ch* ⊠ *Free* ⊗ *Nov.– Mar., daily 8:30–5:30; Apr.–Oct., daily 8:30–6:30.*

WHERE TO EAT

$$ ✕ **Adlerkeller.** The 450-year old cel-
SWISS   lar underneath the Adler Hotel on the edge of Appenzell town is *the* place for fondue in winter. Carved wood-paneled walls, a dark medieval room, and ancient glassed-over cobblestones are a bit chilly and museum-like, but the friendly service and excellent local wine list will warm you right back up. $ *Average main: 27 SF* ⊠ *Weissbadstrasse 2* ☎ *071/7871389* ⊕ *www. adlerhotel.ch* ⚲ *Reservations essential.*

$$ ✕ **Hof.** One of Appenzell's most popular restaurants serves hearty
SWISS   regional meats and cheese specialties, such as *Käseschnitte* (cheese toast)
  ★   and *Käsespätzli* (Spätzli with cheese), to locals and tourists who crowd elbow to elbow along shared tables and talk over the clatter from the bar. The rustic-wood decor, ladder-back chairs, and the display of sports trophies add to the local atmosphere. If you can still move after all that cheese, play skittles at the in-house lanes after dinner. $ *Average main: 28 SF* ⊠ *Engelg. 4* ☎ *071/7874030* ⊕ *www.gasthaus-hof.ch.*

WHERE TO STAY

For expanded hotel reviews, visit Fodors.com.

$ 🛏 **Berggastaus Aescher-Wildkirchli.** Accessible only by cable car and then
HOTEL   a short 20-minute hike, the Berggastaus Aescher-Wildkirchli sits at the
Fodor'sChoice   top of the Appenzeller Alps and treats you to sweeping views of the
  ★   cool, green valley below. **Pros:** quiet, cozy rooms; unique cliff-dwelling design. **Cons:** difficult to get to; isolated; and far from any other services. $ *Rooms from: 90 SF* ⊠ *Weissbadd* ⊕ *www.aescher-ai.ch* ⤳ 6 *rooms* ⊗⊙ *Breakfast.*

$ 🛏 **Freudenberg.** This is a cookie-cutter modern chalet, but its setting on
HOTEL   a velvety green hillside overlooking town is the most scenic and tran-
  ☾   quil you'll find in the area. **Pros:** child-friendly surroundings, including private playground; excellent value; good base camp for hikers. **Cons:** 10 minutes of the trek from town are uphill; some bathrooms

Dressed in traditional garb, these men prepare for a cattle show in Appenzell.

are small. $ *Rooms from: 80 SF* ✉ *Riedstr. 57* ☎ *071/7871240* ⊕ *www. hotel-freudenberg.ch* ➥ *7 rooms* ⦿ *Breakfast.*

$ | B&B/INN | ★ ⬚ **Hotel Appenzell.** Although only built in 1983, this warm, comfortable lodging has all the gabled coziness of its neighbors, with a view over the Landsgemeindeplatz and beyond to the mountains. **Pros:** central location; bakery on the ground floor with fresh breakfast items to choose from; helpful service. **Cons:** restaurant is filled to capacity in summer, and gets a bit loud. $ *Rooms from: 120 SF* ✉ *Landsgemeindepl.* ☎ *071/7881515* ⊕ *www.hotel-appenzell.ch* ➥ *16 rooms* ⦿ *Breakfast.*

$$ | RESORT ⬚ **Hotel Hof Weissbad.** A popular destination among locals seeking a massage or other spa treatment, the sprawling and leafy Hotel Hof Weissbad is perched in the hilltop village of Weissbad. **Pros:** quiet retreat; accommodating service. **Cons:** slightly older guests; chainy decor. $ *Rooms from: 180 SF* ✉ *Parkstrasse 1, Weissbad* ☎ *071/7988080* ⊕ *www.hofweissbad.ch* ➥ *82 rooms.*

$ | HOTEL ⬚ **Romantik Hotel Säntis.** With a crisp and formal ambience, this prestigious hotel has been in business since 1835. **Pros:** large and comfortable with all the amenities; a good choice for both loungers and the activity-happy. **Cons:** front view is onto the Landsgemeinde, which is a parking lot (albeit a small one). $ *Rooms from: 160 SF* ✉ *Landsgemeindepl.* ☎ *071/7881111* ⊕ *www.saentis-appenzell.ch* ➥ *30 rooms, 6 suites* ⊗ *Closed early Jan.–early Feb.*

SHOPPING

Butchers, bakers, and liquor shops up and down the streets offer souvenir bottles of Appenzeller Bitter (Alpenbitter), a very sweet aperitif made in town. A well-balanced eau-de-vie called Appenzeller Kräuter, made with blended herbs, is another specialty. Shops also sell *mostbröckli*, an air-dried beef, *landjäger*, a smoky dried sausage, regional cheeses, locally produced beer and wine, and bottles of peaty Swiss whiskey.

SHOPS AND SPAS

Mösler. Picnickers can sample the different grades of Appenzeller cheese and its unsung mountain rivals at Mösler. ⊠ *Hauptg. 13* 🕾 *071/7871317.*

Naturmoorbad Gontenbad. One of the strange local rituals in Appenzell is to bathe (or wallow) in muddy moor water, which is prized for its minerals and ability to smooth even the roughest skin. The Naturmoorbad Gontenbad is by turns clinic and spa; each treatment room has a private bathtub into which an attendant pours a mixture of herbs and muddy water. Free with the Appenzell Gold Card, it's an ideal experience for a rainy day. ⊠ *Gontenstrasse 53, Gonten* 🕾 *071/7953123* ⊕ *www.naturmoorbad.ch.*

Sutter. This shop has a good selection of locally made cheeses. ⊠ *Marktstr. 8* 🕾 *071/7871333.*

MT. SÄNTIS

Schwägalp cable car is 33 km (21 miles) southwest of Appenzell, 121 km (75 miles) southeast of Schaffhausen.

GETTING HERE AND AROUND

From Appenzell, the take the train Urnäsch or Nesslau and continue on post bus to Schwägalp, where a cable car does the heavy lifting those last 4,400 feet up to the peak.

EXPLORING

★ **Mt. Säntis.** For a pleasurable high-altitude excursion out of Appenzell southwest to the hamlet of Schwägalp, you can ride a cable car that departs every 30 minutes up to the peak of Mt. Säntis. At 8,209 feet, it is the highest in the region, with beautiful views of the Bodensee as well as of the Graubünden and Bernese Alps. The very shape of the summit—an arc of jutting rock that swings up to the jagged peak housing the station—is spectacular. ⊠ *Schwägalp* 🕾 *071/3656565* ⊕ *www.saentisbahn. ch* 🎫 *41 SF round-trip* ⏱ *June–Oct., Sun.–Thurs. 7:30–6, Fri. and Sat. 7:30–6:30; Nov.–Jan., daily 8:30–5; Feb.–mid-Mar., weekdays 8:30–5, weekends 8–5; mid-Mar.–May, weekdays 8:30–5, weekends 8–5:30.*

WALENSEE

40 km (24 miles) northwest of Vaduz, 65 km (36 miles) southeast of Zürich, 127 km (78 miles) southeast of Schaffhausen.

Between Liechtenstein and Zürich, the spectacular, blue-green lake called the Walensee is a deep emerald gash that stretches 16 km (10 miles) through the mountains, reflecting the jagged Churfirsten peaks. Once bypassed by Zürich residents en route to family chalets in Graubunden and Valais, this area is seeing a new life as a weekend getaway because of a new tunnel that has discreetly hidden the cars in a pipeline of half-tunnels. Walenstadt is the region's biggest town and has the most dining options, while the strand of other lakefront villages are incredibly picturesque and read like a Harry Potter witchcraft spell: Weesen, Quinten, Quarten, and Murg.

EXPLORING

Weesen. At the western end of the Walensee, Weesen is a quiet, shady resort noted for its mild climate and lovely lakeside walkway.

EN ROUTE Between the Walensee and Zürich, about 36 km (22 miles) northwest of Weesen, **Rapperswil** is a small town on the Zürcher See (Lake Zürich) with pleasant views, summertime waterfront strolls, and no fewer than three rose gardens, which is why it is known as the "Swiss City of Roses." If it's rainy, go instead to the forbiddingly Gothic 13th-century Schloss Rapperswil. Inside is a museum on Polish immigration to Switzerland. It's open weekends from 1 to 5 in November, December, and March, and daily from 1 to 5 from April to October; admission is 5 SF.

WHERE TO STAY

For expanded hotel reviews, visit Fodors.com.

$ **Loft Hotel.** Located in the quiet town of Murg, this mod new lodging—not affiliated with the chain, but with a remarkably similar vibe—
HOTEL is a high-concept, low-budget boutique hotel overlooking sparkling Lake Wallensee. **Pros:** incredible lake views; steps from the train station; exceptionally friendly staff. **Cons:** weak Wi-Fi in some areas; inexperienced staff. $ *Rooms from: 120 SF* ⊠ *Alte Spinnerei, Murg* ☎ *081/7203575* ⊕ *www.lofthotel.ch* ⤙ *17 rooms* ⦿ *No meals.*

SKIING

Amden. Despite its small size, Amden is a major winter sports center, offering modest skiing in a ruggedly beautiful setting. Easy and medium slopes with unspectacular drops and quick, short-lift runs provide good weekend getaways for crowds of local Swiss families. The highest trails start at 5,576 feet; there are two chairlifts, three T-bars, one children's lift, 25 km (16 miles) of downhill runs, and 8 km (5 miles) of cross-country trails. You can also take advantage of the ski school, a natural ice rink, and walking paths. One-day lift tickets cost 35 SF; six-day passes cost 165 SF. ☎ *055/6111115.*

LIECHTENSTEIN

When you cross the border from Switzerland into the principality of Liechtenstein, you will see license plates marked "FL": this stands for Fürstentum Liechtenstein (Principality of Liechtenstein). You are leaving the world's oldest democracy and entering a monarchy that is the last remnant of the Holy Roman Empire—all 160 square km (59 square miles) of it. If you don't put the brakes on, you'll wind up quickly in Austria.

Made up of 11 communes called gemeinden, this pint-sized principality was created at the end of the 17th century, when a wealthy Austrian prince, Johann Adam von Liechtenstein, bought out two bankrupt counts in the Rhine Valley and united their lands. In 1719 he obtained an imperial deed from Emperor Karl VI, creating the principality of Liechtenstein. The noble family poured generations of wealth into the new country, improving its standard of living, and in 1862 an heir, Prince Johann the Good, helped Liechtenstein introduce its first constitution as a "democratic monarchy" in which the people and the prince share power equally. Today the principality's 32,000 citizens enjoy one of the world's highest per-capita incomes—prosperous (though discreet) local industries range from making jam to molding false teeth—and pay virtually no taxes.

It's hard to not be curious about this little vestige of royalty, but you may find yourself disappointed in the rather sterile capital city of Vaduz. Its one must-see attraction is the bold and beautiful contemporary art museum, housed in a dazzling black terrazzo box and filled with works by lesser-known contemporary greats like Bill Bollinger and Günter Fruhtrunk. You won't be alone, as the streets are packed with package tourists climbing out of tour buses. Quite a few of the newcomers are from Asia, particularly China, and many of Vaduz's restaurants now offer overpriced sweet-and-sour chicken and other dishes.

Outside the capital you'll find some attractive views, including vineyards climbing up the hillsides. Hiking trails and ski slopes provide ample opportunity to glance, perhaps longingly, back at Switzerland.

VADUZ (LIECHTENSTEIN)

31 km (18 miles) southeast of Appenzell, 159 km (98 miles) southeast of Schaffhausen.

GETTING HERE AND AROUND

From Zürich, take the A1 expressway to Sargans, then change to the A13 heading north and take the Vaduz exit. From St. Gallen, follow the A1 northeast to the Bodensee, where it changes into the A13. Follow this south approximately 50 km (31 miles) to the Vaduz exit.

There are no direct trains to Vaduz, Liechtenstein's capital city; you have to stop on the Swiss side of the Rhine and take a bus across the river. From St. Gallen via Buchs, by train and bus, the trip takes 79 minutes. If you're traveling from Zürich, take the two-hour fast train to Sargans, where a connecting bus takes you to Vaduz (travel time 150 minutes).

ESSENTIALS

Visitor Information Liechtenstein ⊠ *Städtle 37,* ☎ *423/2396300* ⊕ *www. tourismus.li.*

EXPLORING

Kunstmuseum Liechtenstein (*Liechtenstein Museum of Art*). The gorgeous black box that is the Kunstmuseum Liechtenstein offers frequently changing exhibitions of modern art. Don't come expecting old Dutch masters, as this collection embraces Basquiat, Warhol, and Donald Judd, as well as lesser-known rising stars like Bill Bollinger and Günter Fruhtrunk. The casual café is one of Vaduz's cooler spots, a great place to relax with a volume from the well-curated bookshop. ⊠ *Städtle 32,* ☎ *423/2350300* ⊕ *www.kunstmuseum.li* 📧 *12 SF* ⏱ *Tues., Wed., and Fri.–Sun. 10–5, Thurs. 10–8.*

Vaduz Castle is home to the reigning prince of Liechtenstein.

Liechtenstein Center. Have your passport stamped for 3 SF at the tourist office's hard-to-miss Liechtenstein Center. ⊠ *Städtle 39,* ☎ *423/2396300* ⊙ *Daily 10–5.*

Liechtensteinisches Landesmuseum (*National Museum*). Housed in a former tavern and customhouse, the Liechtensteinisches Landesmuseum includes a modern annex built into the cliff. The collection covers the geology, history, and folklore of the principality. ⊠ *Städtle 43,* ☎ *423/2396820* ⊕ *www.landesmuseum.li* ⊠ *8 SF* ⊙ *Tues. and Fri.– Sun. 10–5, Wed. 10–8.*

Postmuseum. Liechtenstein's small postal museum demonstrates the principality's history as a maker of beautifully designed, limited-edition postage stamps. ⊠ *Städtle 37,* ☎ *423/2366105* ⊠ *Free* ⊙ *Daily 10–noon and 1:30–5.*

Ski Museum Vaduz. This small shrine to the region's preferred pastime includes numerous variations on the Alpine theme, including skis, sleds, fashion, and literature. ⊠ *Fabrikweg 5,* ☎ *423/2321502* ⊕ *www. skimuseum.li* ⊠ *7 SF* ⊙ *Weekdays 2–6.*

Vaduz Castle. At the top of a well-marked hill road (you can climb the forest footpath between Restaurant Ratskeller and Café Burg) stands Vaduz Castle. Here His Serene Highness Hans-Adam II, prince of Liechtenstein, reigns in a gratifyingly romantic fortress-home with red and white medieval shutters, massive ramparts, and a broad perspective over the Rhine Valley. Originally built in the 12th century, the castle was burned down by troops of the Swiss Confederation in the Swabian Wars of 1499 and partly rebuilt during the following centuries. A complete overhaul that started in 1905 gave it its present form. It is not open to the public, as Hans-Adam II enjoys his privacy. He is the son of the late beloved Franz Josef II, who died in November 1989 after more than a 50-year reign. Franz Josef's birthday, August 15, is still celebrated as the Liechtenstein national holiday. Heir to the throne Prince Alois increasingly has taken over daily business while Hans-Adam II spends his time in Vienna, where the family museum is one of the city's finest cultural jewels. ✉.

WHERE TO EAT AND STAY

For expanded hotel reviews, visit Fodors.com.

$$ FRENCH ★ 🍴 **Real.** Here you'll find rich Austrian-French cuisine in all its buttery glory prepared by Sebastian Fink. The unpretentious former chef, Felix Real, still presides over the 20,000-bottle wine cellar. There's an abundance of game in season, richly sauced seafood, and soufflés. The ambience is old school, and even the salads are prepared at your table. Downstairs, the more casual Stübli atmosphere is just right for *Geschnetzeltes mit Rösti* (veal in cream sauce with hash brown potatoes). [$] *Average main: 33 SF* ✉ *Städtle 21,* ☎ *423/2322222.*

$$ SWISS ★ 🍴 **Wirtschaft zum Löwen.** Though there's plenty of French, Swiss, and Austrian influence, Liechtenstein has a cuisine of its own, and this is the place to try it. In a wood-shingle landmark farmhouse on the Austrian border, the friendly Biedermann family serves tender homemade *Schwartenmagen* (the pressed-pork mold unfortunately known as headcheese in English), tripe in white wine, lovely meats, and the local crusty, chewy bread. For dessert, order the *Kaiserschmarrn*, a caramelized pancake with plum compote. Be sure to try the region's distinctive wines. When driving here on Route 16, keep an eye out for Schellenberg, posted to the left; if you zip past it, you'll end up in Austria. [$] *Average main: 33 SF* ✉ *Im Winkel 5, Schellenberg, Liechtenstein* ✣ *10 km (6 mi) north of Vaduz off Rte. 16* ☎ *423/3731162* 🌐 *www.loewen.li* ⏲ *Closed Wed. and Thurs.*

$$$ HOTEL 🏨 **Park-Hotel Sonnenhof.** With pleasant views of the valley below and mountains beyond, this hillside retreat offers a leafy respite from the crowds. **Pros:** views of the valley; peace and quiet; excellent service. **Cons:** stuffy decor; a hike from town; open balconies offer little privacy. [$] *Rooms from: 289 SF* ✉ *Mareestr. 29,* ☎ *423/2390202* 🌐 *www.sonnenhof.li* 🛏 *17 rooms, 12 suites* ⏲ *Closed late Dec.–early Jan.* 🍽 *Breakfast.*

$$$ HOTEL 🏨 **Residence.** Rice-paper screens and down duvets mingle in a simple Japanese-European style. **Pros:** 21st-century design with all up-to-date conveniences; indulge your inner lazybones: everything is just three minutes away. **Cons:** a little sleek for the Holy Roman Empire experience; the reception desk is hidden away upstairs. [$] *Rooms from: 260 SF* ✉ *Städtle 23,* ☎ *423/2392020* 🌐 *www.residence.li* 🛏 *24 rooms, 5 suites* 🍽 *Breakfast.*

SPORTS AND THE OUTDOORS

BIKING AND MOTORCYCLING

Bike Garage. In Triesen, about 4 km (2½ miles) south of Vaduz, bikes can be rented from Bike Garage. ✉ *Landstr. 256,* ☎ *423/3900390.*

SHOPPING

Liechtenstein is sometimes called the unofficial, per-capita world champion of stamp collecting. To buy some of its famous stamps, whether to send a postcard to a philatelist friend or to invest in limited-issue commemorative sheets, you must line up with the tour-bus crowds at the popular post office on the Städtle. A sharp crumbly cheese called Liechtensteiner Käse räss can be found while visiting its agriculture commune Ruggell, while wines like Chardonnay, Riesling, and Gewürztraminer, are an ideal souvenir upgrade from postage stamps. The country's Hofkellerei "Princely Cellars" in Vaduz is a great place to sample some local varietals. More recently, an excellent beer brewery opened in the commune of Schaan in 2007, and the brewmeister is happy to arrange tours in English or offer flights of their excellent ales and pilsners.

Schaedler Keramik. Though shops on the main street of Vaduz carry samples of the local dark-glaze pottery painted with folksy flowers and figures, the central source is 8 km (5 miles) north of Vaduz at Schaedler Keramik. Simpler household pottery as well as the traditional and often ornate hand-painted pieces are available for sale. Pottery making is demonstrated daily, and the shop is open weekdays 8–5. ⊠ *Rte. 16, Nendeln, Liechtenstein* ☎ *423/3731414.*

4

Graubünden

AROSA, DAVOS, THE ENGADINE, ST. MORITZ

WORD OF MOUTH

"I would suggest . . . staying in the Engadine Valley. [It] hasn't spent the money on PR, [like] the Jungfrau region has, but it also has magnificent mountain peaks, Alpine lakes, and small, quaint villages."

—swandav2000

WELCOME TO GRAUBÜNDEN

TOP REASONS TO GO

★ **Chic, chicer, chicest:** From Arosa to Zuoz, every mountain resort is a place to be seen by the ski elite. Sparkling St. Moritz, Davos, and Klosters are perfect for chilling out, but don't forget your Gucci sunglasses.

★ **Heidi's hideaway:** Shirley Temple immortalized the just-too-cute orphan, but find out just how much her 1937 film differed from Johanna Spyri's beloved book with a visit to Maienfeld's Heidi Village.

★ **Beautiful sgraffiti:** The Lower Inn Valley is home to some picture-perfect villages, famous for their folkloric dwellings graced with sgraffiti wall decorations. For the best close-ups, head to Guarda—so beautiful it is under federal protection.

★ **Keeping body and soul together:** Palatial spa hotels and a landscape that inspired great painters and philosophers is what Graubünden is about.

1 Heidiland. Everybody's favorite little Swiss miss lived here, and today the village of Maienfeld pays homage to the legendary character with a Heidi Village, Heidi-Path, and Heidi-hof hotel. To the south lies Chur, the capital of Graubünden—largely modern, it has, in fact, nearly 11,000 years of history exhibited in the local museums, churches, even the streets. Then strike southeast for Arosa, a high-altitude village perfect for those who find the winter elegance of St. Moritz just a trifle overbearing.

2 Prätigau and Davos. The fertile Prätigau Valley with its abundance of meadows, forests, and panoramic Alpine vistas is home to Klosters, an attractive, chaleted resort perfect for those seeking fantastic skiing in a quieter atmosphere. Lively, neighboring Davos—Europe's highest city—is as renowned for its winter sports as it is for hosting the World Economic Forum.

3 The Lower Engadine. Bustling Scuol has maintained its ancient feel despite modern amenities. Nature lovers will have all wishes fulfilled in the famed Swiss National Park, while art lovers will adore flower-boxed Guarda and

the magnificent fortress at Tarasp, which seems lifted from the pages of a medieval illuminated manuscript.

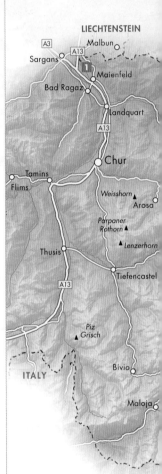

LIECHTENSTEIN

A3 — Malbun

Sargans — A13

Maienfeld

Bad Ragaz

Landquart

A13

Chur

Tamins

Flims

Weisshorn ▲

Arosa

Parpaner Rothorn ▲

▲ Lenzerhorn

Thusis

Tiefencastel

A13

Piz Grisch ▲

Bivio

ITALY

Maloja

4 The Upper Engadine and St. Moritz. Take New York luxury, Paris fashion, a bit of London and Milan, a drop of Munich, a handful of Rome, large swaths of premium ski slopes and crystalline lakes, then add a perfect "champagne climate" of crisp, dry air and plenty of sunshine, mix well, and pour onto a few acres in a gorgeous high-altitude valley. How can anything compare to St. Moritz?

GETTING ORIENTED

Covering about 2,800 square miles, Graubünden is the largest canton in Switzerland, occupying more than one-sixth of the country. With high mountains nestling chic resorts like St. Moritz, Davos, and Klosters, the Grisons (to use the French name) offers as much attitude as altitude. Cross any of the passes southeast to the Engadine Valley for quaint sgraffiti-covered villages and more fresh air than you can imagine.

Updated by
Kati Clinton
Robson

Although the names of its biggest resorts, such as St. Moritz and Davos, register almost automatic recognition, the region wrapped around them remains surprisingly unsung, untouched by the fur-clad celebs who make stages out of its sports centers, aloof to the glamour trends — quirky, resilient, and decidedly set apart.

Nowhere in Switzerland will you find a sharper contrast than the one between the bronzed seven-day citizens who jet into St. Moritz and the stalwart native farmers who nurse archaic dialects and gather their crops by hand, as their Roman-Etruscan ancestors did. Resort life in winter is quite different from everyday existence in Graubünden.

As it straddles the continental divide, its rains pour off northward into the Rhine River, eastward with the Inn River to the Danube River and Black Sea, and south to the River Po. The landscape here is thus riddled with bluff-lined valleys. The southern half basks in crystalline light and, if it weren't for the Italian-speaking Ticino, would receive the most sunshine in the country. Its 150 valleys and 615 lakes are flanked by 937 peaks, among them Piz Buin (10,867 feet) in the north and Piz Bernina (13,307 feet), the canton's highest mountain, in the south.

Like many Swiss cantons, Graubünden is culturally diverse. To the north it borders Austria and Liechtenstein, and in the east and south it abuts Italy. Swiss-German and Italian are widely spoken, and about one-third of the local residents speak Romansh, an ancient regional language. Even the name *Graubünden* itself comes in a variety of forms: Grisons (French), Grigioni (Italian), and Grischun (Romansh). It originates from the "Gray Confederation," one of three leagues that joined together in 1471 to resist the feudal Habsburg rulers. After a period as a "free state," Graubünden became a Swiss canton in 1803. With these dialects and their derivatives cutting one valley culture neatly off from another, it's no wonder the back roads of the region seem so removed from the modern mainstream.

GRAUBÜNDEN PLANNER

WHEN TO GO

Graubünden has essentially two climatic regions. In the lower Rhine Valley (Chur, Heidi-land, etc.), there are normally four distinct and equal seasons. Up in the Engadine, there are four seasons as well, but their distribution is heavily skewed toward winter. Snow can remain until May, and after a brief spring and summer you may experience flurries or frozen dew in August. So even if you're traveling in summer, pack some warm clothing, like a sweater and a windbreaker.

PLANNING YOUR TIME

In Switzerland's largest canton, you can party with the in crowds at Davos or St. Moritz, chill out someplace remote like Guarda or Zernez, or hit the highlights in between. Decide which towns or areas you most want to visit, and then pick one or two hubs. It is certainly possible to embark on a whirlwind tour of many different valleys, but if you want to really experience the unique local culture, feel, and food of Graubünden, then slow down and take your time to explore a place or two in more depth.

GETTING HERE AND AROUND

AIR TRAVEL

Engadine Airport is mainly used by private planes. At 5,600 feet, it's the highest airport in Europe. The closest international airports are Zürich (about 2 hours from Chur) and Lugano (about 2½ hours from St. Moritz).

BUS TRAVEL

You can take the Swiss postbus (postauto) system's *Palm Express* from Lugano in the Ticino to St. Moritz. The four-hour trip passes through a corner of Italy and over the Maloja Pass. Reservations are essential and owners of a Swiss Pass will need to purchase the additional Alpine Ticket for 15 SF. Postbuses are a good way to wind your way up Alpine switchbacks over the region's great passes—that is, if you're not inclined toward motion sickness. The main ski resorts have "sport bus" shuttles, which connect the villages and mountain stations. The service is usually included in the price of your lift ticket or on presentation of a "guest card" (check to see if your hotel offers these discount booklets).

Bus Information Palm Express ☎ 058/4483535 ⊕ *www.postbus.ch.*

CAR TRAVEL

Unless you intend to explore every nook and cranny of Graubünden or some of the more remote valleys, you will not really need a car. In fact, a car might cost more time and irritation than simply using public transportation.

Graubünden is mountainous, with few major highways. Drivers can enter either by way of the San Bernardino Pass from the south or from the north on A13, the region's only expressway, which follows a north–south route. Coming from Austria and Munich, the A27 leads into the Lower Engadine; roads over the Ofen and Bernina passes lead into the Engadine from the South Tyrol and Veltline areas of Italy respectively, and the approach to the Upper Engadine from Italy is over the Maloja

Pass. The Oberalp and Lukmanier passes lead from Uri and Ticino respectively to the Surselva region to join A13.

If you're traveling in winter, make sure to check the status of the passes beforehand. Trains through the Vereina tunnel shuttle cars between Klosters and Sagliains (Susch–Lavin). The tunnel has made the Lower Engadine quickly accessible during the winter, when the Flüela Pass is seldom open.

TRAIN TRAVEL

Thanks to the Swiss Railways (SBB/CFF/FFS) and the affiliated *UNESCO World Heritage Status* narrow-gauge Rhätische Bahn (the Rhaetian Railway, commonly referred to as the "Rhätibahn"), most destinations mentioned here are reachable by train, and Swiss postbuses stop in places where there is no train service.

The *Bernina Express* runs from Chur to St. Moritz via the Albula route and on to Italy past the spectacular Bernina peaks, lakes, and glaciers. The *Engadine Star* makes its way from Klosters to St. Moritz in a couple of hours. The glamorous *Glacier Express,* billed as "the slowest express in the world," connects St. Moritz with Zermatt via the Oberalp Pass, crossing 291 bridges during its 7½-hour journey. The train includes an antique burnished-wood dining car; you can book a table through Rail Gourmino swissAlps.

Reservations for these trains are mandatory and can be made at almost any European rail station. As on the federal railways, a variety of reduced-price passes are available.

Train Information Rail Gourmino swissAlps ✉ *Gürtelstr. 14, Chur* 📠 *081/3001515* ⊕ *www.rgswissalps.ch.* **Rhätische Bahn** 📠 *081/2886565* ⊕ *www.rhb.ch.*

⇨ *For more information on getting here and around, see Travel Smart Switzerland.*

RESTAURANTS

Thanks to all those tourists, restaurants tend to stay open throughout the day for the hungry visitor. The way to be sure is to look for a sign that bears the word *durchgehend*, meaning "without a stop." Some places, however, will serve only snacks—or close entirely—between 2:30 and 5:30. If traveling in the low season (November or April), you may encounter quite a few closed doors. Remember the rugged mountainscape can be deceiving. Hikers and skiers will frequently encounter a cozy *Bergbeizli* ("mountain inn"), where fine locally grown food is served up in a most congenial atmosphere.

Many restaurants in resort towns close from the end of April to mid-June and October to December; there are variations and exceptions, of course, so if you plan a visit during the off-season, check in advance.

Prices in the reviews are the average cost of a main course at dinner or, if dinner is not served, at lunch.

HOTELS

Hoteliers in Graubünden invest fortunes in preserving Alpine coziness on both the outside and inside of their lodgings, which is not always the case in other parts of Switzerland. Therefore, prices in this popular region are comparatively high. Even higher prices are charged for the winter holiday period and in February when most schools are on their winter breaks; during the rest of winter you may find special lower-priced packages that include ski passes. Summer rates are generally lower. Many hotels close between seasons, from April to mid-June and from mid-October to mid-December, but the dates and months vary each year, so be sure to check. In a few winter resorts there are hotels that stay closed all summer; we have not included these in our listings.

Hotels publish tariffs in various ways; double-check to see whether you're paying per person or per room, as well as whether you have *Halbpension* (demi-pension, or half board). If you plan to stay in one place for more than a day or two, half board can cut costs. You may also want to ask about GästeKarte (guest cards), small booklets given by hotels that provide various deals on local transit or attractions. Many places are packed between Christmas and about January 15—so make reservations well in advance for this time.

If you are interested only in sports, you may wish to budget less for hotels by staying in more out-of-the-way villages and commuting to the more expensive areas, such as St. Moritz and Pontresina.

Prices in the reviews are the lowest cost of a standard double room in high season.

TOURS

Arosa, Davos, and Lenzerheide-Valbella offer special hiking packages. You can walk from Davos to Arosa one day and from Arosa to Lenzerheide the next.

The Arosa tourist office offers guided tours and nature walks daily from June through October; you can visit a cheese maker, a regional museum, and a 15th-century chapel. The Davos and Klosters tourist offices arrange guided walks at least once a week from July to September. The Chur tourist office arranges guided tours from April to October every Wednesday at 2 (6 SF). To explore on your own, pick up a map from the tourist office and follow the green and red footprints on the pavement.

The Pontresina tourist office offers guided walking tours of its Old Town from mid-June to mid-October. It also offers guided botanical excursions, glacier treks, and hiking trips to the Swiss National Park, plus mushroom-picking outings in season (August and September). If you are staying in Pontresina, these trips are free; day visitors pay a small fee. Guides for all of the above tours speak English.

Graubünden Holidays. No need to worry about booking a hotel or transporting your luggage, with this service it's all taken care of. Contact local tourist offices or the regional tourist office, Graubünden Holidays. Similar arrangements can be made in the Engadine; call Engadin St. Moritz Tourism Office (☏ *081/8300001* ⊕ *www.engadin.stmoritz.*

ch) for more information. ⊠ *Alexanderstr. 24, Chur* ☎ *081/2542424* ⊕ *www.graubuenden.ch.*

VISITOR INFORMATION
Regional Tourist Office Graubünden Holidays ⊠ *Alexanderstr. 24, Chur* ☎ *081/2542424* ⊕ *www.graubuenden.ch.*

HEIDILAND

The Maienfeld region, with its hills and craggy peaks sloping down to sheltered vineyards, is the gateway from the north into Graubünden, but its claim to fame is that the legendary Heidi lived here. To the west in Surselva, the villages of Flims, Laax, and Falera together form the Alpine Arena, Graubünden's largest connected ski area. Arosa, to the east in the Schanfigg Valley, is a quieter resort village that lies in a bowl at the end of a spectacular, steep, winding road. The transportation hub of the region is Chur, the district capital.

MAIENFELD

102 km (63 miles) southeast of Zurich, 50 km (32 miles) south of Appenzell

Above this graceful little village full of fountains, vineyards, and old stucco houses, the Zürich author Johanna Spyri set *Heidi*, the much-loved children's story of an orphan growing up with her grandfather on an isolated Alpine farm. Taken away to accompany the invalid Clara in murky Frankfurt, she languishes until returning to her mountain home. Nursing her fatally ill son, Spyri spent time in Maienfeld and liked the mountains, but it's unknown whether actual people inspired her tale.

GETTING HERE AND AROUND
Trains connect Chur and Maienfeld; the journey takes no more than 15 minutes.

ESSENTIALS
Visitor Information Heidiland Tourism ⊠ *Bahnhofstr. 1, Maienfeld* ☎ *081/3301800* ⊕ *www.heidiland.com.* **Stadt Maienfeld** ⊠ *Bahnhofstr. 1* ☎ *081/3301912* ⊕ *www.maienfeld.ch/de/tourismus.*

EXPLORING
From Maienfeld you can hike along the **Heidi-Weg** (Heidi Path), either on the short circular route or continuing across steep open meadows and through thick forest to what have now been designated Peter the Goatherd's Hut and the Alm-Uncle's Hut. Here you might meet today's version of that character, who enjoys a chat and can answer Heidi-related questions in English. Along the way you'll take in awe-inspiring Rhine Valley views from flowered meadows that would have suited Heidi beautifully.

☺ **Heididorf** (*Heidi Village*). On both parts of the Heidi-Weg, you pass through Heididorf, in reality the hamlet of Oberrofels. Here you can find the house that was used as a model for the illustrations in the original *Heidi* books. It now houses Heidi-appropriate furnishings

Chur to Davos

KEY

- ← Cable Car/Funicular
- ←•←• Rail lines
- 🎿 Ski Resorts

AUSTRIA

Piz Buin

SILVRETTA GRUPPE

Saglains

Susch

Zernez

Brail

Wisshorn

Schwarzhorn

Grialetsch Glacier

Piz Vadret

Flüelapass

28

Pischa

Jakobshorn

Klosters

Wolfgang

Madrisahorn

Saas

Alp Luzein

Küblis

Fideris

Schiers

Gotschnagrat

Weissfluhjoch

Davos

RHÄTIKON

PRÄTTIGAU VALLEY

Landquart

28

Maienfeld

TO ZÜRICH

Bad Ragaz

Pardiel

Rinerhorn

Frauenkirch

Glaris

Wiesen

Arosa

SCHANFIGG

Weisshorn

Hörnlihütte

Parpaner Rothorn

Lenzerhorn

Wiesen

Alvaneu

GRAUBÜNDEN

Parpan

Valbella

Lenzerheide

Tiefencastel

A13

Chur

Reichenau

3

Albula River

Rhein River

Hinterheim River

Via Mala

Thusis

Zillis

SANKT GALLEN

Illanz

TO OBERALP PASSE AND LUKMANIER

4 mi

4 km

0

The classic children's story of Heidi was set in the peaceful countryside around Maienfeld.

and life-size models of Heidi, Grandfather, and Peter. ☎ *081/3301912* ⊕ *www.heidi-swiss.ch* ✉ *7 SF* ⊙ *Mid-Mar.–mid-Nov., daily 10–5.*

Heidihof Hotel. At the kitsch-happy Heidihof Hotel, a farmhouse that's been expanded, you can have a snack and take in the view or spend the night. For a more genuine Heidi experience, you can sleep in straw at a nearby farm (inquire at the tourist office). ✉ *Bovelweg 16* ☎ *081/3004747* ⊕ *www.heidihof.ch.*

Horse-drawn carriage. As an alternative to walking the route, you can take a two- to three-hour tour in a horse-drawn carriage. The cost is around 30 SF per person, depending on the number in your group. ☎ *081/3301912.*

Schloss Brandis. In Maienfeld, visit a few of the two dozen local wine merchants or enjoy a meal in the Knight's Hall of Schloss Brandis, a castle whose earliest portions date from the 10th century. ☎ *081/ 3022423* ⊕ *www.schlossbrandis.ch* ⊙ *Restaurant daily 11–10* ⊙ *Closed mid-July–mid-Aug.*

SPAS

Tamina Therme. Welcome to the ultimate spa and wellness location in Switzerland, featuring a breathtaking range of treatments and courses designed to relax and invigorate. There are the usual suspects like thermal baths, massages, dermatology, saunas, and fitness classes, and for those who have been working or playing hard, you can choose from burnout prevention courses, detox courses, and a course which can map, treat, and improve your sleeping habits. There is also a two-day medical golf clinic that includes a musculoskeletal system check and mental training with a PGA golf professional. You can even book a private session with a Swiss Olympic marathon trainer or train for a day with Viktor Rothlin, a European marathon champion. Reservations for the bathing and sauna areas are not necessary, but should definitely be considered for the various courses. All the facilities are located in a luxurious, immaculately kept resort complex, with stunning mountain views, two hotels, seven restaurants, an 18-hole golf course, and a casino. ⊠ *Hans Albrecht Strasse, Bad Ragaz* ☏ *081/3032740* ⊕ *www. taminatherme.ch/en* ☾ *Sun.–Thurs. 8 am–10 pm, Fri. 8 am–11 pm*

☞ *Adult weekend day ticket 40 SF (26 SF for 2 hrs on a weekday). Hair salon, hot tubs (indoor and outdoor), sauna, steam room. Gym with: cardiovascular machines, free weights, weight-training equipment. Services: aromatherapy, cellulite treatments, full- and partial-body massages, reflexology. Classes and programs: aerobics, aquaerobics, cycling, dance classes, fitness analysis, flexibility training, massage, meditation, nutritional analysis, nutritional counseling, nutrition lectures, personal training, Pilates, qigong, strength training, stretching, tai chi, weight management, weight training, yoga.*

CHUR

17 km (11 miles) south of Maienfeld

A small city of almost 37,000, with a modern downtown and a busy rail crossroad, the cantonal capital is the oldest continuously settled site north of the Alps. Discoveries of Stone Age tools place Chur's origins back to roughly 11,000 BC. The Romans founded Curia Raetorium on the rocky terrace south of the river; from here, they protected the Alpine routes that led to Lake Constance. By AD 284 the town served as the capital of a flourishing Roman colony, Rhaetia Prima. Its heyday was during the Middle Ages, when it was ruled by bishops and bishop-princes. Narrow streets, cobblestone alleys, hidden courtyards, and ancient shuttered buildings still abound. The southern *föhn* wind that blows up through the Rhine Valley accounts in great part for the wine grapes that grow along the steep slopes around the town.

GETTING HERE AND AROUND

The Swiss Federal Railway trains that enter Graubünden only travel as far as Chur. From here the local Rhätische Bahn (RhB) takes over. Frequent trains arrive in Chur from Zürich (1¼ hours away), Klosters (1 hour), Davos (1½ hours), and Liechtenstein (1 hour).

ESSENTIALS

Visitor Information Chur Tourism Office ⊠ *Bahnhofplatz 3* ☏ *081/2521818* ⊕ *www.churtourismus.ch.*

Romansh

The ancient Romansh (literally, "Roman") language is still predominant in the Lower Engadine and Surselva; roughly 30% of Graubünden residents can speak it. The language dates back to the 1st century BC, when the area was conquered by the Romans and became a province called Rhaetia Prima. An alternative view on this point says the tongue predates the Romans and originated as long ago as 600 BC, when an Etruscan prince named Rhaetus invaded the region.

Anyone versed in a Latin language can follow Romansh's simpler signs (*abitaziun da vacanzas*, for example, is a vacation apartment), but Romansh is difficult to pick up by ear. Nor do the Graubündners smooth the way: Rhaetian Romansh is fragmented into five dialects, which developed separately in formerly isolated valleys, so that depending on where you are, the word for *house* can be seen written on the facades of homes as *casa*, *chasa*, *chesa*, *tga/tgesa*, or *tgea*.

EXPLORING

TOP ATTRACTIONS

★ **Bündner Kunstmuseum.** Collections at Graubünden's art museum include works by well-known artists who lived or worked in the canton, including Angelika Kauffmann; Ferdinand Hodler; Giovanni Segantini; Ernst Kirchner; H.R. Giger; and Giovanni, Augusto, and Alberto Giacometti. There is also a program of rotating exhibitions. The building itself is a majestic Neoclassical structure erected in 1875 as a private residence. ⊠ *Postpl.* ☎ *081/2572868* ⊕ *buendner-kunstmuseum.ch* ▣ *12 SF* ☉ *Tues., Wed., and Fri.–Sun. 10–6, Thurs. 10–8.*

Hof-Torturm (*Citadel Gate Tower*). Opposite the Rätisches Museum, a stone archway under this tower leads into the court of the strong bishop-princes of Chur, once hosts to Holy Roman emperors—sometimes with whole armies in tow—passing through on their way to Italy or Germany. The bishops were repaid for their hospitality by imperial donations to the people. The thick fortifications of the residence aren't for show: they reflect the tendency of inhabitants to dispute the bishops' powers; by the 15th century those who rebelled could be punished with excommunication. The cozy Hofkellerei Stübli, with its warming ceramic stove, is now at the base of the tower. This welcoming restaurant presents visitors with the perfect opportunity to rest weary feet and enjoy superb views of the Kirche St. Martin and nearby square. Head up to the second floor where you can enjoy local specialties and have a drink in the vaulted, paneled room, dating from 1522, which was once used for church meetings. ⊠ *Hof 1* ☎ *081/2523230.*

Obere Gasse. Once the main street through Chur and a major route between Germany and Italy, Obere Gasse is now lined with small shops and cafés. At the end stands the 16th-century Obertor (Upper Gate), guarding the bridge across the Plessur River. ⊠ *Old Town, between the Obertor and Arcaspl.*

A hike through Heidiland offers rewarding views of steep meadows and dense forests.

🕙 **Rätisches Museum.** Displayed in a 1675 mansion, this collection provides a thorough, evocative overview of the canton's development. It includes not only furnishings and goods from that period, but also archaeological finds from the region, both Roman and prehistoric; display texts are in German, but an English-language guidebook is available for 2 SF. There are also exhibitions of special interest on display most of the time. ⊠ *Hofstr. 1* ☎ *081/2574840* ⊕ *www.raetischesmuseum.gr.ch* ✉ *6 SF* 🕙 *Tues.–Sun. 10–5.*

WORTH NOTING

Kathedrale St. Maria Himmelfahrt. The *Cathedral of the Assumption* was built between 1151 and 1272, drawing on stylistic influences from all across Europe. On this same site have stood a Roman castle, a bishop's house in the 5th century, and a Carolingian cathedral in the 8th century. Inside, the capitals of the columns are carved with fantastical beasts; clustered at their bases are less threatening animals, such as sheep and marmots. In the choir is a magnificent late-15th-century altar of gilded wood with nearly 150 carved figures created by Jakob Russ from Ravensburg, Germany. ⊠ *Hof* ☎ *081/2522076* 🕙 *Mon.–Sat. 6 am–7 pm, Sun. 7–7.*

Kirche St. Martin. St. Martin's was rebuilt in 1491 after a fire destroyed the 8th-century original. Since 1526 it has been Protestant. On your right as you enter are three stained-glass windows created in 1919 by Augusto Giacometti, the father of the Graubünden sculptor Alberto Giacometti. The steeple dates from 1917; with permission from the sacristan, you can climb to the top to see the bells. Of note, too, is the 1716 fountain beside the church, whose basin features the signs of the zodiac (the figure on top is a replica of the original). ✉ *Evangel. Kirchgemeinde, Kirchg. 12* ☎ *081/2522292* 🕒 *Mon.–Thurs. 8:30–11:30 and 2–5.*

Rathaus. Chur's Town Hall was built as two structures in 1464, which were connected in 1540. At ground level, under the arches, is the old marketplace. In the open hall on the second floor is a model of the Old Town, which can help you plan a tour of the city. The Grosser Ratsaal (Council Chamber) has a timber ceiling dating from 1493; the Bürgerratskammer (Citizens' Council Chamber) has wall panels from the Renaissance. Both chambers have old ceramic stoves, with the one in the Ratsaal depicting the seven deadly sins. Embedded in the wall beside the door on Reichsgasse 64 is a rod of iron about a foot long—the standard measure of a foot or shoe before the metric system was introduced. Although both chambers are generally closed to the public, very small groups can contact the tourist office to arrange a visit. ✉ *Poststr. 33* 🕒 *Weekdays 8–noon and 1:30–5.*

OFF THE BEATEN PATH

Via Mala. Heading south toward the San Bernardino Pass on the A13, turn off at Thusis and follow the sign for the Via Mala. This "bad road" was used by Romans and traders over centuries. It runs about 6 km (3½ miles) alongside the narrow Hinterrhein gorge. Shortly after the start of the gorge, climb down 321 steps (for a fee of 5 SF) to view the river, rock formations, a mid-18th-century bridge, and the old road itself. Continue to Zillis (*Postpl,* 🌐 *www.zillis-st-martin.ch*) to see the church's renowned 12th-century painted wood ceiling, whose 153 panels mostly depict stories from the Bible. It is one of the world's oldest original artistic works from the Romanesque era. ☎ *081/6509030* 🌐 *www.viamala.ch* 🕒 *Apr. and Oct., daily 9–6; May–Sept., daily 8–7.*

WHERE TO EAT AND STAY

$$ ECLECTIC

🍴 **Calanda.** Young and old meet in this friendly, trendy place with a great big mural featuring the restaurant's specialty: chicken. Thanks to Herbert Max Wesner and his team, you can enjoy a simple charcoal-roasted, free-roaming bird on a bed of salad in mango sauce or a new take on the classic Cordon Bleu, with cheese and cherry tomatoes wrapped in bacon and pork and cooked on skewers. The large, shaded outdoor terrace with a bar playing hit music is a great place to cool off in the summer. The specials menu changes daily, and the popular lunchtime menu is a reasonable 21.50 SF, while the Sunday brunch will only set you back 24.50 SF. [$] *Average main: 30 SF* ✉ *Postpl.* ☎ *081/2530880* 🌐 *www.calanda-chur.ch* 🕒 *Sun.–Thurs. 9 am–11 pm, Fri. and Sat. 9 am–midnight.*

$$ HOTEL

🏨 **Hotel ABC.** This *garni* (without a restaurant) business hotel is just yards from the train station, so you can enjoy the convenience of a central location without worrying about getting a good night's rest, as there are no night trains. **Pros:** central location; free generous breakfast buffet; free business center. **Cons:** with no air-conditioning, it can get stuffy during summer months; requires venturing out for food. [$] *Rooms from: 240 SF* ✉ *Ottostr. 8, off Bahnhofpl.* ☎ *081/2541313* 🌐 *www.hotelabc.ch* 🛏 *44 rooms, 10 apartments (for long-term guests)* 🍽 *Breakfast.*

$$$
HOTEL
Fodor's Choice
★

☷ **Romantik Hotel Stern.** Like many of the good vintages on its wine list, this historic inn, built in 1677, just keeps getting better: the family-owned and -run hotel neighbors the town's main church and features modern, wood-clad guest rooms, a cozy lounge with fireplace, and a rooftop terrace for relaxing. **Pros:** an intimate ambience and welcoming host; finest restaurant in Chur, with both regional and gourmet seasonal dishes. **Cons:** church bells can be a little too close for comfort during the day; some rooms are smaller than average due to dimensions of the old building; some interiors could do with a makeover. $ *Rooms from: 290 SF* ✉ *Reichsg. 11* ☎ *081/2585757* ⊕ *www.stern-chur.ch* ↵ *65 rooms* ⍾ *Multiple meal plans.*

NIGHTLIFE

Giger Bar. The futuristic Giger Bar is a strange space created by Academy Award winner H.R. Giger, a Chur native who designed the monsters and sets for the film *Alien.* ✉ *Comercialstr. 23* ☎ *081/2537506* ⊕ *www. hrgiger.com/barchur.htm* ⊗ *Mon.–Sat. 8–8* ⊗ *Closed Sun.*

SPAS

Therme Vals. Designed by award-winning Swiss architect Peter Zumthor, the Therme Vals is built from local Valser gneiss stone into the side of a mountain in a remote Graubünden valley. Focusing on the serene, primal experience of bathing, the therapies and treatments offered are designed to relieve tension and pamper; think masks, exfoliation, baths, wraps, and massages. Seven different pools are available ranging in temperature, including an exclusive sound bath resonance room linking the rejuvenating powers of water and sound. The special water shiatsu massage combines the positive elements of water therapy with the advantageous properties of shiatsu; while floating weightlessly in warm water, your body will experience reflexive lengthening and stretching, inducing deep relaxation. Double rooms in the on-site hotel are reasonably priced (and convenient given the far-off location), but note that they cost the same as a two-hour massage. ✉ *Vals* ⊹ *51 km (31.5 miles) southwest from Chur; if arriving by public transportation, hotel/ spa pickup from the Therme bus stop can be arranged beforehand* ☎ *081/9268961 baths, 081/9268080 hotel* ⊕ *www.therme-vals.ch/en* ↵ *40 SF baths; 104 SF 50-min water shiatsu massage; 248 SF 2-hr Hawian "Lomi Lomi" massage. Hot tubs (indoor and outdoor), sauna, steam room. Services: aromatheraphy, body wraps, cellulite treatment, exfoliation, facials, manicure, massage, pedicure, waxing. Classes and programs: aquaerobics, flexibility training, meditation, stretching.*

AROSA

★ *29 km (18 miles) southeast of Chur.*

Thanks to its altitude of 5,900 feet, Arosa is a well-known year-round sports center, offering brisk hiking, paragliding, and other activities in summer, and a long skiing or snowboarding season with a guarantee of snow. Its modest size, isolated location, quiet atmosphere, and natural beauty set it apart. There is little of the rush of Davos or the pretension of St. Moritz: this is a friendly, family-oriented spot staffed by upbeat, down-to-earth people. Even the well heeled rarely dress for dinner. On a winter walk you are more likely to be overtaken by sleds and horse-drawn carriages than by cars.

The town has two sections. Inner-Arosa, where the Walsers (immigrants from the Valais) built their wooden chalets in the 14th century, is at the end of the valley. Ausser-Arosa is near the train station and the Obersee (Upper Lake). Between the two is the impossible-to-miss casino, with its mosaic facade of screaming colors (it has now been converted into a theater/cinema). A convenient free bus shuttles through the town, and traffic is forbidden between midnight and 6 am. After you deliver your luggage to your hotel, you probably won't be using your car again while in town.

■ TIP➜ Don't miss the light, water, and music show on the lake at 9:50 pm every Saturday from mid-June to mid-October (except in the event of heavy rain or wind).

GETTING HERE AND AROUND

Arosa lies at the end of a beautiful, winding 29-km (19-mile) road with grades of more than 12% and more than 360 turns. Taking the train from Chur is a lot less nerve-wracking than driving. The Rhätische Bahn (RhB) has frequent departures to and from Arosa. Within town, you can ride the municipal buses for free if you have the Arosa Card, which is available in the summer. At that time, the card is included in all overnight stays. ■ TIP➜ The Arosa Card (free for overnight guests; 13 SF for day-trippers) gives summer visitors free access to many attractions, as well as round-trip rides on the Rhätische Bahn railway between Arosa and Langwies and trips on local mountain lifts and railways, which is great for hikers.

ESSENTIALS

Visitor Information Arosa Tourism Office ✉ *Sport- und Kongresszentrum Arosa* ☎ *081/3787020* ⊕ *www.arosa.ch.*

EXPLORING

Schanfigger Heimatmuseum. Drop into the Egghaus, one of the oldest and best-kept buildings from Arosa's past. It was first mentioned in a 1550 document and now houses the Schanfigger Heimatmuseum. Besides exhibiting the tools of the mountain farmer's difficult trade, this little museum has put together a slide show on local history. The museum building, a mid-16th century wooden farmhouse, is a sight in itself. ✉ *Poststr., Inner-Arosa* ☎ *081/3771731* ⊕ *www.arosa-museum. ch* ▱ *3 SF* ☉ *Late Dec.–mid-Apr., Tues. and Fri. 2:30–4:30; mid-June–mid-Oct., Mon., Wed., and Fri. 2:30–4:30.*

SKIING

Arosa's ski area is small compared with those of the Upper Engadine, Davos-Klosters, and the Alpine Arena (Flims-Laax). Closely screened in by mountains, the 5,900-foot-high resort has runs suitable for every level of skier. Its 13 lifts serve 70 km (43 miles) of trails. The slopes can be accessed directly from the valley at three points: the top of the village, behind the train station, and the Prätschli, a "feeder" lift to the main ski area. The black piste on the **Weisshorn** (8,700 feet) is challenging, but most of the runs there, as well as on **Hörnli** (8,200 feet), range from easy to intermediate.

Swiss Ski and Snowboard School. You can get snow-sports instruction at the official Swiss Ski and Snowboard School. ⊠ *Seeblickstr.* ☎ *081/3787500, 081/3787505* ⊕ *sssa.ch/en.*

ABC Snowsport School. Ski lessons are available at the ABC Snowsport School. ⊠ ☎ *081/3565660.*

Langlauf- und Schneeschuhzentrum Geeser. Cross-country skiers or Nordic walkers will find instruction, guided tours, equipment, and information at the Langlauf- und Schneeschuhzentrum Geeser, the Cross-country and Snowshoe Center. ⊠ ☎ *081/3772215* ⊕ *www.geeser-arosa.ch.*

All schools have English-speaking instructors. At this writing a one-day lift ticket costs 61 SF; a six-day pass costs 284 SF (incremental increases are likely each season). For cross-country skiing or snowshoeing, the Maran and Isla trails have 30 km (18 miles) of groomed trails. There are three official sled runs: Tschuggen, Prätschli, and Litzirüti.

Schlittenkönig. You can rent sleds at the train station or at Schlittenkönig. ⊠ *Seeblickstr.* ☎ *081/3772181* ⊕ *www.aroserschlitten.ch.*

WHERE TO EAT

$ ✕ **Hotel-Restaurant Hold.** Set in a large chalet-style hotel, this busy family
SWISS restaurant sits literally at the foot of the slopes. The menu is mostly traditional fare, including a range of Spätzli specialties—with Graubünden air-dried meat or ham and vegetables, for example—that will put an end to the greatest hunger pangs. Hardly the place for fashionistas, this is a top spot for kids: there are children's meals for 12 SF or less, it's adjacent to the children's ski school, and it even has a small playroom. Ⓢ *Average main: 22 SF* ⊠ *Poststr.* ☎ *081/3784020* ⊕ *www.holdarosa. ch/restaurant* ⊙ *Closed Easter–mid-June and mid-Oct.–early Dec.*

$$$ ✕ **Le Bistro.** The decor fits the name, with a tile floor, old French posters,
FRENCH dried flower bouquets hanging from the ceiling, and newspaper cuttings on the walls. The larger room is flooded with sunlight and bedecked in greenery with an immense view across the valley, but come sundown the call from the cozier warmth of the front parlor draws those looking for romantic lighting and convivial chatter. The menu leans French, with fillet of French Charolais beef or sirloin steak from Limousin beef. For relatively lighter fare, try the fish creations, such as Scottish salmon smoked on-site. Ⓢ *Average main: 45 SF* ⊠ *Hotel Cristallo, Poststr.* ☎ *081/3786868* ⊕ *www.cristalloarosa.ch* ⊙ *Closed early-Apr.–late June and late-Sept.–early Dec.*

WHERE TO STAY

$$$ 🏨 **Alpensonne.** Located about 200 yards from the ski lifts of Inner-Arosa,
HOTEL this family-owned and -run hotel is perfect for those seeking a homey feel that is clean and comfortable. **Pros:** stunning views; accommodating hosts; close proximity to village and ski slopes. **Cons:** some room interiors and balcony furniture need an upgrade; situated on main road through village; busy during the day, but traffic is forbidden at night. Ⓢ *Rooms from: 310 SF* ⊠ *Poststr.* ☎ *081/3771547* ⊕ *www.*

hotelalpensonne.ch 🛏 *30 rooms, 4 apartments* ⏲ *Closed late Apr.–late June and mid-Oct.–end Nov.* 🍴 *Multiple meal plans.*

$$$$ HOTEL ★ 🏨 **Arosa Kulm Hotel & Alpin Spa.** What was once a 19th-century wooden chalet has expanded to become a full-fledged "Alpine lifestyle" destination, and its position on the farthest edge of town, at the base of the slopes, is its biggest draw. **Pros:** cheaper rates in summer; perfect location for views and skiing (ski-in, ski-out); spa packages for a mind, body, and soul revamp. **Cons:** shopping opportunities not as classy as this hotel merits; black-tie is needed for the HB (half board) restaurant gala nights—come prepared. [$] *Rooms from: 444 SF* ✉ *Innere Poststr.* ☎ *081/3788888* 🌐 *www.arosakulm.ch* 🛏 *119 rooms, 24 suites* ⏲ *Closed mid-Sept.–end Nov. and early Apr.–end June* 🍴 *Multiple meal plans.*

$$ HOTEL ★ 🏨 **Sonnenhalde.** The sensor-touch heavy pine door that welcomes you to this *garni* (without a restaurant) chalet-hotel is your first sign of the happy marriage between charm and modern comfort here, followed by the welcoming family and small team of staff offering energetic and reliable service in a cozy space. **Pros:** proximity to ski lifts and village; cheaper rates during the low and summer seasons. **Cons:** dining at the end of a long day's hike requires venturing out. [$] *Rooms from: 222 SF* ☎ *081/3784444* 🌐 *www.gmüetli.ch* 🛏 *22 rooms, 3 suites* ⏲ *Closed late Apr.–late June and mid-Oct.–late Nov.* 🍴 *Breakfast.*

$$$$ HOTEL Fodor's Choice ★ 🏨 **Tschuggen Grand Hotel.** Well-heeled luxury seekers are in seventh heaven as they step into the hushed, welcoming environs of this exclusive hotel where the drive to simply be and do nothing reaches new heights—especially at the Bergoase spa, where the striking modernistic pools offer sensory serenity come rain, snow, or shine. **Pros:** award-winning spa; private mountain railway delivering guests to the heart of the ski area; chic modern furnishings. **Cons:** unfetching stark glass-and-concrete exterior belies the comfort within; very expensive. [$] *Rooms from: 640 SF* ☎ *081/3789999* 🌐 *www.tschuggen.ch* 🛏 *98 rooms, 32 suites* ⏲ *Closed mid-Apr.–July and late Oct.–late Nov.* 🍴 *Multiple meal plans.*

NIGHTLIFE AND THE ARTS

BARS

Disco Nuts. Inside the casino building (called the Kursaal), Disco Nuts plays the latest tunes for young people; it's open 'til the sun comes up. ✉ *Poststr.* ☎ *081/3771940* 🌐 *www.disconuts.ch.*

LOS Café Bar. If you're looking to be at the center of the action, grab a lively game of foosball, or rock the weekend away with a DJ, head to LOS Café Bar, a chill snowboarders' hangout where locals and tourists mix 'n mingle. ✉ *Haus Madrisa* ☎ *081/3565610* 🌐 *www.losbar.ch.*

Strumpf Bar. Located in the Arosa Vetter Hotel, this popular, après-ski bar turns into a smoker's lounge at night and serves a selection of rum, whiskey, and cigars from around the world. ✉ *Seeblickstr.* ☎ *081/3788000.*

Designed by Swiss architect Mario Botta, the sail-shaped skylights of Tschuggen Grand Hotel's Bergoase spa are a colorful beacon against Arosa's snowy backdrop.

MUSIC

Bergkirchli. From Christmas to mid-April and in summer and autumn, concerts are given at 5 pm on Tuesday on the hand-painted organ in Arosa's 500-year-old, wooden-roof Bergkirchli mountain chapel.

Kulturkreis Arosa. A jazz festival takes place in July, and music courses are given from June through October; get the program from Kulturkreis Arosa. ✉ *Poststr.* ☎ *081/3538747.*

SPORTS AND THE OUTDOORS

BALLOONING

Walter Vollenweider. For a balloon flight over Arosa or the Graubünden Alps, call Walter Vollenweider. ☎ *044/3913714.*

Trips are available each weekend from December through March; one-hour flights (three to four hours in total), which start and finish in Arosa, cost 350 SF per person. A special ballooning week is held each February.

GOLF

Maran. Europe's highest tee (6,209 feet) is on the eighth hole of Arosa's 18-hole course at Maran. ☎ *081/3774242* ⊕ *www.golfarosa.ch.*

HIKING AND BIKING

Arosa Tourism Office. Over 200 km (124 miles) of trails are maintained by the Arosa Tourism Office, which also has maps, offers advice on routes, and can arrange hiking or biking trips (including a five-day trek from Davos to Arosa). ☎ *081/3787020* ⊕ *www.arosa.ch.*

SKATING AND CURLING

Eissporthalle. At the indoor Eissporthalle you can watch ice hockey as well as take skating or curling lessons; there's an open-air rink alongside. ☎ *081/3771745.*

PRÄTTIGAU AND DAVOS

The name "Prättigau" means "meadow valley," and it's just that—a lush landscape of alternating orchards, pastures, and pine-covered mountains (though the main through-road is very busy). The predominant language is German, introduced by immigrants from the Valais in the 13th century, though most villages still have Romansh names. Prättigau's most renowned ski resort is Klosters. Its perhaps even more famous neighbor, Davos, lies in the Landwasser Valley, over the Wolfgang Pass. If you prefer something urban, head to Davos; for a quieter village experience, look to Klosters.

KLOSTERS

79 km (49 miles) northeast of Arosa, 49 km (29 miles) east of Chur.

At one time simply a group of hamlets, Klosters has become a small but chic resort, made up mostly of weathered-wood and white-stucco chalets. Author Peter Viertel and his wife, actress Deborah Kerr, made this their home base for decades. The village has two districts: Platz, which is older and busier, and Dorf, which lies on the main road toward Landquart. Klosters is famed for its skiing—British royal family members are faithful visitors—and makes the most of its access to the slopes of the Parsenn, above Davos.

GETTING HERE AND AROUND

The Rhätische Bahn (RhB), or a combination of Swiss railways and the RhB, covers the distance to Klosters in around one hour from Chur.

ESSENTIALS

Visitor Information Information Klosters ✉ *Alte Bahnhofstr. 6*
☎ *081/4102020* ⊕ *www.klosters.ch.*

EXPLORING

Nutli-Hüschi. A brief visit to the folk museum Nutli-Hüschi shows the resort's evolution from its mountain roots. This pretty wood-and-stone farmhouse with a stable was built in 1565. It shows how people lived and worked in the Prättigau in centuries past through exhibits of kitchen utensils, handcrafts, tools, and the spare regional furniture, including a child's bed that could be expanded as the child grew. ✉ *Monbielerstr. at Talstr.* ☎ *081/4102020, 079/4406948* ⊕ *www.museum-klosters.ch* 🎬 *5 SF* ☺ *Late Dec.–mid-Apr. and late June–mid-Oct., Wed. and Fri. 3–5.*

St. Jacob. In Klosters Platz the church of St. Jacob, dating from 1492, is the only remnant of the medieval monastery from which the village took its name. Its windows were painted by Augusto Giacometti.

SKIING

Klosters is known for its vast range of downhill runs, which, together with those of Davos, total 300 km (186½ miles). These are divided almost equally among easy, moderate, and difficult pistes. From the Gotschnagrat (7,494 feet), skiers can connect to the Parsenn slopes and try, for example, the famous Weissflüh run down to the village of Küblis. The sunny Madrisa slopes above Klosters Dorf offer relatively easy skiing and snowboarding, as well as free-ride opportunities.

Lift tickets to the combined Davos/Klosters area cost 69 SF for one day and up to 318 SF for six days, depending on how many and in which areas you want to ski. Bar-coded cards and KeyCards are used; you can activate them online (🌐 *www.davosklosters.ch*). Train or bus transport back to Klosters from other villages within the ski area is included in the price of the regional ski ticket.

TIP→ When booking your hotel, it is worth asking if they offer any special ski-pass deals during your desired travel period. Early and/or late season offers are frequently available.

Nordic Ski School. Never cross-country skied and want to take advantage of the 35 km (21 miles) of tracks? Head to the Nordic Ski School at Bardill Sport. ✉ *Landstrasse 185* ☎ *081/4221040.*

Swiss Ski + Snowboard School. For instruction or to go on a snowshoe trek, contact the Swiss Ski + Snowboard School, which has branches in both Platz (main office, Bahnhofstrasse 4) and Dorf. ☎ *081/4102828* 🌐 *www.sssk.ch/en.*

Swiss Ski & Snowboard School Saas. The Swiss Ski & Snowboard School Saas, located near the train station in Klosters Platz, offers standard instruction plus special courses in carving, slalom skiing, and more; it has branches in both Platz and Dorf. ☎ *081/4202233.*

WHERE TO EAT

$$ SWISS Fodor's Choice ★ 🍴 **Restaurant Gotschna.** A homey rustic eatery slightly outside Klosters offers up traditional Swiss dishes for the whole family without fuss or fanfare. Stone-clad floors and wall-to-ceiling *Arvenholz* (the traditional pinewood interior of the region) ensconce you in the warmth and comfort of a true mountain abode. Prättigauer Knödel (local beef and pork meatballs served in a cream sauce with spätzli) and fondue followed by homemade cakes or apple strudel works wonders on the soul—it's all somehow reminiscent of a family gathering at the kitchen hearth. In the summer months, diners can enjoy a range of Thai and Indian curries—a rarity in this region—as well as the outdoor garden. [$] *Average main: 26 SF* ✉ *Serneuserstr. 63, Serneus (5 km/3 miles north of Klosters)* ☎ *081/4221428* 🌐 *www.restaurant-gotschna.ch* 🕒 *Closed Mon., Tues., end-Sept.–mid-Nov., and after Easter–mid-June.*

$$ SWISS 🍴 **Restaurant Höhwald.** This friendly, touristy restaurant up the hill from Klosters stands proud in its majestic setting, with a large, open terrace offering incredible valley and mountain views. As for the food, there is a wide selection of dishes to choose from, but be sure to try their seasonal game specialties, such as sliced venison with cranberry sauce or the rack of boar with apricot butter. Inside, decor runs to mounted animal trophies and old-world exposed beams; outside is the breathtaking

mountainscape. $ *Average main: 36 SF* ⊠ *Monbielerstr. 171, Klosters-Monbiel* ☎ *081/4223045* ⊕ *www.hoehwald-klosters.ch* ☉ *Closed Tues., Wed., mid-Apr.–May, and mid-Oct.–mid-Dec.*

WHERE TO STAY

$$$$
HOTEL

🖼 **Alpina.** Conveniently located across from the train station, this family-owned and -run property comprised of three buildings with south-facing balconies is rustic yet comfortable. **Pros:** good on-site restaurants; personal, attentive service; DVD players in all rooms; nice wellness area. **Cons:** no minibar; view of the mountainscape is marred by the train station. $ *Rooms from: 430 SF* ⊠ *Bahnhofstr. 1, Klosters-Platz, Klosters* ☎ *081/4102424* ⊕ *www.alpina-klosters.ch* ⇱ *43 rooms, 13 apartments* ☉ *Closed mid-Apr.–mid–June and early Dec.* ¶◎¶ *Multiple meal plans.*

$$$$
HOTEL
Fodor's Choice
★

🖼 **Romantik Hotel Chesa Grischuna.** Located directly in the town center and renovated from a farmhouse in 1938, the Grischuna has one of the most charming settings in Switzerland, making it one of Klosters's landmarks. **Pros:** full of character and a vibrant eclectic social scene; famed restaurant; cheaper rates in summer. **Cons:** rooms are on the small side; no wellness facilities. $ *Rooms from: 430 SF* ⊠ *Bahnhofstr. 12, Klosters-Platz* ☎ *081/4222222* ⊕ *www.chesagrischuna.ch* ⇱ *23 rooms, 19 with bath* ☉ *Closed mid-Apr–end-June and late-Oct.–Dec.* ¶◎¶ *Multiple meal plans.*

$$
HOTEL

🖼 **Rustico.** Good things come in small packages here—guest rooms are petite but very attractive and there are several on-site eateries serving everything from tapas to more complicated Swiss dishes. **Pros:** award-winning cuisine; cooking classes in summer; enchanting personal hospitality. **Cons:** rooms are extremely small; there are no spa or pool facilities. $ *Rooms from: 220 SF* ⊠ *Landstr. 194, Klosters-Platz* ☎ *081/4102288* ⊕ *www.hotel-rustico.ch* ⇱ *10 rooms, 2 apartments* ☉ *Closed mid-Apr.–mid-June and 2 wks in Nov.* ¶◎¶ *Multiple meal plans.*

$$
HOTEL
♻
Fodor's Choice
★

🖼 **Silvapina.** This delightful hotel in an old chalet-style building is family-run and welcoming of other families, with apartments featuring small kitchens and fireplaces perfect for a small clan. **Pros:** comfy and clean budget accommodation for families; four-minute walk to Madrisa cable car; lovely hosts. **Cons:** next to train track, which can be noisy during the day; dated dining area. $ *Rooms from: 184 SF* ⊠ *Silvapinaweg 6, Klosters-Dorf* ☎ *081/4221468* ⊕ *www.silvapina.ch* ⇱ *14 rooms, 4 studios, 2 apartments* ☉ *Closed 3rd wk Apr.–mid-June and mid-Oct–early Dec.* ¶◎¶ *Multiple meal plans.*

NIGHTLIFE

Casa Antica. Revelers dance late into the night at Casa Antica, a 300-year-old converted barn. ⊠ *Landstr. 176* ☎ *081/4221621.*

Chesa Bar. A popular after-dinner spot, Chesa Bar has piano music and several intimate bar areas. ⊠ *Bahnhofstr. 12* ☎ *081/4222222.*

Gaudy's Graströchni. Located at the bottom of run 21, near the Gotschnabahn, the Graströchni is the perfect place to end a day of skiing with a pint (or five). ⊠ *Rütipromenade 2* ⊕ *www.grastroechni.ch.*

Gotschnabar. To find the après-ski crowd, head (or ski) to the bottom of the Gotschnabahn and hit up the Gotschnabar, which is equal parts

Klosters's landmark Romantik Hotel Chesa Grischuna has been attracting A-list stars for decades.

hip and relaxed. Note that it's only open in winter. ⊠ *Gotschnastrasse 21* ⊕ *www.gotschnabar.ch.*

Piano Bar. Lively, late-night action in the center of town can be found downstairs in the Hotel Schweizerhof's Piano Bar—a resort institution. ⊠ *Via dal Bagn 54, St. Mortiz* ☎ *081/8370707* ☉ *Dec.–Easter, 9 pm–2 am.*

SPORTS AND THE OUTDOORS
BIKING AND HIKING
The Klosters area has plenty of trails for exploring the countryside. The 250 km (155 miles) of summer hiking routes are reduced to 35 km (22 miles) of prepared paths in winter. There are 120 km (74½ miles) of mountain-biking routes, including a steep, free-ride track running from the Gotschnabahn mid-station (Gotschnaboden) back down into Klosters Platz—for serious riders only.

Bardill Sport. To rent mountain bikes, try Bardill Sport. ⊠ *Talstation Gotschnabahn* ☎ *081/4225500.*

Bertram's Bike Shop. Another source for mountain bikes is Bertram's Bike Shop. ⊠ *Doggilochstr. 64* ☎ *076/3184264.*

GOLF
Golf Klosters. Not to be outdone by its neighbors, Klosters has also added a relatively tough nine-hole Golf Klosters, including a driving range. An electric golf cart is included in the greens fee and the seventh hole provides the additional handicap of a jaw-dropping view of Klosters. ⊠ *Selfrangastrasse 44* ☎ *081/4221133* ⊕ *www.golf-klosters. ch* ☉ *May–late Oct.*

SKIING IN GRAUBÜNDEN

With Davos, site of the world's first ski lift; St. Moritz, arguably the world's ritziest resort; and other hot spots within its confines, Graubünden has earned its reputation as the ultimate winter destination. You'll find downhill skiing and snowboarding for all skill levels, as well as miles of *Langlauf* (cross-country skiing) trails prepared for both the classic and skating techniques.

Sports shops can outfit you with the necessary equipment; in Davos, you can even rent ski clothing. If you plan to spend a few days in one resort, check with local tourist offices for special packages. If you want to spend a day in a different resort within Graubünden, buy the lift ticket with your train ticket and the return fare will be reduced. Remember that accidents do occur, especially in unmarked zones. Avoid them unless you are suitably equipped and led by a qualified guide.

4

HORSEBACK RIDING
For horseback-riding excursions, contact the tourist office, which can help you locate local operators.

SKATING
Sportszentrum. Klosters's Sportszentrum has rinks for skating, hockey, curling, and ice bowling in season. Skate rentals are available. ⊠ *Doggilochstr. 51, Klosters-Platz* ☏ *081/4102131* ⊕ *www.sportzentrum-klosters.ch.*

SLEDDING
Klosters/Davos is big on sledding, with eight sled runs crisscrossing resort mountains. The 3½-km (2-mile) Rinerhorn run, up the valley from Davos, is lighted up at night. A day card costs 50 SF, while a sled can be rented for 10 SF at the cable-car valley station with a 50-franc deposit; most shops will also accept your passport as a deposit. Evening runs on the lighted slope are open Wednesday and Friday, 7–11 pm, from January to March. They cost 20 SF for an evening.

Day tickets for Schatzalp to Davos Platz cost 30 SF, while night sledding (6–10:30 pm) costs 24 SF. Day cards at Madrisa mountain cost 33 SF. The run here is 8½ km (5 miles) long and ends in Saas, from which you can return by bus to Klosters (buses leave every hour or so until 7:24 pm). Sled rentals at the Madrisa cable-car station are 10 SF. Another sled run begins at the midway station of the Gotschna cable car. Day passes cost 33 SF; sled rentals at the station cost 10 SF.

Andrist Sport. Sleds are available for rental at Andrist Sport. ⊠ *Gotschnastr. 8* ☏ *081/4102080* ⊕ *www.andrist-sport.ch.*

Gotschna Sport. Gotschna Sport also rents sleds. ⊠ *Alte Bahnhofstr. 5, Klosters-Platz* ☏ *081/4221197.*

DAVOS

11 km (7 miles) southwest of Klosters.

At 5,116 feet, this highest "city" (stretching the definition) in Europe is good for cold-weather sports even in the soggiest of winters. Davos is famous for its ice sports and skiing, and almost more celebrated for hosting the annual World Economic Forum every January. The town and its lake lie in the Landwasser Valley, which runs parallel to the Upper Engadine, though they're separated by the vast Albula chain, reaching to more than 9,840 feet. On the opposite side of the valley stands the Strela chain, dominated by the Weissfluhgipfel.

This is a capital for action-oriented sports enthusiasts and not necessarily for anyone seeking a peaceful, rustic mountain retreat (especially at the end of December, when there's an invasion of ice-hockey fans for the international Spengler Cup).

Davos is divided into Platz and Dorf (village), which together are one noisier-than-average urban strip, though Dorf is the calmer of the two. The town's first visitors came to take cures for lung disease in the bracing mountain air. Now, except for a few token historic structures and brightly painted buildings, the town is modern and architecturally undistinguished, and the center of town sometimes fills with the exhaust of city traffic. But no matter how densely populated and fast-paced the town becomes, the slopes are still spectacular, and the regulars return.

GETTING HERE AND AROUND

Davos is 30 minutes from Klosters, 1½ hours from Chur, and 2½ hours from Zürich. When traveling from Zürich or Chur, you'll have to change trains at Landquart. The journey from St. Moritz takes 1½ hours, with a transfer at Filisur. From Scuol, it takes 1 hour, 15 minutes with a change in Klosters Platz. In case you accidentally ski down to the wrong resort, or your après-ski lasts longer than anticipated, it's worth noting that there is at least one train an hour from Klosters to Davos between 5 am and at least 10 pm, though it tends to be 11:30 pm during the ski season.

The Vereina tunnel provides year-round train service from Klosters to Sagliains, near Susch–Lavin. Car-carrying trains leave from just above Klosters—road signs indicate a train carrying cars and the name Vereina.

Once in Davos, there is one train per hour covering the 3 km (1.8 miles) between the villages of Davos Dorf and Platz. Much more convenient is the bus line through town, along Promenade; it's free for overnight guests in summer and for winter guests in possession of a valid lift pass.

ESSENTIALS

Visitor Information Information Davos Dorf ✉ *Bahnhof bldg.*
☎ *081/4152121* ⊕ *www.davos.ch.* **Information Davos Platz** ✉ *Talstrasse 41*
☎ *081/4152121* ⊕ *www.davos.ch.*

Even if you don't ski, Graubünden has fun outdoor activities for the whole family.

EXPLORING

Kirche St. Johann (*Church of St. John the Baptist*). Among the town's few architectural highlights, the late-Gothic Kirche St. Johann stands out by virtue of its windows by Augusto Giacometti. Nearby is the 17th-century Rathaus (Town Hall). ⊠ *Rathausstutz 2.*

Kirchner Museum. The Kirchner Museum boasts the world's largest collection of works by the German artist Ernst Ludwig Kirchner, whose off-kilter lines and unnerving compositions inspired the Expressionist movement. He traveled to Davos in 1917 for health reasons and stayed until his suicide in 1938. ⊠ *Promenade 82, Davos-Platz* ☎ *081/4106300* ⊕ *www.kirchnermuseum.ch* ✉ *12 SF* ⊗ *mid-Apr.–mid-June and late Oct.–Dec., Tues.–Sun. 2–6; late June–late Oct. and Dec.–mid-Apr., Tues.–Sun. 10–6.*

Museum of Medicine. Davos was once famous as a retreat for people suffering from respiratory problems, such as those caused by tuberculosis (its mountain air kept TB bacteria from growing as quickly). Davos was the inspiration for Thomas Mann's novel *The Magic Mountain*. The Museum of Medicine, which exhibits old-fashioned medical equipment, recalls the days when the streets were lined with spittoons. ⊠ *Platzstr. 1, Davos-Platz* ☎ *081/4135259* ⊕ *www.medizinmuseum-davos.ch* ✉ *3 SF* ⊗ *Thurs. 5–7, and by appointment. Closed May and Nov.*

Wintersportmuseum. The Wintersportmuseum has a large collection of well-preserved equipment, including sleds, skis, skates, bindings, and costumes, showcasing the history of winter sports, from their relatively primitive infancy to the modern day. ⊠ *Promenade 43, Davos-*

Platz ☎ 081/4132484 🌐 www.wintersportmuseum.ch 🎟 5 SF ⏲ Late June–mid-Oct. and Dec.–Apr., Tues. and Thurs. 4:30–6:30.

SKIING

Davos can accommodate some 24,000 visitors on 300 km (186½ miles) of runs. The fairly steep slopes of the **Parsenn-Gotschna** are accessed from town by the Parsenn funicular. For an alternative, try the **Rinerhorn,** a 15-minute ride by bus or train. Here the slopes lead to the hamlet of **Glaris,** 7 km (4½ miles) from Davos. A must for the skilled skier is the descent from **Weissfluhgipfel** (9,330 feet) to **Küblis,** in the Prättigau. This magnificent, 13-km (8-mile) piste has a vertical drop of 6,560 feet and is classified as difficult at the top but moderate for most of its length. A real challenge for experts is the three-hour tour across the mountains to Arosa—which requires a guide and good weather conditions. An easy 2-km (1-mile) run is No. 11, the Meierhofer Tälli, which Davosers renamed the Hillary Clinton run, as it's her favorite here. **Jakobshorn,** a ski and snowboard area on the west-facing side, is reached by cable car and lift from Davos Platz. The **Pischa** ski area, on the Flüela Pass road, is a free-ride paradise, and especially suitable for children and families—as is the **Bünda** slope in Davos Dorf.

Lift tickets to the combined Davos–Klosters area cost 69 SF for one day, 318 SF for six days, and include transport between the ski areas.

Lauglauf (Cross-Country Ski) School. There are more than 75 km (47 miles) of prepared cross-country ski trails, for which there is no charge. The Lauglauf (Cross-Country Ski) School is in Davos-Dorf. ✉ *Promenade 157, Davos-Dorf* ☎ *081/4162454* 🌐 *www.ssd.ch.*

PaarSenn. If you need to get outfitted for skiing, including clothing, go to PaarSenn. ✉ *Promenade 159, Davos-Dorf* ☎ *081/4101010* 🌐 *www.paarsennsport.ch.*

Snowsports School Davos. The Snowsports School Davos gives skiing, cross-country, snowboard, and telemark lessons; it also organizes ski touring. ✉ *Promenade 157, Davos-Dorf* ☎ *081/4162454* 🌐 *www.ssd.ch.*

Top Secret Snowboard and Freeski School and Shop. For the expert skier (freestyle, off-piste, and the like), the place to go is Top Secret Snowboard and Freeski School and Shop. ✉ *Brämabüelstr. 11, Davos-Platz* ☎ *081/4137374* 🌐 *www.topsecretdavos.ch.*

WHERE TO EAT

$ ECLECTIC 🍴 **Bar-Bistro Angelo.** If you have had enough Bündner specialties, try this restaurant, which doubles as a shop selling wines and spirits, pasta, and honey. Simple chalkboard fare is on offer, but the vibrant artwork, live piano music, and a well-stocked bar create a cool, modern feel. The menu of the day changes depending on available produce, but exotic meats (crocodile, gazelle, and kangaroo) and a diverse menu of cordon bleu and Rösti are the specialties here, as are affordable prices. A fiery and fun Spanish evening serving up paella with live Spanish music for 30 SF per person is provided sporadically in the winter season (round up 10 people and it's guaranteed). Takeaway is also available. [$] *Average main: 25 SF* ✉ *Promenade 119, Davos-Platz* ☎ *079/2479779* ⏲ *Closed Sun.; closed Sat. Easter–Christmas. No lunch Jan.–Easter.*

$$ SWISS ★ 🍴 **Bistro Gentiana.** A cozy bistro and the region's number one place for fondue, this "café des artistes" dates back to the late 1880s, when it served as the town firehouse. After an Art Deco overhaul, it became a longstanding haunt for those seeking out snails, regional mushrooms, and age-old recipes for cheese and meat fondues. A convivial atmosphere with plenty of regional wines makes for a relaxed dinner. Cheese lovers should try the "Fondue Dinner Gentiana," a three-course extravaganza that includes a platter of local dried meat, as well as a special cheese fondue served with pears, mushrooms, diced ham, pearl onions, bacon, and kirsch. There is also a children's menu. Note there are two dinner services—if you don't want to be hurried out, reserve for the later 8:30 sitting. [$] *Average main: 35 SF* ✉ *Promenade 53, Davos-Platz* ☎ *081/4135649* 🌐 *www.gentiana.ch* ⏲ *Closed Easter–late June and mid-Oct.–early Dec.; closed Wed. in summer. No lunch.*

4

WHERE TO STAY

$$ HOTEL 🏨 **ArtHausHotel Quisisana Davos.** This striking red building exudes a mysterious pull: inside, the walls are brightened by lively abstract paintings created by artist, owner, and manager Diego do Clavadetscher, and the guest rooms are little works of art unto themselves. **Pros:** unique and quirky, with original art throughout; owner welcomes guests with personal service and open-minded conversation. **Cons:** not a high-style hotel with requisite amenities; no sauna or après-ski facilities. [$] *Rooms from: 244 SF* ✉ *Platzstr. 5, Davos-Platz* ☎ *081/4100510* 🌐 *www.arthaushotel.ch* 🛏 *18 rooms, 1 apartment* ⏲ *Closed mid-Apr.–late May and early-Sept.–early-Dec.* 🍽 *Multiple meal plans.*

$$$ HOTEL 👶 🏨 **Bünda Davos.** This hotel, in a typical chalet-style building, is perfectly located right by the beginners' ski slope, the children's slope, and a ski school branch, as well as on the cross-country ski track; in addition, the Parsenn funicular is only a few minutes' walk away. **Pros:** direct access to beginner and kids' skiing; great for families. **Cons:** slightly outside the center; not most characterful of places. [$] *Rooms from: 278 SF* ✉ *Museumstr. 4, Davos-Dorf* ☎ *081/4171819* 🌐 *www.buendadavos.ch* 🛏 *37 rooms, 3 suites* ⏲ *Closed mid-Apr.–May and mid-Oct.–Nov.* 🍽 *Multiple meal plans.*

$$$ HOTEL Fodor's Choice ★ 🏨 **Schatzalp.** About 950 feet above town on a quiet, car-free slope, this spectacular hotel will transport you back to the grand spa days of Davos; once used as a sanatorium, the entire hotel is now decorated in elegant Belle Epoque style, though many salons have been given striking modern touches like exotic fabrics and contemporary furnishings. **Pros:** free ski-pass for the Schatzalp area in winter; peaceful, awe-inspiring location; building has historic charm; boundless activities for all ages. **Cons:** those seeking amazing amenities or modern rooms might be disappointed; no TVs. [$] *Rooms from: 350 SF* ✉ *Schatzalp, Davos-Platz* ☎ *081/4155151* 🌐 *www.schatzalp.ch* 🛏 *92 rooms, Villa Guarda and Chalet* ⏲ *Closed late Mar.–mid-June and mid-Oct.–mid-Dec.* 🍽 *Multiple meal plans.*

$$$$ HOTEL 🏨 **Steigenberger Belvédèrè.** With its Neoclassical stone fireplace, wedding-cake white plaster, and period details, this is a grand hotel in every sense of the word and its packages for sports, the outdoors, and culture lovers help everyone appreciate the equally grand surroundings. **Pros:** central

Many people think Guarda is one of the prettiest villages in the Lower Engadine.

location; outstanding concierge and personal service; half board is a nice way to save a little on the stiff prices. **Cons:** very expensive; reception area is chaotic at times. [$] *Rooms from: 470 SF* ✉ *Promenade 89, Davos-Platz* ☎ *081/4156000* 🌐 *www.steigenberger.com/en/davos* 🛏 *97 rooms, 30 suites* 🕒 *Closed mid-Apr.–mid-June and mid-Oct.–mid-Nov.* 🍴 *Multiple meal plans.*

NIGHTLIFE AND THE ARTS

BARS

Ex Bar. In the Hotel Europe, the Ex Bar is where hipsters gather to listen to DJs. ✉ *Promenade 63, Davos-Platz* ☎ *081/4154141* 🌐 *www.ex-bar-davos.ch* 🕒 *Closed Sun.*

Mountain's Akt. If you want somewhere to chill out or watch live sports via satellite TV, head to Mountain's Akt. On weekends, DJs keep the atmosphere upbeat. ✉ *Promenade 64, Davos* ☎ *081/4132744* 🌐 *www.mountainsakt.com.*

CASINO

Casino. The bright, glassed-in Casino is one of the main socializing places in Davos. It opens at 2 pm daily and does not require formal dress. ✉ *Hotel Europe, Promenade 63, Davos-Platz* ☎ *081/4100303* 🌐 *www.casinodavos.ch.*

DANCING

Cabanna Club. The Cabanna Club lures an energetic crowd with techno music—those on the older side usually head to the "Cava" (under the Cabanna) for more acoustic fare. ✉ *Promenade 63, Davos-Platz* ☎ *081/4154141, 079/6198640* 🌐 *www.cabanna.ch.*

Pöstli Club. The Pöstli Club, in the Morosani Posthotel, is a winter-only institution with a dance floor and music ranging from rock to folk and pop. For the dance starved, the club opens up Friday nights in July. ⊠ *Promenade 42, Davos-Platz* ☎ *081/4154500.*

Rotliechtli Music Club. In the Hotel Davoserhof, the Rotliechtli Music Club attracts a young—or at least young at heart—crowd with somewhat traditional taste in music. ⊠ *Berglistutz 2, Davos-Platz* ☎ *081/4149443* ⊕ *www.rotliechtli.ch* ☉ *Closed Sun.*

MUSIC

The annual **Young Artists in Concert festival** (⊕ *www.davosfestival.ch*) is held in early August. Young musicians from all over the world practice and perform classical music in churches and the Hotel Morosani Schweizerhof.

SPORTS AND THE OUTDOORS

HIKING AND BIKING

Davos is threaded with more than 450 km (280 miles) of well-marked trails perfect for hiking or biking in winter and summer.

Ettinger Sport. Mountain bikes can be rented at the train station or at Ettinger Sport. ⊠ *Promenade 153, Davos-Dorf* ☎ *081/4101212, 081/4106161* ⊕ *www.ettinger.ch.*

Luftchraft Flugschule Davos. Luftchraft Flugschule Davos gives lessons and offers tandem flights during the summer and winter seasons. ⊠ *Mattastr. 9, Davos-Platz* ☎ *079/6231970* ⊕ *www.luftchraft.ch.*

SAILING AND WINDSURFING

Segelschule Davosersee. Sailing and windsurfing are popular on Davos Lake, where there's always a stiff breeze. To rent boats or take a lesson with a sailing school, call Segelschule Davosersee. ⊠ *Flüelastr. 4, Davos-Dorf* ☎ *076/5663130* ⊕ *www.davossail.ch.*

Hans-Martin Heierling. Sailing school instructor Hans-Martin Heierling offers lessons and rents out boats as well. ☎ *076/5663130.*

SKATING

Sports Center Davos. Davos has a long reputation as an important ice-sports center, with its enormous Sports Center Davos and speed-skating rink, the biggest natural ice track in Europe. The Ice Stadium maintains one indoor and two outdoor rinks. ⊠ *Talstr. 41, Davos-Platz* ☎ *081/4153600.*

THE LOWER ENGADINE

This is the most picturesque of Graübunden's many valleys, and like Dorothy landing in Oz, you might be a bit shocked by what you find here. You'll hear people talk of *Schellenursli* (a legendary little boy with a bell), and there's even a sort of Scarecrow—during the *Hom Strom* holiday on the first Saturday in February, the children of Scuol make a figure out of hay to scare winter away. Festivals and folklore abound, as do dense forests and quaint village settings. "Allegra!" is the proper greeting on the street, reflecting the Romansh language and Latinate culture here. The outer walls of houses are decorated using the *sgrafitto* technique—a signature of the Engadine. (First a layer of dark stucco is whitewashed, and then symbols and drawings of local fauna are scraped into the paint revealing the dark stucco beneath—usually the name of the original builder appears with a quote or a poem, and the extent and quality of the sgraffiti suggests the wealth and station of the owner.) Although the Lower Engadine is more enclosed than its upper counterpart, both have a dry, crisp "champagne" climate.

GUARDA

★ *37 km (23 miles) east of Davos.*

The former main road through the Inn Valley (Engadine) was higher up on the slopes than today's road. It passed through Guarda, one of a pleasant chain of small villages that includes Ardez and Ftan. Each has fine sgraffitied homes, but Guarda, where the architecture is government-protected, is particularly well suited for a leisurely exploration along its ancient cobbled streets. The dark-on-light etchings on the facades (contrasting sharply with the bright flowers on the windowsills) draw pedestrians from one photo op to the next. As its name implies, Guarda ("watch") sits high on a hillside looking out over the valley and the peaks to the south, which reach up to 9,840 feet.

WHERE TO STAY

$$ HOTEL ★ **Meisser.** This picturesque, family-owned hotel, made up of three ancient farmhouses, has sgraffiti and flower boxes on the outside, antiques and honey-color pine on the inside, and a luxurious restaurant serving tasty local dishes. **Pros:** unique ambience and style of the renovated farmhouses; special local cuisine; inspired views from the lawn. **Cons:** you are out in the sticks with nowhere to go except the great outdoors; basic amenities (like an ATM) are a 20-minute drive. [$] *Rooms from: 250 SF* ✉ *Dorfstr. 42* ☎ *081/8622132* 🌐 *www.hotel-meisser.ch* 🛏 *20 rooms, 5 suites* 🕓 *Closed early Apr.–early May, and Nov.* 🍴 *Multiple meal plans.*

SCUOL AND TARASP-VULPERA

13 km (8 miles) east of Guarda.

The villages of Scuol and Tarasp-Vulpera effectively form one large resort, although a car or bus is needed to travel between the two. The area owes its popularity to the 20 mineral springs (traditionally used for liver cures), the beautiful surroundings (mountains and dense forests), and the proximity of the Parc Naziunal Svizzer. Previously popular only in summer, the villages now fill up in winter, thanks to skiing on the south-facing slopes of Motta Naluns.

A small town, Scuol has a petite but exemplary Old Town, with five fountains from which you can do a taste-test comparison of normal tap water against spring water.

GETTING HERE AND AROUND

Scuol is connected to Chur (2 hours away) and Klosters (45 minutes) by train. To get here from St. Moritz (1 hour 21 minutes), change at Samedan.

Upper and Lower Engadine

AUSTRIA

Saas

Klosters

Götschnagrat

Weissfluhjoch   Wolfgang

Davos

Pischa

SILVRETTA GRUPPE

Piz Buin

TO SAMNAUN AND AUSTRIA

LOWER ENGADINE

Ftan   Scuol

Guarda   Ardez   Vulpèra

Saglains   Tarasp

Jakobshorn

Lavin

Weisshorn

Rinerhorn

Flüelapass

Susch

Piz d'Arpiglias

Schwarzhorn

Piz Nuna

GRAUBÜNDEN

Zernez

Grialetsch Glacier

Piz Vadret

VAL MÜSTAIR

Brail

Parc Naziunal Svizzer
(Swiss National Park)

ALBULA

UPPER ENGADINE

Piz dal Acqua

TO MÜSTAIR

S-Chanf

Zuoz

Albulapass

Albula Tunnel

La Punt

Corviglia

Bever

Livigno

Piz Nair

Samedan

Muottas Muragl

Celerina

Punt Muragl

St. Moritz   Pontresina

ITALY

Champferer See

Piz Languard

Silvaplana

Piz Rosatsch

Piz Lagalb

Piz Corvatsch

Diavolezza

ilvaplaner See

Piz Tschierva

Piz Morteratsch

Bernina Pass

Piz Bernina

TO POSCHIAVO AND ITALY

ITALY

KEY

Cable Car/Funicular

Rail lines

Ski Resorts

Guarda's preserved sgraffitied houses and vibrant flowering window boxes produce great photo ops.

ESSENTIALS

Visitor Information Scuol ☎ 081/8618800 ⊕ www.scuol.ch.

EXPLORING

Two other villages lie on the opposite side of the river from Scuol. **Vulpera**, whose permanent residents number around 50, has an 1876 Trinkhalle (pump house) with its spring pumping out mineral-rich water that's said to be good for the digestive tract; you can enjoy this water at the nearby Bogn Engiadina spa, since the Trinkhalle is no longer open to the public. From Vulpera, take a 10-minute bus ride up to **Tarasp**, a cluster of houses, inns, and farms around a tiny lake. The Vulpera golf course straddles the road, so if you are traveling by car you may want to close your windows.

Fodor's Choice ★ **Schloss Tarasp.** The village is dominated by the magnificently pictur-esque stronghold Schloss Tarasp, perched 500 feet above. This grand castle lords over the valley with an impressive main tower. The oldest sections date from the 11th century, when the castle was built by the leading family of Tarasp. Tarasp became part of Austria in 1464; the imperial eagle still can be seen on the castle walls. In the early 1800s Napoléon gave Tarasp to Canton Graubünden, newly part of the Swiss federation. The castle went through several owners and subsequent neglect before passing into private hands in the early 20th century. You must join a tour (German-language, with some info in English) to see the interiors, which range from the Romanesque chapel to the opu-lent 19th-century reception rooms; the schedule varies, but there are at least two tours a day from May to October. Call ahead for times. Spe-cial midnight tours are conducted during the full moon. The bus from

Vulpera departs roughly every hour. It's a 1½-hour walk from Scuol, following a well-marked path that goes over the Punt'Ota (high bridge). ⊠ *Tarasp* ☎ *081/8649368* ⊕ *www.schloss-tarasp.ch* 🎫 *12 SF* ⊙ *Mid-May–Oct., daily, times vary; Christmas–Easter, Tues. and Thurs., times vary.*

QUICK BITES

Glatscharia Balnot. For a delicious ice cream or Italian gelato, a good coffee, or a quick email check, stop in at the Glatscharia Balnot. The shop is relaxed and splashed with a riot of color. ⊠ *Stradun 404, near the tourist office and bus station of Scuol* ☎ *081/8600069* ⊙ *Weekdays 8:30–7, Sat. 8:30–6, Sun. 1–6.*

SKIING AND SNOWBOARDING

The region's ski area centers around 14 gondolas and lifts going up Scuol's **Motta Naluns,** at elevations between 4,100 and 9,184 feet. The 80 km (50 miles) of trails include the 10-km (6.2-mile) Traumpiste (Dream Run), a good run of medium difficulty with a few tough areas. There is a wide range of ski passes available for an equally wide range of prices on a sliding scale beginning at 55 SF for a day pass. Tarasp has one short ski lift for beginners. Bus transport between Scuol/Sent and Scuol/Tarasp-Vulpera is free of charge if you have a ski pass.

Snowboarding is extremely popular on these broad, sunny slopes.

Element Snowboard School. Conveniently located close to the train station and valley gondola station, the Element Snowboard School can rent you gear *and* teach you how to shred the pistes. ⊠ *Talstation Bergbahn, Scuol* ☎ *081/8600777* ⊕ *www.element-scuol.ch.*

Schweizer Schneesportschule Scuol. You can also sign up with Schweizer Schneesportschule Scuol for instruction in Alpine and cross-country skiing. ⊠ *Scuol* ☎ *081/8641723* ⊕ *www.snowsportscuol.ch.*

There are 76 km (47 miles) of prepared cross-country tracks around Scuol. Rental equipment is available at sports shops in Scuol and next to the Motta Naluns cable-car station.

Kinderland Nalunsin. As for children, they can find snowy excitement at the Kinderland Nalunsin, a combination ski school and daycare center. It costs 8 SF per hour or 40 SF per day; lunch is an additional 10 SF. ☎ *081/8611414.*

WHERE TO STAY

$$
HOTEL
★

Engiadina. This typical 16th-century Engadine house is located in the heart of Scuol's Old Town and has inviting rooms decorated with Swiss pine, carved ceilings, and exposed beams in beige tones brightened with reds or blues. **Pros:** enchanting location; service with a smile; delicious

CLOSE UP

The Rhätibahn

The Rhätibahn (Rhätische Bahn) is not simply a means of transport but a journey that thousands love to experience every year. In July 2008 it won UNESCO World Heritage status in recognition of its feats of engineering and the wondrous landscapes that it passes through. The track winds its way across glaciers, over viaducts and gorges, and past stupendous Alpine scenery—along the way revealing scenes from a centuries-old way of life that's been all but forgotten in the bigger towns and cities.

The tracks of this wondrous travel experience thread a large section of Graubünden but also reach to other cantons in Switzerland and can even transport you southward across the border to Italy. The network offers special services with named prestige trains—the top three are the Arosa Express, Bernina Express, and the Glacier Express. Each follows its own route, and prebooking is essential. Doing a little research to see which lines fit with your itinerary is well worth it. To ensure your chosen outpost is on one of the varied lines and to avoid disappointment, it is best to check online or call ahead. For more details, call ☎ *081/2886565* or visit 🌐 *www.rhb.ch.*

---

food. **Cons:** Scuol is built on the mountainside, and the Old Town is near the valley bottom, so it's a bit of a hike into town. [$] *Rooms from: 214 SF* ✉ *Rablüzza 152Scuol* ☎ *081/8641421* 🌐 *www.hotel-engiadina.ch* 🛏 *12 rooms, 5 suites* ⏲ *Closed early Apr.–early June and end-Oct.–mid-Dec.* 🍴 *Multiple meal plans.*

$$ HOTEL ★ 🏨 **Hotel Villa Post.** Marked by its distinctive turret topped with a Swiss flag, this former post office provides simply and tastefully decorated guest rooms and a familial atmosphere ideal for those seeking a peaceful home away from home. **Pros:** sense of history; fine dining; grand natural setting. **Cons:** anyone on the lookout for a buzzing social atmosphere should look elsewhere; if traveling by public transport, keep in mind that there's only one bus per hour. [$] *Rooms from: 240 SF* ✉ *Vulpera* ☎ *081/8641112* 🌐 *www.villa-post.ch* 🛏 *25 rooms* ⏲ *Closed end Mar.–early May and mid-Nov.–mid-Dec.* 🍴 *Multiple meal plans.*

$$$ HOTEL Fodor's Choice ★ 🏨 **Schlosshotel Chastè.** While many Swiss hoteliers can claim a second generation of family ownership, this hidden treasure boasts 500 years under the Pazeller family's care, who have preserved the bulging, sgraffitied stucco exterior and modernized much of what's behind the magnificently carved Arvenholz wood door. **Pros:** superb cuisine; enchanting rooms; untouched magical surroundings. **Cons:** Tarasp is a bus ride out of Scuol, so it's not a convenient location for those coming by train; those seeking wild nights may be overwhelmed by the serenity. [$] *Rooms from: 350 SF* ✉ *Tarasp* ☎ *081/8613060* 🌐 *www.schlosshoteltarasp.ch* 🛏 *19 rooms* ⏲ *Apr.–early June and mid-Oct.–mid-Dec.* 🍴 *Multiple meal plans.*

$$ HOTEL 🏨 **Villa Engiadina.** This folly of towers and gables standing guard over Vulpera was built in 1902 and was transformed into a hotel in the late 1990s, introducing visitors to its sprawling views of the valley and vertigo-inducing balconies found in the tower rooms. **Pros:** the views;

proximity to golf course (and a 30% discount); winter evenings in front of the fireplace; kids sleep and eat for free. **Cons:** no elevator and lots of stairs. $ *Rooms from: 220 SF ⊠ Vulpera ☎ 081/8612244 ⊕ www.villa-engiadina.ch ⬌ 15 rooms, 4 suites ⊗ Closed Apr.– mid-May and end-Oct.–mid-Dec.* ¡○¡ *Multiple meal plans.*

WORD OF MOUTH

"We stayed at the Schlossho-tel Chastè last year. It's right by Tarasp Castle, so we got to see the castle all lighted up at night—it was stunning. Schloss-hotel Chastè is also a wonderful place to stay, pricey, but worth it. We found that whole area just beautiful!"—wrenwood

SPAS

★ **Bogn Engiadina Scuol.** For the inside-and-out spa experience, head to the Bogn Engiadina Scuol, one of Europe's most famous spas. Standing in the middle of town tucked against the mountainside, an elevator and a staircase in a silolike modern construction lead you down to the entrance, and the calming blue interior, fantastic aquatic murals, and shifting reflections from backlit pools start relaxing you before your toes even touch the water. Six pools, both indoor and outdoor, range in temperature from 15.5°C (60°F) to 32°C (90°F). There are also saunas, solariums, steam rooms, and a massage area. A special Roman-Irish ritual treatment alternates between moist and dry heat, massage, and mineral baths, and lasts 2½ hours; it's best to reserve 24 hours in advance. A therapy center offers mud baths, gymnastics, tha-lassotherapy (using seawater), and electrotherapy (if you have a doctor's prescription). In addition to steeping in mineral water, you can drink it from four different sources near the entrance; wait for someone to serve you. ⊠ *Town center, Scuol ☎ 081/8612600 ⊕ www.engadinbadscuol.ch ⊗ Fri.–Wed. 8 am–9:45 pm; Thurs. 2–7 ⬌ 25 SF for bathing area with sauna, 66 SF with Roman-Irish baths. Hot tubs (indoor and outdoor), sauna, steam room. Gym with: cardiovascular machines, free weights. Services: acupuncture, aromatherapy, foot reflexology, lymphatic drain-age, underwater massage. Classes and programs: aerobics, aquaerobics, body sculpting, dance classes, Pilates, Spinning.*

SPORTS AND THE OUTDOORS

BIKING

Rental bicycles are available at sports shops in Scuol. For the adventur-ous, bikes can be taken on the cable car; once on the mountain, you can explore on your own or join a guided tour. Contact the tourist office for details.

ICE SPORTS

Sportanlage Trü. Open-air ice rinks for hockey, curling, and skating are available in Scuol from early December to early March at Sportanlage Trü. ☎ *081/8612606.*

Eishalle Gurlaina. Eishalle Gurlaina, in Scuol, has indoor skating facilities that are open to the public in summer; in winter you can watch local ice hockey games and tournaments. ☎ *081/8640272.*

The majestic Tarasp castle lords over this part of the valley.

SLEDDING
There are three main sled runs, between 2½ and 7 km (1½ and 4½ miles) long.

Sport Heinrich. You can rent a sled at the Motta Naluns mountain station or from Sport Heinrich in Scuol. ⊠ *Hauptstr. 400, Scuol* ☎ *081/8641956* ⊕ *www.sport-heinrich.ch.*

WHITE-WATER RAFTING
Swissraft. Swissraft organizes daily white-water rafting expeditions in rubber dinghies on the River Inn from May to late September. ☎ *081/9115250* ⊕ *www.swissraft.ch.*

ZERNEZ

27 km (17 miles) southwest of Scuol.

This friendly little crossroads, the last town before the higher valley of the Inn, lies along the route over the Ofen Pass to the Val Müstair and Italy. Serious hikers sporting loden hats, knickers, and sturdy boots come to stock up on picnic goods and topographical maps before setting off for the Parc Naziunal Svizzer. In winter there are cross-country trails. The Alpine skiing areas of the Lower and Upper Engadine are accessible by public transport.

ESSENTIALS
Visitor Information Zernez ☎ *081/8561300* ⊕ *www.zernez.ch.*

WHERE TO STAY

$$ | ☒ **Chasa–Veglia Hotel Garni.** Located down a quiet side street, "the old
B&B/INN | house"—complete with converted barn—is a town treasure where the
owner's wood-carving skills are on display at every turn, from the doors
and chairs to ceilings and fretwork panels over the lighting fixtures.
Pros: the charming handcrafted interior. **Cons:** you will need to go elsewhere for dinner. $ *Rooms from: 180 SF* ☒ *Runatsch* ☎ *081/2844868*
⊕ *www.chasa-veglia.ch* ⇆ *22 rooms, 9 with bath* ▤ *No credit cards*
⊗ *Closed Apr., May, and Nov.–late Dec.* ⦿ *Breakfast.*

PARC NAZIUNAL SVIZZER

1 km (0.6 mile) east of Zernez

The Swiss National Park is a magnificent federal preserve of virtually
virgin wilderness teeming with local wildlife.

GETTING HERE AND AROUND

There are access roads from Zernez, Scuol, S-chanf, and the Ofen Pass.

EXPLORING

★ **Parc Naziunal Svizzer** (*Swiss National Park*). Established in 1914, the
Parc Naziunal Svizzer covers 173 square km (107 square mi), including
the Macun lakes near Lavin. Although small compared with a U.S. or
Canadian national park, it has none of the developments that typically
hint of "accessibility" and "attraction": no campgrounds, no picnic
sites, no residents, and few rangers. This is genuine wilderness, every
leaf protected from anything but nature itself. Dead wood is left to rot
and insects to multiply. Rangers see that rules are obeyed—no fires,
dogs, bikes, skis, or tents are allowed, and picking plants is forbidden. Although the last bear was shot in the Lower Engadine in 1904,
the park is home to large herds of ibex (the heraldic animal on the
Graubünden flag), chamois (a distant relative of the goat), red and roe
deer, and marmots. Don't forget binoculars; without them you might
not see much fauna—the animals give a wide berth to the 80 km (50
mi) of marked paths. Remember these are wild animals and not likely
to line up for Twinkies by the road. If big game fail to appear, you can
just enjoy the scenery and watch out for a bearded vulture overhead.
Before heading into the park, visit the three-story **Nationalpark-Haus** in
Zernez, where you can view the permanent exhibition with the help of
your English audioguide, stock up on maps, and enjoy the natural history exhibit. Special exhibitions change once or twice each year. Guided
walks in German are available Tuesday through Thursday; reserve one
to two days in advance to join a group (25–35 SF for adults) or book
a private guided walk in English (350 SF).

Trails start out from parking lots off the park's only highway (visitors
are encouraged to take buses back to their starting point)—a series of
wild, rough, and often steep paths. Visitors are restricted to the trails
except at designated resting places. The Il Fuorn–Stabelchod–Val dal
Botsch trail marks botanical and natural phenomena with multilingual
information boards and leads to a spectacular barren ridge at 7,672
feet; the round-trip journey takes about four hours. A three-hour route
from picturesque S-chanf (pronounced ess-*chanff*) takes you into a deep

glacial valley where ibex and chamois often gather; the return, by a riverside trail, passes a snack bar—just across the park border and thus permitted. ⊠ *Nationalpark-Haus, Zernez* ⊹ *Leaving the village toward Ofen Pass* ☎ *081/8514141* ⊕ *www.nationalpark.ch* 🎫 *7 SF* ⊙ *Daily 8:30–6.*

Müstair. If you continue through the National Park over the Ofen Pass to the Münster Valley and Italy, you can visit the Benedictine Convent of St. John at Müstair, a UNESCO World Heritage site on the Italian border. The convent is still active and has fasting weeks in spring and fall. Take time to wonder at the Romanesque frescoes from AD 800–1170; more paintings are being uncovered using laser technology. Admission is free. ⊠ *Müstair* ⊕ *www.muestair.ch.*

Museum. The appealingly simple convent complex also houses a small museum with Baroque statues and Carolingian works. ⊠ *Müstair* ☎ *081/8516228* ⊕ *www.muestair.ch* 🎫 *12 SF* ⊙ *May–Oct., Mon.–Sat. 9–noon and 1:30–5, Sun. 1:30–5; Nov.–Apr., Mon.–Sat. 10–noon and 1:30–4:30, Sun. 1:30–4:30*

WHERE TO STAY

$$
HOTEL
🏨 **Hotel Parc Naziunal, Il Fuorn.** This century-old mountain inn in the Swiss National Park is on the highway and makes an ideal base for hikers. **Pros:** only hotel in the national park; nice outdoor dining terrace; idyllic location for nature lovers, hikers, and bike enthusiasts. **Cons:** rooms are basic. 💲 *Rooms from: 196 SF* ⊠ *Il Fuorn, Zernez* ☎ *081/8561226* ⊕ *www.ilfuorn.ch* 🛏 *37 rooms, 18 with bath* ⊙ *Closed late Oct.–mid-Dec. and mid-Apr.–mid-May* ❢❍❢ *Multiple meal plans.*

THE UPPER ENGADINE

Stretching from Brail to Maloja and with a gate to the Swiss National Park at S-chanf, this is one of the country's highest regions—the highest settlement is at 6,710 feet—and one of its most dazzling. From mountain peaks, such as Piz Corvatsch or Piz Nair, you can swoosh down world-class slopes or simply take in the dizzying views over the lakes and mountains. In addition to sports, winter and summer are both packed tight with cultural programs and events. Summer is also when the lowland farmers send their cows up to the high Alpine pastures to graze.

PONTRESINA

★ *38 km (24 miles) southwest of Zernez.*

On a south-facing shelf along the Flaz Valley, Pontresina is a beautiful resort town. It grew by converting its farmhouses to pensions and hotels for use by summer tourists. Today its climbing school has made a name for itself, and the village has become a popular hiking center. From here you can see clear across to the Roseg Valley, once filled with a glacier that has retreated to the base of Piz Roseg itself. The River Flaz winds through the valley from the Morteratsch glacier, which oozes down from Piz Bernina. Although the main street is built up with restaurants and shops, the resort still has a relaxed atmosphere. Every second Thursday from the end of June until the middle of August there's a street market in the lower part of the village, with locals selling fresh produce and handmade crafts. The altitude of Pontresina (6,000 feet) ensures wintry weather, and skiers have easy access to the slopes of Diavolezza (9,751 feet). In the off-seasons between Easter and mid-June and mid-October through Christmas, many hotels are closed.

GETTING HERE AND AROUND

Trains connecting with Pontresina by and large follow the same schedule as those to and from St. Moritz, with a change in Samedan. Pontresina–Chur trains take two hours, with a change at Samedan. The Scuol–St. Moritz trains also take you to Pontresina, with a transfer at Samedan. Direct trains from Scuol to Pontresina are also possible.

ESSENTIALS

Visitor Information Pontresina Tourist Information ⊠ *Rondo Center, Via Maistra 133* ☎ *081/8388300* ⊕ *www.pontresina.ch.*

EXPLORING

Museum Alpin. The Museum Alpin documents local history and life in the region over the centuries. It also exhibits local flora, fauna, and minerals; be sure to check out the room full of birds whose recorded songs can be heard at the push of a button. The summer and winter seasons bring a revolving schedule of exhibitions. ⊠ *Via Maistra* ☎ *081/8427273* ⊕ *www.pontresina.ch/museumalpin* ⊠ *6 SF* ☉ *June–mid-Oct. and mid-Dec.–mid-Apr., Mon.–Sat. 4–6; open 3–6 when raining or snowing.*

EN
ROUTE

Punt Muragl. At Punt Muragl, off the train line and highway between St. Moritz and Pontresina, you'll find the funicular for Muottas Muragl at 8,055 feet. Up here, summer or winter, walkers can take the Philosophers' Path, which is dotted with quotations from famous minds as well as more modern observations about life. Following the three circular paths takes about 1½ hours. An alternate way back down to the valley is the 4-km (2½-mile) sled run. Sleds can be rented at the valley station for 15 SF. This, together with a large playground, makes Muottas a good excursion for children. During the day, the funicular fare is 33 SF round-trip, or 15 SF for an evening round-trip. To keep body and soul together, visit the rustic chic **Berghotel Muottas Muragl** for a meal with a truly spectacular view. The menu focuses on local specialties such as dried meat, Capuns, and the gnocchilike *Pizokel*, along with a nice selection of meat and fish dishes. ∎ TIP➡ From Muottas Muragl, you can embark on a 3½-hour long traverse to Alp Languard, where you can take a chairlift down to Pontresina. The Segantini Hut (approximately halfway along) offers possibly the most spectacular (and photographed) views of the Upper Engadine and its series of five terraced, serenely azure lakes. Expect moderate difficulty, since parts are rocky and steep; hiking boots are a must. ⊠ *Punt Muragl* ☎ *081/8428232* ☉ *Closed start Apr.–late May and mid-Oct.–mid-Dec.*

Pontresina is a popular hub for climbing and hiking.

SKIING

There's a small beginners' slope in the village at San Spiert. The compact ski areas of Diavolezza (9,768 feet) and, on the other side of the road, Lagalb (9,705 feet), on the Bernina Pass, complement the much more extensive ones at St. Moritz. All three are about 20 minutes away by bus. Lift tickets cost 73 SF for one day, 365 SF for a six-day regional ticket. Individual day passes for Diavolezza and Lagalb cost 62 SF. Rides on the Engadine bus service are included in the price of a regional ski ticket.

Ski and Snowboard School. Newcomers can learn the basics at the Ski and Snowboard School. ⊠ *Rondo/Kongresszentrum Pontresina, Via Maistra 133* ☎ *081/8388383* ⊕ *www.pontresina-sports.ch.*

Cross-Country Ski Center. Below the village, on the Engadine Marathon Trail, is the Cross-Country Ski Center. ⊠ *Langlaufzentrum Cuntschett 1* ☎ *081/8426844* ⊕ *www.pontresina-sports.ch.*

WHERE TO EAT

$
SWISS
★
✕ **Grond Café Pontresina.** This café offers fantastic views down the Roseg Valley, as well as a menu that satisfies all kinds of cravings—from bowls of breakfast muesli to a wide selection of sandwiches, pastas, risotto, and plates of *Rösti*. Locals know to ask for the homemade Engadiner *Nusstorte* (shortbread crust with a dense nut and caramel filling) or a strudel—as well as for a seat on the terrace. $ *Average main: 18 SF* ⊠ *Via da Mulin 28* ☎ *081/8388030* ⊕ *www.grond-engadin.ch.*

$$
SWISS
✕ **Steinbock.** Owned by the Walther family, proprietors of the neighboring Hotel Walther, this 17th-century house has been modernized in keeping with Engadine style—lots of wood and warm colors. The Colani

Stübli serves regional and seasonal specialties, such as polenta "Engadiner Art," a filling cornmeal dish with bacon and local cheese. The game dishes served in autumn are exceptional, especially the *Gempsfeffer* (chamois ragout cooked in wine) with hazelnut spaetzle and red cabbage. For dessert you might try the homemade yogurt with woodruff jelly and lemon crumble. $ *Average main: 30 SF* ✉ *Via Maistra 219* ☎ *081/8393626* ⊕ *www.steinbock-pontresina.ch*.

CARRIAGE RIDES

Horse-drawn carriages and sleighs in Pontresina can be booked through **Helene Riedberger** (☎ *081/8428353*). The Roseg Valley "horse omnibus" is run by **Gina and Wohli Wohlwend** (☎ *078/9447555* ⊕ *www.engadin-kutschen.ch*) as a scheduled service in summer and winter. This trip is very popular, so be sure to make a reservation.

WHERE TO STAY

$$$$ ▦ **Grand Hotel Kronenhof.** A grand Versailles set amid mountain peaks,
HOTEL the Kronenhof is the pinnacle for rest, relaxation, and pampering, with
Fodor's Choice gorgeous designs inside and out that highlight a keen attention to detail
★ and a sprawling lawn perfect for soaking in the sun and admiring the views of Roseg Valley. **Pros:** beautiful grounds and location; activities and facilities galore; top-of-the-line, very cool children's facility; excellent dining options. **Cons:** the price is just about the only negative at this stunning hotel. $ *Rooms from: 770 SF* ✉ *Via Maistra 1* ☎ *081/8303030* ⊕ *www.kronenhof.com* ⇨ *65 rooms, 47 suites* ⊙ *Closed early Apr.– mid-June and late Oct.–early-Dec.* ⫞⊚⫞ *Multiple meal plans.*

$$ ▦ **Hotel Station.** Next to the Roseg Valley entrance, the cross-country
HOTEL skiing center, and the train station, this handy hotel offers dependable, low-key accommodations with simple, tasteful guest rooms decked out in traditional wooden furniture. **Pros:** one of only two hotels in town that are open year-round; easily accessible; affordable; melt-in-your-mouth pizzas. **Cons:** near the train line, so it's a short, uphill walk into town. $ *Rooms from: 210 SF* ✉ *Cuntschett 2* ☎ *081/8388000* ⊕ *www.station-pontresina.ch* ⇨ *21 rooms* ⫞⊚⫞ *Breakfast.*

$ ▦ **Roseg Gletscher.** This isolated hotel is only reachable on foot or by
HOTEL horse-drawn carriage/sleigh (it's about 7½ km [4½ mile] up the ruggedly beautiful Roseg Valley), but its location in this untouched valley at the foot of a majestic glacier makes for a unique hiking or relaxing point. **Pros:** unique, gorgeous location; good food. **Cons:** remote; can be noisy before dawn during hunting season. $ *Rooms from: 160 SF* ☎ *081/8426445* ⊕ *www.roseg-gletscher.ch* ⇨ *15 rooms, 5 with bath, 100-person dormitory space* ⊙ *Closed mid-Oct.–early Dec.* ⫞⊚⫞ *Multiple meal plans.*

★ ## NIGHTLIFE AND THE ARTS
BARS AND LOUNGES
Bar Pitschna Scena. Bar Pitschna Scena has live music Thursday nights in summer and winter seasons. ✉ *Hotel Saratz* ☎ *081/8394000*.

The Pöstlikeller. The Pöstlikeller serves up cocktails, long drinks, and shooters, as well as live music on occasion. ✉ *Hotel Post, Via Maistra* ☎ *081/8389300*.

The spa at the Grand Hotel Kronenhof is a relaxing place to soak in the mountain views.

Winebar. The elegant Winebar with its wood, stone, and fur seat cushions serves a wide range of wines and is conveniently located on the main street. ✉ *Via Maistra 140* ☎ *081/8427090.*

MUSIC

Kurorchester Pontresina. The Kurorchester Pontresina plays chamber concerts daily between mid-June and mid-September at 11 am in the Tais forest. Check with the tourist office for more information.

SPAS

Bellevita. Located in the center of Pontresina, Bellavita (meaning "good life") features indoor and outdoor hot pools, cold plunge pools, and a range of wet and dry saunas. Views of the surrounding mountains are undeniably epic and the wellness area is complemented by a decent range of massage options (reservations required). The spa is family-friendly with a diving board and 75-meter black-hole slide to keep younger (and in some cases, not so young) guests occupied. Prices are reasonable and the baths are open until 10 pm on weekdays and 9 pm on weekends, giving visitors the opportunity to watch the sun dip behind the mountains from the comfort of a relaxing thermal pool. ✉ *Via Maistra 178, Pontresina* ☎ *081/8370037 general, 081/8370038 appointments* ⊕ *www.pontresina-bellavita.ch* ☞ *26.50 SF baths and spa, 80 SF for a 40-min aromatic oil massage, 160 SF for a 90-min hot stone massage. Hot tubs (indoor and outdoor), sauna, steam room. Services: aromatherapy, massage, solarium. Classes and programs: aquaerobics, meditation, personal training.*

SPORTS AND THE OUTDOORS
BIKING
Fähndrich Sport. Touring and mountain bikes can be rented at the Fähndrich Sport. ⊠ *Via Maistra 169* ☎ *081/8427155* ⊕ *www.faehndrich-sport.ch*.

Flying Cycles. Flying Cycles rents all kinds of bikes and can suggest scenic routes. ☎ *081/8426844* ⊕ *www.pontresina-sports.ch*.

HIKING
Pontresina and the top of the Alp Languard chairlift (open only in summer) are good starting points for hikers.

The Muottas Muragl funicular near Pontresina carries you to a high Alpine perch to begin the 9-km (5.6-mile) trek to Alp Languard. You're bound to break a sweat; the trail climbs 912 vertical feet and drops 3,038. The chairlift at Alp Languard brings you back to the valley.

The Diavolezza cable car, which runs in the summer, and the Rhaetian Railway also bring you to good hiking trails. For information on a variety of guided excursions and glacier hiking (60 SF), contact the tourist office. If you're staying overnight in Pontresina, some of the tours are free.

ICE SPORTS
Sportpavilion Eisplatz. There's a large natural ice-skating rink at the Sportpavilion Eisplatz. Rental skates and instruction are available. From December through the end of February, seven curling rinks with instructors are also available. ⊠ *Via Maistra* ☎ *081/8426346*.

MOUNTAIN CLIMBING
Bergsteigerschule Pontresina. Bergsteigerschule Pontresina, the biggest mountain-climbing school in Switzerland, offers instruction in rock and ice climbing for people of all skill levels. The company also leads guided tours and ski tours in English. ⊠ *Via Maistra 163* ☎ *081/8428282* ⊕ *bergsteiger-pontresina.ch*.

ST. MORITZ

Fodor's Choice ★ *5 km (3 miles) west of Pontresina, 85 km (53 miles) southeast of Chur.*

Who put the *ritz* in St. Moritz? Undoubtedly, St. Moritz's reputation was made by the people who go there and who have been going there, generation after generation, since 1864, when hotelier Johannes Badrutt dared a group of English tourists—already summer regulars—to brave the Alpine winter as his guests. They loved it, delighted in the novelty of snowy mountain beauty—until then considered unappealing—and told their friends. By the turn of the century St. Moritz, Switzerland, and snow were all the rage.

The first historical reference to the town dates from 1139, and in 1537 Paracelsus, the great Renaissance physician and alchemist, described the health-giving properties of the St. Moritz springs. St. Moritz gets busy with celebs and socialites around the winter holidays—some New Year's Eve events have guest lists closed a year in advance—but the glitter fades by spring. Very ordinary people fill the streets come summer—the same hikers you might meet in any resort—and hotel prices plummet.

Continued on page 180

Near St. Moritz, Corviglia is a popular
snow sports hub.

Switzerland has some of the best skiing in the world, but that's not all it
has to offer in winter. The Alpine nation's mountain resorts are a wonderland of snow-inspired activities. There are also spas, shopping, and
local food and wine to warm you. Here's a peek into the cool-weather
lifestyle, from first tracks to après ski.

WINTERTIME
in the ALPS

by Kati Clinton Robson

Ever since the birth of Alpine skiing in the late 19th century, when British ski enthusiasts convinced the train conductors of Wengen's cog railway to keep their trains running in winter, skiers have flocked to Switzerland to take advantage of the great snow and breathtaking views. Skiing is a national obsession for the Swiss, who as majority "owners" of the Alps believe it their right to hold all winter sporting titles and bring home Olympic gold every four years. Huge drops are commonplace; many resorts have slopes with vertical descents of over 1,500 meters (4,921 feet), as well as long, undulating, 10-km-plus pistes taking riders from the mountaintop to the valley floor below.

Today's visitors are just as likely to be snowboarding as skiing, and there are numerous options for more indoor-inclined visitors too. Though Switzerland's mountain resorts are glorious destinations year-round, there's something special about a frosty retreat. As the sun moves over the Alps, watch for a reddish hue on the snowy peaks—the bewitching alpenglow that signals the end (or the beginning) of another perfect winter day in the mountains.

TOP SWISS MOUNTAIN-RESORT DESTINATIONS

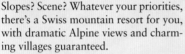

Slopes? Scene? Whatever your priorities, there's a Swiss mountain resort for you, with dramatic Alpine views and charming villages guaranteed.

BEST FOR OVERALL SKIING: Davos/ Klosters. Year after year, ski enthusiasts make this area their preferred destination in droves. From baby hills to black runs—and everything in between—skiers and boarders are spoiled for choice. Klosters is the quieter, quainter option while the neighboring urban sprawl of Davos is more practical than picturesque.

BEST FOR CELEB SPOTTING AND ULTIMATE LUXURY: St. Moritz. There's a reason St. Moritz has a reputation as *the* place to "put on the ritz." Old money and the nouveau riche set mix and mingle with playboys, it girls, and wannabes. With luxurious shopping and tranquil spas, there are many more ways to lighten your wallet than just lift tickets.

BEST FOR FAMILIES: Wengen. With the village on a sunny shelf and views up and down the valley, Wengen has many group-friendly activities, an outdoor ice rink, and long, enjoyable sled runs.

Families will especially appreciate the proximity of the nursery slopes and the quality of the children's ski school.

BEST FOR OFF-PISTE AND APRÈS SKI: Verbier. Ski all day, party all night. Although it has satisfying slopes for intermediate skiers, Verbier has really sealed its reputation with epic, challenging off-piste runs. Hire a guide and get ready to work up an appetite. And there's no letting up when the sun goes down, as this resort has one of Switzerland's wildest après ski and nightlife scenes.

BEST SETTING: Zermatt. Situated at the end of a narrow valley, and capped off by the famed Matterhorn massif, car-free Zermatt just has something magical. Little beats skiing—or simply basking—in the shadow of Switzerland's most iconic peak. And the enchanting village, with its delicious eats, lively after-dark vibe, and cozy firesides can hardly be topped either.

For more on specific resorts and activities, see regional chapters.

(left) Via Serlas, the shopping street in St. Moritz; (top right) Sledding is offered at many resorts; (right bottom) Mountain restaurant and cabin in Verbier.

BEYOND SKIING AND SNOWBOARDING

Even powderhounds and snow bunnies need a break from the slopes once in a while. Cold-weather classics like ice-skating and sledding need not be overlooked, but here are some inspiring ideas for more unique experiences.

SLEIGH AND CARRIAGE RIDES: When your troops tire of ski lessons and lift lines, why not arrange a horse-drawn sleigh ride for the whole group? Kick back, relax, and enjoy a touch of yesteryear, while getting acquainted with the village and the surrounding countryside. From Arosa to Zermatt, rides are available year-round—with carriages when the snow's not plentiful.

AFTER-DARK ACTIVITIES: Just because the sun has set, it doesn't mean you still can't enjoy outdoor adventures. Besides night skiing, many resorts also offer nighttime sledding and moonlit snowshoe walks—both of which usually include an option for a fondue dinner along the way. These events are typically available on Fridays and Saturdays; inquire at the local tourist information office for more details.

IGLOO ACCOMMODATIONS: A unique way to enjoy the slopes is to stay on after the hordes have left for the night. Each year, igloo villages are created on the pistes above Davos, Engelberg, Gstaad, and Zermatt. Open from Christmas until April, rooms range from a standard six-bed to a romantically decorated two-bed suite. Overnight stays include a cheese-fondue dinner, state-of-the-art gear to keep you warm (as the temp inside hovers just above freezing), and a hot breakfast. Added bonus: each village has a sauna or a hot tub. ☎ *041/6122728* ⊕ *www. iglu-dorf.com*

REST AND RELAXATION: Most high-end hotels have their own spas, but spa towns have natural thermal baths that won't break the bank. Davos, Leukerbad, Pontresina, Scuol, and Zernez offer great skiing, as well as the opportunity to soothe those aching muscles once the day is done.

(top left) A horse-drawn sleigh ride through Sertig Valley; (bottom left) Igloo near Gstaad; (right) Alpine spas are a great way to stay warm.

SAVE VS. SPLURGE MOUNTAIN-TRIP TIPS

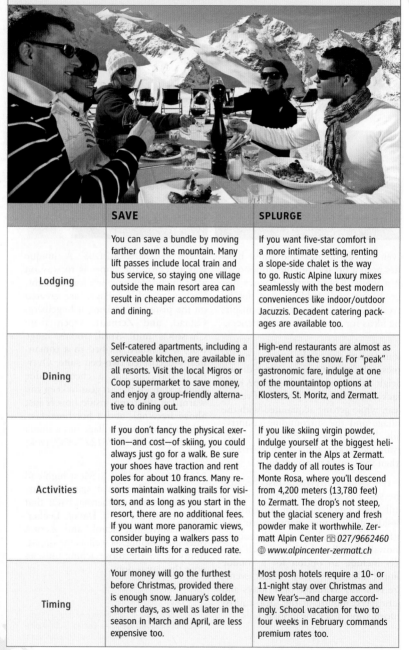

	SAVE	SPLURGE
Lodging	You can save a bundle by moving farther down the mountain. Many lift passes include local train and bus service, so staying one village outside the main resort area can result in cheaper accommodations and dining.	If you want five-star comfort in a more intimate setting, renting a slope-side chalet is the way to go. Rustic Alpine luxury mixes seamlessly with the best modern conveniences like indoor/outdoor Jacuzzis. Decadent catering packages are available too.
Dining	Self-catered apartments, including a serviceable kitchen, are available in all resorts. Visit the local Migros or Coop supermarket to save money, and enjoy a group-friendly alternative to dining out.	High-end restaurants are almost as prevalent as the snow. For "peak" gastronomic fare, indulge at one of the mountaintop options at Klosters, St. Moritz, and Zermatt.
Activities	If you don't fancy the physical exertion—and cost—of skiing, you could always just go for a walk. Be sure your shoes have traction and rent poles for about 10 francs. Many resorts maintain walking trails for visitors, and as long as you start in the resort, there are no additional fees. If you want more panoramic views, consider buying a walkers pass to use certain lifts for a reduced rate.	If you like skiing virgin powder, indulge yourself at the biggest heli-trip center in the Alps at Zermatt. The daddy of all routes is Tour Monte Rosa, where you'll descend from 4,200 meters (13,780 feet) to Zermatt. The drop's not steep, but the glacial scenery and fresh powder make it worthwhile. Zermatt Alpin Center ☎ 027/9662460 ⊕ www.alpincenter-zermatt.ch
Timing	Your money will go the furthest before Christmas, provided there is enough snow. January's colder, shorter days, as well as later in the season in March and April, are less expensive too.	Most posh hotels require a 10- or 11-night stay over Christmas and New Year's—and charge accordingly. School vacation for two to four weeks in February commands premium rates too.

Mountaintop meals are a memorable—and pricey—way to dine.

DID YOU KNOW?

The Philosophers' Trail at Muottas Muragl near Pontresina is open to hikers and snowshoers from December through April. Quotes from famous thinkers are posted along the route.

Funiculars and cable cars whisk hikers and walkers to magnificent trails above St. Moritz.

Then visitors see St. Moritz for what it really is: a busy, built-up old resort city that sprawls across a hillside above an aquamarine lake, the St. Moritzersee, surrounded by forested hills and by graceful, though not the region's most dramatic, peaks. Piz Rosatsch, with its glacier, dominates the view, with Piz Languard (10,699 feet) on the east and Piz Güglia (7,492 feet) on the west.

St. Moritz-Dorf is the most like a downtown, with busy traffic, but outlawing cars in the center of town and building the Serletta car park near the train station has alleviated competitive parking. Other than that, don't expect a picturesque village.

Even a hundred years of hype have not exaggerated its attraction as a winter sports center. The place that twice hosted the Olympic games (1928 and 1948)—and trademarked the shining sun as its logo—is still well set up for sports, with excellent facilities for ice-skating, bobsledding, ski jumping, and horseback riding. But it hardly has a lock on fine skiing: St. Moritz shares a broad complex of trails and facilities with Sils, Silvaplana, Celerina, and Pontresina; only the slopes of Corviglia, Marguns, and Piz Nair are directly accessible from town.

GETTING HERE AND AROUND
Between Chur and St. Moritz, direct trains take about two hours. To get to St. Moritz from Scuol you must change trains in Samedan.

ESSENTIALS
Visitor Information St. Moritz Tourist Information ✉ *Via Maistra 12* ☎ *081/8373333* ⊕ *www.stmoritz.ch.*

EXPLORING

Engadiner Museum. One of the few reminders that contemporary St. Moritz was once an Engadine village is the Engadiner Museum, a reproduction of the traditional sgraffitied home. In a building dating from 1906, the museum has displays of furniture, tools, and pottery in rooms decorated in styles from different periods. ⊠ *Via dal Bagn 39* ☎ *081/8334333* ⊕ *www.engadiner-museum.ch* 🎟 *8 SF* ☉ *June–Oct. and Dec–Apr., Sun.–Fri. 10–noon and 2–5.*

Segantini Museum. The somewhat forbidding stone structure that houses the Segantini Museum showcases the work of Italian artist Giovanni Segantini (1858–99). His huge triptych *La Vita, La Natura, La Morte* hangs in the domed upper floor. Take a seat on the bench to take in the work of this fine Impressionist artist. ⊠ *Via Somplaz 30* ☎ *081/8334454* ⊕ *www.segantini-museum.ch* 🎟 *10 SF* ☉ *Mid-May–mid-Oct. and early Dec.–mid-Apr., Tues.–Sun. 10–noon and 2–6.*

SKIING

Don't let the whirlwind of activities at St. Moritz make you forget that its raison d'être is skiing. You can reach the **Corviglia–Piz Nair, Suvretta,** and **Marguns** slopes, immediately above St. Moritz, from the Chantarella–Corviglia funicular in Dorf, the Signal cableway in Bad, the Suvretta chairlift, and the Marguns gondolas in Celerina. There are 80 km (50 miles) of difficult, intermediate, and easy runs and a half pipe for snowboarders. The Upper Engadine ski region offers 350 km (217 miles) of prepared trails. The views from Corviglia, Piz Nair, and the Suvretta Paradise run are magnificent.

Descents behind Piz Nair (10,026 feet) eventually lead down to Marguns; they are often in shadow in early winter but have the best snow up to the end of the season. With the help of snowmaking equipment, conditions usually remain excellent until late April. The sunny Suvretta slopes are usually less crowded, but they don't have snowmaking equipment. You can join a group and go with an instructor on a free "snow safari" offered by any ski school, which begin in Sils and end in Morteratsch. One-day tickets for St. Moritz are 73 SF; six-day regional passes cost 365 SF. Prices include transportation between ski stations on the Engadine) bus service.

Suvretta Snowsports School. For instruction there are a number of choices, including the Suvretta Snowsports School. ⊠ *Via Chasellas 1* ☎ *081/8366161* ⊕ *www.suvrettasnowsports.ch.*

St. Moritz Ski School. The St. Moritz Ski School, in town, is the oldest in Switzerland. ⊠ *Via Stredas 14* ☎ *081/8300101* ⊕ *www.skischool.ch.*

Ski Service Corvatsch. Rental equipment is available at Ski Service Corvatsch at the Corviglia Valley and mountain stations. ☎ *081/8387777.*

Ski hotline. For reports on daily snow conditions, call the hotline; the English-language version comes last. ☎ *084/4844944.*

▥ TIP➜ **In an effort to attract more visitors, St. Moritz's top hotels have banded together to offer an unbeatable lift-ticket deal: starting with two-night stays, guests can also reserve a one-day lift ticket for just 25 SF (two nights = one-day pass for 25 SF; three nights = two-day pass for 50 SF, and**

so on). The rest of the ticket price is covered by the hotel, which means three-star properties are less likely to participate—the deal is only available when you make your booking, so be sure to inquire up front.

Langlauf School. Cross-country skiing has its base in St. Moritz Bad, where the Langlauf school offers lessons and excursions. You can try out the close-by Engadine Marathon track or the many side valleys. Near the school is a lighted circular trail of 3 km (2 miles) open from 5:30 pm to 9 pm. ✉ *Plazza Paracelsus 2* ☎ *081/8336233.*

WHERE TO EAT

$$$ ITALIAN ★ 🍴 **Chesa Veglia.** When Elizabeth Taylor and many other legendary VIPs headed to St. Moritz, this was their favored watering hole. A 17th-century *Bauernhof* (farmhouse), its raw beams, aged wood, and native carvings have been self-consciously restored and the rustic-luxe restaurant divided into three rooms (an upscale grill, a Stübli, and a pizzeria). The main menu includes good Continental cuisine; you can order melt-in-your-mouth venison with spätzli and red cabbage or beef tournedos with warm foie gras and Périgord sauce at prices that are St. Moritz–high. There are good fruit tarts at teatime, when the atmosphere is at its most convincing. Later you'll find dinner and dancing with live entertainment and piano music in the grill. [$] *Average main: 60 SF* ✉ *Via Veglia 2, St. Moritz-Dorf* ☎ *081/8372800* 🌐 *www.badruttspalace.com/en/geniessen/restaurants/chesa-veglia* ✍ *Reservations essential.*

$ SWISS 🍴 **Engiadina.** With its pine-panelled interior and crackling log fire, this traditional Engadine restaurant has all the coziness of Grandma's house. The specialty is a delightfully decadent champagne fondue, though other favorites are steak with french fries and, in winter, escargots. It's a popular oddity for this ritzy resort—more homespun than glitz and glamour, and a reasonably priced, low-key establishment for couples or a small group of friends. During summer months, there are tables out front that offer partial views of the lake and, as an added bonus, the La Gondla Après Ski bar—located in an old gondola, not 10 steps from the restaurant door—is open daily in both summer and winter. [$] *Average main: 25 SF* ✉ *Via Dimlej 1* ☎ *081/8333000* 🌐 *www.restaurant-engiadina.ch* ⏲ *Closed Mon. and May.*

$$ SWISS Fodor's Choice ★ 🍴 **Meierei.** On a winding, private forest road partway around the lake, this 17th-century *Landgasthof* (country inn) is sought out for its light meals and delicious combinations such as fillet of venison with elderberry dumplings and polenta with mushrooms and Gorgonzola. Formerly both a farm and dairy, its sun terrace attracts day hikers, cross-country skiers, and horseback riders. (If you're not a guest, you'll have a 20–30 minute walk along the lake promenade, as only guests may drive in and park on-site.) If you don't want a full meal, light snacks are also on hand. [$] *Average main: 26 SF* ✉ *Via Dim Lej 52* ☎ *081/8387000* 🌐 *www.hotel-meierei.ch* ⏲ *Closed Mon., Apr.–mid-June, and mid-Oct.–mid-Dec.*

$$$$ MEDITERRANEAN 🍴 **Talvò by Dalsass.** Acclaimed Italian chef Martin Dalsass and his wife Lorena took the helm at St. Moritz's celebrated Talvò at the end of 2011 and have already achieved 18 Gault-Millau points. Though the menu changes seasonally, specialties include summer venison with pea puree and chanterelle mushrooms and the perennial favorite of

DID YOU KNOW?

St. Moritz is arguably the ritziest ski resort in Switzerland. If you're staying at a different resort within Graubünden but still want to try the famed slopes here, buy the lift ticket with your train ticket and the return fare will be reduced.

green-olive gnocchi with shrimp, cherry tomatoes, and basil. To finish off, try the chocolate mousse made with olive oil; the result is a deeply rich, unctuous dessert, which miraculously remains as light in your stomach as it was in your mouth. With a focus on the highest quality ingredients and a simplistic, Mediterranean cooking style that allows each individual taste to shine, dining here is a true culinary experience, though be prepared to spend almost as much on a meal as on a hotel room. At 210 SF, the seven-course tasting menu is an excellent value to à la carte dining. [$] *Average main: 80 SF* ✉ *Via Gunels 15, St. Moritz-Champfèr* ✣ *3 km (2 miles) southwest of St. Moritz, about 330 feet from the postbus stop* ☎ *081/8334455* 🌐 *www.talvo.ch* ✍ *Reservations essential* ⏲ *Closed Apr.–late June and late Sept.–Dec.*

WORD OF MOUTH

"Try to take the [Palm Express] bus from Lugano up to St Moritz—certainly one of the most gorgeous bus rides in all of Europe. From Lugano the bus heads over to Lake Lugano, follows its shores (stopping for a break in Menaggio before negotiating the sinuous Maloja Pass—via a series of hairpin turns with the bus horn blasting at each [one] warning oncoming cars. [It's] a wonderfully scenic trip and a utilitarian way of getting from central Switzerland to St Moritz—Lugano being on the main rail line between Milan, Italy and Zurich/Lucerne."—PalenQ

WHERE TO STAY

$$$$ HOTEL ★ 🏨 **Badrutt's Palace.** With its pseudo-Gothic stone and mismatched sprawl of architectural excess, the Palace is Switzerland at its most glitzy and glamorous, complete with its own ski shop and private instructors, an exlusive spa, and a high-society pedigree. **Pros:** every conceivable desire can be catered to (guests rarely hear the word "no"); your chance to be treated like royalty; excellent ski facilities. **Cons:** sky-high prices; missing a distinct, cohesive atmosphere. [$] *Rooms from: 830 SF* ✉ *Via Serlas 27* ☎ *081/8371000* 🌐 *www.badruttspalace.com* 🛏 *157 rooms, 38 suites* ⏲ *Closed Apr.–mid-June and mid-Sept.–Dec.* 🍴 *Multiple meal plans.*

$$ HOTEL 🏨 **Bellaval.** Simple rooms at good value right at the train station are reason enough for guests to stay here, but expectations are still surpassed time and time again by its unpretentious restaurant and convenient location. **Pros:** next to train station; excellent food; free use of rowboats on Lake St. Moritz; easy on the wallet. **Cons:** no elevator and three flights of stairs; not for those seeking the height of luxury. [$] *Rooms from: 190 SF* ✉ *Via Grevas 55, St. Moritz-Dorf* ☎ *081/8333245* 🌐 *www.bellaval-stmoritz.ch* 🛏 *23 rooms, 15 with bath* 🍴 *Multiple meal plans.*

$$$ HOTEL 🏨 **Corvatsch.** This family-run hotel in the middle of St. Moritz-Bad will make you feel right at home, as the friendly service and a drink by the crackling fire in the cozy "living room" are often all one needs at the end of a long day of hiking or skiing. **Pros:** family hosts are very welcoming and helpful; the food is delicious and rated highly by locals. **Cons:** those who need a "room with a view" should stay elsewhere; beds are not large. [$] *Rooms from: 330 SF* ✉ *Via Tegiatscha 1, St. Moritz-Bad* ☎ *081/8375757* 🌐 *www.hotel-corvatsch.ch* 🛏 *30 rooms, 1 suite* ⏲ *Closed Oct.–Dec. and late Apr.–June* 🍴 *Breakfast.*

$$$$ **Kulm.** This luxury hotel can claim its share of St. Moritz superlatives:
HOTEL it was the first hotel here (1856) *and* the first house to have electricity in all of Switzerland (1878), but modern comfort has come a long way as seen by its top-quality facilities like a nine-hole golf course, putting green, ice skating, and curling in winter.**Pros:** excellent location and views; no desire is too big or too small; free bicycle rental includes Flyer electric bikes. **Cons:** exterior is not the most attractive; dress codes; super expensive. $ *Rooms from: 745 SF ⊠ Via Veglia 18* 📞 *081/8368000* ⊕ *www.kulmhotel-stmoritz.ch* ↩ *132 rooms, 41 suites* ⊗ *Closed mid-Apr.–late June and Sept.–Dec.* ⦿ *Multiple meal plans.*

$$$ **Languard.** Set in the town center, this delightful little hotel shares
B&B/INN the Kulm's lovely mountain views, but not its prices. **Pros:** affordable
★ place with five-star views; central location. **Cons:** no spa or restaurant; bathrooms are a bit dark. $ *Rooms from: 340 SF ⊠ Via Veglia 14(off Via Maistra)* 📞 *081/8333137* ⊕ *www.languard-stmoritz.ch* ↩ *21 rooms, 1 suite.* ⊗ *Closed late Apr.–early June and mid-Oct.–early Dec.* ⦿ *Breakfast.*

$$$$ **Suvretta House.** The Suvretta House encourages visitors to embrace
HOTEL its unique location outside the village and stupendous views of Piz
★ Corvatsch and the Silvaplana Lake, as well as to take advantage of the indoor ski center, rental facilities and ski school, and private access to the Corvilgia slopes just outside the front door. **Pros:** beautiful location and views; state-of-the-art ski facilities; 25-meter pool. **Cons:** not for anyone who hates dress codes; traditional decor of muted browns and dark greens may not be to everyone's liking. $ *Rooms from: 550 SF ⊠ Via Chasellas 1, St. Moritz-Suvretta* 📞 *081/8363636* ⊕ *www. suvrettahouse.ch* ↩ *134 rooms, 37 junior suites, 10 suites* ⊗ *Closed Apr.–June and Sept.–early Dec.* ⦿ *Some meals.*

$$$$ **Waldhaus am See.** Perched on a peninsula overlooking the lake and
HOTEL mountains, this vacation lodge geared to leisurely stays has a merely
Fodor's Choice peripheral view of St. Moritz's urban sprawl across the highway along
★ with a big, sunny balcony, dining rooms with views, and a clientele that includes family groups and senior citizens.**Pros:** peaceful location with stunning views; whiskey bar. **Cons:** dated in places; rooms in the building behind the main hotel have limited views. $ *Rooms from: 390 SF ⊠ Via Dim Lej 6* 📞 *081/8366000* ⊕ *www.waldhaus-am-see.ch* ↩ *47 rooms, 3 apartments* ⦿ *Multiple meal plans.*

NIGHTLIFE AND THE ARTS

To find out what's happening, check the English-language section in the biweekly *Engadine Information* brochure, available at the tourist office, hotels, and shops, or find information online at ⊕ *www.engadin. stmoritz.ch.*

BARS AND LOUNGES

Cava. The après-ski clique favors the Steffani Hotel's Cava. ⊠ *Via Traunter Plazzas* 📞 *081/8369696.*

Devil's Place. Choose from the world's largest selection of whiskeys (2,500 at last count) at the Devil's Place, in the Waldhaus am See. It's mentioned in the *Guinness Book of World Records.* ⊠ *Via Dim Lej 6* 📞 *081/8366000.*

Miles Davis Lounge. Classified as a cigar lounge, midnight jazz and rock concerts make this after-hours venue in the Kulm Hotel a lively weekend option in summer and winter. ⊠ *Via Veglia 18, St. Mortiz* ☎ *081/8368000.*

Verde Couch Bar. Smokers looking to avoid frostbite head to Verde Couch Bar, one of the few places they are still welcome indoors in Graubünden. ⊠ *Plazza dal Mulin 4, St. Mortiz* ☎ *081/8334230.*

CASINOS

Casino St. Moritz. The Casino St. Moritz, in the Kempinski Grand Hôtel des Bains in St. Moritz-Bad, offers roulette, poker, blackjack, and slot machines with a "fantasy jackpot." It's open Sunday through Thursday until 3 am, Friday and Saturday until 4 am. It closes in May and November. ⊠ *Via Mezdi 29* ☎ *081/8375454* ⊕ *www.casinostmoritz.ch.*

DANCING

Anton's Bar. Anton's Bar, open year-round, is a winter-season hot spot at the Suvretta House. Don't forget your jacket and tie. ⊠ *Via Chasellas 1* ☎ *081/8363636.*

Diamond. A combination club, lounge, and restaurant, Diamond has wide appeal for the young and chic. ⊠ *Via Maistra 33* ☎ *081/8349767.*

King's Club. In Badrutt's Palace, the King's Club has a Moorish decor. Open only in winter, it has a steep cover charge on weekends. ⊠ *Via Serlas 27* ☎ *081/8371100.*

Vivai. In the basement of the Steffani Hotel, Vivai is open during the winter season. ⊠ *Via Traunter Plazzas 6* ☎ *081/8369696.*

MUSIC

Engadine Festival. The Engadine Festival takes place from mid-July to late August, with smaller-scale performances throughout the Upper Engadine. ☎ *081/8520588.*

Snow & Symphony Music Festival. The musical highlight in St. Moritz is the Snow & Symphony Music Festival, which takes place over 14 days in early spring. Prize-winning classical and jazz musicians, chamber orchestras, and a symphony orchestra give roughly 20 concerts. The performances are held in hotels and on mountaintops. ☎ *081/8344646* ⊕ *www.snowandsymphony.ch.*

St. Moritz Chamber Orchestra. The St. Moritz Chamber Orchestra gives free daily concerts in summer at 11 am in the spa center's hall or park. Contact the tourist office for more information.

SPAS

Medizinisches Therapiezentrum Heilbad. As a break from all those sports, the town offers relaxation at the Medizinisches Therapiezentrum Heilbad. The local mineral springs have been known for more than 3,000 years; in 1535 the physician and alchemist Paracelsus praised the water, which is the richest in iron and carbonic acid in Europe. Massages and most treatments are done in individual cabins with private baths. Peat baths and packs need a doctor's prescription, but you can take a mineral bath anytime; try one with natural aromas such as pine or rosemary (40 SF) or relax with a glass of Prosecco (44 SF). ⊠ *Plazza Paracelsus 2* ☎ *081/8333062* ⊕ *www.heilbad-stmoritz.ch* ⊘ *Weekdays 8–7, Sat.*

8–noon ☞ *35 SF baths, 82 SF mud pack, 110 SF for a 60-min full-body massage. Hot tub. Gym with: cardiovascular machines, free weights, weight-training equipment. Services: aromatherapy, facials, massage, mud packs, physiotherapy, solarium. Classes and programs: aerobics, aquaerobics, cycling, fitness analysis, flexibility training, massage, personal training, strength training, stretching.*

SPORTS AND THE OUTDOORS

This is the place to see winter sports that were, or still are, found only here, such as polo and cricket played on snow, bobsledding on natural ice, and horse racing on snow, which includes *skijöring* (skiers pulled by riderless horses). The frozen lake acts as the "white arena" for some events and provides the backdrop for others. A tent village complete with grandstands, palm trees, restaurants, bars, and art exhibitions is installed on the lake from late January through February during the White Turf, which includes horse racing and skijöring.

BIKING

Free maps of biking routes are available at the tourist office.

Corviglia Sport Shop. Mountain-bike rentals cost about 30 SF a day (afterwards each additional day is 20 SF) at Corviglia Sport Shop. ⊠ *Via Maistra 21* ☎ *081/8334477* ⊕ *www.corviglia-sport.ch.*

BOBSLEDDING

In 1890 and 1891 the first bobsled races were held on the road between St. Moritz and Celerina. The present-day run, built each year from natural ice, follows roughly the same course; it's the only one of its kind in the world.

Olympia Bob Run. There is no entry fee if you want to watch the regular Olympia Bob Run races. Or you can tear along the run yourself by riding behind an experienced pilot. The ride costs 250 SF; book well in advance. The run is open from late December through early March. ⊠ *Plazza Gunter Sachs* ☎ *081/8300200* ⊕ *www.olympia-bobrun.ch.*

GOLF

Engadine Golf Course. Samedan's 18-hole Engadine Golf Course, the oldest on the continent, is about 10 minutes by car from St. Moritz. It's open from late May to early October. ⊠ *Samedan* ☎ *081/8510466* ⊕ *www.engadin-golf.ch/en.*

St. Moritz Golf Club. The St. Moritz Golf Club has a nine-hole course in the Kulm Park. ☎ *081/8368236* ⊕ *www.stmoritz-golfclub.ch/en.*

HIKING

There are dozens of hiking and walking routes around St. Moritz, all well signposted. Maps are available at the tourist office. All cable cars, funiculars, and some chairlifts run in summer, providing access to higher trails, including the magnificent Via Engiadina path (moderate difficulty), which runs along the mountainside at roughly 6,560 feet to the beginning of the valley. The full walk takes about six hours, but you can descend to valley level earlier if you're tuckered out.

ICE SPORTS

Cresta Run. On the world's one and only Cresta Run, riders on skeletons (metal toboggans) rush headfirst down a winding ice channel from St. Moritz to Celerina, accelerating to about 90 mph. You can watch the runs every morning from the path or the roof of the Junction Hut. If you'd like to try the run, contact the St. Moritz Tobogganing Club. It's a private club, but they do allow temporary memberships (for 600 SF) that will give you five runs. The Cresta is open from late December to the last day of February. Note that the run is not open to women. ⊕ *www.cresta-run.com.*

Ludains Ice Arena. The outdoor Ludains Ice Arena, along the lake, is open from mid-July to late April. Skate rentals are available. ⊠ *Via Ludains 5, St. Moritz-Bad* ☎ *081/8335030.*

Kulm. The skating and curling rinks at the Kulm Hotel are open to the public in winter; rental skates and curling lessons are also available. ☎ *081/8368000.*

Ticino

BELLINZONA, LOCARNO, LUGANO

WORD OF MOUTH

"Lugano makes a good base for exploring the other lakes. You can easily hop on a bus to Menaggio (Lake Como) from where you can take a ferry to Bellagio. Or go by train to Locarno and hop on a ferry for exploring Lake Maggiore."

—Ingo

WELCOME TO TICINO

TOP REASONS TO GO

★ **Luscious Lugano:**
Nowhere in Ticino do Italian chic and Swiss quality mingle so perfectly. But there is more going on here than people-watching and ice-cream tasting: churches, museums, and the restored Old Town also demand attention.

★ **Land o' Lakes:** Gaze at the verdant mountains, cozy villages, and palm-fronted shores from the vantage point of the elegant old ferry boats that ply the waters of the Lago Maggiore and Lago di Lugano.

★ **Castle-topped Bellinzona:**
Old cobblestone streets, shady arcades, and the three fortresses that once upon a time held the line between Italy and the wild Swiss take the visitor back to a time when this region belonged to Milan.

★ **Get a view:** Monte Bré (near Lugano) can be climbed on foot or by funicular, which is faster and far less tiring. Either way, the view from the top is one that will take your breath away.

1 Sopraceneri. Capital of the Ticino, Bellinzona has always been a famous crossroads thanks to three passes—the St. Gotthard, the Lukmanier, and the San Bernardino—from the north. The town's great castles—Castelgrande, Montebello, and Sasso Corbaro—prove that Bellinzona was always in the firing line. To the west along Lago Maggiore lies Locarno, Switzerland's sunniest town, with its bevy of Baroque and Renaissance churches (including the cliff-top Santuario della Madonna del Sasso). Just beyond are the lakeside promenades of Ascona, so beloved by painters, and the Isole di Brissago (Brissage Islands), Switzerland's most beautiful botanical garden.

2 Sottoceneri. South of Monte Ceneri, the Ticino changes. While the countryside shelters many Italianate villages clustered around ancient bell towers, the bustling city of Lugano draws all eyes. There are really two Luganos. Sophisticated, modern Lugano is Switzerland's fourth- most-important financial center; Lugano of the old-world charm is another, its arcades and twisting streets reminiscent of a small Italian town. Fashionable boulevards and art-filled museums compete with the fabled waterside promenade, Il Lungolago, and lose out to its stupendous vistas of the blue lake and bluer peaks. On Lago di Lugano's shores lie a gaggle of gorgeous villages: Gandria, Campione, and Morcote.

5

GETTING ORIENTED

The canton is geographically divided into two regions by the small mountain range (1,817 feet) called Monte Ceneri, which rises up south of the valley below Bellinzona. Extending northeast and northwest of Monte Ceneri in the windswept Sopraceneri region are several mountainous valleys, including Valle di Blenio, Valle Maggia, Valle Verzasca, and Valle Leventina. Included in this region north of or, literally, above Monte Ceneri are Locarno and Ascona, which share a peninsula bulging into Lago Maggiore. The more developed southern region, Sottoceneri ("below Ceneri"), is home to business and resort towns, notably Lugano.

EATING WELL IN TICINO

Ticinese food has strong ties to northern Italian cooking—logically enough, since Lombardy and Piedmont in Italy segue right into Ticino, which became part of the Swiss Confederation in 1803.

Visit a grotto for an authentic taste of Ticinese cuisine—many offer serene settings and lake views. Merlot is a common local wine (above, right)

Italian staples here include cheeses—from semihard *Formaggio d'Alpe Ticinese* to tiny goat's-milk *formaggini*—and sausages from *cicitt* (goat meat and cinnamon) to *zampone* (pork stuffed into an emptied-out pig's trotter and leg). Game is popular in season, and deer or wild boar (also horse) find their way into *salami, salumi, salamelle,* and *salametti.* A major specialty is polenta: cornmeal cooked for a long time and then formed into a cake.

As for markets and festivals: during the pre-Lent (late February or early March) festivities like Rabadan in Bellinzona, there's a *risottata* when huge cauldrons of risotto are stirred in the streets, the air redolent with smells of grilling *luganighe* (pork sausages). Chestnut fests, like the *castagnata* in Ascona, take place all over the canton in October.

—Gail Mangold Vine

DRINK LIKE A LOCAL

When you're here, avoid Swiss-style coffee; opt for a *liscio*, Italian-style espresso. At all hours of the day, you'll hear customers asking for a *corretto*—coffee laced with local brandy, called grappa. Finish off your meal with a shot of *nocino,* a green-walnut liqueur also known as *ratafiá.* The unripe nuts are soaked in alcohol such as grappa and mixed with herbs and spices.

GROTTOS

A grotto is a simple eatery serving local Ticinese cuisine. Grottos usually have tree-shaded outdoor seating in warm weather, and are mostly located off the beaten track. Word to the wise: the food here is seasonal, so some of the dishes described may not be available depending on the time of year you visit. Here are some of our favorites and the best Italian-influenced dishes you can find at each.

Grotto Morchino. Feast on specialties like *bresaola* (Ticinese air-dried beef), *busecca* (tripe soup), and risotto with leeks and rosemary. ⊠ *1 via Carona, Pazzallo* ☎ *091/9946044* ⊕ *www.morchino.ch.*

Grotto Flora. Martin Dalsass of Santabbondio and other top Ticinese chefs call this grotto located near Lugano a favorite. Mushroom and saffron risotto, meat (beef, chicken, lamb, pork) *arrostite sul fuoco* (roasted on an open fire), and *zabaione* (whisked eggs, sugar, wine) are must-haves. ⊠ *Agra* ☎ *091/9941567* ⊕ *www.grottoflora-bnb.ch.*

Grotto del Giuvan. Dine on specialties like *nerveti e barbabietole* (chopped meat and onion with beets); *prosciutto crudo* (raw ham) with pears and mustard; and potato and nettle gnocchi with porcini mushrooms. ⊠ *19 via Stradone, Salorino* ☎ *091/6461161* ⊕ *www.grottodelgiuvan.ch.*

Grotto dell' Ortiga. In this converted craftsman's workshop near Lugano, try the soup of *fagioli e radicchio* (bean and red chicory); *pizzocheri* (buckwheat pasta); or seasonal risotto with nettles, artichokes, asparagus, basil, mushrooms, or pumpkin. ⊠ *35 strada Regina, Manno* ☎ *091/6051613* ⊕ *www.ortiga.ch.*

La Baita. Across Lago Maggiore from Locarno is this popular grotto serving salami, coppa, lardo, pancetta, mortadella, and *salumeria nostrana* (*meaning* "made our way"). To finish, try the *pesche al vino* (peaches in wine). ⊠ *6573 Magadino-Orgnana* ☎ *091/7804343* ⊕ *www.baita.ch.*

TICINO WINE

Roughly 6,000 tons of wine grapes—about 7% of Switzerland's total production—are grown each year in the rolling hills of the Ticino. Leading the way is the popular Merlot grape, introduced in 1905, which now accounts for 80% of the region's wine production. If you appreciate Merlot and the many other white and blush varieties grown here, you should visit in May when locals celebrate **Cantine Aperte**, (which means "Open Cellars"), an open house of wineries across the canton. The occasion, when visitors can stop by for free tastings, marks the launch of wines from the previous autumn's harvest. Dates are posted at ⊕ *www.ticinowine.ch.* In September, don't miss wine-harvest festivals like the **Sagra dell'Uva** in Mendrisio (⊕ *www.sagradelluva.ch*) or **Bacchica** in Bellinzona (⊕ *www.bacchica.ch*), when street life leaps alive with seasonal markets, eating and drinking, parades, music, and dance.

5

TICINO LAKES

They say, "When in Rome . . ." but there's no need to travel so far south for a taste of the good life. Do as the ancient Romans did (and the wealthiest Italians and Swiss still do) and vacation in this balmy corner of paradise.

There are many ways to explore Ticino's lovely lakes: hop on a bike for a leisurely cycle along the water (above), or head for higher ground on a hike with spectacular views (below, right).

Though it's often know as the Italian Lake Country, the shores of Lago Maggiore and Lago di Lugano are also partly Swiss. You won't find white sands or waist-high waves, but its Mediterranean feel has nonetheless earned Ticino a reputation as a summer idyll. From the tall palms and semitropical vegetation that grace the coast to the rounded green mountains that feel a little like Rio, the Ticino lakes are an ideal destination for beachcombers, photographers, and lots of other nature lovers. Sunbathe at Lugano's famous Lungolago. Take a daylong cruise on Lago Maggiore. Hike the many trails that wind from the lakes to the mountains. No matter how you spend your free time, you'll probably want to spend most of it outdoors.

—Alexis Munier

BEST TIME TO GO

In south-of-the-Alps Ticino, you can usually dine alfresco from March onward. By June, there are sunny skies day in, day out. July and August may be hot and crowded, but that means people-watching is at its best and that the water's fine. Autumn brings richly hued leaves and sparser crowds.

WAYS TO EXPLORE

BY WATER

Both Lago di Lugano and Lago Maggiore are crisscrossed by many ferries. By day, choose the scenic tour that whisks you from Lugano around the lake, stopping at Campione d'Italia, Ponte Tresa, and Morcote. By night, a jazz or gin-soaked "booze" cruise on one of the many sleek party boats awaits. Feeling sporty? You can rent a kayak or canoe in nearly every town on Lago Maggiore and paddle your way across the gentle waves to Italy. Bring a picnic lunch and just drift before garnering the strength to make it home. For those who don't fancy a workout, most rental outfits also offer less taxing paddleboats.

BY BIKE

Being so close to Italy means that car traffic can be intense, and biking here is best suited to experienced riders. For a short adventure on two wheels, pedal through Lugano's Old Town and window-shop at the numerous art galleries or designer boutiques before stopping to indulge in creamy gelato.

Brave souls can rent a bike, or one of the hugely popular electrically assisted "e-bikes," and pedal the roughly four-hour, 70-km (50-mile) Locarno–Camedo–Locarno loop. From the Lido, you'll cross the Maggia River to Ascona and ride along the lake, with stunning views of the surrounding mountains and the Isole di Brissago. At Cannòbio, you can head back to Locarno along the same route, or continue through to Camedo and the picturesque Centovalli before arriving back where you began this tiring, thrilling journey.

BY FOOT

Begin in the Castagnola area of Lugano, following the Sentiero (Footpath) di Gandria, which passes by narrow cobblestone streets, manor houses, and silver-hued olive trees. Just past the Sasso (Rock) di Gandria, stairs lead up to the quaint fishing village of Gandria. Time for a cool drink on a balcony overlooking the lake.

BEST PHOTOS

■ Capture the magic of the Ticino lakes region by setting your lens on the following sights:

■ Locarno's Casa dei Canonici and its medieval garden in the heart of the Old Town—and the Madonna del Sasso perched on the hillside above.

■ Campione's otherwordly casino, visible from any point across Lago di Lugano.

■ The more-than-900 varieties of camellia trees in bloom at the Camellia Park in Locarno.

■ Glistening bathing beauties (of both sexes) in skimpy suits at Lugano's Lido.

■ Tiny Gandria's winding streets and stately mansions.

■ The crumbling stone houses and colorful frescoes in Vira, one of the tiny villages that line the Riviera del Gambarogno, a 10-km (7-mile) stretch of Maggiore lakeshore that's across from Locarno.

■ Views of Monte San Salvatore rising lush above the morning fog.

5

Updated by
Alexis Munier

Visitors a bit weak on their geography might hear the names Lugano, Ascona, Locarno, and Bellinzona and assume—quite naturally—that they're in Italy. Color photographs of the region might not even set them straight: nearly every publicity shot shows palm trees and mimosas, azure waters, and indigo skies. Surely this is the Italian Mediterranean or the coast of the Adriatic. But behind the waving date palms are telltale signs: fresh paint, manicured gardens, punctual trains. There's no mistake about it: it's a little bit of Italy, but the canton Ticino is decidedly Swiss.

For the German Swiss, it's a little bit of paradise. They can cross over the St. Gotthard or San Bernardino passes and emerge into balmy sunshine, fill up on gnocchi and polenta in shaded grotti, drink Merlot from ceramic bowls, gaze at the waters of Lago Maggiore (Lake Maggiore)—and still know their lodging will be strictly controlled by the Swiss Hotel Association. They never even have to change currency. The combination is irresistible, and so in spring, summer, and fall they pour over the Alps to revel in low-risk Latin delights.

And the Ticinese welcome them like rich, distant cousins, to be served and coddled and—perhaps just a bit—tolerated. The Italian-speaking natives of the Ticino—a lonely 8% of the Swiss population—are a minority in their own land, dominated politically by the German-speaking Swiss, and set apart from them by language as well as culture.

Their Italian leanings make perfect sense: an enormous mountain chain blocks them from the north, pushing them inexorably toward their lingual roots. Most of the territory of the Ticino belonged to the pre-Italian city-states of Milan and Como until 1512, when the Swiss Confederation took it over by force. It remained a Swiss conquest until 1798, when from the confusion of Napoléon's campaigns it emerged a free canton, and in 1803 it joined the confederation for good.

Ticino remains a canton apart nonetheless, graceful, open, laissez-faire. Here you'll instantly notice differences in manner and body language among people engaged in conversation; you'll also discover fewer English-speaking Swiss. The climate, too, is different: there's an extraordinary amount of sunshine here, more than in central Switzerland and even more than in sunny Italy, immediately across the border. Mountain-sports meccas aside, this is the most glamorous of Swiss regions: the waterfront promenades of Lugano, Locarno, and Ascona, lined with tightly pruned trees, rhododendrons, and bobbing yachts, contain a rich social mix of jet-set resorters. A drive of a few miles brings the canton's impoverished past into view: foothill and mountain villages are still scattered with low-roof stone cabins, although nowadays those cabins often prove to have been gentrified into chic vacation homes.

Although they're prosperous, with Lugano standing third in banking, after Zürich and Geneva, the Ticinese hold on to their past, a mountain-people culture that draws them to hike, hunt, and celebrate with great pots of risotto stirred over open outdoor fires. It's that contrast—contemporary glamour combined with an earthy past—that grants travelers a visit that's as balanced and satisfying as a good Merlot.

5

TICINO PLANNER

WHEN TO GO

No one complains about the weather in the Ticino. Palm trees, magnolia, century plants, and full-bodied wines suggest why so many "northerners" come to the canton for their vacation: the weather is milder in winter than elsewhere in Switzerland, while stark summer temperatures are moderated by the lakes and the mountains.

There can be some surprises, though, since you are in the Alps. Sudden storms and drops in temperature are a possibility. Make sure you have some warmer clothing and something waterproof. If you intend to trek up the valleys or up to the summit of a mountain, you will definitely need sturdy hiking boots and sunglasses.

Lush and Mediterranean, the Ticino is gorgeous in springtime; the season starts as early as mid-March here, making the region a popular late-winter escape. In summertime, lakeside activity surges, and the weather can at times be hot.

PLANNING YOUR TIME

The important parts of the Ticino are all fairly close to one another, but depending on the amount of time you have, you might want to choose one or two home bases. Locarno or Ascona will allow you easy and quick access to the Verzasca and Maggia valleys and to all the sites and sights along Lago Maggiore. Lugano gives you fast access to the Lago di Lugano and the gems of Gandria, Morcote, and Campione. From Bellinzona, you will have good access to everything. And there's a lot to do if you want to. If not, you can enjoy long meditative walks in the mountains or along the lakes. Shopping in Lugano, touring the lakes by ferry, or hopping a funicular up a mountain, followed by a simple meal in a grotto, will give you some classic Ticinese moments. More active types will have lots of sports options available: skiing and snow-boarding in winter, swimming, climbing, and golf during the warmer months. If you find yourself in need of a big city, remember that Milan is at most 1½ hours away by train from Lugano.

GETTING HERE AND AROUND

AIR TRAVEL

The nearest international airport is in Italy. Malpensa, near Milan, is one of the biggest hubs in southern Europe. Shuttle-Bus connects Milan's Malpensa and Linate airports with Lugano. Swiss International Air Lines, known as Swiss, is Switzerland's domestic carrier and has direct connections to Lugano's airport, Aeroporto Lugano-Agno.

To get to Lugano from Aeroporto Lugano-Agno, take one of the frequent shuttle buses or a taxi.

Air Contacts Shuttle-Bus ☏ *091/9676030* ⊕ *www.shuttle-bus.com.*

BOAT AND FERRY TRAVEL

Lago di Lugano and Lago Maggiore are traveled by graceful steamers that carry passengers from one waterfront resort to another, offering excellent views of the mountains. On Lago di Lugano, the Navigazione Lago di Lugano (Navigation Company of Lake Lugano) offers excursions around the bay to Gandria and toward the Villa Favorita. Boats owned by Navigazione Lago Maggiore-Bacino Svizzero (Swiss Navigation Company of Lake Maggiore) cruise Lago Maggiore.

Boat and Ferry Information Navigazione Lago di Lugano ⊠ *Casella Postale 56, Lugano* ☏ *091/9715223* ⊕ *www.lakelugano.ch.* **Navigazione Lago Maggiore-Bacino Svizzero** ⊠ *Lungolago Motta, Locarno* ☏ *091/7516140* ⊕ *www.navlaghi.it.*

BUS TRAVEL

The Palm Express scenic postbus route carries visitors from St. Moritz to Lugano via the Maloja Pass. It takes about four hours and can be arranged at any train station or tourist office.

You can also contact Railtour Suisse.

There's a convenient postbus sightseeing system here that you can use to get around the region, even into the backcountry. You can get booklets with suggested itineraries and prices through the Autopostale Ticino-Moesano or through local tourist and post offices.

Postbus excursion prices are reduced with the Locarno or Lugano Holiday Passes. Even better, they are free with the Swiss Pass.

Bus Information Autopostale Ticino-Moesano ⊠ *Via S. Balestra, Lugano* ☏ *0840/852852* ⊕ *www.autopostale.ch.* **Railtour Suisse** ☏ *031/3780101* ⊕ *www.railtour.ch.*

CAR TRAVEL

There are two major gateways into Ticino: the St. Gotthard Pass, in the northwest, and the San Bernardino Pass, to the northeast. From the St. Gotthard Pass, the swift A2 expressway leads down the Valle Leventina to Bellinzona, where it joins with A13, which cuts south from the San Bernardino. A2 directs the mingled traffic flow southward past Lugano to Chiasso and the Italian border, where the expressway heads directly to Como and Milan.

As an alternative, there's the St. Gotthard Tunnel—if traffic is light, it can cut an hour off your travel time, but if the passes are closed and it's holiday migration time, tunnel traffic can be nasty. A car is a real asset here if you intend to see the mountain valleys—and a hindrance in the congested lakeside resorts.

TRAIN TRAVEL

The St. Gotthard route connects south from Zürich, cuts through the pass tunnel, and heads into Bellinzona and Lugano. Side connections lead into Locarno from Brig, crossing the Simplon Pass and cutting through Italy. Swiss Pass travelers do not have to pay Italian rail fares to cross from Brig to Locarno via Domodossola and the Centovalli. Trains connect out of Zürich's airport and take about three hours to Lugano, Locarno, and Ascona; from Geneva, catch the Milan express, changing at Domodossola, Locarno, and Bellinzona. For information contact the Swiss Federal Railway, here called the Ferrovie Federali Svizzere (FFS).

Secondary rail connections here are minimal and can make all but the most mainstream rail sightseeing a complicated venture; most excursions will require some postbus connections. Nevertheless, there is a regional discount pass called the Holiday Pass available from the Ferrovie Autlinee Regionali Ticinesi. The pass is valid for the Lugano and Locarno areas and gives you unlimited free travel for three or seven consecutive days on bus and train and a 30–50% discount on others.

Train Information Ferrovie Federali Svizzere ☏ *0900/300300 1.19 SF per min* ⊕ *www.sbb.ch.*

⇨ *For more information on getting here and around, see Travel Smart Switzerland.*

RESTAURANTS

From rib-sticking local specialties like *pizzoccheri* to refined fare such as expertly grilled seafood and delicate homemade pasta, Ticino has it all. The Ticinese, like their Italian cousins, believe life is too short for bad food or bad wine. The result is cuisine with simple ingredients that are delicious in any combination. Don't forget to wash it all down with a local Merlot. Restaurants here run the gamut from highbrow four-star establishments to local pizzerias with wood-burning ovens.

Prices in the reviews are the average cost of a main course at dinner or, if dinner is not served, at lunch.

HOTELS

The hotel industry of this Mediterranean region of Switzerland capitalizes on its natural assets, with lakeside views of Lago Maggiore and Lago di Lugano, and swimming pools and terraces that pay homage to the omnipresent sun. As Ticino is at its best in spring and fall, and packed with sun seekers in summer, many hotels close down for the winter. Tourist offices often publish lists of those remaining open, so if you're planning to come in low season—and even in January the lake resorts can be balmy—check carefully.

Keep in mind that most hotels are not air-conditioned, in spite of hot spells in July and August. Vacation resorts don't depend on the demi-pension (half board) system like many of their mountain counterparts, but arrangements can be made. Remember, there are several festivals in all towns in summer, notably in Locarno and Lugano—so expect full hotels. Otherwise, the Ticino is moderately well visited throughout most of the year, except in late fall and after the Christmas/New Year period.

Prices in the reviews are the lowest cost of a standard double room in high season.

VISITOR INFORMATION
Ticino Turismo ⊠ *Pallazzo Civico, Via Camminata 2, Bellinzona* ☎ *091/8252131* ⊕ *www.ticino.ch.*

SOPRACENERI

The mountainous valleys of Valle di Blenio, Valle Maggia, Valle Verzasca, and Valle Leventina reach, like the fingers of a hand, south from the Alps into the basin of Lago Maggiore and Monte Ceneri, in the Sopraceneri. At the tips are the sun-kissed resorts of Locarno and Ascona, both on the northern edge of Lago Maggiore. Here the true spirit of the canton is still evident in the numerous small valley communities, each of which was politically autonomous at fewer than 100 inhabitants. The Sopraceneri reveals a slightly slower-paced, homier side of the Ticino, leaving the flashier offerings to Lugano in the south.

BELLINZONA

Fodor'sChoice *141 km (88 miles) south of Luzern, 150 km (93 miles) south of St.*
★ *Moritz.*

All roads lead to Bellinzona, the fortified valley city that guards the important European crossroads of the St. Gotthard and San Bernardino routes. The capital of the Ticino, its importance through the ages is evident in the three massive fortified castles that rise over its ancient center. As the only example of late medieval military architecture preserved along the Alpine range, the castles and fortifications have been named a World Heritage Site by UNESCO. They were built by the Sforza and Visconti families, the dukes of Milan who ruled northern Italy and its environs for centuries. In the 15th century many of the surrounding valleys began falling into the hands of the expanding Swiss Confederation. Bellinzona, however, remained Italian until Milan itself—as well as Bellinzona—was occupied by the French in 1503. Bellinzona decided to cast its lot with the confederation. Ironically, the names of the castles that had been built in part to keep the Swiss at bay were then changed to Schwyz, Uri, and Unterwalden—the three core cantons of the Swiss Confederation. Eventually the names were changed again, and the fortresses are known today as Castelgrande, Castello di Montebello, and Castello di Sasso Corbaro.

The three castles have been exceptionally well restored, and each merits a visit (a walk along the ramparts at night is particularly appealing), but

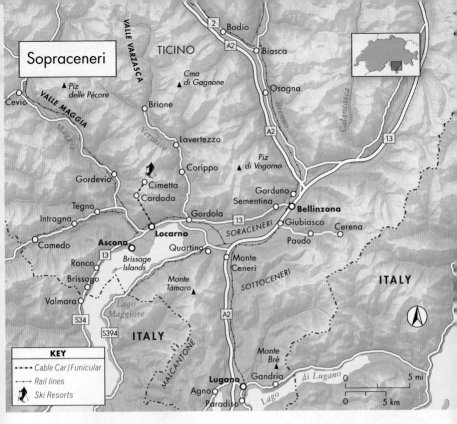

the city itself should not be overlooked: it's a classic Lombard town, with graceful architecture, red cobblestones, and an easy, authentically Italian feel. It's relatively free of tourists and thus reveals the Ticino way of life, complete with a lively produce market on Saturday featuring boar salami, wild mushrooms, and local cheeses.

GETTING HERE AND AROUND

Transportation gateway to the Ticino, Bellinzona is not only on the Zürich–Milan route but also has frequent trains running to and from Locarno (25 minutes away) and Lugano (30 minutes). Buses to smaller villages leave from the bus depot at the train station. Remember, if you have a Swiss Pass or another rail-discounting card, it also applies to the buses.

ESSENTIALS

Visitor Information Bellinzona Turismo ✉ *Palazzo Civico, Via Camminata 2* ☎ *091/8252131* ⊕ *www.bellinzonaturismo.ch.*

EXPLORING

TOP ATTRACTIONS

Castello di Montebello. The most striking of Bellinzona's three castles has a core section that dates from the 13th century. The palace and courtyard, both from the 15th century, are encircled by walls with spectacular walkways on top. The center structure houses an attractive, modern

Museo Civico (Municipal Museum) and the Museo Archeologico (Archaeology Museum), with exhibits on local history and architecture, including an impressive collection of Gothic and Renaissance stone capitals. ⊠ *Salita al Castello di Montebello* ☎ *091/8252131* ⊕ *www. castellodimontebello.com* 📧 *10 SF, 15 SF combination ticket includes Castelgrande and Castello di Sasso Corbaro* ☉ *Easter–Nov., daily 10–6.*

Castello di Sasso Corbaro. This massive and forbidding fieldstone construction's almost complete absence of curves is typical of the Sforza style. It was designed by a Florentine military engineer and built in 1479 for the duke of Milan, who insisted the work be completed in six months, as indeed it was. Temporary art exhibitions are held in the belvedere and in the Emma Paglia Room. Ambitious walkers can reach the castle in about 45 minutes by treading uphill from the Castello di Montebello along a switchback road through woods; if you're driving, follow the signs to Artore. ⊠ *Via Sasso Corbaro* ☎ *091/8255906* 📧 *10 SF, 15 SF combination ticket includes Castelgrande and Castello di Montebello* ☉ *Easter–Nov., Tues.–Sun.10–10, Mon. 10–6.*

Centro Storico. With its heavy-column arcades, wrought-iron balconies, and shuttered facades, Bellinzona's Old Town exhibits the direct influence of medieval Lombardy. The small area is distinguished by red cobblestones.

Chiesa Santa Maria delle Grazie. The earliest records of the Church of St. Mary of Grace date from the 15th century, when it was part of a Franciscan monastery. Now it's a retirement home. The church's most remarkable feature is the huge fresco on a wall segmenting the main nave painted by an unknown Lombard artist some time around 1500. It depicts the Crucifixion in the center, surrounded by 15 vignettes from the life of Christ. ⊠ *Via Convento, Bellinzona-Ravecchia* ☎ *091/8252131.*

Palazzo Civico. This splendid Renaissance structure was rebuilt in the 1920s. Its courtyard is framed by two stacked rows of delicate vaulted arcades decorated with sgraffiti depicting Bellinzona in the 19th century. The top floor consists of an airy loggia. ⊠ *Piazza Nosetto.*

WORTH NOTING

Castelgrande. Although this castle was first mentioned in a document from the 6th century, the current structure dates from the 1200s. The massive exterior is dominated by two heavy, unmatched towers and the remaining portion of a crenellated wall that once stretched all the way to the river. Modern renovations have added an elaborate complex of restaurants and museums that include historical and archaeological exhibitions. The 14th-century ceiling murals, created to embellish the wooden ceiling of a local villa (now demolished), offer a peek at privately commissioned decorative art. A dramatic audiovisual history of Bellinzona and the Ticino Valley is shown in one room. ⊠ *Salita al Castelgrande* ☎ *091/8258145* 📧 *10 SF, 15 SF combination ticket includes Castello di Montebello and Castello di Sasso Corbaro* ☉ *Daily 10–6.*

Chiesa Collegiata di San Pietro e San Stefano. The sober, late-Renaissance facade of the Collegiate Church of St. Peter and St. Stephen, begun in the 16th century, stands across from the Castelgrande. Its Baroque interior is richly decorated with frescoes and stuccowork by a host of

Ticino's Fossil Trove

Rooted firmly on the southern shores of Lago di Lugano, the 3,595-foot Monte San Giorgio has been an irresistible draw for paleontologists since the mid-19th century. Excavations in its five successive strata have regularly yielded extremely well-preserved fossils, allowing scientists to study the evolution of various groups of marine creatures of the Middle Triassic era (245–230 million years ago). Thousands of the reptiles, fish, and invertebrates found here—some of them unique specimens—have made their way into museums of paleontology in Zürich, Lugano, and Milan.

No wonder, then, that UNESCO added the entire region—an area measuring 2,098 acres and extending across the communities of Meride, Riva San Vitale, and Brusino Arsizio—to the list of World Heritage Natural Sites in 2003. This designation for Monte San Giorgio is Switzerland's second such honor, coming two years after that for the glaciers spanning the Jungfrau, Aletsch, and Bietschhorn summits.

Ticino artists. Of particular note is the late-18th century Crucifixion attributed to Simone Peterzano that serves as a central altar painting. ⊠ *Piazza Collegiata* ☎ *091/8252131.*

Chiesa San Biagio. One of Bellinzona's two Italianate churches, St. Biagio is a spare medieval treasure guarded on the exterior by an outsize fresco of a soldierly Christ. The 12th-century late-Romanesque structure suggests a transition into Gothic style. Alternating natural red brick and gray stone complement fragments of exquisitely colored 14th-century frescoes. ⊠ *Via San Biagio 13, Bellinzona-Ravecchia* ☎ *091/8252131.*

Museo Villa dei Cedri. The city's art gallery sporadically mounts worthwhile exhibits of pieces from its collection, donated by private citizens. Behind the garden and grounds, the city maintains a tiny vineyard used to produce its very own Merlot, available for sale inside. ⊠ *Piazza San Biagio 9* ☎ *091/8218520* ⊕ *www.villacedri.ch* ☷ *8 SF* ☉ *Tues.–Fri. 2–6, weekends 11–6.*

WHERE TO EAT

$$$
MODERN ITALIAN
★

✕ **Castelgrande.** Now that the oldest of the city's castles has been renovated, its chic, modern restaurant merits a visit. Don't expect a quick cafeteria lunch served to shorts-clad tourists: this is a serious experience, with daringly cool, postmodern decor and sophisticated efforts from the Italian chef, including fried shrimp tails in a butternut squash and coconut sauce, or smoked lamb served with mint-infused couscous. The wine list has more than 70 Ticino Merlots. Downstairs, there's a lighter atmosphere at the more casual Grotto restaurant. Its stunning summer terrace is a great spot to soak up views and sunshine. $ *Average main: 42 SF* ⊠ *Salita al Castelgrande* ☎ *091/8148781* ⊕ *www. ristorantecastelgrande.ch* ☉ *Closed Mon.*

$$
ITALIAN
★

✕ **Malakoff.** In this small family restaurant uphill from the town center, chef Rita Fuso prepares innovative Italian dishes from high-quality local ingredients. The pasta is homemade, and the vegetables and meats often come from nearby farms. Some of the herbs come from Fuso's own garden. Try seasonal variations on regional fare, such as the exquisite lemon- and ricotta-filled ravioli in a butter-sage sauce. The best bet (and a great value at around 32 SF) is the daily two-course special, such as monkfish carpaccio followed by a beef fillet with grilled seasonal vegetables. $ *Average main: 38 SF* ⊠ *Carrale Bacilieri 10* ☎ *091/8254940* ⊘ *Closed Sun. and Wed.*

$$ ✕ **Osteria Sasso Corbaro.** From the heights of the ancient Castello di Sasso
MEDITERRANEAN Corbaro, this atmospheric restaurant serves meals inside a beautifully restored hall. In the summer you can dine alfresco at sturdy granite tables in the shady, walled-in courtyard. The cooking, Mediterranean with French touches, includes fresh seafood—a top choice is the pan-fried foie gras with caramelized apples. Good local wines round out the experience. Take the 45-minute walk up from the rail station for a stunning view as well as a preparatory workout before indulging in desserts like creamy panna cotta and homemade tiramisu layered with ice cream. $ *Average main: 38 SF* ⊠ *Castello di Sasso Corbaro, Via Sasso Corbaro 44* ☎ *091/8255532* ⊕ *www.osteriasassocorbaro.com* ⊘ *Closed Sun. evening, Mon., and Dec.–Feb.*

WHERE TO STAY

$ ▦ **Grotto Paudese.** Immaculate, friendly, and family-run, this bed-and-
B&B/INN breakfast is perched high above the town in the tiny hamlet of Paudo. **Pros:** a rare traditional experience; hilltop location benefits from much-appreciated cool breezes. **Cons:** avoid the windy road if you suffer from motion sickness; two of the four rooms share a hall shower. $ *Rooms from: 130 SF* ⊠ *Paudo* ☎ *091/8571468* ⊕ *www.osteriapaudese.ch* ⇋ *4 rooms* ⊘ *Hotel closed mid-Dec.–Feb. Restaurant closed Mon.–Thurs.* ❙⦿❙ *Breakfast.*

$$ ▦ **Hotel Internazionale.** Mixing the contemporary with the historic, the
HOTEL century-old hotel is furnished with black-and-white modern pieces set against a gray palette, which contrasts with original stained-glass windows and a wrought–iron staircase. **Pros:** central location; no minibars; two handicapped-accessible rooms. **Cons:** top floor is not accessible by elevator; restaurant is under separate ownership, so there's no room service. $ *Rooms from: 200 SF* ⊠ *Viale Stazione 35* ☎ *091/8254333* ⊕ *www.hotel-internazionale.ch* ⇋ *60 rooms, 3 suites* ❙⦿❙ *No meals.*

$$ ▦ **Locanda Brack.** The shady terrace, discriminating wine list, and excel-
B&B/INN lent homemade pastas using mostly organic ingredients are what attract visitors and locals alike to this osteria perched on the hillside of Gudo, between Bellinzona and Locarno. **Pros:** peaceful, beautiful surroundings; owners are passionate to share their unique philosophy and local wines. **Cons:** remote location; besides the hotel's restaurant, there are limited dining choices. $ *Rooms from: 190 SF* ⊠ *Via Malacarne 26, Gudo-Progero* ☎ *091/8591254* ⊕ *www.osteriabrack.ch* ⇋ *7 rooms* ⊘ *Closed Dec.–Feb. Restaurant closed Tues. and Wed.* ❙⦿❙ *Breakfast.*

Crowds of movie buffs descend on Locarno in August for the town's international film festival.

LOCARNO

25 km (16 miles) west of Bellinzona, 45 km (28 miles) northwest of Lugano.

Superbly placed on the sheltered curve of the northernmost tip of Lago Maggiore and surrounded on all sides by mountains, Locarno is Switzerland's sunniest town. Subtropical flora flourishes here, with date palms and fig trees, bougainvillea and rhododendron, and even aloe vera burgeoning on the waterfront. Don't forget your sunglasses—you don't show your face in Locarno without a stylish set of shades, especially during August, when the town makes worldwide news with its film festival, showcasing the latest cinema on an outdoor screen in the Piazza Grande. It also hosts international artists in concert.

Modern Locarno is actually made up of three communities so tiny and close together that you often don't notice you've moved from one to another: Locarno, Muralto, and Minusio. The town's raison d'être is its waterfront, which has a graceful promenade curving around the east flank of the bay, and a beach and public pool complex along the west. Its clear lake is often as still as glass, reflecting the Ticinese Alps across to the south. Locarno's Lombard-style arcades and historic landmarks continually draw visitors inland as well. There are a few pedestrian-only streets in the heart of the Old Town.

GETTING HERE AND AROUND

From Bellinzona, trains are a 20–30 minute ride. Trains from Bern are frequent. The trip lasts about four hours; trains pass through Luzern and the Gotthard Pass or the Lötschberg tunnel and the Centovalli.

From Geneva, the fastest and most scenic route passes through Domo-dossola and the Centovalli on a trip that takes around 4½ hours. The Centovalli is all twists and turns, so if you suffer from motion sickness, you may wish to avoid these routes. The town is best explored on foot; the traffic can be stifling in the summer. Buses run frequently to Ascona, next door.

ESSENTIALS

Visitor Information Sportello Informativo di Locarno ⊠ *Via Largo Zorzi 1* ☎ *0848/091091* ⊕ *www.ascona-locarno.com.*

EXPLORING
TOP ATTRACTIONS

Chiesa di San Francesco. Harmonious and almost delicate, the Church of St. Francis and its convent stand cheek-by-jowl with the painfully bulky, modern building that houses the city's Department of Education, Culture, and Sports. The history of the parish goes back to the early 13th century, when it was allegedly founded by Saint Anthony of Padua. The current church was begun in 1538, however, on the remains of earlier constructions. Perhaps the most remarkable aspect of the interior is the series of frescoes, which have been restored to their original splendor. Note the fine marble carvings and paintings on the side altars. ⊠ *Via S. Francesco.*

Chiesa Nuova (*New Church*). This exuberantly decorated Baroque church, built in 1630, has a disproportionately large statue of St. Christopher on its facade. ⊠ *Via Cittadella.*

★ **Piazza Grande.** From underneath the crowded arcades of this piazza, shoppers spill onto the square to lounge in cafés and watch each other drink, smoke, and pose.

★ **Santuario della Madonna del Sasso.** With a breathtaking view of Locarno, the Sanctuary of the Madonna of the Rock crowns the hilltop hamlet of Orselina—pilgrims make the steep hike up to it, but most others opt for the short funicular ride that starts close to the train station. The church is open to visitors, but you must reserve ahead to see the rest of the convent, where Brother Bartolomeo da Ivrea had a vision of the Virgin Mary in 1480. Within the sanctuary you'll find several side chapels featuring statues depicting scenes from the New Testament, such as the Last Supper. The church, which was given a neo-Renaissance facade in the late 19th century, is a lavishly decorated affair. Among its artistic treasures are Bramantino's 1520 *The Flight into Egypt* and Ascona-born Antonio Ciseri's *Christ Carried to the Sepulcher,* a dramatic, Caravaggesque procession scene painted in 1870. ⊠ *Via Santuario 2, Orselina* ☎ *091/7436265* ⊕ *www.madonnadelsasso.org* ⛟ *Funicular 7.50 SF round-trip.*

WORTH NOTING

Casa dei Canonici. The House of the Canons has a lovely interior courtyard. It's now a private house, so you'll have to peek inside. ⊠ *Via Cittadella.*

Casa Rusca. Immediately to the left of the Church of St. Anthony stands the city's art gallery, inside what was an 18th-century residence. Its permanent collection includes the work of Jean Arp, and temporary exhibits highlight both Swiss and international artists. ✉ *Piazza Sant'Antonio* ☎ *091/7563185* 🎟 *8 SF* ⏲ *Apr.–mid-Jan., Tues.–Sun. 10–noon and 2–5.*

Chiesa di Sant'Antonio. Built in the 17th century, the Church of St. Anthony stands on a small plaza in the midst of narrow streets lined with splendid old medieval and Baroque houses. ✉ *Piazza Sant'Antonio.*

Museo Civico e Archeologico. The city's Municipal and Archaeological Museum's collection is notable for its Roman relics, including a major glass collection, and Romanesque sculpture. It's housed in a heavily rebuilt version of what was once Castello Visconteo, erected in 1300 as a stronghold of the dukes of Milan. Soon after, it was virtually destroyed by the invading Swiss Confederates. ✉ *Piazza Castello 2* ☎ *091/7563180* 🎟 *7 SF* ⏲ *Apr.–Oct., Tues.–Sun. 10–noon and 2–5.*

WHERE TO EAT

$$ ITALIAN 🍴 **Casa del Popolo.** The politics lean left at this town classic, where the sprawling terrace spills out onto the square and the crowds come more for the ambience than the food. Among the Italian favorites, the amazingly delicate *piccata alla Milanese* (veal cutlets pounded thin, coated in egg, and sautéed) is a standout. Also popular are the spicy *penne all'arrabbiata* (pasta with a spicy tomato sauce) or any of the 20 varieties of pizza. Red-checkered tablecloths and occasional appearances by the local politico round it all out. [$] *Average main: 27 SF* ✉ *Piazza Corporazione* ☎ *091/7511208* 💳 *No credit cards.*

$$$ ITALIAN ★ 🍴 **Osteria del Centenario.** Across from the waterfront, this unashamedly nouvelle restaurant east of the town center serves innovative Franco-Italian cuisine that's absolutely top quality, from its moderately priced business lunch to the lavish five-course *menu de dégustation* (sampling menu). Specialties include lamb steak served on a bed of mint-infused eggplant ratatouille. You can have an aperitif on the lakefront terrace before sitting down to a meal in a chic environment with modern art lining the walls, warm terra-cotta tiles, and dark-wood furnishings. [$] *Average main: 45 SF* ✉ *Viale Verbano 17, Locarno-Muralto* ☎ *091/7438222* 🌐 *www.osteriacentenario.ch* ⏲ *Closed Nov.; Mar.–Oct. and Dec., closed Sun.; Jan. and Feb., closed Sun. and Mon.*

WHERE TO STAY

$ B&B/INN 🏨 **Cittadella.** Perched near Lago Maggiore, this Old Town option has pleasant guest rooms tucked under the rafters with classic tile floors in cream and red. **Pros:** surprisingly peaceful location in the heart of Old Town; tasty local seafood virtually at your feet. **Cons:** top-floor rooms can get stuffy in the summer; reserve online—sometimes it's difficult to get through to the staff by phone. [$] *Rooms from: 170 SF* ✉ *Via Cittadella 18* ☎ *091/7515885* 🌐 *www.cittadella.ch* 🛏 *10 rooms* ⏲ *Restaurant closed Sun. and Mon. in June and July; Mon. in Aug.–May* 🍽 *Breakfast.*

$$ HOTEL 🏨 **Du Lac.** A terrific location makes this friendly hotel a particularly good base for exploring Locarno. **Pros:** friendly, smiling staff; parking garage just steps away. **Cons:** no restaurant. [$] *Rooms from: 200 SF* ✉ *Via Ramogna 3* ☎ *091/7512921* 🌐 *www.du-lac-locarno.ch* 🛏 *30 rooms.*

$$
B&B/INN
Fodor's Choice
★

☷ **Tr3 Terre.** This gorgeously equipped bed-and-breakfast—perhaps the nicest in all of Ticino—has five chic rooms with burnished hardwood floors and tasteful contemporary furnishings. **Pros:** good value; multiple choices for foodie vegetarians. **Cons:** near a firing range that's in use one day a week; outside Locarno. $ *Rooms from: 210 SF* ✉ *Ponte Brolla, Tegna* ☎ *091/7432222* ⊕ *www.3terre.ch* ➤ *5 rooms* ⊙ *Restaurant closed Tues. and Wed.* ⦿ *Breakfast.*

NIGHTLIFE AND THE ARTS

BARS

Bar Lungolago. The Bar Lungolago draws a young and style-conscious crowd. ✉ *Via Bramantino 1* ☎ *091/7515246.*

La Balena. A fun experience on a hot summer night is La Balena, a boat docked beside the Lungolago Giuseppe Motta. Although it has a full menu, thirsty locals pop in regularly for La Balena's wide assortment of cocktails and local wines. ✉ *Porto Regionale, Lungolago Giuseppe Motta, Locarno* ☎ *091/7511386* ⊕ *www.ristorantebalena.ch.*

La Regina. This place has a glass-covered terrace that's popular for cocktail sipping. ✉ *Via Naviglio Vecchio 4* ☎ *091/7514111.*

CASINO

Casinò di Locarno. With 150 slot machines, the Casinò di Locarno has plenty of gambling options. It's open every day from noon to 3 am, and until 4 am on Friday and Saturday nights. ✉ *Via Largo Zorzi 1* ☎ *091/7563030* ⊕ *www.casinolocarno.ch.*

FILM

Locarno International Film Festival. Held since 1946, the Locarno International Film Festival screens prestigious international movies every August on the Piazza Grande. ✉ *Via B. Luini 3a* ☎ *0848/091091* ⊕ *www.pardo.ch.*

MUSIC

Moon and Stars. This series of evening concerts by international pop stars is held the second week of July. ✉ *Piazza Grande* ☎ *0900/800800* ⊕ *www.moonandstarslocarno.ch.*

THEATER

Teatro di Locarno. The Teatro di Locarno hosts theatrical companies from September through May. ✉ *Palazzo Kursaal, Via Largo Zorzi 1* ☎ *091/7597660* ⊕ *www.teatrodilocarno.ch.*

VALLE VERZASCA

12 km (7 miles) north of Locarno, 25 km (15½ miles) north of Lugano.

The Ticino's mountain valleys, set just a short distance from its major cities, are rugged reminders of the region's modest history. Stone homes, called *rustici,* dot the valleys, some of which are so deep that the sun never quite reaches bottom. Driving through these valleys can be disorienting. Time seems to have stopped; you'll encounter whole villages perched on craggy mountainsides in apparent defiance of gravity. A short drive along Route 13 through the wild and rugged mountain gorge of the Valle Verzasca leads to Corippo, where a painterly composition of stone houses and a 17th-century church are all protected as architectural landmarks. The mountain village of Sonogno lies at the end of the 26-km (16-mile) valley.

GETTING HERE AND AROUND

Buses headed to the Verzasca Valley leave from both Ascona and Locarno; to get there you have to change in either Bignasco or Cavergno. The trip takes nearly two hours in all.

EXPLORING

Ponte dei Salti. About 12 km (7 miles) north of Corippo, in the town of Lavertezzo, you'll find this graceful double-arch stone bridge dating from the 16th or 17th century. The bridge was destroyed in a flood in 1906 and rebuilt in 1958.

SPORTS AND THE OUTDOORS

HIKING

The Verzasca River carved an impressive gorge from these jagged peaks, and you can weave along its banks through hardwood grooves and tiny villages. When hunger strikes, stop for wild mushroom risotto in one of the grotto restaurants along the 13-km (8-mile) trail that connects Sonogno and Lavertezzo.

VALLE MAGGIA

4 km (2 miles) northwest of Locarno, 30 km (19 miles) northwest of Lugano.

A drive through this rugged agricultural valley, stretching northwest from Locarno, will give you a sense of the tough living conditions endured for centuries by Ticinese farmers, whose descendants today quarry granite. The deep, dark valleys are a stark contrast to sunny Locarno, only a short distance south. Until the 1920s many Valle Maggia natives emigrated to the United States; some returned, bringing with them several English phrases that still pepper the local dialect. As you pass through Gordevio, Maggia, Someo, and Cevio—the latter, the valley's main village—you feel as if you're in a time capsule. There's little commercialization, and the mostly 17th-century houses call to mind a movie set. Bignasco, just beyond Cevio, is the last village before the valley splits in two as you continue north.

GETTING HERE AND AROUND

Getting into Ticino's valleys usually requires buses, which depart infrequently from the Locarno train station. The trip up Valle Maggia, for example, takes nearly an hour to reach Cevio. (The Ferrovie Autolinee Regionali Ticinesi runs a train into Ponte Brolla at the start of Valle Maggia, but from here you'll still have to take a bus to Cevio.)

OFF THE BEATEN PATH

Chiesa di San Giovanni Battista. In the tiny village of Mogno stands a beautiful modern chapel built in 1994 by world-renowned Ticinese architect Mario Botta (who has also designed such headline-making structures as the San Francisco Museum of Modern Art). Constructed in simple lines, the minimalist chapel is built of granite in two colors, creating remarkable patterns. ⊠ *Mongo.*

ASCONA

3 km (1¾ miles) west of Locarno.

Although it's only a few minutes from Locarno, tiny Ascona has a life of its own. It was little more than a fishing village until the end of the 19th century, when the town was adopted by vegetarians, socialists, mystics, nudists, and other progressive sorts.

GETTING HERE AND AROUND

From Locarno, pick up the bus on the lake end of the Piazza Grande. You can also take the ferry over for a more romantic, 30-minute ride. No trains head to Ascona.

EXPLORING

Monte Verità. A hillside park behind the waterfront, Monte Verità was the site of a utopian, vegetarian artists' colony in the early 1900s. Influenced by Eastern and Western religions as well as the new realms of psychology, its ideals attracted thousands of sojourners, including dancer Isadora Duncan, novelist Hermann Hesse, and psychologist Carl Jung. You can visit the group of Monte Verità buildings on a guided tour, including the unusual flat-roofed Casa Anatta. ⊠ *Via Collina 84* ☎ *091/7854040* ⊕ *www.monteverita.org.*

★ **Piazza Motta.** On the waterfront, the pedestrian-only Piazza Motta is crowded with sidewalk cafés. The promenade on the water's edge is swarming with boats.

Via Borgo. This charming labyrinth of lanes behind Piazza Motta leads uphill past art galleries (not all showing very good works) to Via Borgo, lined with contemporary shops and galleries.

OFF THE BEATEN PATH

Isole di Brissago. Alpine drama and subtropical colors are wed in Brissago, yet another flowery lakefront resort at the lowest elevation in Switzerland. It's an easy excursion by car or bus from Ascona. The main attraction, however, lies offshore: the Brissago Islands, federally preserved as botanical gardens, are set like jewels in the lake. They teem with more than 1,000 species of subtropical plants: plaques identify them in Italian, German, and French, and an English guide to the plants is for sale for 8 SF at the gate. Have lunch or drinks at the restaurant in a beautifully restored 1929 villa. Boats bound for the islands depart regularly from Ascona (20 SF round-trip) and Locarno (34 SF round-trip). You must leave with the last boat back to the mainland— usually around 6 pm—so check the schedule carefully when planning your excursion. ☎ *091/7914361* ⊕ *www.isolebrissago.ch/en* ⊠ *8 SF* ☉ *Easter–mid–Oct., daily 9–6.*

WHERE TO EAT

$ ✕ **Grotto du Rii.** On your way to or from Italy, consider a visit to this beau-

ITALIAN

Fodor's Choice

★

tiful stone grotto-house. With lush flowers pouring out of its window boxes, it's straight out of a fairy tale. The rooms inside cast their spell; they are cozily crammed with all manner of charm—carriage-wheel

Ascona's Piazza Motta is a popular spot for lakeside strolls and dining alfresco.

lamps, mounted animals, small spots to relax by a fireplace. Enjoy the rosemary-infused wine on the terrace, followed by *brasato* (beef shoulder) with polenta and the daring *dolce sorpresa* (surprise dessert). On Tuesday night the four-course meal accompanied by Ticinese musicians is a good deal. The restaurant is a 15-minute walk from the train station in Intragna, 9 km (5 miles) northwest of Ascona. $ *Average main: 25 SF* ⊠ *Via Cantonale, Intraga* ☎ *091/7961861* ⊕ *www.grottodurii. ch* ⊙ *Closed Wed. Sept.–June.*

$$ ✕ **Hostaria San Pietro.** If you're looking for a bite in the Old Town, take
ITALIAN out your map and try your best to find this charming restaurant. Tucked away in a maze of tiny streets, this little gem serves creative Italian-influenced pasta and fish dishes. Sample its fresh local catch (often a fish fillet in lemon-basil sauce), plump ravioli stuffed with vegetables and toasted almonds, or any of the grilled specialties. The most romantic tables are in the intimate garden that's between the walls of neighboring houses. $ *Average main: 35 SF* ⊠ *Passagio San Pietro 6* ☎ *091/7913976* ⊙ *Closed Mon. and Jan.*

$$ ✕ **Osteria Nostrana.** The tables of this bustling restaurant spread into
ITALIAN the piazza overlooking the lake. Inside, rough wooden ceilings, marble-top tables, chandeliers, and a hodgepodge of photos and posters add to its charm. Look for the spaghetti with porcini, bacon, and cream, along with daily and seasonal specials. If you haven't met your weekly pizza quota, try the simple Margherita—a crispy classic that never goes out of style. The wine list, with more than 100 Italian and Swiss vintages, deserves consideration. $ *Average main: 28 SF* ⊠ *Piazza Motta* ☎ *091/7915158* ⊕ *www.ristoranti-ff.ch.*

$$$ ECLECTIC 🍴 **Seven.** Locals and tourists alike flock to Seven for more than just its sleek, minimalist interior. On a Friday or Saturday night, this is *the* place to see and be seen in the area. The restaurant has gone upscale since its opening a few years ago, and now features gastronomic cuisine by well-regarded Swiss chef Ivo Adam. Traditional dishes, such as mushroom ravioli with apricot-teriyaki chicken breast or veal with green-apple quinoa, display very inventive qualities. If you're not in the mood for fine dining, head to the more casual Seven Easy, which serves tasty pizza and lighter fare. Another plus: while Seven closes for the winter, Seven Easy stays open all year. [$] *Average main: 50 SF* ✉ *Via Moscia* ☎ *091/7807777* 🌐 *www.seven-ascona.ch* 🕓 *Closed Nov.–May.*

WHERE TO STAY

$$$ HOTEL ★ 🏨 **Castello Seeschloss.** Dating from 1250, this hotel is certainly romantic—that doesn't even take into account its garden setting and enviable address across from the waterfront. **Pros:** lakeside rooms have original details; deluxe tower rooms start not much higher than standard doubles. **Cons:** the tower loft can be reached only by spiral staircase. [$] *Rooms from: 350 SF* ✉ *Piazza Motta* ☎ *091/7910161* 🌐 *www.castello-seeschloss.ch* 🛏 *45 rooms* 🕓 *Closed Nov.–Mar.* 🍽 *Breakfast.*

$$$$ HOTEL Fodor's Choice ★ 🏨 **Giardino.** The Great Gatsby would feel in his element in this Relais & Châteaux property that's as glamorous as a Mediterranean villa but still fabulously modern. **Pros:** Sunday frequently features ballet recitals or jazz performances; spectacular garden setting. **Cons:** overflowing with German and Swiss-German tourists; room prices vary greatly—call ahead for rates. [$] *Rooms from: 700 SF* ✉ *Via Segnale 10* ☎ *091/7858888* 🌐 *www.giardino.ch* 🛏 *54 rooms, 18 suites, 5 apartments* 🕓 *Closed mid-Nov.–Mar.* 🍽 *Some meals.*

$$ HOTEL 🏨 **Tamaro.** The shuttered windows of this 18th-century patrician house overlook the waterfront; inside, you can lounge in sitting rooms richly furnished with precious antiques, handsome books, and even a grand piano. **Pros:** personable staff isn't afraid to show a sense of humor; private terrace has fine lake views. **Cons:** not all rooms have air-conditioning—be sure to request one that does; some rooms lack Internet access, but free Wi-Fi is available in the lobby. [$] *Rooms from: 250 SF* ✉ *Piazza Giuseppe Motta 35* ☎ *091/7854848* 🌐 *www.hotel-tamaro.ch* 🛏 *51 rooms* 🕓 *Closed mid-Nov.–Feb.* 🍽 *Breakfast.*

NIGHTLIFE AND THE ARTS

The ideals that brought Isadora Duncan here still bring culture to Ascona: every year it hosts a series of world-class jazz and classical music concerts. Almost every day of the summer, the lakefront piazza serves as an open-air stage for entertainment, with mime, theater, and live pop bands. Locarno's August film festival is only a cab ride away across the peninsula.

BARS AND DANCING

Eden Bar. At Hotel Eden Roc, Eden Bar is the place to sip Bellinis and listen to live music. ✉ *Hotel Eden Roc, Via Albarelle 16* ☎ *091/7857171* 🌐 *www.edenroc.ch.*

5

MUSIC

JazzAscona. This joint seeks out performers a cut above the standard jazz and swing groups. It attracts an amazing array of international performers to its open-air bandstands for one week in June. ⊠ *Viale Papio 5* ☏ *091/7910091* ⊕ *www.jazzascona.ch.*

Settimane Musicali. The Settimane Musicali bring in orchestras, chamber groups, and top-ranking soloists to Ascona and Locarno. Events run from late August to mid-October. ☏ *0848/091091* ⊕ *www.settimane-musicali.ch.*

SOTTOCENERI

Although Monte Ceneri is no Everest, it marks the border between the Sopraceneri and its vastly different southern cousin, "below" the Ceneri. The Sottoceneri is the Ticino with attitude, where culture and natural beauty join forces with business and commerce. The resort town of Lugano is an international glamour magnet, but even there the incredible scenery and traditional warmth haven't been completely upstaged.

LUGANO

45 km (28 miles) southeast of Ascona, 39 km (24 miles) southeast of Locarno.

Strung around a sparkling bay like Venetian glass beads, with dark, conical mountains rising out of its waters and icy peaks framing the scene, Lugano earns its nickname as the Rio of the Old World. Of the three world-class waterfront resorts, Lugano tops Ascona and Locarno for architectural style, sophistication, and natural beauty. This isn't to say that it has avoided the pitfalls of a successful modern resort: there's thick traffic right up to the waterfront, much of it in manic Italian style, and it has more than its share of concrete waterfront high-rise hotels with balconies skewed to produce "a room with a view" regardless of aesthetic cost. Yet the sacred *passeggiata*—the afternoon stroll to see and be seen that winds down every Italian day—asserts the city's true personality as a graceful, sophisticated resort. It's not Swiss, not Italian . . . just Lugano.

GETTING HERE AND AROUND

From Bellinzona, trains run frequently and take about 30 minutes. Trains from Locarno run at least once an hour (with a change usually in Bellinzona or Giubiasco); the trip lasts nearly one hour. Lugano is 1–1½ hours away from Milan, with very frequent connections. Trains coming from Geneva pass either through Bern/Luzern or Zürich for five- to six-hour journeys. Postbuses spider out from Lugano to hamlets and main towns from the depot on Via Serafino Balestra. Lugano is particularly difficult to drive through, and the parking garages are usually packed.

Take the funicular from the station to the Old Town—unless you want to carry your suitcases down the steep hill and many steps. It's best to start your tour through the city in the morning, before it gets too hot. Note that the museums are closed on Monday.

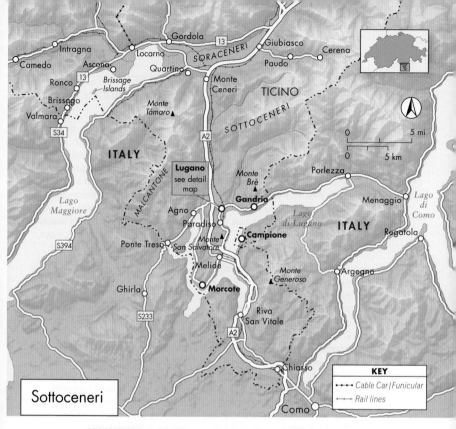

Sottoceneri

ESSENTIALS

Visitor Information Ente Turistico del Lugano ✉ *Palazzo Civico, Riva Albertolli* ☎ *058/8666600* ⊕ *www.luganoturismo.ch.*

EXPLORING

TOP ATTRACTIONS

★ **Chiesa di Santa Maria degli Angioli** (*Church of St. Mary of the Angels*). The simple facade doesn't prepare you for the riches within. Begun in the late 15th century, the church contains a magnificent fresco of the *Passion and Crucifixion*, as well as *The Last Supper* and *Madonna with the Infant Jesus*, all by Bernardino Luini (1475–1532). ✉ *Piazza Luini, Old Town.*

Giardino Belvedere (*Belvedere Gardens*). This lakefront sculpture garden frames a dozen modern works with palms, camellias, oleanders, and magnolias. At the far west end there's a public swimming area. ✉ *Quai Riva Antonio Caccia, near Piazza Luini, Old Town* 🎫 *Free* ⊗ *Daily 24 hrs.*

Herman Hesse Museum. In the tower of the Casa Camuzzi, a fabulous jumble of old houses on a hilltop in Montagnola, the Herman Hesse Museum is tiny but impressive. The Nobel Prize–winning author lived here the last 43 years of his life, writing *Siddhartha* and *Steppenwolf*. His rooms have been meticulously preserved; you can see his papers,

A GOOD WALK: LUGANO

Begin at **Piazza della Riforma,** which is dominated by the **Palazzo Civico,** or town hall. Look up to the gable above the clock to see the city's coat of arms. (The building also houses the tourist office, whose entrance is on the lakeside.)

On the western side of the square, Piazza della Riforma bleeds into Piazza Rezzonico, which contains a large fountain by Otto Maraini dating from 1895.

Heading out of Piazza della Riforma on the north side, onto Via Luvini, you come to Piazza Dante, which is dominated by a large department store and a bank. From here, if you pop over one street east to the busy Via Pretorio, you can get a look at Lugano's oldest building, the Pretorio (1425), at No. 7. Back at Piazza Dante, turn left down Via Pessina, which leads you into Piazza Cioccaro, on your right. Here the funicular from the train station terminates and the typical *centro storico* (Old Town) begins, its narrow streets lined with chic clothing shops and small markets selling mushrooms and pungent local cheeses.

From Piazza Cioccaro, walk up the shop-lined staircase street of Via Cattedrale. The street curves left, ending at the **Cattedrale di San Lorenzo.** Take a moment to enjoy the view from the church square.

Head back and then south along the waterfront promenade known as **Il Lungolago,** and at the Imbarcadero Centrale (Central Wharf) take the underpass to cross the road, coming back up at Piazza della Riforma.

Leave the piazza at the northeast side through a portico onto Via Canova. After crossing over Via della Posta/Via Albrizzi, you come to the **Museo Cantonale d'Arte,** on your right.

Continue straight ahead to the 17th-century church of San Rocco, with its neo-Baroque facade. Turn left onto Via Carducci before you reach the church and you'll find a small orange-tile pedestrian entranceway into the Quartiere Maghetti—a town within a town. It's a tangle of streets full of porticoes, little squares, shops, and offices, a modern take on old forms, created in the early 1980s by the architects Camazind, Brocchi, and Sennhauser.

Exit the Quartiere Maghetti onto Via Canova (you'll be behind the church now) and continue east, crossing Via Stauffacher. On your left is the open Piazza dell'Independenza. Cross over the wide Corso Elvezia to enter the **Parco Civico.** Inside the grounds, in addition to the nearly 15 acres of greenery, you'll find the **Museo Cantonale di Storia Naturale.**

From here you can opt to spend the afternoon at the **Lido,** the city's public beach and pool, just east of the park across the River Cassarate.

Or you can head back to town along the waterfront promenade and take in the stunning mountain views: straight ahead, the rocky top of Monte Generoso (5,579 feet), and flanking the bay at right and left, respectively, Monte San Salvatore and Monte Brè.

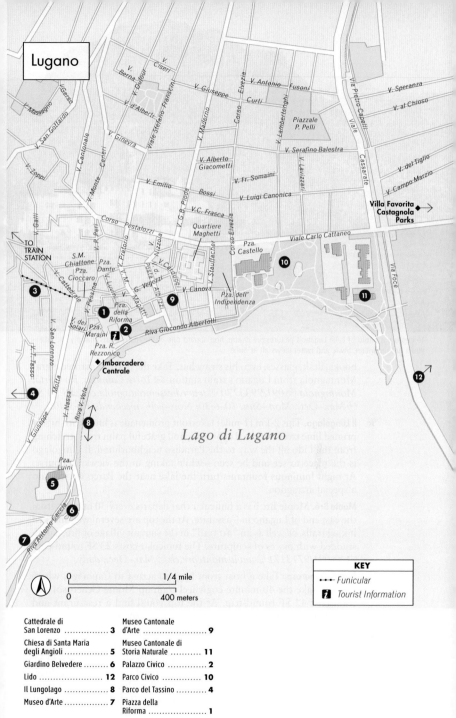

Lugano

TO TRAIN STATION

Lago di Lugano

Imbarcadero Centrale

Villa Favorita Castagnola Parks →

KEY

•••• Funicular

🛈 Tourist Information

0   1/4 mile

0   400 meters

To capture a photo of Lake Lugano's picturesque charm, hop aboard one of the many boats that ply the lake—you'll get mountain, town, and water views all at once.

books, desk, glasses, even his straw hat. Take the postbus marked Agra-Montagnola from Lugano's train station. ✉ *Torre Camuzzi, Ra Cürta, Montagnola* ☎ *091/9933770* ⊕ *www.hessemontagnola.ch* 🎫 *8.50 SF* ⊘ *Mar.–Oct., Mon.–Sun. 10–6:30; Nov.–Feb., weekends 10–5:30.*

★ **Il Lungolago.** This 2-km (1-mile) lakefront promenade is lined with highly pruned lime trees, funereal cypresses, and graceful palm trees stretching from the Lido all the way to the Paradiso neighborhood. Il Lungolago is the place to see and be seen—while taking in the views, of course. At night luminous fountains turn the lake near the Parco Civico into a special attraction.

Monte Brè. Monte Brè has a funicular that departs every 30 minutes from the east end of Lugano in Cassarate. At the top are several well-marked hiking trails, as well as an "art trail" in the summit village of Brè, a path studded with pieces of sculpture. The funicular costs 23 SF round-trip. ✉ ☎ *091/9713171* ⊕ *www.montebre.ch* ⊘ *Mar.–Dec., daily.*

Monte Generoso. Take a boat from Lugano across to Capolago, where you can take the 40-minute cogwheel train up Monte Generoso. The train cost 42 SF round-trip. At the top you'll find a restaurant and lots of marked hiking trails. ✉ *Capolago* ☎ *091/6305111* ⊕ *www. montegeneroso.ch* ⊘ *Mid-Mar.–Dec., daily.*

Monte San Salvatore. Monte San Salvatore can be reached via the funicular in Paradiso. Departing every 30 minutes, the funicular costs 24 SF round-trip. At the top are a huge relief model of the entire Sottoceneri region and marked "nature itinerary" paths, which have signs pointing out flowers and trees. ✉ *Paradiso* ☎ *091/9852828* ⊕ *www. montesansalvatore.ch* ⊘ *Mid-Mar.–mid-Nov., daily.*

Museo Cantonale d'Arte (*Cantonal Art Museum*). Three palaces dating from the 15th to the 19th century were joined to form this museum. Its exhibits include paintings, sculpture, and photography, including some important avant-garde works. The permanent collection holds works by Klee, Turner, Degas, Renoir, and Hodler, as well as contemporary Ticinese artists. Descriptive material is available in English. ⊠ *Via Canova 10, Old Town* ☎ *091/9104780* ⊕ *www. museo-cantonale-arte.ch* ☜ *8 SF, 12 SF includes temporary exhibits* ⊙ *Tues. 2–5, Wed.–Sun. 10–5.*

Museo d'Arte (*Museum of Art*). Consistently outstanding temporary exhibits are the hallmark of this museum. Recent offerings included works by George Baselitz, Egon Schiele, Christo and Jeanne-Claude, and Marc Chagall. Brochures are available in English. ⊠ *Villa Malpensata, Riva Antonio Caccia 5, Lungolago* ☎ *058/8667214* ⊕ *www.mdam.ch* ☜ *12–25 SF* ⊙ *Tues.–Sun. 10–6, Fri.10–9.*

> ## THE PARKS OF CASTAGNOLA
>
> For an idyllic daytime excursion, take a short tram trip out of Lugano's city center to the fabled Castagnola parks, which surround the Villa Favorita (the famous Thyssen-Bornemisza estate, now closed to the public). The Parco degli Ulivi (Olive Park) spreads over the lower slopes of Monte Brè and offers a romantic landscape of silvery olive trees mixed with wild rosemary; you enter it from the Sentiero di Gandria (Gandria Footpath). Parco San Michele (St. Michael Park), also on Monte Brè, has a public chapel and a broad terrace that overlooks the city, the lake, and the Alps.

★ **Piazza della Riforma** (*Reformation Square*). In the early 19th century, several buildings were torn down in order to enlarge the square—providing more room for the present-day café tables. Commonly referred to simply as "La Piazza," it's the social and cultural heart of the city and the site of outdoor markets and open-air concerts. ⊠ *North of the Imbarcadero Centrale, Old Town.*

WORTH NOTING

Cattedrale di San Lorenzo (*Cathedral of St. Lawrence*). Behind this church's early Renaissance facade is a Baroque interior with carefully restored frescoes and a baptismal font dating from 1430. The church has premedieval origins: it became a collegiate church in 1078. Eight centuries later it became a cathedral. ⊠ *Via Cattedrale, Old Town.*

Lido. The city's public beach has two swimming pools and two restaurants. To reach it, you'll have to cross the Cassarate River. Heading east from the Parco Civico, cross Viale Castagnola and then turn toward the lake. The entrance to the main swimming area is ahead on the right. Everyone from families to scenesters comes here to cool off. ⊠ *Via Cassarate 6* ☎ *058/8666880* ☜ *10 SF* ⊙ *May and Sept., daily 9–7; June–Aug., daily 9–7:30.*

Museo Cantonale di Storia Naturale (*Cantonal Museum of Natural History*). A museum since 1854, the Cantonal Museum of Natural History contains exhibits on fossils, animals, and plants, mostly those typical of the region, with all labels in Italian. There's a large section on local

Lugano's Piazza della Riforma is the main site of the city's markets and festivals.

crystals that is especially interesting for people planning long hikes in the mountains. ⊠ *Viale Cattaneo 4, Parco Civico* ☎ *091/8154761* ⊕ *www.ti.ch/mcsn* 🖃 *Free* ⊗ *Tues.–Sat. 9–noon and 2–5.*

Palazzo Civico (*Town Hall*). This Neoclassical Lombard structure dates from 1844. Inside there's a large inner yard surrounded by a four-sided arcade, with a wide vestibule on the piazza side. It houses the town council and tourist office. ⊠ *Riva Albertolli, Old Town.*

Parco Civico (*City Park*). A green oasis in the city center, the park has cacti, exotic shrubs, and more than 1,000 varieties of roses, as well as an aviary, a tiny deer zoo, and a fine view of the bay from its peninsula. ⊠ *South of Viale Carlo Cattaneo, east of Piazza Castello.*

Parco del Tassino (*Tassino Park*). Just behind the train station, this park offers lovely bay views from its rose gardens. A small deer park and playground make it very child-friendly. To get here, take Bus 2 east to the San Domenico stop in Castagnola, or hop aboard the funicular from Old Town. ⊠ *Via Tassino* 🖃 *Free.*

WHERE TO EAT

$$
ITALIAN
Fodor's Choice
★

✕ **Al Portone.** Silver and lace dress up the stucco and stone here, but the ambience is cozy. The chef and owner, Francis Carré, serves refined Franco-Italian cuisine, including inventive dishes like cardomom-poached pears with Gorgonzola mousse and roasted loin of lamb in a Provençal crust. Vegetarians will delight in the special meatless menu, and can feast on homemade chestnut gnocchi with a local mushroom sauce and spinach-mascarpone soufflé. When the summer heat is stifling, ask to dine in the small garden. The restaurant is a true find—nowhere else in Switzerland can you find such an elegant meal at such a reasonable price. $ *Average main: 37 SF* ⊠ *Viale Cassarate 3, Lugano-Cassarate* ☎ *091/9235511* ⊕ *www.ristorante-alportone.ch* ⊘ *Closed Sun. and Mon., and early Jan. and Aug.*

$$$ ✕**Grotto della Salute.** Absolutely authentic, this no-frills place pulls in a
MODERN ITALIAN local crowd for a good bottle of local wine and a satisfying, contemporary spin on old favorites like homemade pasta, roasted meat, and fresh fish. The dedicated owners pride themselves on quality ingredients with absolutely no additives. During the summer guests can dine on the terrace under the shade of centuries-old sycamore trees. $ *Average main: 42 SF* ⊠ *Via Sindicatori 4, Massagno* ☎ *091/9660476* ⊕ *www.grottodellasalute.com.*

$$$ ✕**Il Canvetto di Silvio Galizzi.** Tall, dark, and quirkily handsome celebrity
MODERN ITALIAN chef Silvio Galizzi pursues *nuova cucina* (contemporary Italian cuisine) with ambition and flair in this eatery perched high in the vineyards. Galizzi has made waves in the world of Swiss gastronomy with such dishes as duck liver with mango chutney and pears or grilled tiger shrimp and roasted black garlic in a champagne sauce. The property boasts 100-year old Merlot vines, and was the first vineyard of its kind in Ticino—if you're curious about how the wine is made, ask to see the tiny museum. It's in the Vallombrosa B&B, which has some rustic guest rooms that honor artists with a strong link with Ticino. $ *Average main: 45 SF* ⊠ *Vallombrosa, off Via Castelrotto, Castelrotto* ⊕ *www.vallombrosa.ch* ⊘ *Closed Sun. and Mon. No dinner Tues.–Thurs.*

$ ✕**La Tinera.** Tucked down an alley off Via Pessina, this cozy basement
ITALIAN taverna squeezes loyal locals and tourists onto hard wooden chairs and
★ benches for authentic regional specialties, hearty meats, and pastas. Ticinese wines are served in traditional ceramic bowls—try a strong red to cut through the thick *polenta taragna*, made of cornmeal and buckwheat. (Once you try this polenta, you'll never eat the bland yellow version again.) It's served with *luganighe*, cumin-flavored local sausages. End your meal with strong espresso matched with light, melt-in-your-mouth tiramisu. $ *Average main: 20 SF* ⊠ *Via dei Gorini 2, Old Town* ☎ *091/9235219* ⊘ *Closed Sun. and Aug.*

$$$ ✕**Locanda del Boschetto.** The grill is the first thing you see in this grotto-
SEAFOOD style eatery, a specialist in pure and simple seafood *alla griglia* (grilled). Homemade pasta is another specialty, and when the two are combined, as in the house favorite linguine *allo scoglio* (with shellfish), you'll leave your plate cleaner than a whistle. The decor is a study in refined linen and rustic wood, and the service is helpful and down-to-earth. The restaurant is at the end of a cul-de-sac in a residential neighborhood, not far from the Lugano South exit on the autostrada. $ *Average main: 42 SF* ⊠ *Via Boschetto 8, Paradiso* ☎ *091/9942493* ⌗ *Reservations essential* ⊘ *Closed Mon. and last 2 wks of Aug.*

$$$ ✕**Ristorante Orologio Da Savino.** Snow-white tablecloths and chairs stand
ITALIAN out against shiny, dark hardwood floors in this open, minimalist restaurant. The attentive staff and personable owner are quick to bring you modern Italian dishes and a fine selection of fresh fish, as well as vegetarian-pleasing delights like balsamic-marinated tofu with grilled vegetables. They will also retreat to let you linger over coffee. Favored by locals, it's one of the few greats in town with few or no tourists in sight.

$ *Average main: 45 SF* ✉ *Via Nizzola 2, Old Town* ☎ *091/9232338* ⊕ *www.ristorante-orologio.com* ⊘ *Closed Sun. and 2 wks in Aug.*

WHERE TO STAY

$$ ⊡ **Hotel Lugano Dante.** This friendly, well-decorated lodging is rated by
HOTEL   many travelers as the best deal in town. **Pros:** many repeat customers
call it the best deal in town; exceptionally friendly staff. **Cons:** central
location means throngs of tourists in the immediate area. $ *Rooms from: 240 SF* ✉ *Piazza Cioccaro 5, Old Town* ☎ *091/9105750* ⊕ *www. hotel-luganodante.com* ⇨ *83 rooms* ¶◎¶ *Breakfast.*

$$$ ⊡ **International au Lac.** Next to the Church of St. Mary of the Angels, this
HOTEL   historic hotel has interiors that are exuberantly decorated, with gilded
paintings, ornate antiques, and heavy, sumptuous furniture. **Pros:** you'll
forget you're downtown when lounging at the pool or in the back garden; live classical music. **Cons:** some rooms feel dated; not the place for
up-to-date amenities and luxury toiletries. $ *Rooms from: 275 SF* ✉ *Via Nassa 68, Old Town* ☎ *091/9227541* ⊕ *www.hotel-international.ch* ⇨ *80 rooms* ⊘ *Closed Nov.–Easter* ¶◎¶ *Breakfast.*

$ ⊡ **Pestalozzi.** Right in the middle of town, this older hotel is a few steps
HOTEL   away from the lake and offers excellent value. **Pros:** a favorite among
thrifty travelers; a stone's throw from the Old Town. **Cons:** some rooms
lack air-conditioning and TVs. $ *Rooms from: 175 SF* ✉ *Piazza Indi-pendenza* ☎ *091/9214646* ⊕ *www.pestalozzi-lugano.ch* ⇨ *55 rooms* ¶◎¶ *No meals.*

$ ⊡ **San Carlo.** Ideally located on the main shopping street, this friendly
HOTEL   hotel is owned and managed by one of the nicest families in town.
Pros: each room is uniquely crafted; terrific prices. **Cons:** some decor is
straight out of high-school wood shop; walls tend to be thin. $ *Rooms from: 155 SF* ✉ *Via Nassa 28, Old Town* ☎ *091/9227107* ⊕ *www. hotelsancarlolugano.com* ⇨ *20 rooms* ¶◎¶ *Breakfast.*

$$$$ ⊡ **Splendide Royale.** This local landmark opened its doors in 1888, and
HOTEL   much of the Victorian luster of its public spaces—with their colorful
Fodor's Choice   frescos, crystal chandeliers, and ornate antiques—has been respectfully
★   preserved. **Pros:** the historic suites are showstoppers; even the smallest
rooms feature heated bathroom floors. **Cons:** the 1983 wing feels a bit
more *Miami Vice* than *Pride and Prejudice*; grand interiors miss-
ing a bit of cozy warmth. $ *Rooms from: 474 SF* ✉ *Riva A. Caccia 7, Loreto* ☎ *091/9857711* ⊕ *www.splendide.ch* ⇨ *86 rooms, 7 suites* ¶◎¶ *Breakfast.*

$$$$ ⊡ **Villa Principe Leopoldo and Residence.** Spectacularly perched on a hill-
HOTEL   side overlooking Lake Lugano, this mansion offers an unparalleled loca-
★   tion and old-world service. **Pros:** beautiful views of Lake Lugano and
the surrounding mountains; worlds away from the noise and traffic of
the city. **Cons:** staff as well as guests can be pretentious. $ *Rooms from: 800 SF* ✉ *Via Montalbano 5, Collina d'Oro* ☎ *091/9858855* ⊕ *www. leopoldohotel.com* ⇨ *50 rooms, 24 suites* ¶◎¶ *Breakfast.*

$$$$ ⊡ **Villa Sassa Hotel, Residence & Spa.** Set on a hill overlooking Lugano,
HOTEL   Villa Sassa's lake and mountain views are so pretty you might find
it hard to leave the hotel to make the trek into town. **Pros:** peaceful
grounds; free arrival and departure shuttle; gorgeous views from the
infinity pool. **Cons:** must prearrange kitchen use with apartment rental;

not in town. [$] *Rooms from: 480 SF* ✉ *Via Tesserete 10* ☎ *091/911 41 11* 🌐 *www.villasassa.ch* 🛏 *49 rooms, 71 apartments* 🍴 *No meals.*

NIGHTLIFE AND THE ARTS

BARS

Bottegone del Vino. Just off the Piazza delle Riforma, Bottegone del Vino has a great selection of wine accompanied by good local cheeses and tapas. ✉ *Via Magatti 3, Old Town* ☎ *091/9227689.*

Cafè Retrò. This popular piano bar features both local and international musicians. ✉ *Via Nassa 11, Old Town* ☎ *091/9231233.*

Splendide Royale. For a refined and uncrowded place to enjoy a cocktail, head to the palatial Splendide Royale. ✉ *Riva A. Caccia 7, Lungolago* ☎ *091/9857711.*

CASINO

Casinò Lugano. In addition to slot machines and gaming tables, the three-floor Casinò Lugano has a bar and restaurant. ✉ *Via Stauffacher 1, Old Town* ☎ *091/9737111* 🌐 *www.casinolugano.ch.*

DANCING

Living Room. With a dance floor and lounge, the lively Living Room hosts some of the better European electro and rock up-and-comers. ✉ *Via Trevano 89a, Molino Nuovo* ☎ *091/9233281* 🌐 *www.livingroomclub.ch.*

Morandi. On Friday and Saturday night Morandi is the most popular club catering to the over-30 crowd. It's a great place to dance to songs from the '70s and '80s. ✉ *Via Trevano 56, Molino Nuovo* ☎ *076/3475251* 🌐 *www.56morandiclub.ch.*

MUSIC

Blues to Bop Festival. The free Blues to Bop Festival livens up the Piazza della Riforma at the end of August. 🌐 *www.bluestobop.ch.*

Estival Jazz. July's Estival Jazz brings jazz and world music to the Piazza della Riforma. 🌐 *www.estivaljazz.ch.*

Lugano Festival. From April to June, the city hosts the Lugano Festival, which draws world-class orchestras and conductors. 🌐 *www.luganofestival.ch.*

SHOPPING

Via Cattedrale. Cute novelty shops and antiques stores line the staircase street of Via Cattedrale.

Via Nassa. All the top designers can be found in the shops lining the pedestrian-only Via Nassa.

Fox Town. If it's international designer clothing bargains you're after, explore the factory outlet store Fox Town. It's open daily from 11 to 7. ✉ *Via Angelo Maspoli, Mendrisio* ☎ *0848/828888.*

GANDRIA

Fodor's Choice ★

7 km (4 miles) southeast of Lugano.

Although its narrow waterfront streets are crowded with tourists, the tiny historic village of Gandria still merits a visit, either by boat or by car. Gandria clings vertiginously to the steep hillside; its many stairways and passageways lined with flower-filled balconies hang directly over open water. Souvenir and crafts shops now fill its backstreet nooks, but the ambience of an ancient fishing village remains.

OFF THE BEATEN PATH

Museo Doganale. The thrilling subject of smuggling is brought to life at the Museo Doganale, on the shady southern shore of Lago di Lugano across from Gandria. Known as the "Smuggler's Museum," this place explores the romantic history of clandestine trade between Italy and Switzerland. It bristles with ingenious containers, illicit weapons, and other contraband. You can catch a boat from the jetty in Gandria. ✉ *Cantine de Gandria* 🕾 *091/9239843* ⊕ *www.musee-suisse.ch/e/gandria/index.php* 🎫 *Free* ⊘ *Easter–Oct., daily 1:30–5:30.*

CAMPIONE

18 km (11 miles) south of Gandria, 12 km (7 miles) south of Lugano.

In the heart of Swiss Italy lies Campione. Here, in this southernmost of regions, the police cars have Swiss license plates but the police officers inside are Italian; the inhabitants pay their taxes to Italy but do it in Swiss francs. Its narrow streets are saturated with history, and the surrounding landscape is a series of stunning views of Lago di Lugano and Monte San Salvatore.

In the 8th century the lord of Campione gave the tiny scrap of land, less than a square kilometer (½ square mile) in area, to the monastery of St. Ambrosius of Milan. Despite all the wars that passed it by, Campione remained Italian until the end of the 18th century, when it was incorporated into the Cisalpine Republic. When Italy unified in 1861, Campione became part of the new Kingdom of Italy—and remained so. There are no frontiers between Campione and Switzerland, and it benefits from the comforts of Swiss currency, customs laws, and postal and telephone services. Despite its miniature scale, it has exercised disproportionate influence on the art world: in the Middle Ages a school of stonemasons, sculptors, and architects from Campione and the surrounding region worked on the cathedrals of Milan, Verona, Cremona, Trento, and Modena—even the Hagia Sophia in Istanbul.

NIGHTLIFE AND THE ARTS

Casino Campione. Campione is a magnet for gamblers, thanks to an eye-catching casino designed by star architect Mario Botta. It calls to mind a huge brown UFO landing on the little town. When you're not playing the tables you can dine in the restaurant or enjoy a show. Men are required to wear a jacket, but they don't have to wear a tie in summer. ✉ *Piazza Milano 1* 🕾 *091/6401111* ⊕ *www.casinocampione.it.*

EN ROUTE

Swissminiatur. If you wish to see all of Switzerland's monuments in a few hours, then stop in the town of Melide, 8 km (5 miles) south of Lugano. The Swissminiatur has all the sights and sites you could wish for, including pint-sized versions of the Château de Chillon, Basel's Münster, and Locarno's Madonna del Sasso. Nearly 3.5 km (2 miles) of miniature tracks have been laid out and are busily used by tiny passenger and

Indulge in a room with serene lake views at the Dellago hotel.

freight trains. ⊠ *Melide* ☎ *091/6401060* ⊕ *www.swissminiatur.ch* 🎫 *19 SF* ⊙ *Mar.–Oct., daily 9–6, Nov.–mid. Dec, daily 1–4.*

MORCOTE

11 km (7 miles) northwest of Campione, 10 km (6 miles) south of Lugano.

At the southernmost tip of the glorious Ceresio Peninsula is the atmospheric village of Morcote, its clay-colored houses and arcades looking directly over the waterfront.

GETTING HERE AND AROUND
A half-hour bus ride connects Morcote to Lugano.

EXPLORING
Chiesa di Madonna del Sasso (*Church of the Madonna of the Rock*). A steep and picturesque climb leads up to the Chiesa di Madonna del Sasso, with its well-preserved 16th-century frescoes. Its elevated setting affords wonderful views.

★ **Parco Scherrer.** The Parco Scherrer is a remarkable garden created over a period of decades by the Swiss business executive Arthur Scherrer (1881–1956). This folly rising from the lakeside brings together architectural samples from around the world—including an Egyptian sun temple, a Siamese teahouse, and an Indian palace—within the setting of a carefully landscaped garden. ⊠ *Am See<* ⊕ *www.promorcote.ch* 🎫 *7 SF* ⊙ *Mid-Mar.–Oct., daily 10–5; July and Aug., daily 10–6.*

WHERE TO STAY

$$ HOTEL ★ 🏨 **Carina Carlton.** This family-run hotel has somehow managed to fit pretty and spacious rooms, a lovely restaurant, a generous terrace, and an outdoor pool into the narrow strip between the mountain and the lake. **Pros:** filled with repeat guests, many of them Swiss or Italian; restaurant is definitely worth a try. **Cons:** no air-conditioning, but there's a fan in every room; noisy cars can be heard along the shore road. [$] *Rooms from: 220 SF* ✉ *Riva da Sant' Antoni* ☎ *091/9961131* 🌐 *www.carina-morcote.ch* 🛏 *22 rooms* 🕓 *Closed mid-Oct.–mid-Mar.* 🍴 *Breakfast.*

$$ HOTEL Fodor's Choice ★ 🏨 **Dellago.** Combining a soothing atmosphere, personal service, and unpretentious savoir-faire, this stylish refuge on the lake spoils its guests. **Pros:** breakfast comes with homemade jams, fine teas, and a selection of unusual breads; there's a hotel paddleboat for excursions on the lake; dockside lounge pours outstanding cocktails. **Cons:** rooms facing the busy street are noisy; most rooms do not allow children. [$] *Rooms from: 220 SF* ✉ *Lago di Lugano, Melide* ☎ *091/6497041* 🌐 *www.hotel-dellago.ch* 🛏 *16 rooms, 4 suites* 🍴 *Breakfast.*

Luzern and Central Switzerland

BÜRGENSTOCK, RÜTLI MEADOW, WEGGIS, WILLIAM TELL COUNTRY

WORD OF MOUTH

"Visiting Mt. Pilatus during my stay in Luzern was one of the best day trips I have ever taken! You boat across the lovely lake, then take the world's steepest cog railway up to the top if the mountain and take in the breathtaking alpine views."

—LunaBella

WELCOME TO LUZERN AND CENTRAL SWITZERLAND

TOP REASONS TO GO

★ **Luzern:** The must-see spot on the tour, it offers not only famous sights—the Chapel Bridge, the Lion Monument—but also other treasures, like the Rosengart Picassos and that perfect table for two under the chestnut trees on the lakeside promenade.

★ **Mountain majesty:** Thanks to cable cars and cog railways, hill thrills—and some of the most staggering panoramas—can be yours atop Mts. Pilatus, Titlis, and Rigi.

★ **Wilhelm Tell country:** As with all good legends, the story of the famous archer who shot an apple from his son's head with a crossbow may have little basis in fact, but don't tell that to the crowds who visit his home turf in and around Altdorf.

★ **A paddleboat steamer ride:** Lake Luzern's smart white steamboats—including beautifully kept and picturesque old paddle steamers—offer a voyage back in time.

1 **Luzern.** The little big city, Luzern offers a full cultural palette: wander through the medieval solidity of the Old Town; shop your way through the many boutiques; take a boat cruise to a yodeling beat; and listen to a diva sing in Jean Nouvel's architectural wonder, the Kultur- und Kongresszentrum.

2 **Luzern Environs.** Towering over Luzern, Mt. Pilatus is dramatic and impressive, with a restaurant teetering on its razor-sharp ridge at the top. Take the "golden round-trip," which includes a bus from Luzern, a cable car trip to the top, a cogwheel train back down the other side, and a boat ride back to Luzern. Head south to Engelberg—noted for its outdoor sports—where you can take the gondola up to the top of Mt. Titlis. You'll gasp at the view here, the loftiest in central Switzerland.

3 **Urnersee.** Hallowed by myths, the Urnersee is the southern—and by far most romantic—leg of Lake Luzern. Dramatic mountains run steeply into the lake as sharp peaks stab into the clouds, a landscape that has inspired many a master, including Rossini, Wagner, Schiller, and Twain (bring along your sketchbook or journal). Weggis and Vitznau are the "Riviera" towns, sheltered by coves and beloved by the rich. Farther south, pay your respects to the historic Rütli Meadow; the picturesque Tell Chapel, just across the lake; and Altdorf, where Wilhelm Tell first became a legend.

GETTING ORIENTED

To enter Luzern is to approach the very heart of historic Switzerland, for the sharply indented shoreline of the Vierwaldstättersee (Lake Luzern) was the cradle of the Swiss Confederation, forged here in the 13th century on the Rütli Meadow as one of the world's first democracies. Most-visited Luzern, with its Old Town, sits on one end of the lake; the quieter but equally historic Altdorf, home of Wilhelm Tell, on the other. In between is probably the most beautiful stretch of lakeshore in Switzerland.

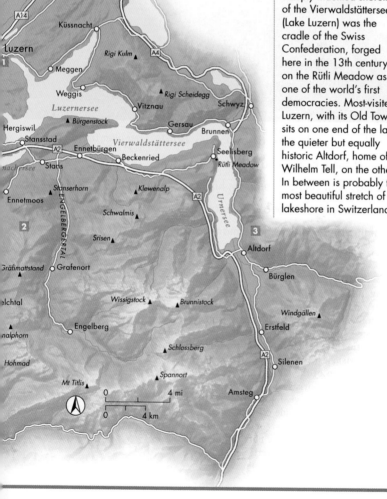

LAKE LUZERN

Towns where travelers used to stop to brush the dust off their clothes have turned into full-service spas with culinary temples, hiking trails, and docks for pleasure boats. What was once a part of the long route from Germany to Italy is now a destination in its own right.

Lake Luzern (above) is in the heart of Switzerland, both geographically and historically. Lake steamers cruise the water (below, right), while photo ops of the surrounding mountains abound (above, right).

The many inlets of Lake Luzern that stretch all over the region vary in size, depth, and wind conditions. They are at some points flanked by gentle green hillsides, and at others by steep mountain cliffs. The lake's lower end is home to gusting winds that thrill windsurfers, while the quiet middle basin is perfect for waterskiing. Boats steam along from the top of the lake to the bottom, carrying lunching locals and tourists snapping shots of imposing peaks that loom high above. Endless trails snake around the region, often with altitude differences of 1,000 feet over just a few miles, while secondary (and some primary) roads along its shores are narrow and winding—the perfect excuse to rent a convertible.

—Katrin Gygax

BEST TIME TO GO

While misty spring or fall can be romantic, the low clouds that winter brings usually obscure the scenery. It's summer you want: hiking trails are free of snow, the lake is a comfortable 73 degrees, restaurant terraces are open, cowbells clang in the distance, and the sky is so blue you're suspicious.

WAYS TO EXPLORE

BY BOAT

If you have the time, the best way to see the sights is on the water. Short 1-hour cruises offer a new angle on the area you're in, but to get the full Technicolor panorama of the lake's character, take the 3½-hour tour of the whole lake: it heads from the hilly and small-scale but busy series of inlets dotted with impressive villas near Luzern; through the quieter basin surrounded by the spa towns of Bürgenstock, Weggis, and Vitznau; to the wilder Urnersee between Brunnen and Flüelen, where the cliffs rise precipitously out of the depths of the lake and high into the sky.

BY BIKE

Whether you prefer an easy ride through the green pastures of cow country or are ready to tackle a steep mountain pass, you'll find both options here, and all levels in between. For easy trips, check out the good network of official bike paths off the main thoroughfares. For something with more altitude, you may have to share a narrow twisting road with a car or two from time to time.

BY FOOT

Switzerland has such an extensive network of hiking trails that you can be sure of getting to wherever you want. Thousands of official yellow *Wanderweg* (trail) signposts can be found all over the country, so you always know where you're going and how long it will take to get there. The map system is also very comprehensive and detailed, so feel free to go exploring up Mt. Pilatus, along the lake, or into the green fields of the lowlands. History buffs will appreciate the Swiss Path, which winds around the Urnersee and passes sites significant to the birth of the nation.

BEST PHOTO OPS

If you're in Luzern early in the morning on a clear day, head for the See-brücke. The lighting will be ideal for postcard-perfect shots of the Chapel Bridge, the Water Tower, and Mt. Pilatus. You may even catch some fishermen trying their luck in the River Reuss. For lake and mountain panoramas, wait until later in the day and walk along the National-quai for the best-lighted views. To get the Old Town rooftops in the picture, you can gain altitude via the old city ramparts, called the Museggmauer.

6

Updated
by Susan
Vogel-Misicka

With the mist rising off the waves and the mountains looming above the clouds, it's easy to understand how Wagner could have composed his *Siegfried Idyll* in his mansion beside the lake. This is inspiring terrain, romantic and evocative. When the waters roil up, you can hear the whistling chromatics and cymbal clashes of Gioacchino Rossini's thunderstorm from his 1829 opera, *Guillaume Tell.*

It was on Lake Luzern, after all, that Wilhelm Tell—the beloved Swiss national folk hero—supposedly leaped from the tyrant Gessler's boat to freedom. And it was in a meadow nearby that three furtive rebels and their cohorts swore an oath by firelight and planted the seed of the Swiss Confederation.

The Rütli Meadow on the western shore of Lake Luzern is the very spot where the confederates of Uri, Schwyz, and Unterwalden are said to have met on the night of November 7, 1307, to renew the 1291 Oath of Allegiance—Switzerland's equivalent of the U.S. Declaration of Independence. With this oath, the world's oldest still-extant democracy was born, as the proud charter territories swore their commitment to self-rule in the face of the Habsburgs' Holy Roman Empire. Every August 1, the Swiss national holiday, citizens gather in the meadow in remembrance of the oath, and the sky glows with the light of hundreds of mountaintop bonfires.

Wilhelm Tell played an important role in that early rebellion and his story, especially as told by German poet and playwright Friedrich von Schiller in his play *Wilhelm Tell* (1805), continues to stir those with a weakness for civil resistance. Here, around the villages of Altdorf, Bürglen, and the stunningly picturesque lakeside Tell Chapel, thousands come to honor the memory of the rebellious archer.

Yet for all its potential for drama, central Switzerland and the area surrounding Lake Luzern are tame enough turf: neat little towns, accessible mountains, smooth roads, virtually glamour-free resorts—with modest, graceful Luzern astride the River Reuss much as it has been since the Middle Ages.

An eminently civilized region, Zentralschweiz (Central Switzerland) lacks the rustic unruliness of the Valais, the spectacular extremes of the Berner Oberland, and the eccentricity of Graubünden. It's also without the sophistication and snob appeal of jet-set resorts or the cosmopolitan mix of Geneva, Basel, and Zürich. Instead, villages here range neatly around their medieval centers; houses are tidy, pastel, picture-book cottages, deep-roofed and symmetrical, each rank of windows underscored with flowers. Luzern, the capital, hosts arts festivals and great shopping but little native industry. Serene and steady as the Reuss that laps at the piers of its ancient wooden bridges, it's an approachable city in an accessible region.

Central Switzerland's popularity with tourists has spawned an infrastructure of hotels, restaurants, museums, excursions, and transportation that makes it one of the easiest places in Switzerland to visit, either by car or by rail—and one of the most rewarding. As Wagner exclaimed, "I do not know of a more beautiful spot in this world!"

6

LUZERN AND CENTRAL SWITZERLAND PLANNER

WHEN TO GO

The geographic heart of Switzerland enjoys four distinct seasons, which are temperate in the valleys and more extreme in the mountains. Spring, summer, and fall are perfect for warm-weather outdoor activities.

Fall becomes crisp around October and winter brings snow to the highlands. Keep in mind that snow can stay as late as May and come as early as August over 6,500 feet.

Avoid walking in creek beds: a hidden rainstorm high in the mountains can turn a trickling brook into a rushing torrent in a matter of seconds and has swept away many a hiker.

If you're going up and down mountains, dress like an onion: in layers. The warmth of the valley can be quickly replaced by a cold breeze 5,000 feet higher.

GETTING HERE AND AROUND

AIR TRAVEL

The nearest airport to Luzern is Zürich Airport, which is approximately 54 km (33 miles) northeast of Luzern.

BOAT AND FERRY TRAVEL

One of the joys of traveling in this region is touring Lake Luzern on one of its time-stained 20th-century paddleboat steamers. These are a slow but extremely scenic and therefore worthwhile mode of transportation; you'll find locals on day trips traveling along with you.

Lake Luzern boasts five historic paddle steamers built between 1901 and 1928, and they connect virtually every community on the lakeside. The larger boats have full restaurant facilities and even the smaller ones offer refreshments. As elsewhere in Switzerland, they link, where practical, with both the train and postbus services. The round-trip/excursion tickets offer best value for the money.

Services are frequent in the peak season, but in the off-peak season services are limited, so check on availability when you arrive. Schifffahrtsgesellschaft des Vierwaldstättersees offers culinary and sightseeing cruises around the lake daily from May to October. Rides on these are included in a Swiss Pass, Swiss Boat Pass, or the discount Tell Pass. Individual tickets can be purchased at Luzern's departure docks; the fee is based on the length of your ride.

Boat and Ferry Information Schifffahrtsgesellschaft des Vierwaldstättersees ⊠ *Werftestr. 5* ☎ *041/3676767* ⊕ *www.lakelucerne.ch/en.html.*

BUS TRAVEL
The postbus network carries travelers faithfully, if slowly, to the farthest corners of the region. It also climbs the St. Gotthard and Furka passes (remember, these are closed in winter).

CAR TRAVEL
Although Mt. Rigi and Mt. Pilatus aren't accessible by car, nearly everything else in this region is.

The descent from Andermatt past the Devil's Bridge, which once carried medieval pilgrims from the St. Gotthard Pass and drew thrill seekers during the 19th century, now exemplifies awe-inspiring Swiss mountain engineering: from Göschenen, at 3,627 feet, to the waterfront, it's a four-lane expressway.

Keep in mind, many of the towns in this region are scattered around the unusually shaped Vierwaldstättersee, so sometimes a ferry will be faster than a freeway.

TRAIN TRAVEL
Swiss National Railways is enhanced here by a few private lines (to Engelberg, Pilatus, the Rigi Kulm) that make it possible to get to most sights.

⇨ *For more information on getting here and around, see Travel Smart Switzerland.*

RESTAURANTS
In this heavily visited region, most restaurants are open all day, sometimes with a more limited menu between lunch and dinner. You'll find outside seating wherever it's possible to create any, including huge gravel-strewn terraces shaded by magnificent chestnut trees as well as tiny sidewalk tables fighting for space with pedestrians. Unless you're eating in one of the upscale hotels where "smart casual" clothing is a must, the unofficial dress code of the rest of the country applies: if you're clean, you're in. Fresh, nonsloppy jeans are preferable to a dirty suit.

Prices in the reviews are the average cost of a main course or equivalent combination of small dishes at dinner or, if dinner is not served, at lunch.

THE TELL PASS

If you don't have a Swiss Pass, there's a central Switzerland regional discount pass, called the Tell Pass, on sale from April to October. The 15-day pass grants you 5 days of unlimited free travel on main routes, 10 days at half fare. The 7-day pass gives you 2 days free, 5 at half fare. The 15-day pass costs 246 SF second class, 284 SF first class; the 7-day pass costs 180 SF second class, 204 SF first class. The ticket can be bought at rail or boat ticket offices, on cruise boats, from travel agencies, or from tourist offices.

Besides the national lines, most private rail lines will also accept the pass. Remember that many routes run by private companies are only half price (not free) with the pass. All boat trips and the private excursions to Rigi and Pilatus are free to holders of regional passes—but getting to the starting point by train or bus may still cost you half the price you'd have to pay without the pass. All this travel adds up. If you plan to cover a lot of ground, however, you may save considerably.

Choose your free days in advance: you must confirm them *all* with the first inspector who checks your pass.

For more information go to ⊕ *www. tellpass.ch.*

HOTELS

In the mountains, high season means the winter ski season; in the valleys, summer is more expensive. As the terrain and climate vary radically between balmy lakefronts and icy heights, check carefully for high and low seasons before booking ahead. Resorts such as Weggis and Vitznau cut back service considerably in winter, just when Engelberg comes alive. Book early for ever-popular Luzern. Prices drop by as much as 25% in winter, approximately November through March. Rates are often calculated on a per-person basis, so it's wise to confirm rates, particularly if you're traveling as anything other than a couple.

Prices in the reviews are the lowest cost of a standard double room in high season, including taxes.

VISITOR INFORMATION

The principal tourist bureau for the whole of central Switzerland, including the lake region, is Vierwaldstättersee Tourismus (⊕ *www. lakeluzern.ch*).

LUZERN

57 km (36 miles) southwest of Zürich.

Luzern city is a convenient base for excursions all over central Switzerland. The countryside here is tame, and the vast Vierwaldstättersee offers a prime opportunity for a lake steamer cruise. Where the River Reuss flows out of Lake Luzern, Luzern's Old Town straddles the narrowed waters.

There are a couple of discount passes available for museums and sights in the city. ■ TIP→ The LucerneCard, which costs 19 SF for one day (27 SF for two days, 33 SF for three days), grants unlimited travel on all public transportation in Luzern and half-pride admission at select museums. If you're staying in a hotel, pick up a special visitor's card; once stamped by the hotel, it entitles you to discounts at most museums and other tourist-oriented businesses. Both passes are available at the tourist office.

DRESS CODE

Although residents appreciate the value of comfortable clothes, this is definitely not the place to let it all hang out: droopy T-shirts, ill-fitting shorts, and baseball caps will get you looks of disdain, service nowhere but McDonald's, and difficulty gaining admission to most churches. Of course we don't mean you in particular, it's those other guys....

GETTING HERE AND AROUND

Luzern's centrally located train station functions as a rail crossroads, with express trains connecting from Zürich, a 46-minute trip, and Geneva, a three-hour trip. Trains enter from the south via the St. Gotthard Pass from the Ticino and via the Furka Pass from the Valais. Directly outside the station's entrance is the quay where lake boats that form part of the public transit system can take you to a variety of towns along the Vierwaldstättersee, including Weggis, Vitznau, Flüelen (with a bus connection to Altdorf), and Brunnen.

It's easy to reach Luzern from Zürich by road, approaching from national expressway A3 south, connecting to A4 via the secondary E41 in the direction of Zug, and continuing on A4, which turns into the A14, to the city. From Basel in the northwest, it's a clean sweep by the A2 to Luzern.

Approaching from the south, take the A2 to Altdorf, where a tunnel sweeps you through to the shores of the lake. If you're heading for resorts on the north shore, leave the expressway at Flüelen and follow the scenic secondary route.

Parking is limited, and Luzern's Old Town is pedestrian-only; it's best to park your car and walk. All the destinations in this region mentioned here are small, reachable by train or boat, and can easily be traveled on foot once you get there.

The main tourist office for the hub city of Luzern is in the Bahnhof, off Track 3.

ESSENTIALS

Visitor Information Bahnhof Luzern ⊠ *Zentralstr. 5* ☎ *041/2271717* ⊕ *www. luzern.com.*

EXPLORING

TOP ATTRACTIONS

Altes Rathaus (*Old Town Hall*). In 1606 the town council held its first meeting in this late-Renaissance-style building, built between 1602 and 1606. It still meets here today. ⊠ *Kornmarkt 3.*

★ **Bourbaki-Panorama.** The panorama was the IMAX theater of the 19th century; its sweeping, wraparound paintings brought to life scenes of epic proportions. The Bourbaki is one of only 30 remaining in

Don't miss the elaborate frescoes inside the Jesuitenkirche (Jesuit Church) in Luzern.

the world. Painted by Édouard Castres between 1876 and 1878 (he was aided by many uncredited artists, including Ferdinand Hodler), it depicts the French Army of the East retreating into Switzerland at Verrières, a famous episode in the Franco-Prussian War. As you walk around the circle, the imagery seems to pop into three dimensions; in fact, with the help of a few strategically placed models, it does. There's a recorded commentary in English. A modern glass cube filled with shops, movie theaters, and a restaurant surrounds its conical wooden structure. ⊠ *Löwenpl. 11* 🕾 *041/4123030* ⊕ *www. bourbakipanorama.ch* 🕾 *12 SF* ☉ *Nov.–Mar., Mon.–Sun. 10–5; Apr.– Oct., Mon.–Sun. 9–6.*

Historisches Museum (*History Museum*). Housed in the late-Gothic armory dating from 1567, this stylish institution exhibits numerous city icons, including the original Gothic fountain that stood in the Weinmarkt. Reconstructed rooms depict rural and urban life. ⊠ *Pfisterg. 24* 🕾 *041/2285424* ⊕ *www.hmluzern.ch* 🕾 *10 SF* ☉ *Tues.–Sun. and most holidays 10–5.*

Fodor's Choice
★

Jesuitenkirche (*Jesuit Church*). Constructed in 1666–77, this Baroque church with a symmetrical entrance is flanked by two onion-dome towers, added in 1893. Inside, its vast interior, restored to its original splendor, is a dramatic explosion of gilt, marble, and epic frescoes. Nearby is the Renaissance **Regierungsgebäude** (Government Building), seat of the cantonal government. ⊠ *Bahnhofstr., just west of Rathaus-Steg* 🕾 *041/2100756* ⊕ *www.jesuitenkirche-luzern.ch* ☉ *Daily 6 am– 6:30 pm.*

Luzern (Lucerne)

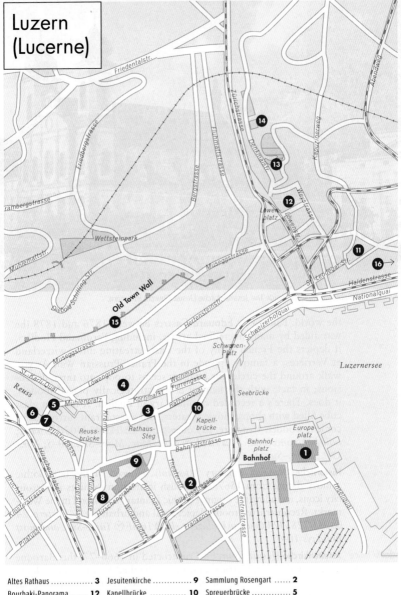

A GOOD WALK

Start at the **Kultur- und Kongresszentrum,** near the train station, which gives you a beautiful view of all the places you'll see in Luzern. Walk down Pilatusstrasse to see the impressive modern-art collection at the **Sammlung Rosengart.**

Cut north to Bahnhofstrasse, taking a left to the modern bridge, the Rathaus-Steg, and head north to the **Altes Rathaus,** across the bridge. This late-Renaissance building is on Rathausquai, the city's main avenue.

Turn left and climb the stairs past the ornately frescoed Zunfthaus zur Pfistern, a guildhall dating from the late-15th and early-16th centuries, to the Kornmarkt, where the grinding din of the grain market was once heard. Cut left to the **Weinmarkt,** a fountain square.

Leave the square from its west end, turn right on Kramgasse, and head west across the Mühlenplatz to the **Spreuerbrücke,** an unlikely exhibition space for dark paintings of the plague.

Crossing the bridge to the left bank you'll find a pair of museums, the **Natur-Museum** and the **Historisches Museum.**

From the end of the Spreuerbrücke, cut back upriver along Pfistergasse, veer left on Bahnhofstrasse, and turn right into Münzgasse to the **Franziskanerkirche.**

Return to Bahnhofstrasse and head to the **Jesuitenkirche.** Continuing east past the Rathaus-Steg Bridge, you'll see the **Kapellbrücke,** the oldest bridge of its kind in Europe.

After crossing the Kapellbrücke, break away from Old Town through thick pedestrian and bus traffic at Schwanenplatz to Schweizerhofquai.

Double back and take the first right, St. Leodegarstrasse, to the **Hofkirche.**

Go back down the church steps, doubling back on St. Leodegarstrasse, turn right, and continue on to Löwenstrasse.

Turn right and walk up to Löwenplatz and the **Bourbaki-Panorama,** which dominates the square with its mix of Victorian and modern architecture.

Beyond the plaza, up Denkmalstrasse, is the **Löwendenkmal,** called by Mark Twain "the most mournful and moving piece of stone in the world."

Immediately adjoining the small park that shades the lion lies the **Gletschergarten.**

Return down Denkmalstrasse and, at Löwenplatz, turn right on Museggstrasse, which cuts through an original city gate and runs parallel to the watchtowers and crenellated walls of Luzern, constructed around 1400. The fifth tower is the **Zytturm.**

TIMING

The Old Town is easy to navigate and ideal for walking. You can take in the sights on this route in about three hours; to this add another hour each to see the Natur-Museum and Historisches Museum, and time to linger at the Kapellbrücke and the Löwendenkmal. Both the Natur-Museum and the Historisches Museum are closed Monday.

6

The Chapel Bridge is the oldest wooden bridge in Europe.

Fodor's Choice ★ **Kapellbrücke** (*Chapel Bridge*). The oldest wooden bridge in Europe snakes diagonally across the Reuss. When it was constructed in the early-14th century, the bridge served as a rampart in case of attacks from the lake. Its shingle roof and grand stone water tower are to Luzern what the Matterhorn is to Zermatt, but considerably more vulnerable, as a 1993 fire proved. Almost 80% of this fragile monument was destroyed, including many of the 17th-century paintings inside. However, a walk through this dark, creaky landmark will take you past polychrome copies of 110 gable panels, painted by Heinrich Wägmann in the 17th century and depicting Luzern and Swiss history; stories of St. Leodegar and St. Mauritius, Luzern's patron saints; and coats of arms of local patrician families. ⊠ *Between Seebrücke and Rathaus-Steg, connecting Rathausquai and Bahnhofstr..*

★ **Kultur- und Kongresszentrum** (*Culture and Convention Center*). Architect Jean Nouvel's stunning glass-and-steel building manages both to stand out from as well as to fuse with its ancient milieu. The lakeside center's roof is an oversized, cantilevered, flat plane; shallow water channels thread inside, and immense glass plates mirror the surrounding views. The main draw is the concert hall, which opened in 1998. Although the lobbies are rich in blue, red, and stained wood, the hall itself is refreshingly pale, with brilliant acoustics. Among the annual music events is the renowned International Music Festival. A museum focuses on rotating exhibits of new international artists. ⊠ *Europapl. 1* ☎ *041/2267070* ⊕ *www.kkl-luzern.ch.*

★ **Löwendenkmal** (*Lion Monument*). The Swiss guards who died defending Louis XVI of France at the Tuileries in Paris in 1792 are commemorated here. Designed by Danish sculptor Berthel Thorwaldsen and carved out of a sheer sandstone face by Lucas Ahorn of Konstanz, this 19th-century wonder is a simple, stirring image of a dying lion. The Latin inscription translates "To the bravery and fidelity of the Swiss." ✉ *Denkmalstr. 4* ⊕ *www.luzern. com/en/sightseeing-fuehrungen/ sightseeing/lion-monument.*

WALKING TOURS

The Luzern tourist office offers English-language walking tours of the city. The usual schedule is daily from May to October and Wednesday and Saturday from November to April. Tours take about two hours and cost 18 SF.

Sammlung Rosengart (*Rosengart Collection*). A father-and-daughter team amassed this amazing group of works by major late-19th- and 20th-century artists. Now housed in a former bank building, the collection reveals their intensely personal approach; the Rosengarts acquired according to their own tastes instead of investment potential. Here you can see Miró's *Dancer,* Léger's *Contraste de formes,* and works by Cézanne, Monet, Matisse, Klee, and Chagall. There's an especially rich selection of Picassos; the artist painted the daughter, Angela Rosengart, five times. ✉ *Pilatusstr. 10, New Town* ☎ *041/2201660* ⊕ *www.rosengart.ch* 🎫 *18 SF* ⊙ *Apr.–Oct., daily 10–6; Nov.–Mar., daily 11–5.*

Weinmarkt (*Wine Market*). What is now the loveliest of Luzern's several fountain squares was famous across Europe for the passion plays staged here in the 15th to 17th century. Its Gothic central fountain depicts St. Mauritius (patron saint of soldiers), and its surrounding buildings are flamboyantly frescoed in 16th-century style. ✉ *West of Kornmarkt.*

WORTH NOTING

Franziskanerkirche (*Franciscan Church*). Since its construction in the 13th century, this church has been persistently remodeled. It still retains its 17th-century choir stalls and carved wooden pulpit. The barefoot Franciscans once held a prominent social and cultural position in Luzern, which took a firm stance against the Reformation and today remains approximately 70% Roman Catholic. ✉ *Franziskanerpl. 1, off Münzg.* ☎ *041/2260080.*

Gletschergarten (*Glacier Garden*). This tourist attraction, excavated between 1872 and 1875, shows stones that have been dramatically pocked and polished by Ice Age glaciers. A private museum on the site displays impressive relief maps of Switzerland and an elaborate 19th-century hall of mirrors. ✉ *Denkmalstr. 4* ☎ *041/4104340* ⊕ *www. gletschergarten.ch* 🎫 *12 SF* ⊙ *Apr.–Oct., daily 9–6; Nov.–Mar., daily 10–5.*

Hofkirche. This sanctuary of St. Leodegar was first part of a monastery founded in 750. Its Gothic structure was mostly destroyed by fire in 1633 and rebuilt in late-Renaissance style, so only the towers of its predecessor were preserved. The carved pulpit and choir stalls date from the 17th century, and the 80-rank organ (1650) is one of Switzerland's finest. Outside, Italianate loggias shelter a cemetery for patrician families of Old Luzern. ✉ *St. Leodegarstr. 6* ☎ *041/4182020* ⏲ *Call for hrs.*

👶 **Natur-Museum** (*Natural History Museum*). Unusually modern display techniques bring nature lessons to life here. The museum focuses on local natural history, with panoramas of early Luzern settlers and live animals for children to meet. ✉ *Kasernenpl. 6* ☎ *041/2285411* 🌐 *www.naturmuseum.ch* 🎟 *8 SF* ⏲ *Tues.–Sun. 10–5.*

Spreuerbrücke (*Chaff Bridge*). This narrow covered bridge dates from 1408. The weathered wood structure's interior gables hold a series of eerie, well-preserved 17th-century paintings by Kaspar Meglinger of the *Dance of Death*. Medieval in style and inspiration, they chronicle the plague that devastated all of Europe in the 14th century. ✉ *Between Geissmattbrücke and Reussbrücke, connecting Zeughaus Reuss-Steg and Mühlenpl.*

OFF THE BEATEN PATH

Verkehrshaus. Easily reached by steamer, car, train, or Bus 6, 8, or 24, the Swiss Transport Museum is almost a world's fair in itself, with a complex of buildings and exhibitions both indoors and out, including live demonstrations, dioramas, and a "Swissorama" (360-degree screen) film about Switzerland. Every mode of transit is discussed, from stagecoaches and bicycles to jumbo jets and space capsules. The museum also houses the country's first IMAX theater. If you're driving, head east on Haldenstrasse at the waterfront and make a right on Lidostrasse. Signs point the way. ✉ *Lidostr. 5* ☎ *041/3704444* 🌐 *www.verkehrshaus.ch* 🎟 *30 SF* ⏲ *Apr.–Oct., daily 10–6; Nov.–Mar., daily 10–5.*

Zytturm (*Time Tower*). The clock in this fifth watchtower was made in Basel in 1535 and still keeps time. ✉ *North of Museggstr.*

WHERE TO EAT

$$ ITALIAN

🍴 **Bellini.** This sleek restaurant brings a taste of Ticino to Luzern's New Town. The menu features hearty and reasonably priced Swiss-Italian dishes like spinach gnocchi, sausage with polenta, and all sorts of pizzas. In addition to beautiful mosaic tiles and a crackling fireplace, the dining room features the work of young local artists, and the lounge hosts live piano music some evenings. From April to October, the restaurant sets up camp in a leafy park across the street. In the winter on Sundays and holidays there's an all-you-can-eat brunch for 49 SF. [$] *Average main: 26 SF* ✉ *Hotel Continental, Murbacherstr. 4* ☎ *041/2289050* 🌐 *www.continental.ch.*

$$ FRENCH

🍴 **Bodu.** A touch of Paris in the heart of Luzern, this restaurant is filled with advertising posters from the '20s and '30s, simple wooden tables, and a green-and-yellow checkered floor. The darker, barlike entrance leads to the bright main room with a terrace overlooking the river. Sumptuous dishes like steamed sea bass with roasted eggplant and spinach-ricotta ravioli, or rack of lamb with thyme, green beans, and scalloped potatoes, are based on fresh market ingredients. Smoking is permitted in the dining room, where the bar is located. [$] *Average main: 38 SF* ✉ *Kornmarkt 5, Old Town* ☎ *041/4100177* 🌐 *www.brasseriebodu.ch.*

Luzern's position on the River Reuss and Lake Luzern offers lakeside dining options galore.

$$ SWISS ★ 🍴 **Galliker.** Step past the ancient facade and into a room roaring with local action. Brisk waitresses serve up the dishes that *Mutti* (Mom) used to make: fresh *Kutteln* (tripe) in rich white-wine sauce with cumin seeds; real *Kalbs-kopf* (chopped fresh veal head) served with heaps of green onions and warm vinaigrette; and authentic Luzerner *Kügelipaschtetli* (puff-pastry nests filled with finely ground beef, savory herbs, and cream sauce). Occasional experiments in a modern mode—such as steak with wasabi sauce—prove that Peter Galliker's kitchen is no museum. Desserts may include raspberries with peppermint ice cream. [$] *Average main: 36 SF* ✉ *Schützenstr. 1* ☎ *041/2401002* 🕓 *Closed Sun., Mon., and mid-July–mid-Aug.*

$$$ SWISS ★ 🍴 **Old Swiss House.** This popular establishment has been feeding travelers since 1931. Originally built as a farmhouse in 1858, it pleases crowds with its beautifully contrived collection of 17th-century antiques, leaded glass, and an old-world style now pleasantly burnished by more than 80 years of service. The standing menu includes specialties from around the country: cubed fillet of beef in a green-pepper mustard sauce with fresh buttered noodles, pike perch with ratatouille and potatoes, and chocolate mousse. In warm weather you can enjoy your meal in the outdoor seating area, which spills out into the pedestrian zone. [$] *Average main: 48 SF* ✉ *Löwenpl. 4* ☎ *041/4106171* 🌐 *www.oldswisshouse.ch/en* 🕓 *Closed Mon. and Feb.*

$$ SWISS 🍴 **Pfistern.** One of the architectural focal points of the Old Town waterfront, this floridly decorated guild house provides an authentic medieval setting in which to sample reasonably priced local fare (the guild's origins can be traced back to 1341). Lake fish with steamed new potatoes or *pastetli* (meat pies with puff pastry) are worthy local options. The

interior is woody and publike; in summer the small first-floor balcony or the airy cobblestone riverside arcade provides one of the best seats in town. $ *Average main: 35 SF* ⊠ *Kornmarkt 4* ☎ *041/4103650* ⊕ *www. restaurant-pfistern.ch.*

$$ ✕ **Rebstock/Hofstube.** Formerly a 16th-century tavern, this spot is a
SWISS favorite meeting place for Luzern's art and media crowd. The lively brasserie hums with locals lunching by the bar, and the more formal old-style restaurant glows with wood and brass under a low-beamed parquetry ceiling. Fresh market ingredients are combined for modern, international fare, including chicken simmered in white wine, rabbit stewed with rosemary, classic garlic snails, and the signature dessert, Vogelheu: batter-fried croissants sprinkled with sugar and cinnamon. There is ample outside seating when it's warm, including a small garden. $ *Average main: 40 SF* ⊠ *St. Leodegarstr. 3, Old Town* ☎ *041/4171819* ⊕ *www.rebstock-luzern.ch/rebstock_02.php.*

WHERE TO STAY

For expanded hotel reviews, visit Fodors.com.

$$$ 🏨 **Hofgarten.** This gracious 12th-century house close to the Hofkirche
HOTEL and the Löwendenkmal has been artfully modernized with an eclectic mix of colors and themes. **Pros:** leafy garden terrace in summer; very quiet. **Cons:** doesn't get as much sun as other hotels. $ *Rooms from: 295 SF* ⊠ *Stadthofstr. 14* ☎ *041/4108888* ⊕ *www.hofgarten.ch* ⇱ *18 rooms* ⦿ *No meals.*

$$$$ 🏨 **The Hotel.** Noted French architect Jean Nouvel, who also designed
HOTEL Luzern's Kultur- und Kongresszentrum, focuses on ultrahip design here; parquet floors are this lodging's only remaining old-world touch. **Pros:** heaven for style junkies; hip restaurant and lounge. **Cons:** the odd staff member is snobby. $ *Rooms from: 370 SF* ⊠ *Sempacherstr. 14* ☎ *041/2268686* ⊕ *www.the-hotel.ch* ⇱ *10 rooms, 20 suites* ⦿ *No meals.*

$$$ 🏨 **Hotel Des Balances.** Built in the 19th century on the site of two ancient
HOTEL guildhalls, this waterfront lodging is full of style. **Pros:** all rooms have
★ great views; the river terrace is exceptional. **Cons:** top-floor rooms are very small. $ *Rooms from: 350 SF* ⊠ *Weinmarkt* ☎ *041/4182828* ⊕ *www.balances.ch* ⇱ *56 rooms, 9 suites* ⦿ *No meals.*

$$$ 🏨 **Krone.** Spotless and modern, this hotel softens its edges with white lin-
HOTEL ens and walls; look in the recessed niche of one of the interior walls for a stone shrine retained from the original structure. **Pros:** very friendly and helpful staff; good central location. **Cons:** restaurant has a no-alcohol policy. $ *Rooms from: 320 SF* ⊠ *Weinmarkt 12* ☎ *041/4194400* ⊕ *www.krone-luzern.ch* ⇱ *25 rooms, 4 apartments* ⦿ *Breakfast.*

$ 🏨 **Löwengraben.** For something completely different, spend a night in
HOTEL jail—which is what this hotel was until as recently as 1998. **Pros:** innovative design; cheerful service. **Cons:** not for claustrophobics or for stays cursed by endless rainy days. $ *Rooms from: 150 SF* ⊠ *Löwengraben 18* ☎ *041/4107830* ⊕ *www.jailhotel.ch* ⇱ *52 rooms, 4 suites* ⦿ *Breakfast.*

$$ ⊞ **Montana.** The luxurious original woodwork, parquet floors, and shin-
HOTEL ing terrazzo are all in superb condition at this 1910 palace. **Pros:** good
jazz concerts in a you-are-there venue; large terrace hovers over the lake.
Cons: off the beaten path; somewhat difficult to find. $ *Rooms from:*
250 SF ⊠ *Adligenswilerstr. 22, Old Town* ☎ *041/4190000* ⊕ *www.*
hotel-montana.ch ⤶ *52 rooms, 14 suites* ¶○¶ *No meals.*

$$$$ ⊞ **National Hotel.** This monumental landmark, founded in 1870, was
HOTEL once home base to Cesar Ritz, the man who invented the world's first
modern luxury hotel. **Pros:** splendid marble-columned breakfast hall;
promenade restaurant under chestnut trees. **Cons:** the adjoining casino
makes for occasional overly boisterous guests. $ *Rooms from: 465*
SF ⊠ *Haldenstr. 4* ☎ *041/4190909* ⊕ *www.national-luzern.ch* ⤶ *29*
rooms, 12 suites ¶○¶ *No meals.*

$$$$ ⊞ **Palace Hotel.** Built in 1906, this brilliantly refurbished waterfront
HOTEL hotel drinks in the broadest possible lake views. **Pros:** lakefront set-
★ ting, right off the promenade; grand interiors. **Cons:** backs onto a main
thoroughfare. $ *Rooms from: 540 SF* ⊠ *Haldenstr. 10, Old Town*
☎ *041/4161616* ⊕ *www.palace-luzern.com* ⤶ *73 rooms, 57 suites*
¶○¶ *No meals.*

$$$$ ⊞ **Park Weggis.** In terms of style, this five-star lakeside resort has mul-
RESORT tiple personalities—its most traditional rooms, for example, are in the
Art Nouveau main building, which dates back to 1875. **Pros:** beautiful
setting; luxe materials. **Cons:** with window between the shower and
the bed, you might feel like a porn star in the Adara suites. $ *Rooms*
from: 400 SF ⊠ *Hertensteinstr. 34, Weggis* ☎ *041/3920505* ⊕ *www.*
parkweggis.ch ⤶ *32 rooms, 20 suites.*

$$ ⊞ **Schlüssel.** This crisp, no-nonsense lodging on the Franziskanerplatz
HOTEL attracts a young crowd in search of a bargain. **Pros:** staff makes that
extra effort. **Cons:** be prepared for insistent morning church bells.
$ *Rooms from: 190 SF* ⊠ *Franziskanerpl. 12* ☎ *041/2101061* ⊕ *www.*
luzern-schluessel.ch ⤶ *10 rooms* ¶○¶ *Breakfast.*

$$$$ ⊞ **Schweizerhof.** Owned by the same family since 1861, this imposing
HOTEL structure has hosted Napoléon III, Leo Tolstoy, and Mark Twain—and
Richard Wagner lived here while his lakefront home at Tribschen was
being completed. **Pros:** top-of-the-line comfort combined with modern
technology. **Cons:** a nearby supermarket looms a little close in the
back. $ *Rooms from: 440 SF* ⊠ *Schweizerhofquai 3a* ☎ *041/4100410*
⊕ *www.schweizerhof-luzern.ch* ⤶ *80 rooms, 21 suites* ¶○¶ *No meals.*

$$ ⊞ **Wilden Mann.** The city's best-known hotel, the gracious and atmo-
HOTEL spheric Wilden Mann has stone walls, coffered ceilings, brass fittings,
★ and burnished wood everywhere. **Pros:** friendly service; medieval archi-
tecture straight out of Middle Earth. **Cons:** some ceilings are a bit low.
$ *Rooms from: 250 SF* ⊠ *Bahnhofstr. 30* ☎ *041/2101666* ⊕ *www.*
wilden-mann.ch ⤶ *42 rooms, 9 suites* ¶○¶ *Breakfast.*

$$ ⊞ **Zum Weissen Kreuz.** In the bustling heart of the Old Town, this hotel
HOTEL has a tongue-in-cheek combination of sleek modern lines and gilded
frames and fat cherubs. **Pros:** free Internet access; hotel guests get
discount at in-house pizzeria; young, enthusiastic staff. **Cons:** some
room views are limited. $ *Rooms from: 220 SF* ⊠ *Furreng. 19, Old*

6

A Carnival party atmosphere takes over Luzern for the seven days of Fasnacht.

Town ☎ *041/4188220* ⊕ *www.hotel-wkreuz.ch* ⇱ *20 rooms, 1 suite* ⵏⵀⵣ *Breakfast.*

NIGHTLIFE AND THE ARTS

For information on goings-on around town, go to the tourist office for a copy of the German/English *Luzern City Guide*, published quarterly by the city. Get it stamped by your hotel for discounts on museums, public transit, and special events.

NIGHTLIFE
BARS AND LOUNGES

Louis Bar. This bar offers live jazz in the style of its namesake, Louis Armstrong. While you're there, sip one of the 80 Scotch whiskies on hand. ⊠ *Hotel Montana, Adligenwilerstr. 22* ☎ *041/4190000* ⊕ *www. hotel-montana.ch.*

Meridiani. The attractive Meridiani bar pours everything from coffee to cognac. ⊠ *Klosterstr. 12* ☎ *041/2404344* ⊕ *www.meridiani.ch.*

Opus. This place specializes in fine wines, many served by the glass. ⊠ *Bahnhofstr. 16* ☎ *041/2264141* ⊕ *www.restaurant-opus.ch.*

Pacifico. Reds dominate the murals and furnishings at this high-ceilinged Mexican cantina, where young locals come for its variety of fancy cocktails. ⊠ *Pilatusstr. 15* ☎ *041/2268787* ⊕ *www.pacifico-luzern.ch/englisch/01.htm.*

Penthouse. With three rooftop terraces, Penthouse has outstanding views and an extensive drink menu. DJs do their thing Friday and Saturday

CARNIVAL: SEVEN DAYS OF MADNESS

Although Carnival (called Fasnacht in German) is celebrated throughout the country, the party aspect is taken most seriously in Luzern. On the first Thursday seven weeks before Easter each year, seven days of madness follow, alive with parades, confetti, dancing, singing, and, of course, drinking. The parades begin with an orderly procession of Guggä—elaborately costumed brass and drums bands that can turn any pop tune into a festive event—that soon devolves into a writhing, rowdy, Old Town festival that goes more or less nonstop throughout the week. Guests are encouraged, if not downright expected, to join in. Many locals take the week off—there's no getting any work done anyway.

night, when the bar is open until 3:30 in the morning. ⊠ *Pilatusstr. 29* ☎ *041/2268888* ⊕ *www.penthouse-luzern.ch.*

Roadhouse. This British-owned pub presents DJs spinning tunes and live rock-and-roll acts. ⊠ *Pilatusstr. 1* ☎ *041/2202727* ⊕ *www.roadhouse. ch/.*

CASINO
Grand Casino Luzern. The most elegant nightlife in Luzern is found in the Grand Casino Luzern, an early-20th-century building on the lake's northern shore near the grand hotels. You can play *boule* (a type of roulette) in the Gambling Room; dance in the Club; watch the cabaret in the Casineum; or have a meal in Olivo, a Mediterranean restaurant with views of the mountains and the lake. In summer, sit outside under the palm trees at the lounge-like Seecafe. ⊠ *Haldenstr. 6* ☎ *041/4185656* ⊕ *www.grandcasinoluzern.ch.*

THE ARTS
FILM
Movie theaters, scattered around town, usually screen films in their original language. You can also catch a show in the Bourbaki-Panorama development.

FOLKLORE
Night Boat. The Night Boat sails from the dock across from Schwanenplatz every evening from May to September. This pleasant lake cruise has meals, drinks, and a folklore show. ⊠ *Schwanenpl.* ☎ *041/3194978* ⊕ *www.nightboat.ch.*

MUSIC
Blue Balls Festival. In July, the eclectic **Blue Balls Festival** brings nine days of indoor and outdoor concerts, plus a lakeside market and a host of food and drink vendors. ⊠ *Schweizerhofquai* ☎ *043/2437323* ⊕ *www. blueballs.ch.*

Lucerne Festival. The cultural hub of central Switzerland, the city hosts the annual Lucerne Festival from mid-August to mid-September in the Kultur- und Kongresszentrum. Outstanding classical performers come from all over the world; past guests have included tenor Jonas Kaufmann and superstar pianist Lang Lang. ⊠ *Hirschmattstr. 13* ☎ *041/2264400* ⊕ *www.lucernefestival.ch.*

Luzerner Symphonieorchester. Performing at the Kultur- und Kongresszentrum, this symphony orchestra has a season that runs from October through June. ⊠ *Pilatusstr. 18* ☎ *041/2260510* ⊕ *www.sinfonieorchester.ch.*

Stadtkeller. Summer performances at the Stadtkeller come with yodelers, dirndled dancers, and more. In the winter, the stage features contemporary sounds, including blues, jazz, and rock. Meals are also available. ⊠ *Sternenpl. 3* ☎ *041/4104733* ⊕ *www.stadtkeller.ch.*

THEATER

Luzerner Theater. Directly on the waterfront, the Luzerner Theater hosts plays in German and operas in their original languages. ⊠ *Theaterstr. 2* ☎ *041/2281414* ⊕ *www.luzerner-theater.ch.*

SPORTS AND THE OUTDOORS

BIKING

Train Station. The Swiss practice of renting bicycles from the train station comes in handy here, as the lake-level terrain offers smooth riding. ⊠ *Bahnhofpl.* ☎ *051/2273261.*

BOATING

Marina Charter. Pedal-, motor-, and sailboats are available through Marina Charter. ⊠ *Alpenquai 13* ☎ *041/3607944* ⊕ *www.bootsvermietung.ch.*

SNG Luzern. This company offers fair-weather boat rentals from April to October and a variety of boat tours throughout the year, some of which include tasty meals. ⊠ *Alpenquai 11* ☎ *041/3680808* ⊕ *www.sng.ch.*

Werft Herzog AG. Werft Herzog AG specializes in motorboats that accommodate up to eight passengers. ⊠ *Nationalquai* ☎ *041/4104333* ⊕ *www.herzog.ch/mieten.html.*

SWIMMING

♙ **Lido Luzern.** Near the Verkehrshaus, the Lido Luzern lets you swim in the lake from May to September. If the lake is too cold, there's a heated pool that's popular with families. Other facilities include a playground and a restaurant with an attractive patio overlooking the waterfront. ⊠ *Lidostr. 6a* ☎ *041/3703806* ⊕ *www.lido-luzern.ch* ⊠ *7 SF.*

SHOPPING

The best shopping in the region is concentrated in Luzern, which has a wide variety of Swiss handicrafts (embroidery, wood figurines, clocks) as well as the luxury goods appropriate to its high profile. The pedestrian zone along Hertensteinstrasse is packed with boutiques and department stores. In Luzern, shops are generally open until 6:30 pm, except on Thursday and Friday, when many stay open until 9 pm. On Saturday, most shops shut their doors at 4 pm and don't reopen until Monday.

From May to October, a **Flohmärt,** or flea market, takes place every Saturday from 8 to 4 at Untere Burgerstrasse, not far from the Franziskanerkirche. For locally made crafts, there's a **Handwerksmarkt** on the

Weinmarkt. It takes place on the first Saturday of every month from April through December.

DEPARTMENT STORES

Globus. The city's most fashionable department store, Globus has a wonderful gourmet supermarket in the basement. ⊠ *Pilatusstr. 4* ☎ *058/5785555* ⊕ *www.globus.ch.*

Manor. A good bet for sporting goods, Manor has a cafeteria-style restaurant on the top floor and a rooftop terrace with great views of Luzern. ⊠ *Weggisgasse 5* ☎ *041/4197699* ⊕ *www.manor.ch.*

Migros. Migros specializes in groceries and inexpensive items. ⊠ *Hertensteinstr. 9* ☎ *041/4170740* ⊕ *www.migros.ch.*

HANDICRAFTS AND GIFTS

Aux Arts du Feu. High-end china and crystal are on offer at Aux Arts du Feu. ⊠ *Schweizerhofquai 2* ☎ *041/4101401* ⊕ *www.auxartsdufeu.ch.*

Bookbinders Design. An upscale stationer, Bookbinders Design stocks quality pens and pencils and brightly colored recycled-paper products. ⊠ *Hertensteinstr. 3* ☎ *041/4109506* ⊕ *www.bookbindersdesign.ch.*

Schmid-Linder. With an extensive line of Swiss embroidery and linen, Schmid-Linder also stocks cuckoo clocks, cowbells, and a large stock of wood carvings from Brienz, in the Berner Oberland. ⊠ *Denkmalstr. 9* ☎ *041/4104346.*

WATCHES

Bucherer. One of the city's poshest jewelry and watch stores, Bucherer sells Audemars Piguet, Piaget, and Rolex. ⊠ *Schwanenpl. 5* ☎ *041/3697700* ⊕ *www.bucherer.com.*

Gübelin. A high-end watch shop, Gübelin is the place for Breguet, Patek Philippe, and its own house brand. ⊠ *Schwanenpl. 7* ☎ *041/4170010* ⊕ *www.guebelin.ch.*

WOMEN'S CLOTHING

Caroline. This shop sells wild, one-of-a-kind hats for all seasons. Even if you're not in the market for one, it's fun to peek in the window and watch Caroline Felber and her apprentices at work. ⊠ *Moosstr. 1* ☎ *041/2105363* ⊕ *www.huete.ch.*

De Boer Plus. This exclusive plus-size boutique has a vast selection of labels and styles. ⊠ *Weggisgasse 29* ☎ *041/4106239* ⊕ *www. maisondeboer.ch/de_boer_plus.*

Rive Gauche. This shop stocks a wide variety of mid-range labels, such as Fabiana Filippi and Odd Molly. ⊠ *Pilatusstr. 14* ☎ *041/2108916.*

SPAS

Fitnesspark National Luzern. This chain of wellness centers extends throughout the country, but the one in Luzern stands out for its extensive pool area, which includes thermal baths, hot tubs, and great views of Mt. Pilatus. Swimsuits are required in the pool, but the men's and women's saunas and steam rooms are textile-free. The Fitnesspark National is good value, especially if you bring along your own soap, towel, and indoor footwear; otherwise you can buy or rent what you need. You can also book a massage, a fitness class, or a session with a personal trainer. ⊠ *Haldenstr. 23* ☎ *041/4170202* ⊕ *www.fitnesspark. ch/luzern/front_content.php?idcat=1304* 🖾 *35 SF* ☞ *46 SF–190 SF massages, 44 SF–210 SF spa packages. Hot tub, sauna, steam room. Gym with: aerobics, aquaerobics, body sculpting, cycling, fitness analysis, kickboxing, nutritional counseling, personal training, Pilates, Spinning, step aerobics, strength training, weight training, yoga. Services: massage.*

Palace Spa. Though petite, the Palace Spa manages to feel grand thanks to its clever layout, elegant fixtures, and generous amenities. On the third floor of the Palace Hotel, the spa has separate men's and women's saunas, steam rooms, and relaxation areas that are free for hotel guests and anyone who books a treatment. Especially relaxing is the signature Palace Massage, which combines long strokes with gentle pressure. Couples can book the spa suite to enjoy side-by-side massages while gazing out at the lake and mountains. There's also a small gym. ∎ **TIP→** The day spa packages are good value. ⊠ *Palace Hotel, Haldenstr. 10* ☎ *041/4161515* ⊕ *www.palace-spa.ch* ☞ *75 SF 30-min foot massage, 240 SF 90-min hot-stone massage, 145 SF–390 SF day spa packages. Hot tub, sauna, steam room. Gym with: cardiovascular machines, free weights, weight-training equipment. Services: aromatherapy, facials, mani-pedi, massage, waxing.*

LUZERN ENVIRONS

Since Luzern doesn't have the sprawling suburbs associated with most cities, bucolic landscapes are just a short day trip away. Craggy mountaintops, lush hills dotted with grazing cows, and peaceful lakeside villages—along with one of the most famous mountains in Switzerland—are easily reached by boat, train, or car.

MT. PILATUS

10 km (6 miles) southwest of Luzern.

Unlike Queen Victoria, who rode to the summit of this 6,953-foot mountain by mule in 1868, you can travel to Mt. Pilatus via cable car. At the top, a grand 19th-century "mountaineer's" hotel is the centerpiece of the surprisingly stroller-friendly mountain peak.

The mountain was named either from the Latin *pileatus* (wearing a cap), to refer to its frequent cloud covering, or, more colorfully, for the ghost of Pontius Pilate, who supposedly haunts the summit. (His body, it was said, was brought here by the devil.) For centuries it was forbidden to climb the mountain and enrage the ghost, who allegedly unleashed deadly storms.

GETTING HERE AND AROUND

If you don't have time for the four-hour hike, there are two ways to get to the top of Mt. Pilatus from Luzern: either a bus and a cable car or a boat ride and a cogwheel train will take you there.

ESSENTIALS

Visitor Information Pilatus Tourist Information ⊕ *www.pilatus.ch/en.*

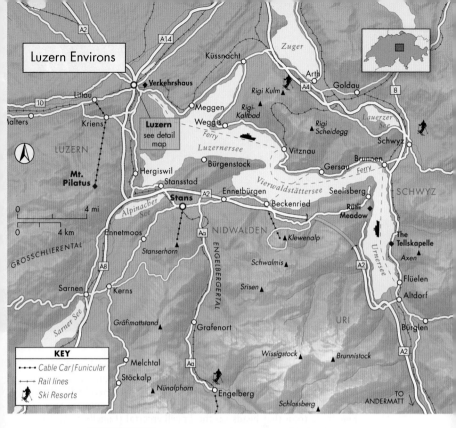

Luzern Environs

Zuger See

Küssnacht
A2
A14
Verkehrshaus
Arth
A4
Goldau
Rigi Kulm
Litlau
10
8
Meggen
Rigi-Kalibad
Walters
Kriens
Weggis
Rigi Scheidegg
Schwyz
Luzern
see detail
map
Ferry
Lauerzer See
LUZERN
Luzernersee
Vitznau
Mt. Pilatus
Hergiswil
Bürgenstock
Gersau
Brunnen
Stansstad
Ferry
Ennetbürgen
Seelisberg
SCHWYZ
Stans
A2
Vierwaldstättersee
0   4 mi
Beckenried
Rütli Meadow
0   4 km
Alpnacher See
NIDWALDEN
The Tellskapelle
Ennetmoos
Aa
Klewenalp
Urnersee
Axen
GROSSCHLIERENTAL
A8
Stanserhorn
Schwalmis
A2
Flüelen
Sarnen
Kerns
ENGELBERGERTAL
Srisen
Altdorf
Bürglen
Gräfimattstand
Grafenort
URI
A2
Sarner See
Wissigstock
Brunnistock
Melchtal
Aa
Stöckalp
TO
Nünalphorn
Engelberg
ANDERMATT
Schlossberg

KEY

•••• Cable Car/Funicular
+—+— Rail lines
⛷ Ski Resorts

EXPLORING

Mt. Pilatus. To reach the mountain by cable car, first take a bus from the train station in Luzern to the suburb of Kriens, where you catch a tiny, four-seat cable car that flies silently up to Fräkmüntegg (4,600 feet). From there, change to the 40-seat cable car that sails through open air up the rock cliff to the summit station (5,560 feet). A 10-minute walk takes you to **Esel**, one of the central peaks that make up Pilatus. From a platform here views unfold over the Alps and the sprawling, crooked Lake Luzern. Once you reach the top, glorious views are everywhere. The flat main trail on the top leads in and out of the mountain, and comes replete with striking cavern windows that offer drop-dead gorgeous vistas. The main view takes in Luzern, which looks like a toy village from way up here. The refurbished mountaineer's hotel, once graced by Queen Victoria, features 27 rooms and three suites done up in alpine chic decor. Meanwhile, it still feels like the 19th century in the restaurant, where the food is spiced up by the views just outside the elegant sash windows.

A super variation for the trip between Luzern and Mt. Pilatus involves riding one of the steepest cogwheel trains in the country—often down gradients inclined nearly 48%—through four tunnels that pierce sheer rock, to Alpnachstad. From there, take the train or the ferry, which

Reach for the heights with a hike around Mt. Pilatus, 10 km (6 miles) from Luzern.

leaves from the jetty across from the train station, back to Luzern. Prices range from 68 SF to 96 SF, depending on the route you take. To go on to Engelberg, get off the Luzern-bound train at Hergiswil, where you can cross the track and climb aboard the small, private Stans–Engelberg train that heads up the Engelbergertal (Engelberg Valley). ☎ 041/3291111 ⊕ *www.pilatus.ch/en.*

STANS

10 km (6 miles) southeast of Mt. Pilatus, 10 km (6 miles) south of Luzern.

In the heart of lush valley terrain and mossy meadows, Stans is an old village whose appealing Old Town center is dotted with the deep-roof houses typical of central Switzerland. This was the home of the beloved Heinrich Pestalozzi, the father of modern education. After the French army invaded the village in 1798, slaughtering nearly 2,000 citizens, it was Pestalozzi who gathered the orphaned children into a school, where he applied his progressive theories in the budding science of psychology to the practice of education. Instead of rote memorization and harsh discipline, Pestalozzi's teaching methods emphasized concrete examples (using plant specimens to teach botany, for example) and moral as well as intellectual development. He also championed the idea of fostering a child's individuality.

ESSENTIALS

Visitor Information Vierwaldstättersee Tourismus ✉ *Bahnhofpl. 4* ☎ *041/6108833* ⊕ *www.lakeluzern.ch/en.*

EXPLORING

Monument to Arnold von Winkelried. On the town square stands this 19th-century monument to Arnold von Winkelried, a native of Stans who died while leading the Swiss Confederates to victory over the Austrians at the battle of Sempach in 1386. The Austrians, armed with long spears, formed a Roman square so that the Swiss, wielding axes and halberds, couldn't get in close enough to do any damage. Shouting, "Forward, confederates, I will open a path!" von Winkelried threw himself on the spears, clasping as many of them as he could to his breast and creating an opening for his comrades. ⊠ *Knirig., facing the Pfarrkirche St. Peter und St. Paul.*

Pfarrkirche St. Peter und St. Paul (*Church of Sts. Peter and Paul*). The bell tower of the Pfarrkirche St. Peter und St. Paul is in Italian Romanesque style, with increasing numbers of arched windows as it rises. The incongruous steeple was added in the 16th century. ⊠ *Knirig. 1* ☎ *041/6109261.*

Stanserhorn. A two-part journey on a nostalgic 1893 funicular and an ultramodern cable car takes you to the Stanserhorn (6,200 feet), from whose peak you can see the Titlis, the highest point in central Switzerland. A "convertible" version of the cable car, unveiled in 2012, lets you feel the wind in your hair. ⊠ *Stansstaderstr. 19* ☎ *041/6188040* ⊕ *www.stanserhorn.ch* 🖃 *68 SF round-trip* ☉ *Early Apr.–early Nov., daily 8:15–5:15.*

OFF THE BEATEN PATH

Mt. Titlis. Set 19 km (12 miles) south of Stans, this is perhaps the most spectacular of the many rocky peaks that surround the Obermatt's long, wide bowl. Thanks to a sophisticated transportation system that benefits skiers, hikers, climbers, and sightseers alike, it's possible to ride a small cable car up to the tiny mountain lake (and famous ski area) called Trübsee (5,904 feet). From there, change and ascend to Stand to catch the famous Rotair cable car, which rotates to give 360-degree panoramas on its way up to the summit station on the Titlis. At the top is a multilevel structure that seems to conjure up Disney's Space Mountain: four rock-embedded, fortress-thick floors lead to shops, an ice grotto (serving drinks from a solid-ice bar), and a restaurant whose views take in the Jura Mountains, the Graubünden, and Bernese Alps. Mt. Titlis looms over the village of Engelberg (3,280 feet), which is an hour from Luzern by train. Engelberg clusters at the foot of its Benedictine Kloster (monastery), founded in 1120. The monastery grounds are open to the public daily and include a dairy. ⊠ *Gerschnistr. 1* ☎ *041/6395050* ⊕ *www.titlis.ch* 🖃 *86 SF round-trip.*

URNERSEE

Perhaps it was destiny that Switzerland was born right here. Take one look at the spectacular mix of snowy peaks, sapphire lakes, and picturesque meadows surrounding the Urnersee—the southern leg of Lake Luzern—and you'll wonder if all of this beauty inspired the pact signed in 1291 between the clans of Schwyz, Unterwalden, and Uri. This Oath

DID YOU KNOW?

The world's steepest cog railway carries visitors to the summit of Mt. Pilatus (6,953 feet). At times, the car travels on gradients inclined 48%, and the track punches through sheer rock in a series of tunnels. The views at the top are truly stunning.

of Eternal Alliance announced the creation of a new realm—the world's longest-running continuous democracy.

This is not the only iconic historical event in the region. Although Wilhelm Tell is considered by some to be mere myth, this is the hallowed ground where he may have been born and where he became a legend. Every year, thousands of Swiss make a pilgrimage here, taking a lake steamer from Luzern all the way down to the Urnersee (or driving the same route along the northern lakefront highway to Brunnen) to find their way to the Rütli Meadow—the birthplace of Switzerland—and to then trace the story of Tell in neighboring lakeside villages. If you want to "go high" and get a bird's-eye view of the area, opt for the excursion up to the top of majestic Rigi Kulm, the summit of Mt. Rigi, by train or cable car.

Lake cruises depart from the main docks by the train station (schedules are available at the ticket and tourist offices); the boat will be marked for Fluelen. First-class seats are on top; each level has a restaurant-café. The exterior seats are only slightly sheltered; if you want to sit inside, you may feel obligated to order a drink. Take advantage of the boat's many stops—you can get on and off at will.

WEGGIS

★   *25 km (15 miles) northeast and across the lake from Bürgenstock, 20 km (12 miles) northeast of Luzern.*

With a pretty waterfront park and promenade, Weggis is a summer resort town known for its mild, almost subtropical climate—little wonder that it is a magnet for Switzerland's retirees. It's far from the highway and accessible only by the secondary road, so you get a pleasant sense of isolation. At 5,900 feet, the famed **Mt. Rigi** is just a cable-car ride away from Weggis: follow signs for the Rigibahn, a station high above the resort (a 15-minute walk). From here you can ride a large cable car to **Rigi-Kaltbad,** a small resort on a spectacular plateau; walk across to the electric rack-and-pinion railway station and ride the steep tracks of the Vitznau–Rigi line to the summit of the mountain. Take an elevator to the **Rigi-Kulm** hotel to enjoy the views indoors or walk to the crest (45 minutes) to see as far as the Black Forest in one direction and Mt. Säntis in the other. Or consider climbing to the top, staying in the hotel, and getting up early to see the sun rise over the Alps—a view that astounded both Victor Hugo and Mark Twain. With Lake Luzern on one side and Lake Zug on the other, Mt. Rigi can feel like an island.

GETTING HERE AND AROUND

During daylight hours, boats arrive here every hour from Luzern (9.20 SF one-way) and Flüelen (19.50 SF one-way). There are also bus and train connections between the two towns, changing in Brunnen. Weggis has a cable car up to the top of the Rigi, while Vitznau has a cogwheel train (each runs approximately once an hour, 40 SF one-way).

You can also approach Rigi via the cogwheel train from Arth-Goldau; the two lines were built by competing companies in the 1870s in a

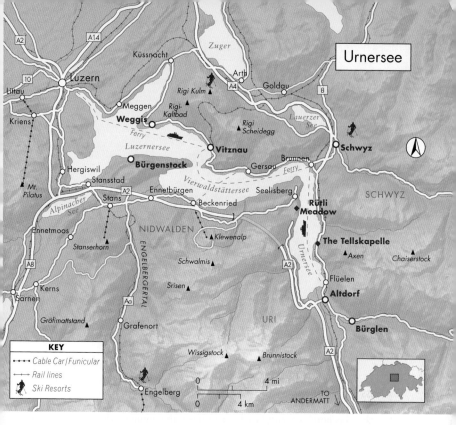

race to reach the top and capture the lion's share of the tourist business. The line rising out of the lakefront resort of Vitznau won, but the Arth-Goldau line gets plenty of business, as its base terminal lies on the mainstream St. Gotthard route. The round-trip fare from Weggis, Vitznau, or Arth-Goldau is 64 SF.

ESSENTIALS

Visitor Information Weggis Tourist Information ⊠ *Seestr. 5* ☎ *041/2271800* ⊕ *www.wvrt.ch.*

SKIING

Mt. Rigi. At 5,900 feet, Mt. Rigi has two cogwheel railways, three cable cars, and a number of small ski lifts that serve its downhill runs as well as its cross-country, ski-hiking, and sledding trails. ⊕ *www.rigi.ch.*

WHERE TO STAY

For expanded hotel reviews, visit Fodors.com.

$$$
RESORT
★
🖼 **Beau-Rivage.** Built in 1908, this attractive business-class resort concentrates its comforts on a small but luxurious waterfront site, with a large restaurant above the manicured lawn, a small swimming pool with mountain views, and comfortable lounge chairs at the lake's edge. **Pros:** a great place to just be; impeccable service. **Cons:** backs onto the main

A steam train heads to the summit of Mt. Rigi on the Vitznau–Rigi railway.

road. [$] *Rooms from: 274 SF* ✉ *Gotthardstr. 6* ☎ *041/3927900* 🌐 *www.beaurivage-weggis.ch* 🛏 *39 rooms* 🕒 *Closed Nov.–Mar.* 🍴 *Breakfast.*

$$$ HOTEL ★ 🏨 **Post Hotel Weggis.** This 1960s-era concrete block has been redesigned within an inch of its life, with excellent results—if Weggis is Florida, this hotel is South Beach. **Pros:** up-to-the-minute style; fabulous bathrooms; top-notch service. **Cons:** no other nightlife in town. [$] *Rooms from: 280 SF* ✉ *Seestr. 8* ☎ *041/3922525* 🌐 *www.poho.ch* 🛏 *45 rooms* 🍴 *No meals.*

$$ HOTEL 🏨 **Rigi-Kulm.** In a 19th-century lodging (think parquet floors, gilt mirrors, and sandstone staircases), this high-altitude hotel mixes clean-lined interior design with well-chosen antique furnishings. **Pros:** a sunny perch above the clouds November–February. **Cons:** once you're here, you're here. [$] *Rooms from: 228 SF* ✉ *Rigi Kulm* ☎ *041/8801888* 🌐 *www.rigikulm.ch* 🛏 *33 rooms* 🍴 *Breakfast.*

VITZNAU

4 km (2½ miles) southeast of Weggis, 26 km (16 miles) east of Luzern.

For a quintessentially scenic spot, stop over in Vitznau, a tiny waterfront resort that competes with Weggis for the balmiest weather. Small as this village may be, it looms large on the tourist radar. Not only is Vitznau the home of the magnificently palatial Park Hotel, it's also the site of Switzerland's first-ever cog railway (opened in 1871); the Mülefluh fortress (the first artillery fortress in the country); and the shipyards where Lake Luzern's fabled paddleboat steamers were first built. Today it's the best place to see the world's largest Swiss flag, proudly displayed in summer on a face of Mt. Rigi overlooking Vitznau.

ESSENTIALS

Visitor Information Vitznau Tourism Information ✉ *Bahnhofstr. 1* ☎ *041/2271810* 🌐 *www.wvrt.ch/en.*

> **WORD OF MOUTH**
>
> "Mt. Rigi is a splendid day trip from Lucerne—take a boat to Vitznau and take the mountain-climbing little train from near the dock to the summit." —PalenQ

WHERE TO STAY

For expanded hotel reviews, visit Fodors.com.

$$$$ HOTEL ★ 🏨 **Park Hotel.** Set in a fairy-tale lakefront palace, this isolated but lavish retreat dominates the tiny village of Vitznau. **Pros:** one-stop vacationing; luxuriously relaxing. **Cons:** off the beaten track. [$] *Rooms from: 540 SF* ✉ *Seestr. 18* ☎ *041/3996060* 🌐 *www.parkhotel-vitznau.ch* 🛏 *75 suites* 🍴 *No meals.*

$ HOTEL 🏨 **Rigi.** This solid lodging has a delightfully old-fashioned facade, modern interiors, and a welcoming atmosphere that comes from being family-owned and -run. **Pros:** centrally located; friendly service; calm atmosphere. **Cons:** some traffic noise in daytime; could use a slight face-lift. [$] *Rooms from: 150 SF* ✉ *Seestr.* ☎ *041/3998585* 🌐 *www.rigi-vitznau.ch* 🛏 *35 rooms* 🍴 *Breakfast.*

$ B&B/INN ★ 🏨 **Schiff.** Dwarfed by the massive Park Hotel across the street, the Hotel Schiff shares much of the same view for a fraction of the cost. **Pros:** friendly atmosphere; the grounds are open to visitors. **Cons:** bathrooms are down the hall. [$] *Rooms from: 84 SF* ✉ *Kantonstr.* ☎ *041/3971357* 🌐 *www.schiff-vitznau.ch* 🛏 *4 rooms without bath* 🕒 *Closed Oct. and Nov.* 🍴 *Breakfast.*

$$$ RESORT 🏨 **Vitznauerhof.** With a lakefront garden, full-service spa, and a restaurant in the former boathouse, you're likely to be tempted to stay a little longer at this Jugendstil hotel. **Pros:** exquisite setting; impeccable service; free use of spa. **Cons:** backs onto a main road. [$] *Rooms from: 350 SF* ✉ *Seestr. 80* ☎ *041/3997777* 🌐 *www.vitznauerhof.ch* 🛏 *48 rooms, 5 suites* 🍴 *Breakfast.*

SPAS

Mineralbad & Spa. The region's mineral springs have been attracting visitors for hundreds of years, and this spa, which opened in 2012, represents the latest wave. Perched at 4,757 feet above sea level, the Mineralbad & Spa offers stunning mountain views and delightful pools both inside and out. Designed by Swiss architect Mario Botta, it's fashioned mostly from Italian granite. The adults-only spa has a steam room, a unisex sauna, and a so-called "crystal bath," which is pretty but only a few inches deep. Despite its lofty location, the spa is easy to reach by cable car from Weggis or cogwheel train from Vitznau. Spontaneous visitors can rent a swimsuit and towel for just 10 SF. ✉ *Rigi Kaltbad* ☎ *041/3970406* 🌐 *www.mineralbad-rigi-kaltbad.ch* ☞ *55 SF–105; SF 25–50-min full-body massage; 95 SF–140 SF packages with massage, towel, and glass of prosecco. Hot tubs, sauna, steam room. Services: massage.*

Sparkling Wellness. The six individually appointed spa cottages at the Park Hotel Weggis are equipped with saunas, steam rooms, whirlpools, bathtubs, power showers, foot baths, tanning beds, and entertainment systems. In addition to the cottages—which are actually arranged in row-house fashion—there is a spa specializing in Tibetan treatments like the "Himalaya Harmony" massage. Five of the therapists are from Tibet, and one is a former monk. Rounding out the facilities are a gym and a heated outdoor swimming pool overlooking Lake Luzern. In summer, you can opt for a massage outside by the lake. ⊠ *Park Weggis, Hertensteinst. 34, Weggis* 🕾 *041/3920505* ⊕ *www.sparklinghealth.ch/en/sparkling-wellness* ⌖ *200 SF 90-min full-body massage; 410 SF spa cottage package with massage. Gym with: cardiovascular machines, free weights, weight-training equipment. Services: aromatherapy, facials, mani-pedi, massage, medical peelings/lifts, permanent makeup, waxing.*

SPORTS AND THE OUTDOORS

SWIMMING

Because of a quirk of climate, Vitznau's bay is warmer than Luzern's Lido, making this a great place to swim.

EN ROUTE From Vitznau, a boat tour will take you across Lake Luzern to **Beckenried**, from which a cable car leads to Klewenalp (5,250 feet), a small resort overlooking the lake. The area is excellent for hiking, with breathtakingly panoramic views of the lake and mountains on clear days. If you're driving, you could also follow the north shore to Gersau, a tiny lake resort that was an independent republic—the world's smallest—from 1332 to 1798. From Gersau the boat snakes around the sharp peninsula of the Seelisberg; the 1980 completion of a 9¼-km (6-mile) tunnel through the peninsula, south of the lake, opened the way for even swifter north–south travel between Luzern and points north and the St. Gotthard route and points south.

RÜTLI MEADOW

Fodor's Choice ★ *14 km (8 miles) southeast of Vitznau, 15 km (10 miles) northwest of Altdorf on Urnersee, 35 km (22 miles) southeast of Luzern.*

At the south end of Lake Luzern, past the gorgeously scenic Seelisberg Peninsula, the narrow, majestic Urnersee accesses some of the most legendary landmarks in the region.

GETTING HERE AND AROUND

The lake steamers from Luzern make frequent stops here.

EXPLORING

The **Schillerstein**, on the right as you cruise past the peninsula, is a spectacular natural rock obelisk extending nearly 85 feet up out of the lake, onto which has been carved a gigantic dedication: "To the author of Wilhelm Tell, Friedrich von Schiller. 1859." About 10 minutes beyond the rock, the lake steamer pulls up at the quaint, 19th-century landing dock for perhaps the most historically significant site in central Switzerland: the Rütli Meadow, where the confederates of Schwyz, Unterwalden, and Uri are said to have met in 1307 to renew the 1291 Oath of Eternal Alliance.

A five-minute walk up the hillside brings you to a grassy plateau where a rock and flagpole mark the sacred location. Nearby is a medieval rock bench nestled by towering trees—the perfect spot to think about

The Rütli Meadow is the birthplace of modern Switzerland, and the world's oldest democracy.

another monumental event that took place here centuries later: amid threats of a 1940 German invasion, General Guisan, Swiss army commander in chief, summoned hundreds of officers to the meadow to reaffirm their commitment to the Swiss Confederation in a secret, stirring ceremony. Afterward, head back down the hill to study the small video presentation (perhaps also take a photo of a costumed historical interpreter) and be sure to stop in the time-burnished, 19th-century chalet snack shop, with its lovely stained-glass salons and picturesque wood verandas.

ALTDORF

20 km (12 miles) south of Rütli Meadow, 35 km (22 miles) southeast of Luzern.

Schiller's play *Wilhelm Tell* sums up the tale for the Swiss, who perform his play religiously in venues all over the country—including the town of Altdorf, just up the road from the Rütli Meadow. Leave the steamer at Flüelen, the farthest point of the boat ride around the lake, and connect by postbus to Altdorf, the capital of the canton Uri and, by popular if not scholarly consensus, the setting for the famous scene in which Tell was forced to use his crossbow to shoot an apple off his own son's head.

Though there are no valid records of Wilhelm Tell's existence, and versions of the legend conflict with historical fact, no one denies the reality of his times, when central Switzerland—then a feudal dependent of Austria but by its own independent will not yet absorbed into the Holy Roman Empire—suffered brutal pressures and indignities

CLOSE UP

The Swiss Path

Central Switzerland is well suited to experiencing the country's history, with landmarks representing facts and legends going back more than 700 years. You can see the sights below in a day by boat, bus, and train; on foot or by bicycle it will take you at least two days. Start at Switzerland's birthplace: catch the boat from Luzern to the Rütli Meadow, where representatives from the three original cantons swore their Oath of Eternal Alliance against the Habsburgs in 1291. A short boat trip down the lake to Flüelen and the bus to Altdorf will take you to the statue of Wilhelm Tell, Switzerland's legendary symbol of independent spirit.

Back in Flüelen, walk the *Weg der Schweiz* (the Swiss Path), which you can locate on the shore right by the train station, and head north along the lake. The path dates from 1991, when it was created to commemorate the 700th anniversary of the signing of the oath of allegiance. The historic footpath covers 35 km (21½ miles) of lakefront lore in 26 sections, each honoring one of Switzerland's cantons. In 14 hours, or better yet spread out over several days, you can trace the mythical steps of Wilhelm Tell and the genuine steps of medieval

forerunners, climb through steep forests and isolated villages, and visit the holiday resort of Brunnen.

As you walk along it, you'll find yourself going through a series of hand-hewn tunnels that form part of the original Axenstrasse, a road built into the mountainside in 1865. This amazing feat of engineering shortened the long voyage from north to south over the Alps. You can walk to the romantic 19th-century lakeside chapel, the Tellskapelle (1 hour each way) or all the way to Brunnen (on foot 5½ hours; by bike 2½ hours) or turn around and head back to Flüelen if you run out of steam.

A side trip to Schywz from Brunnen takes you to the Bethlehemhaus, a wooden structure built in 1287. From Brunnen or Flüelen, you can take the train back to Luzern, where the Bourbaki Panorama depicts the French army's retreat through Switzerland in 1870–71. Up the street, see the moving *Löwendenkmal,* a dying lion sculpted into a cliff in 1821 in memory of Swiss mercenaries who died defending Louis XVI during the French Revolution; and the Gletschergarten, an outdoor park incorporating an expanse of rock shaped by passing Ice Age glaciers.

---

under its local rulers. The mythical Gessler was one of those rulers, and his edict—that the proud Swiss should bow before his hat suspended from a pole in the village square at Altdorf—symbolizes the cruel oppression of the time. Schiller's Tell was a consummate hero: brisk, decisive, a highly skilled helmsman as well as marksman, and not one for diplomatic negotiations. He refused to kneel and provoked his famous punishment: to shoot an apple off his young son's head before a crowd of fellow townsmen. If he refused, both would be killed. Tell quietly tucked an arrow in his shirt bosom, loaded another into his crossbow, and shot the apple clean through. When Gessler asked what the second arrow was for, Tell replied that if the first arrow had struck his child, the second arrow would have been for Gessler and he would not have missed.

For this impolitic remark, Tell was sentenced to prison. While deporting him across Lake Luzern, the Austrians (including the ruthless Gessler) were caught in a violent storm and turned to Tell, the only man onboard who knew the waters, to take the helm. Unshackled, he steered the boat to a rocky ridge, leapt free, and pushed the boat back into the storm. Later he lay in wait in the woods near Küssnacht and shot Gessler in the heart. This act inspired the people to overthrow their oppressors and swear the Oath of Eternal Alliance around a roaring bonfire, laying the groundwork for the Swiss Confederation.

GETTING HERE AND AROUND

On the main train and car route linking the area south of the Alps with the north, Altdorf was a main stop on the journey when it took weeks, not hours, to get from Zürich to Milan. As a consequence, there are hourly train connections from Zürich, Luzern, or Lugano (stop in Flüelen and take the bus into Altdorf's center, the Telldenkmal stop). The lake steamers from Luzern take about three hours to Flüelen. Train and boat tickets to Altdorf will include the five-minute bus trip from Flüelen to Altdorf's Telldenkmal stop.

ESSENTIALS

Visitor Information Altdorf Tourismus ✉ *Schützeng. 11* ☎ *041/874 8000* ⊕ *www.altdorftourismus.ch.*

EXPLORING

William Tell Monument. This often-reproduced monument in the village center shows a proud father with crossbow on one shoulder, the other hand grasping his son's hand. It was sculpted by Richard Kissling in 1895.

SPORTS AND THE OUTDOORS

BIKING

Train Station. You can rent bikes at the train station in Flüelen. ☎ *051/2214532.*

Zweirad Affentranger. Mountain bikes and motorbikes can be rented and serviced in Altdorf through Zweirad Affentranger. ✉ *Gotthardstr. 53* ☎ *041/8701315.*

BÜRGLEN

3 km (1¾ miles) southeast of Altdorf, 40 km (25 miles) southeast of Luzern.

Wilhelm Tell was supposedly from the tiny, turreted town of Bürglen, just up the road from Altdorf.

EXPLORING

Tell-Museum. The Tell-Museum displays documents and art related to the legendary man. ✉ *Postpl.* ☎ *041/8704155* ⊕ *www.tellmuseum. ch* 🖭 *5.50 SF* ⊙ *July–Aug., 10–5; May 15–June, and Sept.–Oct. 15, 10–11:30, 1:30–5. .*

Across the lake from the Rütli Meadow sits the Tellskapelle, a beautiful shrine to Wilhelm Tell.

THE TELLSKAPELLE

14 km (9 miles) north of Altdorf, 41 km (26 miles) southeast of Luzern.

Have your camera ready for this magnificently picturesque lakeside chapel, set at the foot of the Axen mountain.

GETTING HERE AND AROUND

The lake steamer from Luzern stops here as well as at the Rütli Meadow (directly across the lake), making it convenient to see both sites in one shot. Boats leave Luzern hourly in summer, less frequently in winter. You can also take a taxi from Brunnen (about 50 SF each way), but set a time for your driver to pick you up again: there is no stand at the Tellskapelle. The steamer also stops in Brunnen.

EXPLORING

Fodor's Choice **Tellskapelle.** A shrine to Wilhelm Tell, the church is adjacent to the **Tell-**
★ **splatte,** which was the rocky ledge onto which Tell, the rebellious archer, leaped to escape from Gessler's boat, pushing the boat back into the stormy waves as he jumped. Built in 1500, it was restored in High Victorian fashion in 1881. It contains four frescoes of the Tell legend (painted at the time of restoration), showing the taking of the oath on the Rütli Meadow, Tell shooting the apple on his son's head, Tell's escape, and Gessler's death. ⊕ *www.weg-der-schweiz.ch.*

SCHWYZ

20 km (12 miles) south of Rütli Meadow, 35 km (22 miles) southeast of Luzern.

This historic town is the capital of the canton Schwyz, root of the name Switzerland and source of the nation's flag. Switzerland's most precious archives are stored here as well. Traces of an independent settlement at Schwyz have been found from as far back as the Bronze Age (2500 BC–800 BC), but it was its inhabitants' aid in the 1291 Oath of Eternal Alliance that put Schwyz on the map.

Many of Schwyz's splendid houses owe their origin to the battlefield. The men of Schwyz had a reputation as fine soldiers and were in demand in other countries as mercenaries during the 16th and 17th centuries. They built many of the houses you can see today with their military pay.

ESSENTIALS

Visitor Information Schwyz Tourismus ⊠ *Bahnhofstr. 4* ☎ *041/8555950* ⊕ *www.schwyz-tourismus.ch.*

EXPLORING

Bundesbriefmuseum (*Federal Charter Museum*). See the beautifully scripted and sealed original oath of allegiance, as well as battle flags and paintings of the period, in Schwyz's Bundesbriefmuseum. ⊠ *Bahnhofstr. 20* ☎ *041/8192064* ⊕ *www.bundesbriefmuseum.ch* 🖭*4 SF* ⊗ *May–Oct., Tues.–Fri. 9–11:30 and 1:30–5, weekends 9–5; Nov.–Apr., Tues.–Fri. 9–11:30 and 1:30–5, weekends 1:30–5* ⊗ *Closed Mon.*

Fodor's Choice
★ **Ital-Redinghaus.** Schwyz has several notable Baroque churches and a large number of fine old patrician homes dating from the 17th and 18th centuries, not least of which is the Ital-Redinghaus with its magnificent interior, antique stoves, and fine stained glass. A visit to this grand house includes a peek inside the neighboring **Bethlehemhaus**, the oldest wooden house in Switzerland, dating from 1287. There is no parking on the grounds; park on the nearby town square and walk 50 yards to the entrance off Reichstrasse. ⊠ *Rickenbachstr. 24* ☎ *041/8114505* ⊕ *www.irh.ch* 🖭*5 SF* ⊗ *May–Oct., Tues.–Fri. 2–5, weekends 10–noon and 2–5.*

Rathaus (*Town Hall*). Schwyz's most famous landmark is the Rathaus; its richly frescoed exterior (1891) depicts the Battle of Morgarten, the 1315 conflict in which the Swiss defeated the Austrian army. The building is still used as the Town Hall. ⊠ *Hauptpl. 1.*

Basel

WORD OF MOUTH

"There are a LOT of museums in Basel (don't have the exact figures, but it's significant), plus the lovely river walk, and a very interesting and historic Old Town."

—swandav2000

WELCOME TO BASEL

TOP REASONS TO GO

★ **Three corners:** Not many cities offer a more cosmopolitan mix. Here Switzerland merges with Germany and France, and Basel is home to some 150 nationalities.

★ **Art old and new:** This city of the arts has galleries full of old master paintings and some pictures so contemporary the paint is still drying— more than 30 museums cater to every taste.

★ **Fasnacht:** Each spring during its three-day Lenten celebration the city's streets are filled with spectacularly costumed revelers, bands, and pipers.

★ **Münster madness:** Not only is this cathedral an amazing piece of architecture, it also offers fabulous views of the city and the River Rhine.

★ **Noble dust:** A short boat ride from Basel, the Colonia Augusta Raurica is the oldest Roman settlement on the Rhine, complete with a restored 1st-century BC theater.

1 **Altstadt.** Bordering the marketplace, the Altstadt (Old Town) lies in front of the majestic red Town Hall and is host to a thriving consumables market. Winding alleyways lead off to a maze of shopping possibilities.

2 **Kleinbasel.** East of the Rhine on the German side of town, Kleinbasel (Small Basel) is a lively blue-collar center that includes the huge Messe Basel complex, where Art Basel is held every June.

3 **St.** Alban. Combine culture with lunch here: narrow quiet streets wind around patrician houses downhill to the Rhine, where a medieval paper mill is just steps from the Museum of Contemporary Art and two excellent restaurants.

KLEINBASEL
2

Riehenstrasse

Rebgasse

Uferngasse

Rheingasse

Riehentorstr.

Oberer Rheinweg

MEDIEVAL DISTRICT

Wettsteinallee

Wettsteinplatz

Grenzacherstrasse

Theodorsgraben-Anlage

Wettsteinstrasse

Schaffhauser-Rheinweg

Münster

Wettstein-brücke

Rhein

Ritterg.

St. Alban-Rheinweg

St. Alban-Graben

♦ **Kunstmuseum**

Dufourstrasse

KUNSTMUSEUM

Malzgasse

St. Alban-Vorstadt

Museum of Contemporary Art ♦
3
ST. ALBAN

St. Alban-Tal

St. Alban

St. Alban-Tor ♦

5

6

GETTING ORIENTED

Shouldering the Swiss Jura Mountains, the German Black Forest, and the French Vosges, Basel is Switzerland's third-largest city and the central conurbation for the northwest part of the country. Bordering both banks of the Rhine, Basel is 730 feet above sea level—the lowest altitude of any Swiss city north of the Alps. From here the river turns 90 degrees north and widens into a majestic waterway.

7

4 Zoo. A hollow nestled behind the SBB train station is home to about 620 kinds of animals and offers experiences such as penguin walks (in winter), elephant baths, and pelican feedings.

5 Colonia Augusta Raurica (Augst). Painstakingly restored over the past 50 years, this former Roman town includes the original amphitheater and a re-creation of a typical villa, along with a museum of artifacts found during archaeological digs.

6 Basel Environs. Technically not part of Basel but so close that it hardly matters—even if one is just across the German border—the surrounding towns are host to museums and historic sites worth a visit.

Updated by
Rachel Maru-
sak Hermann

Although it lacks the gilt and glitter of Zürich and the Latin grace of Geneva, in many ways Basel (Bâle in French) is more sophisticated than either. Situated at the frontier between two of Europe's most assertive personalities—France and Germany—and tapped directly into the artery of the Rhine, the city has grown remarkably urbane, cosmopolitan, and worldly wise, yet is delightfully eccentric as well.

Its imagination has been fed by centuries of intellectual input: Basel is host to Switzerland's oldest university (1460) and patron to some of the country's—and the world's—finest minds. As a northern center of humanist thought and art, it nurtured the painters Konrad Witz and Hans Holbein the Younger, as well as the great Dutch scholar Erasmus. And it was Basel's visionary lord mayor Johann Rudolf Wettstein who, at the end of the Thirty Years' War, negotiated Switzerland's ground-breaking—and lasting—neutrality.

Each day more than 30,000 French and German commuters cross into Basel, working at leading banks and pharmaceutical firms. Yet Basel's population remains modest, hovering just above 190,000; its urban center lies gracefully along the Rhine, with no building so tall as to block another building's view of the cathedral's twin spires. Two blocks from the heart of the thriving shopping district you can walk along medieval residential streets cloaked in perfect, otherworldly silence to Münsterhügel (cathedral mount), where the Romanesque-Gothic cathedral offers superb views over the Altstadt and the Rhine all the way to the surrounding mountains.

The high number of museums per capita is a reflection of Basel's priorities: the city has more than 30, including the world-class Kunstmuseum, the Museum Tinguely, and the Fondation Beyeler. As high culture breeds good taste, Basel has some of the most varied, even quirky, shopping in Switzerland, all within walking distance. But you can still get a beer and a bratwurst here: natives primarily speak German or their own local version of *Schwyzerdütsch*, called *Baseldytsch*.

BASEL PLANNER

WHEN TO GO

Basel is located in the Rhine Valley, which affords it an agreeably mild climate. Warm Mediterranean air also wafts this way from the Rhône Valley. The average temperature in January, the coldest month, is 1 Celsius (34 F); in July, the warmest, 19 Celsius (66 F). Fog is rare, unlike in other Swiss regions, and the average rainfall is the lowest north of the Rhône.

PLANNING YOUR TIME

If you are in town for just a day, your best bet is to take a stroll through Basel's Altstadt, making sure to see the Münster and the sweeping views from the terrace overlooking the Rhine. Art enthusiasts could decide to circle from here directly to the Kunstmuseum, and shoppers may want to head down one of the winding alleyways into the Freie Strasse or the Marktplatz. A leisurely late-afternoon walk across the Mittlere Rheinbrücke and upstream along the sunny Kleinbasel riverside promenade (Oberer Rheinweg) is a good way to see the town in its best light.

If you are sticking around for longer, then take in some of the city's smaller museums, perhaps in the picturesque St. Alban quarter. From here take a ferry across the river and head east to the Museum Tinguely. Or organize your day around a trip to Riehen; the Fondation Beyeler's stunningly well-rounded (and beautifully presented) collection of 20th-century art can be reached in a mere 20 minutes by tram.

In summer you could opt to take a boat trip to the Roman ruins of Augusta Raurica in Augst, east of Basel. Or take a driving tour of, or catch a local train to, some of the small villages scattered south of the city, such as Balsthal, Holderbank, Oberer Hauenstein, Langenbruck, and Liestal to experience the more rural delights of the area. Cool off in very hot weather like the locals by taking a dip in the Rhine. Dive in after the Wettsteinbrücke and float down to one of three popular refreshment stands where you can watch a seemingly endless stream of locals doing the same.

GETTING HERE AND AROUND

Hotel guests in Basel receive a complimentary Basel Mobility Ticket, which allows free use of all public transportation within the city during their stay. Holders of the Swiss Pass also travel free on all Basel public transport systems.

BASEL TOUR OPTIONS

Basel Tourismus organizes two-hour walking tours of the city, which start from the tourist information office in the Stadt Casino and cater to German, French, and English speakers. Tours take place from May to October, Monday through Saturday at 2:30. From November to April the walking tours are held every Saturday at 2:30. The cost is 15 SF.

7

AIR TRAVEL

Basel uses EuroAirport (just across the border in France), which is shared with Mulhouse in France and Freiburg in Germany. Direct flights link Basel to most major European cities, including Zürich. The nearest intercontinental airport is Zürich Airport.

Regular bus service runs between EuroAirport and the Bahnhof SBB in the center of Basel. The trip takes about 15 minutes and costs 4.40 SF per person.

One-way taxi fare from the airport to the Basel center is approximately 50 SF; it takes about 15 minutes in light traffic and up to 30 minutes at rush hour (around 7:30 am to 8:30 am, noon to 2 pm, and 5 pm to 7 pm). There are normally cabs at the taxi stand, but if you need to call one from the airport, make sure you leave the building on the Swiss side.

CAR TRAVEL

The German autobahn A5 enters Basel from the north and leads directly to the Rhine and the center of the city. From France the autoroute A35 (E9) peters out at the frontier, and secondary urban roads lead to the center. The A2 autobahn leads off to the rest of Switzerland. Since most of the city's sights are within walking distance of downtown, it's advisable to park your car for the duration of your visit. Expect to pay around 25 SF per day for parking at an all-day garage.

TAXI TRAVEL

Unless you need transportation in the middle of the night, taking taxis makes little sense in Basel: most sights are clustered in the pedestrian zone along tram lines or within a maze of one-way streets. Taxis are costly, less efficient, and less available than the ubiquitous tram.

Taxi Contacts 33er Taxi ☎ *061/3333333.* **Mini Cab** ☎ *061/7777777.* **Taxi-Zentrale** ☎ *061/2222222.*

TRAIN TRAVEL

There are two main rail stations in Basel. The Bahnhof SBB in Grossbasel connects to destinations in Switzerland, France, and with the Intercity Express to Germany. The Badischer Bahnhof in Kleinbasel runs services to Germany. If you're coming from Germany and staying in the Old Town, make sure your train goes all the way to the SBB station on Centralbahnstrasse; many a weary traveler has walked an hour from the German side of town.

Train Contacts Badischer Bahnhof ✉ *Schwarzwalderstr. 200, Kleinbasel* ☎ *061/6901215.* **Bahnhof SBB** ✉ *Centralbahnstr., Bahnhof SBB* ☎ *0900/300300.*

TRAM TRAVEL

Most Basel trams run every 6 to 8 minutes all day, and every 15 minutes in the late evening. Tickets must be bought at the automatic machines at every stop. Stops are marked with green-and-white signs; generally the trams run from 5:30 or 6 in the morning until midnight. *Mehrfahrtenkarten* (multi-journey cards) allow you six trips, saving you 10% on each trip. These cards can be purchased from the ticket office at Barfüsserplatz. *Tageskarten* (day cards), from the ticket machines at the tram stops, allow unlimited travel all day within the central zone for 9 SF.

Kids will love watching the Jean Tinguely–designed Carnival Fountain.

⇨ *For more information on getting here and around, see Travel Smart Switzerland.*

VISITOR INFORMATION
The main tourist information desk in Basel is in the Stadt Casino at Barfüsserplatz and is open weekdays 9–6:30, Saturday 9–5, Sunday and holidays 10–3; there is also a branch located in the Bahnhof SBB train station on Centralbahnstrasse.

Basel Tourismus (*Basel Tourism*). ⊠ *Stadt Casino, Steinenberg 14* ☎ *061/2686868* ⊕ *www.basel.com.*

EXPLORING BASEL

The Rhine divides the city into two distinct sections: on the southwestern bank lies Grossbasel (Greater Basel), the commercial, cultural, and academic center, which encompasses the Altstadt and, directly upriver, the quiet winding medieval streets of St. Alban, where you can stroll along the Rhine, peek into antiques shops, then dine in a cozy bistro. Also in Grossbasel is the upscale and leafy residential neighborhood of Bruderholz, home to one of Switzerland's best restaurants, Stucki. The opposite bank, to the northeast, is Kleinbasel (Small Basel), a Swiss enclave on the "German" side of the Rhine that is the blue-collar quarter of the city. Here are the convention center, chain stores galore, artsy boutiques, and hotels with terraces that afford glorious views of the Münster (cathedral).

The best way to see Basel is on foot or by tram, as the landmarks, museums, and even the zoo radiate from the Old Town center on the Rhine, and the network of rails covers the territory thoroughly.

ALTSTADT

If you stand in the middle of the Marktplatz, or even just watch river traffic from the Mittlere Rheinbrücke, it's easy to envision the Basel of centuries ago. On a bend of the Rhine, Basel's historic center is full of majestic Gothic spires and side streets that are largely unchanged since the 1600s. Still, woven through its delicately preserved architecture are impressive state-of-the-art museums and miles of shop-lined pedestrian zones.

To reach the center of the Altstadt from the SBB, head north (left) on Heuwaage-Viadukt, turn right on Steinenvorstadt and continue until you reach the central square, Barfüsserplatz.

TOP ATTRACTIONS

Fasnacht-Brunnen (*Carnival Fountain*). Created by the Swiss artist Jean Tinguely, known for his work in mechanized media, this witty, animated construction was inaugurated by the city in 1977. Its whimsically styled metal figures busily churn, lash, and spray with unending energy. It is especially impressive in winter when the jets of water freeze, creating unique airborne sculptures. ⊠ *Theaterpl.*.

Haus zum Kirschgarten (*Kirschgarten House*). This 18th-century home was built as a palace for a young silk-ribbon manufacturer. Nowadays it contains the 18th- and 19th-century collections of the city's Historical Museum, displayed as furnishings in period rooms. The timepieces, porcelain, and faience are especially outstanding. ■ **TIP→** It's free the first Sunday of the month. ⊠ *Elisabethenstr. 27–29* ☎ *061/2058600* ⊕ *www. hmb.ch* ⊡ *7 SF* ⊙ *Tues.–Fri. and Sun. 10–5, Sat. 1–5.*

★ **Historisches Museum** (*History Museum*). Housed within the 13th-century Barfüsserkirche (Church of the Shoeless Friars), this museum has an extensive collection of Basel's cathedral treasury, wooden sculptures, coins, armor, and other vestiges of the city's past. An underground gallery displays fully reconstructed medieval and Renaissance guild rooms, complete with stained glass, ceramic stoves, and richly carved wood. Upstairs, next to the choir, the Münster Treasury contains priceless reliquaries in gold. Despite its status as one of the finest examples of Franciscan architecture north of the Alps, the church was deconsecrated in the 19th century and turned into a warehouse until it was rescued in 1894 and converted to its present-day use as a museum. General descriptions are in German, French, and English. ⊠ *Barfüsserpl.* ☎ *061/2058600* ⊕ *www.hmb.ch* ⊡ *12 SF* ⊙ *Tues.–Sun. 10–5.*

Kunsthalle (*Basel Art Gallery*). A must-see for lovers of contemporary art, this museum has hosted landmark, precedent-setting exhibits of contemporary art since 1872. In addition to showing the work of several modern masters early in their careers (Klee and Picasso), the gallery was the first in Europe to display works by American Abstract Expressionists. It's renowned as one of the world's most active institutions dedicated to the presentation of contemporary art. Programs include video installations, performances, and artist talks. ✉ *Steinenberg 7* ☎ *061/2069900* ⊕ *www.kunsthallebasel.ch* ✉ *10 SF includes admission to Architekturmuseum* ☉ *Tues., Wed., and Fri. 11–6, Thurs. 11–8:30, weekends 11–5.*

Fodor's Choice
★ **Kunstmuseum** (*Museum of Fine Arts*). In a city known for its museums, the Kunstmuseum is Basel's heirloom jewel. It was built in 1936 to house one of the world's oldest public art collections, owned by the city since 1661. The imposing facade gives way to an inner courtyard studded with statues. Inside is the world's largest assemblage of paintings by members of the Holbein family, an exceptional group of works by Konrad Witz, and, in fact, such a thorough gathering of the works of their contemporaries that the development of painting in the Upper Rhine is strikingly documented. Other Swiss artists are well represented: from Basel's own Arnold Böcklin to Klimt-like Ferdinand Hodler. The museum's other forte is its international 20th-century collection, from Georges Braque to Jasper Johns. ✉ *St. Alban-Graben 16* ☎ *061/2066262* ⊕ *www. kunstmuseumbasel.ch* ✉ *15 SF* ☉ *Tues.–Sun. 10–6.*

★ **Lällekönig.** When a famous gate tower on the Grossbasel side was destroyed, lost along with it was the notorious Lällekönig, a 15th-century gargoyle of a king whose mechanized clockwork caused the apparatus to stick out his tongue and roll his eyes at the "lesser" citizens across the river. Kleinbasel residents seek symbolic revenge even today. During the annual Vogel Gryff festival, a birdlike figure dances to the midpoint of the bridge, gives the Lällekönig a flash of his backside, and takes the party back to Kleinbasel. You can see a working facsimile of the Lällekönig on the corner of what is now a chain restaurant at Schifflände, while the original still ticks and taunts away in the nether regions of the Historical Museum. ✉ *Schifflände.*

Marktplatz (*Marketplace*). Flowers, fruits, and vegetables are sold most mornings from open stands in this central square. In fall and winter passersby purchase bags of hot roasted chestnuts, the savory scent of which wafts through the square. ✉ *South of Marktg.* ☉ *Market: Mon.– Sat. 6 am–1:30 pm.*

★ **Mittlere Rheinbrücke** (*Middle Rhine Bridge*). Basel's most historic bridge is a good metaphor for the city's successful mix of custom and commerce. It is used as a catwalk for many of Basel's centuries-old celebrations, while beneath its span processions of barges continually glide through its low-slung arches. First built around 1225, the bridge made possible the development of an autonomous Kleinbasel and the consequent rivalry that grew between the two half towns. A stone bridge replaced the wooden one at the turn of the 20th century. ✉ *Schifflände.*

★ **Münster** (*Cathedral*). Basel's cathedral evolved into its current form through a combination of the shifts of nature and the changing whims of architects. A 9th-century Carolingian church, it was consecrated as a cathedral by Henry II in 1019. Additions, alterations, and reconstructions in late Romanesque and early Gothic style continued through the 12th and 13th centuries. When Basel's devastating earthquake destroyed much of the building in 1356, subsequent reconstruction,

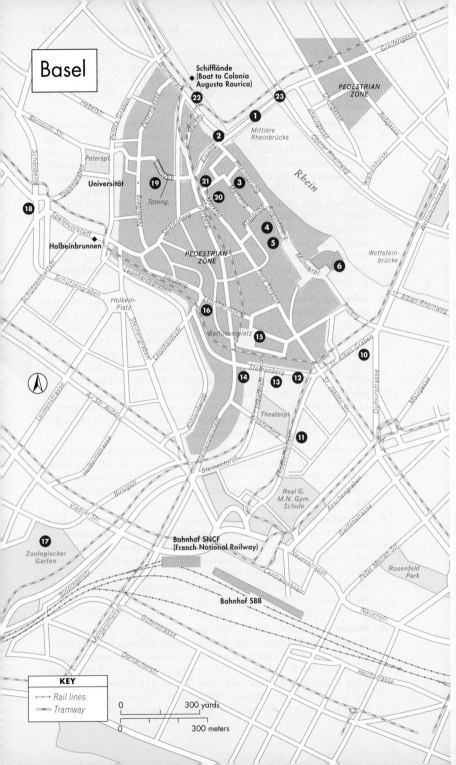

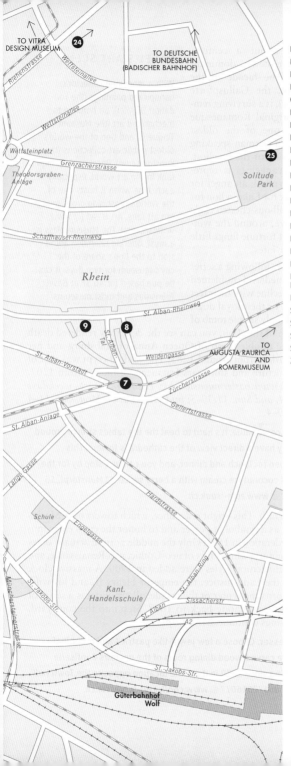

which lasted about a century, adhered to the newly dominant Gothic style. The facade of the north transept, the Galluspforte (St. Gall's Door), is a surviving remnant of the original Romanesque structure. It's one of the oldest carved portals in German-speaking Europe—and one of the loveliest. Each of the evangelists is represented by his symbol: an angel for Matthew, an ox for Luke, a lion for Mark, and a bulbous-chested eagle for John. Above, around the window, a wheel of fortune flings little men off to their fates.

Inside on the left, following a series of tombs of medieval noblemen whose effigies recline with their feet resting on lions or their loyal dogs, stands the strikingly simple **tomb of Erasmus.** North of the choir, you can see the delicately rendered death portraits on the double **tomb of Queen Anna of Habsburg** and her young son, Charles, from around 1285. The vaulted **crypt** was part of the original structure and still bears fragments of murals from 1202. ⊠ *Münsterpl.* ⊕ *www.baslermuenster.ch* ☉ *Easter–mid-Oct., weekdays 10–5, Sat. 10–4, and Sun. 11:30–5; mid-Oct.–Easter, Mon.–Sat. 11–4 and noon 11:30–4.*

> **BASEL'S ART SCENE**
>
> With a renowned collector's handpicked paintings (the Fondation Beyeler), an homage to mechanized art (the Museum Tinguely), and one of the world's oldest public art collections (the Kunstmuseum), Basel earns a high rank in the art world, especially each June when it hosts one of the world's most glamorous modern art fairs, Art Basel (⊕ *www.artbasel.com*). The Museum Pass is a must, offering unlimited admission to the lion's share of the city's museum for two days. It can be purchased for 46 SF at Basel Tourismus and most museums.

QUICK BITES

Zum Isaak. For scenic value, it's hard to beat the the tables strewn around the plaza, as they have a direct view of the cathedral's towers. This friendly place open for lunch and dinner, and you can just stop by for the house dessert of coconut ice cream with a berry sauce. ⊠ *Münsterpl. 16* ☎ *061/2614712* ⊕ *www.zum-isaak.ch.*

★ **Rathaus** (*Town Hall*). This bright red edifice, which towers over Marktplatz, was built as a symbol of power and to honor the city's entry into the Swiss Confederation in 1501. Only the middle portion actually dates from the 16th century; while a mix of neo-Gothic, neo-Renaissance, and art nouveau architectural styles were added in 1900. A massive clock with figures of the Lady Justice, the emperor Henry II, and his wife, Kunegunde, adorns the center of the facade; all around it is a series of colorful oil paintings, dating back to 1608. Step into the courtyard, where the paintings continue. ⊠ *Marktpl..*

QUICK BITES

Confiserie Schiesser. Choose a few jewel-like pastries and order leaf-brewed tea in the carved-wood dining room of the upstairs Confiserie Schiesser, steeping since 1870 in its prime location opposite the Town Hall. ⊠ *Marktpl. 19* ☎ *061/2616077* ⊕ *www.confiserie-schiesser.ch.*

A GOOD WALK

Six bridges link the two halves of the city; the most picturesque is the **Mittlere Rheinbrücke**. On the corner at Schifflände, you can see a facsimile of the infamous **Lällekönig**, a 17th-century gargoyle mechanized to stick out his tongue and roll his eyes at his rivals across the river. Walking across the bridge, you'll see Basel's peculiar, gondola-like ferryboats (you can ride one for 1.60 SF).

Back across the Mittlere Rheinbrücke in the Altstadt, turn left up a steep alley called the **Rheinsprung**, banked with 15th- and 16th-century houses. Turn right at Archivgässlein, and you'll come to the **Martinskirche**, the city's oldest parish church, dating from 1287.

Continue along Martinsgasse to the elegant neighboring courtyards of the **Blaues und Weisses Haus**, meeting place of kings. Just beyond, turn left and head past the basilisk fountain into Augustinergasse; no. 2 is the **Naturhistorisches Museum**, and just beyond is the **Museum der Kulturen Basel**, both of which house great natural history and prehistory collections.

Augustinergasse leads into the Münsterplatz, dominated by the striking red-sandstone 12th-century **Münster**, burial place of Erasmus. Walk around to the cathedral's riverside to the Pfalz terrace for wide views of the river, the Altstadt, Kleinbasel, and the Black Forest.

From the Münsterplatz, head down Rittergasse to the first busy cross street. Ahead of you is St. Alban-Vorstadt, which leads to the **St. Alban-Tor**, one of the original 13th-century city gates. St. Alban-Tal leads from St. Alban-Vorstadt down to St.

Alban-Rheinweg on the Rhine to the **Museum für Gegenwartskunst** (Museum of Contemporary Art).

Take St. Alban-Rheinweg along the riverside, ascend the Wettstein Bridge stairways, and head left onto St. Alban-Graben to find the **Kunstmuseum,** home of one of Europe's oldest public collections. Continue down St. Alban-Graben to the intersection of Steinenberg. A few blocks straight ahead into Elisabethenstrasse will take you to the **Haus zum Kirschgarten**, a showcase of 18th- and 19th-century decorative arts. To circle back into the center of the Altstadt, however, veer right on Steinenberg, which goes by the **Kunsthalle.**

Continue on Steinenberg until it opens out onto the bustling Barfüsserplatz and the Spielzeug Welten Museum Basel and the **Historisches Museum**. Behind the tram concourse on Barfüsserplatz, follow the pedestrian zone to Leonhardsberg, which leads left up the stairs to the late-Gothic **Leonhardskirche**. Continue along the church walk into Heuberg street, the spine of one of the loveliest sections of old Basel. On Spalenvorstadt perches the **Holbeinbrunnen**, styled from a drawing by Hans Holbein. The Spalenvorstadt stretches to the 14th-century **Spalentor** gate.

7

The Kunstmuseum is known worldwide for its collection of statues and paintings by the Holbein family.

WORTH NOTING

Blaues und Weisses Haus (*Blue and White Houses*). Built between 1763 and 1775 for two of the city's most successful silk ribbon merchants, these were the residences of the brothers Lukas and Jakob Sarasin. In 1777 the emperor Joseph II of Austria was a guest in the White House. Adding that to the roster of Blue House visitor names—including Czar Alexander of Russia, Emperor Francis of Austria, and King Friedrich Wilhelm III of Prussia, who met for dinner here in 1814—brings the guest book over the top. The restored houses look more cream and gray these days, but are clearly labeled for curious passersby. ⊠ *Martinsg..*

Grand Hotel Les Trois Rois (*Three Kings Hotel*). The statues on the facade depict the biblical three wise men and are thought to date from 1754. The young general Napoléon Bonaparte lunched here in 1797 and an opulently decorated suite is named after him. Noteworthy guests have included Queen Elizabeth II, Charles Dickens, and Picasso. In 1897 the great Hungarian-born Jewish writer Theodor Herzl stayed here during the first Zionist Congress, which laid the groundwork for the founding of the state of Israel. ⊠ *Blumenrain 8* ⊕ *www.lestroisrois.com.*

Museum der Kulturen Basel (*Basel Museum of Cultures*). After a radical renovation by star architects Herzog and de Meuron, the ethnographic museum held its much-awaited reopening in September 2011. "Expeditions: The World in a Suitcase," the first permanent exhibit to open since the museum's makeover, displays what Basel anthropologists from the 19th and 20th centuries brought back from their expeditions around the globe. Three to four rotating exhibitions explore the history of Switzerland and its neighbors. Descriptions are available

CLOSE UP

Fasnacht

Dating from the Middle Ages, Fasnacht, Switzerland's best-known festival, draws people from all over the world. Beginning at 4 am on the Monday following Ash Wednesday, all lights are turned off and the city is illuminated by the lanterns of the *Cliques* (carnival associations). The event features a blast of fifes and drums, boisterous *Guggemusik* (played by enthusiastic, rather than talented, marching bands), and a covering of confetti. The streets are packed with zillions of onlookers who have fortified themselves against the cold morning with a bowl of the traditional *Mehlsuppe* (flour soup). A colorful masked procession traverses the Old Town until dawn, and continues for the next two days.

in German, French, English, and sometimes Italian. ⊠ *Münsterpl. 20* ☎ *061/2665600* ⊕ *www.mkb.ch* 🎫 *16 SF* ☉ *Tues.–Sun. 10–5.*

☪ **Naturhistorisches Museum** (*Natural History Museum*). All aspects of the natural sciences—from the history of the earth to extinct mammals to interesting insects—are featured here. A tour is like an expedition into the remotest corners of the planet, where natural objects, large and small, wait to be discovered, inspected, and contemplated. Most descriptive materials are in German only. ⊠ *Augustinerg. 2* ☎ *061/2665500* ⊕ *www.nmb.bs.ch* 🎫 *7 SF* ☉ *Tues.–Sun. 10–5.*

Pharmazie-Historisches Museum (*Museum of Pharmaceutical History*). This museum showcases original and re-created pharmacy counters and all kinds of beakers and flacons, and old remedies. To balance out the scientific quota, there is also a look at the history of alchemy. The museum is housed in Zum Vorderen Sessel, a home once frequented by Paracelsus. English-language information sheets are available. ⊠ *Totengässlein 3* ☎ *061/2649111* ⊕ *www.pharmaziemuseum.ch* 🎫 *8 SF* ☉ *Tues.–Fri. 10–6, Sat. 10–5.*

☪ **Spielzeug Welten Museum Basel** (*World Toy Museum Basel*). Bordering on the Barfüsserplatz, this museum has several floors filled with 18th-, 19th-, and 20th-century toys, including a cast of 2,500 teddy bears. The dollhouses, on a 1:12 scale, are all artistically displayed. ⊠ *Steinenvorstadt 1* ☎ *061/2259595* ⊕ *www.spielzeug-welten-museum-basel.ch* 🎫 *7 SF* ☉ *Daily 10–6.*

Spalentor (*Spalen Gate*). Like the St. Alban-Tor, the Spalentor served as one of Basel's medieval city gates. More imposing than graceful, the 14th-century structure has a toothy wooden portcullis; note Basel's coat of arms atop the gate. ⊠ *Spalenvorstadt.*

You can get good views of the Altstadt and the Mittlere Rheinbrücke from Kleinbasel.

KLEINBASEL

More down-to-earth than its "big brother" across the river, Kleinbasel is where you'll see people living rather than visiting. Immigrants from India, Turkey, the Balkans, and beyond mix well with young people on a budget in the narrow streets, which are lined with small shops, corner bars, and eateries. Warm weather attracts a crowd along the banks of the Rhine and the green riverside promenade, and in June the neighborhood transforms completely into hipster central as the rich and famous flock to Art Basel.

Museum Tinguely. As you circle the innovative and quirky installations at Museum Tinguely, you may have a few questions. How do they work? What do they mean? And where did the artist find this stuff? Born in Fribourg, 20th-century master Jean Tinguely is best known for his whimsical *métaméchaniques* (mechanical sculptures), which transform machinery, appliances, and items straight from the junk heap into ironic and often macabre statements. For instance, *Le Ballet des Pauvres*, from 1961, suspends a hinged leg with a moth-eaten sock, a horse tail and a fox pelt, a cafeteria tray, and a blood-soaked nightgown, all of which dangle and dance on command. The wing of the museum projecting over the Rhine has a splendid river view of Basel. Many of the sculptures are activated at preset times, typically every 5–15 minutes, and it pays to wait and see them in action. Admission to temporary exhibitions is included in the entrance fee. Information sheets are available in English. ✉ *Paul Sacher-Anlage 2, Kleinbasel* ☎ *061/6819320* ⊕ *www.tinguely. ch* ⏱ *15 SF* ⊙ *Tues.–Sun. 11–6.*

Statue of Helvetia. What would the woman pictured on most Swiss coins do if freed from the confines of currency? With spear and shield set aside (and with a packed suitcase in hand), this humanistic interpretation shows her seemingly contemplating the possibilities from a perch not far from the border of her homeland and the wide world beyond. ⊠ *On the edge of Mittlere Rheinbrücke, Kleinbasel.*

ST. ALBAN

Just off the very busy crossing of Sankt Alban Graben and Durfourstrasse is quiet St. Alban, also known as Dalbe to locals. A neighborhood of old patrician town houses and villas, it's still home to Basel's oldest affluent families and a pleasant mix of museums and restaurants.

☙ **Basler Papiermühle** (*Basel Paper Mill*). In a beautifully restored medieval mill with a still functioning waterwheel, this museum honoring paper, writing, and printing is surprisingly accessible. Demonstrations of papermaking, typesetting, and bookbinding reveal much about the ancient craft. You can participate in a papermaking process, beginning with the pulpy raw material simmering in the "visitors' vat" and take home a sheet as a unique souvenir. Kids can try out quills and ink or spell out their names in pieces of type for printing. Exhibits are in German, French, and English. ⊠ *St. Alban-Tal 37, St. Alban* 🕾 *061/2259090* ⊕ *www.papiermuseum.ch* 🎫 *14 SF* ☉ *Tues.–Fri., Sun. 11–5, Sat. 1–5.*

Museum für Gegenwartskunst (*Museum of Contemporary Art*). Bringing the city's art collections up to the present, this museum focuses on works from the 1960s onward. The fittingly modern building looks as though it has shouldered its way in between the street's half-timber houses. The language of the exhibition materials typically corresponds to the nationality of the artists. ⊠ *St. Alban-Rheinweg 60, St. Alban* 🕾 *061/2066262* ⊕ *www.kunstmuseumbasel.ch* 🎫 *15 SF* ☉ *Tues.–Sun. 11–6.*

St. Alban-Tor (*St. Alban's Gate*). This original medieval city gate is set amid a lovely garden near remnants of the town's ramparts. Parts of the gate date from the end of the 14th century. ⊠ *St. Alban-Vorstadt, St. Alban.*

ZOO

A zoo with a conscience, its management makes an effort to both educate the public and help save rare species from extinction, making visits an exciting experience, especially for children.

☙ **Zoologischer Garten** (*Zoological Garden*). Referred to by Baslers as *Zolli,* this zoo is famed for its rhinoceroses, hippopotamuses, gorillas, and fabulous vivarium filled with fish and reptiles. Animal enclosures are scattered around and almost hidden by the garden environment. Very child-friendly, the zoo has a handy and enormous restaurant. ⊠ *Binningerstr. 40, Zoo* 🕾 *061/2953535* ⊕ *www.zoobasel.ch* 🎫 *18 SF* ☉ *Nov.–Feb., daily 8–5:30; Mar., Apr., Sept., and Oct., daily 8–6; May–Aug., daily 8–6:30.*

COLONIA AUGUSTA RAURICA (AUGST)

Founded in 44–43 BC, Augst is the oldest Roman settlement on the Rhine, and today has been largely reconstructed as a noted museum of ancient Roman antiquities (one suspects the Swiss might have done the same with Rome's Colosseum if they had gotten their hands on it). The site is reachable by car from Basel in 15 minutes or in summer via a leisurely boat trip up the river. From the Bahnhof SBB take train S1 to Kaiseraugst, or Bus 81 from Basel-Aeschenplatz to Augst; thereafter it takes approximately 10 minutes from either of these stops to walk uphill to the Roman Museum. To view the restoration areas scattered around the almost suburban neighborhood, be prepared for a fair bit of walking.

WORD OF MOUTH

"There is a tourist tram you can catch which gives you a tour of Basel. The hotel gave us a transport pass for the time we were staying in Basel, which we thought was fabulous (how many cities in the world do that?)."
—Kay

★ **Augusta Raurica.** The remains of this 2,000-year-old Roman settlement have been extensively rebuilt, with substantial portions of the ancient town walls and gates, streets, water pipes, and heating systems all in evidence. The 1st-century-BC theater, described as the best-preserved ancient complex north of the Alps, has been gloriously restored in the last few years. ⊠ *Giebenacherstr. 17, Augst* ⊕ *www.augustaraurica.ch* 🎟 *Free* ☉ *Daily 10–5.*

Römermuseum (*Roman Museum*). Roman daily life is vividly depicted in this carefully rebuilt home. Everything, from the thermal baths to the ancient board games in the sitting rooms has been completely re-created. The museum also exhibits the largest trove of Roman silver known to exist, which was unearthed in 1962. The objects, dating mostly from the 4th century, are believed to have been buried by the Romans in 350 to protect them from the ravages of the Alemanni, the German tribes who drove the Romans out of Switzerland. English, French, and German brochures are available. ⊠ *Giebenacherstr. 17, Augst* ☎ *061/8162222* ⊕ *www.augustaraurica.ch* 🎟 *7 SF* ☉ *Mar.–Oct., Mon. 1–5 and Tues.–Sun. 10–5; Nov.–Feb., Mon. 1–5 and Tues.–Sun. 11–5.*

BASEL ENVIRONS

A trip outside Basel is worth it, whether you visit the spectacular grounds of the Fondation Beyeler or cross the border to visit Germany's famous Vitra Design Museum, where private foundations enhance the area's reputation as a center for art.

Fodor's Choice ★ **Fondation Beyeler.** For decades, the world's most prestigious art collectors would journey to Basel to worship at the feet of one of modern art's greatest gallery owners, Ernst Beyeler. At the end of his phenomenal career, he left his incomparable collection to the public and commissioned the noted architect Renzo Piano to build a museum in the town of Riehen, on the outskirts of Basel. The Fondation Beyeler presents an astonishingly well-rounded collection of modern art, and Piano's simple lines direct attention to more than 200 great works. The collection's catalog reads like a who's who of modern artists—Cézanne, Matisse, Lichtenstein, and Rauschenberg.

In this bright and open setting, Giacometti's wiry sculptures stretch toward the ceiling and Monet's water lilies seem to spill from the canvas into an outdoor reflecting pool. Indigenous carved figures from New Guinea and Nigeria stare into the faces on canvases by Klee and Dubuffet. A stellar selection of Picassos is juxtaposed with views of blue skies. Besides the permanent collection, several prestigious art exhibits every year attract art lovers from around the globe. The tram trip from Schifflände takes about 20 minutes. Public tours in English are offered one Sunday each month, or private tours can be arranged. ⊠ *Baselstr. 101, Riehen* ☎ *061/6459700* ⊕ *www.beyeler.com* 🖭 *25 SF* ⊙ *Thurs.– Tues. 10–6, Wed. 10–8.*

OFF THE BEATEN PATH

Vitra Design Museum. In the German town of Weil am Rhein, this museum's main building is a startling white geometric jumble designed by famed architect Frank Gehry. The renowned design museum hosts large-scale temporary exhibits that put architecture, art, and everyday design on display. During guided tours, buildings by architectural masters, including the exquisitely angular Fire Station by Zaha Hadid and the curved symmetry of the Conference Pavilion by Tadao Ando, can be visited. To get here by car, take A5/E35 north from Basel toward Karlsruhe; turn right onto Route 532, then turn left after exiting at Weil am Rhein. The museum is 1½ km (about 1 mile) ahead on the right. Or from either Claraplatz or the Badischer Bahnof train station in Basel, take Bus 55 toward Kandern to the Vitra stop (20 minutes). Bring your passport and get there by noon or 2 for a tour in English. ⊠ *Charles-Eames-Str. 1, Weil am Rhein, Germany* ☎ *07621/7023200* ⊕ *www. design-museum.de* 🖭 *€8* ⊙ *Daily 10–6.*

WHERE TO EAT

Classic but boundary pushing, bank-breaking but exquisite gourmet cuisine has long been one of Basel's fortes. New trends are appearing and disappearing in the blink of an eye. Snuggled between three countries, Basel has inherited the culinary interests of each, and excels with offering its own specialties and those of its neighbors . . . and beyond.

Eating out here, as anywhere in Switzerland, can be a costly delight, and top-of-the-range restaurants are plentiful. Stucki, a landmark establishment, remains a top spot for gourmet dining, especially with the addition of one of Switzerland's top chefs, Tanja Grandits. Zum Goldenen Sternen and Teufelhof never go out of fashion with their French-inflected cuisine. At the other end of the scale, you will never have to go far for a German-style sausage, Italian pasta, or mouthwatering desserts, as reliable local restaurants and cafés can be found on practically every street. Basel is, in fact, full of comfortable haunts. The city's down-to-earth fare owes its roots to the Germanic hordes who

The Fondation Beyeler: an incredible collection of contemporary and modern art housed in a museum designed by Renzo Piano.

arrived here to rout the ancient Romans, bringing with them homey fare like schnitzel and *Spätzli* (tiny flour dumplings), all to be washed down with beer.

As for dining specialties, the proximity of the Rhine means that most Basel restaurants serve a variety of freshwater fish. If the city could claim a regional specialty, it would be salmon. (These days much of it is shipped in from elsewhere, but the Rhine variety is making a comeback.) The meaty fish is best served *nach Basler Art* (Basel-style), meaning in a white-wine marinade with fried onions on top. Try it with a bottle of the fruity local Riesling.

If you're on the Marktplatz, join other hungry shoppers standing in front of mobile kitchens, holding bare *Wienerli* (hot dogs) and dipping them into thick golden mustard. You should also indulge in *Kaffee und Kuchen*—the late-afternoon coffee break the neighboring Germans live for. But locals have their own version: instead of a large slice of creamed cake, they select tiny sweet pastries—two or three to a saucer—and may opt for a delicate Chinese tea instead of a Kaffee.

Refined Indian, Thai, and Turkish restaurants are popping up around town, and there are some fun themed spots worth checking out, such as Das Neue Rialto, which sells food and the designer furniture you sit on to eat it. This is a great concept in a city renowned for its art-filled atmosphere. After all, this is Switzerland, where anything you sit on or see that takes your fancy you should be able to order to go, no?

For a satisfying and budget-friendly lunch, many restaurants offer lunch specials (*Tagesmenu*) that include a dish of the day, a starter or salad, and maybe even a dessert. They are the best way to eat well on a budget.

Smoking is banned in all restaurants in Basel, but there are a few work-arounds. With the purchase of a "Fumoir Card," smokers can light up in participating bars and lounges for 10 SF per year.

Prices in the reviews are the average cost of a main course at dinner or, if dinner is not served, at lunch.

ALTSTADT

$$$
FRENCH
Fodor'sChoice
★
✕ **Bel Étage/Atelier.** This grand old Heuberg mansion has been trans-formed into a cultural center boasting two restaurants, a trendy bar, and even medieval ruins in the basement. The formal Bel Étage showcases chef Michael Baader's masterly culinary inventions, with dishes such as anglerfish saltimbocca with sage, Parmesan gnocchi, and zucchini, or lamb with lavender honey sauce and risotto with artichokes. Sip wines by the glass, then buy the bottles you'd like to take home in the on-site wineshop. The artsy Atelier serves modern cuisine made with regional ingredients and features a mural where patrons can paint during din-ner. [$] *Average main: 59 SF* ⊠ *Hotel Teufelhof, Leonhardsgraben 49* 🕾 *061/2611010* ⊕ *www.teufelhof.com* ⊗ *Bel Étage closed Sun. and Mon. No lunch Sat.*

$$$
ITALIAN
✕ **Chez Donati.** Now under ownership of the Grand Hotel Les Trois Rois, and just a five-minute stroll away, this much-loved establishment has been serving up a selection of Italian standards for more than 50 years, and is famous for its antipasti and to-die-for desserts. Other specialties include osso buco with saffron risotto and scampi with a special house sauce. The traditional, gilt-framed Venetian paintings are supplemented with modern art (world masters have long convened here, including Andy Warhol, Jean Tinguely, and Pablo Picasso). Dine while enjoying the view of the Rhine from your white-draped table. Riverside terrace seating is available. [$] *Average main: 60 SF* ⊠ *Grand Hotel Les Trois Rois, St. Johanns-Vorstadt 48* 🕾 *061/3220919* ⊕ *www.lestroisrois.com* ⊗ *Closed Sun. and Mon. and mid-July–mid-Aug.*

$$
SWISS
✕ **Löwenzorn.** This classic, comfortable gathering place serves typical Swiss food, including the traditional and filling *Kalbsläberli und Rösti* (veal liver with grated, fried potatoes). You can also try the more sophis-ticated grilled pike perch with ratatouille, roasted pine nuts, and rice. Regulars come for a beer, a full plate, and some laughs with the friendly staff. With stained-glass lamps, ceramic stoves, and attractive wood-work, it's a nice mix of bistro and beer hall. In summer, enjoy grilled *Schweinswürstl* (pork sausages) in the beer garden. [$] *Average main: 40 SF* ⊠ *Gemsberg 2–4* 🕾 *061/2614213* ⊕ *www.loewenzorn.ch.*

$
ITALIAN
✕ **Manger & Boire.** Take a break in this quiet little right in the middle of the shopping mayhem of Gerbergasse. Serving smaller portions of dishes from the formal upstairs dining room—a bright, elegantly appointed space that offers elaborate dishes made with market ingre-dients—the friendly staff will bring you tasty inventions like mari-nated beef with beets and a side of horseradish, or squid ink ravioli stuffed with salmon and served with a saffron sauce. In warm weather, outdoor seating at small tables in the cobblestone alley completes the

Take a break from museum hopping at one of Basel's many casual cafés.

medieval feel. $ *Average main: 25 SF* ✉ *Gerberg. 81* ☎ *061/2623160* ⊕ *www.mangerboire.ch.*

$$
INTERNATIONAL

✕ **ONO.** With its floor-to-ceiling windows, vaulted ceilings, and wide-open spaces, this hot spot on the edge of the Old Town offers a cosmopolitan atmosphere where you can find cuisine from around the world. There's also an impressive cocktail bar and music until the wee hours of the morning. The market-fresh menu changes daily, but the *salade de chevre chaud croustillant* (warm and crispy goat cheese salad) with truffle oil and honey is a tasty classic with a twist. The organic beef fillet from Argentina, served with a morel sauce, is a melt-in-your mouth main course. The sidewalk terrace is a perfect spot to lunch and people-watch in warm weather. $ *Average main: 38 SF* ✉ *Leonhardsgraben 2* ☎ *061/3227070* ⊕ *www.ono-lifestyle.ch* ☉ *Closed Sun.*

$$
FRENCH
★

✕ **Schlüsselzunft.** This historic guildhall has been transformed into an airy and elegant dining room. The extremely popular dining room, famous for its traditional ceramic stove, draws a crowd with its business lunches. Dinner features well-executed seasonal cuisine such as pike perch fillets served on red lentils with a parsley root sauce. Another winner is the lamb with rosemary risotto, ratatouille, and balsamic essence. Also on the premises is an inexpensive courtyard café called the Schlüsselhöfli, with a menu that changes daily. $ *Average main: 42 SF* ✉ *Freie Str. 25* ☎ *061/2612046* ⊕ *www.schluesselzunft.ch* ◿ *Reservations essential* ☉ *Closed Sun. in June–Aug.*

KLEINBASEL

$$ ✕ **Brauerei Fischerstube.** If you're serious about sampling the local color,
SWISS stop in here for a cold one. The Fischerstube, a famous local brewery,
★ produces its own lagers and ales in the deep, frothing copper tanks
you see at the end of the room. If you like their Ueli Bier, named for a
Fasnacht jester, you can buy a keg to take home. The look is simple,
with whitewashed walls and sanded wooden tables, offering a range
of tasty snacks like oven-fresh pretzels to heartier local dishes of steak
or sour beef liver with Rösti, which tastes a lot better than it sounds.
In summer, the rooftop beer garden is very popular. $ *Average main:
30 SF* ⊠ *Rheing. 45, Kleinbasel* ☎ *061/6929200* ⊕ *www.restaurant-
fischerstube.ch* ⊰ *Reservations essential.*

ST. ALBAN

$ ✕ **Restaurant/Café Papiermühle.** With the splashing of the paper mill's
CAFÉ waterwheel in the background, this is a restful spot for lunch or after-
★ noon coffee (it's only open until 6 pm, except on Friday when it's open
until midnight). The hand-scrawled chalkboard lists salads, soups, and
pasta dishes. After 3 pm hot food is no longer served, but sandwiches
and other snacks are available. Hand signals are all you need to order a
slice of one of the delicious homemade cakes on display. Sunday morn-
ings find this one of Basel's most popular brunch locations—try the
Birchermüsli, the original, creamy, fruity version of muesli. $ *Average
main: 22 SF* ⊠ *St. Alban-Tal 35, St. Alban* ☎ *061/2724848* ⊕ *www.
papiermuehle.ch* ▭ *No credit cards* ⊘ *Closed Mon.*

$$$ ✕ **St. Alban-Eck.** This neighborhood restaurant, a five-minute walk from
FRENCH the Kunstmuseum, is a well-known landmark in St. Alban. In a half-
timber house, it's a real *petit coin sympa* (friendly little place), with
plank wainscoting in natural wood, framed historic prints, and net
curtains. The cuisine gracefully mixes Swiss and French favorites. Try
the market-fresh grilled catfish with shrimp ragout and a fennel-tomato
sauce, or a locally sourced veal steak with pink pepper and a white balsamic vinegar sauce, both complemented by seasonal vegetables. $ *Av-
erage main: 49 SF* ⊠ *St. Alban-Vorstadt 60, St. Alban* ☎ *061/2710320*
⊕ *www.st-alban-eck.ch* ⊰ *Reservations essential* ⊘ *Closed Sun. and
mid-July–mid-Aug. No lunch Sat.*

$$$ ✕ **Zum Goldenen Sternen.** Dating from 1412, this *Gasthof* claims to be the
FRENCH oldest restaurant in Switzerland, even though the building was moved
Fodor'sChoice to its current riverside site in 1974. Impeccable restoration retained
★ the antique beams, stenciled ceilings, and unvarnished planks of the
original Baroque and Gothic construction. In summer you can opt for
a table on the river terrace out front or in the rear garden. Though it
could easily play a secondary role, the food does its best to live up to
the stunning setting with dishes like roast lamb sirloin with an olive-
and-celery crust, Mediterranean-style vegetables, and praline sweet
potatoes with sesame seeds, or a skewer of monkfish, scallops, and
giant prawns on herb risotto and braised fennel. There's also a seven-
course tasting menu that changes monthly. $ *Average main: €48* ⊠ *St.*

Alban-Rheinweg 70, St. Alban ☎ *061/2721666* 🌐 *www.sternen-basel.ch* ✍ *Reservations essential.*

ZOO

$ ITALIAN ★ 🍴 **Das Neue Rialto.** If you find you're sitting pretty in this trendsetting restaurant, you can always bring your chair home with you. Chef Niggi Rechsteiner allows you to enjoy his culinary creations in a designer space where all the furniture is for sale. Set on the second floor of a swimming pool complex, this lunch-only spot offers plenty of seasonal dishes—grilled pike perch with vegetables wrapped in puff pastry, or pasta with grilled garlic, bell pepper strips, and *merguez* sausage are two tasty options. [$] *Average main: 20 SF* ✉ *Birsigstr. 45, Zoo* ☎ *061/2053145* 🌐 *www.dasneuerialto.ch* ✍ *Reservations essential* ⏲ *Closed weekends. No dinner.*

BRUDERHOLZ

$$$ CONTEMPORARY Fodor's Choice ★ 🍴 **Stucki.** One of Switzerland's top chefs, Tanja Grandits gives her guests a delightful culinary experience in a refined—but not uptight—setting. Contrasting flavors, colors, and textures in delightful creations such as a watermelon rose juice amuse-bouche topped with a cumin croquette, the German-born chef calls her cuisine style "aroma kitchen." Exciting seasonal choices include calamaretti seasoned with chili salt and served on an anise-flavored tomato-and-focaccia salad, and organic salmon in a miso-hollandaise sauce with pistachio pesto. The restaurant is in the residential neighborhood of Bruderholz; take tram No. 15 from Marktplatz toward Bruderholz and get off at Radio Studio Basel. [$] *Average main: 60 SF* ✉ *Bruderholzallee 42, Bruderholz* ☎ *061/3618222* 🌐 *www.stuckibasel.ch* ✍ *Reservations essential* ⏲ *Closed Sun. and Mon.*

WHERE TO STAY

Grand as a palace? Way-cool as a converted prison? An art lover's paradise? Or cozy and comfortably lived-in? The hotel scene in Basel is definitely varied. But with its busy convention center offering a different trade fair most months, this is a city that prides itself on being especially business-friendly. Many hotels pamper their business clientele (a never-ending supply), with leisure travelers taking second place. Signs pointing to meeting rooms and business centers are often more prominent than any paintings on the wall. But don't write off the city's business-oriented hotels—these often drop their prices significantly on weekends and offer superb amenities.

At the top of the pile is the Grand Hotel Les Trois Rois, which feels like a palace and is frequented by visiting heads of state and the glitterati. Originality also abounds, ranging from the converted prison that is now the trendy Au Violon to the artist's canvas known as the Teufelhof. Many hotels offer a river view and a calm, relaxed, designer interior.

Cheaper hotels range from the all-orange extravaganza of Easyhotel to the homely feel of Hecht am Rhein.

When there's a trade fair in town, prices shoot through the roof, and every bed for miles can be filled. This is also true at Fasnacht, during Art Basel, and many of the other festivals. Staying connected is getting easier as hotels are increasingly offering free Wi-Fi. Breakfast tends to be an add-on at budget hotels, while higher-end establishments include it. All Basel hotels equip their guests with free travel passes for use in the city during their stay.

Prices in the reviews are the lowest cost of a standard double room in high season.

ALTSTADT

$$$$ HOTEL Fodor's Choice ★ 🏨 **Grand Hotel Les Trois Rois.** Basel's leading rendezvous for the rich and famous ever since three 11th-century kings (Conrad II, Henry III, and Rudolf III) once convened here, the Trois Rois has long been an integral part of Basel history. **Pros:** regal prices are reflected in regal service; bathrooms have heated floors; wide array of dining choices. **Cons:** ambience of the rooms is somewhat spoiled by the flat-screen TVs. [$] *Rooms from: 515 SF* ✉ *Blumenrain 8* ☎ *061/2605050* 🌐 *www.lestroisrois.com* 🛏 *83 rooms, 18 suites* 🍴 *Breakfast.*

$ HOTEL 🏨 **Hotel Basel.** Just off the market square, this modern hotel is steps from all the attractions of the Old Town. **Pros:** close to the river; friendly and accommodating staff; attractive weekend rates. **Cons:** during the week the clientele means business; streamlined decor can seem somewhat stark. [$] *Rooms from: 190 SF* ✉ *Münzg. 12* ☎ *061/2646800* 🌐 *www.hotel-basel.ch* 🛏 *69 rooms, 3 suites* 🍴 *No meals.*

$ HOTEL ★ 🏨 **Hotel Brasserie Au Violon.** The former residents here—priests and prisoners—never had it so good. **Pros:** fresh breakfast favorites are included and served in a Provençal-style dining room. **Cons:** some small rooms; safes only available at reception. [$] *Rooms from: 160 SF* ✉ *Im Lohnhof 4* ☎ *061/2698711* 🌐 *www.au-violon.com* 🛏 *20 rooms* 🕒 *Closed between Christmas and New Year's* 🍴 *Breakfast.*

$ HOTEL 🏨 **Rochat.** The location of this modest but roomy hotel is a great asset; set across from the university, it's in a quiet area far from the shopping masses. **Pros:** good breakfast buffet; service polite and to the point. **Cons:** try not to get lost in the rabbit warren of corridors; not easily accessible for wheelchair users. [$] *Rooms from: 190 SF* ✉ *Petersgraben 23* ☎ *061/2618140* 🌐 *www.hotelrochat.ch* 🛏 *50 rooms* 🍴 *Breakfast.*

$$ HOTEL 🏨 **Teufelhof.** The Teufelhof is actually two hotels in one: the Art Hotel has nine rooms that are works of art in their own right, as each is regularly redecorated by a different Swiss artist. **Pros:** great location—only three tram stops away from the main station. **Cons:** can be noisy in summer; no air-conditioning. [$] *Rooms from: 250 SF* ✉ *Leonhardsgraben 49* ☎ *061/2611010* 🌐 *www.teufelhof.com* 🛏 *33 rooms, 5 suites* 🍴 *Breakfast.*

KLEINBASEL

$ **EasyHotel.** Less is definitely more at the EasyHotel, where guest rooms
HOTEL   are compact, minimalist, and decorated with up-to-date decor and vivid
colors. **Pros:** for a central location (close to the convention center where
Art Basel and Baselworld are held every year), impeccably clean rooms,
and the ease of booking immediately day or night on the Internet,
this hotel chain is hard to beat. **Cons:** no lobby; rooms can only be
booked online. $ *Rooms from: 70 SF* ✉ *Riehenring 109, Kleinbasel*
☎ *0900/327927* ⊕ *www.easyhotel.com* ↻ *24 rooms* ⦿ *No meals.*

$ **Hecht am Rhein.** Sandwiched between two more expensive hotels, this
HOTEL   budget lodging has guest rooms that seem bigger than in the neighboring
★   establishments. **Pros:** the price is right; great riverside location. **Cons:**
shared bathrooms; common areas are a bit musty. $ *Rooms from: 130*
SF ✉ *Rheing. 8, Kleinbasel* ☎ *061/6901515* ⊕ *www.hotelbasel.ch* ↻ *30*
rooms ⦿ *Breakfast.*

$$ **Krafft.** On the waterfront, Krafft has a can't-get-any-better location
HOTEL   that makes it perfect for people-watching. **Pros:** refreshment station
Fodor'sChoice   on each floor; very friendly staff. **Cons:** loud chatter sometimes drifts
★   up to the rooms. $ *Rooms from: 285 SF* ✉ *Rheing. 12, Kleinbasel*
☎ *061/6909130* ⊕ *www.krafftbasel.ch* ↻ *52 rooms, 11 suites.*

BAHNHOF SBB

$ **City Inn.** If you'd rather do without all the pomp and circumstance,
HOTEL   consider one of the brightly colored, crisply furnished rooms at the City
★   Inn. **Pros:** you can use the excellent facilities of Hotel Euler. **Cons:** eleva-
tor doesn't reach all levels; rooms have a spartan feel. $ *Rooms from:*
108 SF ✉ *Centralbahnpl. 14, Bahnhof SBB* ☎ *061/2758000* ⊕ *www.*
cityinn.ch ↻ *30 rooms* ⦿ *No meals.*

$ **Hotel Euler.** This 150-year-old landmark has been tastefully renovated
HOTEL   throughout to bring out the best of its original features, including elabo-
★   rate gilt-edged mirrors and stucco ceiling moldings. **Pros:** near the train
station and close to the center of town; oversized terrace great for
people-watching. **Cons:** glazed windows reduce noise from the trams
outside, but sometimes not enough. $ *Rooms from: 157 SF* ✉ *Central-*
bahnpl. 14, Bahnhof SBB ☎ *061/2758000* ⊕ *www.hoteleuler.ch* ↻ *60*
rooms, 6 junior suites ⦿ *No meals.*

NIGHTLIFE AND THE ARTS

For a complete listing of events, pick up a copy of *Basel Live,* a book-
let published every two weeks (partially in English). Also note *Events
Highlights,* a flyer printed every six months in English. Both are avail-
able at the tourist office and hotel desks. If you'd like to play it by ear,
the Steinenvorstadt is crowded with bars filled with young people, and
on the Kleinbasel side there are late-night bars along Oberer Rheinweg.

NIGHTLIFE

ALTSTADT
BARS AND LOUNGES
Baragraph. With its back-to-the-1970s feel, the centrally located Baragraph attracts a mixed crowd for its beer and cocktails. The staff is generous with the peanuts. ✉ *Kohlenberg 10* ☎ *061/2618864.*

Campari Bar. Behind the Kunsthalle, Campari Bar pulls in an artsy crowd with its pop-art interior and tree-shaded terrace. ✉ *Steinenberg 7* ☎ *061/2728383.*

Das Café des Arts. The extremely popular Café des Arts, draws an interesting mix of patrons with its leather stools, grand piano, and elegantly spiral staircase. ✉ *Barfüsserpl. 6* ☎ *061/2735737* ⊕ *www.desarts-basel. ch.*

Sperber. With the feel of an English pub, Sperber presents live music some evenings. ✉ *Münzg. 12* ☎ *061/2646800.*

DANCING AND NIGHTCLUBS
Atlantis. DJs spin funk, hip-hop, house, and R&B at Atlantis, one of the city's hottest clubs. ✉ *Klosterberg 13* ☎ *061/2289696* ⊕ *www.atlan-tis. ch.*

Club 59. You have to be at least 25 to enjoy the three floors of music at Club 59, where the DJ rages through disco to reggae. ✉ *Steinenvorstadt 33* ☎ *061/2815950* ⊕ *www.club59.ch.*

KLEINBASEL
BARS AND LOUNGES
Bar Rouge. It began as an arty experiment, but the crimson interior of Bar Rouge has caught on. Looking sleek with its leather sofas, cascading chandeliers, and floor-to-ceiling windows, this club is located on the top floor of a glass tower. ✉ *Messepl. 10, 31st fl., Kleinbasel* ☎ *061/3613031* ⊕ *www.barrouge.ch.*

ZOO
BARS AND LOUNGES
Acqua. Opposite the Zoo, Acqua is known for its "waterfall" artwork in the hallway. It remains trendy, loud, and fun. ✉ *Binningerstr. 14, Zoo* ☎ *061/2716300* ⊕ *www.acquabasilea.ch.*

THE ARTS

ALTSTADT
MUSIC
Musik Akademie Basel. This important music academy draws top-drawer international performers. ✉ *Leonhardsstr. 6* ☎ *061/2645757* ⊕ *www. musik-akademie.ch.*

Stadt-Casino. The Stadt-Casino hosts the Basel Symphony Orchestra, the Basel Chamber Orchestra, and a wide range of visiting performers. ✉ *Steinenberg 14* ☎ *061/2737373* ⊕ *www.stadtcasino.ch.*

Basel's theater scene offers a mix of classical and contemporary plays; many shows are in German.

THEATER

Theater Basel. Theater Basel hosts opera, operetta, and dance performances, as well as dramas, usually in German. The season runs from August to May. ⊠ *Theaterstr. 7* ☎ *061/2951133* ⊕ *www.theater-basel. ch.*

KLEINBASEL

Ticketcorner. You can purchase tickets to all sorts of events, from pop concerts to ballet, at Ticketcorner. ⊠ *On the 5th floor inside Manor department store, Greifeng. 22, Kleinbasel* ☎ *061/6854699.*

THEATER

Musical Theater. The Musical Theater is a popular venue for touring companies. ⊠ *Feldbergstr. 151, Kleinbasel* ☎ *061/6998899* ⊕ *www. musicaltheaterbasel.ch.*

SHOPPING AND SPAS

The major downtown shopping district stretches along **Freie Strasse, Spalenberg,** and **Gerbergasse,** where you can find many one-of-a-kind boutiques. More reasonably priced shops along **Steinenvorstadt** cater to a younger crowd.

ALTSTADT

DEPARTMENT STORES

Coop City. This store carries a wide selection of clothing and household goods, as well as groceries in the lower level. ✉ *Gerberg. 4* ☎ *061/2699250.*

Globus. This upscale department store stocks everything from gourmet edibles to chic clothing. ✉ *Marktpl. 2* ☎ *061/2684545.*

SPECIALTY STORES

BOOKS

Bider & Tanner. Bider & Tanner is Basel's largest international bookstore, with a large selection of English books. You can also book tickets to arts events here. ✉ *Aeschenvorstadt 2* ☎ *061/2069999.*

Erasmushaus. Erasmushaus has one of the city's largest collections of fine antique manuscripts, books, and autographs, mostly in German but including a large selection of multilingual publications. If they cannot help you in the search for a particular tome, they will be happy to supply the names of the other specialist shops in the Basel area. ✉ *Bäumleing. 18* ☎ *061/2289944* ⊕ *www.erasmushaus.ch.*

Thalia Bücher. This shop on one of the city's main shopping strips sells music, movies, stationery, and books. There's a decent English section. ✉ *Freie Str. 32* ☎ *061/2642626* ⊕ *www.thalia.ch.*

CALLIGRAPHY

Abraxas. A great source for fine writing instruments, Abraxas also stocks everything from thick paper and delicate fountain pens to luxurious sealing waxes and reproductions of antique silver seals. ✉ *Rheinsprung 6* ☎ *061/2616070* ⊕ *www.abraxasswitzerland.com.*

Scriptorium am Rheinsprung. Dedicated to the art of calligraphy, Scriptorium am Rheinsprung even mixes its own ink. ✉ *Rheinsprung 2* ☎ *061/2613900* ⊕ *www.kalligraphie.com.*

CRAFTS AND GIFTS

Atelier Baumgartner. Specializing in home furnishings, Atelier Baumgartner also stocks European handicrafts, including handcrafted music boxes and nutcrackers from the Erzgebirge region of Germany. ✉ *Spalenberg 8* ☎ *061/2610843* ⊕ *www.atelierbaumgartner.ch.*

Dianda Basel. With Swiss souvenirs galore, Dianda Basel stocks Fasnacht figurines and other clever crafts. ✉ *Schnabelg. 8* ☎ *061/2611016* ⊕ *www.dianda-basel.ch.*

Heimatwerk. This shop sells a selection of exquisite Swiss crafts. ✉ *Schneiderg. 2* ☎ *061/2619178.*

Johann Wanner. Highly specialized handiwork comes from Johann Wanner, which sells handblown, hand-painted, and hand-molded Christmas ornaments, Victorian miniatures, tartan ribbons, cards, and calendars. ✉ *Spalenberg 14* ☎ *061/2614826* ⊕ *www.johannwanner.ch.*

FOOD SPECIALTIES

Confiserie Bachmann. This shop carries a Basel specialty called *Leckerli,* a chewy cookie made of almonds, honey, dried fruit, and kirsch. There are also branches of Confiserie Bachmann on Blumenrain and Central-bahnplatz. ⊠ *Gerber. 51* ☎ *061/2613583.*

Glausi's. This fine selection of more than 250 types of cheeses comes from the Swiss Alps, the neighboring Jura and Vosges mountains, and beyond. ⊠ *Spalenberg 12* ☎ *061/2618008.*

Läckerli-Huus. The famous Läckerli-Huus sells a variety of sweets, including wonderful Leckerli. A large selection of gift canisters and a shipping service make getting gifts home a cinch. ⊠ *Gerber. 57* ☎ *061/2642323* ⊕ *www.laeckerli-huus.ch.*

Schiesser. A convivial tearoom that opened in 1870, Schiesser sells carefully crafted (and costly) confections in its downstairs shop. ⊠ *Marktpl. 19* ☎ *061/2616077* ⊕ *www.confiserie-schiesser.ch.*

LINENS

Caraco. Handmade Swiss lace and embroidered goods are on offer at Caraco. ⊠ *Gerber. 77, Falknerstr. entrance* ☎ *061/2613577.*

Schlossberg Boutique. All manner of household linens for the bedroom, dining room, and kitchen are for sale at Schlossberg Boutique. ⊠ *Gerber. 26* ☎ *061/2610900* ⊕ *www.schlossberg.ch.*

Sturzenegger. This shop specializes in household items, including table decorations edged with St. Gallen lace. It also carries an extensive line of undergarments with labels such as Hanro. ⊠ *Theaterstr. 4* ☎ *061/2616867* ⊕ *www.sturzeneggerbasel.ch.*

MEN'S CLOTHES

Classic Herrenmode. This shop carries everything for the well-dressed man: formal and casual shirts, cashmere pullovers, and underwear. ⊠ *Fischmarkt 5* ☎ *061/2610755* ⊕ *www.classic-mode.ch.*

SHOES

Müki. Kids will feel like royalty when they try on stylish European-made children's shoes in an oversize red chair at Müki. ⊠ *Münsterberg 14* ☎ *061/2712436* ⊕ *www.mueki.ch.*

Rive Gauche. High-end designer shoes are on offer at Rive Gauche. This is the place to satisfy that Prada, Miu Miu, or Marc Jacobs craving. ⊠ *Schneiderg. 1* ☎ *061/2611080* ⊕ *www.rivegauche.ch.*

TOYS

Bercher & Sternlicht. For the young (or young at heart), Bercher & Sternlicht carries miniature trains and accessories. ⊠ *Spalenberg 45* ☎ *061/2612550* ⊕ *www.berchersternlicht.ch.*

Spielegge. With an emphasis on wooden toys, Spielegge stocks chisel-carved puppets and whimsical watercolor puzzles of fairy-tale scenes. ⊠ *Rümelinspl. 7* ☎ *061/2614488.*

Spielhuus. A good source for board games, Spielhuus also has reasonably priced children's toys and fanciful Fasnacht costumes. ⊠ *Eiseng. 8* ☎ *061/2649898.*

WOMEN'S CLOTHES

Beldona. This boutique stocks classy Swiss lingerie. ⊠ *Freie Str. 103* ☏ *061/2731170* ⊕ *www.beldona.ch.*

Fogal. Swiss hosiery is the specialty at Fogal, a lovely lingerie shop. Look out for the tray of clearance goods. ⊠ *Freie Str. 4* ☏ *061/2611220.*

Le Mouton à Cinq Pattes. You'll find mostly reasonably priced French and Italian styles at Le Mouton à Cinq Pattes. ⊠ *Eiseng. 6* ☏ *061/2620007.*

Trois Pommes. Thsi boutique dominates the high end of fashion, with Jil Sander, Prada, Gucci, and Dolce & Gabbana. ⊠ *Freie Str. 74* ☏ *061/2729255* ⊕ *www.troispommes.ch.*

KLEINBASEL

DEPARTMENT STORE

Manor. Whether you're in need of socks, toothpaste, or chocolate on the cheap, head to Manor. ⊠ *Greifeng. 22, Kleinbasel* ☏ *061/6854699* ⊕ *www.manor.ch.*

Migros. In the main train station, Migros is a great place to put together an impromptu picnic. It stays open until 10 pm seven days a week. ⊠ *Centralbahnpl., Bahnhof SBB* ☏ *058/5758412.*

SPAS

Spas are gaining in popularity all over Switzerland, and new ones seem to be popping up all the time. Basel is no exception, and spas cater to customers who want the latest fitness equipment, a pampering massage, or even waterslide and wave pool.

🕲 **Aquabasilea.** While you enjoy the purifying effects of a mud bath or the serenity of a steam bath, the kids will have a ball zooming around the Turbo Tube slide or free-falling down the nearly vertical Cliff Drop. "Something for everyone" is not an exaggeration at Aquabasilea, located outside Basel in the town of Pratteln. The huge facility houses waterslides, a wave pool, a swimming pool, indoor and outdoor saunas, a full-service spa, and a Turkish-style hammam. Many of the spa services are available for couples at a reduced rate. Look for the spa changing rooms on the second floor to avoid the locker room feel of the main changing area. ⊠ *Hardstr. 57, Pratteln* ☏ *061/8262424* ⊕ *www. aquabasilea.ch* ☉ *Mon.–Thurs. and Sun. 10–8, Fri. and Sat. 10–10* ☞ *15 SF for kids in pool area; 20 SF for adults in pool area; 25 SF for adults in spa area. Indoor and outdoor hot tubs, sauna, steam rooms. Services: aromatic body wrap, facial, lymph drainage, purifying mud bath, sauna infusions, relaxing massages, spa manicure and pedicure.*

Dampfbad Basel. An urban oasis tucked inside a former train station, this Turkish-style hammam has quaint and cozy feel. True to the traditional spa experience in the Middle East, guests are invited to relax in one of two steam rooms, cleanse and exfoliate their skin using a bath mitt and mild olive oil soap, then relax in a warm-water basin. Unlike many Swiss spas, the Dampfbad does not require you to be nude and provides bath sheets to be worn throughout the hammam.

Much-appreciated perks include high-end health and beauty products as well as complimentary herbal tea, fresh fruit, and water in the resting lounge. The Dampfbad offers an extensive menu of excellent massage services, including deep-tissue and reflexology. ⊠ *Vogesenplatz 1, St. Johann* ☎ *061/3221505* ⊕ *www.dampfbadbasel.ch* ☾ *Weekdays 11:30–10, Sat. 10–10, Sun. 10–8* ☞ *32 SF admission to spa area; 39 SF includes a light lunch; 69 SF includes a 30-min massage. Indoor hut tub, steam rooms. Services: acupressure, foot reflexology, massage.*

Migros Fitnesspark. If you're someone who likes to earn your relaxation time, Migros Fitnesspark offers a full gym and a wide range of fitness classes, so you can work out before enjoying the steam room, sauna, hot tub, cold-water plunge pool, and solarium. You'll find three separate areas in the wellness zone: a relaxation pool area where bathing suits are required and a steamy soak in the hot tub or a few laps in the 90-degree water will loosen stiff muscles; a sauna area with separate facilities for men and women, and a mixed nudist sauna area. For the total experience, opt for the 25-minute massage combo. ⊠ *Steinentorberg 8, Heuwagge* ☎ *058/5758150* ⊕ *www.wellnessparc.ch* ☾ *Fitness area weekdays 6:30 am–10 pm, weekends 9–7; wellness zone weekdays 8–10, weekends 9–7* ☞ *35 SF admission to fitness area and wellness zone; 42 SF 25-min massage. Indoor hot tub, sauna, steam room. Gym with: cardiovascular machines, free weights, weight-training. Services: herbal massage, reflexology, sport massage. Classes and programs: aerobics, aquaerobics, body sculpting, cycling, dance classes, fitness analysis, flexibility training, kickboxing, nutritional analysis, nutritional counseling, personal training, Pilates, step aerobics, strength training, stretching, weight training, yoga.*

Fodor's Choice **Sole Uno.** The incredibly relaxing saltwater pool at Sole Uno mimics
    ★   the sensation of floating in the Dead Sea, with the adding advantage of soft music that's audible underwater. About 20 minutes outside of Basel, Rheinfelden became known as a healing haven after natural salt deposits were discovered here in the late 19th century. Wellness seekers still come for the soothing waters, which they can enjoy in peaceful surroundings at the all-season outdoor pool that spirals into a bubbling whirlpool. The sprawling facility includes Finish-style saunas, an authentic Russian banya, and several steam baths. To get here by car, take A3 toward Zurich, then get off at the Rheinfelden East exit. ⊠ *Roberstenstr. 31, Rheinfelden, Germany* ☎ *061/8366763* ⊕ *www. soleuno.ch* ☾ *Daily 8–10:30* ☞ *25 SF includes 2 hrs in wellness park, 38 SF 20-min exfoliating hammam massage, 35 SF 20-min relaxing wellness massage. Indoor and outdoor hot tubs, saunas, and steam rooms. Services: aquatic therapy, baths, massage, scrubs. On-site café and restaurant.*

Fribourg and Neuchâtel

WORD OF MOUTH

"In Neuchatel, the station is located up the hill above the town, but there's a handy funicular railway to take you down to the lakeside and back."

—Gordon_R

WELCOME TO FRIBOURG AND NEUCHÂTEL

TOP REASONS TO GO

★ **Stir the melting pot:** Fondue famously originated in the Neuchâtel area—try the two-cheese *fondue neuchâteloise* that honors the region's fabulous Gruyère and Emmental cheeses or opt for *fondue fribourgeoise*, a delicious Vacherin Fribourgeois delight.

★ **Switzerland's largest lake:** Lac Neuchâtel is a great place for a boat trip, to try out wakeboarding, or to savor the fine fish served on its shores.

★ **You say Schloss:** And I say Château. In either language, this area has some of Switzerland's most impressive castles, from Grandson to Gruyères.

★ **Homegrown talent:** Whether it's the clockwork extravaganzas of Tinguely or the disturbing alien-like creations of Giger, these two sculptors are true knockouts.

★ **Gorgeous Gruyères:** Step into a postcard in this perfect specimen of a medieval stronghold, its single main street cozy within the ramparts.

1 Fribourg. Gateway town to the region, Fribourg is one of Switzerland's best-kept secrets. Have your camera ready for its medieval Old Town, adorned with steep, cobbled streets, and bridges in all styles from wooden to suspension. Get enlightened with the cathedral's noted Art Nouveau stained glass. Then head south to pretty-as-a-picture Gruyères. Looming over its lovely square and centuries-old geranium-clad houses is the town's spectacular hilltop castle. After touring this car-free village, take in modern and traditional cheese-making demonstrations of the famed regional cheeses, Vacherin Fribourgeois and Gruyère. North of Fribourg lies time-burnished Murten, a peaceful lakeside resort.

2 Lac Neuchâtel and Environs. In the heart of "Watch Valley" and flanked by vineyards, this French-accented city on the shores of Lac Neuchâtel celebrates the grape each fall with a weekend of parades and feasting. Enjoy its architecture—Romanesque to Rococo—and discover the Bronze Age lifestyle of stilt-house dwellers at Laténium. South, along the shores of Lac Neuchâtel, discover the grand castle at Grandson.

GETTING ORIENTED

This area is roughly organized like a hand. At the wrist are the Alpine foothills of Fribourg; these curve gently down to the palm of flatter Neuchâtel, with the long ellipse of Lac Neuchâtel. Beyond lie the Jura's rugged fingers, which form valleys in the Jura Mountains and finally come to rest on the plateaus.

8

CHEESE: FRIBOURG'S CALLING CARD

A traveler cruising Switzerland's emerald hills and villages far from industrial turf can't help but notice the damp, fresh, earthy ephemera of the dairy that hangs in the air—a mild, musky tang that scents the cream, thickens the chocolate, and alchemizes the cheese.

La Maison du Gruyère (above) is the starting point for many dairy tours. Here you can watch the production of the region's namesake cheese (below, right), or enjoy a pot of fondue (above, right).

And nowhere else will you smell this as strongly as in the region of Fribourg—the area that gave birth to the famous cheese, Gruyère, a main component of fondue. This region also sits shoulder to shoulder with two other areas that give us great cheeses: Emmentaler (near Bern) and Tête de Moine from the Jura Mountains.

Today, as always, Swiss cheese is most delightfully experienced in that most satisfying of all Swiss dishes, fondue, which first became fashionable in America during the 1950s ski craze. Those who have not acquired the habit may feel uncomfortably replete after only a few mouthfuls.

—Alexis Munier

CRÈME-DOUBLE DE LA GRUYÈRE

Along the Fribourg countryside you can find another dairy delight. Crème-double, a Gruyère specialty, rivals Devonshire cream. A rich, extra-thick, high-fat cream that—without whipping—almost supports a standing spoon; it is served in tiny carved-wood *baquets* (vats), to be spooned over bowls of berries and meringues.

DAIRY TRAIL

In the Gruyère region and surrounding mountains, cattle head uphill in summer, and production of local cheeses—the firm, fragrant Gruyère and Vacherin—soars. They are sold at various stages: young and mild, ripe and savory, or aged to a heady tang. The great commercial cheese factory of Gruyère may have an automated, cheese-turning robot, but head into the hills of Fribourg and you'll still see old copper pots sizzling over wood fires.

The Sentier des Fromageries is an excellent walking path that connects the dairies in Pringy-Moléson. Two routes are available, but each begins at the **Maison du Gruyère** (✉ *Place de la Gare 3* ☎ *026/9218400* ⊕ *www.lamaisondugruyere. ch*) and ends at the lofty **Fromagerie d'Alpage** (✉ *Moléson-sur-Gruyères* ☎ *026/9211044* ⊕ *www.fromagerie-alpage. ch*) in Moléson-Village. The Maison du Gruyère is nestled in the meadows that lie below the Château de Gruyères. Both a museum and demonstration dairy, you can learn the history of the famous cheese and how it retains its AOC standing. Several times a day, from 9 to 11 and 12:30 to 2:30, the cheese makers open their doors and welcome you to their wonderfully pungent world. At the end of the trail at Fromagerie d'Alpage, you can assist in the cheese-making process if you reserve in advance (May to September only). Cheese-making demonstrations are held at 10 am daily. For more information on the Sentier des Fromageries, see the Gruyère Tourism site at ⊕ *www.la-gruyere.ch*.

OFF THE BEATEN PATH

Halfway between the mountain pass that connects Schwartzsee with Charmey, **Alp Balisa** (✉ *Schwartzsee* ☎ *026/4121295* ⊕ *www.alpbalisa.ch*) is a small family-run dairy that operates all summer long. It may be out of the way, but the tiny dairy has a reputation as one of the most charming in Switzerland.

FONDUE

Though fondue is de rigueur in any Alpine setting, Fribourg has a fanatical stronghold. The recipe is surprisingly simple—cheese melted together with white wine, garlic, and a dash of kirsch (brandy distilled from cherries). Aficionados debate the perfect blend of cheeses and whether to include mushrooms or tomatoes. Fribourg is the source of *fondue fribourgeoise*, the combination of the canton's two greatest cheeses—Gruyère and Vacherin Fribourgeois—into a creamy *moitié-moitié* (half-and-half) blend. The Vacherin can be melted alone for an even creamier fondue, and potatoes can be dipped instead of bread. Eat like a local and head to Fribourg's **Café du Midi** (✉ *Rue de Romont 25* ☎ *026/3223133* ⊕ *www.lemidi.ch*), Bulle's **Café de la Gare** (✉ *Av. de la Gare 6* ☎ *026/9127688*), or **Café Tivoli** (✉ *Place d'Armes 18* ☎ *021/9487039* ⊕ *www. cafetivoli.ch*) in Châtel-St-Denis, all of which are famous for their hospitality, decor, and most of all, their fabulous fondue.

8

Updated by
Alexis Munier

Shouldered by the more prominent cantons of Bern and Vaud, the cantons of Fribourg and Neuchâtel are easily overlooked by hurried visitors. If they do stop, it is usually for a quick dip into the environs of Fribourg and Gruyères. That leaves the rest of this largely untouched area to the Swiss, who enjoy its relatively unspoiled nature and relaxed approach to life.

Although the strict cantonal borders are a messy reflection of historic power struggles, the regional boundaries are unmistakable, even to an outsider. Fribourg starts in the pre-Alpine foothills above Charmey and rolls down across green hills, tidy farms, and ancient towns until it reaches the silty shores of the Murten, Neuchâtel, and Biel lakes. The region of Neuchâtel begins in these silt-rich fields (which grow everything from lettuce to tobacco), sweeps across Lac Neuchâtel to its château- and vineyard-lined western shore, and rises up to the Jura Mountains.

The Röstigraben (or "Rösti Divide," named after the buttery, panfried potato cakes Swiss Germans are particularly fond of) is the tongue-in-cheek name for the linguistic border where French meets German. It runs through Fribourg and butts up against the northern borders of Neuchâtel. In some towns you can walk into a *boulangerie* (bread bakery) selling dark *Vollkornbrot* (whole-grain bread) or find a family named Neuenschwand that hasn't spoken German for generations.

Nature's delights take pride of place here. But no matter what aspect of history interests you, you should find something to please you: prehistoric menhirs and the lifestyle of stilt-house people at Laténium, near Neuchâtel; the Roman amphitheater in Avenches; or imagining the Battle of Murten from the city's ramparts. Perhaps you'd prefer Grandson's castle, with Charles the Bold's ridiculously bejeweled hat and life-size, fully armored replicas of jousting knights. If you love Gothic churches and religious art, you can have your fill, especially in

Fribourg and Neuchâtel. There's stained glass at Romont, and the sheer romantic thrill of medieval towns like storybook Gruyères.

FRIBOURGH AND NEUCHÂTEL PLANNER

WHEN TO GO

Spring and fall are beautiful times to visit anywhere in this region. During the summer, temperatures reach an average of 18–20° C (65–68° F), which is comfortable, but crowds tend to pick up, especially in Gruyères. During a heat wave it's not unusual for temperatures to soar to 30° C (86° F). In winter the average temperature is 0–3° C (32–38° F). In the pre-Alps region there can be long periods of snowfall. January is great for winter sports. You can't be sure of snow in December, and in February some canton or other (not to mention the Germans, English, Dutch, and Italians) will invariably have school vacations, so slopes get pretty crowded. When the snow lasts, March can also be great for skiing.

PLANNING YOUR TIME

Though the major sights themselves don't require too much time to visit, they are scattered throughout the region, so it takes a while to get to them. If you have only one or two days, try to take in one or more of the cities. Neuchâtel and Fribourg have very different characters, and a day easily can be spent walking around the city centers, visiting a few museums, and sampling restaurants.

If you cut out the museums, then each of these could be combined with a trip to one of the smaller nearby towns we mention. More time allows you to tour the area and take in its subtle differences. If you start at Fribourg, cut south to the castle at Gruyères, and from there, circle northwest through the ancient town of Murten on your way to Neuchâtel.

From Neuchâtel, head south along the Route du Vignoble (Wine Route) to the château town of Grandson and on to Yverdon-les-Bains. Or spend some time pursuing the many sporting opportunities that the different seasons and towns have on offer. Alternatively, summer is the perfect time to take a long trip on Lac de Neuchâtel or to enjoy a hike.

GETTING HERE AND AROUND

AIR TRAVEL

Fribourg lies between Geneva International Airport, 138 km (86 miles) to the southwest, and Zürich Airport, 180 km (112 miles) to the northeast. Train connections to both are good.

The Bern-Belp Airport is a small international airport 34 km (21 miles) northeast of Fribourg, near Bern.

BIKE TRAVEL

Biking is popular here, and itineraries are varied. You can huff and puff uphill, bounce over mountain-bike trails, or coast along the flatlands around the lakes. Route maps can be picked up in most tourist offices or train stations. Swiss Federal Railways offers reasonably priced rentals at most train stations. Bikes must be reserved at least one day in advance, three in summer. Check with tourist offices for a map of over

20 different biking itineraries called La Broye à Vélo. At Estavayer-le-Lac and Payerne cyclists (and hikers) can also book a "Safari Nature" package with one overnight stay (reserve at least one week in advance).

Biking Information Estavayer-le-Lac Tourisme ☎ *026/6606161* ⊕ *www. estavayer-payerne.ch.*

BOAT AND FERRY TRAVEL

There are frequent boat trips on the lakes of Neuchâtel and Murten in summer, plus usually a host of themed evening trips. Contact La Navigation Lacs de Neuchâtel et Morat for more information.

Boat and Ferry Information Navigation Lacs de Neuchâtel et Morat ☎ *032/7299600* ⊕ *www.navig.ch.*

BUS AND TRAM TRAVEL

Postbus connections, except in the principal urban areas, can be few and far between.

Consequently, you should plan excursions carefully using the bus schedules available at the train station, or phone the local tourist office for advice.

CAR TRAVEL

An important and scenic trans-Swiss artery, the A12 expressway cuts from Bern to Lausanne, passing directly above Fribourg. A parallel route to the northwest extends the A1 between Zürich and Bern, connecting Bern to Murten, Payerne, and Lausanne.

The A5 expressway runs between Neuchâtel and Yverdon, but passes through a lot of tunnels. If you have the time, take the national road for a more scenic view of the lakeshore. The charms of this varied region can be experienced easily by car, and there are scenic secondary highways throughout. Keep in mind that some towns, like Gruyères, are car-free, or have pedestrians-only centers; in these cases, parking lots are easy to find.

TRAIN TRAVEL

The main train route connecting Basel, Zürich, and Geneva passes through the Fribourg station between Bern and Lausanne. Neuchâtel has hourly connections to main Swiss cities. Regional train services to smaller destinations leave from the larger towns of Fribourg and Neuchâtel, though buses may take a more direct route.

RESTAURANTS

Both Fribourg and Neuchâtel have a plethora of top-quality, French-influenced restaurants. They offer far cheaper lunch menus (three or more courses) and sometimes even a plat du jour, although it will cost more than it does in simpler establishments, where the price is typically under 20 SF. No one here lays down strict dress codes: the more upscale the restaurant, the fancier the attire, but you won't be thrown out for not wearing a tie. Restaurants open for dinner at about 6 in the evening, though diners tend to arrive closer to 7:30, and kitchens wind down between 9:30 and 10. Lunch is usually served from 11:30 to 2, but you can often get simple fare even after that. For a quick, cheap meal that still has local flavor, try a crêperie. The closer you are to France, the more of these you'll find.

Prices in the reviews are the average cost of a main course at dinner or, if dinner is not served, at lunch.

HOTELS

As they become more tourist-oriented, Fribourg and Neuchâtel are developing better hotel infrastructures. Fribourg is the best equipped, though there's still only a handful of choices in the Old Town. In Neuchâtel most lodgings sit along the lake. Many hotels don't offer air-conditioning, but do offer more than one meal plan.

Prices in the reviews are the lowest cost of a standard double room in high season.

FRIBOURG

With its landscape of green hills against the craggy peaks of the pre-Alps, Fribourg is one of Switzerland's most rural cantons. Its famous Fribourgeois cows—the Holsteins (black and white, the colors of the cantonal coat of arms)—provide the canton with its main income, although light industry is gradually replacing the cows. Fondue has a long history here, as does Gruyère cheese and Switzerland's famous *crème-double* (double cream, with a fat content of at least 45%).

FRIBOURG

34 km (21 miles) southwest of Bern, 74 km (46 miles) northeast of Lausanne.

Between the rich pasturelands of the Swiss plateau and the Alpine foothills, the Sarine River (called the Saane by German speakers) twists in an S-curve, its sandstone cliffs joined by webs of arching bridges. In one of the curves of the river is the medieval city of Fribourg. The city grew in overlapping layers; it's an astonishing place of hills and cobblestones, ramparts and Gothic fountains, ancient passageways, and worn wooden stairs. Only on foot can you discover its secret charm as one of the finer ensembles of medieval architecture in Europe.

Historic Fribourg is a stronghold of Catholicism; it remained staunchly Catholic even during the Reformation. The evidence is everywhere, from the numerous chapels and religious orders to the brown-robed novitiates walking the sidewalks. Fribourg University, founded in 1889, remains the only Catholic university in Switzerland. It is also the only bilingual institution of its kind and reflects the region's peculiar linguistic agility. Two-thirds of the people of Canton Fribourg are native French speakers, one-third are native German speakers, and many switch easily between the two. In the Basse-Ville neighborhood, old-timers still speak a unique mixture of the two languages, called Boltz. Officially, the city is bilingual, although French predominates.

GETTING HERE AND AROUND

Direct trains connect Fribourg to major Swiss cities: Geneva is 1 hour 25 minutes away, Lausanne is 45 to 50 minutes, Bern is 22 to 35 minutes, and Zurich is 1 hour 24 minutes on a direct train. Buses leave from behind Fribourg's train station for villages in the surrounding canton.

8

If your knowledge of French or German is good, then the Fribourg and Neuchâtel transportation websites will be useful.

From the Place de Tilleul in Fribourg, the Rue de Lausanne climbs upward. Like Rue des Alpes, it, too, is shop-lined, with tightly spaced 18th-century buildings hiding terraced gardens of surprising size. The 19th- and 20th-century section of the city begins at the top of Rue de Lausanne; nearby are the main buildings of the university. The 21st century has arrived in the form of the Fribourg Center shopping mall, close to the station.

ESSENTIALS

Visitor Information Fribourg Tourisme ✉ *1 av. de la Gare* ☎ *026/3501111* ⊕ *www.fribourgtourism.ch.*

EXPLORING

TOP ATTRACTIONS

Basse-Ville (*Lower City*). At Fribourg's very core is the Basse-Ville, tucked into a crook of the river. Here you'll find the 11th- through 16th-century homes of the original village, as well as a lively café and cellar-theater scene.

★ **Cathédrale St-Nicolas** (*St. Nicholas Cathedral*). Fribourg's grand cathedral rears up from the surrounding gray, 18th-century buildings. Its massive tower was completed in the 15th century, two centuries after construction began in 1283. Above the main portal, a beautifully restored tympanum of the Last Judgment shows the blessed few headed toward Peter, who holds the key to the heavenly gates; those not so fortunate are led by pig-faced demons into the cauldrons of hell. Inside you can see the famous 18th-century organ, as well as the restored 1657 organ. The exceptional stained-glass windows, installed between 1873 and 1983, are executed in a number of styles, including Pre-Raphaelite and Art Nouveau. In the **Chapelle du St-Sépulcre** (Chapel of the Holy Sepulchre), a group of 13 figures dating from 1433 portrays the entombment of Christ. If you can handle the 368 steps, climb to the tower for a panoramic view. ▮**TIP➔** During services, you won't be allowed in. ✉ *Rue St-Nicolas* 🎫 *Free, tower 3.50 SF* 🕙 *Mon.–Sat. 7:30–7, Sun. 8:30 am–9:30 pm. Tower Mar.–Nov., weekdays 10–noon and 2–5, Sat. 10–4, and Sun. 2–5.*

Église des Cordeliers (*Church of the Franciscan Friars*). This imposing 13th-century church is attached to a Franciscan friary. Its pale walls and the rose-, gray-, and alabaster-colored ceiling contrast with the Gothic darkness of the interior. A 16th-century polyptych by an anonymous Nelkenmeister, or Maître à l'Oeillet (one of a group of painters who signed their works only with red and white carnations), hangs over the high altar. A carved-wood triptych, believed to be Alsatian, and a 15th-century retable of the temptation of St. Anthony painted by the Fribourg artist Hans Fries adorn the side walls. At the entrance to the cloister leading to the friary is a 13th-century five-panel fresco depicting the birth of the Virgin Mary. ✉ *Place de Notre-Dame* ☎ *026/3471160* 🎫 *Free* 🕙 *Mon.–Sat. 9–6, Sun. noon–6.*

☾ **Espace Jean Tinguely–Niki de Saint Phalle.** Once the city's tram terminal, this is one of the premier modern-art spaces in Switzerland. It houses

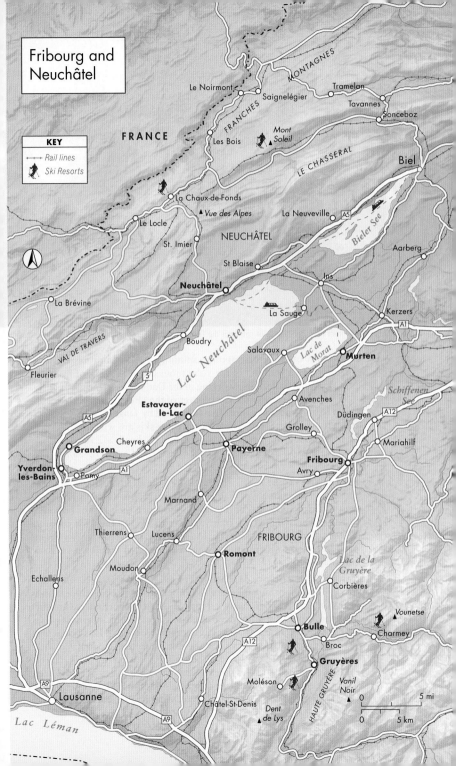

All that cheese comes from right here: herds of cows dot the Fribourg countryside.

a selection of whirring, tapping, spinning metal sculptures by Jean Tinguely and a wall full of the voluptuous, colorful work of his wife, Niki de Saint Phalle. After working in the Dadaist movement, Tinguely (1925-91) made headlines as a pioneer of the "kinetic art" movement. Kids (16 and under free) are often fascinated by Tinguely's work; something is happening somewhere all the time: skis are walking, a potted plant is turning, a toy rabbit is being hit on the head. ⊠ *2 rue de Morat* ☎ *026/3055140* ⊕ *www.mahf.ch* 🖂 *6 SF* ☾ *Wed. and Fri.–Sun. 11–6, Thurs. 11–8.*

Hôtel de Ville (*Town Hall*). The Hôtel de Ville (Rathaus in German) is the seat of the cantonal parliament, built on the foundations of the château of Berthold IV of Zähringen, who founded the town of Fribourg in 1157. The symmetrical stairways were added in the 17th century, as were the clockworks in the 16th-century clock tower. A vibrant produce market sets up on the square in front of the Town Hall on Saturday mornings.

Musée d'Art et d'Histoire de Fribourg (*Fribourg Museum of Art and History*). This important museum is housed in the Renaissance Ratzé Mansion and, incongruously, an old slaughterhouse connected to the mansion proper by an underground passage. The mansion displays 12th- to 19th-century art, including several works by Hans Fries. The 19th-century slaughterhouse, a stark stone structure modernized with steel-and-glass blocks, provides the setting for a provocative mix of sacred sculptures and the kinetic, scrap-iron whimsies of native son Jean Tinguely. The attic gallery displays 19th- and 20th-century paintings from Swiss artists, as well as from Delacroix, Courbet, and others.

Take a breather in the quiet sculpture garden overlooking the river. Limited descriptive material in English is available upon request, and guided tours in English can be booked in advance. ✉ *12 rue de Morat* ☎ *026/3055140* ⊕ *www.mahf.ch* 🎟 *6–8 SF* ⊙ *Tues., Wed., and Fri.– Sun. 11–6, Thurs. 11–8.*

Planche-Supérieure. As Fribourg expanded from the Basse-Ville, it crossed the river over the Pont du Milieu (Middle Bridge) to a narrow bank, the Planche-Inférieure, where picturesque, terraced houses abound. As the town prospered, it spread to the statelier 16th- and 17th-century Planche-Superiéure, a large, sloping, open triangular *place* (square) that was once the busy livestock market. It is now lined with several upscale restaurants and cafés. From here you can walk up to the Chapelle de Lorette (Loreto Chapel), once a favored pilgrimage site, for the best view of Fribourg.

Pont de Zähringen (*Zähringen Bridge*). From St. Nicholas Cathedral, slip through the rue des Épouses to the Grand-Rue, lined with 18th-century patrician homes. Near the end of this street is the historic Zähringen Bridge, with views over the Pont de Berne, the Pont de Gottéron, and the wooden remains of the ancient towers that once guarded the entrance to the city. You're now in the area where Duke Berthold IV first established his residence and founded the city in 1157.

NEED A BREAK?

Le Café du Belvédère. The terrace of Le Café du Belvédère has a fabulous view up the river to the Planche-Supérieure. Inside it's a *café littéraire* by day and a lively bar and meeting spot at night. An eclectic mix of '70s plastic furniture and a huge, rounded plastic bar contrast wonderfully with the wood-beamed interior. The friendly staff serves a selection of teas, coffees, and homemade syrups as well as alcohol, and you can enjoy Asian delights from the excellent Tam's Kitchen restaurant upstairs. ✉ *36 Grand-Rue* ☎ *026/3234407.*

WORTH NOTING

Musée Suisse de la Machine à Coudre (*Swiss Sewing Machine Museum*). An example of almost every sewing machine ever built (more than 250) is on exhibit here. There's also a collection of contraptions created to ease the life of handworkers and housewives before the age of electricity, including useful household firsts such as vacuum cleaners and washing machines. A side room is packed with curiosities from bygone days, such as chestnut-hulling boots. Owner Edouard Wassmer will charm you with anecdotes and history. ✉ *58 Grand-Rue* ☎ *026/4752433* ⊕ *www.museewassmer.com* 🎟 *7 SF* ⊙ *By appointment only.*

Neuve-Ville (*New Town*). When the Pont St-Jean was built in the 17th century, making the northern bank of the river readily accessible, the merchant houses and walled cloisters of the Neuve-Ville popped up.

Pont de Berne (*Bern Bridge*). In this city of bridges, the Pont de Berne is the oldest. Set to the north of the Basse-Ville, it is made entirely of wood and was once the only access to the city.

EN ROUTE

Maison Cailler. On the way from Fribourg to Gruyères, chocoholics should consider stopping at this tantalizing chocolate factory in the

8

otherwise unassuming town of Broc. A name in Swiss chocolate since 1819, Cailler offers a 90-minute tour complete with chocolate tasting. ✉ *7 rue Jules Bellet, Broc* ☎ *026/9215960* 🌐 *www.cailler.ch* 🎟 *10 SF* 🕓 *Apr.–Nov., Mon.–Sun. 10–6; Dec.–Mar., Mon.–Sun. 10–5.*

WHERE TO EAT

$$$ FRENCH Fodor's Choice ★ 🍴 **Des Trois Tours.** If you have a penchant for innovative food that's superbly presented, try Alain Bächler's award-winning restaurant just outside town. The focus is on gloriously fresh market cuisine, ranging from wild-mushroom lasagna to strawberry tarts. Enjoy your meal in the sunny bistro, the main dining room, or on the chestnut-tree-shaded terrace in summer. The decor is rather pared-down, but retains features of the original 19th-century patrician house. To reach the hamlet of Bourguillon (Bürglen in German) take a bus from Fribourg train station; a cab costs around 25 SF. Either way, it's a 10-minute ride. When you call for reservations, get more transportation how-tos from the staff. [$] *Average main: 60 SF* ✉ *15 rte. de Bourguillon, Bourguillon* ☎ *026/3223069* 🌐 *www.troistours.ch* ✍ *Reservations essential* 🕓 *Closed Sun. and Mon., late July–early Aug., and late Dec.–early Jan.*

$$ FRENCH 🍴 **Hôtel de Ville.** Centrally located, this is one of the top Fribourg restaurants, thanks to owner/chef Frédérik Kondratowicz's superlative take on seasonal cuisine. Fresher-than-fresh are such delights as lamb with an herb crust, vegetable moussaka with candied orange, and asparagus and spinach risotto. Swiss and French wines are the focal point of the thoughtful wine list. The ambience in this one-floor-up spot is bourgeois bistro with arty notes, and there are some great views of Fribourg from the windows. [$] *Average main: 35 SF* ✉ *6 Grand-Rue* ☎ *026/3212367* 🌐 *www.restaurant-hotel-de-ville.ch* ✍ *Reservations essential* 🕓 *Closed Sun. and Mon., and late-July–Aug. No lunch Tues.*

$$ FRENCH 🍴 **L'Epée.** It's a good idea to make reservations at this popular brasserie in the Basse-Ville. The food is delicious and reasonably priced, the staff is friendly, and the view up to the cathedral is a real draw—from inside or the terrace, by day or night. Options could include prawn and orange salad, veal medallions with lemon sauce, or the warm chocolate cake with a lushly decadent melted center. [$] *Average main: 33 SF* ✉ *39 Planche-Supérieure* ☎ *026/3223407* 🌐 *www.brasserie-epee.ch* 🕓 *Closed Mon. and Tues., and a few wks in midsummer. No dinner Sun.*

$$$ FRENCH 🍴 **Le Pérolles.** On Fribourg's main street, this restaurant's severe lines are softened by art-filled walls and, in nice weather, the leafy vistas from the sun-dappled balcony. One bite here reveals why chef/owner Pierre-André Ayer has earned so much praise. In a summer incarnation, his menu showstoppers include local lake fish drizzled with herb and shallot butter, grilled beef fillet accompanied by a fricassee of tomatoes and dates, and poached peaches with lavender honey and raspberry sorbet for dessert. [$] *Average main: 55 SF* ✉ *18A bd. de Pérolles* ☎ *026/3474030* 🌐 *www.leperolles.ch* ✍ *Reservations essential* 🕓 *Closed Sun.–Tues., 3 wks in July and Aug., and 2 wks in Dec. and Jan.*

$ FRENCH 🍴 **Xpresso Café.** On the fourth floor of the Fribourg Center, this café does waffles and crepes—both savory and sweet. You can also choose from a wide selection of teas and coffees. Set in a shopping center, this outpost of a popular Swiss chain offers a perfect time-out from heavy-duty retail therapy. $ *Average main: 15 SF* ✉ *12 av. de la Gare* ☎ *026/3417808* 💳 *No credit cards* 🕒 *Closed Sun. No dinner.*

WHERE TO STAY

For expanded hotel reviews, visit Fodors.com.

$$ B&B/INN Fodor's Choice ★ 🏨 **Auberge aux 4 Vents.** Guests reserve months ahead for this quirky, high-style country inn noted for its fabulous gardens and fanciful themed rooms. **Pros:** individuality and unique quirky character of venue; personal style of the owners. **Cons:** traditionalists may feel out of place here; outside central Fribourg. $ *Rooms from: 180 SF* ✉ *124 rue de Grandfey* ☎ *026/3473600* 🌐 *www.aux4vents.ch* 🛏 *8 rooms* 🕒 *Closed first 3 wks of Jan.* 🍴 *Breakfast.*

$ HOTEL 🏨 **Hôtel de la Rose.** In a typical 17th-century sandstone house, this hotel is within walking distance of museums, churches, the cathedral, and the Old Town. **Pros:** excellent central location; high-quality service; friendly disposition of staff. **Cons:** the lack of air-conditioning can be a nuisance in summer months. $ *Rooms from: 160 SF* ✉ *1 rue Morat* ☎ *026/3510101* 🌐 *www.hoteldelarose.ch* 🛏 *40 rooms* 🍴 *Breakfast.*

$ HOTEL 🏨 **Hotel du Faucon.** At this seven-story lodging, you are treated to modern, quiet, attractive, and spacious studio-like rooms at very good prices. **Pros:** friendly staff; pedestrian zone means no traffic noise. **Cons:** breakfast is overpriced; reception desk is unstaffed at night; parking adds a slice to the tab. $ *Rooms from: 125 SF* ✉ *76 rue de Lausanne* ☎ *026/3213790* 🌐 *www.hotel-du-faucon.ch* 🛏 *23 rooms.*

$$$ HOTEL Fodor's Choice ★ 🏨 **Romantik Hotel Restaurant Au Sauvage.** A cloister in the 17th century, then an inn during the cattle-market days of the 18th and 19th centuries, this sophisticated auberge now has a striking blend of minimalist furnishings and medieval details. **Pros:** enchantingly steeped in medieval history; central location. **Cons:** staff does not always speak English willingly (if at all). $ *Rooms from: 280 SF* ✉ *12 Planche-Supérieure* ☎ *026/3473060* 🌐 *www.hotel-sauvage.ch* 🛏 *17 rooms* 🍴 *Breakfast.*

NIGHTLIFE

BARS

La Cave de la Rose. To get a feel for Fribourg's nightlife, try one of the cellar bars scattered throughout the Old Town, such as La Cave de la Rose. This convivial place stays open into the wee hours of the morning. ✉ *1 rue de Morat* ☎ *026/3220755.*

Elvis et Moi. With a kitschy, Elvis-inspired interior, this place offers both live bands and DJ sets. It's open Tuesday to Saturday. ✉ *13 rue de Morat* ☎ *026/3220755* 🌐 *www.elvis-et-moi.ch.*

Planet Edelweiss. Seemingly in the middle of nowhere, this 19th-century inn has been transformed into a lively *restaurant de nuit* and disco. The diverse crowd (ranging from bankers to farmers) at this haven of rural hipsterdom doesn't arrive until after 10, but stays until 2 am during the week and 4 am on weekends. The 12-minute taxi ride from town runs about 25 SF. ✉ *Mariahilf 1, Düdingen* ☎ *026/4920505* 🌐 *www.planet-edelweiss.ch.*

8

CASINO

Casino Barrière de Fribourg. Near the northern autoroute exit, the Casino Barrière de Fribourg has roulette, blackjack, poker, and 100 slot machines, as well as a bar and restaurant and regular shows. A five-minute taxi ride from town costs around 17 SF. ⊠ *11 rte. du Lac, Granges-Paccot* ☎ *026/4677000* ⊕ *www.lucienbarriere.com.*

GRUYÈRES

Fodor's Choice ★ *35 km (21 miles) south of Fribourg.*

Rising above the plain on a rocky crag and set against a backdrop of Alpine foothills, the castle village of Gruyères seduces from afar. This perfect specimen of a medieval stronghold comes complete with a cobbled main street, stone fountains, and well-preserved houses whose occupants try to outdo each other with picturesque facades and geranium displays in summer. The town was once the capital of the Alpine estates of the Burgundian counts of Gruyères, and its traditional crest bears a stylized crane (*grue*), a motif that adorns countless pieces of the town's famed blue-and-white or dark-red-and-white pottery. Gruyères is car-free, so you'll have to park in one of three lots outside town and walk up from the Maison du Gruyère.

GETTING HERE AND AROUND

To connect with Gruyères via public transport, buses from Fribourg are your best bet. Take a bus to Bulle, and change to another bus that heads directly to Gruyères (a trip of 1 hour 15 minutes). Alternatively, take the bus to Bulle, then change to a train and get off at the town of Gruyères in front of the cheese dairy La Maison du Gruyère. Walk up to the town (approximately 15 minutes). This option takes one hour, and there are hourly connections. If training from Lausanne or Zürich, transfer to a local train at Palézieux—this rail journey takes up to about five hours.

ESSENTIALS

Visitor Information Gruyère Tourisme ⊠ *Village Center* ☎ *0848424424* ⊕ *www.la-gruyere.ch.*

EXPLORING

★ **Château de Gruyères.** Crowning the storybook village of Gruyères is the town's famed château. Between 1080 and 1554, 19 counts held political power over this region, and they built and expanded this medieval castle. Little is known about them except for the last one, Michel. A lover of luxury and a big spender, he expanded the estates and then fled his creditors in 1555. In 1849 a wealthy Geneva family bought the castle and encouraged painter friends to decorate a room now known as Corot's Room, as it features four of the great painter's landscapes. Also worth seeing is the Knights' Room with its impressive 19th-century fresco cycle depicting local legends, and the aptly named Fantastic Art

Room, hung with contemporary work. An 18-minute multimedia show called *Gruyères,* which brings to life the history of the castle in animated form (available in eight languages), shown daily in the old caretaker's lodge, is worth your time. ☎ 026/9212102 ⊕ *www.chateau-gruyeres.ch* ⊠ *10 SF* ☉ *Apr.–Oct., daily 9–6; Nov.–Mar., daily 10–4:30.*

Giger Museum. This museum houses the largest collection of paintings, sculpture, furniture, and film designs by the enormously talented but equally tormented H.R. Giger. The Swiss surrealist won an Academy Award for his set design for the horror film *Alien;* he's not likely to win any prizes for his cheerful, healthy outlook on life (or women). That said, a few of his sculpture/furniture pieces are very good. Most people will get enough of an idea about the artist just by sitting in the Giger Bar, opposite the museum. Here you can admire ceiling buttresses that look like elongated backbones with ribs, and his ingenious trademark chairs: yet more spines and ribs, with pelvises for headrests. ⊠ *Château St. Germain* ☎ *026/9212200* ⊕ *www.hrgigermuseum.com* ⊠ *12.50 SF* ☉ *Apr.–Oct., daily 10–6; Nov.–Mar., Tues.–Fri. 1–5, weekends 10–6, closed Mon.*

Maison du Gruyère. Before going up to town, you can visit the very touristy Maison du Gruyère, a demonstration *fromagerie* (cheese dairy) where the famous cheese is produced with fully modernized equipment. Demonstrations are given two to four times a day, depending on the season. There's also a shop and a restaurant that offers every variation on a cheese dish you ever dreamed of (including three-course "Gruyère cheese menus" for 20 to 38 SF). ⊠ *Pringy-Gruyères* ☎ *026/9218400* ⊕ *www.lamaisondugruyere.ch* ⊠ *7 SF* ☉ *June–Sept., daily 9–7; Oct.–May, daily 9–6.*

Tibet Museum. Housed in an artfully converted chapel, this museum run by the Alain Bordier Foundation boasts an important collection of some 300 Buddhist sculptures, paintings, and ritual objects, mainly Tibetan or otherwise Himalayan, but also some from northern India and Myanmar. ⊠ *4 rue du Château* ☎ *026/9213010* ⊕ *www.tibetmuseum.info* ⊠ *10 SF* ☉ *Apr.–Oct., daily 11–6; Nov.–Mar., Tues.–Fri. 1–5, weekends 11–6.*

OFF THE BEATEN PATH

Fromagerie d'Alpage. For a more authentic, historical perspective on cheese making than at the Maison du Gruyère, visit this facility on the edge of Moléson-sur-Gruyères. Watch Gruyère, the true Vacherin d'Alpage, or Petit Moléson being made in a cauldron over an open fire in the low-roofed chalet, just as it has been made for centuries. A small restaurant serves traditional local dishes. Reservations advised. ⊠ *12 pl. de l'Aigle, Moléson-sur-Gruyères* ☎ *026/9211044* ⊕ *www.fromagerie-alpage.ch* ⊠ *5 SF* ☉ *May–Sept., daily 9–7.*

SKIING

Moléson. At 3,609 feet, Gruyère's "house mountain" of Moléson offers skiing and wraparound views of the pre-Alps and Lake Geneva. There are 30 km (18 miles) of downhill runs. Ascend via funicular, cable car, or T-bar. Sledding and snowshoeing are also popular here.

WHERE TO EAT AND STAY
For expanded hotel reviews, visit Fodors.com.

The cobbled streets, fountains, and absence of cars in Gruyères evoke a medieval atmosphere.

$$
SWISS

✕ **Auberge de la Halle.** Set amid Gruyères's most historic buildings, the exterior of this medieval structure welcomes guests with cheerful flower boxes and green-and-white-striped awnings. Inside, a warm woody interior with raftered ceiling and smooth stone floors offers an appealing setting in which to enjoy traditional dishes such as a moitié-moitié (half Gruyère, half Vacherin Fribourgeois) fondue or the definitely-worth-trying signature dish called Soupe du Chalet, a meal unto itself. Sit in the section called "the verandah" to enjoy great views with your meal. $ *Average main: 28 SF* ✉ *24 rue de Bourg* ☎ *026/9212178* ⊕ *www.auberge-halle.ch* ⊗ *Closed Tues. Oct.–Apr.*

$
B&B/INN

⌂ **Hostellerie des Chevaliers.** Standing outside the gates of Gruyères, this family-friendly hotel shares the same views of the valley and the castle as in-town lodgings, but without the noise. **Pros:** quiet location; friendly, personal service. **Cons:** no restaurant or elevator in-house. $ *Rooms from: 160 SF* ✉ *1 ruelle des Chevaliers* ☎ *026/9211933* ⊕ *www.chevaliers-gruyeres.ch* ⥗ *34 rooms* ⦿ *Breakfast.*

$$
B&B/INN
Fodor's Choice
★

⌂ **Hostellerie St-Georges.** Breathtaking mountain and valley views make this hotel a treat. **Pros:** copious breakfasts; atmospheric dining is second to none; stunning views. **Cons:** flies can be a problem during summer months; no elevator; small and noisy rooms are at front of house. $ *Rooms from: 180 SF* ✉ *22 rue du Bourg* ☎ *026/9218300* ⊕ *www.st-georges-gruyeres.ch* ⥗ *14 rooms* ⊗ *Closed Nov.–Mar.* ⦿ *Breakfast.*

$$$
B&B/INN
Fodor's Choice
★

⌂ **Hôtel De Ville.** Set on cobblestoned Rue du Bourg, this beckoning small hotel has large, airy rooms that tastefully mix bright Tuscan colors with traditional pine furnishings. **Pros:** traditional country hotel in enchanting medieval setting; sidewalk terrace for fair-weather dining. **Cons:** rich fondue smell in the restaurant may be too pungent for the faint-hearted;

La Désalpe

When the Alpine grass thins out in the fall, the cows of Haute Gruyère are led down to the village stables—in style, with huge bells around their necks and flowers and pine branches wound through their horns. Not to be outdone by their beasts, the cowherds wear their Sunday best: typically, a dark blue jacket embroidered with edelweiss motifs and puffy short sleeves that optically double the width of the wearers' shoulders. With their black-trimmed straw caps, fancy pipes, and bushy beards, the men are the real stars of the day. The women, in red-checked aprons and flat straw hats, stay in the background. To avoid two weeks of continual congestion on the roads, the foothill villages of Charmey (last Saturday in September) and Albeuve (first Saturday in October) have the herds descend together,

making a folk festival of it. Decorated cows, heifers, sheep, goats, and even pigs are paraded through the streets from 9 am until about 3 pm. The partying goes on all day, with flag throwing, marching bands, alpenhorn playing, and stalls selling Bénichon specialties. (Originally a benediction of the church, Bénichon has become a harvest celebration.) Watch for the *poyas* adorning the front walls of Gruyères farmhouses. These are naive-style paintings of cows filing up to the high pastures in spring. They advertise which breed the farmer owns and symbolize hope for a productive summer. (Before the 1820s, cheese was only made up on the Alps, where the cows had the lushest grass, so farmers had four months a year to make their living.)

no elevator. $ *Rooms from: 280 SF* ✉ *29 rue du Bourg* ☎ *026/9212424* ⊕ *www.hoteldeville.ch* 🛏 *8 rooms* ⦿ *Breakfast.*

8

BULLE

5 km (3 miles) northwest of Gruyères, 31 km (19 miles) southwest of Fribourg.

With more than 17,000 inhabitants, the town of Bulle has many attractions worthy of a larger destination: a castle (not open to the public), three-storied patrician houses lining the cobblestone main street, and a scenic backdrop so perfect you might think it has been painted. Bulle is also the site of the annual Salon Suisse des Goûts et Terroirs, a big-deal food fair held in October.

GETTING HERE AND AROUND

Trains from Fribourg to Bulle change in Romont and take 45 minutes. There is direct bus service from Fribourg station; the ride is 37 minutes.

EXPLORING

Musée Gruérien. Learn about regional traditions at the Musée Gruérien, which contains displays of folk costumes, handicrafts, and farm tools—it even has full reconstructions of the interiors of rural dwellings and a mountain cheese-making facility. Renovated in 2011, the museum boasts reserves of more than 25,000 items. ✉ *25 rue de la Condémine*

☎ *026/9161010* ⊕ *www.musee-gruerien.ch* ✉ *8 SF* ⊙ *June–Sept., Tues.–Sat. 10–5; Oct.–May, Tues.–Sat. 10–noon and 2–5, Sun. 2–5.*

ROMONT

15 km (9 miles) northwest of Bulle, 49 km (30 miles) southwest of Fribourg.

The best way to approach this 13th-century town of two broad streets is to leave the highway and drive up to its castle terrace. The fortress's 13th-century ramparts surround the town, forming a belvedere from which you can see the Alps—from Mont Blanc to the Berner Oberland. You'll also find a 12th-century Cistercian convent, the 17th-century Capuchin monastery, and the lovely 13th-century Collégiale, one of the purest examples of a Gothic church in Switzerland, with period (and modern) windows, sculptures, choir stalls, a screen, and an altarpiece.

GETTING HERE AND AROUND
By train, it takes 17 minutes to reach Romont from Fribourg.

EXPLORING
Vitromusée (*Stained-Glass Museum*). Inside the castle, the Vitromusée shimmers with crisscrossing shafts of colored light from its glass panels, both ancient and contemporary. A slide presentation traces the development of the craft, and a workshop area demonstrates current techniques. The museum now includes a donated collection of reverse painting on glass. ☎ *026/6521095* ⊕ *www.vitromusee.ch* ✉ *10 SF* ⊙ *Apr.–Oct., Tues.–Sun. 10–1 and 2–6; Nov.–Mar., Thurs.–Sun. 10–1 and 2–5.*

PAYERNE

15 km (9 miles) north of Romont, 18 km (11 miles) west of Fribourg.

The meandering streets in this market town are filled with pastel-painted 18th-century buildings, now converted to shops and restaurants. The star attraction, however, remains the town's celebrated abbey church, a landmark of the Swiss Romanesque style.

GETTING HERE AND AROUND
The train from Fribourg to Payerne takes 26 minutes; from Neuchâtel to Payerne, change at Yverdon (52 minutes).

ESSENTIALS
Visitor Information Payerne Tourisme ✉ *10 pl. du Marché* ☎ *026/6769922* ⊕ *www.payerne.ch.*

EXPLORING
Eglise Abbatiale (*Abbey Church*). The magnificent 11th-century Eglise Abbatiale, built on the site of an ancient Roman villa, is one of the finest examples of Romanesque art in Switzerland. Of particular note in its austere, restored interior is the impressively engineered barrel vaulting; the frescoes and primitive carvings on the capitals of stone pillars are also of interest. Organ concerts are frequent attractions, and exhibitions are staged in both the church and an adjoining museum.

☎ *026/6626704* 🖃 *12 SF* ☉ *May–Oct., Tues.–Sun. 10–noon and 2–6; Nov.–Apr., Tues.–Sun. 10–noon and 2–5.*

ESTAVAYER-LE-LAC

7 km (4 miles) northwest of Payerne, 30 km (19 miles) northwest of Fribourg, 51 km (32 miles) southeast of Neuchâtel.

Along with its history-soaked and highly picturesque Old Town (in summer, don't miss the Saturday morning market bursting with local produce), lakeside Estavayer is a haven for walkers, cyclists, boaters, and water-sports enthusiasts. In addition, it is a beloved base for nature lovers who head here to enjoy Grande Cariçaie, one of Europe's premier nature reserves, which nestles along the southern flank of Lac Neuchâtel.

The tiny town can still be navigated using a map drawn in 1599. It has retained much of its medieval architecture, from the arcades of the town center to the gracious, multi-towered medieval **Château de Chenaux**, which now houses its government offices.

GETTING HERE AND AROUND

Estavayer-le-Lac is 35 minutes from Fribourg by train; from Neuchâtel, change trains at Yverdon (41 minutes).

ESSENTIALS

Visitor Information Estavayer-le-Lac Tourisme ⊠ *16 rue de L'Hôtel de Ville* ☎ *026/6631237* ⊕ *www.estavayer-payerne.ch.*

EXPLORING

Musée des Grenouilles (*Frog Museum*). For something completely different, visit the quirky Musée des Grenouilles. Here are displays of 108 embalmed frogs posed like people in scenes of daily life from the 19th century. Other exhibits include an authentic 17th-century kitchen, military artifacts, and household objects dredged from Lac Neuchâtel. ⊠ *13 rue du Musée* ☎ *026/6648065* ⊕ *www.museedesgrenouilles.ch* 🖃 *5 SF* ☉ *Mar.–June, Sept., and Oct., Tues.–Sun. 10–noon and 2–5; July and Aug., daily 10–noon and 2–5; Nov.–Feb., weekends 2–5.*

WHERE TO STAY

For expanded hotel reviews, visit Fodors.com.

$

B&B/INN

🏨 **My Lady's Manor.** Listed in all the "charming small hotels in Switzerland" books, and consequently a very popular option, this bed-and-breakfast is set in a Neoclassical manor built in 1910. **Pros:** unique private house; owner is a font of information about the area. **Cons:** shared bathrooms; none of the usual hotel amenities; limited availability. $ *Rooms from: 130 SF* ⊠ *7 rte. de St-Pierre* ☎ *026/6632316* ⊕ *www.myladysmanor.org* 🛏 *10 rooms* ⦿ *Breakfast.*

8

If you climb to Murten's ramparts you'll get a nice view of Lake Murten over the town's rooftops.

MURTEN

★ *19 km (12 miles) northeast of Estavayer-le-Lac, 17 km (11 miles) north of Fribourg.*

The ancient town of Murten, known in French as Morat, is a popular resort on the Murtensee/Lac de Morat (Lake Murten). The bilingual town has a boat-lined waterfront, windsurfing rentals, a lakeside public pool complex, grassy picnic areas, and a promenade as well as a superbly preserved medieval center. From the town's 13th-century gates, take a stroll through the fountain-studded cobblestone streets. Climb up the worn wooden steps to the town ramparts for a view of the lake over a charming montage of red roofs and stone chimneys.

While a small town, Murten looms large in the history of Switzerland. Its most memorable moment came on June 22, 1476, when the Swiss Confederates—already a fearsomely efficient military machine—attacked with surprising ferocity and won a significant victory over the Burgundians, who were threatening Fribourg under the leadership of Duke Charles the Bold. Begun as a siege 12 days earlier, the battle cost the Swiss 410 men, the Burgundians 12,000. The defeat at Murten prevented the establishment of a large Lotharingian kingdom and kept Switzerland's autonomy unchallenged for decades. Legend has it that a Swiss runner, carrying a linden branch, ran from Murten to Fribourg to carry the news of victory. He expired by the town hall, and a linden tree grew from the branch he carried. Today, to commemorate his dramatic sacrifice, some 15,000 runners participate annually on the first Sunday in October in a 17-km (11-mile) race up the steep hill from Murten to Fribourg. As for the linden tree, it flourished in Fribourg for some 500 years until 1983, when it was ingloriously felled by a drunk driver. It has been replaced with a steel sculpture.

GETTING HERE AND AROUND

Murten is 29 minutes from Fribourg by train; from Neuchâtel, change at Kerzers (37 minutes). If arriving by car, leave it in the parking area in front of the town's 13th-century gates.

ESSENTIALS

Visitor Information Murten Tourisme ✉ *6 Franz-Kirchg.* ☎ *026/6705112* 🌐 *www.murtentourismus.ch.*

EXPLORING

Musée de Morat (*Murten Museum*). Complete with two water-powered mill wheels, the Musée de Moratis in the town's old mill. On view are prehistoric finds from the lake area, military items, and trophies from the Burgundian Wars. ✉ *4 Ryf* ☎ *026/6703100* 🌐 *www.museummurten.ch* 🎫 *6 SF* 🕒 *Apr.–Nov., Tues.–Sat. 2–5 and Sun. 10–5.*

Aventicum. One of the most notable ancient Roman settlements of Switzerland's "Roman era" is the Aventicum, which dates from 58 BC to AD 400. Pride of place goes to the famous Musée et Théâtre Romain (Roman Museum and Theater), where you can still see the remains of an ancient Roman forum, a bathhouse, and an amphitheater where bloodthirsty spectators once watched the games. The collection of Roman antiquities at the town museum is noteworthy, particularly the gold bust of emperor Marcus Aurelius. To get here from Murten, head 8 km (5 miles) southwest to Avenches. ✉ *Rue Centrale* ☎ *026/6751727* 🌐 *www.aventicum.org* 🎫 *4 SF* 🕒 *Apr.–Sept., Tues.–Sun. 10–5; Oct., Feb., and Mar., Tues.–Sun. 2–5; Nov.–Jan., Wed.–Sun. 2–5.*

8

WHERE TO EAT

$$$ FRENCH Fodor's Choice ★

🍴 **Auberge des Clefs.** This is a very special restaurant, so if you're traveling by car and can book well ahead you should definitely stop by to see why it gets such high praise from top food critics. The à la carte fare at the ground-floor bistro looks simple at first—tuna tartare, bouillabaisse, even Wiener schnitzel—but in the hands of owner/chef Werner Rätz the results will amaze. For the full experience, opt for the bistro's five-course prix-fixe Menu du Marché for 110 SF. Upstairs in the restaurant, there are just two set-price menus: one with five courses for 110 SF (different from the bistro), and one with seven courses for 140 SF. Restaurant or bistro, the atmosphere is laid back, the staff on the ball and friendly, and the views of lake and mountains from the terrace are divine. The place is in Lugnorre, 5 km (3 miles) northwest of Murten. [$] *Average main: 41 SF* ✉ *4 rte. de Chenaux, Lugnorre* ☎ *026/6733106* 🌐 *www.aubergedesclefs.ch* ✍ *Reservations essential* 🕒 *Closed Wed. and Thurs.*

WHERE TO STAY

For expanded hotel reviews, visit Fodors.com.

$$ HOTEL 👶 Fodor's Choice ★

🏨 **Hotel de l'Ours.** Talk about having it all: this converted 19th-century winegrower's home has stylish rooms with marble bathrooms, a waterfront location, to-die-for terrace and garden, and even an indoor pool. **Pros:** near train station and boat landing; kid-friendly atmosphere; romantic ambience. **Cons:** hard to leave. [$] *Rooms from: 220 SF* ✉ *5* *rte. de l'Ancien Pont, Sugiez Vully* ☎ *026/6739393* 🌐 *www.hotel-ours.ch* 🛏 *8 rooms* ⏲ *Closed 3 wks beginning mid-Oct. and late Dec.–early Jan.* 🍴 *Breakfast.*

$ HOTEL 🏨 **Hotel Murtenhof & Krone.** In the heart of Murten's Old Town, this cluster of patrician houses dating back to 1428 conjures images of centuries gone by. **Pros:** individuality and heritage of establishment very much cherished; in the heart of the peaceful Old Town; kindly and quirky staff. **Cons:** some say the walls are a tad too thin. [$] *Rooms from: 160 SF* ✉ *1–3 Rathausg.* ☎ *026/6729030* 🌐 *www.murtenhof.ch* 🛏 *57 rooms, 5 suites* 🍴 *Breakfast.*

$$$$ HOTEL 🏨 **Le Vieux Manoir au Lac.** Truly worthy of Relais & Châteaux status, this stately, turreted mansion sits in a manicured park on Lac de Morat. **Pros:** within walking distance of medieval Murten; romantic candlelit dinner on the pier—book a few days ahead. **Cons:** frequent functions can disturb the prevailing tranquillity; restaurants are somewhat pricey. [$] *Rooms from: 520 SF* ✉ *18 rue de Lausanne, Murten-Meyriez* ☎ *026/6786161* 🌐 *www.vieuxmanoir.ch* 🛏 *36 rooms* 🍴 *Breakfast.*

LAC NEUCHÂTEL AND ENVIRONS

The region of Neuchâtel belonged to Prussia from 1707 to 1857, with a brief interruption caused by Napoléon and a period of dual loyalty to Prussia and the Swiss Confederation between 1815 and 1857. Yet its French heritage remains untouched by Germanic language, diet, or culture. Some boast that the inhabitants speak "the best French in Switzerland," which is partly why so many summer language courses are taught here.

NEUCHÂTEL

★ *28 km (17 miles) northwest of Murten, 48 km (30 miles) northwest of Fribourg.*

At the foot of the Jura Mountains, flanked by vineyards and facing southeast, the city of Neuchâtel enjoys panoramic views of Lac Neuchâtel and the range of the middle Alps, including the majestic mass of Mont Blanc and the Berner Oberland. Lac Neuchâtel, at 38 km (24 miles) long and 8 km (5 miles) wide, is the largest lake located entirely within Switzerland. (The much larger lakes of Geneva and Constance are shared with France and Germany, respectively.) A prosperous city, Neuchâtel has a reputation for precision work, beginning with watchmaking in the early 18th century. In fact, the region is often referred to by locals as "Watch Valley." The city itself lies on the Watchmaking Route—a 200-km (125-mile) heritage trail with 27 stops running from Geneva to Basel. There are traditional workshops, museums, and countless other insights into the ingenuity of this craftsmanship and time itself.

Visitors to Neuchâtel city will note that broad avenues in the lower part of town bordering the lake are lined with neo-Romanesque yellow-sandstone buildings, which inspired author Alexandre Dumas to call Neuchâtel "a city with the appearance of an immense *joujou* (toy) dressed in butter." The collegiate church and the 12th-century castle, which today houses the cantonal government, sit gracefully above the city's bustling old marketplace. You can stroll (or cycle) along the lakeside promenade as far as Hauterive, the next village to the north.

Neuchâtel's biggest annual festival is the winemakers' three-day celebration of the grape harvest, the *fête des vendanges.* It's celebrated the last weekend of September with parades and fanfare throughout the city. Also of note are the many absinthe distilleries in the area. Absinthe originated in Val-de-Travers, 26 km (16 miles) to the west of Neuchâtel city, in the 18th century and since 2005 (when Switzerland re-legalized absinthe) the regional distillers have become famous for brewing some of the best absinthe in the world. At a restaurant in town, it's worth ordering this local specialty just to observe the elaborate serving ritual.

GETTING HERE AND AROUND

Neuchâtel has direct trains to and from major Swiss cities: Geneva is 1 hour 10 minutes away, Lausanne is 41 minutes, Bern is 33–50 minutes, Basel and Zürich are both 1½ hours away. Trains run frequently between Fribourg and Neuchâtel (with transfers) and take at least 1 hour.

Take Bus No. 7 to Place Pury to get Littoral Neuchâtel buses to countryside villages. Bus information can be found on the town website.

ESSENTIALS

Visitor Information Neuchâtel Tourisme ✉ *Hôtel des Postes* ☎ *032/8896890* ⊕ *www.neuchateltourisme.ch.*

EXPLORING

TOP ATTRACTIONS

Église Collégiale (*Collegiate Church*). The French influence in Neuchâtel is revealed in its monuments and architecture, most notably the Église Collégiale. The handsome Romanesque and Burgundian Gothic structure, with a colorful tile roof, dates from the 12th century. The church contains a strikingly realistic and well-preserved grouping of life-size painted figures called *le cénotaphe,* or monument. Dating from the 14th and 15th centuries, this is considered one of Europe's finest examples of medieval art. From April through September there are free guided tours (usually between 10 and 4) of the Château de Neuchâtel(Neuchâtel Castle) adjoining the church; check at the château entrance to learn when the next one in English starts. Anyone not wanting to climb steep streets can reach the church from the Promenade Noire off the Place des Halles by an inconspicuous elevator—*ascenseur publique.* ✉ *3 rue de la Collégiale* ⊕ *www.collegiale.ch* 🎫 *Free* ☉ *Weekdays 8–noon and 1:30–5.*

🔁 **Laténium.** Located at water's edge, this interactive archaeological ★ museum is the largest in Switzerland. In the nearby community of Hauterive, it displays artifacts found in and around Lac Neuchâtel and explains how they were recovered. The lifestyles of Bronze Age lake dwellers are skillfully depicted, with pride of place going to a sculpted standing stone from Bevaix, a village southwest of Neuchâtel, which resembles a man. Inside the museum you can also see the remains of a 60-foot-long Gallo-Roman barge; outside in the park, its reconstruction is moored near a full-scale wooden Bronze Age house on stilts. There is a pamphlet in English, and for 5 SF you can rent an hour-long audio-guide in English. ■TIP➡ There is a free shuttle boat service to Hauterive from the port in Neuchâtel that runs Friday–Sunday in April and May and Tuesday–Sunday June–September. ⊠ *Espace Paul Vouga, Hauterive* ☎ *032/8896917* ⊕ *www.latenium. ch* ⌨ *9 SF* ⊙ *Tues.–Sun. 10–5.*

★ **Musée d'Art et d'Histoire** (*Museum of Art and History*). Thanks to a remarkable curator, the Musée d'Art et d'Histoire displays a striking collection of paintings gathered under broad themes—nature, civilization—and mounted in a radical, evocative way. The 15th-century allegories, early Impressionist paintings, and contemporary abstractions pack the walls from floor to ceiling, interacting, conflicting, and demanding comparison. You may climb a platform (itself plastered with paintings) to view the higher works. This aggressive series of displays is framed by the architectural decorations of Neuchâtel resident Clement Heaton, whose murals and stained glass make the building itself a work of art.

This novel museum also has the honor of hosting three of this watchmaking capital's most exceptional guests: the **automates Jaquet-Droz**, three astounding little androids, created between 1768 and 1774, that once toured the courts of Europe like young mechanical Mozarts. Pierre Jaquet-Droz and his son Henri-Louis created them, and they are moving manifestations of the stellar degree to which watchmaking had evolved by the 18th century. Le Dessinateur (the Draughtsman) is an automated dandy in satin knee pants who draws graphite images of a dog, the god Eros in a chariot pulled by a butterfly, and a profile of Louis XV. La Musicienne (the Musician) is a young woman playing the organ. She moves and breathes subtly along with the music and actually strikes the keys that produce the organ notes. L'Écrivain (the Writer) dips a real feather in real ink and writes 40 different letters. Like a primitive computer, he can be programmed to write any message simply by the change of a steel disk. The automatons come alive only on the first Sunday of the month, at 2, 3, and 4 (more often in summer; days and times are posted on the museum's website), but the audiovisual show re-creates the thrill. ⊠ *1 esplanade Léopold-Robert* ☎ *032/7177925* ⊕ *www.mahn.ch* ⌨ *8 SF* ⊙ *Tues.–Sun. 11–6.*

WORTH NOTING

Centre Dürrenmatt. Named after the Swiss writer and artist Friedrich Dürrenmatt (1921–90), the Centre Dürrenmatt, perched high above Neuchâtel, houses an exhibition devoted to modern literature and visual arts. One of Switzerland's (and the world's) top architects, Mario Botta, designed a curving, skylighted underground space connected to Dürrenmatt's former home (now a private library and offices). Many of Dürrenmatt's paintings are disturbing, reflecting a bleak worldview that tends to be softened by the humor, albeit acerbic, in his writing. Letters and excerpts of his books are also on display, with each artwork accompanied by a quote. ✉ *74 chemin du Pertuis-du-Sault* ☎ *032/7202060* 🌐 *www.cdn.ch* 🎫 *8 SF* ⏲ *Wed.–Sun. 11–5.*

Galeries de l'Histoire (*History Gallery*). This gallery houses scale models of Neuchâtel from the year 1000 to 2000. ✉ *7 av. DuPeyrou* ☎ *032/7177925* 🌐 *www.mahn.ch* 🎫 *Free* ⏲ *Wed. and Sun. 1–5.*

Old Town. The architecture of the Old Town presents a full range of French styles. Along Rue des Moulins are two perfect specimens of the Louis XIII period, and—at its opposite end—a fine Louis XIV house anchors the Place des Halles (market square), also notable for its turreted 16th-century Maison des Halles. The Old Town has several fine patrician houses, such as the magnificent Hôtel DuPeyrou, home of the friend, protector, and publisher of Jean-Jacques Rousseau, who studied botany in the nearby Val-de-Travers. Most of the Old Town is a pedestrian-only zone, though public buses do rumble through. You can stroll as far as Marin-Epagnier (east side) and Vaumarcus (west side).

Tour des Prisons (*Prison Tower*). This tower, which adjoins the Collegiate Church, has panoramic views from its turret. On your way up, stop in one of the original wooden prison cells. ✉ *Rue Jehanne-de-Hochberg* 🎫 *2 SF* ⏲ *Apr.–Oct., daily 8–6.*

EN ROUTE

Musée Cantonale de la Vigne et du Vin. Neuchâtel is part of what is known as the Three Lakes wine region, the smallest of Switzerland's six winegrowing areas. The famous Pinot Noir rosé wine, Oeil de Perdrix, originated in Neuchâtel and the canton produces many other excellent wines, including traditional-method sparkling wine made by the Mauler winery in an old Benedictine monastery in Val-de-Travers. Amid the vineyards that fan out to the west of Neuchâtel city and slope gently down to the lake sits Château Boudry, which houses the Musée Cantonale de la Vigne et du Vin (Cantonal Museum of Vine and Wine). ✉ *Château Boudry, Sentier du Château, Boudry* ☎ *032/8421098* 🌐 *www.chateaudeboudry.ch* 🎫 *Museum 7 SF* ⏲ *Wed.–Sun. 2–6.*

8

WHERE TO EAT

$ FRENCH Fodor's Choice ★

🍴 **Bach & Buck.** This simply furnished crêperie-cum-tearoom opposite the Jardin Anglais is an ideal spot to grab a cheap but tasty meal. Its location close to the university ensures a young crowd, many of whom head here to enjoy a choice from more than 120 types of crepes: sweet or savory, meat or vegetarian. Gluten-free, wheat, and buckwheat varieties cater to many diets. A selection of more than 30 teas also can be enjoyed while playing one of the video games or perusing one of the comic books they have on offer. Make a quick visit to the neighboring shop, Art' Thé, to pick up a bag of tea and associated utensils for a charming memento to take home. [$] *Average main: 12 SF* ✉ *29 av. du 1er-Mars* ☎ *032/7256353* 🌐 *www.artthe.ch* 💳 *No credit cards* ⏲ *Closed Sun. and 2 wks in July. No dinner.*

$$ ITALIAN

🍴 **Le Banneret.** Owner/chef Angelo de Marco often emerges to greet diners in the ground-floor brasserie of this popular restaurant, housed in a late-Renaissance building at the foot of the Rue du Château. But whether you eat on the ground floor, in the room upstairs, or outside next to a fountain, the menu is the same and the homemade pasta and fish dishes for which de Marco is particularly well known are utter delights. Ⓢ *Average main: 32 SF* ✉ *1 rue Fleury* ☎ *032/7252861* ⊕ *www.restaurantlebanneret.ch* ⊘ *Closed Sun. and Mon., 1 wk each in Apr. and Sept. and mid-Dec.–early Jan.*

$$$ ✕ **Le Bocca.** Despite its proximity to the lake, there's neither a terrace nor
FRENCH   a view at Le Bocca, and charming owner/chef Claude Frôté wants it that
Fodor's Choice   way: customers should come to this spot for his innovative food. Set
★   just north of Neuchâtel, this restaurant offers an array of menus in its brasserie and main dining room. If you're a fan of organ meats such as tripe—long popular in Neuchâtel—you can eat for a lot less: Le Bocca's contemporary takes on these traditional dishes only run you 32 SF to 44 SF. Hand in hand with the fine food (past delights have included foie gras with passion fruit or beef fillet with olives and pistachios) is a great wine list with 25,000 bottles in stock. Ⓢ *Average main: 44 SF* ✉ *11 av. Bachelin, St-Blaise* ☎ *032/7533680* ⊕ *www.le-bocca.com* ⌃ *Reservations essential* ⊘ *Closed Sun. and Mon. and around Easter and Christmas.*

$$ ✕ **Le Cardinal Brasserie.** Enjoy a perfect café crème or a whole meal along
FRENCH   with the Neuchâtelois at one of the most authentic cafés in the Old Town. This place models itself on a traditional Parisian brasserie, and the striking Art Nouveau interior certainly helps: the molded ceiling, etched windows, and blue-and-green decorative tiles all date from 1905. Fish is a specialty, and large platters of *fruits de mer* (shellfish) in season are a delicious treat. A "menu of the day" special usually costs 18 SF. Ⓢ *Average main: 35 SF* ✉ *9 rue du Seyon* ☎ *032/7251286* ⊕ *www. lecardinal-brasserie.ch* ⊘ *Closed Sun. and 2 wks in July.*

WHERE TO STAY
For expanded hotel reviews, visit Fodors.com.

$$ ⊡ **Alpes et Lac.** This modest 19th-century hotel across from the train
HOTEL   station overlooks the tile rooftops, sparkling lake, and white-capped Alps. **Pros:** welcoming staff willing to help you with your French; just steps from the station. **Cons:** some rooms are on the small side; rooms facing the station can be noisy. Ⓢ *Rooms from: 190 SF* ✉ *2 pl. de la Gare* ☎ *032/7231919* ⊕ *www.alpesetlac.ch* ⇗ *30 rooms* ⦿ *Breakfast.*

$$$$ ⊡ **Beau-Rivage Hotel.** This thoroughly elegant, gracefully restored 19th-
HOTEL   century hotel has a perfect perch on the lakeshore; on a clear day there's
★   a splendid view of the Alps. **Pros:** high standard of service and facilities rare in region; outstanding views; lakeside location. **Cons:** a tad too corporate and lacking in character for some; fourth-floor rooms are darker and smaller than the rest. Ⓢ *Rooms from: 410 SF* ✉ *1 esplanade du Mont Blanc* ☎ *032/7231515* ⊕ *www.beau-rivage-hotel.ch* ⇗ *66 rooms.*

$$ ⊡ **Café-Hôtel de L'Aubier.** In the pedestrian zone at the foot of the château,
HOTEL   this delightful, entirely no-smoking hotel offers light, modern, spacious
★   guest rooms with warm color schemes inspired by the spices for which they are named. **Pros:** central location in pedestrian zone; bright, light, and modern atmosphere. **Cons:** can tend toward noisiness on weekends due to central location; not well suited to those traveling by car. Ⓢ *Rooms from: 180 SF* ✉ *1 rue du Château* ☎ *032/7101858* ⊕ *www. aubier.ch* ⇗ *9 rooms, 3 with bath.*

Set on an eponymous lake, Neuchâtel is a bustling city with a strong French influence.

$$$$ **Hôtel Palafitte.** Unique in Europe, this one-level hotel is partly built on
HOTEL   piles on Lac Neuchâtel, giving it unbeatable clear-day views that include
Fodor's Choice   the distant Alps. **Pros:** romantic getaway; dig that golf-cart-style vehicle
★   that shuttles you to your room. **Cons:** despite air-conditioning, strong
sun may heat your room up; some glitches in maintenance; breakfast is
expensive. $ *Rooms from: 540 SF* ⊠ *2 rte. des Gouttes d'Or, Monruz*
☏ *032/7230202* ⊕ *www.palafitte.ch* ⤶ *40 suites.*

$ **La Maison du Prussien.** In the gorge of Vauseyon, 10 minutes from
B&B/INN   Neuchâtel, this restored 18th-century brewery is nestled alongside a
roaring woodland stream. **Pros:** traditional old-world charm; authentic
restoration; quiet location. **Cons:** no elevator. $ *Rooms from: 175 SF*
⊠ *Au Gor du Vauseyon, 11 rue des Tunnels* ☏ *032/7305454* ⊕ *www.
hotel-prussien.ch* ⤶ *8 rooms, 2 suites* ☉ *Closed mid-July–mid-Aug.
and late Dec.–early Jan.*

NIGHTLIFE

Neuchâtel has an ever-changing selection of *restaurants de nuit* and
bars musicaux, establishments that pulse with hot sounds until the
wee hours of the morning and sometimes serve food—along the lines
of steak-*frites* (steak and fries)—to keep you going.

Café Trio. With sleek furnishings and a long zinc-topped bar, the Café
Trio is open until 2 on Friday and Saturday. ⊠ *3 rue des Moulins*
☏ *032/7242224.*

SPORTS AND THE OUTDOORS

SWIMMING

There are public beaches at many villages and resorts on the lake.

Lac Neuchâtel is the largest lake located entirely within Switzerland's borders.

Piscine du Nid-du-Crô. Right on the lake, this extensive municipal complex has outdoor and indoor pools. ⊠ *30 rte. des Falaises* ☎ *032/7226222* ⊕ *www.lessports.ch.*

GRANDSON

29 km (18 miles) southwest of Neuchâtel.

A tour of the Old Town of Grandson is eminently worthwhile. The church, tower, fountains, and narrow streets lined with extraordinary facades make this a truly time-burnished spot. For guided strolls, stop in at the tourist office in the Maison des Terroirs (open daily 11–6). This lakeside village in Canton Vaud has a long history. It is said that in 1066 a member of the Grandson family accompanied William of Normandy (better known as "William the Conqueror") to England, where he founded the English barony of Grandson. Otto I of Grandson took part in the Crusades.

EXPLORING

○ **Château de Grandson** (*Grandson Castle*). When the Burgundian Wars
★ broke out in the late-15th century, the Château de Grandson, built in the 11th century and much rebuilt during the 13th and 15th centuries, was in the hands of Charles the Bold of Burgundy. In 1475 the Swiss won it by siege, but early the next year their garrison was surprised by Charles, and 418 of their men were captured and hanged from the apple trees in the castle orchard. A few days later the Swiss returned to Grandson and, after crushing the Burgundians, retaliated by stringing up their prisoners from the same apple trees. After being used for three

centuries as a residence by the Bernese bailiffs, the castle was bought in 1875 by the de Blonay family, who restored it to its current impressive state, with high, massive walls and five cone turrets. Inside, you can see reproductions of Charles the Bold's Burgundian war tent and two jousting knights astride their horses—in full armor. There are also *oubliettes* (dungeon pits for prisoners held *in perpetua*), torture chambers, and a model of the Battle of Grandson, complete with a 20-minute slide show (in English if you get in quickly enough to push the right button). The dungeons now house an extensive vintage-car museum, displaying the prized beauties of Greta Garbo and Winston Churchill. ⊠ *Pl. du Château* ☎ *024/4452926* ⊕ *www.chateau-grandson.ch* ✉ *12 SF* ⊙ *Apr.–Oct., daily 8:15–6; Nov.–Mar., daily 8:15–5.*

YVERDON-LES-BAINS

6 km (2½ miles) southwest of Grandson, 38 km (24 miles) southwest of Neuchâtel.

With a center closed to traffic, Yverdon-les-Bains is a charming, bustling place. Located at the southernmost tip of Lac de Neuchâtel, this pastel-colored lakefront town has been appreciated for its thermal waters and sandy, willow-lined shore since the Romans first invaded and set up thermal baths here. In the 18th century its fame spread across Europe. Today, along the waterfront, you'll find parks, promenades, a shady campground, and a 2-km (1¼-mile) stretch of little beaches.

GETTING HERE AND AROUND

Trains from Fribourg to Yverdon-les-Bains take 54 minutes; from Neuchâtel to Yverdon-les-Bains the trip is 18 minutes.

ESSENTIALS

Visitor Information Yverdon-les-Bains Tourisme ⊠ *2 av. de la Gare* ☎ *024/4236101* ⊕ *www.yverdonlesbainsregion.ch.*

EXPLORING

Château de Yverdon-les-Bains. In the center of the Old Town sits the turreted, mid-13th-century Château de Yverdon-les-Bains. Most of the castle is now a museum, with exhibits on locally discovered prehistoric and Roman artifacts, Egyptian art, natural history, and, of course, local history. A special room is dedicated to the famous Swiss educator Johann Heinrich Pestalozzi (1746–1827), who spent 20 years here. His influential ideas on education led to school reforms at home and in Germany and England. ⊠ *Place Pestalozzi 1* ☎ *024/4259310* ⊕ *www. musee-yverdon-region.ch* ✉ *8 SF* ⊙ *June–Sept., Tues.–Sun. 11–5; Oct.– May, Tues.–Sun. 2–5.*

Hôtel de Ville (*Town Hall*). In front of Yverdon's Hôtel de Ville—an 18th-century building notable for its French-inspired Neoclassical facade—stands a bronze statue of Swiss educator Johann Heinrich Pestalozzi (1746–1827), grouped with two children. ⊠ *Place Pestalozzi 1.*

Maison d'Ailleurs. While Yverdon has a lot of history, it also has a special place in its heart for the future thanks to this fanciful "Museum of Science Fiction, Utopia, and Extraordinary Journeys." While mainly a research center and library for scholars, the "House of Elsewhere"

8

mounts fascinating exhibitions for the general public, including such recent shows as the ones devoted to the popular "Return to Dinotopia" books and H. P. Lovecraft. ✉ *14 pl. Pestalozzi* ☎ *024/4256438* ⊕ *www. ailleurs.ch* 📧 *12 SF* ⊘ *Wed.–Fri. 2–6, weekends 11–6.*

Thermal Center. The municipal Thermal Center is completely up to date, with indoor and outdoor pools, whirlpools, and massage jets, as well as numerous massage, beauty, and relaxation treatments. Swim caps are mandatory, and children under three are not permitted. ✉ *22 av. des Bains* ☎ *024/4230232* ⊕ *www.thermes-yverdon.ch* 📧 *19 SF* ⊘ *Mon.– Sat. 8–10, Sun. 8–8.*

Bern

WORD OF MOUTH

"I have to speak up for Bern—love it! Nice amble, especially on a cloudy or rainy day, with all the arcaded shops and cafés for people-watching. We always go up to the rose gardens and sit on the terrace for a drink, watch those few souls brave enough to float down the Aare River."

—mokka4

WELCOME TO BERN

TOP REASONS TO GO

★ **Lived-in history:** UNESCO only made Bern a World Heritage Site in 1983, but the city's cobblestone arcades and clock towers have been beautifully preserved since the 1400s.

★ **Feats of Klee:** The spectacular Zentrum named for Paul Klee—the whimsical painter who hopscotched across art—is a tour de force of vibrant creativity.

★ **Undercover shopping:** Bern's got it all—from couture fashion to artisan chocolatiers—and, thanks to those famous arcaded streets, you can even enjoy window-shopping in rainy weather.

★ **The Zibelemärit:** Think of an object—a train car, an alarm clock, a teddy bear—and you will likely see it rendered in onions at November's city-wide celebration of the vegetable.

★ **Those sunbathing Swiss:** Warm summer days lure swimmers to the Marzili's sweeping lawns and swift, icy stretch of river below the Federal Parliament Building.

Map labels

Universität
Hedlerstr.
Speicherg.
Waisenhaus-platz
Schuttestr.
Kornhausbr.
Parkterrasse
Aarbergerg.
Bollwerk
Neuengasse
Zeughausg.
Brunngasshalde
Haupt-bahnhof
Kornhauspl.
CITY CENTER
Spitalgasse
Bären-platz
Marktgasse
1
Bubenbergpl.
Schauplatzg.
Bundes-platz
Theater-platz
Casinoplatz
Christoffelg.
Bundeshaus
Kochergasse
Bundesgasse
Bundes-
Münzgraben
Kirchenfeldbr.
Kleine Schanze
Münztrain-terrasse
Aare
4
Sulgeneckstr.
Brückenstrasse
Marzilistr.
Aarstrasse
Dalmaziquai
MUSEUM DISTRICT **3**
Schweizerisches ◆ Alpines Museum
Helvetia-platz
Bernisches Historisches Museum
Bernastr.
Marzilistr.
Naturhistorisches Museum

1 **Altstadt (Old Town) and City Center.** Today the historic Rathaus, Münster, painted fountains, and 18th-century guildhalls rub shoulders with arcades and cellars full of restaurants and quirky boutiques. The swath of land between the Zytglogge and the Haupt-bahnhof is Bern's most commercially vibrant, a dense warren of narrow streets and pedestrian passageways studded with shops, hidden alleys, grand architecture, and the Swiss Federal Government complex.

2 **Bärengraben and Rosengarten.** The eastern end of Bern's Old Town houses the BearPark on the slopes of the River Aare. Up the hill is the Rose Garden, with an impressive collection of flora and stunning views over the city.

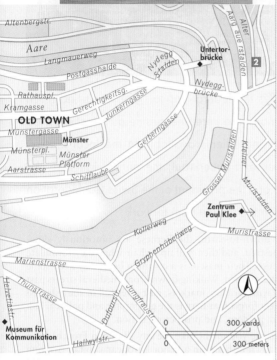

OLD TOWN

Münster

Zentrum
Paul Klee

Museum für
Kommunikation

| 0 | 300 yards |
| 0 | 300 meters |

GETTING ORIENTED

Few capital cities are as charming and compact as Bern, Switzerland's political nerve center. Alluring medieval streets, frolicsome fountains, and palpable history coexist so easily with outdoor markets and traditional cheese-and-potatoes that it's easy to forget this is actually a fully wired, surprisingly young 21st-century urban center.

9

3 **Museum District: Kirchenfeld.** The Kirchenfeld neighborhood is a masterpiece of late 19th-century urban planning, where a top array of Bern's museums is grouped together in a tight, easy-to-visit cluster on the south bank of the River Aare.

4 **Greater Bern.** Just north of the center are neighborhoods that stray from the medieval feel of the Old Town, be it modern, funky, or artistic, each is charming in its own way. The Paul

Klee Center, an easy bus ride away, is in the eastern suburbs and well worth the detour.

Updated
by Susan
Vogel-Misicka

Although Bern is the federal capital, you won't find much cosmopolitan nonsense here: the *cuisine du marché,* based on the freshest ingredients available in the local market, features fatback and sauerkraut; the annual fair fetes the humble onion; and the president of the Swiss Confederation has been known to take the tram to work.

Warm, friendly, down-to-earth, the Bernese are notoriously slow-spoken; ask a question, and then pull up a chair while they formulate a judicious response. Their mascot is a common bear; they keep some as pets in the center of town. Walking down broad medieval streets past squares crowded with farmers' markets, past cafés full of shirt-sleeved politicos, you might forget that Bern is the geographic and political hub of a sophisticated, modern, and prosperous nation.

In fact, at first glance you might take the city (Berne in French) for a thriving country town rather than a major European capital. Arriving in the city center, either by car or by train, most visitors see only its Old Town and miss altogether the modern sprawl of banking and industry that surrounds it. Although Bern is full of patrician houses and palatial hotels, there is no official presidential residence: the seven members of the coalition government, each of whom serves a year as president, have to find their own places to live when in Bern.

Bern wasn't always so self-effacing. It earned its pivotal position through a history of power and influence that dates from the 12th century, when Berchtold V, Duke of Zähringen, expanded his fortress at the tip of a sharp meander in the River Aare. He named his new city for the first animal he killed in the local woods (an unlucky but now immortalized brown bear).

Over the years Bern stayed on top, and when the Swiss Confederation took its contemporary, federal form in 1848, Bern was a natural choice for its capital.

Yet today it's not the massive Bundeshaus (Federal Parliament Building) that dominates the city, but instead its perfectly preserved arcades, fountains, and thick, sturdy towers—all remnants of its heyday as a medieval power. Bern owes its architectural unity to a major fire that swept through town in 1405, destroying most of the houses, then mainly of wood. It was rebuilt in sandstone, and its arcades stretch on for some 6 km (4 miles). They're the reason UNESCO granted Bern World Landmark status.

BERN PLANNER

WHEN TO GO

Architecture can be a big tip-off: covered stone arcades, dark underground cellars, small windows, and thick stone walls were all medieval coping tactics in the face of bad weather. Bern can be cold and wet and miserable in winter, its indoor spaces warmed with fires and packed with people.

But it is mild and sunny from spring through autumn, when every restaurant that can sets up camp in the street, windows are thrown open, and people take to the river by the Marzili with unrestrained glee. Summer is warm, and July through mid-August is vacation season. Note that many restaurants close up shop for vacation for a few weeks during the summer season.

PLANNING YOUR TIME

The Bernese do not scurry around their city, and neither should you— its considerable charms are best discovered at a slow, steady pace with a plan to get from A to B but no fixed idea how. The most efficient, flexible, cheap, and enjoyable way to navigate Bern's cobblestones is on foot. The city is easy to navigate: count on 10 minutes to walk at a steady clip from the Hauptbahnhof to the Bärengraben; about 5 to take the bus.

It is technically possible to see the major sights in a day, but you'd miss seeing the sun set over medieval rooftops, you wouldn't be able to linger in restaurants, and this is a city that comes out at night. Do pace yourself as you wander the streets, do visit the museums at a steady clip, and do get a running start on the narrow curved steps up the Münster steeple. Indulge any urges to explore Marzili or Matte, to pursue your curiosity at the markets, to take a sudden chocolate break, to watch the bears, or to admire the fountains—although it is indeed strange to find the latter sitting in the middle of main-street traffic.

GETTING HERE AND AROUND

AIR TRAVEL

Bern-Belp Airport is 10 km (6 miles) from the city center. A shuttle bus ride to the Hauptbahnhof takes 30 minutes and costs 10 SF. Costing about 6 SF, another option is go via train and bus, which takes about the same amount of time. A taxi to the Hauptbahnhof costs about 50 SF.

CAR TRAVEL

Bern sits squarely on the map of Swiss expressways. The A1 connects the city with Basel and Zürich to the north, with Lac Léman and Geneva to the south, and via Lausanne with the Valais. The A6 to the Berner Oberland runs just east of the city. Downtown pedestrian zones make parking in city garages a virtual necessity; electric signs on major incoming roads post current numbers of empty spaces.

BUS AND TRAM TRAVEL

Trams and buses are handy for getting outside the Altstadt. Service by Bernmobil is extensive, with city center fares costing between 2 SF and 4 SF. An unlimited day ticket is about 11 SF. Buy tickets from the dispensers at every stop by finding the name of the stop closest to your destination on the map, then selecting the fare listed for it. Swiss Pass holders travel free.

Bus Contact Bernmobil ☎ 031/3218844 ⊕ www.bernmobil.ch.

TAXI TRAVEL

Bernese taxis are clean and plentiful, but circuitous downtown traffic routing renders them cumbersome and expensive; a ride from the Hauptbahnhof to the Bärengraben costs about 20 SF.

Taxi Contacts Bären Taxi ☎ 031/3711111 ⊕ www.baerentaxi.ch. **Nova Taxi** ☎ 031/3313313 ⊕ www.novataxi.ch.

TRAIN TRAVEL

Bern is a train-based city with high-speed connections to Berlin, Paris, and Milan. Bern's Hauptbahnhof is also a major hub for trains within Switzerland. Count an hour to reach Zürich or Basel, less than two for Geneva, four hours to Lugano. A tight network of local and regional trains keeps Bern connected to surrounding communities.

⇨ *For more information on getting here and around, see Travel Smart Switzerland.*

VISITOR INFORMATION

Bern Tourismus, based in the Hauptbahnhof, distributes free brochures and maps, publishes Bern Guide, and operates a 3-D multimedia history presentation called *BernShow* at its satellite information center next to the Bärengraben.

Its guides also lead 90-minute English-language walking tours of the Altstadt at 11 am daily between April and October, on Saturday the rest of the year. Upon request they also organize group tours conducted by bus or down the Aare in rafts. Reserve at the tourist center in the Hauptbahnhof.

Bern Tourismus ✉ *Hauptbahnhof, Bahnhofplatz 10a, City Center* ☎ *031/ 3281212* ⊕ *www.bern.com.*

EXPLORING BERN

From the time it was built on a high, narrow peninsula above the rushing Aare, Bern's streets have followed the river's flow. The original town began by what is now the Nydegg bridge—it controlled the ferry crossing there—and spread westward, uphill to the *Zeitglockenturm* (known locally as the *Zytglogge*), a clock tower constructed in 1191 to mark Bern's first significant western gate. Further expansion in 1256 stretched the city to where the Käfigturm now stands; one last medieval growth spurt, hot on the heels of a resounding victory over the Burgundians

The best way to explore Bern is to take your time meandering through the city's markets and arcades.

in 1339, moved the city walls west yet again to the present-day train station, the Hauptbahnhof

The bustling, commercial city center radiates out from that train station. To get to the Altstadt, follow the trams across Bärenplatz and through the Käfigturm. Marzili and Matte, former working-class and still flood-prone neighborhoods, lie together along the riverbed of the Aare. All of these areas are easily explored on foot, but in Marzili and Matte you may want to take your cue from the locals: walk down, ride the funicular up. The cluster of museums in Kirchenfeld, on the south side of the river, is a short (spectacular) walk or tram ride away.

ALTSTADT (OLD TOWN) AND CITY CENTER

Fire destroyed the original, predominantly wooden structures that comprised the Altstadt, the historical heart of the city that perches above the Aare. The Bernese rebuilt using local sandstone, and today's arcaded, cobblestone streets radiate medieval appeal. Eclectic upscale boutiques inhabit some of the oldest buildings downhill from the Zytglogge; Marktgasse and Spitalgasse favor chain and department stores.

TOP ATTRACTIONS

Bundeshaus (*Houses of Parliament*). Conceived as a national monument and the beating heart of the Swiss Confederation (the 7-member Federal Council, the 46-member Council of States, and the 200-member National Council all meet here), this massive, majestic domed complex built between 1852 and 1902 takes its symbolism seriously. The 26 fountains out front represent the Swiss cantons; solemn statues inside

A GOOD WALK

Bern's downtown is not large, but it can be steep and there's a lot to absorb. To begin the walk, exit the main hall of the Hauptbahnhof, following signs for the Altstadt.

On the far side of Spitalgasse is the **Heiliggeistkirche**. Duck inside for a peek at its colorful Baroque ceiling, then follow the trams left past the cheerful Pfeiferbrunnen (Bagpiper Fountain) to the first intersection, Bärenplatz.

Keep following the trams (carefully) through the **Käfigturm**, a 17th-century prison tower built on the site of the city's 13th-century main gate, and continue down Marktgasse. At the end, follow the trams to the left to the Kindlifresserbrunnen, atop which an ogre (most likely a Fasnacht character) sits munching on several small children.

Dominating the town center is the mighty **Zytglogge**, Bern's original western gate and communal horological reference point since 1530. Continue down Kramgasse, the medieval main street. The painted figures and insignia above some houses indicate their connections to specific guilds; others date from the city's 18th-century height of prosperity.

At No. 49, the **Einsteinhaus** is where a young man named Albert struggled to make his name in physics. Take nearby Kramgasse (called Gerechtigkeitsgasse from this point on) and continue down the hill. The Gerechtigkeitsbrunnen (Justice Fountain), considered the jewel of Bern's fountains, depicts the emperor, the pope, the sultan, and the mayor of Bern.

As you pass the Hotel zum Goldenen Adler, the 18th-century successor to the city's oldest guesthouse, veer left where the main street becomes Nydeggasse and aim downhill into Nydeggstalden.

The **Nydeggkirche**, set back from the road on your right, occupies the site of Duke Berchtold's original fortress and thus represents the oldest part of the city.

From the church courtyard, head for the far end of the church and take the covered Burgtreppe stairs down to Mattenenge, turning left then right when you get to the bottom.

Both routes will leave you facing Bern's oldest river crossing, the Untertorbrücke, or Lower Gate Bridge, with the Läuferbrunnen (Messenger Fountain) and its bear-human duo sheltering under a tree to your left.

Cross the swift, blue-green Aare and head left past the Landhaus to the paved footpath marked "Rosengarten" and zigzag to the right on Lerberstrasse. When you reach Aargauerstalden you will be rewarded with a fetching view of the Altstadt. From here, head back down the hill to the traffic circle and cut directly across it to the new **BearPark**.

Walk straight through the carefully tended **Rosengarten** to see the best view of all—the city's bridges, rooftops, and, on clear days, the **Gurten**, Bern's local hill.

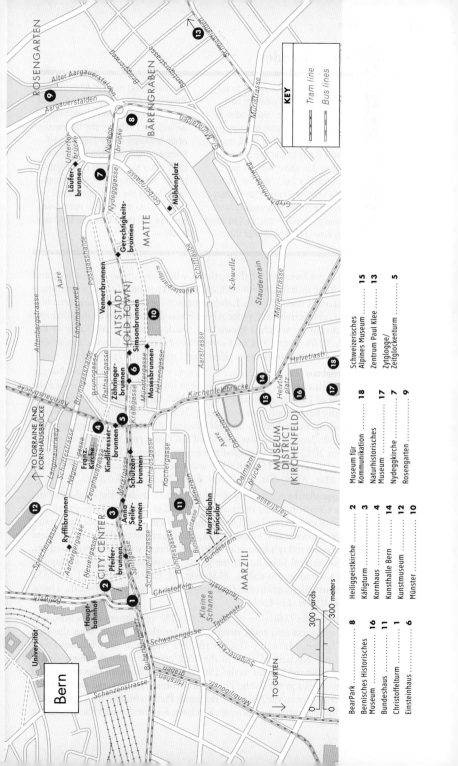

Bern

KEY

Tram line

Bus lines

CLOSE UP

Bern's Arcades

As Albert Einstein discovered to his delight in 1902, the weather has been bested in Bern. "Both sides of the road are completely lined by old arcades so that one can stroll from one end of the city to the other in the worst downpour without getting noticeably wet," he wrote to his fiancée in 1902. Sturdy 15th-century pillars support the low vaulted roofs of these picturesque *Lauben* (arcades), which extend to the edge of the sidewalk along miles of Altstadt streets. Steeply angled cellar doors at street level lead down to additional underground eateries and businesses, while brilliantly colored and carved *Brunnen* (fountains), historically the city's water sources and congregation points, punctuate the main thoroughfares. Ten of the most prominent fountains are the work of Hans Gieng, who created them between 1542 and 1549.

depict the swearing of the oath on which the union is founded; and two huge murals, one in each chamber, represent the Vierwaldstätter-see (Lake Lucerne) and a Landsgemeinde (outdoor cantonal assembly) scene, respectively the place where Swiss democracy was founded and the means by which it flourished. Guided tours are available in English. ⊠ *Bundespl. 3, City Center* ☎ *031/3228522* ⊕ *www.parlament. ch* ☎ *Free* ☉ *Guided tours Mon.–Sat., usually at 11:30 and 3.*

★ **Einsteinhaus** (*Einstein's House*). The sofa comes from Princeton, but the rest of this genteel apartment has been lovingly re-created to evoke the world of 1905, the miracle year in which then-tenant Albert Einstein, a badly paid, newly married young clerk in Bern's Patent Office, developed and published his *Special Theory of Relativity.* All signage is in English. Note: The museum closed after suffering serious water damage in 2012 and is expected to reopen sometime in 2013. ⊠ *Kramg. 49, Altstadt* ☎ *031/3120091* ⊕ *www.einstein-bern.ch* ☎ *6 SF* ☉ *Feb. and Mar., Mon.–Sat. 10–5; Apr.–Dec. 23, daily 10–5.*

Heiliggeistkirche (*Church of the Holy Ghost*). Built in the shadow of the huge Christoffelturm on the site of a disused monastery hospital, this Baroque church, laid out like a Huguenot temple, turned out to be a survivor as town walls, houses, gates, and fountains crashed down around it to create today's busy transport hub. Serenity does still reign within, where natural light floods the green sandstone supporting a magnificent vaulted stucco ceiling. ⊠ *Spitalg. 44, City Center* ☎ *031/3701552* ⊕ *www.heiliggeistkirche.ch* ☎ *Free* ☉ *Tues. and Wed. 11–6:30, Thurs. 11–8:30, Fri. 11–4:30.*

★ **Kunstmuseum** (*Museum of Fine Arts*). The permanent collection, one of the largest and most diverse in Switzerland, begins with the Italian Trecento (notably Duccio and Fra Angelico) then follows Swiss art from Niklaus Manuel in the 15th century through Albert Anker and Ferdinand Hodler in the 19th and on to Giovanni Giacometti and Cuno Amiet in the 20th. The Impressionists are covered from Manet through Monet; the Nabis, by Bonnard. Picasso bridges the gap between Toulouse-Lautrec and Braque; Kirchner, Kandinsky, and Klee represent

Carved figures of angels stand above the main door of the Bern Münster.

German Expressionism through Blue Rider to Bauhaus. Mondrian and Meret Oppenheim round out the 20th century. Temporary exhibits often take it from there. ⊠ *Hodlerstr. 8–12, City Center* ☎ *031/3280944* ⊕ *www.kunstmuseumbern.ch* ✉ *7 SF (collection only)* ⊘ *Tues. 10–9, Wed.–Sun. 10–5.*

Fodor's Choice ★ **Münster** (*Cathedral*). Master Builder Matthäus Ensinger already had Strasbourg's cathedral under his belt when he drew up plans for what became the largest and most artistically important church in Switzerland. The city broke ground in 1421 on the site of a smaller church that was dismantled once the cathedral's choir could accommodate Sunday worshippers, and work continued, with minor interruptions, for about 180 years. The finishing touch, the tip of the open, octagonal, 328-foot **steeple,** was added almost 200 years after that, in 1893. Today Switzerland's highest church tower houses two tower keepers (in an apartment below the spire) and presents wraparound views of Bern and the surrounding mountains.

The Reformers dismantled much of the Catholic Münster's interior decoration and paintings (dumping them in the Münsterplattform, next door), but the exterior 15th-century representation of the Last Judgment above the **main portal** was deemed worthy and spared. The archangel Michael stands between ivory-skinned angels with gilt hair (heaven) on the left and green demons with gaping red maws (hell) on the right; painted images of the Annunciation and the Fall of Man flank the carved figures as you pass through the doors. Elaborately carved pews and choir stalls within are crowned by 15th-century **stained-glass** windows that show an easy mix of local heraldry and Christian iconography. The organ, above the main entrance, is often used for concerts. ⊠ *Münsterpl. 1, Altstadt* ☎ *031/3120462* ⊕ *www.bernermuenster.ch* ☜ *Steeple 5 SF* ☉ *Easter–mid Oct., Mon.–Sat. 10–5, Sun. 11:30–5; mid Oct.–Easter, Mon.–Sat. noon–4, Sun. 11:30–4 (tower closes 30 mins before church).*

Nydeggkirche (*Nydegg Church*). A plaque on the outside wall of the church indicates where vestiges of Duke Berchtold's 12th-century Nydegg Castle (destroyed about

WORD OF MOUTH

"Bern to me is one of Europe's most underrated large cities—a unique look and feel due to the arcades over many of its sidewalks (good for a rainy-day trip from either Lucerne or Interlaken). If into museums, the new Paul Klee Museum is raved about as much for its avant-garde architecture of the building itself as the contents." —PalenQ

1270) still poke through the landscape; the church itself was begun in 1341, and its wooden pulpit dates from 1566. ⊠ *Nydegghof 2, Altstadt* ☎ *031/3520443* ⊕ *www.nydegg.ch* ☉ *Daily 8–5.*

★ **Zytglogge/Zeitglockenturm** (*Clock Tower*). Though its exterior dates from 1771, the internal walls of Bern's first western gate reach back to the 12th century and represent the city's core. The calendar clock on the Kramgasse side began keeping Bern's official time in 1530; the gilded rooster to the left of the mechanical figures crows four minutes before every hour to begin the sequence of marching bears, fools, and gilded knights who strike the bells. The astronomical clock to the rooster's right keeps track of the day, the month, the zodiac, and the moon. Tours of the horological masterpiece behind it all are conducted in English. ⊠ *Kramg. at Hotelg., Altstadt* ☎ *031/3281212* ⊕ *www.zeitglockenturm.ch* ☜ *Tour 15 SF* ☉ *Tours Apr.–Oct., daily 2:30; Nov.–Mar., by request* ☞ *Reservations recommended.*

WORTH NOTING

Christoffelturm (*Christoffel Tower*). The 14th-century maps, 19th-century photographs, and St. Christopher's huge limewood head give context to the thick stone foundations of Bern's third city gate. The tower was built between 1344 and 1366 and destroyed in 1865 after a tight vote in favor of the train station. Its ruins have been incorporated into the underground shopping mall of the train station. ⊠ *Christoffel-unterführung, City Center.*

Käfigturm (*Prison Tower*). This tower, completed in 1643, served as the city's prison until 1897. Reconfigured as the Confederation's Political Forum in 1999, it now hosts political events and exhibitions. ⊠ *Marktg. 67, City Center* ☎ *031/3227007* ⊕ *www.kaefigturm.admin.ch* ☜ *Free* ☉ *Weekdays 8–6, Sat. 10–4 during exhibitions.*

Kornhaus (*Granary*). Wine stocked the cellar and grain filled the top three floors of this granary for 100 years during Bern's Golden Age. Then the 1814 Vienna Congress separated the city from its territories, and this monumental Baroque storage depot lost its function overnight. The cellar was renovated in 1893 and painted four years later; today it houses a restaurant. The **Kornhausforum** (Media and Design

DID YOU KNOW?

The Zähringer Fountain, in front of Bern's Clock Tower, portrays an armored bear. The Duke of Zähringen established Bern in the 12th century, naming the city after a bear he killed in the forest nearby. Bern's association with the animal is evident today in the statues, flags, and live bears that live in the city's BearPark.

Center) organizes contemporary design, architecture, video, photography, and applied art exhibits upstairs. ⊠ *Kornhauspl. 18, Altstadt* ☎ *031/3129110* ⊕ *www.kornhausforum.ch* ⊠ *Free, occasional charge for special events* ⊘ *Tues.–Fri. 10–7, Sat. 10–5.*

QUICK BITES

Kornhaus Café. Outdoor tables, a sunny central location, light meals, homemade pastries, several kinds of coffee, and open doors from 8 am (9 am on Sunday) until midnight give the Kornhaus Café a constant, marketlike buzz. ⊠ *Kornhauspl. 18, Altstadt* ☎ *031/3277270* ⊕ *www.kornhauskeller.ch.*

BÄRENGRABEN AND ROSENGARTEN

⟳ ★ **BearPark.** Bern almost certainly gets its name from the local contraction of the German *Bären,* due to Berchtold V's supposed first kill in the area, and the image of a bear is never far away, from the official coat of arms to chocolate morsels. The city has kept live bears since 1513, when victorious Bernese soldiers brought one back from the Battle of Novara and installed it in a hut on what is now Bärenplatz. Björk, Finn, and their twin daughters Ursina and Berna feel at home in this closed-in area just off the Aare River, complete with quasi forest, shrubs, and cave, where they can play, swim, climb, and sleep all day. Photos and plaques in English describe the bears and their lifestyle. The park is open all hours, every day. ⊠ *Grosser Muristalden 4, Bärengraben* ☎ *031/3571515* ⊕ *www.baerenpark-bern.ch* ⊠ *Free.*

QUICK BITES

Restaurant Rosengarten. Open from early March to late November, the Restaurant Rosengarten serves dishes such as salmon tartare with crème fraîche and wasabi, tandoori chicken kebabs, veal saltimbocca, and Brie sandwiches against a backdrop of panoramic Altstadt views. ⊠ *Alter Aargauerstalden 31b, Rosengarten* ☎ *031/3313206* ⊕ *www.rosengarten.be.*

⟳ ★ **Rosengarten** (*Rose Garden*). The lower Altstadt's hilltop cemetery was converted to a public park in 1913. Today its lawns, arbors, playground, and formal gardens draw leisurely couples and families with young children. The gardens are planted with azaleas, irises, rhododendron, and rose varieties such as Ingrid Bergman (deep velvet red), Maria Callas (bright magenta), Christopher Columbus (peach), Cleopatra (red tips, orange interior), and Lady Di (small and pink). ⊠ *Alter Aargauerstalden/Laubeggstr, Rosengarten* ☎ *031/3281212* ⊠ *Free.*

MUSEUM DISTRICT: KIRCHENFELD

Kirchenfeld is a quiet, leafy neighborhood due south of the Altstadt, with radial streets and unexpected vistas. It was constructed in 1881 according to a district plan and quickly filled with embassies, consulates, and the bulk of Bern's museums.

Bernisches Historisches Museum (*Bern History Museum*). Indonesian shadow puppets, Japanese swords, Polynesian masks, Indian figurines,

CLOSE UP

Paul Klee: Bern's Artistic Son

It's ironic that Expressionist painter Paul Klee (1879–1940), one of Switzerland's most prolific and talented artists, wasn't a Swiss citizen during his life. Though he was born near Bern and spent most of his life in the country, his nationality was determined by the lineage of his father, who was German.

Born into a family of musicians, Klee filled his schoolbooks with caricatures and images copied from magazines. At age 19 he left Bern to study drawing in Munich, but he couldn't support himself with his art and returned to his parents in 1902. Four years later he had saved enough from his work as a violinist with the Bern Music Society to marry pianist Lily Stumpf and move to Munich, where they lived until 1926.

A trip to Tunisia in 1914 clarified Klee's artistic calling. "Color has taken possession of me," he wrote, upon encountering desert light. "I am a painter." His signature became color—rendered in oil, watercolor, ink, or all three—and almost childlike paintings with a highly developed sense of poetry, music, and dreams. Recognition followed in the 1920s, with exhibitions in Paris and New York and a teaching position at the Bauhaus from 1921. In 1933 the Nazis labeled him a degenerate, his academic position in Düsseldorf was terminated, and he and Lily moved to Switzerland. The apartment they took the following year in Bern's Elfenau district became his studio for the rest of his life.

In 1935 Klee began to show symptoms of severe fatigue and what was misdiagnosed as the measles turned out to be scleroderma (determined after his death). He continued to paint, however, and produced more than 1,000 works the year before his death in the Ticino, where he had gone to convalesce. His ashes are buried in Bern's Schosshalde cemetery, next to today's Zentrum Paul Klee.

9

and Celtic jewelry fill the ground floor, and the Islamic collection is exquisite, but head to the basement for the real focus: Bern and its place in Swiss history. Armor and arms, lavish church treasure (including sculptures from the Münster), magnificent silver, tapestries "acquired" in 1476–77 when the Bernese pushed Charles the Bold back into France, and several of Hans Gieng's original fountain statues lead the charge. The second floor is devoted to Einstein; major signage is in English. ✉ *Helvetiapl. 5, Kirchenfeld* ☏ *031/3507711* ⊕ *www.bhm.ch* 🎟 *13 SF* ✆ *Tues.–Sun. 10–5.*

Kunsthalle Bern (*Bern Art Gallery*). A completely different animal from the Kunstmuseum across town, this groundbreaking contemporary art venue built in 1918 by and for artists (among them Kirchner, Klee, and Giacometti père) seeks to confront, provoke, and engage viewers with the artistic phenomena of today. This translates each year to between six and seven exhibits of work by living artists; they become part of a history that includes Wassily Kandinsky, Henry Moore, Jasper Johns, Sol LeWitt, Bruce Nauman, Christo, and Grandma Moses. ✉ *Helvetiapl. 1, Kirchenfeld* ☏ *031/3500040* ⊕ *www.kunsthalle-bern.ch* 🎟 *8 SF* ✆ *Tues.–Fri. 11–6, weekends 10–6.*

☺ **Museum für Kommunikation** (*Museum of Communication*). This resolutely
★ interactive museum keeps its focus on the act of communication rather
than the means. Exhibits examine body language across cultures, the
views of Switzerland's minority populations, the history of the Swiss
postal service, and the evolution of telecommunication through to the
Internet. The world's largest collection of postage stamps is also here.
All signage is in English. ⊠ *Helvetiastr. 16, Kirchenfeld* ☎ *031/3575555*
⊕ *www.mfk.ch* ✉ *12 SF* ⊙ *Tues.–Sun. 10–5.*

☺ **Naturhistorisches Museum** (*Museum of Natural History*). The biggest
draw here is the stuffed body of Barry, a St. Bernard who saved more
than 40 people in the Alps between 1800 and 1812, but start with the
Alpine minerals, diamonds, and fossils in the basement, working up to
wild animals in the city. Birds' nests, skeletons large and small, interactive temporary exhibits, and more than 200 wildlife dioramas round out
the highlights. Basic signage is in English. ⊠ *Bernastr. 15, Kirchenfeld*
☎ *031/3507111* ⊕ *www.nmbe.ch* ✉ *8 SF* ⊙ *Mon. 2–5, Tues., Thurs.,
and Fri. 9–5, Wed. 9–6, weekends 10–5.*

★ **Schweizerisches Alpines Museum** (*Swiss Alpine Museum*). A slide show
overview of Switzerland's relationship with its mountains acts as an
introduction to this detailed museum. Exhibits include massive topographical models and relief maps; audiovisual consoles covering top-
ics such as the Roman introduction of viticulture, power generation,
and global warming; Alpine farming implements, toys, and skis; frank
descriptions of mountain life; ceremonial masks; and Hodler's seven-
part mural of the Matterhorn's conquest. You'll leave with a hearty
appreciation for Swiss tenacity. All signage is in English. ⊠ *Helvetiapl.
4, Kirchenfeld* ☎ *031/3500440* ⊕ *www.alpinesmuseum.ch* ✉ *12 SF*
⊙ *Tues., Wed., and Fri.–Sun. 10–5; Thurs. 10–8.*

**OFF THE
BEATEN
PATH**
Gurten. Bern's very own hill rises 1,000 feet above the city and presents
a delightful alternative to the city on clear afternoons. The view moves
from the Jura Mountains in the west to the Alps in the east by way of
Bern itself; multiple lawns, terraces, and restaurants allow for picnics,
cafeteria service, or formal dining as you gaze. The bright red funicular
to the top takes three minutes; head left to the east for a diagram label-
ing more than 200 distant peaks or right for a 360-degree view from
the top of the Gurtenturm. You can also walk up from Wabern. ⊠ *Wabern* ⊹ *Tram No. 9 to Gurtenbahn* ☎ *031/9612323 funicular* ⊕ *www.
gurtenpark.ch* ✉ *Funicular 10.50 SF round-trip* ⊙ *Funicular Mon.–Sat.
7 am–11:45 pm, Sun. 7 am–8:15 pm.*

GREATER BERN

☺ **Zentrum Paul Klee** (*Paul Klee Center*). Engaged creativity are the watch-
Fodor'sChoice words in this undulating, light-filled complex inspired by the life and
★ art of Paul Klee and designed by Renzo Piano. The permanent collection is the world's largest of works by Klee (about 200 are on display
at any given time); temporary exhibits focus on his artistic environment and legacy. The Ensemble Paul Klee performs regular, varied, and
colorful short concerts in the auditorium; guest artists from the worlds
of theater and dance present productions, readings, and workshops (in

German) with a pictorial slant. The Kindermuseum Creaviva, a sunny, paint-spattered area visible from the Restaurant Schöngrün on the north end of the interior Museum Street, is open to children over four and anyone else who would like to make art. A sculpture garden and multilingual audio tours of the permanent collection round out the possibilities—come early and plan to spend the day. Basic signage is in English. To get to the Zentrum from the city's central Hauptbahnhof, ride the No. 12 bus for 10 minutes to the end of the line. ⊠ *Monument im Fruchtland 3, Schöngrün* ☎ *031/3590101* ⊕ *www.zpk.org* 🖃 *20 SF* ☉ *Collection, Tues.–Sun. 10–5; Museum Street, Tues.–Sun. 9:30–5:30.*

WHERE TO EAT

Traditionally, dining in Bern has been a pretty grounded affair, characterized by Italian home cooking and German-style meat and potatoes. Two favorite local dishes are the *Bernerplatte*—great slabs of salt pork, beef tongue, smoked bacon, pork ribs, and mild pork sausage cooked down in broth then heaped on top of juniper-scented sauerkraut, green beans, and boiled potatoes—and *Berner Rösti*, shredded potatoes panfried with onions, butter, and chunks of bacon. But newer options include creative vegetarian cuisine, refined gastronomic delicacies, fresh fish—often caught in the nearby Aare River—and myriad ethnic foods. Most menus change with the seasons, featuring asparagus in spring, berries in summer, and wild game in fall; food presentation can be sophisticated; and service is almost universally friendly.

Many of Bern's established restaurants are dark, often underground, and accessible through a kind of cellar storm door that looks much like the one Dorothy just missed getting to when the tornado hit her Kansas farm. But once you're down there, you'll find the atmosphere cozy and warm, with a hint of the medieval—especially in the simpler, beer-hall-type venues. Another option is sitting at one of the few tables that are usually outside each restaurant, but under the famous Bernese arches, so you're sheltered from summer showers on a hot July evening, say, or a biting spring breeze. As soon as the weather permits, indoor restaurants are abandoned—but still open—as diners flock outdoors.

Be sure to make reservations, especially if you want to eat outside in warm weather. Popular garden restaurants that attract both tourists and locals will be packed at lunch, so you might try arriving a little before noon—but don't try the other extreme and come late, as most kitchens switch to the snack menu after 2 pm—if they're still open.

Prices in the reviews are the average cost of a main course or equivalent combination of smaller dishes at dinner or, if dinner is not served, at lunch.

Fans of Paul Klee's colorful paintings should not miss the extensive collection of his work at Zentrum Paul Klee.

ALTSTADT (OLD TOWN) AND CITY CENTER

$$ SWISS Fodor's Choice ★

🍴 **Della Casa.** Beloved by Swiss politicians, this institution is affectionately nicknamed "Delli" and has been operating nearly as long as the Federal Parliament Building down the street. It may be the ultimate place to sample a Bernerplatte, luscious veal liver with Rösti, and hearty oxtail stew with fried macaroni. The yellowed "Säli" on the ground floor and the wood-paneled restaurant upstairs share the same big, generous kitchen; the veteran waitresses shepherd you through the menu; and there's no need to rush—your second portion awaits on a warming table nearby. [$] *Average main: 30 SF* ✉ *Schauplatzg. 16, City Center* ☎ *031/3112142* 🌐 *www.della-casa.ch* 🕒 *Closed Sun.*

$$ MODERN ASIAN

🍴 **Fugu-Nydegg.** Modern Thai and Japanese cuisine are the two pillars of this sleek two-level restaurant in the Old Town. In addition to curry, noodle, beef and fish dishes, the menu offers innovative desserts like bananas in fried dough smothered in chocolate sauce. The restaurant provides shady sidewalk seating in summer; in winter, try to get a seat upstairs where it's brighter. At lunchtime, you can get meals to go for a mere 11 SF. [$] *Average main: 28 SF* ✉ *Gerechtigkeitsg. 16, Altstadt* ☎ *031/3115125* 🌐 *www.fugu-nydegg.ch.*

$$ SWISS

🍴 **Harmonie.** Fondue is Harmonie's raison d'être. Whether classic (Gruyère), *moitié-moitié* (half Gruyère, half Vacherin), or gussied up with truffles and champagne, pots of hot cheese arrive trailing copious amounts of bread and, ideally, a carafe of Vaudois white. *Käseschnitte* (open-face sandwiches with melted cheese), *Chäshörnli* (macaroni and cheese), traditional pork sausage, veal, beef, rack of lamb, and sides of crispy brown Rösti or *Spätzli* (dumplings) complete the picture of a nation well fed. The family-run establishment, open since 1915, is warm and simply decorated with wood-paneled walls and colorful tablecloths. [$] *Average main: 30 SF* ✉ *Hotelg. 3, Altstadt* ☎ *031/3131141* 🌐 *www.harmonie.ch* 🕑 *Closed weekends.*

$$$ FRENCH 🍴 **Jack's Brasserie.** Time moves a little more slowly here amid the civilized elegance of chandeliers and china teapots. Picture windows face the train station; gilt ceiling details, grapevine motifs, and striped banquettes warm up the wood paneling; and the day's papers hang from lampposts at discreet intervals between tables. The menu changes seasonally, but the classic French theme is constant—expect tartares and minestrone in summer, cassoulet or veal liver in winter, and Jack's giant Wienerschnitzel year-round. There's an excellent selection of Swiss wines and expensive but top-flight French reds. [$] *Average main: 46 SF* ✉ *Hotel Schweizerhof Bern, Bahnhofpl. 11, City Center* ☎ *031/3268080* 🌐 *www.schweizerhof-bern.ch.*

$$ EUROPEAN 🍴 **Kornhauskeller.** Entering the Kornhauskeller is akin to entering a cathedral, except that the stunning vaulted ceilings and frescoes are underground and the lounge-bar in the gallery stocks an incredible array of whiskeys, rums, and bourbons. The building has focused on food throughout its long life, first as a wine cellar/granary, then as a beer hall, now as a classy, popular restaurant where Italian dishes like buffalo mozzarella crostini and lemon risotto with king prawns share the menu with Swiss dishes, including a regal Bernerplatte. [$] *Average main: 34 SF* ✉ *Kornhauspl. 18, Altstadt* ☎ *031/3277272* 🌐 *www.kornhauskeller.ch.*

$$ ITALIAN ★ 🍴 **Lorenzini.** This complex of bars and a restaurant is a popular gathering place for stylish patrons looking for an Italy fix. Three specialty bars serve coffee, wine, and cocktails, and the restaurant offers delectable homemade pastas and desserts, with a signature dish of veal escalope with ham and sage, paired with saffron risotto. Cushioned brown benches and black wooden chairs surround white-clad tables with silver bread bowls. Eclectic photos, prints, and paintings adorn the walls, and marble statues stand tucked in alcoves. The staff exudes the barest hint of attitude, and Tuscany and Piedmont jostle for space on the wine list. The open-air atrium, crammed with tables and summer diners, is decorated with olive trees, grape vines, and pink geraniums. [$] *Average main: 30 SF* ✉ *Hotelg. 10, Altstadt* ☎ *031/3185067* 🌐 *www.lorenzini.ch.*

$ VEGETARIAN 👶 Fodor's Choice ★ 🍴 **Tibits.** Everything on the menu can be ordered to go, and its integration into the train station building makes this airy space a favorite with travelers. But linger in the wicker chairs or claim a space on one of the long communal tables. For families, the children's corner has toys, storybooks, a blackboard, and high chairs. The food is 100% vegetarian and sold by weight from a buffet that can yield three courses; homemade sandwiches and soups such as pumpkin, lentil, or green pea with peppermint fill in the gaps. To drink: fresh fruit and vegetable juices, organic wine, flavored coffee, herbal tea, and cocktails such as rooibos tea–infused vodka. [$] *Average main: 24 SF* ✉ *Bahnhofpl. 10, City Center* ☎ *031/3129111* 🌐 *www.tibits.ch.*

Head to Tibits for a satisfying meal that's kid-friendly and easy on the wallet.

$$ ITALIAN ★ 🍴 **Verdi.** Music is a leitmotif along walls studded with opera posters, paintings, programs, scores, photos, and clippings; there are also low ceilings, wooden beams, gilt mirrors, velvet drapes, stone walls, and a newly renovated balcony with three working fireplaces. The real star, however, is the menu, which sees cold-weather ingredients like truffles, cream, and polenta transition to tomatoes, basil, and fennel as the weather warms up. Rack of lamb with a caponata of eggplant, onions, capers, olives, and tomatoes is a year-round favorite. The wine cellar, visible through glass doors off the dining room, ranges all over Italy. [$] *Average main: 28 SF* ✉ *Gerechtigkeitsg. 7, Altstadt* ☎ *031/3126368* 🌐 *www.bindella.ch.*

$$ FRENCH ★ 🍴 **Zimmermania.** A deceptively simple local favorite and one of the most typically French bistros in Bern, this cultural transplant tucked away on a backstreet near the Rathaus has been serving classics like *entrecôte Café de Paris* (beef in butter sauce) with french fries, escargots in herb garlic butter, and calf's head since 1848. In a city that celebrates the onion, this is a good place to try onion soup. Lunch specials are under 20 SF; wines come from Switzerland, Italy, and France. [$] *Average main: 38 SF* ✉ *Brunng. 19, Altstadt* ☎ *031/3111542* 🌐 *www.zimmermania.ch* ⏲ *Closed Sun. and Mon.*

BÄRENGRABEN AND ROSENGARTEN

$$ SWISS 🍴 **Altes Tramdepot.** This restaurant is a beer hall at heart. Dark, light, and "normal" varieties are brewed in copper vats behind the bar and specialty beers appear at Easter, in October, or during the full moon. Filling dishes like Bernerplatte with homemade Spätzli, cordon bleu,

Weisswurst, and warm pretzel filled with ham pair perfectly with the house brews. There are also a few vegetarian dishes. Don't miss the outdoor beer garden overlooking the Altstadt. The kitchen stays open from 11 am to 11:30 pm every day of the year. $ *Average main: 26 SF* ⊠ *Grosser Muristalden 6, Bärengraben* ☎ *031/3681415* ⊕ *www. altestramdepot.ch.*

KORNHAUSBRÜCKE AND LORRAINE

$$$$
MEDITERRANEAN

✕ **Meridiano.** The curved gold ceiling, white baby grand, brown suede bench nooks, and sweeping view of the Altstadt complete with operatic Alpine backdrop make this chic, modern restaurant a wonderful spot for a romantic meal. Chef Markus Arnold's cooking is creative, modern, French-inspired, and always market fresh. Try specialties like his fried duck liver served with duck-liver ice cream, and blueberry clafouti, or lamb with eggplant "caviar" and butternut squash. Ask for a seat on the terrace in summer—the view is spectacular. $ *Average main: 66 SF* ⊠ *Hotel Allegro, Kornhausstr. 3, Kornhausbrücke* ☎ *031/3395245* ⊕ *www.kursaal-bern.ch* ⊗ *Closed Sun. and Mon. No lunch Sat.*

MARZILI AND MATTE

$$
ECLECTIC

✕ **Gartenrestaurant Marzilibrücke.** The menu at this casual bohemian spot on the Marzili side of the river reaches to the far corners of the globe. Expect Indian curries, Thai dishes, Italian pasta, German schnitzel, and Greek salads to share the menu. In summer, a shaded gravel garden and the gourmet-pizza zone more than double the restaurant's size. Indoors, red-and-yellow pillows punctuate the simple white benches and wood tables. Italian and Spanish wines dominate; Sunday brunch is served from 10 am to 2 pm. $ *Average main: 32 SF* ⊠ *Gasstr. 8, Marzili* ☎ *031/3112780* ⊕ *www.taberna.ch* ⊗ *No lunch Sat.*

$$
MEDITERRANEAN

✕ **Schwellenmätteli.** A chest-high glass barrier stands between you and white water at the tip of this stylish, sun-soaked restaurant and bar. Built like a ship's prow past the edge of the Matteschwelle weir, the unique establishment maintains a hip, beachlike atmosphere with its chaise lounges, teak bar stools, and cushioned wicker chairs. The dining area, indoors or outside beneath a retractable roof, serves Mediterranean-inspired dishes like lemongrass-cream soup, rhubarb-strawberry chutney with baked Vacherin, red snapper with lemon risotto and grilled vegetables, and *cabillaud* (cod) saltimbocca with saffron potatoes. $ *Average main: 34 SF* ⊠ *Dalmaziquai 11, Matte* ☎ *031/3505001* ⊕ *www.schwellenmaetteli.ch* ⊗ *Closed Mon.*

$$$
MEDITERRANEAN
Fodor's Choice
★

✕ **Zum Zähringer.** This restaurant has four distinct areas: a formal, elegant salon, a casual bistro, a covered terrace overlooking the River Aare, and a garden that hosts barbecues in summer. All share the same kitchen, which serves up excellent, mostly Mediterranean dishes such as lamb carpaccio with Parmesan and arugula, veal scaloppine with truffle cream, and *sauerbraten* (beef marinated in red wine) with mashed potatoes. The history of Zum Zähringer dates back to the time when Badgasse (Bath Street) was Bern's red-light district and the inn on the

9

corner was a favorite with Giacomo Casanova. $ *Average main: 48 SF* ⊠ *Badg. 1, Matte* ☎ *031/3120888* ⊕ *www.restaurant-zaehringer.ch* ☉ *Closed Sun. No lunch Sat.*

WHERE TO STAY

Bern has plenty of top-quality hotels, many of them with magnificent 19th-century characteristics: towering ceilings ornately accented with stucco moldings; balconies with curlicue Belle Epoque iron railings; domed corner turrets; and miles of marble floors. A step or two below, price-wise, are some older venues that tend toward the generic. But today's owners and managers are waking up to the fact that flowered prints and dusty blue carpeting are just a little too 1980s, even if they're spotlessly clean. These new entrepreneurs are ripping up old flooring to expose and polish up the often centuries-old parquet underneath; they're whitewashing the walls; installing state-of-the-art entertainment systems; upgrading the bathrooms (or just plain adding them); and fixing up the rooms with simple, modular furniture that keeps the prices at a level the average traveler can afford.

Given Bern's geographical characteristics, almost all the hotels listed in this chapter are located within the same medieval central-city core—which easily can be crossed on foot in 10 minutes at most. Most of the streets are pedestrian, or "traffic-calmed" to the extent that most drivers don't venture into the Old Town at all. In fact, you can leave your car in a parking lot for the duration of your stay and easily explore the area by foot—it's the best way to get acquainted with the city's charming nooks and crannies.

One truism here is that most, if not all, of Bern's hotel staffers are professional, cheerful, and accommodating. And most of them speak at least three languages comfortably, one of which is sure to be English. If you can, book in advance as music festivals, trade conventions, sports events, and parliamentary sessions (March, June, September, and December) can fill rooms fast. Rates drop on weekends, when there is less demand.

Prices in the reviews are the lowest cost of a standard double room in high season, including taxes.

ALTSTADT (OLD TOWN) AND CITY CENTER

$ 🖳 **Ador.** Nicely appointed and located just west of the Hauptbahn-
HOTEL hof, this boxy hotel is a good deal if you're price conscious but still want something stylish. **Pros:** well-designed modern interiors; close to everything. **Cons:** uninspiring exterior located on a block heavy with early-1970s concrete. $ *Rooms from: 170 SF* ⊠ *Laupenstr. 15, City Center* ☎ *031/3880111* ⊕ *www.hotelador.ch* ⊃ *57 rooms* ⦿❘ *Breakfast.*

$$ 🖳 **Belle Epoque.** Pay close attention to the walls in this boutique gem,
HOTEL they're furnished entirely with Belle Epoque originals: Steinlen graces
★ the bathrooms and breakfast area, Hodler and Klimt spice up suites named for them, and the bar has photos of Toulouse-Lautrec standing

next to the Moulin Rouge poster behind you. **Pros:** well-stocked breakfast buffet; located on a charming and quiet cobblestone street. **Cons:** live jazz on Sunday 7 pm–10 pm (October to May) draws a boisterous crowd. $ *Rooms from: 240 SF* ✉ *Gerechtigkeitsg. 18, Altstadt* ☎ *031/3114336* ⊕ *www.belle-epoque.ch* ⤳ *14 rooms, 3 junior suites* ❏|❍❏ *Some meals.*

$$$$ ⛱ **Bellevue Palace.** A pretension-free mix of Belle Epoque elegance and
HOTEL contemporary ease defines this impeccable hotel built in 1913 to accom-
Fodor's Choice modate government visitors. **Pros:** two loungeable lobbies great for
★ decompressing; fabulous Alpine views from south-facing rooms and outdoor dining terrace; elegant design; free Wi-Fi. **Cons:** modern rooms may seem spare; no in-room coffee/tea facilities. $ *Rooms from: 524 SF* ✉ *Kocherg. 3–5, Altstadt* ☎ *031/3204545* ⊕ *www.bellevue-palace. ch* ⤳ *108 rooms, 18 suites* ❏|❍❏ *Breakfast.*

$$ ⛱ **Best Western Bären.** Occupying much of a city block between the
HOTEL Hauptbahnhof and the Bundeshaus, this business-class hotel (along with its twin next door, the Bristol) is a favorite with parliament officials and bankers because it's perfectly placed at the heart of Bern's commercial district. **Pros:** good value; very central; practical desks for working. **Cons:** a bit clunky compared to the elegant hotels in the area. $ *Rooms from: 225 SF* ✉ *Schauplatzg. 4, City Center* ☎ *031/3113367, 800/780–7234 in U.S.* ⊕ *www.baerenbern.ch* ⤳ *57 rooms* ❏|❍❏ *Breakfast.*

$ ⛱ **Goldener Schlüssel.** This 500-year-old property—the oldest in Bern—is
HOTEL within earshot of the Zytglogge bells. **Pros:** good bang for the buck; quiet location. **Cons:** small rooms. $ *Rooms from: 188 SF* ✉ *Rathausg. 72, Altstadt* ☎ *031/3110216* ⊕ *www.goldener-schluessel.ch* ⤳ *34 rooms* ❏|❍❏ *Breakfast.*

$$ ⛱ **Hotel Bern.** This energetic property, located on a busy street behind
HOTEL the Kornhaus, has an imposing facade that looks like a 19th-century
⟳ bank. **Pros:** kids stay free; expert service. **Cons:** compared with the guest rooms, the restaurants might seem staid. $ *Rooms from: 275 SF* ✉ *Zeughausg. 9, City Center* ☎ *031/3292222* ⊕ *www.hotelbern.ch* ⤳ *99 rooms* ❏|❍❏ *Breakfast.*

$$$$ ⛱ **Hotel Schweizerhof Bern.** After two years of renovations, this five-star
HOTEL hotel reopened to great acclaim in 2011. **Pros:** luxe rooms and design
Fodor's Choice elements; lovely rooftop terrace; free in-room beverages. **Cons:** location
★ across from train station isn't very glamorous; views from rooms and lobby bar are limited. $ *Rooms from: 455 SF* ✉ *Bahnhofplatz 11, City Center* ☎ *031/3268080* ⊕ *www.schweizerhof-bern.ch* ⤳ *84 rooms, 15 suites* ❏|❍❏ *Some meals.*

$$ ⛱ **Kreuz.** There aren't many frills at this spartan property, but that is
HOTEL counterbalanced by the up-to-date modern furnishings in well-outfitted guest rooms, personable service, and a housekeeping team that works hard upholding the stereotype of the Swiss as a people with a penchant for cleanliness. **Pros:** excellent location; efficient staff. **Cons:** the gym is very small; front rooms may catch noise from the street. $ *Rooms from: 200 SF* ✉ *Zeughausg. 39/41, City Center* ☎ *031/3299595* ⊕ *www. kreuzbern.ch* ⤳ *103 rooms* ❏|❍❏ *Breakfast.*

9

$ HOTEL 🏨 **Nydeck.** Mirrors work magic in this small, tidy corner hotel near the Nydeggbrücke, an excellent location near the BearPark and main attractions of the Old Town. **Pros:** cheerful environment; perfect medieval neighborhood setting. **Cons:** the bed barely fits in some of the rooms. [$] *Rooms from: 170 SF* ✉ *Gerechtigkeitsg. 1, Altstadt* ☎ *031/3118686* 🌐 *www.hotelnydeck.ch* 🛏 *12 rooms* 🍴 *Breakfast.*

$$ HOTEL 🏨 **Savoy.** This neatly tailored hotel is just minutes from the main train station, as well as the city's markets and arcaded shopping streets. **Pros:** rooms have soundproofed windows; very friendly staff. **Cons:** interiors could use a bit of an overhaul. [$] *Rooms from: 280 SF* ✉ *Neueng. 26, City Center* ☎ *031/3114405* 🌐 *www.hotel-savoy-bern.ch* 🛏 *48 rooms, 6 suites* 🍴 *Breakfast.*

GREATER BERN

$$$ HOTEL 🏨 **Allegro.** In a town renowned for its antiquites, the Allegro stands out as thoroughly modern. **Pros:** heated tile floors in bathrooms; upper south-facing rooms with Alpine views; spa/gym. **Cons:** slightly off the beaten path. [$] *Rooms from: 320 SF* ✉ *Kornhausstr. 3, Greater Bern* ☎ *031/3395500* 🌐 *www.allegro-hotel.ch* 🛏 *167 rooms, 4 suites.*

$$$ HOTEL 🏨 **Innere Enge.** Art Nouveau accents, pristine Alpine views, exposed beams, and jazz memorabilia from greats like Lionel Hampton, John Lewis, Hazy Osterwald, and Clark Terry punctuate the spacious, sunny rooms in this half-timbered inn that dates to the early 1700s. **Pros:** lush private park; large outdoor terrace. **Cons:** far from the city center. [$] *Rooms from: 333 SF* ✉ *Engestr. 54, Greater Bern* ☎ *031/3096111* 🌐 *www.innere-enge.ch* 🛏 *9 rooms, 17 suites* 🍴 *Breakfast.*

NIGHTLIFE AND THE ARTS

Twice a year, Bern Tourismus widely disseminates *Bern Guide,* a free, pocket-size, bilingual (German/English), and comprehensive guide to what's on in the city (exhibits, nightlife, festivals, shopping, excursions, and useful telephone numbers). The website 🌐 *www.bern.com* fills in any remaining gaps.

NIGHTLIFE

The Bernese like to party, and nightlife options accordingly run the gamut from plush velvet seating and Belle Epoque refinement to jazz lounges, casual sidewalk bars, and plugged-in clubs where DJs spin the latest. Bärenplatz and Kornhausplatz bubble over with revelers on summer evenings; many restaurants transition into bars as the night wears on.

ALTSTADT (OLD TOWN) AND CITY CENTER

BARS

Adriano's. This friendly, glassed-in coffee bar serves fresh croissants from 7 am (10 am on Sunday), sandwiches throughout the day, and wine or beer to a sidewalk crowd come nightfall. ✉ *Theaterpl. 2, Altstadt* ☎ *031/3188831* 🌐 *www.adrianos.ch.*

Bar Toulouse-Lautrec. Exquisite Belle Epoque paintings and outdoor jazz grace the Bar Toulouse-Lautrec. ✉ *Hotel Belle Epoque, Gerechtigkeitsg. 18, Altstadt* ☎ *031/3114346* ⊕ *www.belle-epoque.ch.*

Bellevue Bar. Well-heeled travelers (and local politicians) come to see and be seen at the wood-paneled Bellevue Bar. ✉ *Hotel Bellevue Palace, Kocherg. 3–5, Altstadt* ⊕ *www.bellevue-palace.ch.*

Klötzlikeller. This wood-paneled Weinstube dates from 1635, making it Bern's oldest basement restaurant and the city's last true wine cellar beneath the arcades. ✉ *Gerechtigkeitsg. 62, Altstadt* ☎ *031/3117456* ⊕ *www.kloetzlikeller.ch.*

DANCING
Du Théâtre. Smart young professionals stop after work for a mellow glass of wine and stay until 3:30 am for weekend dance parties at Du Théâtre. ✉ *Hotelgasse 10, Altstadt* ☎ *031/3185067* ⊕ *www.dutheatre.ch.*

Shakira. This place specializes in Latin music, salsa dancing, and tropical drinks. ✉ *National Hotel, Maulbeerstr. 3, City Center* ☎ *031/3817767* ⊕ *www.shakira.ch.*

KORNHAUSBRÜCKE
CASINO
Grand Casino Bern. All 261 slot machines and 11 gaming tables at the Kursaal's Grand Casino Bern function until 4 am from Thursday through Saturday. ✉ *Kornhausstr. 3, Kornhausbrücke* ☎ *031/3395555* ⊕ *www.grandcasino-bern.ch.*

MATTE
BARS
Martini Terrazza. The Riviera vibe at the outdoor Martini Terrazza and indoor Lounge, both part of the Schwellenmätteli restaurant complex, lure thirtysomething hipsters down to the river. ✉ *Dalmaziquai 11, Matte* ☎ *031/3505001* ⊕ *www.schwellenmaetteli.ch.*

DANCING
Wasserwerk Club. The Prodigy, Moby, and The Roots all played the sophisticated Wasserwerk Club early in their careers. ✉ *Wasserwerkg. 5, Matte* ⊕ *www.wasserwerkclub.ch.*

THE ARTS

Bern's three-pronged arts scene covers opera and symphonic classics, seasonal festivals, and cubbyhole theaters buried underground.

ALTSTADT (OLD TOWN) AND CITY CENTER
MUSIC AND THE PERFORMING ARTS
Bern Billett. Bern Billett handles ticket sales for the Bern Symphonie-Orchester and the Stadttheater. ✉ *Nägelig. 1a, Altstadt* ☎ *031/3295252* ⊕ *www.bernbillett.ch.*

Berner Puppentheater. Marionettes, stick puppets, hand puppets, shadow puppets, and masks come to life on stage at the Berner Puppentheater. ✉ *Gerechtigkeitsg. 31, Altstadt* ☎ *031/3119585* ⊕ *www.berner-puppentheater.ch.*

Berner Symphonie-Orchester. The Berner Symphonie-Orchester performs orchestral work and chamber music. ☎ *031/3282424* ⊕ *www. bsorchester.ch.*

Kultur-Casino. These events are primarily held in the Kultur-Casino. ✉ *Herreng. 25, Altstadt* ☎ *031/3280228* ⊕ *www.kultur-casino.ch*

Gurten Festival. Altstadt streets empty briefly in mid-July as A-list rockers like James Blunt, Billy Idol, and Lenny Kravitz draw crowds to the four-day open-air Gurten Festival. ⊕ *www.gurtenfestival.ch.*

Stadttheater. The Stadttheater presents at least seven full-scale operas, 10 dramas, and three contemporary dance pieces each year. ✉ *Kornhauspl. 20, Altstadt* ☎ *031/3295111* ⊕ *www.konzerttheaterbern.ch.*

Theater am Käfigturm. The Theater am Käfigturm, three levels below Spitalgasse, presents pantomime, modern dance, avant-garde plays, and the occasional piece aimed at children. ✉ *Spitalg. 4, City Center* ☎ *031/ 3116100* ⊕ *www.theater-am-kaefigturm.ch.*

FILM

If a film was made in English, Bernese cinemas generally show it in English. Local newspapers list screening times (look for "E" to confirm the language) and most theaters advertise current programs on big boards underneath the Käfigturm and in the Christoffelunterführung.

OrangeCinema. The open-air OrangeCinema sets up camp in front of the university each July and shows recent mainstream favorites through August. ✉ *Grosse Schanze, City Center* ☎ *0800/078078* ⊕ *www. orangecinema.ch.*

GREATER BERN

Marians Jazzroom. This popular place hosts top international jazz, blues, and gospel artists between September and May. ✉ *Engestr. 54, Länggasse* ☎ *031/3096111* ⊕ *www.mariansjazzroom.ch.*

SPORTS AND THE OUTDOORS

BIKING

Bern Rollt. There are about 300 km (185 miles) of marked trails in and around Bern. Leave ID and a 20 SF deposit with Bern Rollt between May and October and you can ride for free from 7:30 am to 9:30 pm. ✉ *Hirschengr. and Zeughausg., City Center* ☎ *079/2772857* ⊕ *www. bernrollt.ch.*

SPAS

Oktogon Hammam. Housed in a former gasworks, the three-story building follows the Middle-Eastern hammam tradition. You pass through a series of serene rooms where you steam, scrub, shower, and soak. Admission includes an exfoliation mitt and a linen sheet to wear for modesty's sake. At the end of the process, you recline on a bed under the wooden eaves. You can also book extras like a soapsuds massage. The on-site café serves free tea and sells light snacks. On Tuesday only women can visit the spa. ✉ *Weihergasse 3* ☎ *031/3113101* ⊕ *www.hammam-bern.ch* ☞ *46 SF 25-min oil massage; 95 SF packages. Steam room.*

The Spa at Hotel Schweizerhof. Though fairly compact, this underground refuge features a wealth of facilities. There's a sauna, steam bath, plunge pool, and a relaxation pool with bubble jets—not to mention a fitness room for those who want to do more than just relax. The spa offers massages and a variety of cosmetic treatments; a quiet room with water beds extends the pampering. The spa is free for hotel guests, and the public can gain access by booking spa services. Guests are asked to wear a swimsuit or a towel at all times. ⊠ *Hotel Schweizerhof Bern, Bahnhofplatz 11* ☎ *031/3268080* ⊕ *www.schweizerhofbern.ch* ☞ *60 SF for a 20-min head and neck massage, 240 SF for a 90-min Abhyanga massage; 195 SF to 300 SF for day spa packages. Hot tub, sauna, steam room. Gym with: cardiovascular machines, free weights, weight-training equipment. Service: facials, massages.*

SWIMMING

Swimmers have headed into the cold, swift Aare just before its U-turn around the Altstadt since Bern was founded. These days a hot Sunday may see scantily clad (or, in certain sections, naked) crowds of more than 10,000 sprawled on beach towels on the grass, swimming laps in the pools, or bobbing happily in the river (a system of handrails projected over the water prevents bathers from traveling too far downstream).

Marzili. Known universally as The Marzili, this sunny stretch of riverbank below the Bundeshaus presents a unique, and entirely free, take on the city. ⊠ *Marzilistr. 29, Marzili* ☎ *031/3110046* ⊕ *www.aaremarzili.ch.*

Solbad Schönbühl. Heated mineral-rich indoor baths, open-air saltwater pools, underwater massage jets, bubble beds, whirlpools, a mushroom fountain, eucalyptus steam baths, and a sauna park are highlights at the sprawling Solbad Schönbühl, open year-round to the north of Bern. Bathing suits and towels can be rented on-site; admission to the baths is 28 SF. ⊠ *Mattenweg 30, Schönbühl* ☎ *031/8593434* ⊕ *www.solbad.ch.*

SHOPPING

Bern's official store hours are 9 to 7 weekdays and 8 to 5 on Saturday. Thursday hours are extended to 9; stores in the Hauptbahnhof may open on Sunday. Smaller stores, particularly in the Altstadt, may stay shuttered Monday morning, close for lunch, close before 9 pm on Thursday, and/or open as late as 10 am.

SHOPPING STREETS

No street or side alley in downtown Bern is without interest to shoppers, and you never know what fabulous discovery may await at the end of an intriguing passageway or the bottom of cellar stairs. **Spitalgasse** and **Marktgasse** form the city center's main shopping drag; parallel streets such as **Neuengasse**, **Aarbergergasse**, and **Amthausgasse** can also be very rewarding. The Altstadt, from **Brunngasse** to **Junkerngasse** by way of

Kramgasse and **Gerechtigkeitsgasse,** is lined and honeycombed with fine specialty boutiques.

ALTSTADT (OLD TOWN) AND CITY CENTER

BOOKS

Stauffacher. It is easy to get lost in the sprawling trilingual Stauffacher, emporium of books, maps, and multimedia, but there are far worse fates. The substantial English Bookshop occupies the third floor of the west wing; regular readings (some in English) are held in the Café Littéraire. ✉ *Neueng. 25–37, City Center* ☎ *031/3136363* ⊕ *www. stauffacher.ch.*

Thalia. At this German-language chain store lodged in the basement of the Loeb department store, globes, dictionaries, multilingual travel guides, English-language fiction and biographies, a play area for kids, and a sizable selection of books about Switzerland are highlights. ✉ *Spitalg. 47–51, City Center* ☎ *031/3202020* ⊕ *www.thalia.ch.*

CHOCOLATE

Abegglen. Chocolate-covered plums and truffles made with Bailey's, kirsch, or coconut white chocolate lead the charge at Abegglen. ✉ *Spitalg. 36, City Center* ☎ *031/3112111* ⊕ *www.confiserie-abegglen.ch.*

Beeler. The specialty at Beeler is the Caramelina, where truffle meets caramel, in seven flavors including mocha-cardamom and cassis. ✉ *Spitalg. 29, City Center* ☎ *031/3112808* ⊕ *www.confiserie-beeler.ch.*

Eichenberger. Find an assortment of pralines and truffles, as well as hazelnut gingerbread emblazoned with the iconic bear, at Eichenberger. ✉ *Bahnhofpl. 5, City Center* ☎ *031/3113325* ⊕ *www.confiserie-eichenberger.ch/.*

Tschirren. The self-styled prince of Bernese chocolatiers, Tschirren, has been making its divine assortment of artfully rough-hewn truffles since 1919. ✉ *Kramg. 73, Altstadt* ☎ *031/3111717* ⊕ *www.swiss-chocolate.ch.*

DEPARTMENT STORES

Globus. Good quality, stylish, often vibrantly colorful home accessories and cooking gear fill the upper stories at Globus. On the lower levels, luscious hats and scarves, cosmetics, and designer labels give way to foodstuffs—from specialty oils through cheese—in the upscale supermarket downstairs. ✉ *Spitalg. 17–21, City Center* ☎ *058/5784040* ⊕ *www.globus.ch.*

Loeb. Legos, model trucks, and children's clothing are found on the top floor of Loeb, descending through craft supplies, luggage, and housewares to assorted stationery, hosiery, and Swiss-themed souvenirs on the ground floor. ✉ *Spitalg. 47–51, City Center* ☎ *031/3207111* ⊕ *www. loeb.ch.*

GIFTS AND SOUVENIRS

Boutique Nelli. The warrenlike Boutique Nelli has a whimsical selection of glassware, jewelry, candles in rainbow colors, and imaginative kitchen gadgets. ✉ *Gerechtigkeitsg. 3, Altstadt* ☎ *031/3111040.*

9

Heimatwerk. Victorinox, Wenger, and Swiss Military knives dominate the window at Heimatwerk, a high-quality emporium of Swiss-made music boxes, toys, handicrafts, textiles, and ceramics. ⊠ *Kramg. 61, Altstadt* ☎ *031/3113000* ⊕ *www. heimatwerk-bern.ch.*

Holz Art. Colorful handmade wooden figures and candelabras, delicate shaved-wood trees, and lacy wooden cutouts pull focus at Holz Art. ⊠ *Münsterg. 36, Altstadt* ☎ *031/3126666* ⊕ *www.holz-art-bern.ch.*

> **SUNDAY TEA**
>
> Many chocolatiers' shops have tearoom areas at the back and are, therefore, allowed to open on Sunday. If you go, be sure to try the Bernese specialty *Lebkuchen*, a dense, flat spice cake made with hazelnuts, honey, and almonds.

HOME ACCESSORIES

Cachet. This unusual shop stocks culturally resonant items such as iron Japanese teapots, colored grass baskets, camel rugs, Turkish lamps, multicolored bottles, whimsical mobiles, and soulful carved-wood furniture from India, Indonesia, and Pakistan. ⊠ *Amthausg. 22, City Center* ☎ *031/3118466* ⊕ *www.cachet.ch.*

Depot. Clean, livable, often joyously colorful and affordable designs channel faraway locales at Depot, where the focus is on decorative items like candles and vases, plus necessities like towels, sheets, and dishes. ⊠ *Spitalg. 4, City Center* ☎ *058/5762400* ⊕ *www.depot-online.com.*

MARKETS

Weihnachtsmarkt (*Christmas Market*). Throughout December, hot mulled wine adds spice to the arts and crafts, colorful decorations, and seasonal produce lining the stall set up around Old Town during the Weihnachtsmarkt, which keeps regular shop hours. ⊠ *Münsterplatz and Waisenhausplatz, Altstadt.*

Zibelemärit (*Onion Market*). The Zibelemärit is a Fasnacht-tinged remnant of a 15th-century Autumn Market that lasted two weeks; 19th-century farmers' wives, notably from Fribourg, developed the habit of coming to Bern on the first day of the market to sell their excess produce, in particular onions. Today half the 700 stalls that line the City Center on the fourth Monday in November display a vast assortment of items made with onions—everything from wreaths to alarm clocks to soup. Some say the best time to browse the annual market is just after it opens at 4 am on the fourth Monday in November, when stalls are candlelit; you may be treated to a predawn dusting of snow, and confetti battles—a major part of the festivities—do not yet rage. ⊠ *Bundesplatz, Altstadt.*

Tuesday and Saturday are Bern's formal year-round market days, with most of the action concentrated in the morning along Bundesplatz, Bärenplatz, Waisenhausplatz, Schauplatzgasse, Gurtengasse, and Bundesgasse in the center of town.

Bern has been a market town since the Middle Ages, and seasonal outdoor markets are still an integral part of daily life.

Produce Market. The Bundesplatz and Bärenplatz are filled with fresh produce, herbs, and flowers every day between May and October. ⊠ *Bärenplatz, Altstadt.*

Meat and Cheese Market. Münstergasse, near Bärenplatz, offers meats and dairy products every Tuesday and Saturday. ⊠ *Münstergasse.*

Trader's Market. This awning-covered warren is the place for handmade soaps, antique copper pots, silver jewelry, handmade hammocks, tie-dyed scarves, and incongruous objects like Panama hats. It adds late-night hours on Thursday between April and October. ⊠ *Waisenhausplatz, Altstadt.*

Crafts Fair. Arts and crafts stalls fill the Münsterplatz on the first Saturday of the month between March and December. ⊠ *Münsterplatz, Altstadt.*

Flea Market. Held on Matte's Mühleplatz the third Saturday of the month from May to October, this market has the look and feel of an antiques-laden tag sale. ⊠ *Mühleplatz, Matte.*

TOYS

Bilboquet. The old red cash register works at Bilboquet. Kid-sized umbrellas have animal handles, and the plush toys range from snow owls to llamas. ⊠ *Münsterg. 37, Altstadt* ☎ *031/3113671.*

Chlätterbär. This shop sells fully stocked wooden kitchens, xylophones, beaded jewelry, drum sets, hand puppets, and wooden dollhouse furniture. ⊠ *Amthausg. 3, City Center* ☎ *031/3111196* ⊕ *www.chlaetterbaer.ch.*

Puppenklinik. The owner of the Puppenklinik has a passion for restoration; the result is a huge collection of vintage dolls, toys, teddy bears, and puppets from around the world. ✉ *Gerechtigkeitsg. 36, Altstadt* ☎ *031/3120771.*

U-Tiger. There are very few hard edges at U-Tiger, where cloud sofas, green-dragon bean bags, quilted soccer fields, and fuzzy sheep hot-water bottles headline the creative selection of room furnishings and other accoutrements for children. ✉ *Gerechtigkeitsg. 69, Altstadt* ☎ *031/ 3279090* ⊕ *www.utiger-kindermoebel.ch* ⊙ *Closed Mon.*

Berner Oberland

GSTAAD, INTERLAKEN, JUNGFRAUJOCH,
LAUTERBRUNNEN, MÜRREN, WENGEN

WORD OF MOUTH

"Trummelbach Falls: Amazing spectacle that sadly does not allow
for good photos. It is like indoor waterfalls and was absolutely
worth the visit."

—Duvies

WELCOME TO BERNER OBERLAND

TOP REASONS TO GO

★ **Top of the world:**
At 11,333 feet, the Jungfraujoch isn't the highest place on the planet, but it certainly feels like it, with the Alp's longest glacier and scores of snow-slathered peaks so close.

★ **Twin peaks:** The upwardly mobile head to the adjacent mountain-top villages of Wengen and Mürren to find the Switzerland of cheese, chalet, and chic cliché.

★ **Shangri-la found:** Complete with 72 cascading waterfalls (among Europe's highest), the Lauterbrunnen Valley is like a massive version of Yosemite National Park.

★ **Gilded Gstaad:** Money attracts money, and there's certainly a lot of it here. Mere mortals can indulge in exquisite meals, skiing, and overnight stays in paradise.

★ **Old Switzerland, in a nutshell:** Ballenberg is a delightfully reconstructed Swiss village—à la America's Colonial Williamsburg—with traditional crafts on show.

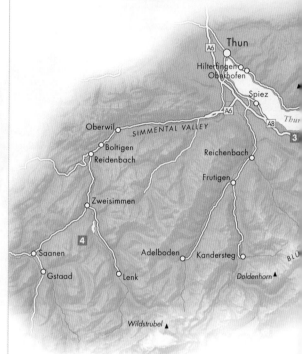

1 Jungfrau Region. A transportation hub, bustling Interlaken has upward of 130 hotels and makes the perfect base camp (it also has a lively nightlife). A short ride away are the magnificent summits of summits—the Eiger, Mönch, and Jungfrau (with the highest train station in Europe). Nestled below are the villages of Grindelwald, Lauterbrunnen, Wengen, and

Mürren, all chalets and geraniums. In winter they have the ambience that every North American "alpine village" resort aims for—and misses.

2 Brienzersee. In the Oberland a wide variety in altitude creates a great diversity of scenery, so you can bathe comfortably in Lake Brienz after skiing on the Jungfrau slopes in July. Waterfront Brienz is home

GETTING ORIENTED

Blessed with nine valleys, the lovely lakes of Thun and Brienz, jet-set Gstaad, and the ageless grandeur of the Jungfrau, this compact region contains a universe of sights. No wonder Switzerland's tourist industry began here in the early 1800s, with English gentry flocking to gape at its gorgeous Alpine scenery.

10

to famed wood carvers and the storybook museum village of Ballenberg. Nearby, the plot thickens in Meiringen—Sherlock Holmes nearly met his match here at Reichenbach Falls.

3 Thunersee. This idyllic lake is named for Thun, a resort town of medieval dignity. Between bouts of waterskiing and wakeboarding, castle-hop to your heart's content: the shoreline villages of Spiez, Hilterfingen, and Oberhofen all have fairy-tale-worthy extravaganzas.

4 Simmental and Gstaad. From Spiez, the highway leads southwest into the Simmental valley, where forest gorges hide Gstaad, a chic and modish winter resort.

Updated
by Susan
Vogel-Misicka

There are times when the reality of Switzerland puts post-card idealization to shame, surpassing advertising-image peaks and skies. Those times happen most often in the Berner Oberland, for this rugged region concentrates some of the best features of rural Switzerland: awesome mountain panoramas, massive glaciers, crystalline lakes, gorges and waterfalls, chic ski resorts, dense pine forests, and charming gingerbread chalets.

Before the onslaught of visitors inspired many locals to switch from farming to innkeeping, agriculture was the prime industry—this is still true today, evidenced by the frequent sight of brown-and-white cows dotting the hillsides, as though conveniently placed for photo ops. The houses of the Berner Oberland are classics: the definitive Swiss chalet, whose broad, eaved roofs cover fancifully scalloped and carved gables. Facades are painted with the family dedication on wood that has weathered to dark sienna. From early spring through autumn, window boxes spill torrents of well-tended geraniums and petunias, and adjacent woodpiles are stacked with mosaic-like precision in readiness for dropping temperatures.

The region is arranged tidily enough for even a brief visit. Its main resort city, Interlaken, lies in green lowlands between the gleaming twin pools of the Brienzersee and the Thunersee, which are linked by the River Aare. Behind them to the south loom craggy, forested foothills, and behind those foothills stand some of Europe's noblest peaks, most notably the snowy crowns of the Eiger (13,026 feet), the Mönch (13,475 feet), and the fiercely beautiful Jungfrau (13,642 feet).

Because nature has laid the region out so conveniently, it has become the most popular in Switzerland for tourism. Its excursion and transportation systems carry enormous numbers of visitors to its myriad viewpoints, overlooks, and wonders. The railroad to the Jungfraujoch transports masses of tour groups to its high-altitude attractions, and on a peak-season day its crowded station can look like the Sistine Chapel in

August or the Chicago Board of Trade. But the tourist industry handles the onslaught with ease, offering such an efficient network of boats, trains, and funiculars, such a variety of activities and attractions, and such a wide range of accommodations, from posh city hotels to rustic mountain lodges, that every visitor can find the most suitable way to take in the marvels of the Bernese Alps.

PLANNING

WHEN TO GO

The Oberland has four distinct seasons, each more beautiful than the last. Valley springs and summers are perfect for outdoor activities, from hiking and biking to swimming. Falls becomes crisp around October and winter brings snow. Keep in mind that snow can stay as late as May and come as early as August at over 6,500 feet.

Winter versus summer? Everyone loves the magic of snow, but all that white can easily lend a sameness to all those mountains—something you avoid if you enjoy an Alpine summer. Warm weather can also mean haze, which can taint your photos of spectacular valleys, so be sure to pack your camera's polarizer filter. If crowds aren't your thing, try the early spring/late fall off-season. Cultural offerings are limited to traditional arts and crafts, although Gstaad hosts the Yehudi Menuhin Music Festival every summer.

No matter the season, sports enthusiasts will be in their element: hiking, biking, waterskiing, sailing, parasailing and gliding, bungee jumping, skiing, snowboarding, and sledding are just a few activities available.

GETTING HERE AND AROUND

AIR TRAVEL

Within 90 minutes, Belp Airport in Bern brings you via train to Interlaken, the hub of the Berner Oberland. Near Basel, EuroAirport (across the border in France) is under 2½ hours by train or bus. The Zürich Airport is also less than a 2½ hour train ride away. Geneva's Cointrin is just under three hours away.

BOAT AND FERRY TRAVEL

In warmer months, round-trip boat cruises around Lake Thun and Lake Brienz provide an ever-changing view of the craggy foothills and peaks. Boats run in winter, too, though on a reduced schedule.

The round-trip from Interlaken to Thun takes about four hours; the trip one way takes about two hours and includes stops for visits to the castles of Oberhofen, Spiez, and Hilterfingen. A round-trip from Interlaken to Brienz takes around 2½ hours, to Iseltwald about 1¼ hours. These boats are public transportation as well as pleasure cruisers; just disembark whenever you feel like it and check timetables when you want to catch another.

Tickets are flexible and coordinate neatly with land transit: you can cruise across to Thun and then take a train home for variety. Buy tickets and catch boats for Lake Thun at Interlaken West station. For Lake Brienz, go to Interlaken Ost (East).

10

Boat and Ferry Information BLS Schifffahrt Berner Oberland ✉ *Lachenweg 19, Thun* ☎ *058/3274811* ⊕ *www.bls.ch.*

BUS TRAVEL

Postbuses (also called postautos or postcars) travel into much of the area not served by trains, including most smaller mountain towns.

CAR TRAVEL

Driving in the Berner Oberland allows you the freedom to find your own views and to park at the very edges of civilization before taking off on foot or by train. If you are confining yourself to the lakefronts, valleys, and lower resorts, a car is an asset.

But several lovely resorts are beyond the reach of traffic—and train, funicular, and cable-car excursions take you to places ordinary tires can't tread; sooner or later, you'll leave the car behind and resort to public transportation. Remember that Wengen and Mürren are car-free. The site ⊕ *www.route.search.ch* offers detailed driving directions and maps in English.

TRAIN TRAVEL

The Berner Oberland is riddled with federal and private railways, funiculars, cogwheel trains, and cable lifts designed with the sole purpose of getting you closer to its spectacular views.

⇨ *For more information on getting here and around, see Travel Smart Switzerland.*

DISCOUNTS AND DEALS

Berner Oberland Regional Pass. If you're traveling extensively in this region, be sure to invest in a seven-day Berner Oberland Regional Pass, which offers 450 km (279 miles) of free rail, bus, and boat travel for any three days of your visit, with reduced fares for the remaining four days, as well as discounts on some of the pricey private excursions into the heights (half off the trip to the Jungfraujoch, for instance). The cost is 282 SF for first-class travel, 233 SF for second class. ☎ *058/3274750* ⊕ *www.regiopass-berneroberland.ch.*

RESTAURANTS

Eating in the Berner Oberland can be a tasty lesson in the local dialect. Take *Gstampfti Chrugli, Suure Mocke,* and *Chalbsläberli mit Röschti.* Fortunately, these traditional meals—that's mashed potatoes, braised beef, and sliced calf liver with butter hash browns to us—taste much better than they sound. Although no Swiss citizen would think of eating fondue in summer, the region teems with restaurants full of wood-and-cowbell decorations that serve exactly what tourists want, which includes melted cheese in its many forms. Other restaurants go sleek, with 20 SF cocktails, dim track lighting, and duck à la European fusion. There's no shortage of pizza and pasta joints either, though the better ones will have wood-fired ovens and homemade dough. Like the rest of Switzerland, eating out is slow time—there's no rushing in for a quick bite before your train. Your check won't come until you ask for it, and it's polite to tack on a few francs—just round the bill up a bit—if the service was good.

Prices in the reviews are the average cost of a main course at dinner or, if dinner is not served, at lunch.

HOTELS

This is the most-visited region in Switzerland, so book as early as possible. High season here means winter, with summer making up a second-place high season.

Decide on which experience you want: the townie feel of a place like Interlaken, which has many bars, night clubs, restaurants, and movie theaters; the much quieter Grindelwald, with fewer venues; or the cliff-top-secluded Mürren or Wengen, where you'll be getting most of your evening's entertainment from the hotel—usually including meals.

Prices in the reviews are the lowest cost of a standard double room in high season.

VISITOR INFORMATION

Berner Oberland Tourismus is a good place to start, as its website lists a number of regional tourist boards.

Contact Berner Orberland Tourismus ⊕ *www.berneroberland.ch.*

THE JUNGFRAU REGION

The thriving resort town of Interlaken lies between two spectacularly positioned lakes, the Brienzersee (Lake Brienz) and the Thunersee (Lake Thun), and is the gateway to two magnificent mountain valleys, one leading up to the popular sports resort of Grindelwald, the other to Lauterbrunnen and the famous car-free resorts of Wengen and Mürren. Looming over both valleys, the Jungfrau and its partner peaks—the Eiger and Mönch—can be admired from various high-altitude overviews.

INTERLAKEN

58 km (36 miles) southeast of Bern.

Often touted as a town without character, Interlaken has patiently borne the brunt of being called "the best place in Switzerland to get away *from*"—but this, it turns out, is a tribute to the town's proximity to many of the wonders of the Bernese Alps. This bustling Victorian resort town is a centrally located home base for travelers planning to visit the region's two lakes and the mountains towering behind them. Those who want up-close mountain views more than nightlife, however, will want to consider staying in one of the smaller resort towns. The name *Interlaken* has a Latin source: *interlacus* (between lakes). At 1,860 feet, Interlaken dominates the Bödeli, the branch of lowland between the lakes that Interlaken shares with the nearby towns of Unterseen, Wilderswil, Bönigen, Goldswil, and Matten. The town's two train stations, Interlaken Ost (East) and Interlaken West, are good orientation points; most sights are just a few minutes' walk from one of the stations. There are unlimited excursion options, and it is a pleasant, if urban, place to stay.

10

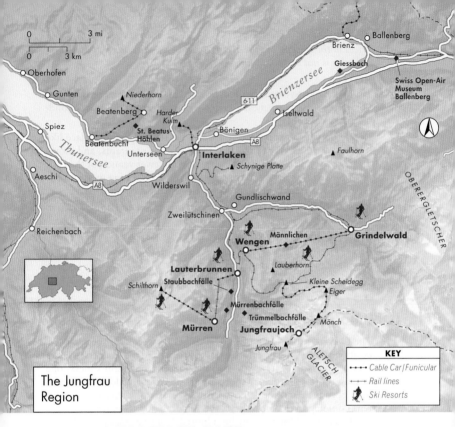

The Jungfrau Region

KEY

•···• Cable Car / Funicular
————— Rail lines
⛷ Ski Resorts

GETTING HERE AND AROUND

Interlaken has two train stations: Interlaken West, where trains arrive from Bern, Thun, and Spiez, and Interlaken Ost (East), which connects you to Brienz and the Jungfrau region. West is the more central station, but check with your hotel—some of the town's fine hotels are clustered nearer the East station, and all Brienzersee boat excursions leave from the docks nearby. The direct train that comes from Bern stops at both stations. From Zürich, a line leads through Bern to Interlaken and takes about two hours; a more scenic trip over the Golden Pass route via Luzern takes about three hours.

Buses to nearby towns leave from the train stations, both of which have taxis to help you schlep your luggage to your hotel; there are also carriage rides for the romantically inclined.

Swift and scenic roads link both Bern and Zürich to Interlaken. From Bern, take A6 leads to Spiez, then A8 to Interlaken. From Zürich, travel by Highway A3 south to pick up first A4 and then A14 in the direction of Luzern. South of Luzern, pick up the A8 in the direction of Interlaken.

The Interlaken Tourist Office, at the foot of the Hotel Metropole, provides information on Interlaken and the Jungfrau region. Arrange your excursions here.

BERNER OBERLAND TOUR OPTIONS

Oberland Tours offers customized van tours within the Berner Oberland. You can take excursions to Mürren and the Schilthorn, to Grindelwald and Trümmelbach Falls, to Kandersteg and the Blausee, and to Ballenberg. You can also devise your own itinerary, and the company will arrange it for you.

Guests are picked up at one of the Interlaken train stations or at their hotels. Some tours are available with English commentary with advance notice, preferably at least a week. The tourist office is the best source of information.

For a nostalgic tour of the streets of greater Interlaken by horse-drawn carriage, line up by the Interlaken West train station.

ESSENTIALS

Visitor Information Interlaken Tourismus ⊠ *Höheweg 37* ☎ *033/8265300* ⊕ *www.interlaken.ch.*

EXPLORING

TOP ATTRACTIONS

Fodor's Choice
★ **Schynige Platte.** For a most splendid overview of the region, head to this 6,454-foot plateau for a picnic, or wander down any of its numerous footpaths, or visit its Alpine Botanical Garden, where more than 600 varieties of mountain flowers grow. A cogwheel train dating from 1893 takes you on the round-trip journey, though you may opt to walk either up or (more comfortably) down. Make sure to specify when you buy your ticket. Trains run from approximately 7:25 am to 4:45 pm. To get here, take the four-minute ride on the Bernese Oberland Railway from Interlaken East to Wilderswil. ⊠ *Wilderswil* ☎ *033/8287233* ⊕ *www. jungfrau.ch* 🎫 *35 SF one-way, 60 SF round-trip* ☉ *Late May or early June–late Oct., daily, depending on snow conditions.*

☾
★ **St. Beatus-Höhlen.** Lovers of Old Swiss style should consider the 8-km (5-mile) trek to the St. Beatus caves. Their legend goes back to the 6th century, when the missionary St. Beatus arrived on the Thunersee to find the local population terrorized by a dragon that lived in the lake and surrounding grottoes. Exorcised by Beatus, the fleeing dragon fell to his death on the rocks. Today you can see the stalagmites, stalactites, and pools inside, as well as a replica of Ponzo, the dragon, for children to explore. Take a jacket, as it's cold inside the caves. You can reach the caves by taking Bus 21 from either train station or by crossing by boat from the Interlaken West station to Sundlaunen, then a 20-minute hike to the caves. ⊠ *Seestr., Sundlauenen* ☎ *033/8411643* ⊕ *www. beatushoehlen.ch* 🎫 *18 SF* ☉ *Late Mar.–late Oct., daily 9:30–5.*

★ **Victoria-Jungfrau Grand Hotel & Spa.** Mark Twain once stayed at this landmark, which was designed to take in the view of the snowy Jungfrau. Topped by a magnificent Victorian-style cupola and spire, and lushly appointed with glittering salons, the hotel originated as two humbler inns, the Jungfrau (1807) and the Chalet Victoria (1810). These were merged and expanded, and the facade redesigned and landmark tower

10

The Berner Oberland rewards hikers with spectacular vistas, like this one of the Jungfrau.

added in 1899. (Only two rooms, including the 19th-century restaurant, survived all this renovation.) Enjoy a drink in one of the hotel's many bars or dine on its grassy terrace—this is as luxe as Interlaken gets. ⊠ *Höheweg 41* ☎ *033/8282828* ⊕ *www.victoria-jungfrau.ch.*

Victoria-Jungfrau Spa. An architecturally splendid indoor swimming pool with columns rising from the water is the anchor of the Victoria-Jungfrau spa, a sprawling wellness playground spanning 59,000 square feet. Whether it's sunny or snowy, the outdoor hot tub with a view of Harder Kulm is a particular treat. Adjacent to the pool, the "heat experience zone"—referring to the saunas and steam baths—features walnut trim, iridescent tiles, and flickering candles. Nearby, two distinct spas provide a comprehensive array of treatments: skin is the focus at the Sensai Select Spa, while total well-being is the raison d'être at Espa Spa. In addition to treatment rooms, it has its own saunas, steam baths, and relaxation rooms where guests are encouraged to unwind before or after a treatment. There are separate facilities for men and women, but couples can reserve the private spa and enjoy a few romantic hours together. A gym, tennis courts, and fitness studios provide the chance to exercise, while a small bistro serves light meals. ⊠ *Victoria-Jungfrau Grand Hotel & Spa, Höheweg 41* ☎ *033/8282730* ⊕ *www.victoria-jungfrau-spa.ch* ☞ *90 SF 25-min back and neck massage, 150 SF 55-min body wrap. Day spa packages from 280 SF. Hair salon, hot tubs, sauna, steam room. Gym with: cardiovascular machines, free weights, weight-training equipment. Services: aromatherapy, facials, hair removal, mani-pedi, massage. Classes and programs: aerobics, body sculpting, fitness analysis, personal training, step aerobics, strength training, weight training, yoga.*

WORTH NOTING

Harder Kulm. With a newly built scenic overlook, this 4,337-foot peak can be reached via an eight-minute funicular ride. From the top you'll enjoy views south over the city, the lakes, and the whole panorama of snowy peaks. The chalet-style restaurant offers sumptuous traditional dishes on a sunny terrace. On Thursday evenings in July and August, you an enjoy *Ländler* (traditional dance) music. The funicular station is north of River Aare, across Beaurivagebrücke. ☎ *033/8287339* ⊕ *www. jungfrau.ch* ✉ *Funicular: 27 SF round-trip* ⊙ *Funicular: May–late Oct., Mon.–Sat. 9:10–6:40, Sun. 8:10–6:40.*

Heimwehfluh. An old-fashioned funicular railway chugs to the top of this 2,194-foot mountain, where you get views of both lakes as well as a peek at the Jungfrau, the Eiger, and the Mönch. There's the usual terrace restaurant at the top, along with a children's playground and a model-train show with music and lights. On the way down you can opt for a ride on the a 985-foot-long bobsled run. The funicular station is a 5-minute walk from the Interlaken West station down the Rugenparkstrasse, with departures every 15 minutes between 10 and 5. The train show costs 9 SF. ☎ *033/8223453* ⊕ *www.heimwehfluh.ch* ✉ *14 SF* ⊙ *Apr.–Oct., daily 10–5.*

Höheweg. The tree- and flower-lined walkways on the city's main promenade cut through the edge of the broad green parklands of the Höhematte. This 35-acre park once provided pasture ground for herds of the Augustinian monastery that dominated medieval Interlaken. Cows still graze in fenced-off areas.

Schlosskirche (*Castle Church*). A monastery, founded in 1133, once stood on this site. All that remains are a 14th-century chancel and a wing of the cloister. The rest was incorporated into a private castle in 1745. ✉ *End of Höhematte, south of Hotel du Nord.*

Touristik-Museum der Jungfrau Region. This museum traces the history of tourism in the area over the last 200 years. Exhibits include models of early transportation and primitive mountain climbing and skiing equipment. ✉ *Obere Gasse 26, Unterseen* ☎ *033/8229839* ⊕ *www. touristikmuseum.ch* ✉ *5 SF* ⊙ *May–Oct., Tues.–Sun. 2–5.*

Unterseen. On the north side of the River Aare is this tiny town, founded in 1279 on land rented from the Augustinians. Unterseen retains some of the region's oldest buildings, including the 17th-century Stadthaus (city hall) and the 14th-century church, its steeple dating from 1471. The Schloss Unterseen (Unterseen Castle), built in 1656, stands at the opposite end of the square from these structures, near a medieval arched gateway. You can get here via a 10-minute bus ride from the center of Interlaken, or by walking from the Interlaken West train station. ⊕ *www.unterseen.ch.*

WHERE TO EAT

$$

SWISS

★

Alpenblick. This carved wood-and-shingle 17th-century landmark attracts both locals and travelers with its two restaurants. The Dorfstube serves old-style Swiss cuisine—try the *Felchen* (a kind of whitefish) from nearby Lake Brienz, or an Alpenblick Rösti. The Gourmetstübli, a showcase for chef Richard Stöckli's renowned international fare, may include fish and mussels in a saffron pepper sauce or veal ravioli and vegetables. The established wine cellar offers Swiss and international wines; should you have a few too many glasses there is always the option of staying over, as the Alpenblick is also a hotel, with rooms spread over two chalets. The place is in Wilderswil, 2 km (1 mile) south of Interlaken. $ *Average main: 36 SF* ✉ *Oberdorfstr. 8, Wilderswil* ☎ *033/8283550* ⊕ *www.hotel-alpenblick.ch* ⊘ *Closed Mon. and Tues.*

$$
ECLECTIC ✕**Krebs.** Established in 1875, this old-world spot offers a well-balanced mix of tradition and modern comfort, with starched-collar service. Along with the renovated decor, the traditional Swiss cuisine and homey daily plates have been updated, and now upscale French and Asian creations are also available—tenderloin of pork with balsamic reduction and panfried shiitake noodles could be a good place to start. A sunny front porch overlooks the street, but head for the more formal dining room, opening onto the main promenade. $ *Average main: 28 SF* ✉ *Bahnhofstr. 4* ☎ *033/8260330* ⊕ *www.krebshotel.ch.*

$ ✕**Pizzeria Horn.** On a quiet, nondescript street behind the Victoria-
PIZZA Jungfrau Grand Hotel & Spa, Pizzeria Horn is well worth the trouble it may take to get here. The first pizzeria in Interlaken to have a wood-burning oven, this charming, wood-and-brick outpost has pleasant outdoor seating. Numerous pizza variations, include the one with pears and Gorgonzola, don't disappoint, but don't be afraid to venture toward the meatier dishes like the succulent pork cutlet. The 40-odd Italian vintages that round out the wine list set this pizzeria apart from many of the others. $ *Average main: 22 SF* ✉ *Harderstrasse 35* ☎ *033/8229292* ⊕ *www.pizzeriahorn.ch* ⊘ *Closed Mon. and Tues.*

$$
SWISS ✕**Restaurant Bären.** In the late 1600s, postal workers traveling the Ober-
★ land needed a place to eat and swap horses. They found what they needed in this lumbering wood chalet, one of the oldest buildings in the area. Today the Amacher-Uetz family taps into its 10 generations of experience running the place to serve outstanding Swiss specialties. Don't miss what could arguably be the country's best *Suure Mocke,* a tangy braised-meat dish that's marinated in wine and vinegar for two weeks. More than half of the guests are locals who gather among the thick, lumpy walls of plastered river rock to sample about 30 wines, many of which are Swiss. Yummy desserts like apple pies and meringues are hard to pass up. $ *Average main: 30 SF* ✉ *Seestr. 2, Unterseen* ☎ *033/8227526* ⊕ *www.baeren-unterseen.ch* ⊘ *Closed Mon. No lunch Tues.–Thurs.*

$ ✕**Schuh.** With a luxurious shady terrace spilling into the Höhematte
ECLECTIC in summer and mellow piano sounds enhancing the classicly elegant interior, this café-restaurant serves rich, hot Swiss meals (as well as some Chinese and Thai dishes). The recipes may date all the way back to 1818, but most of the dishes are freshly made in-house on a daily basis. Leave room for the chocolate specialties and pastries, like the glossy strawberry tarts, which you'll also find in the adjoining shop. $ *Average main: 22 SF* ✉ *Höheweg 56* ☎ *033/8888050* ⊕ *www.schuh-interlaken.ch* ⊘ *Closed Mon.*

$$ SWISS ★ 🍴 **Stellambiente.** For something nicely out of the ordinary, try this family-run gem that defies its outdated '60s exterior and residential setting. Along with marvelous, friendly service you'll enjoy modern, flavorful cuisine: order the "surprise" menu and be treated to six inventive courses served on beautiful, individually selected pieces of china. Several vegetarian options take advantage of locally grown ingredients. In summer, the attractive terrace, complete with fountain, turns dining into a garden idyll. [$] *Average main: 34 SF* ✉ *Stella Swiss Quality Hotel, General-Guisan-Str. 2* ☎ *033/8228871* 🌐 *www.stella-hotel.ch.*

WHERE TO STAY

For expanded hotel reviews, visit Fodors.com.

$$ B&B/INN ★ 🏨 **Alphorn.** Completely renovated in 2011, this modern bed-and-breakfast sits on a quiet side street between Interlaken West and the Heimwehfluh. **Pros:** free Internet in every room; peaceful location; pets stay free. **Cons:** some rooms are tiny. [$] *Rooms from: 180 SF* ✉ *Rothornstrasse 29a* ☎ *033/8223051* 🌐 *www.hotel-alphorn.ch* 🛏 *13 rooms* 🕒 *Closed early Jan.-early Mar.* 🍽 *Breakfast.*

$$ HOTEL 🏨 **City Hotel Oberland.** The exterior of this hotel's main building is bristling with mansard windows and stucco trim, while the wing across the street is pierced by a life-size statue of a cow. **Pros:** central location for shopping and nightlife; the breakfast fills you up for sightseeing. **Cons:** noisy neighborhood; limited parking given the number of rooms. [$] *Rooms from: 192 SF* ✉ *Höheweg 7* ☎ *033/8278787* 🌐 *www.city-oberland.ch* 🛏 *192 rooms* 🍽 *Breakfast.*

$$ HOTEL Fodor's Choice ★ 🏨 **Hotel Interlaken.** The oldest hotel in town, the Hotel Interlaken has been hosting overnight guests since 1323—first as a hospital, then as a cloister, and by the early 15th century as a tavern. **Pros:** in the historic part of Interlaken, close to the train station; friendly, helpful service. **Cons:** no air-conditioning. [$] *Rooms from: 224 SF* ✉ *Höheweg 74* ☎ *033/8266868* 🌐 *www.interlakenhotel.ch* 🛏 *55 rooms, 5 suites* 🍽 *Breakfast.*

$$$ HOTEL 🏨 **Hotel Royal–St. Georges.** If you are a fan of Victoriana, this impeccably restored 100-year-old grand hotel is for you, with original moldings, built-in furnishings, and fantastical bath fixtures. **Pros:** enjoyable for architecture lovers; staff recommends a wealth of nearby excursions. **Cons:** artwork and color schemes in modern rooms won't appeal to everyone. [$] *Rooms from: 250 SF* ✉ *Höheweg 139* ☎ *033/8227575* 🌐 *www.hotelroyal.ch* 🛏 *93 rooms, 3 suites* 🍽 *Breakfast.*

$$$$ RESORT ★ 🏨 **Lindner Grand Hotel Beau Rivage.** Set well back from the road and surrounded by gardens, this elegant hotel maintains an unruffled sense of calm. **Pros:** good location; fabulous views; extremely friendly staff. **Cons:** some rooms on the small side; needs some renovation; rooms at the back are very close to train tracks. [$] *Rooms from: 439 SF* ✉ *Höheweg 211* ☎ *033/8267007* 🌐 *www.lindnerhotels.ch* 🛏 *88 rooms, 13 suites* 🍽 *Breakfast.*

$$$$ RESORT Fodor's Choice ★ 🏨 **Victoria-Jungfrau Grand Hotel & Spa.** Restoration has taken this 1865 grand dame firmly into the 21st century, with glitzy touches such as the burled-wood entryway and a vast Belle Epoque lobby that spirals off into innumerable bars and tea salons. **Pros:** location with view of Jungfrau; wonderful spa. **Cons:** so gargantuan that you can feel like a

mouse among many; some call this place overpriced. $\boxed{\$}$ *Rooms from: 650 SF* ✉ *Höheweg 41* ☎ *033/8282828* ⊕ *www.victoria-jungfrau.ch* ⇆ *212 rooms, 95 suites* ⦿ *Multiple meal plans.*

NIGHTLIFE AND THE ARTS

BARS

Brasserie 17. You'll always find a lively mixed crowd at Brasserie 17. ✉ *Happy Inn Lodge, Rosenstr. 17* ☎ *033/8223225* ⊕ *www.brasserie17.ch.*

CASINO

Casino Interlaken. The Casino Interlaken has American roulette, as well as more than 125 slot machines. Las Vegas it's not, but it's congenial and pleasant. ✉ *Strandbadstr. 44* ☎ *033/8276210* ⊕ *www.casino-interlaken. ch* ▭ *5 SF.*

DANCING

High-Life. Near the Interlaken West train station, High-Life brings back classic rock-and-roll. ✉ *Rugenparkstr. 2* ☎ *079/4150907* ⊕ *www.highlife-interlaken.ch.*

Johnny's Club. This has been the definitive after-hours club for years. Don't get here too early, as the place doesn't come alive until midnight. ✉ *Carlton Europe Hotel, Höheweg 92* ☎ *033/8216109* ⊕ *www.johnnys-interlaken.ch.*

Metro Bar. This place attracts the college-age set and the slightly older. ✉ *Hauptstr. 23* ☎ *033/8221961* ⊕ *www.metrobar-interlaken.com.*

Wineart. This classy wine bar has leather furnishings and lovely architectural flourishes. In warm weather, there's sidewalk seating with a view of the Höhematte. Mediterranean snacks are on the menu along with a good variety of wines. ✉ *Jungfraustr. 46* ☎ *033/8237374* ⊕ *www.wineart.ch.*

THEATER

Kursaal Interlaken. Surrounded by beautifully landscaped grounds between the Höheweg and the River Aare, the the Kursaal was built in 1859 in a dramatic combination of Oberland-chalet and Victorian styles. Plays and concerts are often presented here, mostly during the high season. ✉ *Strandbadstr. 44* ☎ *033/8276100* ⊕ *www.congress-interlaken.ch.*

Fodor's Choice
★

Tellfreilichtspiele. For a real introduction to the local experience, don't miss the Tellfreilichtspiele, an outdoor pageant presented in Interlaken every summer by a cast of Swiss amateurs. Wrapped in a rented blanket and seated in a 2,200-seat sheltered amphitheater that opens onto illuminated woods and a permanent "medieval" village set, you'll see 250 players in splendid costumes acting out the epic tale of Swiss hero Wilhelm Tell. The text is Schiller's famous play, performed in German with the guttural singsong of a Schwyzerdütsch accent—but don't worry; with galloping horses, flower-decked cows, bonfires, parades, and, of course, the famous apple-shooting climax, the operatic story tells itself. Tickets range from 35 SF to 58 SF. ☎ *033/8223722* ⊕ *www.tellspiele.ch.*

Laced with waterfalls, including the 941-foot Staubbach Falls (pictured) Lauterbrunnen Valley is one of the most beautiful spots in Switzerland.

SPORTS AND THE OUTDOORS

SAILING

Lake Thun offers the area's best sailing.

Von Allmen Sailing School. From April to August, Interlaken's Von Allmen Sailing School offers courses and boat rentals. ☎ *033/8225693* ⊕ *www. motor-segelbootschule.ch.*

LAUTERBRUNNEN

Fodor's Choice ★ *10 km (6 miles) south of Interlaken.*

Acclaimed by Lord Tennyson as "the stateliest bit of landstrip," the Lauterbrunnen Valley is often ranked as one of the five most beautiful places in Switzerland (we give it the number-one spot). A Swiss Shangri-la, it encloses a nearly perfect set piece of earth, sky, and water. The mountains here seem to part like the Red Sea as two awesome, bluff-lined rock faces line the vast valley, where grassy meadows often lie in shadow as 1,508-foot rocky shoulders rise on either side. What really set this mountainous masterpiece apart are the more than 70 waterfalls (*Lauterbrunnen* means "only springs") that line the length of the 3-km-long (2-mile-long) valley. Some plummet from sky-high crags, others cascade out of cliff-face crevasses, while many are hidden within the rocks themselves; the largest, the Staubbach Falls, were immortalized by Goethe, Wordsworth, and Byron, who described them as "the tail of a white horse blowing in the breeze." For scenery supreme, Lauterbrunnen can't be topped.

The relentlessly picturesque panorama opens up as you get off the train. This tidy town of weathered chalets also serves as a starting point for the region's two most famous excursions: to the Schilthorn and to the Jungfraujoch. Superefficient parking and a rail terminal allow long- and short-term parking for visitors heading for Wengen, Mürren, the Jungfraujoch, or the Schilthorn. To save a lot of money on hotels, consider choosing this valley as a home base for day trips by train, funicular, or cable. But don't ignore its own wealth of hiking options through some of the most awe-inspiring scenery in Europe. Several lovely trails line the valley, including the **Panorama Spazierweg,** which connects Lauterbrunnen with Wengen. Get a map of it (and lots of brochures) from the tourist office on the main street.

HELICOPTER TOUR

Air-Glaciers. If you have the stomach for it, hop on a breathtaking helicopter tour of the amazing mountain ranges from Air-Glaciers. The heliport is south of town off the main road. ✉ *Lischmaad* ☎ *033/8560560* 🌐 *www.airglaciers.ch.*

GETTING HERE AND AROUND

The Bernese Oberland Railway runs trains once or twice an hour from Interlaken Ost station to the village of Lauterbrunnen; the trip takes 20 minutes and stops in such hamlets as Wilderswil and Zweilütschinen.

ESSENTIALS

Visitor Information Lauterbrunnen Tourism ✉ *Stutzli 460* ☎ *033/8568568* 🌐 *www.mylauterbrunnen.com.*

EXPLORING

Staubbachfälle (*Staubbach Falls*). Magnificent waterfalls adorn the length of the Lauterbrunnen Valley, the most famous being the 941-foot Staubbachfälle, which are illuminated at night and visible from town. These falls draw you like a magnet through the village of Lauterbrunnen itself, past a bevy of roadside cafés and the town center (marked by a church and a small Museum of the Lauterbrunnen Valley). Just opposite the falls is a centuries-old graveyard.

Trümmelbachfälle (*Trümmelbach Falls*). A series of 10 glacier waterfalls hidden deep inside rock walls make up the spectacular Trümmelbachfälle, which you can access by a tunnel lift. Approach the departure point via a pretty, creek-side walkway and brace yourself for some steep stair climbing. Be sure to bring along a light jacket—the spray can seem less than refreshing in the cool Alpine air. ☎ *033/8553232* 🌐 *www.truemmelbachfaelle.ch* 🎟 *11 SF* 🕘 *Apr.–early Nov., daily 9–5; July and Aug., daily 8:30–6.*

WHERE TO STAY

For expanded hotel reviews, visit Fodors.com.

$ B&B/INN 👍 🏨 **Chalet Rosa.** Housed in a 350-year-old chalet, this B&B is charming yet modern. **Pros:** bright and modern bathrooms; orthopedic beds; free Wi-Fi. **Cons:** right on main road. [$] *Rooms from: 140 SF* ✉ *Hauptstr.*

☎ 033/8551073 🌐 *www.chaletrosabb.com* 🛏 *11 rooms* 🍴 *Multiple meal plans.*

$$ HOTEL ★ 🏨 **Hotel Silberhorn.** Across from the train station and next to the cable car to Mürren, this wonderful family-owned hotel, set in a lovely garden, is surprisingly quiet option. **Pros:** excellent cuisine; peaceful vibe; amazing views. **Cons:** lacks services of a modern hotel (e.g., room service or an elevator). [$] *Rooms from: 195 SF* ✉ *Zuben* ☎ *033/8562210* 🌐 *www.silberhorn.com* 🛏 *30 rooms* 🕒 *Closed late Oct.–mid-Dec.* 🍴 *Multiple meal plans.*

$ B&B/INN 👶 🏨 **Staubbach.** Across from the Staubbach Falls, this excellent lodging opens directly onto Lauterbrunnen's main street, which is handily lined with shops and cafés. **Pros:** views of Staubbach Falls; children's play area; free tea and coffee all day. **Cons:** no restaurant; in-room facilities are limited. [$] *Rooms from: 160 SF* ✉ *Hauptstr.* ☎ *033/8555454* 🌐 *www.staubbach.com* 🛏 *27 rooms* 🕒 *Closed Nov.–early Jan.* 🍴 *Breakfast.*

MÜRREN

Fodor's Choice ★ *7 km (4 miles) southwest of Lauterbrunnen, 16 km (10 miles) south of Interlaken, plus a five-minute cable car ride from Stechelberg.*

Mürren is perched on a mountaintop shelf—5,361 feet high, to be precise. This village, along with neighboring Wengen, has always lured the rich and famous. The birthplace of downhill and slalom skiing (in the 1920s), Mürren offers extraordinarily peaceful mountain nights and an unrivaled panorama of the Jungfrau, Mönch, and Eiger, all set so close you feel you can almost reach out and touch them. Skiers may want to settle here for daredevil skiing at the top (the annual Inferno Race in January is the largest amateur downhill in the world). Hikers can combine bluff-top trails with staggering views. This is a car-free resort, so no parking lots spoil the scenery.

GETTING HERE AND AROUND

Mürren is usually accessed via a cable car from the center of Lauterbrunnen and then a cogwheel train from Grütschalp (20.80 SF round-trip for both), but these may be shut down for maintenance (global warming's permafrost melt has increased closings). Alternatively, take the bus to Stechelberg—located at the far end of the valley—where two even more dizzying cable cars (round-trip 29.20 SF) have you reaching for the sky in no time. Upon arrival, Mürren splays out along a long mountain ridge road lined with hotels, restaurants, shops, a few historic chalets, and a large *Sportzentrum* (sports center).

ESSENTIALS

Visitor Information Mürren Tourism ✉ *Postfach, across from Alpin Palace Hotel* ☎ *033/8568686* 🌐 *www.mymuerren.ch.*

EXPLORING

Schilthorn. Mürren boasts some of the longest downhill runs because it is at the foot of the Schilthorn (9,748 feet) mountain, famed for its role in the James Bond movie *On Her Majesty's Secret Service*. The peak of this icy megalith is accessed by a four-stage cable-lift ride past bare-rock cliffs and stunning slopes. At each level you step off the

When the Cows Come Home

It's difficult to grow more than grass on the steep slopes of the Alps, so much of the area has traditionally been used to graze sheep, goats, and, of course, dairy cattle, who supply fresh milk to the cheese and chocolate industries that make up such an important part of the country's agricultural economy. Brown Swiss, said to be the oldest breed in the world, has been a reliable producer of dairy products for centuries. Browns are highly prized in the region, as they adapt to all kinds of weather, have strong feet and legs, and produce more milk (which also happens to be higher in protein than that from other cows). Their robust nature has made them increasingly popular throughout the world.

The seasonal movement of livestock from lowland pastures to Alpine meadows is a tradition that goes back to ancient times. In spring, herders in regional costume spruce up their animals with flowers and embroidered bell collars and move them up to the grazing areas in a ceremony known as the *Alpaufzug* (Alpine ascent). In fall they come down the same way in the *Alpabfahrt* (Alpine descent). All cows are fitted with bells to help make them easier to find if they wander away from the rest of the herd, and the collective clang can echo through an entire valley. If you're driving along during one of the ceremonies, be prepared to pull over for a half hour or more while the cows lumber past, taking up the entire road.

cable car, walk across the station, and wait briefly for the next cable car. At the top is the much-photographed revolving restaurant Piz Gloria, where you can see clips of the film. The cable-car station is in the town of Stechelberg, near the spectacular Mürrenbachfälle (Mürrenbach Falls). ⊠ *Stechelberg* ☎ *033/8260007* ⊕ *www.schilthorn.ch* ⌚ *Cable car 94.80 SF round-trip* ☉ *Departures daily year-round, twice hourly 7:25–4:25.*

SKIING

Swiss Ski & Snowboard School. For lessons, contact Mürren's Swiss Ski & Snowboard School at Chalet Finel, directly behind the Hotel Jungfrau. ⊠ *Chalet Finel* ☎ *033/8551247.*

WHERE TO STAY

For expanded hotel reviews, visit Fodors.com.

$$
HOTEL
★
Alpenruh. Clad in time-burnished pine, fitted with gables, and sporting some great gingerbread trim, the Alpenruh is as picturesque a hotel as you can get in Mürren. **Pros:** views straight out of a postcard; tasteful interiors at relatively low prices. **Cons:** nearby cable-car girders mar the view from some rooms; only three bathrooms have bathtubs—if you like a long hot soak après-ski be sure to book one of them. $ *Rooms from: 240 SF* ⊠ *Eggli* ☎ *033/8568800* ⊕ *www.alpenruh-muerren.ch* ⌂ *26 rooms* ⏦ *Multiple meal plans.*

$
HOTEL
★
Hotel Bellevue. Distinguished by its lovely yellow-brick-and-shutter facade, this longtime landmark is a traditional ski lodge with full modern comforts. **Pros:** a welcome "home away from home" abode; small and perfectly fitted to suit the scene outside; handy coin laundry. **Cons:**

Murren is a picturesque village with unbeatable views of the Jungfrau, Mönch, and Eiger peaks.

one room lacks a balcony—be sure to avoid it. $ *Rooms from: 170 SF* ✉ *Lus* ☎ *033/8551401* ⊕ *www.muerren.ch/bellevue* ⇗ *19 rooms* ⊘ *Closed mid-Apr.–early June and end of Oct.–early Dec.* ⊧⊙⊦ *Multiple meal plans.*

$$$

RESORT

Fodor's Choice

★

🏨 **Hotel Eiger.** With a front-row perch directly across from the Eiger, Mönch, and Jungfrau, this is the most stylish hotel in Mürren. **Pros:** fantastic views; plush and cozy environment; adjacent to the Bergbahn cliff-top station. **Cons:** the location is all about peace and tranquillity, not excitement. $ *Rooms from: 288 SF* ✉ *Aegerten* ☎ *033/8565454* ⊕ *www.hoteleiger.com* ⇗ *39 rooms, 10 suites* ⊧⊙⊦ *Multiple meal plans.*

10

WENGEN

Fodor's Choice

★

10 km (6 miles) north of Mürren.

Lord Byron, Consuelo Vanderbilt (the Duchess of Marlborough), and other posh folks put Wengen on the map, spreading the word about its incomparable eagle's-nest perch on a plateau over the Lauterbrunnen Valley. Few places offered such magnificent panoramas and such elegant hotels. And because of its setting, its *Alpenglühen* ("Alpine glow," in which mountains turn pink in the sunset) was said to be the prettiest in all of Switzerland. Alas, success breeds its own problems. Today you can barely drink in the famous view 4,180 feet over the valley, as hundreds of chalets are now in the way. Innerwengen, the town center, is crowded with large buildings and shops with plate-glass windows. But once up on your hotel balcony—the higher the better, of course—you may experience the wonder of yore.

The cozy bar at the Hotel Eiger is a nice place to warm up over a pot of fondue.

What draws most visitors today is some of the Oberland's most challenging skiing (it connects with the trail network at Grindelwald), choicest hotels, and pinkest sunsets. You can aim for centrally located upscale hotels, near shopping and nightlife options, or head downhill to pleasant, more isolated lodging, all artfully skewed toward the view. Half board is just short of obligatory, as only a few restaurants are not attached to a hotel. It's a car-free town; most hotels have porters that meet the trains.

GETTING HERE AND AROUND

Famously, cars cannot drive to Wengen, and the only transport is provided by the little Wengernalp Mountain Railway, or Wengernalpbahn. This departs and arrives from the lower-valley-floor town of Lauterbrunnen and chugs up the mountainside to Wengen every quarter hour, with departures as early as 4:50 am and as late as 12:58 am, depending on the season.

ESSENTIALS

Visitor Information Wengen Tourism ⊠ *Dorfstr.* ☎ *033/8568585* ⊕ *www. wengen.ch.*

SKIING

Wengen. Just over the ridge from Grindelwald, Wengen is nestled on a sheltered plateau high above the Lauterbrunnen Valley. From there a complex transport system connects to Grindelwald, Kleine Scheidegg, and Männlichen. From Wengen you can take a cogwheel train towards Jungfraujoch or Lauterbrunnen. There's also a cable car to Männlichen plus numerous lifts to serve the ski slopes. The Lauberhorn run is tough; it's used for World Cup ski races in January. One-day lift tickets for

Grindelwald-Wengen cost 62 SF, and a two-day pass costs 112 SF. Lift passes for the Jungfrau–Top-Ski-Region are available only for two or more days. A two-day ticket costs 129 SF. 🌐 *www.jungfrauwinter.ch.*

WHERE TO STAY

For expanded hotel reviews, visit Fodors.com.

$$ HOTEL 👶 🏨 **Bären.** This family-run chalet just below the center of town has bright interiors and good views. **Pros:** hosts are top-notch, and so is the food; free Wi-Fi. **Cons:** this is a modest establishment, so don't look for any in-room luxuries. [$] *Rooms from: 220 SF* ✉ *Am Acker* ☎ *033/8551419* 🌐 *www.baeren-wengen.ch* 🛏 *18 rooms* ⏲ *Closed mid-Oct.–mid-Dec. and for 2 wks after Easter* 🍴 *Multiple meal plans.*

$$$$ RESORT 🏨 **Beausite Park Hotel.** On the hill above Wengen (a bit of a hike from the town center, but that may be a virtue), this lodging offers the kind of views that made Wengen world-famous—a vista of mountain majesty with the nearby buildings nearly hidden by trees. **Pros:** peaceful location; perfect location for skiing; family run. **Cons:** 10-minute walk uphill from cable car; back rooms can be dark due to trees. [$] *Rooms from: 436 SF* ✉ *Wengi* ☎ *033/8565161* 🌐 *www.parkwengen.ch* 🛏 *37 rooms, 3 suites* 🍴 *Multiple meal plans.*

$$ HOTEL ★ 🏨 **Hotel Alpenrose.** One of Wengen's first lodgings, this welcoming inn—downhill and away from the center—has been run by the same family for more than a century. **Pros:** traditional family-run business; relaxing salon for tired skiers or hikers. **Cons:** not in central Wengen; no wellness or spa facilities. [$] *Rooms from: 224 SF* ✉ *Roossi 1371C* ☎ *033/8553216* 🌐 *www.alpenrose.ch* 🛏 *40 rooms* ⏲ *Closed early Apr.–mid-May and early Oct.–Christmas* 🍴 *Multiple meal plans.*

$$$$ HOTEL 🏨 **Hotel Falken.** Built in 1895, soon after train tracks reached this mountain retreat, the Hotel Falken maintains its turn-of-the-20th-century feel and its family-run friendliness. **Pros:** sociable atmosphere prevails; generous amenities in bathroom. **Cons:** some textiles could use a face-lift; no spa services. [$] *Rooms from: 360 SF* ✉ *Gruebi* ☎ *033/8565121* 🌐 *www.hotelfalken.com* 🛏 *44 rooms* ⏲ *Closed Nov.–early Dec.* 🍴 *Multiple meal plans.*

$$$$ HOTEL 🏨 **Hotel Regina.** At this genteel Victorian hotel, you sense the genuinely familial mood as soon as you enter the plush and handsome lobby. **Pros:** luxurious, modern interiors; fine award-winning cuisine; welcoming hosts. **Cons:** the hotel's two restaurants, wine bar, and shop close along with the hotel. [$] *Rooms from: 490 SF* ✉ *Schonegg* ☎ *033/8565858* 🌐 *www.hotelregina.ch* 🛏 *72 rooms, 8 suites* ⏲ *Closed mid-Oct.–mid-Dec. and late Apr.–early May* 🍴 *Multiple meal plans.*

GRINDELWALD

Fodor's Choice ★ *19 km (12 miles) southeast of Interlaken.*

Grindelwald (3,393 feet) may be surrounded by the peaks of the Wetterhorn, Schreckhorn, Mönch, and Jungfrau, but it is best known as the "Eiger village"—it faces the terrifying north face of the peak that has claimed so many mountain climbers' lives that some call it the "death wall." In the summer of 2006 the Eiger almost claimed Grindelwald itself as its newest victim: headlines around the world described the

The only way to reach the charming village of Wengen is on the Wengernalp Mountain Railway.

large chunk of rock face that broke off (due to unseasonably warm temperatures) and plummeted down the mountainside, covering Grindelwald in dust for several days.

Not counting its sheer Alpine beauty, the town remains among the most popular in the Berner Oberland for the simple reason that it is one of the most accessible of the region's mountaintop resorts. Strung along a mountain roadway with one main train station (and another used mainly for excursions to and from the mountains), it makes an excellent base for skiing, shopping, and dining—if you don't mind a little traffic. Once you get off the main road, there are gorgeous Alpine hikes in all directions.

GETTING HERE AND AROUND
Bernese Oberland Railway trains run the 35-minute route between Grindelwald and the Interlaken Ost station twice per hour.

ESSENTIALS
Visitor Information Grindelwald Tourism ⊠ *Dorfstr. 110* ☎ *033/8541212* ⊕ *www.grindelwald.ch.*

EXPLORING
Firstbahn. Among the greatest attractions in Grindelwald is the Firstbahn, a 30-minute gondola ride that is one of Europe's longest lifts and offers lovely views of the wide valley below. From the top, you can engage in all sorts of outdoor thrills, from soaring on a zip line in summer to sledding down in winter. Firstbahn is the starting point for an easy 3-km (2-mile) walk to the Bachalpsee. ☎ *033/8287711* ⊕ *www. jungfrau.ch.*

★ **Gletscherschlucht** (*Glacier Gorge*). Travel down into the valley to Grund, below Grindelwald, and visit the Gletscherschlucht. You can either drive or take the bus to the hotel of the same name. From there you can walk a trail along the river and over bridges about 1 km (½ mile) into the gorge. Although you can't see the glacier itself while walking along the edges of the spectacular gorge it sculpted, you'll get a powerful sense of its slow-motion, inexorable force. ✉ *Grund* 🎫 *7 SF* ⏲ *Late May–mid-Oct.*

★ **Oberer Grindelwaldgletscher.** From Grindelwald you can take a 20-minute drive, hop aboard a postbus, or hike up to the Oberer Grindelwaldgletscher, a craggy, steel-blue glacier—act fast though, because 30% of it has melted since 1963, and forecasts have it shrinking another 20% by 2030. You can approach its base along wooded trails, where there's an instrument to measure the glacier's daily movement.

SKIING

An ideal base for the Jungfrau ski area, Grindelwald provides access to the varied trails of Grindelwald First and Kleine Scheidegg–Männlichen. From here you'll have access to a whopping 45 lifts, cable cars and funiculars that service no less than 213 km (132 miles) of downhill runs. Some slopes go right down to the village; there are special areas for snowboarders and beginning skiers. One-day lift tickets that cover the First-Kleine Scheidegg–Männlichen areas (plus Wengen) cost 62 SF. A two-day pass costs 112 SF. A two-day pass for the entire region, which adds Mürren and the Schilthorn, costs 129 SF.

WHERE TO EAT

$ ECLECTIC 🍴 **Bistro Memory.** A no-fuss, family-style bistro, this welcoming place is known for its youthful, smiley staff. With a well-stocked bar, varied menu, and street-side tables for watching the world go by, it has the relaxed feel of an English pub. Mexican and American dishes are served alongside such traditional Swiss fare as potato-garlic soup and a dozen kinds of Rösti. A kid's menu is also on offer. This joint is open all year round. [$] *Average main: 22 SF* ✉ *Hotel Eiger, Dorfstr. 133* ☎ *033/8543131* 🌐 *www.eiger-grindelwald.ch* ✍ *Reservations not accepted.*

$ PIZZA ★ 🍴 **Onkel Tom's Hütte.** Set in a rustic A-frame cabin on the main drag, this tiny pizza parlor is as cozy as they come. Rough-hewn floors accommodate ski boots, and a smattering of wooden tables share space with a huge iron cook stove where the young owner produces fresh pizzas in three sizes (the smallest of which is more than enough for most people). In warmer weather you can sit in an attractive garden with mountain views. There are also generous salads, freshly baked desserts, and a 400-bottle wine list. Its popularity outstrips its size, so enjoy the delicious smells while you wait. [$] *Average main: 22 SF* ✉ *Hauptstr., near the cable car station* ☎ *033/8535239* ⏲ *Closed Wed., Nov., and May. No lunch Thurs.*

WHERE TO STAY

For expanded hotel reviews, visit Fodors.com.

$$ HOTEL 🏨 **Gletschergarten Chalet-Hotel.** An expanded version of the standard chalet-style lodging, the Gletschergarten has been in the same family

Continued on page 400

THE BERNESE ALPS
TOURING THE SUMMITS

by Tim Neville and Heidi Hagemeier

A veritable chorus line of soaring peaks—the Jungfrau, Mönch, Eiger, Männlichen, and Schilthorn—are among Switzerland's mightiest mountains. To take your sightseeing to new heights, use this mini-guide to the cable-cars, gondolas, and trains that scale these sky-high Alps.

The Jungfrau mountain as seen from the Lauterbrunnen hinterlands

THE SUMMIT OF SUMMITS
CHOOSE YOUR BEST TRIP

THE JUNGFRAU: A Train Ride to the Top of the World.

You can't see the whole continent from the Jungfraujoch, Europe's highest accessible peak, but it sure seems like you can. It took some 16 years of work to dig the tunnel through the Eiger that today makes it possible for passengers aboard the **Jungfraujochbahn** to reach the "Top of Europe" in just 30 minutes from Kleine Scheidegg. During its ascent to the 11,333-foot-high station at the icy saddle, or "joch," that links the Mönch and the Jungfrau peaks, the train stops to afford terrifying views down the treacherous Eiger North Face and across yawning crevasses. At the top, hike over the Alps' longest glacier if the elevation (and scenery) haven't taken your breath.

THE WENGERNALP: One of Europe's Longest Rack-Railways.

The Wengernalp train runs from Lauterbrunnen up the Männlichen Ridge and down to Kleine Scheidegg and Grindelwald. In between, this train route offers a fine first-act in acquainting visitors with the

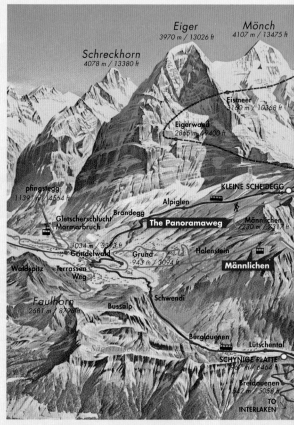

Wengen–Männlichen cable car

Bernese Oberland because it stretches through 12 miles of Switzerland's most beautiful ecozones.

THE MÄNNLICHEN: Europe's Longest Aerial Ride.

Männlichen, a cluster of buildings perched overlooking a vista so spectacular it inspired Lord Byron's "Manfred," is accessible from both Grindelwald and Lauterbrunnen. From Grindelwald the **Männlichen**

gondola stretches an amazing 3¾ miles to an airy station at 7,317 feet. From the Lauterbrunnen side, first take a train to Wengen, then board the cable car to Männlichen.

THE PANORAMAWEG: Switzerland's Most Hiker-Friendly Trail.

No matter how travelers get to the top of the Wengernalp or the Männlichen Ridge, many opt to descend by foot along the relatively easy

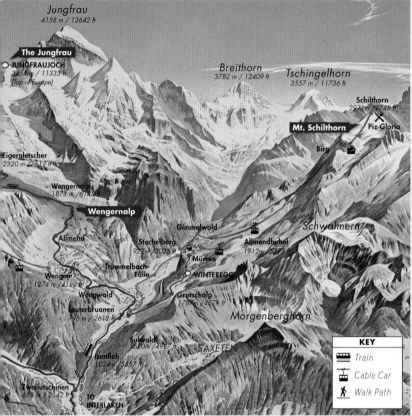

Jungfrau
4158 m / 13642 ft

The Jungfrau
○ JUNGFRAUJOCH
3454 m / 11333 ft
[Top of Europe]

Breithorn
3782 m / 12409 ft

Tschingelhorn
3557 m / 11736 ft

Schilthorn
2971 m / 9748 ft

Mt. Schilthorn ✕ Piz Gloria

Eigergletscher
2320 m / 7612 ft

Birg

Wengernalp
1873 m / 6145 ft

Wengernalp

Gimmelwald

Schwalmern

Allmend

Stechelberg
922 m / 3025 ft

Allmendhubel
1912 m / 5273 ft

Mürren

Trümmelbach-Fälle

○ WINTEREGG

Wengen
1274 m / 4189 ft

Wengwald

Grutschalp
1783 m / 4879 ft

Lauterbrunnen
796 m / 2612 ft

Morgenberghorn

Sulwald
1520 m / 4987 ft

SAXETEN

Isenfluh
1024 m / 3557 ft

Zweilütschinen
688 m / 2142 ft

TO
INTERLAKEN

KEY	
🚃	*Train*
🚠	*Cable Car*
🚶	*Walk Path*

but spectacular **Panoramaweg** trail. This unforgettable hike heads over to Kleine Scheidegg, where trains will then take you down to Grindelwald or Wengen or sky-high up the Jungfrau.

MT. SCHILTHORN: Sky-high Dining at James Bond's Piz Gloria. A dizzying, four-stage cable-car ride up the Schilthorn whisks visitors up to 9,748 feet, where the dominating peaks of

the Bernese Oberland offer a far more memorable spectacle than the Bond movie filmed here in 1969, *On Her Majesty's Secret Service*. Head up early for the James Bond breakfast at the revolving Piz Gloria restaurant or linger in the warm afternoon light on the 360-degree deck that affords views so splendid your photos may look fake.

Skiing at Männlichen

THE JUNGFRAU: A TRAIN-RIDE TO THE "TOP OF EUROPE"

The otherworldly landscape (or maybe it is just the lack of oxygen?) will make you feel like you're on the moon.

WHERE IT STARTS

Granddaddy of all high-altitude excursions is the famous journey to the **Jungfraujoch**—site of the highest railroad station in Europe—and is one of the most popular adventures in Switzerland. From the station at Lauterbrunnen you take the green cogwheel Wengernalp Railway as it grinds steeply up the wooded mountainside.

Get a seat on the right side of the car and watch the valley and the village shrink down below. On the hilltop, the resort town of Wengen pops into view but the train continues to climb and reaches Kleine Scheidegg, a tiny, isolated settlement above the timberline and surrounded by vertiginous scenery.

Top, Jungfraujoch—or the "Top of Europe"—leads to unforgettable vistas of the Aletsch Glacier from the Sphinx Terrace.

WHAT YOU SEE

At Kleine Scheidegg you change to the Jungfraubahn train, which tunnels straight into the rock of the **Eiger,** notorious as one of the most deadly ascents for mountain-climbers. If possible, for the 30- minute train ride up, snag a seat (again, one on the right-hand side) on one of the modern trains, which feature televisions screening a documentary about how the track was built. The train also stops twice, briefly, for icy views down the Eiger North Face and then again for tumbling glaciers framed by enormous picture windows blasted through the mountain's stony face. These are well worth the sprint out of the train for photos (even if someone grabs your seat). These stops only occur on the upward journey. Finally, you reach the **Jungfraujoch terminus** at 11,333 feet. Follow signs to the Top of Europe restaurant, a gleaming white glass-and-steel pavilion. The expanse of rock and ice you will see from here is simply blinding—bring your sunglasses.

FROM THE SPHINX TERRACE

Want to go even higher? Ride a high-tech, high-speed elevator up another 364 feet to the **Sphinx Terrace**: to the south crawls the vast **Aletsch Glacier,** to the northeast stand the Mönch and the Eiger, and to the southwest—almost close enough to touch—towers the tip of the Jungfrau herself. Hope that the outside Sphinx Terrace is open when you visit, as it is a delight to bathe in the sun and, if you're lucky, only a light mountain breeze (toast the moment with a glass of prosecco from the bar near the elevator). If the weather is good, a one-hour hike across a vast snow field lets you reach the **Mönchsjochhütte,** a hiker's dorm with refreshments and grand views.

SKY-HIGH ACTIVITIES

From June to mid-September sign up for a beginner's ski lesson, a dogsled ride, or tour the chill blue depths of the **Ice Palace,** a novelty attraction reminiscent of a wax museum, full of incongruous, slightly soggy ice sculptures.

Top, railway passes below the notorious Eiger North Wall.

TRIP TIP

Return trains, especially toward the end of the day, can be standing room only. You can possibly beat the crowds and get a cheaper price if you go really early in the morning or very late in the afternoon. Even if this isn't an exercise in solitude—the Jungfraujoch restaurants combined can seat 700 people at once—the touch-the-sky experience is worth it.

Admission to the attraction is included in the price of the excursion.
☎ *033/8287233* ⊕ *www.jungfrau.ch*
🚋 *Round-trip Interlaken Ost–Lauterbrunnen–Wengen–Jungfraujoch 190.20 SF, 140 SF for journeys by 6:35 am or after 2 pm from Interlaken Ost, called a Good Morning or a Good Afternoon ticket ⊙ April–Oct., daily 6:35 am (first train up)–5:45 pm (last train down); Nov.–March, daily 6 AM (first train up)–4:40 PM (last train down). The schedule is weather-dependent in winter: call ahead.*

FROM THE WENGERNALP
TO THE PANORAMAWEG

For breathtaking views of Switzerland's mountain heavyweights, nothing beats the gondola or cable-car up the Wengernalp and Männlichen or the famous hike along the Panoramweg.

UP THE WENGERNALP

The Wengernalp train chugs from the relatively balmy flats of the Lauterbrunnen Valley, through the quiet village of Wengen and up to the wind-swept mountainsides of the Kleine Scheidegg. From there the tracks drop down to bustling Grindelwald and more spectacular views. For many, a trip on this rack railway—one of the planet's longest—is just the first stage of the train journey up to the otherworldly ice fields of the Jungfraujoch. Yet it remains a worthy pursuit in itself because the Wengernalp ridge is sensational: the vista here (toward the 6,464-foot peak of Schynige Platte) inspired Lord Byron to write "Manfred" (the poem which kickstarted the Romanticism move-

ment). The trip from either side up to Kleine Scheidegg takes 30-45 minutes. ☎ 033/8287233 ⊕ *www.jungfrau.ch* ✉ *Round-trip from Lauterbrunnen to Kleine Scheidegg, 53.80 SF; Round-trip from Grindelwald to Kleine Scheidegg, 54 SF; Round-trip from Grindelwald to Lauterbrunnen via Kleine Scheidegg, 107.80 SF* ☉ *Departures about every 25 mins from 7 AM–5:40 PM. Schedules are weather-dependent in winter: call ahead.*

Top, couple hiking the Männlichen Panoramaweg. Above, the car–free resort of Wengen sits on a mountainside below the notorious Eiger.

ACROSS THE MÄNNLICHEN RIDGE

Ready to stretch your legs? The Männlichen lifts in summer provide access to a bevy of well-marked trails bathed in glorious views and punctuated by quaint mountain restaurants. Männlichen, a collection of buildings near the Jungfrau, Mönch, and Eiger peaks, can be accessed from lifts on either side—Lauterbrunnen or Grindelwald—of the ridge it sits on. One of the longest gondola rides in the world departs from the Grindelwald side, traveling 6 kilometers (3¾ miles) in 30 minutes. Or, take the five-minute zip up by cable car from Wengen. A spectacular view of both valleys, as well as the Berggasthaus Männlichen (Mountain Guest House), which offers food and guest accommodations, greets you upon arrival.

ALONG THE PANORAMAWEG TRAIL

From Männlichen, warm the legs up by climbing more than 100 meters in elevation to the Männlichen Gipfel (or Männlichen summit), at the edge of the ridge, for great views. Or, if you're reasonably fit, tackle the famous Panoramaweg trail from Männlichen to Kleine Scheidegg, taking about an hour-and-30-minutes on a mild descent along a well-maintained but uneven path. As this is one of the classic hikes in Europe, you will not be alone but there are enough rugged views to go around. The trail curves around the ridge by the Lauberhorn (where World Cup ski races are held); benches about halfway along the route make for a perfect picnic break. When you reach the hamlet of Kleine Scheidegg, catch a train toward either Grindelwald, or Wengen and Lauterbrunnen. ■ TIP→ For the ultimate loop, first ride the gondola from Grindelwald to Männlichen, then hike over to Kleine Scheidegg, and hop trains back to Lauterbrunnen or Grindelwald.

TIMES AND PRICES

Check the Web or the lift stations for full details about times and prices; various offers combine lifts and trains if you plan on hiking between points. ☎ 033/8552933 Wengen-Männlichen, ☎ 033/8548080 Grindelwald-Männlichen ⊕ www.maennlichen.ch

BY TRAIN ⊠ Trains from Lauterbrunnen Train Station to Kleine Scheidegg Train Station ☎ 0900/300300 ⊕ www.sbb.ch ⊠ 53.80 SF roundtrip from Lauterbrunnen ☉ Departures daily about every 25 mins 7 AM–5:40 PM.

BY GONDOLA AND CABLE-CAR: ⊠ Wengen to Männlichen 24 SF (one-way)/41 SF (round-trip); Grindelwald-Männlichen via gondola 32 SF (one-way)/54 SF (round-trip) ☉ Gondola rides between Grindelwald-Männlichen every 30 mins, roughly 8 AM–5:15 PM in summer, roughly 8 AM–4 PM in winter. Cable-car between Wengen-Männlichen: June–Sept., every 15 minutes, 8 AM–5:15 PM; Oct.–May every 15 mins, roughly 8 AM–4 PM.

10

Top, Wengen–Männlichen cable car.

BREAKFAST WITH BOND: ATOP MT. SCHILTHORN

James Bond had to use all of his wits to scale the Schilthorn but all you need is a ride up a string of the world's highest cable cars.

Second only to the Jungfraujoch for jaw-dropping views, the trip up the **Schilthorn** (9,748 feet) is truly a must for visitors to the Berner Oberland. Cue the Hallelujah chorus as you rise beside Yosemite-esque cliffs, past idyllic alpine farms, and at last rise to a mountain pinnacle that normally only the most hearty would ever set foot upon. From there not only are the Jungfrau, Mönch, and Eiger in full view, but a 360-degree riot of ragged peaks are as well.

"VIEWTIFUL" MÜRREN
The ride up is a four-stage cable-car extravaganza. From Lauterbrunen take the postbus toward Stechelberg and its Schilthornbahn station. Head up to a real cliff-hanger of a village, **Mürren**. Packed with Gemütlichkeit, it has superb hiking trails (⊕ *www.schilthorn. ch/en/hiking/*), beautiful hotels, and the Allmendhubel funicular. After a sky-high lunch on a terrace over the Lauterbrunnen valley, change cars once more at Birg for the final cable-car ascent.

Top, cable car ascending the Schilthorn.

The Piz Gloria revolving restaurant offers great views of the Eiger, Mönch, and Jungfrau.

IN THE PIZ GLORIA

The last lap soars across impossible heights to reach the Schilthorn peak, famed for its role in the 1969 James Bond action-film *On Her Majesty's Secret Service*. Here sits the flying-saucer-like lair of the film's villain, Ernest Blofeld, now known as the revolving restaurant **Piz Gloria**. Die-hard fans head here for the James Bond breakfast (no martinis, however), but visitors anytime can enjoy clips of the film in the Touristorama or the metal deck around the circular building for staggering 360-degree views of the scenery. A special combo ticket (transportation/breakfast) leaving from Stechelberg goes for 96.20 SF. Hiking down from the Schilthorn is a knee-smashing affair, so it is best to return to earth via cable-car.

☎ *033/8260007* ⊕ *www.schilthorn.ch* 🚡 *Round-trip cable car Stechelberg–Schilthorn 94.80 SF; 71.20 SF 7:25 AM–8:55 AM or after 3:25 PM in May and mid-Oct.–mid-Nov.* ☉ *Departures yr-round, twice hourly 7:25 AM–4:25 PM; last departure from the top 6:03 PM in summer, 5:03 PM in winter.*

TRIP TIPS

Remember these tips and you won't get into a pique over peaks.

■ Prices for many cable-car and rack train rides can be as high as the peaks themselves. So wallet-watchers may want to consider a Jungfraubahnen Pass (⊕ *www.myjungfrau.ch/en/welcome.cfm?* 🚡 *220 SF*). Valid for 6 consecutive days, it entitles the holder to unlimited trips within the Jungfrau district network. For another 56 SF, you can add the trip to Jungfraujoch. Pass prices are cheaper for those who already have a Swiss Pass or Half-Fare Card. Another euro-stretcher are the special "Good Morning" rates that are offered for the first (as early as 6:30 AM, and also sometimes second) departures of the day, with returns by 12 noon during the peak summer months, or returns any time of the day during November–April.

■ Don't let high altitude sickness get you down. If you might suffer from a mild headache (the usual malady) atop the Jungfrau or Schilthorn peaks, consider taking aspirin before heading skyward. Move slowly. Breathing at the top nets just 67 percent oxygen. Plus: drink plenty of liquids (but not alcohol).

■ Cable cars close twice annually for servicing—usually at the end of April and the end of November.

■ Get a fix on the weather before heading out. Check with your hotel concierge or get clued in with Web cams like ⊕ *www.swisspanorama.com*. Make sure you pick a good-weather day, as the views are the thing when you are up high. Take sunglasses, warm clothes, and sturdy shoes with good tread.

for four generations. **Pros:** homey feel; friendly hosts; magnificent views over glacier. **Cons:** some of the bathrooms would benefit from a makeover. [$] *Rooms from: 230 SF* ✉ *Obere Gletscherstr. 1* ☎ *033/8531721* 🌐 *www.hotel-gletschergarten.ch* 🛏 *26 rooms* 🕒 *Closed mid-Apr.–mid-May and mid-Oct.–mid-Dec.* 🍴 *Multiple meal plans.*

$$$$ RESORT ★ 🏨 **Hotel Belvedere.** The rooms in this hotel offer great views of the Eiger and surrounding peaks, and the staff radiates genuine warmth and professionalism. **Pros:** excellent facilities and cuisine; astounding views; peaceful surroundings. **Cons:** expensive rates; food is so good it may be hard to leave the hotel environs and go farther afield. [$] *Rooms from: 418 SF* ✉ *Dorfstr. 53* ☎ *033/8889999* 🌐 *www.belvedere-grindelwald.ch* 🛏 *56 rooms* 🍴 *Multiple meal plans.*

$$ HOTEL 🏨 **Hotel Cabana.** Brimming with personal warmth, this family-run hotel has become a favorite among those who value tranquillity and convenience. **Pros:** good value; quiet setting. **Cons:** no restaurant, so it's a short walk into town for lunch and dinner. [$] *Rooms from: 232 SF* ✉ *Dorfstr. 46* ☎ *033/8545070* 🌐 *www.cabana-grindelwald.ch* 🛏 *15 rooms* 🕒 *Closed Easter–mid-May, Oct., and Nov.* 🍴 *Breakfast.*

$$ B&B/INN 🏨 **Hotel-Restaurant Wetterhorn.** Overlooking the magnificent ice-blue glacier—as well as a sprawling parking lot—this pretty, wood-trimmed inn offers generous lunches on the terrace and good regional dining inside the comfortable restaurant. **Pros:** perfect base location for skiing and hiking; popular stop for meals. **Cons:** the crowds are also savoring the sights. [$] *Rooms from: 200 SF* ✉ *Obere Gletscherstr. 159* ☎ *033/8531218* 🌐 *www.hotel-wetterhorn.ch* 🛏 *10 rooms, 3 dormitories* 🕒 *Closed late Oct.–late Nov. and 2 wks around Easter* 🍴 *Multiple meal plans.*

$$$$ RESORT ★ 🏨 **Romantik Hotel Schweizerhof.** Behind its dark-wood, red-shuttered chalet facade dating from 1892, this big, comfortable hotel has been expanding rapidly in recent years—it's now twice the size it was in 2007. **Pros:** nothing is rushed, so you can truly relax; small library has books in seven languages; large garden. **Cons:** rooms are well appointed but not lavish. [$] *Rooms from: 510 SF* ✉ *Off Dorfstr.* ☎ *033/8545858* 🌐 *www.hotel-schweizerhof.com* 🛏 *30 rooms, 10 suites* 🕒 *Closed mid-Oct.–mid-Dec. and for a month around Easter* 🍴 *Multiple meal plans.*

THE DEADLY EIGER

Landmarked by its famous "White Spider" (the conjunction of snow fields and icy chutes), the Eiger's notorious north face was first climbed in summer in 1938 via a wandering route. It was not until 1961 that the first group of climbers successfully conquered the almost vertical rock face by climbing straight up its middle. As you look up from the Jungfrau Railway train, the surprise is not that more than 45 people have lost their lives on the north face, but that anyone should have succeeded. Rumor has it that townspeople used to make bets on who would make it and who would not.

NIGHTLIFE AND THE ARTS

Avocado. Artfully furnished with thrift shop treasures, the Avocado serves up whiskey, beer, and the occasional shot of live music. ⊠ *Dorfstr. 158* ☎ *079/9552704.*

Challibar. This cool dance club has a DJ who is happy to play requests. ⊠ *Hotel Kreuz, Dorfstr.* ☎ *033/8545492* ⊕ *www.kreuz-post.ch.*

Gepsi. Open late into the evening, this place has a fun crowd and weekly live music. ⊠ *Hotel Eiger, Dorfstr. 133* ☎ *033/8543131* ⊕ *www.eiger-grindelwald.ch.*

Kings and Queens. In the Grand Hotel Regina, Kings and Queens offers live music nightly in the high season and on weekends the rest of the year. ⊠ *Grand Hotel Regina, Dorfstr. 80* ☎ *033/8548600* ⊕ *www.grandregina.ch.*

Mescalero. Dance until the wee hours of the morning at this dimly lighted dance palace. Occasionally there are live concerts and other events. ⊠ *Hotel Spinne, Hauptstr.* ☎ *033/8548888* ⊕ *www.spinne.ch.*

Plaza Disco. With trippy murals and a horseshoe-shaped bar, the Plaza Disco plays music that attracts an enthusiastic younger crowd (no yodeling here). ⊠ *Dorfstr. 168* ☎ *033/8534240* ⊕ *www.plazadisco.com.*

SPORTS AND THE OUTDOORS

HIKING

Grindelwald is a hiker's paradise, both in summer and winter. Detailed maps of mountain trails are available at the tourist office.

Eiger Trail. The 6-km (3¾-mile) Eiger Trail extends from Alpiglen (near Grindelwald) to Eigergletscher (above Kleine Scheidegg). It abruptly climbs 2,300 vertical feet through cool copses of firs and spruce. Strategically placed benches offer a welcome breather or the perfect spot for lunch. Using only hand tools, the trail was built in 1997 in just 39 days. *Moderate.*

GrindelwaldSports. Head into the mountains with a guided hike lead by GrindelwaldSports. With a day or two's notice, you can set out with a local, trained guide who can talk terrain as you cross beneath those lofty peaks. The Grindelwald tourist office also sometimes organizes outings. The tourist office and GrindelwaldSports are both located at Grindelwald's Sportszentrum on Dorfstrasse. ⊠ *Dorfstr. 110* ☎ *033/8541280* ⊕ *www.grindelwaldsports.ch.*

10

BRIENZERSEE

One of the cleanest lakes in Switzerland—which surely means one of the cleanest in the world—the magnificent bowl that is the Brienzersee mirrors the mountain-scape and forests, cliffs, and waterfalls that surround it. Along the shore are some top attractions: the wood-carving center of Brienz, the wonderful open-air museum village of Freilichtmuseum Ballenberg—Switzerland's Colonial Williamsburg—and Meiringen, the site of Reichenbach Falls, where Sherlock Holmes fought with Moriarty. You can cruise alongside Lake Brienz at high speed on the A8 freeway or crawl along its edge on secondary waterfront roads. You can also

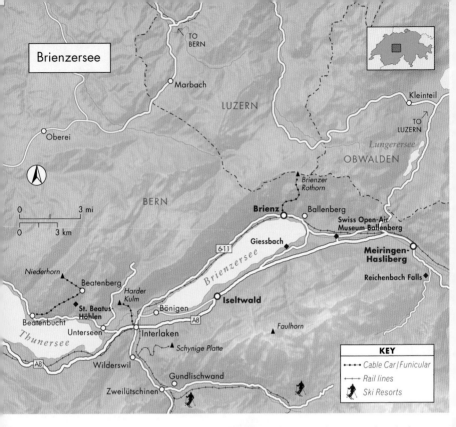

cut a wake across it on a steamer, exploring each stop on foot before cruising to your next destination.

ISELTWALD

9 km (6 miles) northeast of Interlaken.

Set on a lovely and picturesque peninsula jutting out into the quiet waters of the lake, Iseltwald has a bevy of cafés, rental chalets, and hotels clustered at the water's edge. And every restaurant prides itself on its fish dishes.

GETTING HERE AND AROUND

By land, the most scenic route to Iseltwald from Interlaken is via the south-shore road; follow the black-and-white "Iseltwald" signs. You can also take the A8 expressway, following the signs for Meiringen.

EXPLORING

Giessbach. From the edge of Iseltwald, an idyllic forest walk of about 1½ hours brings you to the falls of the Giessbach, which tumble in several stages down rocky cliffs to the lake. They are easy to find, being right next to the 19th-century extravaganza that is the Grand Hotel Giessbach. You can also get to the falls via the Brienzersee steamer, which departs from Brienz or Interlaken Ost. ⊠ *Giessbach.*

WHERE TO STAY

For expanded hotel reviews, visit Fodors.com.

$$
HOTEL
Fodor's Choice
★

Grandhotel Giessbach. Overlooking the famed Giessbach Falls, this 19th-century Belle Epoque showplace trimmed with fancy woodwork and topped with turrets offers lovely scenic views from almost any vantage point. **Pros:** stunning location; old-world charm; all-round experience is one of utter relaxation. **Cons:** day-trippers come for lunch at the terrace, so it can be crowded; isolated location. $ *Rooms from: 240 SF* ⊠ *Am Brienzersee, Brienz* ☎ *033/9522525* ⊕ *www. giessbach.ch* 🛏 *65 rooms, 5 suites* ⊗ *Closed late-Oct.–late Apr.* ❍ *Multiple meal plans.*

BRIENZ

★ *12 km (7 miles) northeast of Iseltwald, 21 km (13 miles) northeast of Interlaken.*

The romantic waterfront village of Brienz, world renowned for its wood carving, is a favorite stop for people traveling by boat as well as by car. Several artisan shops display the local wares, which range in quality from the ubiquitous, winningly simple figures of cows to finely modeled nativity figures and Hümmel-like portraits of Wilhelm Tell. Brienz is also a showcase of traditional Oberland architecture, with some of its loveliest houses (at the west end of town, near the church) dating from the 17th century.

GETTING HERE AND AROUND

Brienz is on the direct rail line with Interlaken, with very frequent train connections.

ESSENTIALS

Visitor Information Brienz Tourismus ⊠ *Hauptstr. 148* ☎ *033/9528080* ⊕ *www.brienz-tourismus.ch.*

EXPLORING

Fodor's Choice
★

Brienzer-Rothorn Bahn. Switzerland's last steam-driven cogwheel train runs from the waterfront of Brienz up to the summit of Brienzer-Rothorn, 7,700 feet above the town. The ride takes an hour and rolls under huge craggy peaks and through verdant meadows to afford stunning views of the lake. (The town will be so far below you'll need pictures to remember the whole excursion wasn't fake.) A restaurant up top serves decent soups and sandwiches on a terrace that makes the most of the views. Trains depart at least once an hour, but to avoid long waits at peak times, purchase your timed ticket in advance on the day you will make the trip. ⊠ *Hauptstr.* ☎ *033/9522222* ⊕ *www.brienz-rothorn-bahn.ch* 🎫 *80 SF round-trip* ⊗ *Mid-May–late Oct., Mon.–Sat. 8:30–5:40, Sun. 7:30–5:40.*

Fuchs Holzschnitzkurse. At Brienz you may want to try your hand at wood carving. From May to October, you can learn to carve the typical Brienzer cow during a two-hour lesson at the atelier of Paul Fuchs. Make a reservation through the tourist office in Meiringen for classes between May and October. His workshop is in Hofstetten, between

10

The train up to Brienzer-Rothorn is the last steam-driven cogwheel in the country.

Brienz and Ballenberg. ⊠ *Scheidweg 19D, Hofstetten* ☎ *033/9725050* ⊕ *www.fuchs-holzschnitzkurse.ch* 🖃 *28 SF.*

Schweizer Holzbildhauerei (*Swiss Woodcarving Museum*). To learn about the history of traditional Swiss woodworking, stop by the Schweizer Holzbildhauerei, where you can also buy locally carved pieces. ⊠ *Hauptstr. 111, Hofstetten* ☎ *033/9521317* ⊕ *www.museum-holzbildhauerei.ch* 🖃 *5 SF.*

Ⓒ **Swiss Open-Air Museum Ballenberg.** Just east of Brienz, a small road leads
Fodor's Choice to the magnificent Swiss Open-Air Museum Ballenberg. More than
★ 100 typical houses from virtually every part of Switzerland are on display in this outdoor exhibit. Dotting the meadows are 19th-century barns, pastel-shuttered houses, antique lace-making shops, traditional haberdasheries, and plenty of carefully reconstructed chalets. Even the gardens and farm animals are true to type. Spinning, forging, and lace making are demonstrated using original tools. The settlement, between the villages of Hofstetten and Brienzwiler, ranges over many acres, and you can easily spend at least a half day here. Via public transport, take the train to Brienz or Brünig and then a short bus ride to Ballenberg. ⊠ *Museumsstr. 131, Hofstetten* ☎ *033/9521030* ⊕ *www.ballenberg.ch* 🖃 *20 SF* ⊙ *Early Apr.–late Oct., daily 10–5.*

WHERE TO EAT AND STAY
For expanded hotel reviews, visit Fodors.com.

$$ ✕ **Restaurant Bären.** It may be next to a parking lot, but this establish-
ECLECTIC ment is a lovely spot for a meal. Mature trees strung with lights shade a brick terrace perched above the lake. The lighter fare includes poached whitefish in a white wine sauce. And if you want a break from Swiss

cuisine, the restaurant's chef from southern India has created a full menu of South Asian fare. On summer evenings you might catch live music—acts that grace the Montreux Jazz Festival often stop here before heading home. [$] *Average main: 28 SF* ✉ *Hauptstr. 72* ☎ *033/9512412* 🌐 *www.seehotel-baeren-brienz.ch.*

$$ SWISS ★ 🍴 **Steinbock Brienz.** At this carved-wood chalet dating from 1787, you can sit out on the flower-lined terrace and choose from among no fewer than 10 interpretations of Lake Brienz whitefish and perch. The menu also has a range of veal classics. There are also nine guest rooms, all with a bright and cheery feel. [$] *Average main: 30 SF* ✉ *Hauptstr. 123* ☎ *033/9514055* 🌐 *www.steinbock-brienz.ch* ⏲ *Closes for a month in Feb. and Mar.*

$$ RESORT 👶 ★ 🏨 **Hotel Lindenhof.** Families often settle in for a week or two at this hotel high above the lakefront, their evenings often spent by the immense stone fireplace, in the panoramic winter garden, or on the spectacular terrace. **Pros:** welcoming to families; manicured gardens; quirky decor. **Cons:** standard rooms are fairly small; may be too cutesy for some. [$] *Rooms from: 180 SF* ✉ *Lindenhofweg 15* ☎ *033/9522030* 🌐 *www.hotel-lindenhof.ch* 🛏 *40 rooms* ⏲ *Closed Jan.–mid-Mar. and Mon. and Tues. in late Mar., Apr., Nov., and Dec.* 🍽 *Multiple meal plans.*

SHOPPING

Brienz is the place for good selections of local wood carvings, including cows, plates, and Nativity figures.

MEIRINGEN–HASLIBERG

12 km (7 miles) northeast of Iseltwald, 21 km (13 miles) northeast of Interlaken.

Set apart from the twin lakes and saddled between the roads to the Sustenpass and the Brünigpass, Meiringen is a resort town with more than 300 km (186 miles) of marked hiking trails and 60 km (37 miles) of ski slopes at the Hasliberg ski region. Historically, its claim to fame is as the place where meringue was invented—the (dubious) legend is that the resident chef had too many egg whites left over and decided to do something different for visiting celeb Napoléon. But there is little history left here, and today Meiringen is merely a pleasant town whose main street is lined with shops selling all sorts of kitschy Swiss merchandise (don't laugh—this stuff is hard to find in many parts of the country).

GETTING HERE AND AROUND

Frequent trains run the 35-minute route between Meiringen and Interlaken.

ESSENTIALS

Visitor Information Tourism Information Meiringen ✉ *Bahnhofstr. 12* ☎ *033/9725050* 🌐 *www.haslital.ch.*

EXPLORING

Reichenbachfälle (*Reichenbach Falls*). Meiringen's one showstopper is the Reichenbachfälle, where Sir Arthur Conan Doyle's fictional detective Sherlock Holmes and his archenemy, Professor Moriarty, plunged into the "cauldron of swirling water and seething foam in that bottomless

Kids love the historic reenactments and animals at Brienz's Swiss Open-Air Museum Ballenberg.

abyss above Meiringen." This was the climax of the "last" Holmes story, *The Final Problem* (the uproar over the detective's untimely end was such that the author was forced to resurrect his hero for further fictional adventures). The falls, 2,730 feet up a mountain a little way outside of town, can be visited via a funicular. ☎ *033/9729010* ⊕ *www. reichenbachfall.ch* 🎫 *10 SF* ⊙ *Closed mid-Oct.–earlyMay; funicular runs every 15 mins daily.*

Sherlock Holmes Museum. Buffs of the famous detective will like the Sherlock Holmes Museum in the center of town. Housed in a small chapel, it contains a replica of the fictional sleuth's front room at 221B Baker Street. ✉ *Kreuzgasse 4* ☎ *033/9714141* ⊕ *www.sherlockholmes.ch* 🎫 *4 SF* ⊙ *May–Oct., Tues.–Sun. 1:30–6; Dec.–Apr., Wed. and Sun. 4:30–6.*

THUNERSEE

If you like your mountains as a picturesque backdrop and like to relax on the waterfront, take a drive around the Thunersee (Lake Thun) or crisscross it on a leisurely cruise boat. More populous than Lake Brienz, its allures include the marina town of Spiez and the large market town of Thun, spread at the feet of the spectacular Schloss Zähringen (Zähringen Castle). There are other castles along the lake, and yet another high-altitude excursion above the waterfront to take in Alpine panoramas—a trip up the Niederhorn.

SPIEZ

19 km (11¾ miles) west of Interlaken.

With its mild climate and lakeside location, Spiez provides a striking contrast to the snowy Alps. A good reason to visit might be the nearby vineyards, which produce about 75,000 bottles of wine per year.

GETTING HERE AND AROUND

A rail line connects this summer lake resort with Thun and Interlaken.

Visitor Information Thun-Thunersee Tourismus ⊠ *Bahnhofstr.* ☎ *033/6559000* ⊕ *www.thunersee.ch.*

EXPLORING

Schloss Spiez. The town's enormous waterfront castle, Schloss Spiez, was home to the family Strättligen and, in the 13th century, its great troubadour, Heinrich. The structure spans four architectural epochs, starting with the 11th-century tower. Its halls contain beautiful period furnishings, some dating back to Gothic times. The early Norman church on the grounds is more than 1,000 years old. ⊠ *Schlossstr. 16* ☎ *033/6541506* ⊕ *www.schloss-spiez.ch* 🖅 *10 SF* ⊗ *Mid-Apr.–mid-Oct., Mon. 2–5, Tues.–Sun. 10–5; July and Aug., Mon. 2–6, Tues.–Sun. 10–6.*

WHERE TO EAT AND STAY

For expanded hotel reviews, visit Fodors.com.

$$
ITALIAN
✕ **Hotel Seegarten Marina.** Choose between a marble-columned pizzeria in one wing and two dining rooms that stretch comfortably along the waterfront. The lake fish specialties are excellent, but there is also a huge range of steaks, pastas, and salads, plus a children's menu—you will be spoiled for choice. Guest rooms upstairs are spare and modern, yet a nice retreat should you have too many cocktails in the Pirate Bar. Ⓢ *Average main: 25 SF* ⊠ *Schachenstr. 3* ☎ *033/6556767* ⊕ *www. seegarten-marina.ch.*

$$$
RESORT
🏨 **Strandhotel Belvédère.** Set on beautiful lawns and gardens, this graceful old mansion has its own manicured beach for secluded swimming. **Pros:** elegant dining; lakeside location; sparkling spa. **Cons:** tour groups can dissolve the peace and tranquillity. Ⓢ *Rooms from: 350 SF* ⊠ *Schachenstr. 39* ☎ *033/6556666* ⊕ *www.belvedere-spiez.ch* 🛏 *29 rooms, 7 suites* ⏇⃝ *Breakfast.*

THUN

10 km (6 miles) north of Spiez, 29 km (18 miles) northwest of Interlaken.

Built on an island in the River Aare as it flows from Lake Thun, this picturesque market town is laced with rushing streams crossed by wooden bridges, and its streets are lined with arcades. On the Old Town's main shopping thoroughfare pedestrians stroll along flowered terrace sidewalks built on the roofs of the stores' first floors and climb down stone stairs to visit the "sunken" street-level shops.

GETTING HERE AND AROUND

A rail line connects Thun, Spiez, and Interlaken. From Bern you can catch A6 south, toward Thun.

10

Set against a beautiful mountain backdrop, the Thunersee is studded with castles.

ESSENTIALS

Visitor Information Thun Tourismus ✉ *Bahnhof, Seestr.* ☎ *033/2259000*
🌐 *www.thuntourismus.ch.*

EXPLORING

★ **Schloss Thun** (*Thun Castle*). From the charming medieval Rathausplatz, a covered stairway leads up to the great Schloss Thun, its broad *donjon* (inner tower) surrounded by four stout turrets. Built in 1186 by Berchtold V, Duke of Zähringen, it houses the fine Schlossmuseum Thun (Thun Castle Museum) and provides magnificent views from its towers. The Knights' Hall has a grand fireplace, an intimidating assortment of medieval weapons, and tapestries, one from the tent of Charles the Bold. The Hall is often the imposing venue for concerts. Other floors display local Steffisburg and Heimberg ceramics, 19th-century uniforms and arms, and Swiss household objects, including charming Victorian toys. ✉ *Schlossberg 1* ☎ *033/2232001* 🌐 *www. schlossthun.ch* 💰 *8 SF* 🕐 *Feb. and Mar., daily 1–4; Apr.–Oct., daily 10–5; Nov.–Jan., Sun. 1–4.*

OFF THE BEATEN PATH

Niederhorn. The trip up the 6,397-foot Niederhorn lets you sit back and soak in the glory of the entire region. From the summit, you can appreciate not only the Jungfrau's splendor but also the rugged terrain surrounding the Gemmi Pass to the west and Grosse Scheidegg to the east. The journey can begin with a funicular from the lakeside town of Beatenbucht (get here via boat or postbus from Thun). If you'd rather, you can catch a gondola in the hamlet of Beatenberg (accessible by postbus from Interlaken). You'll change to a cable car at Vorsass, where you'll find a lovely restaurant, on your way to the Niederhorn. Keep

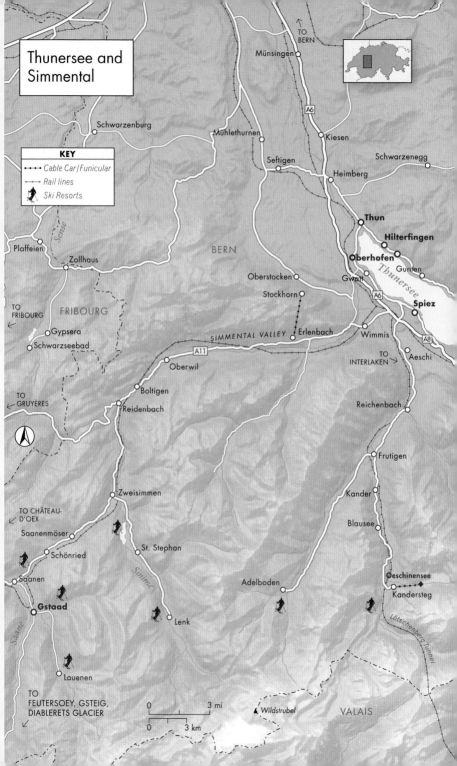

Thunersee and Simmental

TO BERN

Münsingen

A6

Schwarzenburg

Mühlethurnen

Kiesen

Seftigen

Schwarzenegg

Heimberg

Thun

Hilterfingen

BERN

Oberstocken

Oberhofen

Gunten

Plaffeien

Zollhaus

Gwatt

Thunersee

A6

Stockhorn

Spiez

Sense

FRIBOURG

TO FRIBOURG

SIMMENTAL VALLEY

Erlenbach

Wimmis

A8

Gypsera

Oberwil

A11

Aeschi

Schwarzeebad

TO INTERLAKEN

Boltigen

TO GRUYÈRES

Reidenbach

Reichenbach

Frutigen

Zweisimmen

Kander

TO CHÂTEAU- D'OEX

Saanenmöser

Blausee

Schönried

St. Stephan

Saanen

Simme

Adelboden

Øeschinensee

Gstaad

Kandersteg

Lenk

Lötschenberg Tunnel

Saane

Lauenen

TO FEUTERSOEY, GSTEIG, DIABLERETS GLACIER

0   3 mi

0   3 km

▲ Wildstrubel

VALAIS

your eyes peeled for chamois along the ridge. ☎ *033/8410841* ⊕ *www. niederhorn.ch* 🖅 *40–70 SF round-trip* ⊘ *Late Apr.–late Dec.; trips from Beatenbucht depart every 20 mins 8–8.*

WHERE TO STAY
For expanded hotel reviews, visit Fodors.com.

$$
HOTEL
🏨 **Krone.** On the lovely Town Hall Square, this landmark hotel has some fine river views. **Pros:** historic character and central location; bountiful breakfast buffet. **Cons:** paid parking is limited; can be noisy during the busiest times. 💲 *Rooms from: 225 SF* ✉ *Obere Hauptg. 2* ☎ *033/2278888* ⊕ *www.krone-thun.ch* 🛏 *25 rooms, 2 suites* 🍴 *Breakfast.*

$
HOTEL
🏨 **Zu Metzgern.** At the base of the castle hill, this shuttered and arcaded *Zunfthaus* (guildhall) overlooks the Town Hall Square. **Pros:** simple pleasures of life are to be indulged here—food, laughter, conversation; central location in the Old Town. **Cons:** bathrooms are down the hall; parking is awkward; breakfast not included in rates. 💲 *Rooms from: 118 SF* ✉ *Untere Hauptg. 2* ☎ *033/2222141* ⊕ *www.zumetzgern.ch* 🛏 *10 rooms* 🍴 *No meals.*

SHOPPING
Erlebnis-Töpferei. A good spot for traditional pottery, Erlebnis-Töpferei is located just north of Thun. ✉ *Bernstr. 295, Heimberg* ☎ *033/4371472* ⊕ *www.danielhowald.ch.*

HILTERFINGEN

★ *5 km (3 miles) southeast of Thun.*

Lake Thun is famous for its waterside castles, and Hilterfingen and Oberhofen, a little farther along the shore, have two of the best.

Schloss Hünegg. Hilterfingen's castle, Schloss Hünegg, was built in 1861 and furnished over the years with a bent toward Art Nouveau. The stunning interiors have remained unchanged since 1900. Outside is idyllic parkland. ✉ *Staatsstr. 52* ☎ *033/2431982* ⊕ *www.schlosshuenegg.ch* 🖅 *9 SF* ⊘ *Mid-May–mid-Oct., Mon.–Sat. 2–5 , Sun. 11–5.*

OBERHOFEN

★ *2 km (4 miles) southeast of Hilterfingen.*

Schloss Oberhofen. Even Walt Disney would have a hard time topping Schloss Oberhofen for sheer fairy-tale splendor. The jewel of the village, this delightful hodgepodge of towers and spires sits on the waterfront. Begun during the 12th century, it was repeatedly altered over a span of 700 years. Inside, a museum has a display of the lifestyles of Bernese nobility, along with salons done up in the plushest 19th-century style, plus a Turkish "smoking room," a display of magical medieval stained glass, and a 13th-century chapel with noted Romanesque frescoes. ■**TIP**➜ In the Seetürmchen is a lovely, candlelit chamber where all eyes are drawn to an extraordinary carved-wood mermaid chandelier. Those in the know touch the mermaid's belly for good luck.

✉ *Schlossgasse* ☎ *033/2431235* ⊕ *www.schlossoberhofen.ch* 🎫 *10 SF* ☉ *Mid-May–mid-Oct., Mon. 2–5, Tues.–Sun. 11–5.*

SIMMENTAL AND GSTAAD

Separate in spirit and terrain from the rest of the Berner Oberland, this craggy forest gorge follows the Lower Simme into the Saanenland, a region as closely allied with French-speaking Vaud as it is with its Germanic brothers. Here the world-famous resort of Gstaad has linked up with a handful of neighboring village resorts to create the almost limitless outdoor opportunities of the Gstaad "Mountain Rides" region. From Gstaad it's an easy day trip into the contrasting culture of Lake Geneva and the waterfront towns of Montreux and Lausanne. From Interlaken, take A8 toward Spiez, then cut west on A11, following the signs toward Zweisimmen, which leads to Gstaad. The forest gorges of the Simmental Valley lead you through Zweisimmen to the Saanenland and Gstaad.

GSTAAD

49 km (30 miles) southwest of Spiez, 67 km (42 miles) southwest of Interlaken, 68 km (43 miles) northwest of Montreux.

The four fingerlike valleys of the Saanenland find their palm at Gstaad, the Berner Oberland's most glamorous resort. Linking the Berner Oberland with the French-speaking territory of the Pays-d'Enhaut of Canton Vaud, the holiday region of Gstaad blends the two regions' natural beauty and cultures, upholding Pays-d'Enhaut folk-art traditions such as *papier découpage* (paper silhouette cutouts) as well as decidedly Germanic ones (cowbells, wood carvings, and alpenhorns).

In Gstaad, neither culture wins the upper hand—in fact, both cultures take a backseat to a more cosmopolitan attitude. During high season the folksy *Gemütlichkeit* of the region gives way to jet-set international style. Although weathered-wood chalets are the norm (even the two tiny supermarkets are encased in chalet-style structures), the main street is lined with designer boutiques. Prince Rainier of Monaco, Roger Moore, and Elizabeth Taylor have all owned chalets in Gstaad, as well as the late musician and conductor Yehudi Menuhin, who founded his annual summer music festival here. (The Menuhin festival takes place from mid-July through early September, and hotels fill quickly then—as they do for the Swiss Open tennis tournament, held every July.)

Gstaad is a see-and-be-seen spot, with equal attention given to its plentiful skiing and its glamorous gatherings—après-ski, après-concert, après-match. The Christmas–New Year's season brings a stampede of glittering socialites. But you can escape the social scene. There are several unpretentious inns, hotels, and vacation apartments, and dozens of farmhouses that rent rooms, either in Gstaad itself or in one of the nearby Saanenland hamlets (Gsteig, Feutersoey, Lauenen, Turbach, Schönried, Saanenmöser, Saanen). What paradoxically defies and maintains Gstaad's socialite status is its setting: richly forested

10

slopes, scenic year-round trails, working dairy farms, and, for the most part, stubbornly authentic chalet architecture keep it firmly anchored in tradition.

GETTING HERE AND AROUND

There are train connections from Bern; change in Spiez and Zweisimmen. There's also a narrow-gauge train from Montreux every hour that costs 24 SF one-way. The center of Gstaad itself is reserved for pedestrians. You can leave your car at the parking facilities at either end of the main street.

ESSENTIALS

Visitor Information Gstaad Saanenland Tourismus ⊠ *Promenade 41* ☎ *033/7488181* ⊕ *www.gstaad.ch.*

EXPLORING

Museum der Landschaft Saanen (*Saanenland Museum*). On Saanen's main street near the Heimatwerk (handicrafts shop), the tiny Museum der Landschaft Saanen traces the history of the area through tools, costumes, furniture, and decorative pieces. ⊠ *Dorfpl., Saanen* ☎ *033/7447988* ⊕ *www.museum-saanen.ch* 🎫 *6 SF* ☽ *Late May–mid-Oct. and mid-Dec.–Easter, Tues.–Sun. 2–5.*

Saanen Church. The first recorded mention of the Saanen Church, the oldest building in the region, was in 1228, and it is no doubt older than that. Just off Saanen's main street, the church is open daily for visits unless a service is being held. This Romanesque structure was renovated in the 20th century to reveal portions of medieval frescoes on the interior walls. ⊠ *Bortgässli.*

SKIING

Powder hounds and snow bunnies alike will find what they're looking for in Gstaad-Saanenland. Since the building of the one-track railroad from Montreux at the beginning of the 19th century, the holiday region of Gstaad has been popular, both for its ideal location at the confluence of several valleys as well as for the sunny mildness of its slopes. Runs start at 3,608 feet and soar up to 7,217 feet.

Skiing in Gstaad-Saanenland is, in terms of numbers, the equivalent of Zermatt: 57 lifts can transport more than 50,000 skiers per hour to its network of 220 km (136 miles) of marked runs. In fact, these lifts are spread across an immense territory, 20 km (12 miles) as the crow flies, from Zweisimmen and St-Stefan in the east to Château-d'Oex in the west, and 20 km (12 miles) to the Diablerets Glacier in the south. There are also more than 50 km (30 miles) of well-groomed cross-country trails in the area.

Gstaad's expansive area means that most of its lifts are not reachable on foot, and since parking is in short supply, public transport, either by the train or the postbus, is the best option. The flip side is that except in very high seasons (Christmas and February) and in certain places, such as the lift for the Diablerets, waits for lifts are tolerable. A one-day ticket costs between 35 SF and 62 SF, depending on the sector; a six-day pass costs 321 SF.

Gstaad Snowsports. Head here if you want lessons in snowboarding, downhill, or cross-country skiing. ✉ *Promenade 63* ☎ *033/7441865* 🌐 *www.gstaadsnowsports.ch.*

WHERE TO EAT

$$$$ MODERN FRENCH Fodor's Choice ★ 🍴 **Die Chesery.** Brie stuffed with truffles, lobster "cappuccino" (a foamy bisque), and le pigeon "royal": with such showstoppers as these, award-winning chef Robert Speth scales the summits of culinary excellence. He masterfully marries exotic flavors with local ingredients, and his results have foodies and millionaires fighting for reservations; book way ahead in high season. Set in a decorator-perfect chalet (originally built by Prince Sadruddin Aga Khan), this has been a landmark ever since it opened in 1962. Save room for dessert, perhaps the signature hot chocolate cake with kumquats. [$] *Average main: 70 SF* ✉ *Lauenenstr. 9* ☎ *033/7442451* 🌐 *www.chesery.ch* 🕒 *Closed Mon. and Tues., Easter–early June, and early Oct.–mid-Dec.*

WHERE TO STAY

For expanded hotel reviews, visit Fodors.com.

$$$$ RESORT ★ 🏨 **Grand Hotel Park.** A little bit of Vail comes to the Alps in this enormous hotel, which mixes old chalet style with contemporary flair. **Pros:** truly top-notch wellness program and facilities; modern luxe combined with a modern-chalet abode is a winning combination. **Cons:** you may never want to leave (which could break the bank). [$] *Rooms from: 820 SF* ✉ *Wispilestr.* ☎ *033/7489800* 🌐 *www.grandhotelpark.ch* 🛏 *84 rooms, 10 suites* 🕒 *Closed mid-Sept.–late-Dec. and mid-Mar.–early June* 🍽 *Some meals.*

$$$$ HOTEL 🏨 **Le Grand Chalet.** A 10-minute walk from the center of Gstaad, The hilltop Grand Chalet commands a spectacular view of the surrounding mountains and village below. **Pros:** fine food in the restaurant; amazing views. **Cons:** lacks spa facilities; not close to Gstaad nightlife. [$] *Rooms from: 450 SF* ✉ *Neueretstr. 43* ☎ *033/7487676* 🌐 *www.grandchalet.ch* 🛏 *21 rooms, 2 suites* 🕒 *Closed mid-Oct.–mid-Dec. and Apr.–mid-May* 🍽 *Multiple meal plans.*

$$$$ HOTEL ★ 🏨 **Olden.** At the eastern end of the main thoroughfare, this charming Victorian-style inn has an elaborately painted facade and intricately carved woodwork in every interior niche. **Pros:** unique but traditional hotel. **Cons:** no elevator; no spa. [$] *Rooms from: 450 SF* ✉ *Promenade 35* ☎ *033/7484950* 🌐 *www.hotelolden.com* 🛏 *16 rooms* 🕒 *Closed mid-Apr.–early June and late Oct.–mid-Dec.* 🍽 *Breakfast.*

$$$$ RESORT Fodor's Choice ★ 🏨 **Palace.** Towering over tiny Gstaad, this fantasyland castle is as costly as it looks. **Pros:** total hedonism throughout; plethora of amenities—many unique to this establishment. **Cons:** so expensive it hurts; 15-minute walk uphill from town. [$] *Rooms from: 720 SF* ✉ *Palacestr.* ☎ *033/7485000* 🌐 *www.palace.ch* 🛏 *78 rooms, 26 suites* 🕒 *Closed late Mar.–mid-June and mid-Sept.–mid-Dec.* 🍽 *Multiple meal plans.*

$$$ HOTEL ★ 🏨 **Posthotel Rössli.** This comfortable inn, dating back to 1845, combines down-home knotty-pine decor with soigné style. **Pros:** low-key traditional hotel that's a refreshing escape from more overblown places nearby; great atmosphere. **Cons:** limited parking; no bar area.

DID YOU KNOW?

Gstaad is known for its après-ski scene and high-profile vacationers. If you want to arrive in style, book a room at the Palace, an extravagantly appointed castle-like hotel perched above the resort—you might be chauffeured in a Rolls-Royce to check in.

[$] Rooms from: 300 SF ✉ Promenade 10 ☎ 033/7484242 🌐 www.posthotelroessli.ch 🛏 18 rooms 🍴 Multiple meal plans.

NIGHTLIFE AND THE ARTS

BARS

Pinte. This is where people gather after a day on the slopes. Belly up to the beautiful wooden bar or huddle around the stone fireplace. ✉ *Hotel Olden, Promenade 35* ☎ *033/7484950* 🌐 *www.hotelolden.com.*

CONCERTS

Les Sommets Musicaux de Gstaad. Les Sommets Musicaux de Gstaad presents two weeks of classical music from late January to early February. ☎ *022/7386675* 🌐 *www.sommets-musicaux.com.*

Menuhin Festival Gstaad. The Menuhin Festival Gstaad hosts a series of world-class concerts from mid-July to early September. ✉ *Postfach 65* ☎ *033/7488338* 🌐 *www.menuhinfestivalgstaad.ch.*

DANCING

GreenGo. The bar is crowded, but the focal point of this nightclub is the massive dance floor fitted over the Palace Hotel's pool. ✉ *Palace Hotel, Palacestr.* ☎ *033/7485000* 🌐 *www.palace.ch.*

SPAS

Palace Spa. Gorgeous wood, stone, and other materials are the hallmark of the spa at the Gstaad Palace, where you might indeed feel like royalty. The facilities include separate steam baths and saunas for men and women, who can reunite for a swim in the indoor or outdoor pools or to enjoy the warmth of the fireplace-in-the-round at the heart of the 19,000-square-foot facility. There's also a private spa suite, plus a seven-room hammam that can be reserved for private use. The varied treatment menu includes massages, body exfoliations, and anti-aging oxygen facials. Sports enthusiasts will appreciate the squash court as well as the Pilates and fitness studios. ✉ *Palacestr.* ☎ *033/7485000* 🌐 *www.palace.ch/palace-spa* ☞ *80 SF 25-min foot massage, 170 SF 50-min Shiatsu massage, 325 SF 2-hr package. Hot tubs, sauna, steam room. Gym with: cardiovascular machines, free weights, weight-training equipment. Services: aromatherapy, facials, hair removal, mani-pedi, massage. Classes and programs: Pilates.*

SPORTS AND THE OUTDOORS

MOUNTAIN CLIMBING

Great treks and climbs are a stone's throw from Gstaad.

Alpinzentrum. The Alpinzentrum can supply you with mountain guides and snow-sports teachers. ☎ *033/7484161* 🌐 *www.alpinzentrum.ch.*

Valais

CRANS-MONTANA, VERBIER, LEUKERBAD, ZERMATT, AND THE MATTERHORN

WORD OF MOUTH

"Zermatt is like a lot of other alpine ski villages except that it offers a somewhat unique extra: a view of the Matterhorn (on the days it isn't shrouded in clouds)."

—Dukey1

WELCOME TO VALAIS

TOP REASONS TO GO

★ **The Matterhorn:** Shutter-snap this glorious enigma from all angles, be it a luxury hotel room at its base or the sky-high Gornegrat–Monte Rosa Bahn.

★ **Great downhill skiing:** In Valais there's a ski resort for everyone, from family-friendly Saas-Fee to tourist-beloved Zermatt to chic Crans-Montana and Verbier.

★ **Cantonal capital:** Presided over by the castle of Tourbillon, Sion is a fortified link in the giant web of precipitous passes.

★ **Mineral baths:** Known for its natural thermal baths, the year-round destination of Leukerbad lets you dip into Switzerland's healing mineral-rich waters.

★ **Wine route:** Bike-friendly Valais offers a verdant landscape with centuries-old vineyards and unique varietals grown nowhere else.

1 Bas Valais and Sion. If you have to pick one Valais wild valley to explore, head to the Val d'Entremont. Martigny is a treasure trove of art and history, Verbier has great facilities, and the famous Col du Grand St-Bernard pass connecting Switzerland to Italy is, weather permitting, unforgettable. Sion, the canton's capital, is marked by two rocky hills that materialize in front of you like a fairy-tale landscape, one crowned by the Tourbillon castle.

2 Conversion de la Vallée. The adjoining modern ski resorts of Crans-Montana are attractively perched 5,000 feet up on a sunny plateau among woods, grasslands, and small lakes. In nearby Val d'Anniviers, tiny villages are noted for their folkloric *mazots* (small wooden barns balanced on stone disks and columns).

ITALY

GETTING ORIENTED

Switzerland's third-largest canton, Valais is a complex network of valleys, rivers, and peaks harboring an A-to-Z of ski resorts. Its bottom half, a wide, fertile riverbed flanked by bluffs, is the region's most characteristic and imposing. It's fed from the north and south by remote, narrow valleys that snake into the mountains and peter out in Alpine wilderness or lead to the region's most famous landmarks—including that Swiss superstar, the Matterhorn. Not all of Valais covers Alpine terrain, however. The western stretch—between Martigny and Sierre—comprises one of the two chief sources of wine in Switzerland (the other is in Vaud, along Lac Lèman). Valaisan wines come from ancient vineyards that grace the hillsides flanking the Rhône.

3 **Zermatt and Saas-Fee.** Feast your eyes on the Matterhorn in tourist-beloved Zermatt, where you can amble through the bustling village's streets before taking a lift or a train to even higher elevations. Allow half a day to get here and back, enjoying spectacular views from the train en route. Nearby is Saas-Fee, famed for its snowboarding, tamed marmots, glacier skiing, and a lower-key vibe favored by Swiss families and more serious hikers.

4 **Brig and the Alpine passes.** All mountain passes lead to or through Brig. Traffic and rail lines pour into and out of Italy, the Ticino, central Switzerland, and the Berner Oberland via the Simplon, Nufenen, Furka, and Grimsel passes.

Updated by
Adam H.
Graham

For many visitors, Valais is the only part of Switzerland they will ever see—and for good reason. After all, 40 of the 52 4,000-meter-high peaks in the Alps can be found here, making it a skiing, snowboarding, and hiking paradise. With more than 300 sunny days a year, it's also the country's premiere wine region. There are more than 22,000 vineyards, most of them family-owned and -operated. Add to the mix a handful of medieval castles, ancient mountain passes, natural thermal springs, and a network of bike trails, and you've got the best of Switzerland packed into 2,000 square miles (5,180 square km).

More than 500 km (310 miles) of mountains and glaciers span the Bietschhorn, Aletsch, and Jungfrau summits. In 2001, UNESCO named this area a World Heritage Site, joining such other natural wonders as the Galapagos Islands, Yellowstone National Park, and the Serengeti Desert. Today, Valais remains a region where Italian-, French-, and German-speaking cultures converge and the predominant language can change from valley to valley. But nearly everyone speaks English and is exceptionally welcoming to travelers from all over the world.

The Matterhorn is the region's most iconic site, and many newcomers will feel unsatisfied if they don't get a glimpse of Switzerland's most photographed peak. Though it's definitely an image to behold, the Matterhorn is just one of many otherworldly jewels in the Imperial Crown, along with Monta Rosa, Weisshorn, and Dame Blanche—each a gem in its own right. If you must see the Matterhorn, the best place to witness it is from the lovely resort town Zermatt.

To best experience Valais, don't try to explore every valley that ribs out from the Rhône; better to choose one region and spend a few days hiking, driving, or skiing. Enter from Lac Léman and visit the Gianadda museum in Martigny. Spend the night and next day exploring the citadel and Old Town of Sion. Be sure to get up high in the mountains at magnificent resorts like Saas-Fee, Verbier, Zermatt, Leukerbad, and Crans-Montana.

The broad upper valley of the mighty Rhône is a region still wild, remote, beautiful, and slightly unruly. Its *raccards* (typical Valaisan barns balanced on stone disks) still dot the slopes where meadow-grazing cows live at vertiginous angles. For the prettiest scenery, opt for the slow switchback crawl over the mountain passes rather than the more efficient tunnels. And as always, trains are preferable over cars, offering consistently better views and a stress-free and more affordable way to travel.

VALAIS PLANNER

WHEN TO GO

Valais is at its sunny best in high summer and midwinter; foggy dampness overwhelms in late autumn and spring. Mountain weather is impetuous, embracing with its warmth one day and obliterating views and trails the next. Take your cues from local forecasts and mountain operators who have an experienced sense about shifting patterns. Misty clouds move away in short order opening up the path or vista for those who are patient.

Some of the best skiing and hiking can be had in March and September when crowds are the lightest and the sun is at its perfect arc. May, June, and November to mid-December are renovation, repair, and getaway times for locals. Facilities rotate closing periods, though, so you will always find a fluffy bed and good meal.

GETTING HERE AND AROUND

AIR TRAVEL

For international arrivals, you can choose between two airports when flying to Valais: Geneva International Airport or Zürich Airport. Connecting service through London and Paris makes Geneva preferable for those heading to the west (French) end of Valais. Zürich brings passengers closer to the east (German) side, but the Alps are in the way; you must connect by rail tunnel or drive over one of the passes, which will take two to three hours.

BUS TRAVEL

As in other parts of the country, an efficient network of postbuses covers the region, even to the most remote hamlets. If you're staying in a car-free resort, traveling by bus allows you to avoid finding a place to keep your car. Inquire about special bus passes for the region, including the Valais Central Pass for 48 SF (three days of travel within the same week).

Buses are also a convenient way to return to starting points from long-distance hikes. Resorts like Verbier, Crans-Montana, and Saas-Fee, with its contingent valleys, have free shuttles that loop a circuit for skiers and snowboarders, as well as for summer guests.

CAR TRAVEL

Valais is something of a dead end by nature: a fine expressway (A9) carries you in from Lac Léman, but to exit—or enter—from the east end, you must park your car on a train and ride through the Furka Pass tunnel to go north or take the train through the tunnel under the Simplon Pass to go southeast. (The serpentine roads over these passes are open in summer; weather permitting, the Simplon road stays open all year.) You also may cut through from or to Kandersteg in the Berner Oberland by taking a car train to Goppenstein or Brig. A summer-only road twists over the Grimsel Pass as well, heading toward Meiringen and the Berner Oberland or, over the Brünig Pass, to Luzern.

If you want to see the tiny back roads, you'll need a car. The A9 expressway from Lausanne turns into a well-maintained highway at Sierre that continues on to Brig. Additional tunnels and expanded lanes are being carved out of existing highways. Distances in the north and south valleys can be deceptive: apparently short jogs are full of painfully slow switchbacks and distractingly beautiful views. Both Zermatt and Saas-Fee are car-free resorts, though you can drive all the way to a parking lot at the edge of Saas-Fee's main street. Zermatt must be approached by rail from Täsch, the end of the line for cars (there's a garage).

TRAIN TRAVEL

There are straightforward rail connections to the region by way of Geneva and Lausanne to the west and Brig to the east. The two are connected by one clean rail sweep that runs the length of the valley. The run to main connections mid-valley takes about two hours. Add on another hour to arrive at mountain destinations. Routes into smaller tributary valleys are limited, although most resorts are served by post-buses running directly from train stations. The Mont Blanc/St. Bernard Express, with its signature red and white cars, passes through Le Châble for connections to Verbier on its way from Martigny to Chamonix. In Le Châble, take the cableway or bus for the 10- to 20-minute ride.

Train Information: Mont Blanc/St. Bernard Express ☎ 027/7216840 ⊕ www.tmrsa.ch.

⇨ *For more information on getting here and around, see Travel Smart Switzerland.*

RESTAURANTS

For Valaisans, the midday meal remains the mainstay. Locals gather at a bistro for a hearty *plat chaud* (warm meal) that includes meat, vegetable or pasta, and salad for under 20 SF. The evening meal is lighter, perhaps comprising an *assiette* (platter) of cheese and cold cuts shared by the table, accompanied by another bread basket and fruit.

Keep in mind that most eateries do not offer continuous service; lunch winds down around 2 and dinner does not begin before 6. Unless a host greets you or you have a reservation, it is fine to take a seat at an open table.

Multiple dining options can share the same entrance and kitchen. A brasserie, or Stübli, is the homey casual section just inside the doorway, with paper place mats, straightforward dishes, and lively conversation.

The quieter *salle à manger* (dining room) has tables dressed in linen and a *carte* (menu) of multicourse meals and more complicated preparations. If cheese specialties are served, a *carnotzet,* a cozy space in the cellar or a corner away from main dining, is designated to confine the aroma and foster conviviality.

Prices in the reviews are the average cost of a main course or equivalent combination of small dishes at dinner or, if dinner is not served, at lunch.

HOTELS

Valais hotels are in a constant state of flux, and every year at least one old hotel is given a makeover. The most appealing hotels in Valais seem to be old. That is, historic sites have maintained their rustic ambience; postwar inns, their lodgelike feel. Most of those built after about 1960 popped up in generic, concrete-slab, balconied rows to accommodate the 1960s ski boom. They are solid enough but, for the most part, anonymous, depending on the personality of their owners.

Valais is home to some of Switzerland's most famous resorts, and prices vary widely between top-level lodgings and simple auberges (inns) in humbler towns. Remember that many resorts shut down during the lulls in May and from November to mid-December.

Prices in the reviews are the lowest cost of a standard double room in high season, including taxes.

VISITOR INFORMATION

The main tourist office for the entire Valais region is located in Sion.

Visitor Information Valais Main Cantonal Tourist Office ✉ *6 rue Pré-Fleuri, Sion* ☎ *027/3273570* ⊕ *www.valais.ch.*

BAS VALAIS AND SION

As you cross from the canton of Vaud into Bas Valais (Lower Valais), the Rhône and its valley start to lose their broad, flat, deltalike character. The mountains—the Dents du Midi to the west and the Dents de Morcles to the east—begin to crowd in. The river no longer flows placidly but gives a taste of the mountain torrent it will become as you approach its source. And at the Martigny elbow, the most ancient of Alpine routes leaves the Rhône and ascends due south to 8,098 feet at the Col du Grand St-Bernard before descending into Italy's Valle d'Aosta. The Rhône Valley is most fertile just east of Martigny, its flatlands thick with orchards and vegetable gardens, its south-facing slopes quilted with vineyards. This patch of Valais demonstrates the region's dramatic contrasts. Over the fertile farmlands looms the great medieval stronghold of Sion, its fortress towers protecting the gateway to the Alps.

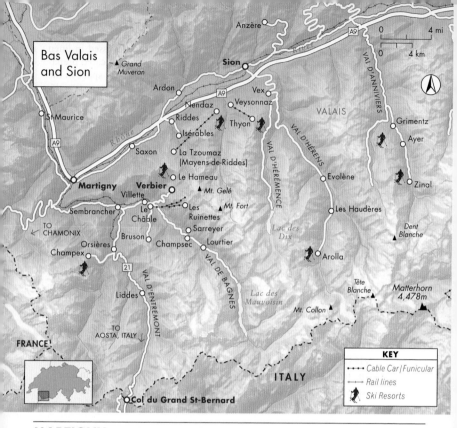

MARTIGNY

23 km (14 miles) southwest of Sion.

At the foot of the Col du Grand St-Bernard, Martigny has long been a commercial crossroads. Testimony to this are the Gallo-Roman ruins discovered in 1976 by engineer Leonard Gianadda. When Gianadda's brother Pierre died in a plane crash, Leonard created a cultural center in his memory.

GETTING HERE AND AROUND

Martigny is the transportation hub for the Lower Valais. Trains often stop at its rail station on the line running between Lausanne (50 minutes away) and Brig (one hour away). Postbuses connect all the towns of the Lower Valais.

ESSENTIALS

Visitor Information Martigny Tourist Information ⊠ *6 ave. de la Gare* ☎ *027/7204949* ⊕ *www.martigny.com.*

EXPLORING

Fodor's Choice **Fondation Pierre Gianadda.** The Fondation Pierre Gianadda rises in bold geometric shapes around the Roman ruins on which it is built. Recent retrospectives have spotlighted works by Renoir and Monet, and the permanent holdings include works by Van Gogh, Cézanne, and Picasso.

Be sure to check out the outdoor sculpture garden at the Fondation Pierre Gianadda.

The **Musée Gallo-Romain** displays Gallo-Roman relics excavated from a 1st-century temple: striking bronzes, statuary, pottery, and coins. A marked path leads through the antique village, baths, drainage systems, and foundations to the fully restored 5,000-seat amphitheater, which dates from the 2nd century. In the gracefully landscaped garden surrounding the foundation, a wonderful **Parc de Sculpture** displays works by Rodin, Brancusi, Miró, Arman, Moore, Dubuffet, and Max Ernst. There's also a sizable **Musée de l'Automobile,** which contains some 50 antique cars, all in working order. They include an 1897 Benz, the Delaunay-Belleville of Czar Nicholas II of Russia, and a handful of Swiss-made models. You may also spot posters for concerts by international classical stars such as Cecilia Bartoli or Itzhak Perlman—the space doubles as a concert hall. ☒ *59 rue du Forum* ☎ *027/7223978* ⊕ *www.gianadda.ch* ▰ *15–25 SF* ☺ *June–Nov., daily 9–7; Dec.–May, daily 10–6.*

☺ **Musée et Chiens du St-Bernard.** Storyboards and films at the Musée et Chiens du St-Bernard praise the lifesaving work of a breed of dog that has come to symbolize the Alpine zone straddling Switzerland and Italy. Eight female St. Bernard dogs live year-round at the museum, which is in a restored arsenal adjacent to Martigny's Roman amphitheater. Visitors may watch the dogs in their grassy outdoor enclosure from both inside the museum and the park outside, and occasionally a handler will bring one of them out to meet and greet. Cuddly toy St. Bernards are sold in the museum shop. Le Collier d'Or (Gold Collar), the museum's terraced café, stays open for at least an hour after the museum itself closes. ☒ *34* *rue du Levant* ☎ *027/7204920* 🌐 *www.museesaintbernard.ch* 🎫 *10 SF* 🕑 *Museum daily 10–6.*

WHERE TO EAT

$$ ECLECTIC 🍴 **L'Olivier.** Stop in here for way better-than-average vittles—owner/chef Olivier Vallotton oversees two separate dining rooms in the same restaurant, one of which, with its wood-backed chairs, is slightly more casual than the other, which has upholstered chairs and table cloths, but the same food is served in both. Menus change often, but dishes might include dandelion salad; poached egg with white asparagus cream and grated dried morels; lasagna of scallops with tomatoes, olives, mozzarella, and basil; or beef fillet flavored with mustard and tarragon served with new potatoes and garden vegetables. A terrace is open in season. There are 29 comfortable guest rooms (all no-smoking) should you wish to spend the night. [$] *Average main: 27 SF* ✉ *Hôtel du Forum, 72bis av. du Grand-St-Bernard* ☎ *027/7221841* 🌐 *www.hotel-forum.ch* 🕑 *Closed Sun.*

TAKE A HIKE

As skiing is to winter, hiking is to summer in Valais, and the valleys that radiate north and south of the Rhône provide almost infinite possibilities. Sociable hikers can join the crowds on trails out of Saas-Fee and Zermatt, but don't overlook alternatives in the less-developed Val d'Anniviers. Skilled trekkers opt for multiday hut-to-hut excursions into the higher elevations, skirting mountains that fail to recognize official borders with France and Italy. Wine enthusiasts can explore the Martigny Wine Path, which offers incredible views of the city, the Rhône Valley, and the Valais Alps as it bypasses several vineyards.

VERBIER

28 km (18 miles) east of Martigny, 54 km (34 miles) southwest of Sion.

A big part of Verbier's appeal is the skiing on sunny slopes and the fact that it's a high-tech, state-of-the-art sports complex that links Quatre Vallées (four valleys) and multiple ski areas, including Thyon, Veysonnaz, Nendaz, and La Tzoumaz. Verbier has a huge aerial cableway, with a cabin that accommodates 150, plus 89 smaller transportation installations. There is plenty of vertical drop, to which the extreme ski and snowboard competitions can attest.

Summer sports here are equally serious: hiking, mountain biking, and hang gliding and its variations compete with golf as the principal activities. Perched on a sunny shelf high above the Val de Bagnes, with wraparound views and the 10,923-foot Mont-Fort towering above, Verbier is protective of its picturesque wooden chalet architecture, yet stays current with modern amenities and comforts. Thanks to its compact layout and easygoing locals, the town has a friendlier feel than the traffic-snarled sprawl of Crans-Montana or hotel-packed Zermatt. But don't be surprised to hear a lot of English spoken in Verbier—it's a haven for moneyed Brits who are big into chalet rentals.

11

GETTING HERE AND AROUND

Verbier is a compact resort town with excellent shuttle service between hotels, chalets, and the lifts. In high season, unless there is parking space at your lodging, a car will be an additional expense and nuisance, so public transportation is recommended. From Martigny, the train trip takes about an hour: take the St. Bernard Express bound for Orsières, its bright red rail cars emblazoned with the region's famous mascot. Disembark in Le Châble, where a connecting bus takes you up the steep, winding road to the post office in the center of Verbier. If you are traveling light, there is a gondola cable car that departs from this base station.

Another option is to drive to Le Châble and leave your car in the large parking lot, then transfer to the resort using the bus or cableway; this way, you can avoid driving the switchback roads to the resort. Once here, you can easily navigate the village on foot or by shuttle bus, and all hotels are clearly signposted.

> ### WATCH A COW FIGHT
>
> In fall, the annual Foire de Martigny celebration hosts the "Combat des Reines," or cow fights, in Martigny's ancient Roman amphitheater. Massive, bell-wearing, naturally combative Hérens cows lock horns (but do not hurt each other) to establish dominance. Smaller fights like this take place in rural areas of Valais during the summer. With other activities like flag throwing, *lutte suisse* (Swiss wrestling), alpenhorn playing, *Hornussen* (like golf and baseball in one), and *Steinstossen* (stone hurling), it just doesn't get any more Swiss than this. For more information, visit ⊕ *www.foireduvalais.ch.*

ESSENTIALS

Visitor Information Verbier Tourist Information ✉ *Pl. Centrale* ☎ *027/7753888* ⊕ *www.verbier.ch.*

EXPLORING

Les Musées du Val de Bagnes. This museum is a collection of seven installations, some within easy walking distance of each other, in the villages of La Châble, Villette, Champsec, Lourtier, Sarreyer, Le Hameau, and Verbier. Most open their doors only in July and August for a historical perspective of life in this isolated area. A restored home, blacksmith forge, grain and logging mill, soapstone masonry, and contemporary art gallery make up the eclectic displays. Open days and hours vary; check the brochure (in French) available from the tourist office. ☎ *027/7761525* ⊕ *www.museedebagnes.ch.*

SKIING

Televerbier. Verbier is the center of Switzerland's famous transit network, Televerbier, which consists of 12 gondolas, five cable cars, 32 chairlifts, and 44 other ski lifts, giving access to 410 km (253 miles) of marked pistes. From this hub an immense complex of resorts has developed—some more modest, others more exclusive—covering four valleys in an extended ski area whose extremities are 15 km (9 miles) or so apart as the crow flies and several dozen kilometers apart by way of winding mountain roads. ⊕ *www.televerbier.ch.*

Verbier is connected to multiple ski areas, and has preserved its charming wooden chalets.

Adrenaline. Sign up for skiing lessons at the Adrenaline counter in the Hardcore Snow and Fashion Shop, which rents ski and snowboarding equipment. It's in the Galerie Alpina, on the main square opposite the post office. ⊠ *Galerie Alpina, rue de la Poste 11* ☎ *027/7717459* ⊕ *www.adrenaline-verbier.ch.*

Ecole Suisse de Ski. If you're looking for a private instructor to fine-tune your ski or snowboard technique, book at the Ecole Suisse de Ski. ⊠ *Rue de Médran 2* ☎ *027/7753363* ⊕ *www.ski-school-verbier.ch.*

Mont-Fort. Les Ruinettes, one of Verbier's four ski areas, gives access to Verbier's entire upper ski area, which culminates at Mont-Fort, at 10,923 feet. This is reached by an aerial tram, *Le Jumbo,* equipped with a cab that accommodates 150. La Chaux Express, a chondola (combination chair lift and gondola on the same cable) sweeps skiers to the upper station. You decide whether to keep your skis or snowboard on for the chair, or take them off to enter the gondola. This entire sector is crisscrossed by a dense network of astonishingly varied pistes. There are several strategic passes, including Les Attelas, Chassoure, Col des Gentianes, and Tortin. Swiss freestyle snowboarder Alex Zillio assisted with the design of the jumps, rails, and pipes at 1936 Neipark at La Chaux. One-day lift tickets for all four valleys cost 66 SF; six-day passes, 343 SF. If you ski only Verbier, Bruson, or Savoleyres/La Tzoumaz, expect to save 12% to 35%. Automated ski passes streamline the lift check-in process; free tickets and discounts for children are available. ⊕ *www. televerbier.ch.*

Toboggan Track. For a different Alpine experience, rent a sled at any of the village sports outlets and take a run down the 10 km (6 mi) toboggan track from Savoleyres to La Tzoumaz. ✉ *Verbier.*

WHERE TO EAT

$$ ITALIAN ✕ **King's Restaurant.** A corner fireplace, wood paneling, and elegant table settings come together here to create a warm, inviting atmosphere that is laid-back and sophisticated at the same time. You'll find some of the most creative and skilled cooking in town—at reasonable prices, by Swiss restaurant standards. Menu options might include slow-cooked duck ravioli with baby beetroot, sherry vinegar, and walnuts; pan-roasted bream with crayfish, potato, and pea-and-tomato sweet-wine vinaigrette; or fig and frangipane tart with limoncello and thyme ice cream. The venue, located in the King's Parc Hotel, also has a good wine list focused on Valais, French, and, of course, Italian vintages. [$] *Average main: 32 SF* ✉ *King's Parc Hotel, Rte. de la Poste* ☎ *027/7752035* 🌐 *www.kingsverbier.ch* ⏲ *Open winter season only.*

$$$ FRENCH ✕ **La Grange.** At rustic-chic La Grange the lofty epicurean choices on the menu might include foie gras with plum sauce or Asian-inspired turbot with saffron and vegetable pearls—saffron from Mund being a Valais specialty. Chef Thierry Corthay's cuisine is not only seasonal (read: frequent menu changes) but also *terroir*, which is to say he serves regional products with pride. Other treats here include the beautiful way each dish is presented on the plate, the entirely smoke-free environment, and the wine list's excellent selection of local vintages. It's best to call ahead; in low season it may close on some days. The terrace is open in season. [$] *Average main: 48 SF* ✉ *70 rte. de Verbier Station* ☎ *027/7716431* 🌐 *www.lagrange.ch* ⏲ *Closed in June.*

$$ SWISS ✕ **L'Ecurie.** Locals and chalet dwellers in the know gather at this central, no-smoking restaurant on the ground floor of the Ermitage. Eccentric owner Jean-Marc, known as *Babouin* (baboon), mans the stoves while his wife Lisette welcomes diners. Lunch has a casual vibe, with paper place mats on the wooden tables. In between meals place settings are removed to create a café where you can order coffee or other beverages, and then the tables are set again—this time with linen and candles—for dinner. Wood-fire grill specialties and homemade pasta are staples, but the daily specials are equally tempting. During the week, lunchtime plats du jour are a good value. **TIP→ In a region where chicken is difficult to find, the poussin with fries is a treat.** [$] *Average main: 26 SF* ✉ *Ermitage, 18 Carrefour Central* ☎ *027/7712760* 🌐 *www.ermitage-verbier.ch.*

WHERE TO STAY

For expanded hotel reviews, visit Fodors.com.

$$ HOTEL **Central Hotel Verbier.** Finding this hotel is easy: you'll see exterior signage on the honey-colored building standing on Verbier's traffic circle. **Pros:** hot tubs and plasma TVs in every room; smoke-free venue; perfect central location. **Cons:** noise can be disruptive; no full-service restaurant; minimum stay of seven nights preferred. [$] *Rooms from: 180 SF* ✉ *Pl. Centrale* ☎ *027/7715007* 🌐 *www.verbiercentralhotel.com* *8 rooms* 🍽 *Breakfast.*

$$$$ B&B/INN Fodor's Choice ★ 🏨 **Chalet d'Adrien.** Named for the owner's grandfather, a baron who discovered the village in the early 1900s, this luxury Relais & Château inn is packed with antiques and collectibles from old farmhouses and châteaux. **Pros:** private ski-mansion feel; friendly, personalized service. **Cons:** 15-minute walk uphill from village; teddy-bear collection in lobby may prove too cutesy for some. [$] *Rooms from: 460 SF* ✉ *Rte. des Creux* ☎ *027/7716200* 🌐 *www.chalet-adrien.com* 🛏 *20 rooms, 8 suites, 1 apt* ⏲ *Closed late Apr.–early July and late Sept.–early Dec.*

$ B&B/INN 🏨 **Ermitage.** Centrally located, this traditional mainstay features compact guest rooms with south-facing balconies that offer views of the Combin mountains (and be sure to request one, because rooms on the north side look out at the slow crawl of cars and people along the main street). **Pros:** one of the best deals in town; well-known restaurant L'Ecurie is in the same building; free Wi-Fi. **Cons:** depressing dark green carpet throughout hotel; small rooms. [$] *Rooms from: 125 SF* ✉ *18 Carrefour Central* ☎ *027/7716477* 🌐 *www.ermitage-verbier.ch* 🛏 *25 rooms, 1 apt* ⏲ *Closed mid-Sept.–mid-Oct., May, and June* 🍴 *Breakfast.*

$$$ HOTEL 🏨 **Nevaï.** This sleek, contemporary hotel is the perfect choice for vacationing cosmopolites who want in-room iPod docks, flat-screen TVs, a restaurant and bar with DJs spinning tunes, and a spa. **Pros:** good location; bars and grill have become a destination on their own. **Cons:** poor noise insulation; level of service and size of spa don't quite live up to what you'd expect at these prices. [$] *Rooms from: 275 SF* ✉ *55 rte. de Verbier* ☎ *027/7754000* 🌐 *www.nevai.ch* 🛏 *33 rooms, 2 suites* ⏲ *Closed May, June, and Sept.–Nov.* 🍴 *Breakfast.*

NIGHTLIFE AND THE ARTS

DANCING

Casbah. If you don't plan to hit the slopes early, you can party at Moroccan-themed Casbah. ✉ *Hôtel Farinet, 6 Carrefour Central* ☎ *027/7716626* 🌐 *www.hotelfarinet.com.*

Coup d'Etat. Open in winter only, Coup d'Etat attracts an English-speaking clientele and is known for its martinis. ✉ *20 rue de la Poste* ☎ *078/6529760* 🌐 *www.coupdetat.ch.*

Crock No Name. The popular Crock No Name—also known as Chez Marie—has live music or DJs nightly. ✉ *22 rte. des Creux* ☎ *027/7716934* 🌐 *www.crock-bar.com.*

Farm Club. The Farm Club is the place to be seen in Verbier—it stays open until 4 am in the winter season. ✉ *King's Parc Hotel, Rte. de la Poste* ☎ *027/77540001* 🌐 *www.kingsverbier.ch.*

MUSIC

Verbier Festival. For more than two weeks overlapping July and August, the Verbier Festival hosts an impressive classical music festival of performances and master classes. Musical director Charles Dutoit assembles the two Verbier Festival Orchestras and soloists of the caliber of Elisabeth Leonskaya, Evgeny Kissin, and Gidon Kremer into a stunning 17-day, 60-concert program that plays out in various venues all over Verbier. ☎ *027/7718282* 🌐 *www.verbierfestival.com.*

SPORTS AND THE OUTDOORS

Verbier offers a variety of summer and winter high-altitude sports, ranging from rock and ice climbing to rafting and snow tubing, all led by specialist outfitters.

BIKING

About 250 km (188 miles) of trails range from difficult distance rides across the passes to simpler runs closer to town.

Médran Sports. This company offers a choice of equipment and gear at competitive rates. ⊠ *Rue de Médran 59* ☏ *027/7716048* ⊕ *www. medransports.ch.*

No Bounds. The pros at No Bounds will help you plan your entire outing, plus rent standard or high-performance bikes, helmets, and shells. ⊠ *Rue de Médran* ☏ *027/7715556* ⊕ *www.nobounds.ch.*

GOLF

Verbier Golf Club. With two two 18-hole courses, Les Moulins and Esserts, the Verbier Golf Club is open for play May through November. ⊠ *Les Esserts* ☏ *027/7715314* ⊕ *www.verbiergolfclub.ch.*

HIKING AND CLIMBING

Trails thread from ridgeline to valley floor in 400 km (300 miles) of pathways that cross nature reserves, highland streams, and historic villages. Sign up at ⊕ *www.guideverbier.com*, **La Fantastique** (☏ *027/7714141*), or **Verbier SportPlus** (☏ *027/7753363*) for everything from hut-to-hut trekking tours to technical rock climbing and rappelling sessions.

COL DU GRAND ST-BERNARD

40 km (25 miles) south of Martigny, 69 km (43 miles) southwest of Sion.

GETTING HERE AND AROUND

The opening of the Col du Grand St-Bernard, the pass connecting Switzerland and Italy, is weather dependent. This ancient high-mountain crossing is closed to cars during the winter months, when it makes an excellent snowshoeing or skiing course. But the roadway also can be shut down in summer due to random snowfalls. On a clear day the drive on narrow twisting roads that thread in and out of avalanche breaks is unforgettable. The traffic on the approach to the pass dramatically reduces once vehicles driving through to the Italian city of Aosta leave the highway at the tunnel entrance.

During summer, public transport to the Hospice St-Bernard is available from Martigny. The journey starts with train service to the village of Orsières, terminus of the rail line, and then switches to bus. It's a one-hour drive by car; add an additional half hour for the rail-bus connection.

EXPLORING

★ **Col du Grand St-Bernard.** Breasting the formidable barrier of the Alps at 8,101 feet, this pass is the oldest and most famous of the great Alpine crossings, and was the first to join Rome and Byzantium to the wilds of the north. Used for centuries before the birth of Christ, it has witnessed an endless stream of emperors, knights, and simple travelers—think of Umberto Eco's *The Name of the Rose,* with its two friars crossing on donkey back in howling winter winds. Napoléon took an army of 40,000 across it en route to Marengo, where he defeated the Austrians in 1800.

L'Hospice du Grand St. Bernard. In operation since the Middle Ages, L'Hospice du Grand St. Bernard has played host to kings, princes, and famous writers like Charles Dickens and Alexandre Dumas. Within these walls you'll find cozy guest rooms and a stone dining hall where you can revive yourself over bowls of soup, slabs of creamy cheese, honey-sweetened tea, and carafes of red wine produced in the Valais. The facility includes an excellent museum with exhibits about the history of the pass and the devoted monks of the Order of St. Augustine who have lived here. Displays of church treasures—chalices, crosses, and altar clothes in gold, silver, and jewels—are on view in another wing. The fresco-bedecked chapel remains open for daily prayers. Behind the hospice is **Chenil au Col du Grand St-Bernard,** a kennel full of the landmark's enormous, furry namesakes: the famous St. Bernard dogs who for centuries helped the monks find travelers lost in the snow. They supposedly came to Switzerland with silk caravans from central Asia and were used by Romans as war dogs; today they're kept more for sentimental than functional reasons. In winter the dogs are boarded at **Fondation Barry du Grand St-Bernard** (☎ 027/7226542 ⊕ *www.fondation-barry.ch*) in Martigny. The foundation is named after the most famous St. Bernard of them all: Barry, who saved more than 40 people in the 19th century and today stands stuffed in Bern's Naturhistorisches Museum (Museum of Natural History). Souvenir stands sell plush versions of St. Bernards, and there are a handful of dining options on either side of the pass. ☎ 027/7871236 ⊕ *www. gsbernard.net* ✉ *Museum 10 SF* ☉ *June and Sept., daily 10–6.*

SION

54 km (34 miles) northeast of Verbier.

Rearing up in the otherwise deltalike flatlands of the western Valais, two otherworldly twin hills flank the ancient city of Sion. The two hills together are a powerful emblem of the city's 1,500-year history as a bishopric and a Christian stronghold. From the top of either hill are dramatic views of the surrounding flatlands and the mountains flanking the valley.

Sion folk are fiercely proud and independent, as reflected in the fanatical support for their soccer team and their dogged attempts to host the Winter Olympics. (There was bitter disappointment when they lost the bid for the 2006 games to rivals across the border in Turin, Italy.) A shortage of high-quality hotels gives the impression that the town is not as hospitable to travelers as the tourist-oriented ski resorts, but don't be deterred; there are ample reasons to spend time here.

GETTING HERE AND AROUND

Sion is a main stop on the railway running between Lausanne (one hour) and Brig (40 minutes); many postbuses threading the region stop at the train station. The town itself can be comfortably explored on foot in an afternoon, unless you lose yourself in one of its museums or labyrinthine antiques shops. In summer a trolley called Le P'tit Sédunois (3 SF) shuttles between the Place de la Panta and the elevated sights.

ESSENTIALS

Visitor Information Sion Tourist Information ✉ *Pl. de la Planta* ☎ *027/3277727* ⊕ *www.siontourism.ch.*

EXPLORING
TOP ATTRACTIONS

★ **Château de Tourbillon.** Crowning Tourbillon, the higher of Sion's hills, the ruined château was built as a bishop's residence at the end of the 13th century and destroyed by fire in 1788. If you take the rugged walk uphill, try to time it for a visit to the tiny chapel with its ancient, layered frescoes. ▣ *Free* ☉ *Oct.–May, daily 11–5; June–Sept., daily 10–6.*

★ **Église-Forteresse de Valère** (*Church-Fortress of Valère*). On Valère, Sion's lower hill, the Église-Forteresse de Valèreis a striking example of sacred and secular power combined—reflective of the Church's heyday, when it often subjugated rather than served its parishioners. Built on Roman foundations, the massive stone walls enclose both the château and the 11th-century **Église Notre-Dame de Valère** (Church of Our Lady of Valère). This structure stands in a relatively raw form, rare in Switzerland, where monuments are often restored to perfection. Over the engaging Romanesque carvings, 16th-century fresco fragments, and 17th-century stalls painted with scenes of the Passion, there sits a rare organ, its cabinet painted with two fine medieval Christian scenes. Dating from the 14th century, it's the oldest playable organ in the world, and an annual organ festival celebrates its musical virtues.

The château complex also houses the **Musée Cantonal d'Histoire** (History Museum), which displays a wide array of medieval sacristy chests and religious artifacts. Expanded exhibits trace daily life and advances in the canton from these early centuries to the present day, including soccer championships. Explanations are in three languages, including English, as are guided tours. ■TIP➜ To reach the Musée Cantonal d'Histoire, you'll have to trek up uneven stone walkways and steep staircases, but you won't regret it. ✉ *Rue des Châteaux 24* ☎ *027/6064715* ⊕ *www.musees-valais.ch* ▣ *Church free, guided tour 4 SF; museum 8 SF* ☉ *Church June–Sept., Mon.–Sat. 10–6, Sun. 2–6; Oct.–May, Tues.–Sat. 10–5, Sun. 2–5. Museum June–Sept., daily 10–6; Oct.–May, Tues.– Sun. 10–5. Tours of the museum June–Sept., daily 2:30; Oct–May, Sun. 2:30.*

QUICK BITES

Le Verre à Pied. It's a tight squeeze to get into Old Town's popular *caveau-oenothèque* (wine bar cum store) Le Verre à Pied, where 150 regional vintages are poured seven days a week. For a few francs you can join winemakers and enthusiasts who swill and sip (often while taking advantage of the free Wi-Fi connection). ✉ *29 rue du Grand-Pont* ☎ *027/3211380.*

Maison Supersaxo (*House of Supersaxo*). This grand old home, tucked into a passageway off Rue Supersaxo, was built in 1505 by Georges

Cycling around Sion's two hills puts the term "mountain biking" into perspective.

Supersaxo, the local governor, to put his rivals to shame. This extravagantly decorated building includes a Gothic staircase and a grand hall whose painted wood ceiling is a dazzling work of decorative art. ⊠ *Passage Supersaxo* 🖾 *Free* 🕑 *Weekdays 8–noon and 2–5.*

Notre-Dame du Glarier (*Our Lady of Glarier*). The cathedral is dominated by its Romanesque tower, built in the Lombard, or Italian, style and dating from the 12th century. The rest of the church is late Gothic in style. ⊠ *Rue de la Cathédrale.*

OFF THE BEATEN PATH

High up in the bluffs and valleys to the south of Sion are scores of isolated eagle's-nest towns, including **Isérables.** Set on a precarious slope that drops 3,280 feet into the lowlands, the town has narrow streets that weave between crooked old stone-shingle mazots. Since the arrival of the cable car, Isérables has prospered and modernized itself. Yet the inhabitants of this village still carry the curious nickname *Bedjuis.* Some say it's derived from "Bedouins" and that the people are descended from the Saracen hordes who, after the battle of Poitiers in 732, overran some of the high Alpine valleys. Excursions to the sights and villages of this *haute vallée* (high valley) can be accomplished in a day, with a little time to hike and explore before returning to Sion.

WORTH NOTING

Espace d'Archéologie (*Archaeology Space*). This space keeps a dozen impressive steles (ancient stone slabs) on permanent display, but otherwise houses temporary exhibits focusing on archaeological finds. Its collection of excavated pieces, including fine Roman works found in Valais, has been moved to the Musée Cantonal d'Histoire. The narrow, cobbled Rue des Châteaux, which leads up to Sion's twin fortifications, passes graceful old patrician houses. ✉ *12 rue des Châteaux* ☎ *027/6064700* ⊕ *www.musees-valais.ch* 🖃 *4 SF* ⊙ *June–Sept., Tues.–Sun. 1–6; Oct.–May, Tues.–Sun. 1–5.*

Hôtel de Ville (*Town Hall*). The imposing Town Hall has extraordinary historic roots: though it was built in the 1650s, it has transplanted stones in the entrance bearing Roman inscriptions, including a Christian symbol from the year AD 377. The 17th-century doors are richly carved wood, and the tower displays an astronomical clock. The interior is only accessible on walking tours run by the tourism office. ✉ *Rue de Conthey and Rue du Grand-Pont.*

Old Town. The Old Town, up Rue de Lausanne, is a blend of shuttered 16th-century houses, modern shops, and a host of sights worth seeing.

Tour des Sorciers (*Sorcerers' Tower*). Just across from the cathedral, this tower is the last remnant of the walls that once ringed the town. ✉ *Rue de la Tour.*

WHERE TO EAT AND STAY
For expanded hotel reviews, visit Fodors.com.

$$
SWISS
✕ **Au Cheval Blanc.** Set on one of Sion's Old Town cobblestone streets, this congenial bistro is bustling around noon, when locals take their midday meal accompanied by a glass of *Dôle* (a Pinot Noir and Gamay blend unique to Valais) or *bière valaisanne*. Top billing on the menu goes to Valais beef and seafood, but traditional dishes such as *civet de chevreuil* (venison stew) with spaetzle may appear during hunting season. For dessert, try wonderfully aromatic Mara strawberries (in season) or the lemon tart served only on Friday and Saturday. This is a great place to sample Valais wines; there is a nice selection served by the glass. 💲 *Average main: 28 SF* ✉ *23 rue du Grand-Pont* ☎ *027/3221867* ⊕ *www.au-cheval-blanc.ch* ⊙ *Closed Sun., Mon., and last 2 wks of Dec.*

$$
FRENCH
✕ **L'Enclos de Valère.** If you've worked up an appetite climbing Sion's Tourbillon or Valère, you may want to stop in at this Old Town eatery on your way back down. Unfussy service, fine French cuisine, and a rustic-cottage setting make it a sentimental favorite. Seasonal items—mushrooms, asparagus, shellfish, and game—lend variety to the upscale menu. When it's not mealtime, drop in for a coffee or a bottle of wine. The garden is open in season. 💲 *Average main: 26 SF* ✉ *18 rue des Châteaux* ☎ *027/3233230* ⊕ *www.enclosdevalere.ch* 🖃 *Reservations essential* ⊙ *Closed Sun. evening and Mon; no lunch Sun. Oct.–Apr.*

$
HOTEL
🏨 **Hôtel des Vignes.** For a hotel with character, head a few kilometers east of Sion to the village of Uvrier to find this sienna-colored palazzo flanked by vineyards. **Pros:** surrounded by a gloriously landscaped park; all rooms are nonsmoking. **Cons:** a 10-minute drive from Sion; restaurant can be disappointing, and there aren't many other dining options nearby. 💲 *Rooms from: 150 SF* ✉ *9 rue du Pont, Uvrier* ☎ *027/2031671* ⊕ *www.hoteldesvignes.ch* 🛏 *33 rooms, 10 suites* ⊙ *Closed end Dec.–mid-Jan.* ⦿*Breakfast.*

$
HOTEL
🏨 **L'Hôtel du Rhône.** Decorated with a mix of old and new, this hotel combines stone, wood, and glass. **Pros:** clean and comfortable; helpful

staff; no-frills base; convenient location. **Cons:** dated feel; not much local charm. [$] *Rooms from: 165 SF* ✉ *10 rue de Scex* ☎ *027/3228291* 🌐 *www.durhonesion.ch* 🛏 *45 rooms* 🍴 *Breakfast.*

NIGHTLIFE AND THE ARTS

Sion attracts world-class musicians and scholars to its festivals celebrating the medieval organ in its church-fortress.

Festival International de l'Orgue Ancien Valère (*International Festival of the Ancient Valère Organ*). One of the region's most popular events, the Festival International de l'Orgue Ancien Valère takes place from mid-July through late August. ☎ *027/3235767* 🌐 *www.orgueancien-valere.ch.*

CONVERSION DE LA VALLÉE

Secured above the plateau north of Sierre and Leuk are the ski towns of Crans and Montana and the hot springs resort of Leukerbad, each with a different personality. Crans-Montana offers expansive skiing, name-brand boutiques, and clubby restaurants. Though Leukerbad also has first-class hotels and ski runs (albeit fewer), it is the restorative pools and spas and authentic Alpine village that attract visitors. Along this stretch of the Rhône, the switchback of language and culture begins. Valais, as it is referred to by French speakers, is called Wallis by locals with Germanic ties. To the south the remote Val d'Anniviers offers a glimpse of a simpler life before high-speed lifts and Internet cafés.

CRANS-MONTANA

12 km (7 miles) northwest of Sierre, 19 km (11 miles) northeast of Sion.

This French-speaking resort rises above the valley on a steep, sheltered shelf at 4,904 feet. It commands a broad view across the Rhône Valley to the peaks of the Valaisan Alps, and its grassy and wooded plateau gets the benefit of Sierre's sunshine and fresh air. Behind the towns, the **Rohrbachstein** (9,686 feet), the **Gletscherhorn** (9,653 feet), and the **Wildstrubel** (10,637 feet) combine to create a complex of challenging ski slopes.

The resort towns themselves—basically one town, with two areas—have an American-style ambience marked by golf courses, chain fashion boutiques, and 1970s architecture that's likely to disappoint those seeking cozy charm. The crowds are young, wealthy, and international, roving in cocoons of the fit, fun loving, and fashionable.

GETTING HERE AND AROUND

From the train station in Sierre, follow the painted red line on the sidewalk to the SMC (Sierre Mollens Crans-Montana) station, where a steep funicular connects the town of Sierre with the resort area of Crans-Montana. The 12-minute ride delivers you to the Montana side of town, where free shuttle buses head to hotels and chalets. Once you're here, car traffic is almost always heavy, so it's best to get around on foot or shuttle bus. As in other resorts, signs point the way to the hotels.

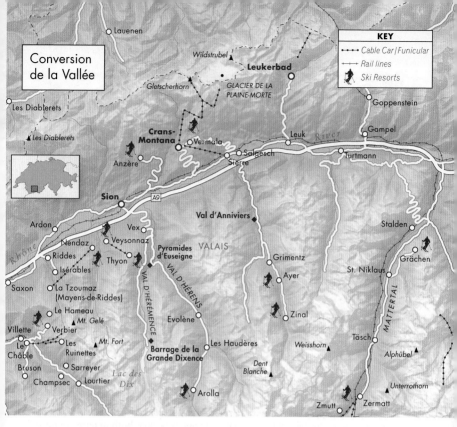

Conversion
de la Vallée

KEY
•••• *Cable Car/Funicular*
━━┿━━ *Rail lines*
⛷ *Ski Resorts*

ESSENTIALS

Visitor Information Crans-Montana Tourist Information ✉ *22 av. de la Gare, Montana* ☎ *027/4850404* ⊕ *www.crans-montana.ch.*

Transportation Information SMC ☎ *027/4813355* ⊕ *www.cie-smc.ch.*

SKIING

Plaine Morte. The pearl of the region is the Plaine Morte, a flat glacier that's perched like a pancake at an elevation of 9,840 feet. A 12-km (7½-mile) cross-country ski trail is open seven months of the year, although there's snow year-round.

Violettes Plaines-Morte. The ascent on the gondola from Violettes Plaines-Morte, virtually under assault by crowds during the high season, will in itself justify your stay in Crans-Montana.

La Toula. The incredibly steep-pitched La Toula is a challenge for pros.

Piste Nationale. Expert skiers may prefer the Piste Nationale, site of previous world championships.

Petit Bonvin. The eastern section of the ski area connects to Aminona, where a park for snowboarders and a bobsled run drop from 7,874-foot-tall Petit Bonvin. A one-day lift ticket costs 63 SF; a six-day pass costs 307 SF, permitting access to 160 km (100 miles) of runs and more than

The cross-country ski trails at Plaine Morte, near Crans-Montana, are open seven months a year.

30 ways to ride to the top. There are several classic cross-country ski circuits atop the golf courses and around the village lakes.

WHERE TO EAT

$$ SWISS 🍴 **Le Mayen.** On Montana's shopping promenade, this restaurant is a successful mix of traditional and contemporary, both in terms of decor and food. It is one of the village's favorite spots for specialty fondues, raclette, platters of air-dried meat, and *Rösti* (grated parboiled potatoes panfried into a buttery cake). Steak tartare is another major attraction. The food is presented with style, there's a good list of Valais wines, and there's a sidewalk terrace that's great for people-watching. It's so popular with locals that it doesn't close between seasons. [$] *Average main: 29 SF* ✉ *Olympic Hotel, 9 rue Louis-Antille, Montana* ☎ *027/4812985* 🌐 *www.amadays.ch.*

$$$$ SWISS Fodor's Choice ★ 🍴 **Restaurant Didier de Courten.** Travelers bound for the uphill resorts detour to chef-hotelier Didier de Courten's contemporary hot spot in Sierre's historical Hôtel Le Terminus. One of the country's highest-rated chefs fills the tables of his gourmet restaurant and upscale brasserie with food and wine enthusiasts who admire his creativity in seasonal dishes like peppered venison medallions with red cabbage and spiced pear marmalade. L'Ampelos, the wine bar, offers an extensive sampling of top Swiss and international vintages. Sleek design elements from the restaurant are repeated behind the 19 red-door guest rooms outfitted with crisp white-on-white linens and colorful leather seating. [$] *Average main: 62 SF* ✉ *1 rue du Bourg, Sierre* ☎ *027/4551351* 🌐 *www.hotel-terminus.ch* ✍ *Reservations essential* ⏲ *Closed Sun. and Mon.; closed late June–mid-July and Christmas–mid-Jan.*

$$
CAFÉ
✕**Taillens.** This overflowing tearoom with exquisite pastries is a must-stop before or after an activity-packed day. Run today by the third generation of the Taillens family, this landmark is beloved by locals and visitors alike. Light meals—salads, soups, and sandwiches—keep service clipping along at a fast pace. Toss aside the calorie counter and peruse the dessert cases for a decadent concoction of chocolate, sugar, and whipped cream. There's a second location at Rue du Grand-Place in Crans. $ *Average main: 27 SF* ✉ *Av. de la Gare, Montana* ☎ *027/4817362* ⊕ *www.boulangerietaillens.ch.*

WHERE TO STAY

For expanded hotel reviews, visit Fodors.com.

$$$
RESORT
★
🏨 **Hotel Guarda Golf.** This newcomer hits a trifecta: comfortable American-style accommodations, impeccable Swiss service, and warm Brazilian hospitality. **Pros:** halcyon views of the Alps; excellent service, including a knowledgeable waitstaff; prompt pick-up and drop-off shuttle. **Cons:** food can be hit or miss; art gallery space could be put to better use. $ *Rooms from: 350 SF* ✉ *Rte. des Zirès 14, Crans* ☎ *027/4862000* ⊕ *www.hotelguardagolf.com* 🛏 *25 rooms* ❖❙ *No meals.*

$$$$
B&B/INN
🏨 **Le Crans Hotel & Spa.** Located high above Crans-Montana's luxury shop–lined streets, this hotel remains a chic perch for deep-pocketed travelers. **Pros:** warm, modern design; excellent restaurant; sybaritic spa. **Cons:** theme rooms seem silly when the Alpine views dominate; location is far away from everything. $ *Rooms from: 400 SF* ✉ *Plans Mayens, Crans* ☎ *027/4866060* ⊕ *www.lecrans.com* 🛏 *7 rooms, 6 suites, 1 apartment* ⊘ *Closed late Apr.–early June and Nov.* ❖❙ *Breakfast.*

$$
B&B/INN
🏨 **Le Mont-Paisible.** One of the hotel directors, an architect, lent his design expertise and eye for interiors to this lookout lodge, which takes in the sweep of Valaisan mountains—indeed, the south-facing guest rooms are blessed with clear-day panoramic views all the way to the Matterhorn. **Pros:** the glassed-in veranda restaurant has a sensational view. **Cons:** hallways filled with dingy silk flowers need updating; rates may go up during peak periods. $ *Rooms from: 250 SF* ✉ *12 ch. du Mont-Paisible, Montana* ☎ *027/4802161* ⊕ *www.montpaisible.ch* 🛏 *40 rooms* ❖❙ *Breakfast.*

$$$
B&B/INN
Fodor's Choice
★
🏨 **L'Hostellerie du Pas de l'Ours.** In a town known for blocklike towers, this petite Relais & Chateaux-listed auberge with its preserved wooden facade stands out. **Pros:** plush rooms rich with amenities; magnificent wellness center with indoor-outdoor pool. **Cons:** somewhat of a walk into the town center. $ *Rooms from: 350 SF* ✉ *41 rue du Pas de l'Ours, Crans* ☎ *027/4859333* ⊕ *www.pasdelours.ch* 🛏 *2 rooms, 14 suites* ⊘ *Closed May and Nov.* ❖❙ *Breakfast.*

NIGHTLIFE

BARS AND DANCING

Amadeus. The small but convivial Amadeus, beneath the Olympic Hotel in Montana, is a popular après-ski venue. ✉ *Olympic Hotel, Rue Louis Antille 4* ☎ *027/4812495* ⊕ *www.amadays.ch.*

Le Pacha. The dance floor buzzes at Le Pacha, a popular spot in Crans. ✉ *Rue du Prado 2, Crans* ☎ *027/4801394* ⊕ *www.lepacha.ch.*

Le Tirbouchon. Run by oenophile Patrick Jenny, this no-frills wine shop, vino bar, and sidewalk café is a refreshing alternative to Crans's overdose of chic. The chummy local go-to houses more than 250 wines, including many lesser-known varieties of Valais wines like Humagne Rouge and Petit Arvine. Tables spill out onto the sidewalk, shared irregularly by a street market where vendors hawk local honey, meat, and cheese. ⊠ *Rte. du Petit Signal 6, Montana* ☎ *027/4802608.*

> ## RIDE A BIKE
>
> Switzerland's high-perched hills, vertiginous vineyards, and steep-sloped trails were once the domain of spandex-clad cyclists, but the introduction of battery-enhanced e-bikes have given casual cyclists reason to rejoice, and new trails have opened from Appenzell to Zug. Many train stations offer an excellent assortment of bikes, including e-bikes.

Monk'is. If music, videos, and shots interest you, Monk'is is a hot, primate-themed venue in Crans. ⊠ *Rue Centrale 19, Crans* ☎ *079/4093285* ⊕ *www.monkis.ch.*

Xellent Club. If you've ever wondered what Salvador Dalí would have produced if he'd illustrated a vodka ad, then head for the Xellent Club, a Crans nightclub that doesn't get started until after 11 pm. ⊠ *Rue Centrale 17, Crans* ☎ *027/4814439.*

CASINO
Casino Crans-Montana. Roulette, blackjack, poker, and an abundance of slot machines are among the games you can play at the high-stakes Casino Crans-Montana, in Montana. You can also just stop in for a drink or dinner, as there is no pressure to play. You'll need your passport for admission. ⊠ *Allée Katherine Mansfield 1, Montana* ☎ *027/4859040* ⊕ *www.casinocransmontana.com.*

SPORTS AND THE OUTDOORS
BOATING
Lac Grenon and Lac Moubra. Lac Grenon and Lac Moubra, two crystalline lakes near the connected villages, are filled with pedal boats and windsurfers on long summer days. Rentals are available at shoreside kiosks.

Etang Long. Wakeboarding and waterskiing services are available on Etang Long.

GOLF
Golf Club de Crans-sur-Sierre. The 18-hole Golf Club de Crans-sur-Sierre, designed by Severiano Ballesteros and Jack Niklaus, is where the Omega European Masters takes place annually. ⊠ *Rue du Prado 20, Crans* ☎ *027/4859797* ⊕ *www.golfcrans.ch.*

HIKING
About 280 km (215 miles) of well-marked trails branch out from both villages, sometimes intersecting but more often leading in opposite directions. Unless you want to scale higher peaks, all that is needed is a good pair of boots and a map to guide you to signed pathways through open terrain, forests, or along the *bisses* (irrigation channels), beloved by butterflies and wildflowers in the summer. Keep an eye out for fast-paced Nordic walkers (power hikers using ski poles).

Bureau Officiel des Guides. If it's an extreme challenge you're looking for, contact the pros at Bureau Officiel des Guides for guidance. ☎ *027/4804466* ⊕ *www.sms04.ch.*

SHOPPING

At times the streets of stylish Crans can feel like a fashion runway, with the leather and fur-trimmed crowd hidden behind logo sunglasses and cashmere hats. This tiny village has taken a cue from Gstaad and St Moritz, assembling the most high-end shops and designer boutiques in the entire region. Though the usual suspects of luxury fashion can be found here—Louis Vuitton, Bulgari, Chanel, Hublot, Moncler, and Prada to name but a few—the streets also offer family-owned shops and an outdoor market which remain affordable spots to sample local wines, meats, and cheeses.

Alex Sports. Don't be deceived by its name: Alex Sports stocks such labels as Bogner, Escada, Ralph Lauren, and Zegna. And, yes, you can buy a down jacket or rent a pair of skis. ⊠ *31 rue du Prado, Crans* ☎ *0274814061* ⊕ *www.alexsports.ch.*

VAL D'ANNIVIERS

25 km (16 miles) south of Sierre.

If you drive east of Sierre and south of the Rhône, following signs for Vissoie, you enter a wild and craggy valley called Val d'Anniviers. The name is said to come from its curious and famous (among anthropologists, at least) nomads, known in Latin as *anni viatores* (year-round travelers).

A stopover in any one of these windswept mountain hideouts to walk, climb, ski, or relax by the fire is a reward. In late September, when herds of bell-toting cows are brought down from the mountains, there's a clangy seasonal celebration called Désalpe.

ESSENTIALS

Visitor Information Sierre Salgesch and Environs Tourist Information ☎ *027/4558535* ⊕ *www.sierre-salgesch.ch.*

EXPLORING

Grimentz. In summer you can drive down a narrow forest road to Grimentz. With a population of 450, this ancient 13th-century village has preserved its weathered-wood houses and mazots in its tiny center. It is particularly known for its *vin du glacier*, or glacier wine, which is traditionally drunk directly from the barrel rather than bottled. ⊕ *www.grimentz.ch.*

St-Luc. Head up a switchback road to the tiny village of St-Luc for a taste of rural life and celestial viewing at the observatory.

WHERE TO STAY

For expanded hotel reviews, visit Fodors.com.

$$$
B&B/INN
🏨 **Grand Hôtel Bella Tola.** Stepping stones lead to the wrought-iron entry of this stately mansion perched above St-Luc's main thoroughfare. **Pros:** feels like staying with an old friend; beautiful location with stunning views. **Cons:** some say the haute cuisine falls flat; many rooms are no

bigger than a breadbasket. [$] *Rooms from: 300 SF* ✉ *Rue Principale, St-Luc* ☎ *027/4751444* 🌐 *www.bellatola.ch* 🛏 *32 rooms* 🕒 *Closed mid-Apr.–mid-June and mid-Oct.–mid-Dec.* 🍴 *Some meals.*

$ B&B/INN 🏨 **Hôtel de Moiry.** This family-run country inn is draped in a profusion of geraniums in summertime and bundled in snowbanks in winter. **Pros:** Swiss kitsch at its best—dig the hand-painted murals of fighting cows in the restaurant. **Cons:** high season requires mandatory half board. [$] *Rooms from: 140 SF* ✉ *Grimentz* ☎ *027/4751144* 🌐 *www.hotel-grimentz.ch* 🛏 *17 rooms* 🍴 *Breakfast.*

SPORTS AND THE OUTDOORS

HIKING

Le Chemin des Planètes. Walk through the universe on an astronomically themed 6-km (4-mile) trail called Le Chemin des Planètes. The Tignousa funicular (round-trip 15 SF) delivers you to the starting point at 7,218 feet. Models of the planets are set along a pathway that begins at the base of the **Observatoire François-Xavier Bagnoud** (*027/4755808* 🌐 *www.ofxb.ch*). Allow two hours to make the ascent from there, past the Hotel Weisshorn. For 10 SF you can view the night sky through the reflecting and refracting telescopes at the observatory. Call ahead to make sure it is open.

LEUKERBAD

21 km (13 miles) northeast of Sierre.

At 4,628 feet, Leukerbad, called Loèche-*les-Bains* in French, is Europe's highest spa village; travelers have been ascending to this Alpine retreat for centuries to take the curative waters and fill their lungs with cleansing mountain air. With 90 km (43 miles) of downhill and cross-country runs of varying difficulty, including some used for World Cup training and testing, Leukerbad is a pleasant alternative to the larger resorts, and its rejuvenating hot mineral pools are a soothing après-ski option. The Torrent cable car whisks skiers to slopes; a one-day ski pass including a visit to one of the public spas is 77 SF; from June to October the price is reduced to 46 SF.

Summer brings hikers who love the combination of trekking and soaking. High-altitude crossings via the Gemmi Pass go back to 500 BC. The ancient connection between the Valais and the Berner Oberland can be traversed easily in a day.

Calcium sulfite hot springs flow beneath the village, filling stone troughs with warm vapor, keeping thoroughfares free of snow, and circulating to private tubs and public pools daily. In the late 1960s an arthritis and rheumatism treatment facility was established, but it has since been overshadowed by upscale wellness hotels and sports clinics. The two largest bath facilities in Leukerbad are Burgerbad and Alpentherme. Both have pools, fountains, whirlpools, jets, and sprays of thermal waters. Towels and robes can be rented at the reception desk.

GETTING HERE AND AROUND

To get to the thermal village of Leukerbad by public transportation, you'll need to transfer to a bus from the Leuk-Susten train station. If you arrive by car, the road from Leuk-Susten to Leukerbad is an easy drive all year round.

DRINK TO YOUR HEALTH

Don't forget to drink a glass of water from the tap in Leukerbad—it's touted to have added health benefits.

ESSENTIALS

Visitor Information Leukerbad Tourist Information ✉ *Rathaus, Rathausstr.* ☎ *027/4727171* 🌐 *www.leukerbad.ch.*

Transportation Information LLB ☎ *027/4702052* 🌐 *www.llbreisen.ch.*

EXPLORING

Burgerbad. With its indoor and outdoor pools, this multilevel facility is more water park than thermal bath. It's usually packed with families, so don't come expecting peace and quiet. But the views of Leukerbad's mountains are terrific, though no better than at Lindner Alpentherme, which is better suited to those seeking tranquillity. Burgerbad has exercise rooms, a sauna, solarium, and snack bar, as well as a giant slide that corkscrews its way down into the one of the thermal baths. ✉ *Rathausstr.* ☎ *027/4722020* 🌐 *www.burgerbad.ch* 🎟 *35 SF includes sauna* 🕒 *Daily 8–8.*

Keller zur Grotte. Just outside Leukerbad is this cozy winery has a tasting room where you can sample its wonderful Humagne Rouges, Fendants, Walliser Roses, and Cornalins, among other unique Valais varietals. The town makes for a great half-day bike ride from Leukerbad, and it is downhill all the way. For those who don't want to climb up again, you can easily throw your bike on the bus as you head back uphill. ✉ *Kegelplatz 7, Varen* ☎ *027/4733647* 🌐 *www.kellerzurgrotte.ch.*

★ **Lindner Alpentherme.** Sporting expansive Palladian windows set in marble, the Lindner Alpentherme looks like a temple perched on the hill. Annexes contain a Clarins beauty center, medical complex, and shopping arcade that includes a pharmacy specializing in natural remedies and juice bar. The unique spa treatment here is the *Bain Romano-Irlandais* (Roman-Irish bath), a two-hour succession of hot and cold soaks and vapor treatments (74 SF). Massage, herbal wraps, scrubs, and medical consultations are also on the menu. For safety reasons, parents are advised not to bring children under eight. ✉ *Dorfpl.* ☎ *027/4721010* 🌐 *www.alpentherme.ch* 🎟 *23 SF for 3 hrs in thermal baths; 53 SF day pass for baths and sauna* 🕒 *Daily 8–8.*

WHERE TO STAY

For expanded hotel reviews, visit Fodors.com.

$ HOTEL Fodor's Choice ★ 🏨 **Hotel Waldhaus.** With the friendliness that comes from a family-run establishment, this chalet-style guesthouse and restaurant is set on a quiet street overlooking the village. **Pros:** quiet location; the town's best restaurant. **Cons:** rooms feel a bit dated; breakfast service somewhat stiff and regimented. [$] *Rooms from: 139 SF* ✉ *Promendae 17* ☎ *027/4703232* 🌐 *www.hotel-waldhaus.ch* 🛏 *15 rooms* 🍴 *No meals.*

$$ HOTEL [H] **Lindner Hotels & Alpentherme Leukerbad.** In the shadow of a stunning mountain range, three hotels—Maison Blanche, Grand Bain, and the Hotel de France—are merged beneath one banner. **Pros:** there's also a private spa for guests only; packages include Alpentherme admission. **Cons:** pleasant service can be hard to come by. [$] *Rooms from: 200 SF* ✉ *1 Dorfpl.* ☎ *027/4721000* 🌐 *www.lindnerhotels.ch* 🛏 *123 rooms, 12 suites* 🍴 *Breakfast.*

SPORTS AND THE OUTDOORS

Sportarena Leukerbad. In the middle of town, this sports arena plays host to practicing Russian hockey players in the summer. It's a great place to rent power-assisted e-bikes, as well as play tennis or squash. ✉ *Römerweg 2* ☎ *027/4701037* 🌐 *www.sportarenaleukerbad.ch.*

ZERMATT AND SAAS-FEE

Immediately east of Sierre you'll notice a sharp change: *vals* become *Tals,* and the sounds you overhear at your next pit stop are no longer the mellifluous tones of the Suisse Romande but the sharper Swiss-German dialect called Wallisertiitsch. Welcome to Wallis (*vahl*-is), the Germanic end of Valais. This sharp demographic frontier can be traced back to the 6th century, when Alemannic tribes poured over the Grimsel Pass and penetrated as far as Sierre.

ZERMATT AND THE MATTERHORN

Fodor's Choice ★ *28 km (18 miles) south of Visp, plus a 10-km (6-mile) train ride from Täsch.*

Despite its fame—which stems from that iconic peak, the Matterhorn, and from its excellent ski facilities—Zermatt is a resort with its feet on the ground. It protects its regional quirks along with its wildlife and its tumbledown mazots, which crowd between glass-and-concrete chalets like old tenements between skyscrapers. Streets twist past weathered-wood walls, flower boxes, and haphazard stone roofs until they break into open country that slopes, inevitably, uphill. Despite the throngs of tourists, you're never far from the wild roar of the silty river or a vertiginous mountain path.

In the mid-19th century Zermatt was virtually unheard of; the few visitors who came to town stayed at the vicarage. The vicar and a chaplain named Joseph Seiler persuaded Seiler's little brother Alexander to start an inn. Opened in 1854 and named the Hotel Monte Rosa, it's still one of five Seiler hotels in Zermatt. In 1891 the cog railway between Visp and Zermatt took its first summer run and began disgorging tourists with profitable regularity—though it didn't plow through in wintertime until 1927. Today the town remains a car-free resort (though electric carts run by the hotels clog the streets). If you're traveling primarily by car, you can park it in the multistory terminal connected to the station in Täsch, where you catch the train into Zermatt.

GETTING HERE AND AROUND

Zermatt, the world's most famous car-free Alpine village, requires that residents and guests leave their vehicles in the village of Täsch. The Matterhorn Gottard Bahn ferries passengers from Brig and Visp to Zermatt, and operates frequent shuttle service from Täsch to the village on a private railway system. It also connects with the Glacier Express, a very touristy train that runs between Zermatt and St. Moritz. Once in Zermatt, another arm of the network, the pricey Gornergrat Bahn (80 SF for round-trip ticket) takes over to sweep skiers and day-hikers to the Gornergrat.

In Täsch, five-star hotels like those in the Seiler group have separate valet terminals plus private transfer that can be booked with your room reservation. In addition, there are open lots where the rates are less expensive, but plan to add at least 13 SF per day for parking to your vacation expenses. If you don't want to make the half-hour drive on mountain roads into the Matter Valley, use rail service that connects through Visp. The scenic ride will take about an hour.

If the weather is clear when you arrive, hustle to the end of the village to see the mountain. Then split your day of exploring between taking a lift or the train to higher elevations and strolling the narrow streets and shops, being sure to stop at one of the local restaurants for raclette.

ESSENTIALS

Visitor Information Zermatt Tourist Information ✉ *5 Bahnhofpl.* ☎ *027/9668100* ⊕ *www.zermatt.ch.*

Transportation Information Gornergrat Bahn ☎ *027/9214711* ⊕ *www. gornergrat.ch.* **Matterhorn Gottard Bahn** ☎ *027/9277474* ⊕ *www.mgbahn.ch.* **Matterhorn Terminal Täsch** ⊕ *www.matterhornterminal.ch.*

EXPLORING

Gornergrat–Monte Rose Bahn. It's quite simple to gain the broader perspective of high altitudes without risking life or limb. A train trip on the Gornergrat Bahn functions as an excursion as well as a ski transport. Part of its rail system was completed in 1898, and it's the highest open-air rail system in Europe (the tracks to the Jungfraujoch, though higher, bore through the face of the Eiger). It connects out of the main Zermatt train station and heads sharply left, at a right angle to the track that brings you into town. Its stop at the **Riffelberg**, at 8,469 feet, offers wide-open views of the Matterhorn. Farther on, from **Rotenboden**, at 9,246 feet, a short downhill walk leads to the **Riffelsee**, which obligingly provides photographers with a postcard-perfect reflection of the famous peak. At the end of the 9-km (5½-mile) line, the train stops at the summit station of **Gornergrat** (10,266 feet), and passengers pour onto the observation terraces to take in the majestic views of the Matterhorn, Monte Rosa, Gorner Glacier, and an expanse of scores of peaks and 24 other glaciers. Make sure to bring warm clothes, sunglasses, and sturdy shoes, especially if you plan to ski or hike down. ✉ *Bahnhofplatz* ☎ *027/9214711* ⊕ *www.gornergratbahn. ch* 🎫 *76 SF round-trip, 38 SF one-way* ⊙ *Departures daily every 24 mins, 7–7, but it's season dependent so check schedules (also online).*

CLOSE UP

The Matterhorn

Matterhorn. At 14,685 feet, the Matterhorn's peculiar snaggletooth form rears up over the village of Zermatt, larger than life and genuinely awe-inspiring. As you weave through crowds along Bahnhofstrasse, the town's main street, you're assaulted on all sides by Matterhorn images—on postcards, sweatshirts, calendars, beer steins, and candy wrappers—though not by the original, which is obscured by resort buildings (except from the windows of pricier hotel rooms). But break past the shops and hotels onto the main road into the hills, and you'll reach a slightly elevated spot where you'll probably stop dead in your tracks. There it is at last, its twist of snowy rock blinding in the sun. Surely more pictures are taken from this spot than from anywhere else in Switzerland.

It was Edward Whymper's spectacular—and catastrophic—conquest of the Matterhorn, on July 14, 1865, that made Zermatt a household word. After reaching the mountain's summit, his climbing party began its descent, tying themselves together and moving one man at a time. One of the climbers slipped, dragging the others down with him. Though Whymper and one of his companions braced themselves to stop the fall, the rope

between climbers snapped and four mountaineers fell nearly 4,000 feet to their deaths. One body was never recovered, but the others lie in modest graves behind the park near the village church, surrounded by scores of other failed mountaineers.

In summer the streets of Zermatt fill with sturdy, weathered climbers. They continue to tackle the peaks, and climbers have mastered the Matterhorn thousands of times since Whymper's disastrous victory.

CLIMBING THE MOUNTAIN
This climb must be taken seriously; you have to be in top physical condition and have climbing experience to attempt the summit. You also need to spend 7 to 10 days acclimatizing once in the area. Less-experienced climbers have plenty of alternatives, though, such as a one-day climb of the Riffelhorn (9,774 feet) or a half-traverse of the Breithorn (13,661 feet). For those wanting a challenge without such extreme altitudes, try a guided trip across the rugged Gorner gorge.

Zermatt Alpin Center. For detailed information, advice, instruction, and climbing guides for the Matterhorn, contact the Zermatt Alpin Center. ✉ *Bahnhofstr. 58* ☎ *027/9662460* ⊕ *www.alpincenter-zermatt.ch.*

↻ **Matterhorn Museum.** To get a sense of life in this high-altitude region and the risks involved in climbing, visit the Matterhorn Museum, a sunken village of chalets, mazots, and dwellings depicted as an archaeological site that visitors walk through, experiencing different periods of time along the way. The personal accounts of local docents liven up the displays of antiquated equipment, clothing, and historical documents about those who lived and climbed here. There is a farmer's cottage, hotel, and church interior, plus stuffed and mounted animals. ✉ *Kirchpl.* ☎ *027/9674100* ⊕ *www.zermatt.ch* 🎟 *10 SF* ⊙ *Easter–June and Oct., daily 2–6; July–Sept., daily 11–6; mid-Dec.–Easter, daily 3–7.*

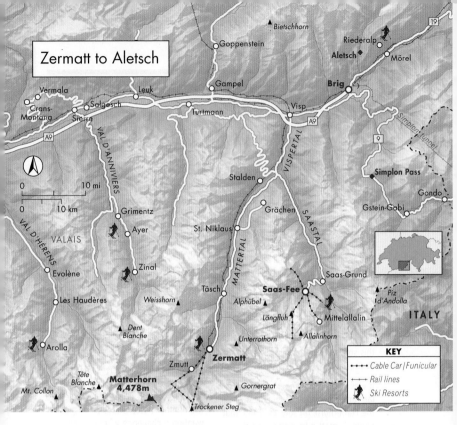

St. Peter's (*The English Church*). Climb the winding pathway behind the ski and snowboard school to the white church on the hill, St. Peter's. Anglican services are still held in the tiny sanctuary established by the British who ignited a climbing fervor to conquer the Matterhorn and other towering peaks in the region. Take time to pause in the cemetery that holds the graves of those who were not fortunate enough to return safely and others who remained in this beloved community to live out their lives.

SKIING

Zermatt's skiable terrain lives up to its reputation: the 63 lift installations, 73 lifts, and mountain railways are capable of moving well above 50,000 skiers per hour up to its approximately 360 km (224 miles) of marked pistes—if you count those of Cervinia in Italy. Among the lifts are the cable car that carries skiers up to an elevation of 12,746 feet on the Matterhorn Glacier Paradise (previously known as Klein Matterhorn), the small Gornergratbahn that creeps up to the Gornergrat, and a subway through an underground tunnel that gives more pleasure to ecologists than it does to sun-loving skiers.

The skiable territory on this royal plateau was once separated into three separate sectors, but the installation of a gondola to Riffelberg has linked the three together. The first sector is **Sunnegga-Blauherd-Rothorn,** which culminates at an elevation of 10,170 feet. **Gornergrat-Stockhorn** (11,155 feet) is the second. The third is the region dominated by the **Matterhorn Glacier Paradise,** which goes to Italy. The best way to prioritize your ski day is still to concentrate on one or two areas, especially during high season. Thanks to snowmaking machines and the eternal snows of the Klein Matterhorn Glacier, Zermatt is said to guarantee skiers 7,216 feet of vertical drop no matter what the snowfall—an impressive claim. Gravity Park, a snowboarding center on Theodul glacier, has pipes, kickers, and rails to thrill. A one-day lift ticket costs 75 SF and a six-day pass costs 371 SF; if you want to ski to Italy it costs 86 SF and 423 SF, respectively. Ask for the hands-free "Swatch Access Key" with computer chip gate activation; you buy a Swatch watch with built-in memory (from 34 SF), and they load your ticket data into it.

WORD OF MOUTH

"Keep in mind there is no guarantee you will even see the Matterhorn if the weather is socked in. Not to discourage you, but I stayed two extra days until the summit cleared. To me it was worth it, but I had two more weeks left on my vacation. Zermatt's tourist office has live cameras of the Matterhorn if anyone is connected." —glaciermeadows

Swiss Ski and Snowboard School. This outfit runs classes from mid-December until mid-April, but can provide private instruction all year. ✉ *Bahnhofstr.* ☎ *027/9662466* 🌐 *www.skischulezermatt.ch.*

WHERE TO EAT

$$ SWISS 🍴 **Elsie's Bar.** This tiny log cabin of a ski haunt, directly across from the church in Zermatt, draws an international crowd as soon as it opens its doors at 4 pm (sometimes as early as noon in peak season). They come to select from an extensive list of aged Scotches and mixed cocktails. Light meals include oysters, escargots, and even a 115 SF plate of spaghetti with caviar and crème fraîche. The doors stay open until 2 am. [$] *Average main: 27 SF* ✉ *Kirchpl. 16* ☎ *027/9672431* 🌐 *www.elsiebar.ch* ⏲ *Closed May–mid-Nov.*

$ SWISS Fodor's Choice ★ 🍴 **Findlerhof.** Ideal for long lunches between sessions on the slopes or for a panoramic break on an all-day hike, this place is perched in tiny Findeln, between the Sunnegga and Blauherd ski areas. The Matterhorn views are astonishing. The food is decidedly fresh and creative, and Franz and Heidi Schwery tend their own Alpine garden to provide lettuce for their salads and berries for vinaigrettes and hot desserts. The fluffy *Matterkuchen,* a bacon-and-leek quiche, will fortify you for the 30- to 40-minute walk down to the village. [$] *Average main: 24 SF* ✉ *Findeln* ☎ *027/9672588* 🌐 *www.findlerhof.ch* ⏲ *Closed May–mid-June and mid-Oct.–Nov.*

$$$ SWISS 🍴 **Grill-Room Stockhorn.** The moment you step across the threshold into this low-slung, two-story restaurant decked with mountaineering memorabilia, the tantalizing aroma of melting cheese should sharpen your appetite. Downstairs you can watch meat roasting on the wood-fired grill while enjoying the chalet-style decor. Upstairs a mélange of Mediterranean tiles and traditional Valaisan exposed darkwood beams creates a romantic atmosphere. This is a great place for

regional dishes and meat specialties like juicy chateaubriand grilled
to perfection and dripping with a
creamy béarnaise sauce, served by
lively staff. $ *Average main: 42
SF* ✉ *Hotel Stockhorn, Riedstr.
11* ☎ *027/9671747* ⊕ *www.grill-
stockhorn.ch* ⊗ *Closed Mon., mid-
May–mid-June, and Oct.*

$$ ✕ **Whymper-Stube.** At this little res-
SWISS taurant in the Hotel Monte Rosa,
plates of melted raclette and bub-
bling pots of fondue are delivered
to tightly packed tables by an agile
waitstaff. Be sure to try the unusual variations on cheese dishes like
the fresh mushroom or pear-laced fondue. The restaurant is named for
Edward Whymper, the first man to reach the Matterhorn summit—
imagine the climbers' stories that must have echoed within these walls.
In the winter season the place stays open until 1 am. $ *Average main:
26 SF* ✉ *Hotel Monte Rosa, Bahnhofstr. 80* ☎ *027/9672296* ⊕ *www.
whymper-stube.ch* ⌕ *Reservations essential* ⊗ *Closed May and last 2
wks of Oct.*

$$ ✕ **Zum See.** In the hamlet (little more than a cluster of mazots) of the
SWISS same name, this restaurant turns out inventive meals that merit acclaim.
A half hour's walk from Zermatt, it overflows until late afternoon with
diners sunning on the terrace or packed into the 400-year-old log house.
(The quickest way to get here is to walk or ski down from Furi.) Hosts
Max and Greti Mennig masterfully prepare such seasonal specials as
venison salad with wild mushrooms and handmade tortelloni with
nettle-ricotta filling. The selection of wines and brandies sets skiers
aglow. $ *Average main: 27 SF* ✉ *Zum See* ☎ *027/9672045* ⊕ *www.
zumsee.ch* ⌕ *Reservations essential* ⊗ *Closed mid-Apr.–June and mid-
Oct.–mid-Dec. No dinner.*

WHERE TO STAY

Many Zermatt hotels, especially larger ones, decide on a year-by-
year basis to close during low season, which lasts from "meltdown"
(anywhere from late April to mid-June) until "preseason" (November
through mid-December). If you plan to travel during the low season,
be sure to call ahead. That noted, the summer "low season" can prove
more popular than the winter ski season, with rates and availability
to match.

For expanded hotel reviews, visit Fodors.com.

$ ⌂ **Hotel Admiral.** An easygoing anglophone owner makes it a snap to
HOTEL check in at this fastidious lodging along Zermatt's riverfront promenade. **Pros:** convivial clientele; laid-back atmosphere makes it easy
for solo travelers to meet new friends. **Cons:** phony chalet exterior;
odd blue carpeting throughout the hotel; "garni" means only breakfast served. $ *Rooms from: 125 SF* ✉ *Matterstr. 23* ☎ *027/9669000*
⊕ *www.hotel-admiral.ch* ⇄ *24 rooms, 1 suite* ⦿ *Breakfast.*

$
HOTEL

⬚ Hotel Mirabeau. Old and new merge at this two-part hotel with a traditional building and contemporary addition. **Pros:** personable personnel; winning mix of old and new; light-filled rooms. **Cons:** mixed reviews for the kitchen; spa facilities a far cry from those of other nearby hotels. **⑊** *Rooms from: 175 SF* ⊠ *Untere Mattenrstr. 12–14* ☎ *027/9662660* ⊕ *www.hotel-mirabeau.ch* ⇶ *44 rooms, 18 suites* ⦿*l Breakfast.*

$$$
HOTEL

⬚ Hotel Monte Rosa. Alexander Seiler founded this historic hotel, expanding it over the years to its current size. **Pros:** near all the entertainment hot spots; historical significance sets a unique, inspiring mood—you'll feel like conquering the Matterhorn yourself. **Cons:** no in-house pool or spa facilities; though trendy, the bar is narrow and uncomfortably cramped. **⑊** *Rooms from: 280 SF* ⊠ *Bahnhofstr. 80* ☎ *027/9660333* ⊕ *www.monterosazermatt.ch* ⇶ *26 rooms, 15 suites* ⊗ *Closed mid-Apr.–mid-June and Oct.–mid-Dec.* ⦿*l Breakfast.*

$$$
HOTEL
Fodor's Choice
★

⬚ Mont Cervin Palace. After a complete renovation in 2012, this Leading Hotels of the World property remains luxurious, genteel, and one of Zermatt's grandes dames. **Pros:** station pickup in a red antique horse-drawn carriage; wellness and spa facilities that are tops. **Cons:** big-city luxury removes you somewhat from the village atmosphere. **⑊** *Rooms from: 350 SF* ⊠ *Bahnhofstr. 31* ☎ *027/9668888* ⊕ *www.seilerhotels.ch* ⇶ *89 rooms, 62 suites, 14 apartments* ⊗ *Closed May–mid-June, Oct., and mid-Nov.* ⦿*l Breakfast.*

$$$
HOTEL

⬚ Omnia Mountain Lodge. At this sophisticated glass-and-steel hotel on the hillside above the Kirchplatz, the only concession to local architecture is the wooden panels that cap each end. **Pros:** Bose soundsystems and designer toiletries; laptops loaned to guests on request. **Cons:** set apart high above the village; staggered building layout can be disorienting. **⑊** *Rooms from: 320 SF* ⊠ *Auf dem Fels* ☎ *027/9667171* ⊕ *www.the-omnia.ch* ⇶ *18 rooms, 12 suites* ⊗ *Closed late Apr.–May* ⦿*l Breakfast.*

$
HOTEL

⬚ Pollux. Despite its hideous 1960s exterior, this hotel has a surprisingly elegant interior, with stone walls, wood floors, and artistic tilework. **Pros:** sparkling clean; après-ski cocktails at the fireside bar. **Cons:** street outside can be noisy; no view from the wellness zone. **⑊** *Rooms from: 135 SF* ⊠ *Bahnhofstr. 28* ☎ *027/9664000* ⊕ *www.hotelpollux.ch* ⇶ *35 rooms* ⦿*l Breakfast.*

$$
HOTEL
Fodor's Choice
★

⬚ Riffelalp Resort 2222m. Set at 7,288 feet amid open fields and dense forests, this mountaintop option offers direct views of the Matterhorn—especially breathtaking in the orange glow of early morning—and enchantingly stylish decor. **Pros:** far from the village hubbub; no better skiing location in Zermatt. **Cons:** dining is limited to the hotel's three options; 10-night minimum stay in peak season; dinner not included in summer rates. **⑊** *Rooms from: 250 SF* ⊠ *Riffelalp* ☎ *027/9660555* ⊕ *www.riffelalp.com* ⇶ *65 rooms, 5 suites, 2 apartments* ⊗ *Closed mid-Apr.–late June and Oct.–mid-Dec.* ⦿*l Breakfast.*

$$
HOTEL

⬚ Walliserhof Hotel. This cozy charmer, a five-minute walk from the main train station, has been a favorite since it opened in 1896 (back then it was called the Touristenhotel Perrin). **Pros:** central location right in town; spacious rooms. **Cons:** the cramped spa feels like an

Guests at the Mont Cervin Palace are picked up at the Zermatt station and driven to the hotel in horse-drawn sleighs in winter.

afterthought. $ *Rooms from: 200 SF* ✉ *Bahnofstr. 30* ☏ *027/9666555* ⊕ *www.walliserhof-zermatt.ch* 🛏 *34 rooms* ◯ *Multiple meal plans.*

NIGHTLIFE

GramPi's Bar. Located in what locals call the "Bermuda Triangle" because of its concentration of nightspots, this is a lively bar where you can get into the mood for dancing downstairs with a Lady Matterhorn cocktail. ✉ *Bahnhofstrasse 70* ☏ *027/9677788* ⊕ *www.grampis.ch.*

Hexen Bar. A great place for après-ski drinks, this chatty witch-themed bar and pub has a subtle gay vibe. *Gespritzer weissers* (white wine spritzers) are a local favorite., but the dark wood paneling and cozy booths might make you want to sample something from the extensive whiskey menu. ✉ *Bahnhofstr. 43* ☏ *027/9675533* ⊕ *www.grampis.ch.*

Josef's Wine Lounge. For excellent wines served with a modern flair, head down the pathway beside the Hotel Mirabeau to Josef's Wine Lounge. ✉ *Hotel Mirabeau, Untere Mattenrstr. 12–14* ☏ *027/9662560* ⊕ *www.hotel-mirabeau.ch.*

Unique Hotel Post. Across the cobblestones from GramPi's is the Unique Hotel Post, which houses a concert hall, a lounge where a DJ spins tunes for late-night revelers (both open only in winter), a disco with a high-energy beat, a cigar lounge, and a mellow pub serving chicken wings and burgers. ✉ *Unique Hotel Post, Bahnhofstr. 41* ☏ *027/9671931* ⊕ *www.hotelpost.ch.*

Schwyzer Stübli. A double dose of regional song and dance can be had at the Schwyzer Stübli. Be prepared for rowdy sing-alongs and accordion music. It's incidentally also a great place to sample traditional Swiss food. ⊠ *Hotel Schweizerhof, Bahnhofstr. 5* ☎ *027/9660000* ⊕ *www. schweizerhofzermatt.ch.*

SPORTS AND THE OUTDOORS

HIKING

With 400 km (248 miles) of marked trails available, you'll have plenty of options for exploring the mountains on foot. Outfitted with scarred boots, rucksacks, and walking sticks, trekkers strike out in all directions for daylong excursions ranging from easy to exhausting. Free route guides are available at the tourist office. Be sure to pack rain gear and a warm jacket along with sunscreen, as the weather changes quickly. Multiday lift passes will ease the way up and leave some change in your pocket for an after-hike beer.

Zermatt Lake Trail. While any hike with views of the Matterhorn is worth the effort, particularly special is a 9-km (6-mile) route from Blauherd to Riffelalp, passing lakes like Stelli, Grindji, and Grüen along the way. A funicular and cable car ride to Blauherd at 8,200 feet brings you to the start, while a train ride on the Gornergratbahn takes you back to town. The route is relatively easy, but you'll still climb 800 vertical feet.

MOUNTAIN BIKING

Mountain biking is closely monitored by Zermatt authorities to prevent interference with hiking on trails. To keep pace with other resorts, about 25 km (15 miles) have been set aside for dedicated downhill tracks with challenging features. A map is available at the tourist office (10 SF).

Slalom Sport. A wide variety of bikes can be rented at Slalom Sport. ⊠ *Kirchstr. 17* ☎ *027/9662366* ⊕ *www.zermattbike.com.*

SHOPPING

Zermatt is Switzerland's souvenir capital, offering a broad variety of junk: scarves, watches, knives, logo clothing, and Matterhorn-in-a-box stones. Popular folk crafts and traditional products include large grotesque masks of carved wood, and lidded *channes* in pewter or tin, molded in graduated sizes; they're sold everywhere, even in grocery stores.

You'll see lots of stores offering state-of-the-art sports equipment and apparel, from collapsible grappling hooks for climbers to lightweight hiking boots in brilliant colors to walking sticks—pairs of lightweight, spiked ski poles for hikers to add a bit of upper-body workout to their climb.

Bayard. Bayard has sporting-goods shops scattered throughout the village, including this one on the Bahnhofstrasse. This is an ideal place to rent ski gear or shop for a a new pair goggles for downhill racing. ⊠ *Bahnhofpl. 2* ☎ *027/9664950* ⊕ *www.bayardzermatt.ch.*

Glacier Sport. This popular shop specializes in ski and climbing equipment and accessories. ⊠ *Bahnhofstr. 19* ☎ *027/9681300* ⊕ *www.glacier-intersport.ch.*

The Riffelalp Resort 2222m boasts Europe's highest outdoor pool; it's heated to 95°F (35°C) year-round.

SAAS-FEE

36 km (22 miles) south of Visp.

Quieter and more low-key than Zermatt is the village of Saas-Fee, a car-free mountain resort with a family-friendly vibe. Saas-Fee also offer a fantastic network of trails that allow you to get up close and personal with the wild marmots who live in subterranean dwellings on the mountain. At the end of the switchback road from Saas-Grund lies a parking garage where you must abandon your car for the length of your stay. But even by the garage you'll be amazed, for the view on arriving at this lofty (5,871 feet) plateau is humbling. (In true Swiss-efficient fashion, you can drop off your bags curbside and call an electric shuttle that will arrive to fetch you in the time it takes to park your car.)

GETTING HERE AND AROUND

Car-free Saas-Fee is on a bus line connection with Brig (about 1 hour 20 minutes) and Visp (1 hour); take the train here from Brig by transferring at Visp or connect with Zermatt by rail with a transfer at Stalden-Saas.

ESSENTIALS

Visitor Information Saas-Fee Tourist Information ⊠ *At the entrance to the village* ☎ *027/9581858* ⊕ *www.saas-fee.ch.*

EXPLORING

Dom. Saas-Fee is at the heart of a circle of mountains called the Mischabel, 13 of which tower to more than 13,120 feet. Among them is the Dom (14,908 feet), the highest mountain entirely on Swiss soil.

★ **Eis Pavillon** (*Ice Pavilion*). Considered the largest in the world, the Eis Pavillon combines fascinating construction with a dash of kitsch. More than 25 feet below the ice pack, the cavernous facility provides an impressive view of the surreal, frozen environment inside glacial formations. There are ice sculptures, exhibits on glaciology and crevasse rescue, and even a chapel-like room for meditation, concerts, and art shows. In winter, the ticket for the cable car and underground funicular is pricey, but if you are up on the mountain, spring for the entrance fee and have a look below the frozen surface of the earth. It's free in summer with Saas-Fee Visitor's Passport. ✉ *Mittelallalin* ☎ *027/9573560* 🎟 *5 SF* 🕓 *Daily 10–approx. 3:30, depending on the season (when the last cable car leaves).*

Fee Glacier. Saas-Fee lies in a deep valley that leaves no doubt about its source—it seems to pour from the vast, intimidating Fee Glacier. *Fee* can be translated as "fairy," and this primordial landscape could illustrate a fairy tale.

SKIING

The first glacier to be used for skiing here was the **Längfluh** (9,414 feet), accessed by gondola, then cable car. The run is magnificent, sometimes physically demanding, and always varied.

From the Längfluh you can take a lift to reach *the* ski area of Saas-Fee, the **Felskinn-Mittelallalin** sector (9,840–11,480 feet). Felskinn harbors its own surprise: in order to preserve the land and landscape, the Valaisans have constructed a subterranean funicular, the Métro Alpin, which climbs through the heart of the mountain to Mittelallalin, that is, halfway up the Allalinhorn (13,210 feet). Tourists debark in a rotating restaurant noted more for the austere grandeur of its natural surroundings than for its food. Felskinn-Mittelallalin's exceptional site, its high elevation, its 15 km (9 miles) of runs, and its ample facilities (cable car, funicular, and three ski lifts) have made Saas-Fee the number one summer-skiing resort in Switzerland. It's also one of two official European snowboard centers sanctioned by the International Snowboard Federation. Lifts don't connect with other resorts in the valley—Saas-Almagell, Saas-Balen, or Saas-Grund. However, good days of skiing can be found a bus ride away, and hiking trails open in winter and summer link all four valleys. A one-day lift ticket costs 67 SF; a six-day pass costs 341 SF. If you buy a six-day pass, you become eligible to purchase a day pass to ski in Zermatt at the reduced price of 20 SF.

WHERE TO EAT

Saas-Fee has always been known for good food, but it's really come into its own in terms of culinary excellence in the last few years. Chefs here provide much more than the usual fondue and raclette.

$$ **SWISS** 🍴 **Bergrestaurant Spielboden.** The views aren't bad at this lunch-only mountaintop restaurant, which received a top-to-toe makeover in 2012. Focusing on Valais wines, this elegant lodge is decidedly upscale, offering a lot more than the usual fondue and raclette. Braised duck leg with mashed potatoes and cabbage, and yak ragout with späetzlis and buttery carmelized onions and Swiss truffles up the ante for mile-high cuisine. [$] *Average main: 40 SF* ✉ *Postfach 97* ☎ *027/9572212* 🌐 *www.spielboden.ch* 🕓 *No dinner.*

$ ✕ **Restaurant Skihütte.** During the winter high season you'll have to be
SWISS quick in order to snag a table on the sun-filled deck of this traditional restaurant on the main drag. A great location at the bottom of the lift, it's perfect for a cold after-ski brewski or tummy-warming Williamine pear schnapps. Inexpensive yet well-prepared Walliser favorites and tasty snacks hold you for another drink and a few more rays. $ *Average main: 25 SF* ✉ *Unter den Bodmen* ☎ *027/9589280.*

$$$ ✕ **Restaurant-Vinothek Fletschhorn.** Markus Neff presides over this gour-
FRENCH mand's paradise, located in the Waldhotel Fletschhorn. The vibe is
Fodor's Choice innovative, the flavors superb, and the dishes rotate seasonally and
★ are heavily based on local products. Among the winners: seafood soup with saffron, panfried duck liver with caramelized red beets, or roasted Alpine lamb chops with rye-bread crust and creamy potato gratin. Lunch is a great time to sample the gourmet team's talents at a more favorable price: they serve straight through from 11:30 to 5:30, and there are mains starting at 25 SF. The expansive vinothek stocks some 45,000 bottles, many local Valasian wines, that match the cuisine's high style. $ *Average main: 55 SF* ✉ *Waldhotel Fletschhorn* ☎ *027/9572131* ⊕ *www.fletschhorn.ch* ✍ *Reservations essential* ⊗ *Closed late Apr.– early June and late Oct.–early Dec.*

WHERE TO STAY

For expanded hotel reviews, visit Fodors.com.

$$$ ⌂ **Dom Hotel.** After an extensive and thoughtful rennovation, Saas-Fee's
HOTEL oldest hotel has embraced a winning mixture of old and new. **Pros:**
Fodor's Choice homey touches blend with discreet high-tech amenities; location in the
★ center of town can't be beat. **Cons:** mediocre restaurant didn't get the memo on Saas-Fee's culinary upgrades; standard rooms are slightly cramped. $ *Rooms from: 275 SF* ✉ *Dorfpl. 2* ☎ *027/9587700* ⊕ *www. thedom.ch* ✍ *28 rooms* ⦿ *Breakfast.*

$$ ⌂ **Ferienart Resort & Spa.** In the center of town, this wood-chalet hotel
RESORT offers some of the best views around. **Pros:** top-of-the-line wellness
Fodor's Choice facilities; babysitting and day-care center a plus for families; gor-
★ geous restaurants. **Cons:** rooms vary drastically; inconsistent service; kitchy mega-resorty vibe. $ *Rooms from: 210 SF* ✉ *Dorfweg 1* ☎ *027/9581900* ⊕ *www.ferienart.ch* ✍ *73 rooms, 11 suites, 2 apartments* ⦿ *Some meals.*

$$ ⌂ **Hotel Schweizerhof.** This hotel has the town's best spa, not to men-
HOTEL tion lofty views of the mountains and glaciers. **Pros:** the town's best spa; secluded hilltop locale. **Cons:** rooms are overdecorated and stuffed with granny-style decor. $ *Rooms from: 245 SF* ✉ *Hallenstr. 10* ☎ *027/9587575* ⊕ *www.schweizerhof-saasfee.ch* ✍ *44 rooms* ⦿ *Breakfast.*

$$$ ⌂ **Waldhotel Fletschhorn.** A member of the Relais & Chateaux collection
B&B/INN of hotels, this sophisticated *Landgasthof* (country inn) is set apart from town at the end of a woodsy lane. **Pros:** staff will pick you up at the station; half board is a steal at only 105 SF per person. **Cons:** 25-minute walk from the village; no spa. $ *Rooms from: 275 SF* ☎ *027/9572131* ⊕ *www.fletschhorn.ch* ✍ *12 rooms, 1 suite* ⊗ *Closed late Apr.–early June and mid-Oct.–early Dec.* ⦿ *Breakfast.*

NIGHTLIFE AND THE ARTS
BARS AND DANCING

Nesti's. Patrons squeeze into Nesti's, a perennial après-ski favorite. ✉ *Am Biel* ☎ *027/9574211.*

Popcorn Bar. A younger crowd congregates for drinks at Popcorn Bar. The all-in-one spot features a shop stuffed with übercool snowboard clothes and gear and a smoking lounge. ✉ *Obere Dorfstr. 6* ☎ *027/9585000* ⊕ *www.popcorn.ch.*

SPORTS AND THE OUTDOORS
HIKING

Larch forests, flower and herb-filled meadows, and glacial zones offer a huge variety of trails (350 km [218 mi]) at all levels of difficulty. Historic routes cross passes into Italy and extend outbound along ridgelines toward the river. Bus and lift services make it easy to return to the village in time for dinner. Most hotels will pack a lunch for the outing, or you can stop at *buvettes* (snack bars) scattered along the trails. **Sentier des Chapelles** (Trail of the Chapels) is a timeworn pilgrimage route from Saas-Fee to Saas-Grund featuring 15 shrines with costumed wooden statues strung along the path like beads on a rosary.

MOUNTAIN CLIMBING

Bergfürerbüro. This mountain-climbing company conducts daily guided forays throughout the year and rents season-appropriate equipment. A popular activity is gorge crossing, which uses safety cables and pulleys to traverse the valley's deep divide. There are also a few *via ferrata* (iron way), preset routes with ladders and cables secured in place to challenge climbers at all stages of competence. ☎ *027/9574464* ⊕ *www. saasfeeguides.ch.*

SLEDDING

☺ **Feeblitz.** Your stay won't be complete without a few runs on the Feeblitz Toboggan Run, the curved and looped track of the *Rodelbobbahn* (bobsled) near the Alpin Express cable-car station. ☎ *027/9573111* ⊕ *www. feeblitz.ch.*

SPORTS CENTER

☺ **Bielen Leisure Center.** The Bielen Leisure Center has a four-lane swimming pool, a children's pool with a whirlpool, a sauna, and two indoor tennis courts. ✉ *Panorama Brücke 1* ☎ *027/9572475* ⊕ *www.super-dome.ch.*

BRIG AND THE ALPINE PASSES

This region is the Grand Central Station of the Alps. All mountain passes lead to or through Brig, as traffic and rail lines pour in from Italy, the Ticino, central Switzerland, and the Berner Oberland. It is also a transit link for Paris, Brussels, London, and Rome. The Simplon, Nufenen, Grimsel, and Furka passes provide exit options and stunning vistas dependent on destination. Northeast of this critical junction the spectacular Aletsch Glacier, the largest in Europe and a UNESCO World Heritage Site, straddles the cantons of Valais and Bern. The Rhône River becomes increasingly wild and silty until you arrive at its source in Gletsch, at the end of the valley called Goms.

The imposing Stockalperschloss is a must-see if you're passing through Brig.

BRIG

19 km (12 miles) southeast of Leukerbad.

A rail and road junction joining four cantons, this small but vital town for centuries has been a center of trade with Italy. Often overlooked as merely a transit point, the town has a legacy that can be appreciated in a couple of hours: a restored core with cobblestone streets, shops, cafés, and the main attraction, a fairy tale–worthy merchant's castle.

ESSENTIALS

Visitor Information Brig Tourism Information ⊠ *Bahnhof 1* ☏ *027/9216030* ⊕ *www.brig-belalp.ch.*

EXPLORING

Fodor's Choice ★ **Stockalperschloss.** The fantastical Stockalperschloss, a massive Baroque castle, was built between 1658 and 1678 by Prince Kaspar Jodok von Stockalper und Thurm (1609–91), a Swiss tycoon who made his fortune in Italian trade over the Simplon Pass. Soaring spectacularly with three towers topped with gilt onion domes and containing a courtyard lined by elegant Italianate arcades, it was once Switzerland's largest private home and is now restored. Inside are libraries, archives, and some Baroque period rooms. Group tours in English are available upon request. To get here from the station, walk up Bahnhofstrasse to Sebastienplatz, then turn left onto Alte Simplonstrasse. ⊠ *Alte Simplonstr. 28* ☏ *027/9216030* 🎟 *8 SF* ⊗ *June–Sept., Tues.–Sun., guided tours at 9:30, 10:30, 1:30, 2:30, 3:30, and 4:30; May and Oct., no tour at 4:30.*

Aletsch: Europe's Longest Glacier

Aletsch's famous glacier—24 km (15 miles)—was at its longest 150 years ago, but now recedes 100 to 165 feet per year. Concern about the recession of the earth's ice formations has made preserving the Aletsch Glacier internationally significant. So UNESCO designated a 250-square-km (97-square-mile) area around the glacier, shared between the cantons of Valais (77%) and Bern (23%), as a protected site. Generations ago the Swiss sensed the need to safeguard the area and began placing parts in conservationist hands.

The glacier's starting point, Concordia Platz, is the confluence of three ice masses that move down from the Bernese Alps. Here the ice has been measured as deep as 2,952 feet—over twice the height of the Empire State Building. Another magnificent formation, the Märjelensee is a lake with icebergs floating on top, carved into the glacier field with walls of ice and stone. As the glacier's ice recedes, nature reclaims the land,

first with moss and small plants, then forest. Pro Natura, the conservation organization that oversees the region, describes the process as "forest emerging from ice." Though some of the area's pine and larch are 600 to 700 years old, extreme conditions keep them short. Animals thought to be extinct thrive here; chamois, martens, badgers, lizards, and birds have adapted to the elevation and temperature.

Cable cars ferry tourists to ridge tops above Ried and Fiesch, where 360-degree views of the sweep of ice are framed by extraordinary peaks. You can see the Bernese Alps, including the Sphinx station on the Jungfraujoch called the "Top of Europe"; the Valaisan Alps; and even into Italy and France. Hiking trails lead to the glacier's edge, and guides take trekkers across parts of the ice field. All around are places to admire nature's grandeur and be grateful that it is being protected.

SIMPLON PASS

23 km (14 miles) southeast of Brig.

Beginning just outside Brig, this historic road meanders through deep gorges and wide, barren, rock-strewn pastures to offer increasingly beautiful views back toward Brig. At the summit (6,593 feet), the **Hotel Bellevue Simplon-Kulm** shares the high meadow with the **Simplon Hospitz** (Simplon Hospice), built 150 years ago at Napoléon's request and now owned by the monks of St. Bernard. Just beyond stands the belltowered **Alt Spital,** a lodging built in the 17th century. Beyond the pass, the road continues through Italy, and it's possible to cut across the Italian upthrust and reenter Switzerland in the Ticino, near Ascona.

■ TIP➔ From the summit of Simplon Pass you can still see parts of the old road used by traders and Napoleon. Look north toward the Bernese Alps to see a portion of the massive Aletsch Glacier.

OFF THE BEATEN PATH

Simplon Tunnel. If you'd rather ride than drive, you can hop aboard (or load your car on) the train that goes through this tunnel, which starts above the eastern outskirts of Brig and runs nearly 20 km (12 miles) before ending in Italian daylight. The first of the twin tunnels—once the world's longest railway tunnels—was started in 1898 and took six years to complete.

ALETSCH

★ *13 km (8 miles) north of Brig.*

Ice-capped peaks with small mountain resorts staggered up their spines rim the Aletsch, a glacier that shares its name with the area surrounding it, paralleling the valley floor. A variety of ecological zones—from deep, frozen expanses in the center to forests emerging at the fringes—are part of a wilderness region that is now firmly in the hands of conservationists, protected as a UNESCO international nature site. In contrast to these extreme expanses, sunny south-facing slopes are active with skiers and hikers staying in the villages of Riederalp, Bettmeralp, and Fiesch-Eggishorn.

GETTING HERE AND AROUND

The Fiesch-Eggishorn cable car takes you to the village of Eggishorn. Bettmeralp is reached via gondola from the Betten train station. Riederalp's link from the Rhône Valley is a giant gondola that lifts passengers from the village of Mörel. The Riederalp Bahnen is located across the street from the Mörel train station, a stop on the Matterhorn Gornergrat line. The 16-minute ride covers nearly 6,500 feet and costs 18 SF round-trip.

ESSENTIALS

Transportation Information Bettmeralp ✉ *Postfach 16, Bettmeralp* ⊕ *www.bettmeralp.ch.* **Fiesch-Eggishorn** ⊕ *www.eggishorn.ch.* **Riederalp Bahnen** ⊕ *www.riederalp.ch.*

SKIING

The three resorts of **Riederalp, Bettmeralp,** and **Fiescheralp** are connected by trails, lifts, and shuttle buses. There are 35 lifts and 104 km (65 miles) of runs, a quarter of which are expert and peak at 9,415 feet. A one-day lift ticket for access to the whole Aletsch ski area costs 55 SF; a six-day pass costs 273 SF. All the essentials are in place in these picture-book villages, but don't expect lots of amenities, varied dining choices, or glitzy nightlife.

Schweizer Schneesport Schule. Anyone requiring a ski school up here should contact the Schweizer Schneesport Schule ☎ *027/9271001* ⊕ *www.skischule-riederalp.ch.*

SPORTS AND THE OUTDOORS

HIKING

Aletsch Panorama Trail. From Brig catch a train to the Betten Talstation cable car, which will whisk you up to Bettmeralp. A gondola takes you to about 8,700 feet up the Bettmerhorn. From there, expect to climb about 1,300 vertical feet and drop more than 2,700 on this 11-km (7-mile) route, arriving at a cable car to take you back to train service in Fiesch. The trail takes you along the massive Aletsch Glacier, through a valley dotted with pristine Alpine lakes. Along the way, stop at the

Gletscherstube, a rustic hut set near the Märjelensee, at 8,640-feet, where you can get a bed for the night to prolong the adventure.

Fiesch cable car. If the day is clear, grab the chance for a spectacular ride to the top of one of the lofty peaks that shadow the roadway by taking the Fiesch cable car up to Eggishorn (9,303 feet). The panoramic views of Alps and glaciers will leave you breathless. As the cable car rotates 360 degrees, you can tick off famous Bernese and Valaisan peaks from your to-see list. The Jungfrau, Eiger, Matterhorn, and Dom are clearly visible, as are peaks that lie across the border in Italy and France. ☏ *027/9712700.*

Vaud

LAUSANNE, ROUTE DU VIGNOBLE, MONTREUX, AND VEVEY

WORD OF MOUTH

"The Saturday morning farmers' market is my very favorite thing I've done in Vevey. I just love it! I've sent other Fodor's folks there and everyone always enjoys it. There's also a Tuesday morning market but it's smaller and in a different location. Both are interesting and fun, and the real thing."

—suze

WELCOME TO VAUD

TOP REASONS TO GO

★ **Montreux's Promenade du Lac:** Walk three magical miles along Lac Léman (Lake Geneva) to the Château de Chillon, Switzerland's most beautiful castle.

★ **Tramping with Charlie Chaplin:** Vevey commemorates its celebrated citizen in bronze at its lake rose garden and is designing a museum in his honor in Corsier.

★ **Lausanne's table for two:** Acolyte of superchef Philippe Rochat, Benoit Violier is the new culinary king to watch.

★ **The grape escape:** From La Côte to Chablais, vineyards and wine cellars allow you to sip vintages that seldom make it beyond the border.

★ **Palatial pursuits:** Grandes dames of luxury, the Beau-Rivage Palace and Montreux Palace hotels even synchronize their gilded awnings to the sun's daily tour over the lake.

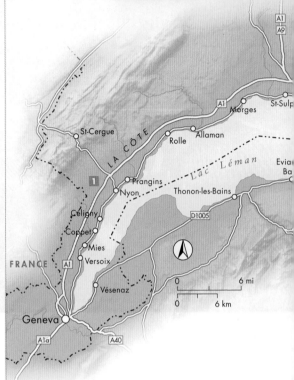

1 La Côte. Studded with wine villages, this region is famed for its châteaux—Prangins displays Swiss history and Morges has 10,000 miniature lead soldiers in residence. But don't miss waterside Nyon, founded by Julius Caesar.

2 Lausanne. Not quite the city it was when Voltaire, Rousseau, and Victor Hugo waxed passionate about its beauty, Lausanne is largely a modern maze, but here and there you'll enjoy a burnt-orange jumble of medieval rooftops, shuttered windows with flower boxes, and misty Lac Léman and the Alps. Happily, the art and nightlife scenes are lively.

3 Lavaux Vignobles and Riviera. Set amid wine villages, the gorgeously picturesque Corniche de Lavaux heads toward Vevey, home to food giant Nestlé.

12

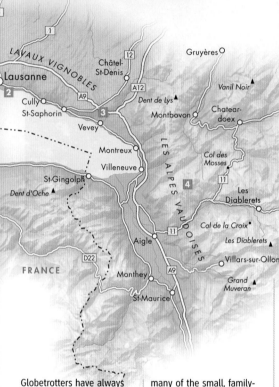

GETTING ORIENTED

Lac Léman is a graceful swelling in the Rhône River, which passes through the northern hook of the Valais and channels between the French and Vaudoise Alps before breaking into the open at Bouveret, west of Villeneuve. The lake is shared by three of Switzerland's great French cities, grandes dames of the Suisse Romande: Lausanne, Montreux, and Geneva. Though the lake's southern shore lies in France's Haute-Savoie, the green hillsides of the north portion and the cluster of nearby Alps that looms over its east end are all part of the canton of Vaud.

Globetrotters have always loved this romantic town—Rousseau, Henry James, and Hemingway are just a few who enjoyed taking walks here. More modern is Montreux: spilling down the hill to a sunny bay, this usually tranquil city goes hot-cool when the Jazz Festival takes over in July.

4 Les Alpes Vaudoises. Framed by a stunning castle, Aigle is the gateway to

many of the small, family-friendly resort towns high in the mountains above. Just across the steep summit of the Col des Mosses lies Château d'Oex, home to hot-air balloons and richly carved wooden chalets unique to the Pays d'Enhaut highlands.

LAC LÉMAN (LAKE GENEVA)

One of western Europe's largest lakes, Lac Léman (also called Lake Geneva) is shared by Switzerland and France. Swiss cantons Geneva and Vaud border it on the west, north, and east; canton Valais and France (Haute-Savoie) are to the south.

Lakeside gardens (above) bloom in spring and summer. Many enjoy biking around the lake (below, right); Château de Chillon (above, right) is one of the most photographed sites in Switzerland.

The lake is comprised of two parts: from Geneva to Yvoire (France) and Nyon (Vaud) is the "Petit Lac," which then opens out into the "Grand Lac."

The Musée du Léman in Nyon, Vaud, is devoted entirely to the lake, and has aquariums featuring lake fish. On land, from May through September the shorelines of cities and larger towns on the lake's Swiss side—Geneva, Nyon, Rolle, Morges, Lausanne, Vevey, and Montreux—take on a Riviera feel, their promenades, leisure harbors and port cafés teeming with life. During the cold months, when CGN boats don't even service smaller stops, port life everywhere quiets down, and off-season bleakness sets in.

—Gail Mangold-Vine

WHEN TO GO

The best time to visit Lac Léman is May through October. These are the months when your chances of getting sunny weather to cruise, swim, sunbathe, water-ski, and to see distant snowy Alpine peaks clear as a bell, are highest. It's also when the CGN and other boat companies run full schedules, so you'll have the biggest selection of stops and themed cruises to choose from.

WAYS TO EXPLORE

HARBORS AND BEACHES

You'll find small, usually free, grass and pebble beaches along the lakeshore. Some leisure harbors offer boat rentals (including paddleboats) and water sports. There are port cafés all along the lake—a summertime must is an after-dark lakeside dinner. Some eateries pride themselves on serving *only* Léman perch—the fish may otherwise come from lakes farther afield so if this is important to you, ask.

BY BOAT

Clear-day mountain views from the lake are breathtaking. Out of Geneva, Swiss Boat runs Petit Lac themed tours like "Parks and Famous Residences." You can cruise the Petit Lac or whole lake with CGN (the latter option takes a day). These are commuter boats, so you can also hop on in Montreux and cruise to Lausanne, or Geneva and go to Morges, whatever combo takes your fancy. Look into lunch and dinner cruises leaving from both Lausanne and Geneva: some gastronomic highflyers may be doing the catering. And don't forget France. Go to Yvoire to enjoy its Garden of the Five Senses or to Evian (of mineral water fame).

BY BIKE

If you wish to bike around the whole lake, count on a week to complete the loop. You can't cycle all the way; stretches by train or boat are inevitable. Most people prefer to do just a short portion. To begin planning, go to ⊕ *www.veloland.ch.* Check out sections six and seven of the Rhône Route from Montreux to Geneva via Morges (100 km [60 miles]); if leaving from Geneva, you'll be traveling the sections in reverse. Veloland gives you all the necessary info (in English), including where to rent bikes and recommended places to spend the night.

12

BEST PHOTO OPS

Photographically speaking, Lac Léman offers four big-ticket lens magnets. The first is quite simply the shoreline, as seen from an approaching boat: piers and promenades festooned with flags and strings of lights, geraniums tumbling out of window boxes, small boats, and swans and ducks bobbing on sparkling wavelets. **Geneva's Rade**, after dark, is a whole festival of twinkling lights. The second: those distant mountain peaks or the up-close-and-personal Chablais cliffs rising out of the south flank of the Grand Lac. The third is without a doubt the **Château de Chillon**, a medieval castle on the lake near Montreux, but spurring as many and maybe even more oohs and aahs is the fourth magnet nearby, a UNESCO World Heritage site: the terraced **Lavaux vineyards**, stepped steeply downwards to the gleaming blue water of the lake.

EATING WELL IN VAUD

The marvelous culinary delights of the region range from the elaborate concoctions of star chefs to the simplest fare.

Vaud's French influences are evident in the region's dishes, from fish caught in Lac Léman (above), to wines from the lakeside slopes (above, right). Sausages (below, right) are part of many traditional meals.

What's the common denominator? In any eatery worth its salt, it'll be *cuisine du marché:* cooking based on fresh market produce. Seasonal is the name of the game.

Like the rest of Switzerland, this region was part of France's Helvetic Republic in 1798 through 1803 and—although Vaud did some time under the House of Burgundy, and borders France to the west—French cooking here, as in *la cuisine française*, does not come out of historical tradition, but out of the relatively recent, essentially 20th-century, phenomenon that saw French restaurants spring up around the globe.

Which is not to say there aren't cross-influences, French and otherwise, in Vaudois cooking, best sampled in cozy *pintes* (wine pubs that serve food) that feature the finest local wines.

MALAKOFFS

The villages of Vinzel and Bursins are the best sources for a very local specialty, the *Malakoff*, which consists of a slice of Gruyère on a piece of toast that is then deep fried. These cheesy delights have always been a favorite of the Vaudois, but after the Crimean Wars they were renamed after a beloved officer who led his army of Vaud-born mercenaries to victory in the siege of Sebastopol.

12

PAPET VAUDOIS

The highlight of Vaudois cuisine, this dish is the unbeatable combination of slowly stewed leeks and potatoes, white wine, and spices, served with the classic pork-and-cabbage-stuffed sausage, *saucisse aux choux*.

FILETS DE PERCHE

Whether dusted with flour and fried in sweet cream butter à la meunière, or sautéed in a simple white wine sauce, this local fish has a ubiquitous place on every lakeside restaurant menu. There is a reason folks order it year-round—when served with thin, crispy frites and washed down with a chilled Chasselas, your taste buds will find themselves in seventh heaven. Beware that some perch in less trustworthy establishments comes from Eastern Europe, so be sure to ask for the real deal.

SAUSAGES

Legend has it that the occupied Vaudois chopped up the biggest hanks of ham to avoid giving them to their Bernese rulers. With copious small pieces of meat on their hands, it is only natural that charcuterie reigns supreme in the canton of Vaud. From the traditional Easter or Pentecôte *boutefas* (sausage stuffed in a pork bladder), to the famous cabbage-stuffed *saucisse aux choux* typically enjoyed from September to April, there is a smoked sausage to suit all tastes.

SWEETS

Desserts here are some of the best, and most unusual, in the country. The *salée au sucre* is a popular breakfast item for special occasions. A yeasty, salty doughnut of sorts, it is topped with a deliciously sweet, creamy filling—a Vaudois "cheese Danish" if you will. Real sweet tooths will prefer the *carac*, a miniature pie filled with dense chocolate ganache and glazed with neon green icing. And if you're tempted by historic desserts of yore, the *gâteau à la raisinée* or *gâteau au vin cuit*—sweetened with a thick syrup of reduced pear or apple juice—is a must-try.

WINE

Chasselas is to Vaud what Fendant is to Valais—a light, often slightly sparkling, white wine whose popularity is unparalleled in the region. While some say it lacks complex aromatic notes, crisp, clean Chasselas is a perfect match for buttery regional specialties like *filets de perche*. Be sure to try Chasselas in all its incarnations—the prestigious Dézaley, Mont-sur-Rolle, or Yvorne all make fine additions to any wine cellar.

Updated by
Alexis Munier

In just one region, you can experience a complete cultural, gastronomic, and scenic sweep of Switzerland. Vaud (pronounced Voh) has a stunning Gothic cathedral (Lausanne) and one of Europe's most evocative châteaux (Chillon), palatial hotels and weathered-wood chalets, sophisticated culture and ancient folk traditions, snowy Alpine slopes and balmy lake resorts, simple fondue and the finesse of some of the world's great chefs. Everywhere there are the roadside vineyards with luxurious rows of vines and rich, black loam.

This is the region of Lac Léman, a grand body of water graced by Lausanne and Montreux. The lake's romance—Savoy Alps looming across the horizon, steamers fanning across its surface, palm trees rustling along its shores—made it a focal point of the budding 19th-century tourist industry and an inspiration to the arts. In a Henry James novella the imprudent Daisy Miller made waves when she crossed its waters unchaperoned to visit Chillon; Byron's Bonivard languished in chains in the fortress's dungeons. In their homes outside Montreux, Stravinsky wrote *The Rite of Spring* and Strauss, his transcendent *Four Last Songs*. And perhaps going from the sublime to the ridiculous, film fans of James Bond will remember Sean Connery's car chase through the hillsides around Lac Léman in hot pursuit of Auric Goldfinger's Rolls as it swept its way to the villain's Swiss factory, neatly tucked in the mountains north of the lake.

Throughout the canton French is spoken, and the temperament the Vaudois inherited from the Romans and Burgundians sets them apart from their Swiss-German fellow citizens. It's evident in their humor, their style, and—above all—their love of their own good wine.

VAUD PLANNER

WHEN TO GO

The lake sparkles and clouds lift from Mont Blanc from spring to fall; November tends to be drizzly gray, and then winter brightens things up above the plain (as they call the flatter terrain surrounding the lake).

Crowds monopolize Montreux and Chillon year-round, but overwhelm them in July (jazz festival time) and August (Europe-wide vacations).

It's worth aiming for the concert and dance season in Lausanne: from September through May.

Remember that at these latitudes summer daylight extends until 9 pm, allowing you to pack a lot into one day; the reverse is true in winter.

PLANNING YOUR TIME

To experience the highlights of lake and mountain, reserve five days. Spend two savoring Lausanne and its Old Town, museums, and hyper-active waterfront. The Corniche route winds its way through the vine-yards and hamlets of the Lavaux. Pull-offs are strategically interspersed for photo ops and to steady the nerves of drivers not used to narrow, cantilevered roadways. Get out and walk a section of the wine trail and definitely taste a glass of white wine. A few hours in the harbor-front town of Vevey, especially its older section, and the glitzy, Riviera-like city of Montreux will suffice. A visit to the region would be incomplete without a tour of Chillon—the fabled fortress that inspired Lord Byron to pen his famous poem "Prisoner of Chillon."

GETTING HERE AND AROUND

AIR TRAVEL

Geneva International Airport is the most convenient hub for Vaud. Trains connect the airport to Nyon, Lausanne, Morges, Vevey, and Montreux—if you're heading to one of the smaller lakeside villages, you will likely have to make a connection in one of these towns. Taxis abound, but fares are steep—the one-way fare to Lausanne runs approximately 220 SF for the 45-minute ride. A *navette,* or shuttle, bus runs twice an hour to major cities in Vaud; most fares are under 50 SF.

Ground Transportation Contact Navette Leman ☎ *0800/107107* ⊕ *www.navetteleman.ch.*

BUS TRAVEL

A useful network of postbus routes covers the region if you want connections to outlying villages and hamlets. Throughout the Riviera, bus service is provided by *VMCV* (Vevey-Montreux-Chillon-Villeneuve). The Line 1 trolley bus parallels the lakefront and is the most heavily used. **▥TIP➜** Hotel guests receive a Riviera Card that allows gratis rides on buses and reduced fares on other modes of transportation.

Bus Contact VMCV ☎ *021/9891811* ⊕ *www.vmcv.ch.*

BOAT AND FERRY TRAVEL

Like all fair-size Swiss lakes, Lac Léman is crisscrossed with comfortable and reasonably swift steamers, here run by the Compagnie Générale de Navigation. In summer they sometimes run more often than the trains that parallel their routes. You can embark and disembark freely at ports along the way. The trip from one end of the lake to the other will take the better part of a day, as routes are designed to serve a third of the lake per circuit, connecting towns on both the French and Swiss sides. Shorter trips like the one from Lausanne to Vevey will take an hour.

Boat and Ferry Information Compagnie Générale de Navigation (*CGN*) ☎ *0848/811848* ⊕ *www.cgn.ch.*

CAR TRAVEL

There are two major arteries leading to Lac Léman, one entering from the north via Bern and Fribourg (A12), the other arcing over the north shore of Lac Léman from Geneva to Lausanne (A1), then to Montreux and on south through the Alpes Vaudoises toward the Col du Grand St-Bernard (A9) in Canton Valais. They are swift and often scenic express-ways, and the north-shore artery (A1 and A9) traces a route that has been followed since before Roman times.

Secondary highways parallel the expressways, but this is one case where, as the larger road sits higher on the lakeside slopes, the views from the expressway are often better than those from the highway. Be sure, however, to detour for the Corniche road views between Laus-anne and Vevey.

Rent the smallest car your physique and luggage will allow, as narrow lanes in wine villages and parking in cities are headaches. Although expensive, opt for public garages that are clearly signed whenever pos-sible. Take the ticket with you after entry, as payment is made via auto-mated machines at the pedestrian entrance; many locations accept credit cards. The ticket returned after payment is your access card to exit.

TRAIN TRAVEL

Lausanne lies on a major train route between Bern and Geneva, with express trains connecting from Basel and Zürich. Regional trains along the waterfront, connecting major lake towns, are frequent and swift unless you board one of the S-trains that stop at every village. Travel time between centers like Geneva and Nyon, or Lausanne and Vevey, is about 15 minutes; count on doubling that on an S-train.

There are also several private rail systems leading into small villages and rural regions, including the Montreux–Oberland–Bernois (MOB) Railroad's Golden Pass, which climbs sharply behind Montreux and cuts straight over the pre-Alps toward Château-d'Oex and the Berner Oberland. Reserve space in one of their glass-dome, panoramic cars and take in the countryside with food and beverage service brought to your seat. The historic Blonay–Chamby Railroad has steam-powered seasonal excursions, as does the Rochers-de-Naye line.

Train Contacts Blonay–Chamby Railroad ☎ *021/9432121* ⊕ *www.blonay-chamby.ch.* **Montreux–Oberland–Bernois Railroad** (*MOB*) ☎ *0840/245245* ⊕ *www.goldenpass.ch.*

⇨ *For more information on getting here and around, see Travel Smart Switzerland.*

12

RESTAURANTS

As in all great wine regions, *dégustation* (wine tasting) and *haute gastronomie* (refined cuisine) go hand in hand here. In inns and auberges throughout La Côte and Lavaux (the two stretches of vineyard-lined shore), you'll dine beside ascot-wearing oenophiles who lower their half lenses to study a label, then go on to order a multicourse feast to complement their extensive tastings.

To experience Vaud's best cuisine, look for *déjeuners d'affaires* (business lunches), plats du jour, and prix-fixe menus, which can offer considerable savings over à la carte dining.

Of course, you will be spoiled for choice by the quality of Lausanne's restaurants. Prices can be high, but if you wander through the backstreets you will see that the less affluent in Lausanne eat well, too.

Prices in the reviews are the average cost of a main course at dinner or, if dinner is not served, at lunch.

HOTELS

It's a pleasure unique to Vaud to wake up, part floor-length sheers, and look out over Lac Léman to Mont Blanc. A series of 19th-century grand hotels with banks of balconied lake-view rooms were created to offer this luxury, yet there's no shortage of charming inns offering similar views on an intimate scale. The hotels of Lausanne and Montreux are long on luxury and grace, and low prices are not easy to find. Especially at peak periods—Christmas to New Year's and June to August—it's important to book ahead. Small auberges in the villages along the lake and in the vineyards offer traditional dishes and simple comforts.

Prices in the reviews are the lowest cost of a standard double room in high season.

VISITOR INFORMATION

The main regional tourist office is located in Lausanne.

Visitor Information Office du Tourisme du Canton de Vaud ⊠ *60 av. d'Ouchy, Lausanne* ☎ *021/6132626* ⊕ *www.lake-geneva-region.ch.*

LA CÔTE

Just northeast of Geneva, La Côte (the shore) of Lac Léman has been settled since Roman times, with its south-facing slopes cultivated for wine. It is thus peppered with ancient waterfront and hillside towns, castles, and Roman remnants. Train and bus service connects most towns and villages, but a car is a must if you want to wind through tiny wine villages. Do get out and walk—if only to hear the trickling of any number of Romanesque trough fountains and to saunter along a lakefront promenade. Be willing to travel back and forth from the slopes to the waterfront a few times if you're determined to cover all the region's charms; sticking exclusively to either the diminutive Route du Vignoble or the shore road deprives you of some wonderful sights.

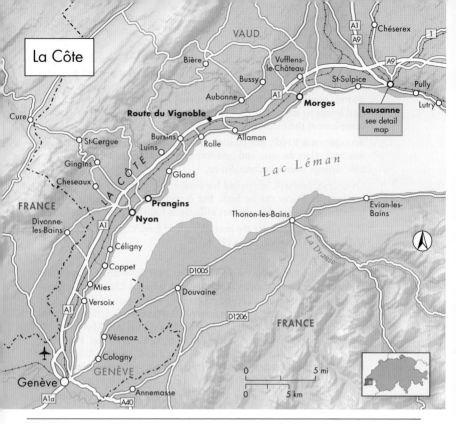

NYON

27 km (17 miles) southwest of Lausanne.

Lovely Nyon, with its waterfront drive, shops, museums, and a castle dominating its cliff-top Old Town, was founded by Julius Caesar around 45 BC as a camp for war veterans. Lovely views can be had from the château-museum's terrace and the town's waterfront promenade, where boats and swans bob in the waves.

GETTING HERE AND AROUND

Nyon is one of the primary stations of the main rail line that goes along the shore of Lac Léman, served by all trains (regional and interregional). There are multiple arrivals and departures every hour. Most sights can be easily reached by foot, as the station is centrally located and just a five-minute walk from the historic Old Town.

ESSENTIALS

Visitor Information Nyon Région Tourisme ⊠ *8 av. Viollier* ☎ *022/3656600* ⊕ *www.nyon-tourisme.ch.*

EXPLORING

Château de Nyon. Dominating Nyon's hilltop over the waterfront is the Château de Nyon, a magnificent 12th-century multispire fortress with a terrace that takes in sweeping views of the lake and Mont

VAUD TOUR OPTIONS

Walking tours led by local historians in Lausanne, Vevey, and Montreux are increasingly popular. They are organized by the towns' tourist offices and are given daily between April and September.

English-speaking guides are often available, but you should call in advance to check. Most local tourist offices offer daily general tours in summer to Gruyères, to Chamonix and Mont Blanc, and to Les Avants and Château-d'Oex by the

Montreux–Oberland–Bernois railroad line's panoramic train. There is also a chocolate excursion to the Cailler factory in Broc. To ensure a tour with English commentary, reserve in advance.

The Lausanne tourist office runs a daily two-hour coach trip into the Old Town, including a visit to the cathedral and an extended city coach tour that takes in the Lavaux vineyards.

Blanc. Its spacious rooms hold the collection of the **Musée Historique,** which traces the history of the castle inhabitants from residence by the Dukes of Savoy (1293–1536) through occupation by the Bernese (1536–1798) to reclamation by the canton following the Vaud revolution. The upper floors held prisoners until 1979, while the city council and courts met in chambers here until 1999. Exhibits throughout highlight the city's position as a renowned porcelain center. Modern-day conversions include a marriage salon and a *caveau des vignerons* (wine cellar) featuring wines of local growers. ⊠ *Pl. du Château* 022/3638351 ⊕ *www.chateaudenyon.ch* 8 SF, includes *Musée du Léman and Musée Romain* ⏱ Apr.–Oct., Tues.–Sun. 10–5; Nov.–Mar., Tues.–Sun. 2–5.

Musée du Léman. Nestled in a charming floral park that parallels the water, the Musée du Léman has interactive exhibits about the fragile ecosystems of the lake, recreational boating activities, and coast-guard rescue techniques. There's a sizable aquarium, housed in a shuttered 18th-century hospital. ⊠ *8 quai Louis-Bonnard* 022/3610949 ⊕ *www.museeduleman.ch* 8 SF, includes *Musée Romain and Château de Nyon* ⏱ Apr.–Oct., Tues.–Sun. 10–5; Nov.–Mar., Tues–Sun. 2–5.

★ **Musée Romain** (*Roman Museum*). Graced by a statue of Caesar, the Musée Romain contains an attractively mounted collection of sumptuously detailed architectural stonework, fresco fragments, statuary, mosaics, and earthenware. The museum was built atop the foundation of a 1st-century AD basilica; a pristine miniature model inside and an excellent trompe l'oeil palace on an outside wall evoke the remarkable original structure. A listing of the exhibits is available in English, as are guided tours. ⊠ *Rue Maupertuis* 022/3617591 ⊕ *www.mrn.ch* 8 SF, includes *Musée du Léman and Château de Nyon* ⏱ Apr.–Oct., Tues.–Sun. 10–5; Nov.–Mar., Tues.–Sun. 2–5.

La Château de Nyon sits prominently above the lakeside town's waterfront.

WHERE TO EAT AND STAY

$$
ITALIAN
✕ **Auberge du Château.** This Italian eatery, just steps from Nyon's château, serves straightforward fare, well-priced plats du jour, and specialty items like shrimp and vegetables on a pillow of saffron cream. In fall the menu expands to include an assortment of game and locally picked mushrooms. An expansive terrace lets diners study the château; in winter broad windows reveal the comings and goings on the municipal plaza. $ *Average main: 26 SF* ⊠ *8 pl. du Château* ☎ *022/3610032.*

$$
HOTEL
🖼 **Hôtel Ambassador.** Terra-cotta stucco and peaked dormers set off this petite hotel on Nyon's main thoroughfare. **Pros:** in upper part of town, which provides best access to sights and shopping; easy parking across the street. **Cons:** nicely laid-out rooms are on the small side; standard fare at the restaurant. $ *Rooms from: 200 SF* ⊠ *26 rue St-Jean* ☎ *022/9944848* ⊕ *www.hotel-ambassador-nyon.ch* ⇌ *18 rooms* ⊫ *Breakfast.*

PRANGINS

3 km (2 miles) northeast of Nyon.

You'll see the elegant hillside château that's home to the national museum before you reach this little commune, where the pace of life moves gently between the *boulangerie* (bakery), post office, and café.

GETTING HERE AND AROUND

Take a train to the Nyon station and switch to local bus service that picks up passengers outside the main entrance. The ride takes seven minutes to the village stop; from there it is a three-minute walk to the château.

EXPLORING

★ **Musée National Suisse** (*Swiss National Museum*). The 18th-century Château de Prangins is home to the Suisse Romande branch of the Musée National Suisse. The castle once had land holdings that stretched all the way to Rolle. Its four floors detail (in four languages, including English) Swiss life in the 18th and 19th centuries. Surrounded by parks and gardens (take note of the extensive culinary plantings set according to ancient documents), the museum is also a major venue for cultural events and regional celebrations. A café with terrace is open for lunch and refreshments. ⊠ *Av. Général Guiguer* ☎ *022/9948890* ⊕ *www. musee-suisse.ch* ⊠ *10 SF* ☉ *Tues.–Sun. 11–5, Thurs. 11–7.*

QUICK
BITES

Rapp Chocolatier. After strolling the galleries and gardens of the National Museum, head to Rapp Chocolatier, a petite chocolate shop in the heart of town. Here handmade confections are stacked in perfect pyramids, and a school and demonstration kitchen are adjacent, so if your timing is right you'll see artisans shaping molten cocoa and plying their forms with heavenly fillings. ⊠ *6 rue des Alpes* ☎ *022/3617914* ⊕ *www.chocolaterie-rapp. com* ☉ *Closed Sun.*

WHERE TO STAY

$$$
HOTEL

La Barcarolle. Hidden in a parklike setting off the lake road, this mustard-colored *relais* (inn) sits amid historic châteaux and country homes. **Pros:** secluded idyllic retreat; grand rooms with lots of amenities. **Cons:** must have a car to cover the distance to other villages. $ *Rooms from: 330 SF* ⊠ *Rte. de Promenthoux* ☎ *022/3657878* ⊕ *www.labarcarolle.ch* ⊃ *36 rooms, 3 suites* ⊗ *Breakfast.*

EN
ROUTE

Rolle. About 12 km (7 miles) northeast of Nyon, the lakefront village of Rolle merits a detour for a look at its dramatic 13th-century château, built at the water's edge by a Savoyard prince. While in town you can visit the Moinat Antiques and Decoration shop for a sample of what it takes to furnish a grand country home. ⊠ *Rolle* ⊕ *www.tourisme-rolle.ch.*

ROUTE DU VIGNOBLE

36 km (22 miles) between Nyon and Lausanne.

Parallel to the waterfront highway, threading through the steep-sloping vineyards between Nyon and Lausanne, the Route du Vignoble (Vineyard Road) unfolds a rolling green landscape high above the lake, punctuated by noble manors and vineyards.

Luins, home of the flinty, fruity white wine of the same name, is a typical pretty village.

Just up the road, the village of **Vinzel** develops its own white wines on sunny slopes and sells them from the *vin-celliers* (wine cellars) that inspired its name.

The route continues through **Bursins,** home of an 11th-century Romanesque church, and goes all the way to **Morges.** The road is clearly signposted throughout.

MORGES

23 km (14 miles) northeast of Prangins, 8 km (5 miles) west of Lausanne.

On the waterfront just west of the urban sprawl of Lausanne, Morges is a pleasant lake town favored by sailors and devotees of its **Fête de la Tulipe** (Tulip Festival), held annually in April and May.

ESSENTIALS

Visitor Information Morges Région Tourisme ⊠ *2 rue du Château* ☎ *021/8013233* ⊕ *www.morges-tourisme.ch.*

EXPLORING

☙ *La Liberté.* The oar-powered warships of the Greeks, Romans, and Phoenicians once crossed the waters of Lac Léman. Now you can follow in their wake on *La Liberté,* a reconstruction of a 17th-century galley. This brainchild of historian Jean-Pierre Hirt is part public works project, part historical re-creation. The 183-foot ship sails the lake Saturday evening and twice Sunday afternoon from mid-May to mid-October; the two-hour tour costs 38 SF. You must book space in advance. ⊠ *45 rue de Lausanne* ☎ *021/8035031* ⊕ *www.galere.ch.*

Musée Alexis Forel. In the heart of town, a 16th-century courtyard-centered mansion, once home to renowned engraver Alexis Forel, displays the holdings of the Musée Alexis Forel. Although most of Forel's exceptional engravings are in the Musée Jenisch, in Vevey, here you can experience his home surroundings. Thick-beamed salons filled with high-back chairs, stern portraits, and delicate china remain as they were in the 1920s, when musicians and writers such as Stravinsky, Paderewski, and Rolland gathered for lively discussions and private concerts. An attic room has a selection of 18th-century puppets and porcelain dolls. ⊠ *54 Grand-Rue* ☎ *021/8012647* ⊕ *www.museeforel. ch* ☎ *10 SF* ☉ *Mid Mar.–early Dec., Wed.–Sun. 2–6.*

Musée du Château. The town's castle, built by the duke of Savoy around 1286 as a defense against the bishop-princes of Lausanne, now houses the Musée du Château. The eclectic collection includes weapons, military uniforms, and 10,000 miniature lead soldiers. In the Salle Général Henri Guisan, you'll find memorabilia of this World War II general, much honored for keeping both sides happy enough to leave Switzerland safely alone. ⊠ *Rue de Château* ☎ *021/3160990* ⊕ *www. musees-vd.ch* ☎ *10 SF* ☉ *Mar.–Nov., weekdays 10–noon and 1:30–5, weekends 1:30–5; July and Aug., Tues.–Sun. 10–5.*

OFF THE BEATEN PATH

Vufflens-le-Château. This village, 2 km (1 mile) northwest of Morges, is known for its namesake château, a 15th-century Savoyard palace with a massive donjon and four lesser towers, all trimmed in fine Piedmont-style brickwork. It's privately owned, but the grounds are open to the public. ✉ *Vufflens-le-Château.*

WHERE TO EAT AND STAY

$$$$ FRENCH ★ 🍴 **L'Ermitage des Ravet.** A multicourse gastronomic treat awaits at the restaurant in this 17th-century farmhouse set beneath old, draping trees. Chef Bernard Ravet and his family serve the classics with modern twists. Son Guy, who trained at top addresses in France and the United States, is prepping to step into his father's shoes, while daughter and sommelier Nathalie pours carefully paired vintages. Pastry magic is in the hands of another daughter, as the chef's wife presides over the dining room. Artistry on the plate includes four styles of duck and goose foie gras or saddle of venison with truffles and chanterelles. The business lunch is a gem. Chic guest rooms beg a stay for the night. [$] *Average main: 65 SF* ✉ *26 rte. du Village, Vufflens-le-Château* ☎ *021/8046868* ✍ *Reservations essential* 🕒 *Closed Sun. and Mon., late Dec., and Aug.*

$$$$ HOTEL 🏨 **Hotel Fleur du Lac.** This lakefront retreat, just outside town on the main route to Lausanne, is surrounded by abundant gardens and stately old trees. **Pros:** resort feel, with private dock and lake access; connected to town by lakefront pathway. **Cons:** not close to the train station. [$] *Rooms from: 358 SF* ✉ *70 rue de Lausanne* ☎ *021/8115811* 🌐 *www.fleur-du-lac.ch* 🛏 *31 rooms, 7 suites.*

LAUSANNE

66 km (41 miles) northeast of Geneva, 108 km (67 miles) southwest of Bern.

"Lausanne is a block of picturesque houses, spilling over two or three gorges, which spread from the same central knot, and are crowned by a cathedral like a tiara. On the esplanade of the church . . . I saw the lake over the roofs, the mountains over the lake, clouds over the mountains, and stars over the clouds." Such was Victor Hugo's impression of this grand and graceful tiered city. Voltaire, Rousseau, Byron, and Cocteau all waxed equally passionate about Lausanne—and not only for its visual beauty. It has been a cultural center for centuries, the world drawn first to its magnificent Gothic cathedral and the powers it represented, then to its university, and during the 18th and 19th centuries to its vibrant intellectual and social life. Today the Swiss consider Lausanne a most desirable city in which to live.

Rising in tiers from the lakeside at Ouchy, Lausanne covers three hills that are separated by gorges that once channeled rivers. The rivers have been built over, and huge bridges span the gaps across the hilltops. On one hill in particular, modern skyscrapers contrast brutally with the beautiful proportions of the cathedral rising majestically from its crest. Atmospheric alleys and narrow streets have mostly been demolished, yet the Old Town clustered around the cathedral has been painstakingly restored.

Below the Old Town spreads the commercial city center, and in the bottom of the hollow between Avenue Jules Gonin and Rue de Genève is

Visit Palace de la Palud in Lausanne on Wednesday or Saturday to browse the market.

the Flon, a neighborhood with plenty of nightspots. Still farther south, along the lake, is the separate township of Ouchy, an animated resort area dominated by the Château d'Ouchy, with a tower dating from the Middle Ages.

GETTING HERE AND AROUND

Lausanne serves as gateway to the region and connector for the east–west routes across the Alps to Milan (three hours) and the TGV to Paris or Avignon (four hours). From Geneva, trains take about 30 minutes and arrive in Lausanne up to four times an hour; from Bern they take a little more than an hour and arrive twice an hour.

While you're here, you will exhaust yourself if you attempt to walk the hillsides of Lausanne from lakefront Ouchy to hilltop Old Town. So do what the locals do and use the Transports Publics de la Région Lausannoise, a subway, rail, and bus network. The Métro subway is the quickest vertical ride from lake to suburbs with stops at the main train station, trendy Flon, and Bessières (cathedral) before terminating in Epalinges. The automated ticket machines can be confusing, as they list all routes.

There are two handy branches of Lausanne Tourisme, one at the main train station and other at the subway station in Ouchy. The former is open daily 9–7, while the latter has the same hours April–September and closes an hour earlier October–March. The main office is open weekdays 9–5. *Mobilis*, a pass that combines all rail and bus services, starts at 8.60 SF for a daily pass. ■ TIP➔ The Lausanne Transport Card provided to all hotel guests is free, and so are your rides on local buses, trains, and the Metro.

ESSENTIALS

Visitor Information Lausanne Tourisme ✉ *2 av. de Rhodanie* ☎ *021/6137373* ⊕ *www.lausanne-tourisme.ch.*

EXPLORING

TOP ATTRACTIONS

Fodor's Choice ★ **Cathédrale de Notre-Dame** (*Cathedral of Our Lady*). A Burgundian Gothic architectural treasure, this cathedral is Switzerland's largest church—and probably its finest. Begun in the 12th century by Italian, Flemish, and French architects, it was completed in 1275. Pope Gregory X came expressly to perform the historic consecration ceremony—of double importance, as it also served as a coronation service for Rudolf of Habsburg as the new Holy Roman Emperor.

Viollet-le-Duc, a renowned restorer who worked on the cathedrals of Chartres and Notre-Dame-de-Paris, brought portions of the building to Victorian Gothic perfection in the 19th century. His repairs are visible as paler stone contrasting with the weathered local sandstone.

Streamlined to the extreme, without radiating chapels or the excesses of later Gothic trim, the cathedral wasn't always so spare; in fact, there was brilliant painting. Zealous Reformers plastered over the florid colors, but in so doing they unwittingly preserved them, and now you can see portions of these splendid shades restored in the right transept. The dark and delicate choir contains the 14th-century tomb of the crusader Otto I of Grandson and exceptionally fine 13th-century choir stalls, unusual for their age alone, not to mention their beauty. The church's masterpiece, the 13th-century painted portal, is considered one of Europe's most magnificent. A tribute to 21st-century technology, the 7,000-pipe organ fills the sanctuary with swells of sacred music.

Holding fast to tradition, the cathedral has maintained a *guet,* or "look-out," since 1405. The guet sleeps in the belfry and is charged with crying out every hour on the hour between 10 pm and 2 am.

Protestant services (the cathedral was reformed in the 16th century) exclude nonworshipping visitors on Sunday at 10 am and 8 pm. You may want to come instead for the evening concerts given on an almost weekly basis in spring and autumn. Guided tours are given July to mid-September. ✉ *Pl. de la Cathédrale, Old Town* ☎ *021/3167161* ☉ *Apr.–Oct., weekdays 7–7, weekends 8–7; Sept.–Mar.., weekdays 7–5:30, weekends 8–5:30.*

Château St-Maire. The fortresslike elements of this 15th-century stone cylinder certainly came into play. The castle was built for the bishops of Lausanne; during the 16th century the citizens wearied of ecclesiastical power and allied themselves with Bern and Fribourg against the bishops protected within. Before long, however, Bern itself marched on Lausanne, put a bailiff in this bishops' castle, and stripped the city fathers of their power. Today the Château St-Maire is the seat of the cantonal government. ✉ *Pl. du Château, Old Town.*

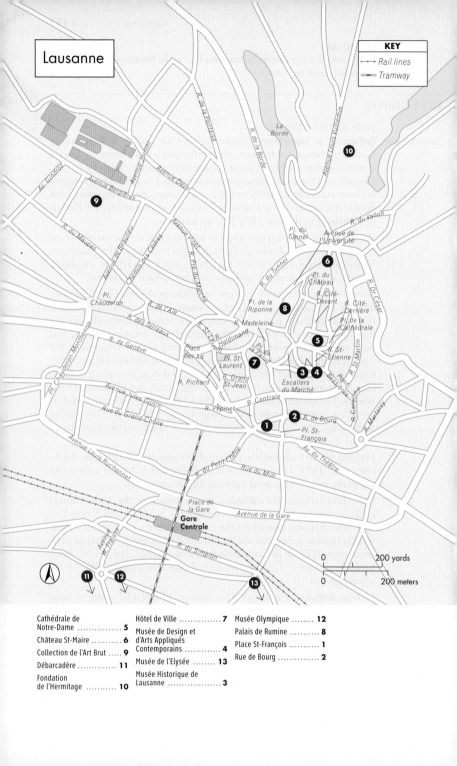

Lausanne

La Borde

R. de la Pontaise

R. de la Borde

R. du Vallon

Avenue Louis Vulliemin

Av. Gindroz

Avenue Jomini

Avenue Dape

Avenue Bergières

9

R. du Maupas

R. de Beaulieu

Chemin des Cèdres

Avenue Villet

R. Préd. Marché

Pl. du Tunnel

Avenue de l'Université

R. du Tunnel

R. Dr. César

Pl. Chauderon

R. de l'Ale

R. des Terreaux

R. St-Jean

R. Haldimand

R. Madeleine

Pl. de la Riponne

Pl. du Château

R. Cité-Devant

R. Cité-Derrière

Pl. de la Cathédrale

6

8

5

R. St-Martin

R. St-Étienne

Pont Bessières

R. César

R. Mariaux

Pl. Chauderon-Montbenon

R. de Genève

Place Bel-Air

Pl. St-Laurent

Pl. de la Palud

7

R. Grand St-Jean

R. Pichard

3 **4**

Escaliers du Marché

Avenue Jules Gonin

Rue du Grand-Chêne

R. Pépinet

R. Centrale

1 **2** R. de Bourg

Pl. St-François

Avenue Louis Ruchonnet

R. du Petit Chêne

Rue du Midi

Av. du Théâtre

Place de la Gare

Gare Centrale

Avenue de la Gare

Avenue W. Fraisse

R. du Simplon

11 **12**

13

0 ____ 200 yards

0 ____ 200 meters

A self portrait of Viollet-le-Duc, restorer of the Cathédrale de Notre-Dame, appears in the face of King David to the right of the main portal.

x

OFF THE BEATEN PATH

Cimetière du Bois-de-Vaux. Always adorned with white flowers, as was her signature style, the grave of Coco Chanel lies within a large wooded cemetery park on the western edge of the city. Urban legend has it that Madame Chanel's beloved companion, her dog, is buried not far away in the pet cemetery on the grounds of the stately Beau-Rivage Palace. The cemetery is accessible by the No. 25 bus toward Bourdonnette, or the Nos. 1 and 6 toward Maladière. ⊠ *2 rte. de Chavannes* ☉ *Daily dawn–dusk.*

★ **Collection de l'Art Brut.** This singular museum focuses on the genre of fringe or "psychopathological" art, dubbed *l'art brut* (raw art) in the 1940s by French artist Jean Dubuffet. His own collection forms the base of this ensemble of raw material from untrained minds—prisoners, schizophrenics, or the merely obsessed. Strangely enough, the collection is housed in the Château de Beaulieu, a former mansion of Madame de Staël, she of the sophisticated salons. The exhibits range from intricate yarn and textile pieces to a wall full of whimsical seashell masks. One of the most affecting works is a panel of rough carvings made by an asylum patient in solitary confinement; it was shaped with a broken spoon and a chamber-pot handle. You can get here by walking up Avenue Vinet or by taking Bus No. 2 from Place St-François in the direction of Désert. ⊠ *11 av. des Bergières, Beaulieu* ☎ *021/3152570* ⊕ *www.artbrut.ch* 🖅 *10 SF, free the 1st Sat. of month* ☉ *July and Aug., daily 11–6; Sept.–June, Tues.–Sun. 11–6.*

A GOOD WALK: LAUSANNE

Begin in the commercial hub of the city, the **Place St-François** (nicknamed "Sainfe" by the Lausannois), where you'll see the former Franciscan Église St-François. Behind the church, take a near hairpin turn right onto the fashionable main shopping street, the ancient **Rue de Bourg.** At the top of Rue de Bourg, Rue Caroline leads you left and left again over the Pont Bessières, where you can see the city's peculiar design spanning gorges and covered rivers.

Crossing the bridge and bearing right brings you up into the Old Town. On your left, the imposing palace of the Old Bishopric now houses the **Musée Historique de Lausanne.**

Adjacent is the **Musée de Design et d'Arts Appliqués Contemporains,** known as the "Mudac" to locals. Straight ahead, at the top of Rue St-Étienne, towers the tremendous **Cathédrale de Notre-Dame,** which is on par with some of Europe's finest churches.

With the cathedral on your left, walk up the narrow passage of Rue Cité-Derrière to the Place du Château and its eponymous monument, the **Château St-Maire.** As you face the château, turn left and walk down the Rue Cité-Devant.

As you pass the cathedral again, veer right toward a flight of wooden steps that leads down to the dramatic Escaliers du Marché, a wood-roof medieval staircase, and the Place de la Palud and the **Hôtel de Ville,** the seat of the municipal and communal councils. Turning right, just up Rue Madeleine, you will come upon the Place de la Riponne and the imposing **Palais de Rumine.**

A long hike up Avenue Vinet, northwest of the Old Town, will take you to the **Collection de l'Art Brut,** an unusual museum of fringe.

South of the Old Town, Ouchy's **Débarcadère** has typical quayside attractions—vendors and people strolling on a promenade. It can be easily reached by the steep subway Métro; there are stations across from the Gare Centrale and under the Rue du Grand-Chêne in the Flon. (There's also a large underground parking garage, a boon in this space-pressed city.)

Just east of Ouchy, on a hillside overlooking the lake, the dramatic **Musée Olympique** tells about the history and sports of the Olympic Games. At this writing the museum is closed for renovations, but is slated to reopen by the end of 2013. It's less than half a mile from the Débarcadère along the Quai de Belgique, which turns into the Quai d'Ouchy.

Uphill and connected by garden pathways, the **Musée de l'Elysée** is a photography museum housed in a restored 18th-century *campagne* (country manor home).

The Collection de l'Art Brut features "psychopathological" art from a variety of nontraditional artists.

🕅 **Débarcadère** (*Wharf*). In fine weather the waterfront buzzes day and night—strollers, diners, concertgoers, in-line skaters, artisans selling their wares—while the white steamers that land here add to the traffic. ⊠ *Pl. du Port, Ouchy.*

★ **Fondation de l'Hermitage.** A 15-minute bus ride from Old Town takes you to this beautifully set 19th-century country home. The estate is now an impressive art gallery with a fine permanent collection of Vaudois artists and headline-grabbing, yet seriously presented, blockbuster shows. Exhibits have included the works of Picasso, Giacometti, and the American Impressionists. Details of the elegant villa have been preserved, including intricate moldings, carved fireplaces, and multipatterned parquet floors. Allow time for a walk on the grounds and coffee at L'esquisse, the café surrounded by the outlying orangery. To get here, take Bus No. 3 from Gare Centrale to the Motte stop or Bus No. 16 from Place St-François to Hermitage. ⊠ *2 rte. du Signal, Sauvabelin* ☎ *021/3125013* ⊕ *www.fondation-hermitage.ch* ⊠ *18 SF* ☉ *Tues., Wed., and Fri.–Sun. 10–6, Thurs. 10–9.*

Hôtel de Ville (*Town Hall*). Constructed between the 15th and 17th century, this is the seat of municipal and communal councils. A painted, medieval **Fontaine de la Justice** (*Justice Fountain*) draws strollers to lounge on its heavy rim. Across the street you can watch the modern **animated clock,** donated to the city by local merchants; moving figures appear every hour on the hour. A street market is held in the square every Wednesday and Saturday morning. ⊠ *2 pl. de la Palud, city center* ☎ *021/3152556* ⊠ *Free.*

Musée Historique de Lausanne (*Lausanne History Museum*). The Ancien-Évêché (Old Bishopric) holds a wealth of both temporary and permanent historical exhibits about the city. Don't miss the 250-square-foot scale model of 17th-century Lausanne, with its commentary illuminating the neighborhoods' histories. Also look for the re-created 19th-century shop windows. ⊠ *4 pl. de la Cathédrale, Old Town* ☎ *021/3154101* ⊕ *www.lausanne.ch/MHL* ⊠ *8 SF* ☺ *July and Aug., Mon.–Thurs. 11–6, Fri.–Sun. 11–5; Sept.–June, Tues.–Thurs. 11–6, Fri.–Sun. 11–5.*

Place St-François (*St. Francis Square*). The stone-paved square is dominated by the massive post office and the former Franciscan **Église St-François** (*Church of St. Francis*), built during the 13th and 14th centuries. From 1783 to 1793, Edward Gibbon lived in a house on the site of the post office and there finished his work on *The Decline and Fall of the Roman Empire.* ⊠ *St-François.*

Café Saint François. This casual gathering spot opposite the church serves decadent pastries and inventive light meals year-round on the heated terrace. If you're famished, head upstairs to the Brasserie for the signature beef entrecôte and frites—the best in town—washed down with a glass of full-bodied local Cornalin. ⊠ *5 pl. St-François* ☎ *021/3202751.*

Rue de Bourg. Once a separate village isolated on a natural ridge, this is now Lausanne's fashionable main shopping street. Narrow and cobblestoned, it's lined with platinum-card stores such as Hermès and Louis Vuitton. Boutiques have been built into the centuries-old buildings, though some have added fittingly modern facades. ⊠ *St-François.*

WORTH NOTING

Musée de Design et d'Arts Appliqués Contemporains (*Museum of Contemporary Design and Applied Arts*). A museum of contemporary design seems amiss in this ancient quarter of the city, but it demonstrates the passion for art in everyday life. Temporary and permanent installations in the restored Maison Gaudard feature glassworks, textiles, and graphics. Creative and performing arts merge in multimedia shows. ⊠ *6 pl. de la Cathédrale, Old Town* ☎ *021/3152530* ⊕ *www.mudac.ch* ⊠ *10 SF* ☺ *Tues.–Sun. 11–6.*

☺ **Musée de l'Elysée.** Stark white walls and parquet floors form an inviting backdrop for the changing array of contemporary photography assembled by this museum in an 18th-century country manor. Wander the rooms, cellar, and attic spaces to view multiple exhibitions—some interactive and designed especially for children. The park surrounding the estate is a quiet place to find a shaded bench and critique the current show. ⊠ *18 av. de l'Elysée, Ouchy* ☎ *021/3169911* ⊕ *www.elysee.ch* ⊠ *8 SF* ☺ *Tues.–Sun 11–6.*

☺ **Musée Olympique** (*Olympic Museum*). With high-tech presentations and touching mementos, this complex pays tribute to the athletic tradition in ancient Greece, the development of the modern Games, the evolution of the individual sports, Paralympic competitions, and to the athletes themselves. There are art objects—an Etruscan torch from the 6th century BC, Rodin's *American Athlete*—as well as archival

12

films and videos, interactive displays, photographs, coins and stamps, and medals from various eras throughout Olympic history. A sculpture park, museum shop, and lovely café overlooking the lake complete this ambitious, world-class endeavor. Brochures and guided tours are available in English. The museum is closed for renovations until late 2013. ⊠ *1 quai d'Ouchy, Ouchy* ☎ *021/6216511* ⊕ *www.olympic.org* 🎫 *15 SF* ⊘ *Apr.–Oct., daily 9–6; Nov.–Mar., Tues.–Sun. 9–6.*

🐾 **Palais de Rumine.** Built at the turn of the last century, this enormous neo-Renaissance structure houses several museums, all with a local spin. The top exhibit at the **Musée Cantonal d'Archéologie et d'Histoire** (Cantonal Archaeology and History Museum) is the gold bust of Marcus Aurelius discovered at nearby Avenches in 1939. The **Musée Cantonal de Géologie** (Cantonal Geology Museum) has an excellent fossil collection, including a mammoth skeleton. Besides its collection of regional fauna, the **Musée Cantonal de Zoologie** (Cantonal Zoology Museum) has a rare collection of comparative anatomy. The **Musée Cantonal des Beaux-Arts** (Cantonal Museum of Fine Arts) has an enlightening collection of Swiss art, not only by the Germanic Hodler and Anker but also by Vaud artists—especially Bocion, whose local landscapes are well worth study during a visit to this region. Each museum has some descriptions or an abbreviated guide in English. Combination tickets cost 8 SF, so if you buy a ticket for one museum, you'll get free entry to the others. ■ **TIP→ All museums offer free admission the first Saturday of the month.** ⊠ *6 pl. de la Riponne, city center* ⊕ *www.musees.vd.ch* ⊘ *Tues.–Thurs. 11–6, Fri.–Sun. 11–5.*

WHERE TO EAT

$$$
SWISS
★

✕ **Café Beau-Rivage.** As if turning its back on star sibling Anne-Sophie Pic and the aristocratic Beau-Rivage Palace, which shelters both, this young, lively brasserie-café faces the lake and the Ouchy waterfront scene. Its flashy brass-and-Biedermeier dining area and bar fill with smart Lausannois and internationals enjoying trendy cuisine du marché. In summer the pillared terrazzo terrace (protected from embarcadero traffic by rose gardens) is the place to go; dine on Tandoori prawns with lemongrass chop suey or sea bream with Niçoise potatoes. Ⓢ *Average main: 50 SF* ⊠ *17–19 pl. du Port, Ouchy* ☎ *021/6133330* ⊕ *www.brp. ch* ⚐ *Reservations essential.*

$
SWISS
★

✕ **Café Romand.** All the customers seem to know each other at this vast, smoky dining institution, where shared wooden tables and clattering china create the perfect ambience for fondue, mussels, sausage, or *choucroûte* (sauerkraut). Prominent members of Lausanne's arts community swarm here after rehearsals and concerts, as service continues until 11 pm—late by Swiss standards. Ⓢ *Average main: 24 SF* ⊠ *2 pl. St-François, St-François* ☎ *021/3126375* ⊘ *Closed Sun.*

$$
ECLECTIC
★

✕ **Étoile Blanche.** This hip café, bar, and restaurant is beloved by students, business executives, and artists alike. Appetizers such as tempura zucchini flowers and main courses like chicken tagine with apricots are deliciously refined—their humble prices make this popular eatery a rare bargain. Brunch is served on Sunday afternoon, while Sunday evening offers the "Table de George"—the chef's special menu of appetizer, main course, and cheese selection for around 26 SF. The simple yet eclectic decor features vintage advertisements and polished wood seating, and several tables are available outside during the summer months. The bar boasts seven beers on tap, a dizzying number by Swiss standards. $ *Average main: 30 SF* ⊠ *Place Benjamin-Constant, city center* ☎ *021/3512460* ⊕ *www.etoileblanche.ch.*

$
FAST FOOD

✕ **Holy Cow!.** Lausannois can feast on freshly grilled, juicy burgers while avoiding the town's three McDonald's. At this self-proclaimed gourmet burger bar, you can chow down on the Elvis burger with blue cheese and bacon or the veggie burger with warm goat cheese, arugula, and spicy chutney. The management has a refreshing "go-local" philosophy, and most ingredients are produced within a 40-km (25-mile) radius. $ *Average main: 14 SF* ⊠ *Rue des Terreaux 10, city center* ☎ *079/8197050* ⊕ *www.holycow.ch* ⌲ *Reservations not accepted* ▭ *No credit cards* ⊙ *Mon.–Thurs. 11–10, Fri. and Sat. 11–11.*

$$$
ECLECTIC

✕ **La Pomme de Pin.** Behind the cathedral, this winsome *pinte* (wine pub)—one of Lausanne's oldest—produces an eclectic menu ranging from French to Italian to Swiss (rabbit and Rösti, anyone?), along with reasonably priced *plats du jour,* served in the casual café and the adjoining linen-decked restaurant. The glass-panel door is often left ajar by neighbors dropping in for a glass of wine or espresso and a quick round of gossip. $ *Average main: 42 SF* ⊠ *11–13 rue Cité-Derrière, Old Town* ☎ *021/3234656* ⊕ *www.lapommedepin.ch* ⊙ *Closed Sun. No lunch Sat. No dinner Wed.*

$$
MODERN FRENCH

✕ **Nomade.** This trendy restaurant-wine bar is one of Lausanne's rendezvous spots for the 30-and-over crowd. Chic yet comfy decor prevails in the cocktail area, while tall communal tables in the wine bar allow for easy mixing and mingling. A top-notch wine list features more than 30 wines served by the glass, with both local and imported varieties. If you're famished, try the tortellini stuffed with prawns and a basil coulis, or panfried scallops drenched in a seafood sauce. $ *Average main: 38 SF* ⊠ *Pl. de l'Europe 9, Flon* ☎ *021/3201313* ⊕ *www.restaurantnomade. ch* ⊙ *No lunch Sun.*

$$$$
FRENCH
Fodor's Choice
★

✕ **Restaurant de l'Hôtel de Ville–Benoit Violier.** Chef Benoit Violier is already winning hearts—and stomachs—with his fresh twist on haute cuisine. Secure in his position as heir to Philippe Rochat, Violier draws on his decade of experience with the famed chef to ensure the restaurant's well-earned reputation as one of the best in Switzerland. It's a quick drive west from Lausanne to this understated manse. The service is spectacular, the staff is friendly, and the food is absolutely stellar. Violier's style is superluxe French, and he is famed for his imaginative combinations of flavors plus stunningly refined presentations. For these finely orchestrated prix-fixe menus the ingredients are key—lamb raised in the Pyrenees, cardoons (an artichoke-like vegetable) grown in the village. Pace yourself, making sure to leave time and room for selections from the immense cheese cart or celestial desserts. Reserve as far ahead as possible—lunch may be your only option. $ *Average main: 95 SF* ⊠ *1 rue d'Yverdon, Crissier* ⊹ *7 km (4 miles) west of Lausanne* ☎ *021/6340505* ⊕ *www.restaurantcrissier.*

com ✍ *Reservations essential* ⏲ *Closed Sun. and Mon. and late July–mid-Aug., end Dec.–early Jan.*

$$ MODERN ITALIAN
🍴 **Restaurant du Théâtre.** Locals come to this upscale spot for oven-fired pizzas—without a doubt the best in town. Inventive Italian dishes like fusilli with red tuna and veal filet mignon with a morel mushroom sauce are robust and flavorful. The elegant dining room is a year-round hit with locals; in summer there is nothing more delightful than sitting under the garden's sprawling trees and umbrellas. Entrances connect to the opera house, making it a natural for pre- and post-performance dining. [$] *Average main: 38 SF* ✉ *12 av. du Théâtre, city center* ☎ *021/3515115* 🌐 *www.restaurant-du-theatre.ch* ⏲ *Closed Sun.*

12

WHERE TO STAY

$$ HOTEL
🏨 **Alpha Palmiers.** Behind this historical facade you'll find a courtyard hotel of modern proportions. **Pros:** family-run operation eschews chain feel; garage parking a godsend in this hilly city. **Cons:** access via a one-way street is tricky to navigate; popular for group meetings. [$] *Rooms from: 200 SF* ✉ *34 rue du Petit-Chêne* ☎ *021/5555599* 🌐 *www.fassbindhotels.com* 🛏 *210 rooms* 🍽 *No meals.*

$$$$ HOTEL Fodor's Choice ★
🏨 **Beau-Rivage Palace.** Of the scores of luxury hotels in Switzerland, this gleaming grande dame stands apart—its Neoclassical flourishes seamlessly restored to period opulence, its vast waterfront grounds manicured like a country estate. **Pros:** old-world elegance with modern flair; park setting with lake views is incomparable. **Cons:** grand interiors missing a personal touch; staff formality adds to upper-crust ambience. [$] *Rooms from: 540 SF* ✉ *17–19 pl. du Port, Ouchy* ☎ *021/6133333* 🌐 *www.brp.ch* 🛏 *155 rooms, 13 suites* 🍽 *No meals.*

$$$ HOTEL Fodor's Choice ★
🏨 **Hôtel Angleterre & Résidence.** Within four graceful 18th- and 19th-century villas and a historic hotel near the waterfront, this small complex has been modernized without ruffling its gentility or disturbing its graceful stone arches, marble floors, or discreet gardens. **Pros:** hip urban feel steeped in history; part of energetic lakefront scene. **Cons:** alley entrance to garage and reception difficult to find; hard to snag a table on the patio for lunch or a sunset cocktail. [$] *Rooms from: 270 SF* ✉ *11 pl. du Port, Ouchy* ☎ *021/6133434* 🌐 *www.angleterre-residence.ch* 🛏 *63 rooms, 12 suites* 🍽 *No meals.*

$ HOTEL
🏨 **Hôtel Regina Garni.** The owners of this friendly lodging spent more than a decade in the United States, so the language barrier is nonexistent. **Pros:** sights and shopping just outside the front door; well priced in an expensive lodging city. **Cons:** while driving up to the entrance is hypothetically possible, it's hard to find the way. [$] *Rooms from: 175 SF* ✉ *18 rue Grand-St-Jean, city center* ☎ *021/3202441* 🌐 *www.hotel-regina.ch* 🛏 *36 rooms* 🍽 *Breakfast.*

$ HOTEL
🏨 **Lausanne Guest House.** This tidy 19th-century town house not far from the train station tends to attract a young crowd, meaning everyone from college students on holiday to families traveling with small children. **Pros:** helpful staff; homey atmosphere. **Cons:** front desk not staffed around the clock. [$] *Rooms from: 140 SF* ✉ *4 Epinettes* ☎ *021/6018000* 🌐 *www.lausanne-guesthouse.ch* 🛏 *25 rooms, 6 with bath* 🍽 *No meals.*

$$$$ 🏨 **Lausanne Palace & Spa.** This Edwardian landmark, distinctly urbane
HOTEL in setting and style, stands on a hill high over the lake, with layers of
★ city scenery draped behind. **Pros:** top-drawer address sure to impress;
easy access to nightlife of the Flon. **Cons:** staid linens in some rooms;
doorman and concierge are quick to size you up. Ⓢ *Rooms from: 540
SF* ✉ *7–9 rue du Grand-Chêne, city center* ☎ *021/3313131* ⊕ *www.
lausanne-palace.ch* ↝ *121 rooms, 31 suites.*

$$ 🏨 **Nash Carlton.** A quiet tree-lined street in one of Lausanne's nicest
HOTEL neighborhoods masks this lodging's close proximity to the train sta-
tion. **Pros:** residential setting is a respite; well-priced neighborhood
eateries within easy walking distance. **Cons:** location not on the lake;
uninspired breakfast buffet. Ⓢ *Rooms from: 190 SF* ✉ *4 av. de Cour,
Sous-Gare* ☎ *021/6130707* ⊕ *www.nashotels.com* ↝ *38 rooms, 6 suites*
🍽 *No meals.*

NIGHTLIFE AND THE ARTS

NIGHTLIFE

BARS

Bar du Palace. An after-hours crowd heads to the stately Bar du Palace.
If it's not your thing, the stylish, pared-down LP Bar is just a corridor
away. ✉ *Lausanne Palace & Spa, 7–9 rue du Grand-Chêne, city center*
☎ *021/3313131* ⊕ *www.lausanne-palace.ch.*

Le Bar. One of the city's choicest and liveliest gathering spots is sophis-
ticated Le Bar. There's an armchair-filled lounge and a tiny wine bar
where you can sip your favorite cocktail or wine. Upstairs, Bar Anglais
offers spectacular lake views from its clubby setting and terrace chaises.
✉ *Beau-Rivage Palace, 17–19 pl. du Port, Ouchy* ☎ *021/6133333*
⊕ *www.brp.ch.*

Le Chorus. Look for a range of styles at Le Chorus, a renowned jazz
cellar that serves food and drinks. ✉ *3 av. du Mon-Repos, city center*
☎ *021/3232233* ⊕ *www.chorus.ch.*

Swiss Wine Bar. To explore the vintages of the country, drop in at the
Swiss Wine Bar where they pour more than 400 different wines and
host tasting events. ✉ *9 rue St-Laurent, Old Town* ☎ *021/3230133.*

DANCE CLUBS

Since most nighttime activity is centered on the Flon and Place St-
François areas, it's easy to sample several hot spots. Things don't get
going until midnight and rock on until 5 am. If you pass a crowded
club where the music is to your taste, duck inside.

Atelier Volant. Latin and tropical music dominate, but funk, rock, and
disco also have their aficionados at Atelier Volant. The crowd is twenty-
somethings out to have a good time. ✉ *12 rue des Côtes-de-Montbenon,
Flon* ☎ *021/6248428* ⊕ *www.ateliervolant.ch.*

D! Club. Inside a converted cinema, this nightspot is a mix of film, fash-
ion, and music. ✉ *Pl. Centrale, city center* ☎ *021/3515140* ⊕ *www.
dclub.ch.*

Lausanne is an ideal place for shopping, from luxury boutiques to department stores.

Loft Electroclub. Special-effect lighting and video screens lend a high-tech feel to Loft Electroclub, whose multiple floors and bars come to life Wednesday through Saturday. ⊠ *1 pl. de Bel-Air, Flon* ☎ *021/3116463* ⊕ *www.loftclub.ch.*

MAD. Clubbers come from as far away as Zürich and Basel to hear their favorite DJs and live bands at MAD. On Sunday night the club hosts a gay crowd. ⊠ *23 rue de Genève, Flon* ☎ *021/3406969* ⊕ *www. madclub.ch.*

THE ARTS

Lausanne is one of Switzerland's arts capitals. Event seasons generally run from September to May, though summer brings outdoor concerts and more casual events. A listing of free and ticketed offerings can be found in *Allons-y,* while monthly updates appear in *Reg'art* (in French). Check out the daily newspaper *24 Heures* for listings as well.

Ticket Corner. Tickets for many performances can be purchased through Ticket Corner. ☎ *0900/800800* ⊕ *www.ticketcorner.ch.*

Billetnet. The Billetnet website is a good source for tickets to event throughout Vaud. ⊕ *www.billetnet.ch.*

Salle Métropole. The Orchestre de Chambre de Lausanne shares the stage at Salle Métropole with the riveting experiments of the Maurice Béjart ballet company. ⊠ *1 pl. Bel-Air, city center* ☎ *021/3450025* ⊕ *www. sallemetropole.ch.*

Théâtre de Beaulieu. Across from the Collection de l'Art Brut, the Théâtre de Beaulieu hosts full-scale musical performances. Keep an eye out for appearances by the Orchestre de la Suisse Romande, which Lausanne shares with Geneva. ✉ *10 av. des Bergières, Beaulieu* ☎ *021/6432110* ⊕ *www.theatredebeaulieu.ch.*

SPORTS AND THE OUTDOORS

BIKING

Gare CFF de Lausanne. The train station, Gare CFF de Lausanne rents bikes. It's best to make a reservation at least one day in advance; in summer three days is recommended. ✉ *5a pl. de la Gare, city center* ☎ *051/2242162.*

Guy Delessert. For a lakefront ride, check out a set of wheels at Guy Delessert. Bikes are available March through November. ✉ *2 pl. du Vieux Port, Ouchy* ☎ *079/6223918.*

Lausanne Roule. This shop provides free bike rentals in year-round—all you need is a 20 SF deposit. It's first-come, first-serve. ✉ *Pl. de l'Europe 1b, Flon* ☎ *021/5330115* ⊕ *www.swissroule.ch.*

SWIMMING

Bellerive. You have access to the lake and three pools at Bellerive, which has generous lawns that are perfect for lounging and a self-service restaurant. ✉ *23 av. de Rhodanie, Ouchy* ☎ *021/3154860.*

Mon-Repos. The indoor pool at Mon-Repos is open year-round. ✉ *4 av. du Tribunal-Fédéral, city center* ☎ *021/3154888.*

Piscine de Montchoisi. The pool at Piscine de Montchoisi makes artificial waves, so it's popular with kids. It's open from mid-May through August. ✉ *30 av. du Servan, Montchoisi* ☎ *021/3154962.*

SHOPPING

High-end designer names and funky boutiques are found on **Place St-François, Rue St-François, Rue de Bourg,** and **Rue du Grand-Pont.** Less expensive shopping is along **Rue St-Laurent** and **Rue de l'Ale.** Generally, store hours are weekdays 9:30–7, 9:30–6 on Saturday, closed Sunday.

BOOKS

FNAC. For magazines, travel guides, and other reading material, FNAC is *the* superstore. It even has a hyperactive coffee bar and a ticket kiosk. ✉ *6 rue de Genève, Flon* ☎ *021/2138585* ⊕ *www.fnac.ch.*

DEPARTMENT STORES

Bongénie. This department store has clusters of designer areas on several levels. ✉ *10 pl. St-François, St-François* ☎ *021/3452727* ⊕ *www. bongenie-grieder.ch.*

Globus. This upscale department store has a splendid food hall on the lower level. ✉ *Rue Centrale at Rue du Pont, city center* ☎ *021/3429090* ⊕ *www.globus.ch.*

Manor. Value-priced Manor stocks a full range of merchandise, including souvenirs. It has bountiful food offerings, too. ✉ *7 rue St-Laurent, city center* ☎ *021/3213699* ⊕ *www.manor.ch.*

MARKETS

There are fruit and vegetable markets in Lausanne along **Rue de l'Ale, Rue de Bourg,** and **Place de la Riponne** every Wednesday and Saturday (8–2:30). **Place de la Palud** adds a flea market to its Wednesday and Saturday produce markets and is the site of a handicrafts market the first Friday of the month from March through December. A weekly flea market sets up on Thursday on **Place Chauderon.** Seasonal additions include summer produce found Sunday along the **Allée Bacounis** in Ouchy, and the Marché Noël (Christmas Market) in December on the transformed **Place St-François** and **Place de la Riponne.**

WATCHES

Most watch shops specialize in brands and are clustered in the St-François neighborhood. Large Swatch boutiques are located in the Globus and Manor department stores.

Bucherer. Rolex, Tag Heuer, and Baume & Mercier are on offer at Bucherer. ⊠ *1 rue de Bourg, Centre* ☎ *021/3123612* ⊕ *www.bucherer.com.*

Boutique Tourbillon. When you're in the market for a watch, this shop sells high-end brands like Blancpain and Omega. ⊠ *8 pl. St-François, Centre* ☎ *021/3235145* ⊕ *www.tourbillon.com.*

Guillard. If you are searching for brands like Ebel, go to Guillard. ⊠ *1 pl. du Palud, Centre* ☎ *021/3126886* ⊕ *www.guillard.ch.*

LAVAUX VIGNOBLES AND RIVIERA

To the east of Lausanne stretches the Lavaux, a UNESCO-designated World Heritage Site with remarkably beautiful vineyards that rise up the hillsides all the way from Pully, on the outskirts of Lausanne, to Montreux—a distance of 24 km (15 miles)—and then beyond to the fortress-crowned town of Aigle. Brown-roof stone villages in the Savoy style, old defense towers, and small baronial castles stud the green-and-black landscape. The vineyards, enclosed within low stone walls, slope so steeply that all the work has to be done by hand. Fertilizer is carried in containers strapped to workers' backs. In early October pickers harvest the fruit, carrying the loads to the nearest road and driving them by tractor to the nearest press. Some Lavaux vintages are excellent and in great demand, but unfortunately, as with so much of Switzerland's wine, the yield is small, and the product is rarely exported. Throughout the year, especially on weekends, winegrowers' cellars and some of the private châteaux-vignobles open for tastings (and, of course, sales). A listing of cave open hours, festivals, and eateries can be found at ⊕ *www.lavaux.ch.*

ST-SAPHORIN

★ *5½ km (3 miles) southeast of Lausanne.*

At the end of the Corniche Road, just west of Vevey, St-Saphorin is perched above the water. With its impossibly narrow, steep cobbled streets and ancient winemakers' houses crowded around fountains and crooked alleys, this is a village that merits a stop. It lies along the ancient

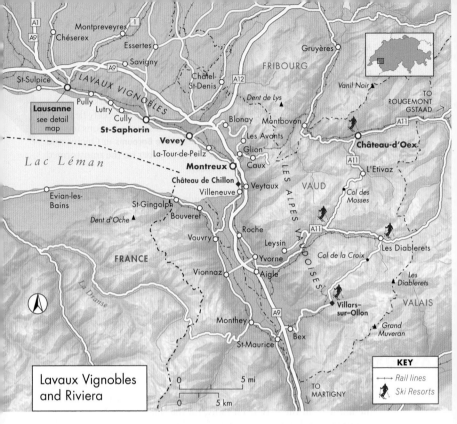

Lavaux Vignobles
and Riviera

Roman highway, and its small church sits atop Roman foundations. There's a tiny **museum** of Roman artifacts (including a sizable millstone) in the church. Go through the low door near the altar; you can see the museum whenever the church is unlocked and services are not being held. The explanations are all in French, but it's easy to chart the church's expansion through its ruins.

For additional vineyard explorations accompanied by jaw-dropping vistas, take the vertical grade uphill—on foot or by car—to Chexbres. ■**TIP**→ **Be attentive, as the close-walled street relies on tight pull-offs to pass oncoming vehicles.** The reward is a different orientation on the working wine village, complete with rail connections to whisk you back down to the active waterfront via Vevey.

EN
ROUTE

The scenic **Corniche de Lavaux** stretches some 17 km (10 miles) through Lavaux, threading above the waterfront from Lausanne to Vevey, between the autoroute and the lakeside Route 9. This is Switzerland at its most Franco-European, reminiscent in its small-scale way of the Riviera or the hill towns of Alsace. You'll careen around hairpin turns on narrow cobbled streets, with the Savoy Alps glowing across the sparkling lake and the Dents du Midi looming ahead. Stop to gaze at the scenery from roadside overlooks or wander down a side lane into the vineyards of Riex, Épesses, Rivaz, or Dézaley, the sources of some of Switzerland's loveliest white wines and all part of the Lavaux UNESCO heritage site.

WHERE TO EAT AND STAY

$$$
SWISS
★

✕ **L'Auberge de l'Onde.** Once the main *relais* (stagecoach stop) between the Simplon Pass and Geneva, this vineyard stop is out of central casting, groaning with history and heady with atmosphere: Igor Stravinsky and Charlie Chaplin were among the artists loyal to its charms. The tiny wood-paneled *pinte* (café), where winemakers come to read the daily papers with a pitcher of St-Saph, as they call it, and devour the upscale plat du jour, is enticing, as are the adjacent, white-tablecloth salons and upstairs-attic beamed grillroom. The staff hovers while day-tripping connoisseurs and repeat faithfuls sniff and roll perfumed wine over their tongues and savor exquisite dishes from the top-notch kitchen. $ *Average main: 47 SF* ⊠ *Centre Ville* ☎ *021/9254900* ⊕ *www.aubergedelonde. ch* ⊗ *Closed Mon. and Tues. late Dec.–mid-Jan., and 1 wk at Easter.*

$$$
B&B/INN
★

☷ **L'Hôtel Baron Tavernier.** Lodging high up on the Corniche Road yields superlative views with elegant comfort. **Pros:** jaw-dropping views of lake, vineyards, and mountains; solitude adjacent to wine trails and cellar doors. **Cons:** overflow crowds drawn to outdoor restaurant on weekends; complicated to access without a car. $ *Rooms from: 320 SF* ⊠ *Rte. de la Corniche, Chexbres* ☎ *021/9266000* ⊕ *www. barontavernier.com* ⤶ *11 rooms, 7 suites* ⦿❘ *Breakfast.*

SPORTS AND THE OUTDOORS

HIKING

Lavaux Vineyard Terraces Trail. This 11-km (6.8-mile) route connects Lutry and St. Saphorin, offering stunning views of Lac Léman, the steep walled terraces of the Lavaux wineries, and a glimpse of snowy peaks in the distance. Portions of the train can be steep, but a lot of it is paved, too. No roughing it here: stop to sample Chasselas, Gamays, and other *vins*, as tasting rooms and bistros flourish in achingly picturesque villages along the route.

VEVEY

4 km (2.5 miles) east of St-Saphorin, 7 km (4.3 miles) west of Montreux, 19 km (12 miles) east of Lausanne.

In the 1870s Henry James captured this waterfront town's mood of prim grace while writing (and setting) *Daisy Miller* in the Hôtel des Trois Couronnes. Indeed, despite its virtual twinning with glamorous Montreux, Vevey retains its air of isolation and old-world gentility. Loyal visitors have been returning for generations to gaze at the Dent d'Oche (7,288 feet), across the water in France, and make sedate steamer excursions into Montreux and Lausanne. Today there are some who come just to see the bronze statue of Charlie Chaplin in a rose garden on the lakefront quay, and to take the funicular or mountain train up to Mont Pèlerin. Vevey is also a great walking town, with more character in its shuttered Old Town; better museums, landmarks, and shops; and more native activity in its wine market than cosmopolitan Montreux can muster.

Many of Lavaux's famous wines are not available outside Switzerland.

GETTING HERE AND AROUND

The regional and local S-trains linking the adjacent cities Vevey and Montreux have departures every 10 to 15 minutes, but the trolley bus that snakes along the lake road is more scenic—its route extends from Villenuve to the Vevey Funicular and is the best way (other than by car) to reach Château de Chillon.

ESSENTIALS

Visitor Information Montreux-Vevey Tourisme ⊠ *29 Grand-Pl.* ⊕ *www. montreux-vevey.com.* **Transports VMCV Publics** ⊕ *www.vmcv.ch.*

EXPLORING

🕐 **Alimentarium.** The Nestlé Foundation, a dynamic force in the region,
★ sponsors this unconventional museum devoted to the celebration and study of food. In a stainless-steel kitchen, chefs demonstrate their skills, and displays on food preparation cover everything from the campfire to futuristic equipment. Other sections focus on merchants, supermarkets, food presentation, and marketing; you can also stroll through herb and vegetable gardens. The exhibits have material in English; some are interactive. ⊠ *Quai Perdonnet* ☎ *021/9244111* ⊕ *www.alimentarium. ch* 🎫 *12 SF* 🕐 *Tues.–Fri. 10–5, weekends 10–6.*

Musée Historique du Vieux Vevey (*Historical Museum of Old Vevey*). This grand 16th-century manor house, briefly home to Charlotte de Lengefeld, wife of Friedrich von Schiller, retains some original furnishings as well as collections of arms, art, keys, and wine-making paraphernalia. ⊠ *2 rue du Château* ☎ *021/9210722* ⊕ *www.museehistoriquevevey.ch* 🎫 *Free* 🕐 *Apr.–Oct., Tues.–Sun. 11–5.*

Musée Suisse de l'Appareil Photographique (*Swiss Camera Museum*). The Musée Suisse de l'Appareil Photographique displays an impressive collection of cameras, photographic equipment, and mounted work. ✉ *99 Grande-Pl.* ☎ *021/9253480* ⊕ *www.cameramuseum.ch* 🎫 *8 SF* ⊙ *Tues.–Sun. 11–5:30.*

QUICK BITES

Yatus. Pause for a glass of a local or imported vintage at this storefront wine bar on a side street. The owner's friendly enthusiasm adds to the pleasure of time spent toasting, chatting, or people-watching. ✉ *24 rue des Deux-Marchés* ☎ *021/9223033* ⊕ *www.yatus.ch.*

CELEBRITY SIGHTINGS

Among the notables who have been drawn to Vevey are Graham Greene, Victor Hugo, Jean-Jacques Rousseau (who set much of his *Julie, ou la Nouvelle Héloïse* here), Fyodor Dostoyevsky, Gustave Courbet, Oskar Kokoschka, Charlie and Oona Chaplin (buried in the cemetery at Corsier), and Swiss native Édouard Jeanneret, known as Le Corbusier. By following an excellent brochure-map published by the tourist office, you can travel to the homes and haunts of some 40 luminaries.

Poyet. If sweets are on your mind, pick up a handcrafted chocolate in the shape of Charlie Chaplin's shoes from Poyet, on a pedestrian walkway near the tourist office. ✉ *8 rue du Théâtre* ☎ *021/9213737* ⊕ *www.confiserie-poyet.ch.*

Musée Suisse du Jeu (*Game and Toy Museum*). Just east of town, the Musée Suisse du Jeu fills a 13th-century castle. Games of strategy and chance, ranging from dice to video games, are represented in displays spanning centuries. Tours are available in English. Its excellent gift shop is stocked with puzzles and board games. The courtyard eatery, in a former gardener's cottage, serves snacks and light meals. ✉ *Rte. 9, 1½ km (1 mile) east of Vevey, Au Château, La Tour-de-Peilz* ☎ *021/9772300* ⊕ *www.museedujeu.com* 🎫 *9 SF* ⊙ *Tues.–Sun. 11–5:30.*

OFF THE BEATEN PATH

Blonay–Chamby Railroad. From Vevey and Montreux, a number of railways climb into the heights, which in late spring are carpeted with an extravagance of wild narcissus blooms. If you like model railroads, you will especially enjoy a trip on the Blonay–Chamby Railroad, whose real steam-driven trains alternate with electric trains. You can depart from either end (parking is more plentiful in Blonay); trains make a stop at a small museum of railroad history in between. The trip takes about 20 minutes each way, not including a browse in the museum. ✉ *Case Postale 366, Lausanne* ☎ *021/9432121* ⊕ *www.blonay-chamby.ch* 🎫 *20 SF round-trip* ⊙ *May–Oct., weekends 10–6:30.*

WHERE TO EAT

$$
SWISS

✕ **Le Mazot.** At this tiny eatery, regulars favor the tender steak—entrecôte of beef or *cheval* (horse)—accompanied by an overflowing plate of fries or a half-moon of crispy Rösti. After years of overseeing bubbling pots of fondue, the other popular draw, hand-painted murals and mirrors set in dark frames have a smoky patina. It's a casual neighborhood place where local wines are poured from pewter pitchers and the people at

Continued on page 506

The Vineyards of
Lavaux

Switzerland's most stunning wine-producing region is the Lavaux, where vine-yards and villages perch on steep terraces that zigzag down to the shoreline of Lac Léman. The UNESCO World Heritage site comprises 10,000 terraces of Chasselas, Gamay, and Pinot Noir vines spread over 40 levels. The area is also full of cellars and wineries worth visiting. Here's how to get the most out of a day trip to wine country from Lausanne.

Hiking trails in the vineyards between Lausanne and Vevey

WINE-TASTING DAY TRIP FROM LAUSANNE

A terrace overlooking Lac Léman

Scenic Lavaux—a 19-mile stretch from Lausanne to Chillon overlooking Lac Léman—overwhelmingly produces Chasselas from the white variety native to this area.

❶ AU CLOS DE LA RÉPUBLIQUE

A 13th-generation winemaker whose stunning cellars hold wines from across Lavaux. The wines bear witness to its different soil types. *Try: Passerillé de Lavaux, a Chasselas dessert wine.*
- ✉ Ruelle du Petit-Crêt, Epesses
- ☎ 021/7991444
- ⊕ www.patrick-fonjallaz.ch

❷ VINOTHÈQUE TESTUZ

The Testuz winery's tasting room offers wines from all of Vaud's wine regions: Pinot Noir, Gamay, and Chasselas predominate. *Try: a full-bodied Pinot Noir and Gamay St Saphorin AOC blend.*

Vineyards abut the tracks in Dézaley

- ✉ Route du Lac, Dézaley
- ☎ 021/7999911
- ⊕ www.testuz.ch

❸ ARC EN VINS

Featuring a range of wines from Lavaux and other Swiss regions, this winery also makes blends combining less prevalent varieties. *Try: an unusual white, Charmont de Lavaux, which is a cross of Chasselas and Chardonnay.*
- ✉ Le Verney D, Puidoux
- ☎ 021/9463344
- ⊕ www.arc-en-vins.ch

❹ LAVAUX VINORAMA

Most Lavaux wineries have meager opening hours or are open by appointment, so this center featuring a savvy selection of some 200 Lavaux wines is a boon. *Try: a red with a hint of black cherry and spice made from an ancient local variety, Plant Robert.*
- ✉ 2 route du Lac, Rivaz
- ☎ 021/9463131
- ⊕ www.lavaux-vinorama.ch

Grapes ready to harvest in Dézaley

❺ ASSOCIATION VITICOLE DE CORSEAUX

Worth a visit for the lake-and-mountain views alone—and while this group of winemakers presents fewer than 20 selections, they offer pleasant surprises. *Try: Pinot Noir Le Corsalin, powerfully structured yet silky.*
- ✉ 20 rue du Village, Corseaux
- ☎ 021/9213185
- ⊕ www.avc-vins.ch

The Train des Vignes   A winepress in Cully

STOP FOR A BITE

✕ AUBERGE DU VIGNERON

Many Vaudois say this terrace boasts the best view in all Lavaux. Stop here, in the dining room or bistro, for Lavaux wines paired with light French cuisine or traditional Swiss dishes, or just come by for a drink between mealtimes.

✉ *14 route de la Corniche, Epesses* ☎ *021/7991419*
🌐 www.aubergeduvigneron.ch

✕ AU CHALET

Part of the hyper-luxurious spa hotel Le Mirador Kempinski Lake Geneva, this Swiss chalet set amid vineyards offers breathtaking views, and excellent food—fondue, *rösti*, pan-fried tomme cheese and more, including local wines.

✉ *5 chemin de l'Hôtel du Mirador, Mont-Pelerin*
☎ *021/9222761*
🌐 www.kempinski.com

❻ OBRIST VINARIA

Obrist makes its own wines and distributes bottles for several international wineries. *Try: Château de Chardonne's Grand Cru Chardonne as an afternoon apéritif.*

✉ 26 avenue Reller, Vevey
☎ 021/9259925
🌐 www.obrist.ch

❼ LA CAVE VEVEY-MONTREUX

This is the tasting venue of a winegrowers' association producing Vevey-Montreux and Chardonne bottlings. *Try: Montreux Entre-Bourgs Chasselas has a floral bouquet and a rich mouth feel.*

✉ 28 avenue Belmont, Montreux
☎ 021/9631348
🌐 www.lacave-vevey-montreux.ch

❽ HENRI BADOUX

Aigle, in the Chablais region, is home to wine and label museums and the Badoux winery, renowned for its Chasselas. *Try: Aigle Les Murailles Chasselas has intriguing mineral and cream notes.*

✉ 18 avenue du Chamossaire, Aigle
☎ 021/4686888
🌐 www.badoux-vins.ch

LAVAUX TOURING TIPS

Local vintners welcome visitors year-round, except during harvest, which is usually in October. If there is a particular winemaker you want to visit, phone ahead for an appointment. You can also keep an eye peeled for hand-painted signs announcing "*caveau ouvert*" or "*dégustation*"; this indicates that a cellar owner or cooperative is pouring wine. (Designate a driver; laws are strict.)

Some wineries have sophisticated tasting rooms; others feature a tasting barrel within the working cellar. These are communal gathering spots so you may be tasting with the locals.

Most cellars charge for tasting, and if you occupy the winemaker's time beyond a casual pour, it is appropriate to buy a bottle unless you find it not to your liking.

Interconnected hiking trails (signposted in several languages, including English) span the length of the shore from Ouchy to Chillon, traversing vineyards and traffic arteries from the lakefront to hillside villages. Walking the entire 32-km (19-mile) *parcours viticole* (wine route) takes about 8½ hours,

GETTING THERE

BY TRAIN: From Lausanne, there are tracks along the lake to Vevey, Montreux, and Aigle. Another track, the Train des Vignes (vineyard train) rolls through the vineyards. Check ⊕ *www.rail.ch* for schedules.

BY CAR: From Lausanne-Ouchy, head straight along the lake road to Vevey/Montreux/Aigle. Turn off (and up) into wine villages, then back down. Signage abounds; you won't get lost.

BY BIKE AND FOOT: You can walk or bike along the wine trail. Download the map at ⊕ *www.montreuxriviera.com*

but you can also break it into smaller segments, allowing time for wine tastings and meals at local restaurants.

Tourist offices can provide a copy of the specialized map that identifies the route and cellars open for tastings. If you're doing a portion of the hiking trail, you can easily catch a vineyard train back to your starting point, as there are hourly stops in every village along the lakefront.

Conne wine cellar in Chexbres

WINE-TASTING PRIMER

Ordering and tasting wine—whether at a winery, bar, or restaurant—is easy once you master a few simple steps.

LOOK AND NOTE

Hold your glass by the stem and look at the wine in the glass. Note its color, depth, and clarity.

For whites, is it greenish, yellow, or gold? For reds, is it purplish, ruby, or garnet? Is the wine's color pale or deep? Is the liquid clear or cloudy?

SWIRL AND SNIFF

Swirl the wine gently in the glass to intensify the scents, then sniff over the rim of the glass. What do you smell? Try to identify aromas like:

- **Fruits**—citrus, peaches, berries, figs, melon
- **Minerals**—earth, steely notes, wet stones
- **Flowers**—orange blossoms, honey, perfume
- **Dairy**—butter, cream, cheese, yogurt
- **Spices**—baking spices, pungent, herbal notes
- **Oak**—toast, vanilla, coconut, tobacco
- **Vegetables**—fresh or cooked, herbal notes
- **Animal**—leathery, meaty notes

Are there any unpleasant notes, like mildew or wet dog, that might indicate that the wine is "off?"

SIP AND SAVOR

Prime your palate with a sip, swishing the wine in your mouth. Then spit in a bucket or swallow.

Take another sip and think about the wine's attributes. Sweetness is detected on the tip of the tongue, acidity on the sides of the tongue, and tannins (a mouth-drying sensation) on the gums. Consider the body—does the wine feel light in the mouth, or is there a rich sensation? Are the flavors consistent with the aromas? If you like the wine, try to pinpoint what you like about it, and vice versa if you don't like it.

Take time to savor the wine as you're sipping it— the tasting experience may seem a bit scientific, but the end goal is your enjoyment.

the next table eavesdrop. $ *Average main: 28 SF* ✉ *7 rue du Conseil* ☎ *021/9217822* ⊘ *Closed Wed. No lunch Sun.*

$$$$ ✕ **Le Montagne.** This elegant, intimate restaurant is set in a restored
FRENCH home in the wine village of Chardonne. Perched high on a hill, it offers a view of the lake (from part of the dining room) that is worthy of a champagne toast. Traditional French dishes like beef medallions and oven-roasted pigeon are straightforward, smartly garnished, and paired with fresh herbs and vegetables. A well-composed wine list of Swiss and international selections offers breadth to match. Those who like a stroll before and after dinner can take the mostly flat five-minute walk to the funicular, an easy way to access these upper reaches. $ *Average main: 65 SF* ✉ *21 rue du Village, Chardonne* ☎ *021/9212930* ⊕ *www. le-montagne.com* ⊘ *Closed Sun. and Mon. and 3 (varying) wks in Aug. and Jan.*

$$ ✕ **National.** A frequently changing menu combines fresh ingredients with
ECLECTIC a twist on standards like veal carpaccio with artichokes or porc massalé wrapped in a banana leaf. The trendy vibe overflows onto the patio, with seating under twinkling lights—a respite from the serious smoking crowd. A thriving bar with extended service hours and proximity to the cinema attracts late diners of all ages. $ *Average main: 34 SF* ✉ *9 rue du Torrent* ☎ *021/9237625* ⊕ *www.natio.ch.*

WHERE TO STAY

$$$$ 🏨 **Grand Hôtel du Lac.** Anita Brookner set her novel *Hotel du Lac* in this
HOTEL lakefront doyenne where readers find an abundance of refinement and
★ global sophistication proffered beneath the Relais & Châteaux banner. **Pros:** historically elegant; pool and garden plus harbor access are sensational in summer. **Cons:** at the outer edge of town; lakefront festivals and neighborhood block parties can engulf. $ *Rooms from: 500 SF* ✉ *1 rue d'Italie* ☎ *021/9250606* ⊕ *www.grandhoteldulac.ch* 🛏 *41 rooms, 9 suites* ⦿❘ *Breakfast.*

$$ 🏨 **Hostellerie Bon Rivage.** This hotel blends right in with the estates fac-
HOTEL ing the lake on the main road between Vevey and Montreux. **Pros:** price/value relationship is tops; picturesque marina setting on the main transportation line. **Cons:** no air-conditioning necessitates closed shutters against the afternoon sun; most guest rooms have only a shower. $ *Rooms from: 205 SF* ✉ *18 rue de St-Maurice, La Tour-de-Peilz* ☎ *021/9770707* ⊕ *www.bon-rivage.ch* 🛏 *50 rooms* ⦿❘ *Breakfast.*

$$$$ 🏨 **Hôtel des Trois Couronnes.** Honeycombed by dramatic atrium stair-
HOTEL wells that look down on marble columns and gleaming floors inlaid
Fodor'sChoice with golden coronets, this regal landmark was Henry James's home
★ base when he wrote (and set here) the novella *Daisy Miller.* **Pros:** from valet to spa attendant, the staff is superb; perfect balance of modern refinement and history. **Cons:** noise wafts up into rooms from terrace parties; even the best face-lifts show a few age lines. $ *Rooms from: 420 SF* ✉ *49 rue d'Italie* ☎ *021/9233200* ⊕ *www.hoteltroiscouronnes. com* 🛏 *46 rooms, 25 suites.*

NIGHTLIFE

Despite its quiet, small-town appearance, Vevey has gathering spots where the music is loud and revelers dance until dawn.

Epsylon Club. Patrons warble karaoke nightly at Epsylon Club, with offers full-throttle clubbing on the weekend. ⊠ *30 av. General Guisan* ☎ *021/9212196* ⊕ *www.epsylon-club.ch.*

Il Baretto. Gays and straights gather for music and cocktails plus imaginative theme parties at Il Baretto, an enclave near the town theater. ⊠ *3 rue du Théâtre* ☎ *021/9212281* ⊕ *www.baretto.ch.*

SPORTS AND THE OUTDOORS

As you drive along the highway, you will see sunbathers lounging on rocks jutting out into the lake and swimmers playing on the stony beaches. It's difficult to tell if they are on private property or have public access. There *are* swimming areas open to everyone that include a mix of facilities—toilets, showers, changing cabins, and snack bars—but lifeguards are only at the pools, so be careful. Slippery rocks, drop-offs, and water traffic on the lake require special attention.

Jardin Doret. Access to the lake, a generous lawn with a children's play area, and a snack bar are among the pluses at Jardin Doret. ⊠ *Off Pl. du Marché* ☎ *0848/868484.*

Vevey/Corseaux Plage. West of Nestlé headquarters, the Vevey/Corseaux Plage has both lake swimming and two large pools, one indoors, the other out. ⊠ *19 av. de Lavaux, Corseaux* ☎ *021/9212368.*

SHOPPING

Boutiques and galleries in the Old Town east of Place du Marché deserve your attention.

La Laiterie de la Grenette. The town's best cheese shop, La Laiterie de la Grenette sells coveted double-crème from a dairy in Gruyéres that locals line up to purchase before the limited daily supply runs out. ⊠ *27 rue des Deux-Marchés* ☎ *021/9212345.*

Saint-Antoine. A modern, multilevel complex diagonally across from the train station, Saint-Antoine clusters large and small retailers within its glass panels. The underground parking is a smart alternative to the cramped, restricted parking in Old Town. ⊠ *1 av. Général-Guisan.*

Tuesday and Saturday bring neighbors, politicians, and foodies to the center of Old Town for the **Vevey Open-Air Bazaar** where wagons circle and stalls fill tidy rows, each piled high with produce from nearby farms, meats cut to order, or seafood netted at dawn. As Vevey is a marketing center for regional wines, the local white is sold in summer at the Saturday market, adding to the spirit of a folkloric festival; you buy your own glass and taste *à volonté* (at will).

The iconic Château de Chillon is one of the most photographed sights in Switzerland.

MONTREUX

4 km (2 miles) southeast of Vevey, 21 km (13 miles) southeast of Lausanne.

Montreux might be called the Cannes of Lac Léman—though it might raise an eyebrow at the slur. Spilling down steep hillsides into a sunny south-facing bay, its waterfront thick with magnolias, cypresses, and palm trees, the historic resort earns its reputation as the capital—if not the pearl—of the Swiss Riviera. Unlike the French Riviera, it has managed, despite overwhelming crowds of conventioneers, to keep up appearances. Its Edwardian-French deportment has survived considerable development, and though there are plenty of harsh modern high-rises with parking-garage aesthetics, its mansarded landmarks still unfurl yellow awnings to shield millionaires from the sun.

Famed for the nearby lakeside Château de Chillon, Montreux is where Stravinsky composed *Petrouchka* and *Le Sacre du Printemps*, and where Vladimir Nabokov resided in splendor. Indeed, Montreux and its suburbs have attracted artists and literati for 200 years: Byron, Shelley, Tolstoy, Hans Christian Andersen, and Flaubert were drawn to its lush shoreline. The resort is best known for its annual jazz festival, which lately has strayed from its original focus to include rock, R&B, Latin, and hip-hop. Each July, Montreux's usually composed promenade explodes in a street festival of food tents, vendor kiosks, and open band shells, which complement standing-room-only concert hall venues.

12

GETTING HERE AND AROUND

Montreux is accessible via regional and local trains on the rail line that runs from Lausanne to the Valais. It is a 20- to 30-minute ride from Lausanne. By car it takes approximately half an hour on the A9 motorway; Exit 19 from the elevated roadway winds down to the lakefront road and into the center of town. Montreux is easily explored on foot, as traffic on Grand Rue can be bumper to bumper during the city's many festivals.

ESSENTIALS

Visitor Information Montreux-Vevey Tourisme ⊠ *5 rue du Théâtre* ☎ *084/8868484* ⊕ *www.montreux-vevey.com* ⊠ *Pl. de l'Eurovision* ⊕ *www.montreuxriviera.com.*

EXPLORING

Fodor'sChoice **Château de Chillon.** One of Switzerland's must-sees is the Château de
★ Chillon, the awe-inspiringly picturesque 12th-century castle that rears out of the water at Veytaux, down the road from and within sight of Montreux. Chillon was built on Roman foundations under the direction of Duke Peter of Savoy with the help of military architects from Plantagenet England. For a long period it served as a state prison, and one of its shackled guests was François Bonivard, who supported the Reformation and enraged the Savoyards. He spent six years in this prison, chained most of the time to a pillar in the dungeon before being released by the Bernese in 1536.

While living near Montreux, Lord Byron visited Chillon and was so transported by its atmosphere and by Bonivard's grim sojourn that he was inspired to write his famous poem "The Prisoner of Chillon." Like a true tourist, Byron carved his name on a pillar in Bonivard's still-damp and chilly dungeon; his graffito is now protected under a plaque.

In high season visitors to Chillon must now file placidly from restored chamber to restored turret, often waiting at doorways for entire busloads of fellow tourists to pass. Yet the 19th-century Romantic-era restoration is so evocative and so convincing, with its tapestries, carved fireplaces, period ceramics and pewter, and elaborate wooden ceilings, that even the jaded castle hound may become as carried away as Byron was. While you're waiting your turn, you can gaze out the narrow windows over the sparkling, lapping water and remember Mark Twain, who thought Bonivard didn't have it half bad. Proceeds from the purchase of a bottle of Clos de Chillon, the white wine from estate vineyards, goes to restoration activities. ⊠ *Veytaux* ☎ *021/9668910* ⊕ *www. chillon.ch* ⊠ *12 SF* ☉ *Mar. and Oct., daily 9:30–5; Apr.–Sept., daily 9–7; Nov.–Feb., daily 10–5.*

Maison Visinand. Montreux's cultural center, the Maison Visinand is housed in a restored mansion in the Old Town. Its calendar of events mixes exhibitions and performances with classes and studios for painting, photography, and dance. ⊠ *32 rue du Pont* ☎ *021/9630726* ⊕ *www.maisonvisinand.ch* ⊠ *Free* ☉ *Wed.–Sun. 3–6.*

The majestic Fairmont Le Montreux Palace is one of the grand dames on Switzerland's hotel scene.

QUICK
BITES

Zurcher. The lunch-and-tearoom set (ladies with poodles, Brits in tweeds, fashionistas in Gucci) regularly descends on Zurcher, the irresistible confiserie on Montreux's main drag. A green salad, the *potage du jour* (soup of the day), and a chocolate torte make a great quick meal. The café is closed on Monday. ✉ *45 av. du Casino* ☎ *021/9635963* ⊕ *www.confiserie-zurcher.ch.*

Musée de Montreux (*Museum of Montreux*). Above the train station, a cluster of 17th-century homes once belonging to the town's successful winemakers is now the Musée de Montreux. This historical museum traces regional development from the time when Roman coins were used as tender, focusing on agricultural life and the shift to tourism. Profiles of famous residents and visitors who lived and worked in the area are highlighted. The museum's cellar restaurant, open from 6 pm, is a good place to sample typical local cuisine. ✉ *40 rue de la Gare* ☎ *021/9631353* ⊕ *www.museemontreux.ch* ✉ *6 SF* ☉ *Apr.–Nov., daily 10–noon and 2–5.*

OFF THE
BEATEN
PATH

Les Avants. The Montreux–Oberland–Bernois railroad leads to the resort village of Les Avants and then on to Château-d'Oex, Gstaad, and the Simmental. Noël Coward bought his dream home in Les Avants, and Ernest Hemingway wrote to his family and friends of the village's fields of daffodils—and, more in character, of its bobsled track. ✉ *Les Avants.*

WHERE TO EAT

$$$$
FRENCH
★

✕ **L'Ermitage.** Freestanding on its own waterfront-garden grounds, this genteel, intimate retreat offers top-drawer haute gastronomie and a few luxurious rooms upstairs. Chef Étienne Krebs's exceptional menu

12

may include duckling with quinoa and foie gras or royal sea bream with ginger and Kaffir lime. You won't go wrong with suggested wine pairings, many from select Swiss vineyards. On-cue service overseen by the chef's wife is calm and elegant. A bit less formal than the dining room is the canopied terrace, open daily in summer for alfresco dining. $ *Average main: 75 SF* ✉ *75 rue du Lac, Clarens* ☎ *021/9644411* ⊕ *www.ermitage-montreux.com* ⊘ *Closed Sun. and Mon.*

$$ ✕ **La Rouvenaz.** If it's an oven-fired pizza or plate of pasta you crave,
ITALIAN there's no place more convivial or convenient than this trattoria on the main drag. The atmosphere is warmed by terra-cotta walls with bold blue accents and endless pitchers of wine. Fresh seafood is a specialty of the house, whether atop a piecrust or a mound of linguine. There is a satellite location serving light fare and desserts across the street on the lakefront promenade. $ *Average main: 35 SF* ✉ *1 rue du Marché* ☎ *021/9632736* ⊕ *www.rouvenaz.ch.*

$$$ ✕ **La Vieille Ferme.** Follow the winding road into the village of Chailly-
SWISS sur-Montreux, where you'll see the stone facade of a 14th-century farmhouse said to be the oldest in the region. Dining rooms that were once stalls and family quarters have stucco and wooden beams. The owner's philosophy—*a bon manger, bon boire* (good food and good drink)—is carved above the raised fireplace that doubles as a grill. The cuisine is true to the heritage of the homestead: beef Stroganoff, chicken simmered in honey and lemon. If it's a fondue or raclette you prefer, a separate *carnotzet* (room beside the wine cellar) serves these cheese specialties. $ *Average main: 41 SF* ✉ *40 rue de Bourg, Chailly-sur-Montreux* ☎ *021/9646465* ⊕ *www.laferme.ch* ⊘ *Closed Mon. and Tues.*

$$ ✕ **Mai Thai.** Weary of regional cuisine? Freshly made spring rolls, satays,
THAI and spicy dishes from this storefront eatery on the edge of Clarens will lighten up the program. Traditional pad thai, multicolor curries, and seafood preparations are superb. This longtime resident of the neighborhood draws locals to its Asian-accented dining room, but at the first hint of warmth they scurry to tables on the terrace built directly on the water. It's not an inexpensive meal, but it is one that will leave you feeling a continental shift. $ *Average main: 36 SF* ✉ *40 rue du Lac, Clarens* ☎ *021/9642536* ⊘ *Closed Mon.*

WHERE TO STAY

$$$$ ⊡ **Fairmont Le Montreux Palace.** Silver mansards and yellow awnings flag
HOTEL this vast institution as a landmark, and the guest rooms' fruitwood
Fodor's Choice furniture, bold accessories, and whirlpool tubs trimmed in granite and
★ marble don't disappoint. **Pros:** halls and salons are replete with history and decorative architecture; discreet staff can handle any request. **Cons:** easy to feel lost in the shuffle of high-end conferences; prices are steep for basics like breakfast and parking. $ *Rooms from: 400 SF* ✉ *100 Grand-Rue* ☎ *021/9621212* ⊕ *www.fairmont.com* ⇶ *185 rooms, 51 suites.*

$$ ⊡ **Masson.** If you enjoy being away from the downtown resort scene,
B&B/INN look up this demure little inn on a hillside in Veytaux, between Chillon and Montreux. **Pros:** serene old family-estate feel; genial hostess is an accomplished innkeeper. **Cons:** need a car unless you want to trek uphill

from the bus stop; no other restaurants nearby. [$] *Rooms from: 200 SF* ✉ *5 rue Bonivard, Veytaux* ☎ *021/9660044* 🌐 *www.hotelmasson.ch* 🛏 *31 rooms* ⏰ *Closed Oct.–Apr.* 🍴 *Breakfast.*

$$$ HOTEL 🏨 **Tralala Hotel.** In a town of world-renowned musical heritage the rooms of this small modern inn tucked in the sharp curve of an Old Town thoroughfare are themed for jazz, rock, and blues stars. **Pros:** refreshing contrast to the town's stately hotel scene; attracts a well-heeled thirtysomething crowd. **Cons:** limited kitchen requires that you dine elsewhere; public street or pay garage parking can be a headache and costly. [$] *Rooms from: 280 SF* ✉ *Rue du Temple 2* ☎ *021/9634973* 🌐 *www.tralalahotel.ch* 🛏 *32 rooms, 3 suites* 🍴 *Breakfast.*

NIGHTLIFE AND THE ARTS

Montreux's famous festivals and arts events are listed in a seasonal booklet published by the tourist office; tickets are sold from its booth at the waterfront. In summer Montreux offers a variety of free outdoor concerts from its bandstand on the waterfront near the landing stage.

Montreux Jazz Festival. The renowned Montreux Jazz Festival takes place every July in the ultramodern Auditorium Stravinski and other lakeside venues. Popular events sell out in hours. ✉ *95 Grand-Rue* 🌐 *www.montreuxjazzfestival.com.*

Ticket Corner. Ticket Corner sells tickets to concerts, sports, and other events. ☎ *0900/800800* 🌐 *www.ticketcorner.com.*

BARS

Harry's New York Bar. The swank Harry's New York Bar has a pianist who tickles the ivories starting in the late afternoon. ✉ *Fairmont Le Montreux Palace, 100 Grand-Rue* ☎ *021/9621200* 🌐 *www.fairmont.com.*

La Vinoteca. Adjacent to a popular Italian restaurant, eclectic La Vinoteca is the smallest bar in town. Look for an excellent selection of Italian wines. ✉ *1 rue du Marché* ☎ *021/9632736* 🌐 *www.rouvenaz.ch.*

Mayfair House. An urbane, designer-clad crowd flocks to the Mayfair House to take in the afternoon sun and make plans for the evening. ✉ *52 Grand-Rue* ☎ *021/9667978* 🌐 *www.mayfair.ch.*

CASINO

Casino Barrière. Slot machines, table games, and multiple dining venues distinguish the Casino Barrière. Be sure to bring your passport, as no other ID will get you in. The casino is open most days from 10:30 am to 3 am, except Friday and Saturday, when it doesn't close until 5 am. ✉ *9 rue du Théâtre* ☎ *021/9628383* 🌐 *www.lucienbarriere.com.*

DANCING

Black Pearl. Techno and Latin sounds accompanied by colorful lighting pulse at Black Pearl, where weekend partying goes until 5 am. ✉ *92 Grand-Rue* ☎ *021/9635288* 🌐 *www.leblackpearl.ch.*

Millésime Club. Rotating DJs attract a young crowd to Millésime Club, which has all-white designer couches for a swank, Miami Beach-feel. ✉ *Grand Rue 100* ☎ *079/5091067* 🌐 *www.millesime-club.ch.*

SPORTS AND THE OUTDOORS
BOATING
Water sports are popular along Montreux-Vevey's waterfront. Lessons and rentals are available at locations in marinas and from docks that rim the lake.

Nautic Loisirs. All types of equipment, from paddle- to motorboats, kayaks to windsurfers, can be rented at Nautic Loisirs. ⊠ *Quai du Casino* ☎ *078/6061588* ⊕ *www.nauticloisirs.ch.*

SHOPPING
Souvenir shops, tony boutiques, and jewelry stores are interspersed randomly along the Grand-Rue.

Forum. This modern complex is topped with shops and restaurants. Underground parking is connected to the Place du Marché, a large covered pavilion where the weekly open-air food market is held every Friday morning. ⊠ *6 pl. du Marché.*

CHÂTEAU-D'OEX

64 km (40 miles) east of Lausanne.

At the crossroads between the Col des Mosses highway to Aigle and the Valais and the route to the Berner Oberland lies Château-d'Oex (pronounced *day*), a popular sports resort that connects with the greater Gstaad ski region. Its perhaps even greater claim to fame these days is ballooning, with hot-air-balloon competitions that draw mobs of international enthusiasts and fill hotels throughout the region.

Separated from the high-altitude Alpine resorts by the modest Col des Mosses (4,740 feet), the Pays-d'Enhaut (Highlands) hereabouts offer an entirely different culture from that of its Vaud cousins. Here the architecture begins to resemble that of the Berner Oberland, with deep-eaved wooden chalets and a mountain-farm air.

This is still Gruyère cheese country. A style known as L'Etivaz is made from milk drawn exclusively from cows grazed on pastures at elevations between 3,280 feet and 7,216 feet. The sweet, late-blooming flowers they eat impart a flavor that lowland cheeses can't approach. The highlands are also the source of one of Switzerland's most familiar decorative arts: *papier découpé,* delicate, symmetrical paper cutouts. They are cut in black, often with simple imagery of cattle and farmers, and fixed on white paper for contrast. The real thing is a refined craft and is priced accordingly, but attractive prints reproducing the look are on sale at reduced prices throughout the region.

GETTING HERE AND AROUND
In any season the train trip to the Alpine village of Château-d'Oex is one of the most picturesque in the country. Board the standard rail cars of the Montreux Oberland Bernois or pay 15 SF extra for reserved seats on the luxurious Golden Pass coaches (discounted with a Swiss Pass). There is a separate MOB ticket office and platform on the upper level of the Montreux station.

DID YOU KNOW?

The first hot air balloon to circumnavigate the world was launched from Château-d'Oex in 1999. Every year the resort hosts "Balloon Week," a festival in January dedicated to the sport.

12

ESSENTIALS

Visitor Information Pays-d'Enhaut Tourisme ⊠ *La Place* ☎ *026/9242525* ⊕ *www.chateau-doex.ch.* **MOB** ⊕ *www.mob.ch.*

EXPLORING

Espace Ballon. The technical and sporting elements of hot-air ballooning that put this tiny village on the world map are highlighted at Espace Ballon, a museum and exhibition space run by professional pilots. Permanent and changing shows follow the history of avionics, challenges shared by flying enthusiasts, and flight records that have been broken by adventurers like Bertrand Piccard and Brian Jones, whose Breitling *Orbiter* set off from a nearby meadow. In addition, there are 3-D movies that take the viewer along for a ride, or you can schedule your own voyage into the thermals.

The annual hot-air ballooning festival gets off the ground in late January in a spectacle featuring over one hundred vibrant balloons. On Friday night a nightglow is held. Scramble to the top of the hill that has the church (look for the steeple) for a stunning view of brilliantly colored, backlit balloons choreographed to music. A lively village fair follows. ⊠ *La Place* ☎ *026/9242220* ⊕ *www.espace-ballon.ch* ⊠ *6 SF* ⊘ *Dec.–Oct., Tues.–Sun 2–6.*

★ **Musée Artisanal du Vieux Pays-d'Enhaut** (*Artisan and Folklore Museum of the Old Highlands*). In Château-d'Oex's tiny center, the Musée Artisanal du Vieux Pays-d'Enhaut gives insight into life in these isolated parts. An old farmhouse reproduces interiors from a farmer's home, a cheese-maker's cottage, and a carpenter's studio. ⊠ *Grand-Rue* ☎ *026/9246520* ⊕ *www.musee-chateau-doex.ch* ⊠ *8 SF* ⊘ *Dec.–Oct., Tues.–Sun. 2–5.*

WHERE TO STAY

$$
B&B/INN
🛏 **Hostellerie Bon Accueil.** In beautifully proportioned 18th-century weathered-wood farmhouses on the outskirts of town, this is the quintessential French-Swiss country inn. **Pros:** peaceful surroundings; unexpected top-notch kitchen. **Cons:** a hike to village shops, restaurants, and the train station; rooms in the main house more appealing. $ *Rooms from: 185 SF* ⊠ *La Frasse* ☎ *026/9246320* ⊕ *www.bonaccueil.ch* ⤴ *17 rooms* ⊘ *Closed Nov.–mid-Dec.* ⦿ *Breakfast.*

Geneva

WORD OF MOUTH

"A boat ride on Lake Geneva is a wonderful must-see experience. You could ride a public boat or one of the tour boats."

—despirited

WELCOME TO GENEVA

TOP REASONS TO GO

★ **Falling water:** The feathery Jet d'Eau, Geneva's iconic harbor fountain, is visible for tens of miles in every direction.

★ **Time on your hands:** Chances are good you'll leave this city of watchmakers with a new timepiece—for glorious old ones, visit the Patek Philippe Museum.

★ **City of God:** The Protestant Reformation moved through Geneva like a hurricane almost five centuries ago; the city's churches still bear scars.

★ **Block party:** The Fêtes de Genève gives everyone a midsummer break by turning La Rade into a 10-day smorgasbord of international foods.

★ **Exclusive baubles:** To wander the Rue du Rhône is to take a roll call of the world's finest jewelers—only here many are homegrown.

★ **Clink glasses:** Swiss wines aren't widely available outside the country, so take the opportunity to explore Gamays from Geneva and Merlots from Montreux at a café, wine bar, or restaurant.

1 Rive Droite (Right Bank). Clustered around a central downtown area (Centre Ville) that includes Cornavin, the main train station, are the business, shopping, and mixed-market residential areas of St. Gervais and Les Pâquis. Both neighborhoods boast waterfronts and a host of across-the-range lodgings (including most of Geneva's five-star hotels) and eateries. To the north, about 10 minutes from the train station by tram, is the International Area, home to the UN's European headquarters and other international organizations.

2 Rive Gauche (Left Bank). Crossing over from the Right Bank on any of several bridges, you'll link up with the Centre Ville Rive Gauche, which includes the shopping streets known as Rues Basses. If you take the Ponts de l'Ile, the Rues Basses are to your left; the Vieille Ville (Old Town) is straight ahead; and to your right is the Plainpalais banking, university, and art-and-theater district. Crossing over on Pont du Mont-Blanc gives you access to the Eaux-Vives waterfront area, behind which a residential, business, and shopping neighborhood opens up.

GETTING ORIENTED

13

Well-groomed and graceful, crowned with a cathedral and draped around the southwestern tip of Lac Léman (also called Lake Geneva), Geneva is a postcard waiting to happen. Headquarters of the 16th-century Calvinist Reformation and an independent crossroads of people and trade from the beginning, the Vieille Ville harbors three millennia of history; today the city of Geneva also hosts the United Nations and the 282-square-km (109-square-mile) canton, or state, of Geneva shares most of its borders with France.

RUES BASSES SHOPPING

Geneva's principal shopping streets, known collectively as the Rues Basses, run along the Left Bank. You'll see everything from limo-loads of body-guarded, burka-clad women shopping for sexy footwear, to jeans-wearing camera-toters seeking a glimpse of the high life.

Geneva's Rue-Basses comprise the heart of the city's shopping scene. Don't forget to pick up some Swiss chocolate at one of the city's top confectioners (below, right).

In true Swiss democratic style, the Rues Basses' sidewalk mix ranges from Mr. and Ms. Everybody to jet-setters. On two parallel streets linked by smaller ones, the Rues Basses (or Low Streets, in relation to the Old Town perched on a hill above) have something for everyone. Rue du Rhône, closer to the river, marks the epicenter of luxury shopping, from heavy-glitz brand boutiques—Chanel, Hermès, Vuitton, et al—to homegrown deluxe watchmakers like Chopard and Piaget. One block in is the more popular thoroughfare known as Rue de Rive, which then becomes Rue de la Croix d'Or, then Rue du Marché, and finally Rue de la Confédération. Up the hill, galleries, antiques shops, home-accessories emporia, and chic boutiques line the Old Town's Grand-Rue.

—Gail Mangold-Vine

BEST TIME TO GO

Hit the area on bustling weekday afternoons when all the stores are sure to be open. The Rues Basses get crowded on Saturday, too, but many watch and jewelry stores are closed then—and they remove window bling so shoppers have nothing but empty display stands to take in. Sunday you'll have the place to yourself; everything except a few eateries is closed tight as a drum.

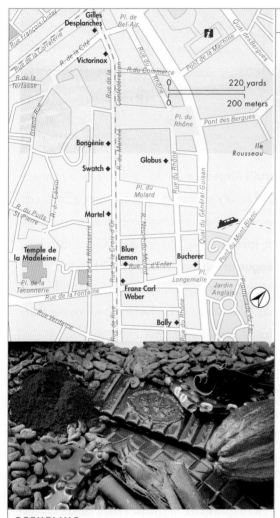

BEST FOR

ALL-AROUND FINDS
Globus: has everything, including a yummy food hall and fab Swiss wines. ✉ *48 rue du Rhône* ☏ *022/3195583*

Franz Carl Weber: come here for toys, backpacks, Swiss flag T-shirts, caps, mugs—you name it. ✉ *12 rue de la Croix d'Or* ☏ *022/3104255*

Victorinox: maker of the original Swiss Army knife—some now come with a USB. ✉ *2 rue du Marché* ☏ *022/3186340*

SWISS DESIGN
Bally: hits include unisex red-and-white trimmed leather bags, and cashmere scarves. *47 rue du Rhône* ☏ *022/3102287*

Blue Lemon: learn the meaning of "soft" when you touch the fabric this sexy feminine apparel is made from. There's a men's line, too. ✉ *10 rue de la Croix d'Or* ☏ *022/3113022*

Bongénie: made-in-Geneva Mizensir candles and sprays—a class act in home perfumery.

Bucherer: a good place to buy another locally produced brand: Rolex. Rolex's own boutique, Chrono-Time, is nearby.

Swatch: Trendy watches (and jewelry), mostly under 100 francs. ✉ *40 rue du Marché* ☏ *022/3114542*

13

REFUELING

Two ideal places for chocolate sampling are **Martel** (✉ *4 rue de la Croix d'Or* ☏ *022/3103119*) and **Gilles Desplanches** (✉ *Corner of Rue de la Corraterie and Rue de la Confédération* ☏ *022/8103028*), where sumptuously sinful pralines and truffles await: white, black, pile after neat little pile; you can buy just the one or a bagful. Stay for lunch or tea—there's seating in both venues and bountiful selections of savory tartlets, meat pasties, and rolls with fillings more likely to be crabmeat and sprouts than ham-and-cheese.

Updated by
Kelly DiNardo

Today the world's largest center for multilateral diplomacy and a hotbed of luxury shopping, Geneva was a postcard-perfect city known for enlightened tolerance long before Henry Dunant founded the International Red Cross here (1864), the League of Nations moved in (1919), the World Health Organization (WHO) set up shop after World War II, or the World Wide Web was invented here at the European Center for Nuclear Research (CERN).

Once a place of refuge for the religious reformers Jean Calvin and John Knox, it has sheltered Voltaire, Victor Hugo, Alexandre Dumas, Lord Byron, and Mary Shelley, offered safe haven to Richard Wagner and Franz Liszt, and expelled its native son Jean-Jacques Rousseau for being liberal way before his time.

Today a whopping 40% of the city's roughly 185,000 inhabitants are not Swiss, but the more than 150 countries that maintain permanent missions to the United Nations Office in Geneva represent merely the most recent group of foreigners to descend on the city. Four hundred years ago it was wave after wave of Protestant refugees: the English fled Bloody Mary, Protestant Italians the wrath of the pope, Spaniards the Inquisition, French Huguenots the oppressive French monarchy—and Geneva flourished, under the iron yoke of its 16th-century reformer, as a multilingual stronghold of Protestant (specifically Calvinist) reform.

The city's history as a crossroads stretches back further still. The Genevois controlled the only bridge over the Rhône north of Lyon when Julius Caesar breezed through in 58 BC; the early Burgundians and bishop-princes who succeeded the Romans were careful to maintain this control. The strategically placed (and wealthy) city-state fell to the French in 1798, then made overtures to Bern as Napoléon's star waned. Geneva finally joined the Swiss Confederation as a canton in 1815. But don't get too carried away with Swiss stereotypes here—they are as foreign to the Genevois as risotto or gnocchi might be to a resident of Bern.

Geneva's museums have drawn particular benefit from the city's unique perspective on history and cultural exchange: you can visit a military exhibit up the hill from the Red Cross's examination of the horrors of war; weigh the extremes of ancient and contemporary ceramics; browse archaeological finds from Egypt and the Far East; compare pre-Christian primitive art with its modern incarnation; relive the Reformation; or explore the fruits of human thought and creativity as expressed on paper, in science, and inside the case of a tiny pocket watch. The Palais des Nations forms the ultimate living (and working) museum of 20th-century history.

The early December celebration of the Escalade, a 17th-century military victory that marked a turning point in Geneva's history, offers a unique peek at the city's core character; the early-August Fête de Genève showcases a different, more easily accessible modern identity and culminates in a fireworks extravaganza set to music that perfectly exploits the beauty of Geneva's physical setting. Mary Shelley conceived of Frankenstein's monster during a dark and stormy night in Geneva, letting him escape over the cliff face of the Salève, to the southeast of the city. But on a beautiful summer night with an ice cream in hand, the Alps glowing pink in the sunset and the harbor lights ablaze, it's hard to imagine anything but bliss.

GENEVA PLANNER

WHEN TO GO

Hot and sunny with a slight breeze in summer, crisp and clear in spring and autumn, rainbow-prone in June—Geneva's weather, when it's good, is spectacular. The Alps glow pink and the Jura fades to silhouette at the end of the day; restaurants set tables outside from March through October.

There are other days—whole weeks of them in winter—when stratus clouds coagulate between the mountains and gray out everything in sight. But relief comes from La Bise, the often bitingly cold north wind that blows in off the lake, clears away *la grisaille* (the grayness), and reveals sparkling snow-covered peaks.

PLANNING YOUR TIME

A curious tension exists in Geneva between dour intellectual concepts and breathtaking physical beauty, and you will probably find yourself torn between the urge to wander the quays and the sense that you ought to hit the museum trail. Don't choose: try to divide whatever time you have in the city equally between an extended stroll along the waterfront and a thorough exploration of the Vieille Ville.

Make time for the International Area if it interests you—never mind if it doesn't. Do not, however, skip Carouge, the creative, convivial warren of craftspeople and artists to the south of the city. Try to see some specialist collections (the Fondation Bodmer and the Patek Philippe Museum are stars), check out the Rues Basses shopping scene, and make sure that you go somewhere—Port Noir, the tip of the Jet d'Eau jetty, the cathedral towers, La Perle du Lac, Cologny—where you can see distance: Geneva genuinely does look equally good from up close and far away.

GETTING HERE AND AROUND

AIR TRAVEL

Geneva International Airport, Switzerland's second largest, lies 5 km (3 miles) northwest of downtown Geneva, in Cointrin. ■ **TIP→ When you arrive, pick up a free ticket from the dispensers in the baggage hall just before customs.** The ticket is valid for 80 minutes and gives you free transportation on trains, buses, trams, and *mouettes* (water shuttles).

GROUND TRANSPORTATION

There's no easier way to get from the airport to the city than the trains that depart every few minutes for the Gare Cornavin, Geneva's main train station. Amazingly, the trip takes just six minutes. The Nos. 5 and 10 buses connect the airport and downtown in about 20 minutes. Taxis are plentiful but expensive: expect to pay 35 SF or more to reach the city center.

BIKE TRAVEL

Bike lanes, indicated by a yellow line and a yellow bicycle symbol on the pavement, are ubiquitous downtown. Yellow signs indicate routes elsewhere in the canton. Genèv'Roule "lends" bicycles from May to October in all their locations, which include Place du Rhône in Centre Ville Rive Gauche, Ruelle des Templiers in Eaux-Vives, Bains des Pâquis in Pâquis, Plaine de Plainpalais in Plainpalais, and Place de l'Octroi in Carouge. Show valid identification, pay a deposit of 20 SF, and the bike is yours for four hours and must be returned the same day.

Bike Rental Information Genèv'Roule ⊠ *17 pl. Montbrillant, Centre Ville Rive Droite* ☎ *022/7401343* ⊕ *www.geneveroule.ch* ⊠ *Across from Rue Barton, Les Pâquis.* ⊠ *Plaine de Plainpalais, Plainpalais* ⊠ *4 ruelle des Templiers (Terrassière), Eaux-Vives.*

BOAT AND FERRY TRAVEL

The Compagnie Générale de Navigation operates steamship connections between Geneva and lake towns in Vaud and France. Swiss Pass holders travel free; those with a Swiss Boat Pass pay half price. Smaller-scale lake travel, including a shuttle service across Geneva's harbor, is entrusted to the Mouettes Genevoises.

Boat and Ferry Information Compagnie Générale de Navigation (*CGN*). ☎ *0848/811848* ⊕ *www.cgn.ch.* **Mouettes Genevoises** ⊠ *4–8 quai du Mont-Blanc, Les Pâquis* ☎ *022/7322944* ⊕ *www.mouettesgenevoises.ch.*

BUS AND TRAM TRAVEL

Local buses and trams operate every few minutes on all city routes from 5 or 6 am to around midnight (depending on the day of the week and the route). On Friday and Saturday, the Noctambus night-bus service kicks in between 2 and 4 am.

The standard one-ride fare is 3.50 SF. Day passes, known as *cartes journalières,* are available from vending machines, Unireso sales points, and the Transports Publics Genevois (TPG) booths at the train station and Rond-point de Rive. Unlimited city-center travel between 9 am and the last bus costs 7 SF; 10 SF will buy you a ticket that allows two people to travel for the price of one on weekends.

Bus and Tram Information Transports Publics Genevois (*TPG*). ☎ *0900/022021* ⊕ *www.tpg.ch.*

CAR TRAVEL

Geneva's long border with France makes for easy access from all points French. The Swiss A1 expressway, along the north shore, connects Geneva to the rest of Switzerland by way of Lausanne. Traffic along the quays clogs easily, and parking in town is both restricted and expensive; look for electric signs on major incoming roads that note the whereabouts of (immaculate) municipal parking garages and their current number of empty spaces.

GENEVA TRANSPORT CARD

Canton-wide public transport is clean, punctual, ubiquitous, and cheap. In fact, it's free if you're staying at a hotel or hostel, or if you're camping. Ask for your **Geneva Transport Card** at your lodging's front desk; it will give you free use of trains, buses, trams, and shuttle boats for the length of your stay.

TAXI TRAVEL

Taxis are clean and drivers are polite, but be prepared to pay a 6.30 SF minimum charge plus 3.20 SF per kilometer (about half a mile) traveled. In the evening and on Sunday, the rate climbs to 3.80 SF per kilometer. Cabs won't stop if you hail them; go to a designated taxi stand (marked on the pavement in yellow) or call.

Taxi Information Taxi-Phone ☎ *022/3314133* ⊕ *www.taxi-phone.ch.*

TRAIN TRAVEL

Express trains from most Swiss cities arrive at and depart from the Right Bank Gare Cornavin every hour. Regional trains leave every 15 minutes en route to Nyon and Lausanne.

⇨ *For more information on getting here and around, see Travel Smart Switzerland.*

VISITOR INFORMATION

Genève Tourisme is headquartered inside the large post office building halfway between the Pont du Mont-Blanc and the Gare Cornavin. Additional information booths serve the airport and, from June through September, the train station. The Arcade d'Information de la Ville de Genève, run by the city on the Pont de la Machine, is another excellent, multilingual source of information about all things Geneva.

Contact Genève Tourisme ✉ *18 rue du Mont-Blanc, Centre Ville Rive Droite* ☎ *022/9097070* ⊕ *www.geneve-tourisme.ch.*

EXPLORING GENEVA

The *République et Canton de Genève* (Republic and Canton of Geneva) commands sweeping views of the French Alps and the French Jura from its fortuitous position at the southwestern tip of Lac Léman. The water flows straight through the city center and into the River Rhône en route to Lyon and the Mediterranean, leaving museums, shops, restaurants, and parks to jostle for space on its history-laden south shore, known as Rive Gauche. Busy shopping streets underline the hilltop Vieille Ville, the Plaine de Plainpalais lies to its west, and Eaux-Vives stretches along the quays to the east.

The *quartier international* (International Area), the Gare Cornavin, and sumptuous waterfront hotels dominate the north shore, or Rive Droite. St-Gervais, just north of the Ponts de l'Ile, was once a watchmaking quarter. Les Pâquis, a mix of artists, ethnic communities, and scrappy pleasure seekers, extends north from the Pont du Mont-Blanc. The International Area, on the outer edge of the city, is a short tram ride from Gare Cornavin; all other neighborhoods are easily toured on foot.

> ### LOCAL CELEBRATIONS
>
> Nothing is too insignificant, it would seem, to be feted in Geneva: it enthusiastically supports a stream of celebrations, including wine harvest, jazz, and cinema-arts festivals. The three-day Fête de la Musique marks the summer solstice with more than 500 open-air concerts; the Fête de l'Escalade rolls back the clock to 1602 each December. The flamboyantly raunchy Lake Parade grinds its way along the quays in July. The 10-day Fêtes de Genève fill the waterfront each August with Ferris wheels, open-air discos, international foods, and a massive display of fireworks set to music.

RIVE DROITE (RIGHT BANK)

INTERNATIONAL AREA

The Palais des Nations, 10 minutes north of the Gare Cornavin by tram, is the focal point of Geneva's humanitarian and diplomatic zone. Modern structures housing UN agencies dominate streets leading to it; embassies, 19th-century villas full of nongovernmental organizations, and museums surround them.

To get to this sector, take Tram No. 13 or No. 15 from the Gare Cornavin to the end of the line (Nations), and disembark onto the recently renovated pedestrian Promenade des Nations. Towering over the 84 computer-managed water fountains is Swiss artist Daniel Berset's *Broken Chair*, a memorial to land-mine victims.

TOP ATTRACTIONS

Jardin Botanique (*Botanical Garden*). These 69 peaceful acres of winding paths and streams bear witness to Geneva's early-19th-century fascination with botany. They also include tropical greenhouses, beds of irises and roses, rock gardens, an aviary, a deer park, a garden of scent and touch, a living catalog of economically useful and medicinal plants, a seed bank, and a formidable research institute. Several of the trees predate 1700. The main entrance is opposite the World Trade Organization. ✉ *154 rue de Lausanne, International Area* ☎ *022/4185100* ⊕ *www.ville-ge.ch/cjb* ✇ *Free* ⊙ *Apr.–Sept., daily 8–7:30; Oct.–Mar., daily 9:30–5.*

★ **Musée d'Histoire des Sciences** (*Museum of the History of Science*). Walk-around glass cases display age-old sundials and astrolabes, microscopes and telescopes, barometers and ornate globes that collectively document the evolution of modern science. Descriptions are in in English. The Neoclassical Italianate jewel that houses the collection, the Villa Bartholoni, dates from 1830. ⊠ *128 rue de Lausanne, International Area* ☎ *022/4185060* ⊕ *www.ville-ge.ch/mhs* ⊠ *Free* ☉ *Wed.–Mon. 10–5.*

Musée International de la Croix-Rouge et du Croissant-Rouge (*International Red Cross and Red Crescent Museum*). This carefully nonjudgmental museum buried in the hillside beneath the world headquarters of the International Committee of the Red Cross traces the history of the struggle to provide emergency care in the face of disaster. At this writing, the museum is closed for a complete renovation and is scheduled to reopen in 2013. The new permanent exhibition will be organized around several themes, including defending human dignity and reviving family ties. An interactive globe will show the latest news from the field. ⊠ *17 av. de la Paix, International Area* ☎ *022/7489525* ⊕ *www.micr.org* ⊠ *10 SF* ☉ *Wed.–Mon. 10–5.*

★ **Palais des Nations** (*Palace of Nations*). Built between 1929 and 1936 for the League of Nations, this monumental compound became the European office of the United Nations in 1946 and quickly evolved into the largest center for multilateral diplomacy in the world. Today it hosts some 9,000 conferences and 25,000 delegates each year; it is also the largest nexus for United Nations operational activities after New York.

Security is tight: be prepared to show your passport. Points of particular interest include the **Assembly Hall,** the largest of 34 conference rooms, where the UN General Assembly and scores of world leaders have met, and the ornate **Council Chamber,** home to the Conference on Disarmament, which glows with allegorical murals. Tours last about one hour and are conducted in 15 languages, including English. ⊠ *14 av. de la Paix, International Area* ☎ *022/9174896* ⊕ *www.unog.ch* ⊠ *12 SF* ☉ *Sept.–Mar., weekdays 10–noon and 2–4, tours: 10:30, noon, 2:30, and 4; Apr.–June, daily 10–noon and 2–4, tours: 10:30, noon, 2:30, 4; July and Aug., daily 10–5, tours: 10:30.*

WORTH NOTING

Musée Ariana. An architectural anachronism when it was completed in 1887, this serene Italianate structure now houses the Musée Suisse de la Céramique et du Verre (Swiss Museum of Ceramics and Glass). Stoneware, earthenware, porcelain, and glass covering 700 years of East–West exchange populate the upper floors; contemporary work rotates through the basement. ⊠ *10 av. de la Paix, International Area* ☎ *022/4185450* ⊕ *www.ville-ge.ch/ariana* ⊠ *Free* ☉ *Tues.–Sun. 10–6.*

Musée Militaire Genevois (*Geneva Military Museum*). The humble setting adds authenticity to this detailed look at a neutral but thoroughly competent military force. Uniformed models, weapons, prints, and documents proceed in chronological order through the eventful history of la Garde Genevoise from 1814 to the present, including a Napoleonic officer's outfit, Guillaume-Henri Dufour's personal effects, and a full-scale re-creation of a Genevois border post during World War II. ⊠ *18*

13

The International Red Cross has a museum with powerful exhibits dedicated to the institution's work and subject matter.

chemin de l'Impératrice, Chambésy, International Area ☎ *022/7344875* ⊕ *museemilitaire.tripod.com* ✉ *Free* ⊙ *Tues.–Sat. 2–5, Sun. 10–noon and 2–5.*

LES PÂQUIS

The Rive Droite neighborhood known as Les Pâquis is lively and diverse, with luxury hotels and expensive apartments lining the waterfront. The crisscrosses of narrow streets opening up behind the five-star glamour have a multiethnic character and house everything from quirky boutiques, bars, and restaurants to the Red Light District.

Beau-Rivage. Jean-Jacques Mayer's descendants still own and operate the hotel he built in 1865. It has discreetly witnessed the birth of a nation (Czechoslovakia, in 1918), the death of an empress (Empress Elisabeth of Austria, in 1898), the sale of royal treasure (the Duchess of Windsor's jewels, in 1987), and the passage of crowned heads from around the world. Sotheby's commandeers its conference rooms for jewelry auctions twice a year. ✉ *13 quai du Mont-Blanc, Les Pâquis* ☎ *022/7166666* ⊕ *www.beau-rivage.ch.*

★ **Mont Blanc.** At 15,767 feet, Mont Blanc is the highest mountain in Europe and the crown jewel of the French Alps. Geneva's Right Bank—particularly its waterfront parkland—has a front-row view framed by three less-lofty acolytes: Les Voirons, to the left; Le Môle, in the center; and Le Salève, to the right.

Monument Brunswick. Charles d'Este-Guelph, the famously eccentric (and deposed) Duke of Brunswick, died in Geneva in 1873 and left his vast fortune to the city on condition that his mausoleum, the Gothic design of which is based on the 14th-century Scaligeri tombs in Verona, be given prominence. No one is sure why his sarcophagus faces inland. ⊠ *Bounded by Rue des Alpes, Quai du Mont-Blanc, and Rue Adhémar-Fabri, Les Pâquis.*

Palais Wilson. The largest of Geneva's grand dames, this former hotel leaped to international prominence on April 28, 1919, when the peace negotiators in Paris chose Geneva to host the newborn League of Nations. International civil servants began work here in November 1920, and the building was renamed in honor of U.S. President Woodrow Wilson in 1924. By 1936 the faltering League had run out of space and moved to the custom-built Palais des Nations. Ten years later it was dismantled. The Palais Wilson was gutted by fire in 1987, meticulously restored in 1998, and now houses the headquarters of the United Nations High Commissioner for Human Rights. It is not open to the public. ⊠ *51 rue des Pâquis, Les Pâquis.*

RIVE GAUCHE (LEFT BANK)

CENTRE VILLE RIVE GAUCHE

Unlike its Right Bank counterpart, which extends vertically down towards the lake and river from the main train station, Cornavin, the Centre Ville Rive Gauche is aligned horizontally with the Rhône and comprises Quai du Général Guisan and the Rues Basses shopping area. Both parts of downtown Geneva—Rive Droite and Rive Gauche—are business, shopping, and to some extent residential areas. Geneva's equivalent to 5th Avenue, or Rodeo Drive, is the Left Bank's Rue du Rhône.

Horloge Fleurie (*Flower Clock*). The city first planted this gigantic, and accurate, floral timepiece in 1955 to highlight Geneva's seminal role in the Swiss watchmaking industry. Some 6,500 plants are required four times a year to cover its 16-foot-wide surface. ⊠ *Quai du Général-Guisan and Pont du Mont-Blanc, Centre Ville Rive Gauche.*

Ile Rousseau. Jean-Jacques Rousseau, the son of a Genevois watchmaker, is known to history as a liberal *French* philosopher in part because Geneva's conservative government so thoroughly rejected his views. His statue on this former city bastion, erected reluctantly in 1835 (57 years after his death), was surrounded by trees and deliberately hidden from view until the 1862 construction of the Pont du Mont-Blanc gave Rousseau the last laugh. In 2012, for Rousseau's 300th birthday, the statue was turned so visitors can once again see his face. ⊠ *Off Pont des Bergues, Centre Ville Rive Gauche.*

Temple de la Fusterie. Designed by Huguenot refugee Jean Vennes and completed in 1715, Geneva's first specifically Calvinist church was built to accommodate the flood of French Protestants that followed the 1685 revocation of the Edict of Nantes. The Baroque facade blended into the secular landscape around it; the well-lighted and whitewashed galleries within allowed 750 people to hear every word the minister said. ⊠ *Pl. de la Fusterie, Centre Ville Rive Gauche.*

Tour de l'Ile. On the border of the Rive Gauche's Plainpalais and Centre Ville neighborhoods is the lone surviving fragment of a 13th-century

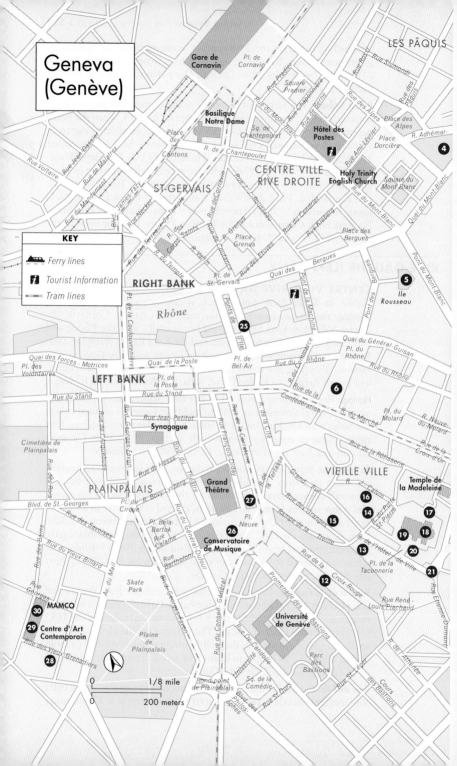

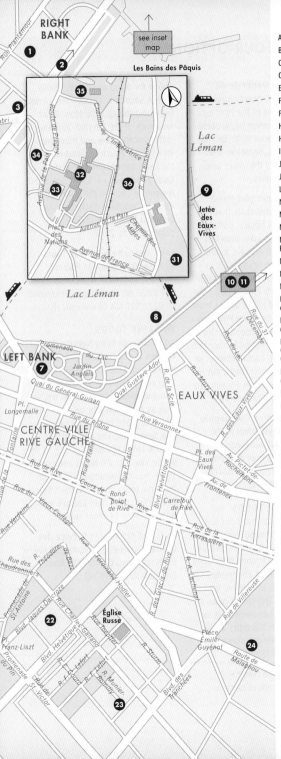

GENEVA TOUR OPTIONS

BOAT TOURS

The **Compagnie Générale de Navigation** (CGN) boards passengers on both sides of the Pont du Mont-Blanc and serves multicourse meals aboard special Belle Epoque steamship cruises. Separate, hour-long CGN loops of the lower lake point out local sights.

Swissboat operates year-round smaller-scale guided tours that take in castles, famous homes, ports, and parkland along the lake. Trips last anywhere from 40 minutes to two hours; recorded commentary is in English. The boats leave from Jardin Anglais on the Left Bank, and, on the Right Bank, board either across from the Beau-Rivage or at the Port des Mouettes. Swissboat also operates a nearly three-hour natural-history tour of the Rhône. Live commentary is in French, but on request they'll put on recorded commentary in English. The boats depart from Place de l'Ile.

Fees and Schedules Compagnie Générale de Navigation (*CGN*). ☎ 0848/811848 ⊕ *www.cgn.ch*. **Swissboat** ✉ *4–8 quai du Mont-Blanc, Les Pâquis* ☎ *022/7324747* ⊕ *www.swissboat.com*.

BUS AND TRAIN TOURS

Key Tours conducts two-hour bus tours of the city, leaving from Place Dorcière daily at 1:30 pm as well as at 10:30 am May–October. It's a good idea to arrive at least 15 minutes early, as the Swiss are known for their punctuality. The circuit costs 45 SF, and recorded commentary is in English. Afternoon bus tours of the Geneva countryside are also available May through October.

Between March and December you can also opt to catch an STT-operated minitrain at Place du Rhône for a trip around the Vieille Ville. A second minitrain leaves from there and the Quai du Mont-Blanc for a tour of the International Area with its scenic lake and mountain views. From March to October, a third minitrain departs from the Quai du Mont-Blanc for a "parks and residences" ride to the Botanical Gardens and back. Each loop lasts between 35 and 75 minutes; the cost is 8.90 to 25 SF.

Fees and Schedules Key Tours ✉ *7 rue des Alpes, Les Pâquis* ☎ *022/7314140* ⊕ *www.keytours.ch*. **STT** ✉ *36 bd. St-Georges, Plainpalais* ☎ *022/7810404* ⊕ *www.sttt.ch*.

WALKING TOURS

An English-speaking **Service des Guides** at the Genève Tourisme lead a two-hour walk through the Vieille Ville every Saturday at 10 am. Additional weekday circuits at 10 am, as well as an 11 am tour on Sunday, take place between June and late September. The cost is 15 SF. English-language audio guides to the Vieille Ville last 2½ hours and cost 18 SF. You can arrange tailor-made thematic tours that trace the history of watchmaking, Jean Calvin's legacy, or any one of 14 other subjects.

Fees and Schedules Service des Guides ✉ *Genève Tourisme, 18 rue du Mont-Blanc, Centre Ville Rive Droite* ☎ *022/9097030*.

Carouge: La Citè Sarde

13

Carouge (from *quadruvium*) began life in the Roman era as a crossroads next to a bridge over the River Arve. It remained a mere hamlet until 1754, when the Duke of Savoy, by then also King of Sardinia, annexed it with intent to create a rival commercial hub for Geneva. That never happened, courtesy of the French Revolution, but the town grew so fast that the royal planners in Turin drew up five separate development plans between 1772 and 1783; their harmonious architecture, plazas, and courtyard gardens still recall Mediterranean ways unheard of in Geneva. Colorful shop windows, sidewalk cafés, friendly restaurants, hole-in-the-wall galleries,

tree-lined fruit-and-vegetable markets (on Wednesday and Saturday), open doors, and working artists infuse Rue St-Joseph, Rue Ancienne, Rue St-Victor, and Place du Marché with vibrant creative energy. For more information go to ⊕ *www.carouge.ch*.

WHEN TO GO
Don't miss the outdoor street fairs in late August or early September (Vogue de Carouge) or the December Christmas Market.

GETTING HERE AND AROUND
Trams 12 and 13 from Rive and Gare Cornavin run on average every 5 minutes and get you here in 15 to 20 minutes.

castle built by Bishop Aymon de Grandson to protect Geneva from attack via the bridge. The castle was demolished in 1677; this carefully preserved lookout tower now houses the Banque Safdié. It is not open to the public. ⊠ *Rue de la Tour-de-l'Ile, Centre Ville Rive Gauche.*

EAUX-VIVES

Overall a tad more sedate in feel than the heart of Pâquis, which lies across the water, Eaux-Vives is nevertheless a bustling mix of residential, commercial, and business life. Quai Gustave-Ador echoes some of the grandeur of the opposite shore with fine old apartment buildings and prestigious office space.

Fodor's Choice ★ **Fondation Martin Bodmer** (*Martin Bodmer Foundation*). The library that sources this humbling exhibition of original texts—from cuneiform tablets, papyrus scrolls, and parchment to a dizzying array of first editions—maps the history of human thought. Dramatic displays of bas-reliefs and dimly lighted Egyptian books of the dead give way to Homer's *Iliad*; handwritten Gospels according to Matthew and John; exquisite copies of the Koran; a perfectly preserved Gutenberg Bible; Shakespeare (the complete works, published in 1623); an autographed score by Mozart; *Oliver Twist*; the *Communist Manifesto*; and *Alice in Wonderland*. A comprehensive printed guide is available in English. Energetic sightseers can get here on foot; otherwise, take the A bus from Rond-point de Rive and get off at Cologny-Temple. The ride takes 12 minutes. ⊠ *19–21 rte. du Guignard, Cologny* ☎ *022/7074433* ⊕ *www. fondationbodmer.org* ⊠ *15 SF* ☉ *Tues.–Sun. 2–6.*

The landmark Jet d'Eau shoots water 459 feet into the air.

Jet d'Eau (*Water Jet*). The direct descendant of a late-19th-century hydroelectric safety valve, Europe's tallest fountain shoots 132 gallons of water—the equivalent of four standard bathtubs—459 feet into the air every second at 125 mph (wind conditions permitting). The water is aerated by a special nozzle, making it white. ⊠ *Off Quai Gustave-Ador, Eaux-Vives.*

Fodor's Choice ★

La Neptune. Old photos of Geneva show scores of black masts and graceful, cream-colored sails crowding the lake. Now *La Neptune*, the only authentic traditional barge still in existence, is hired out for day sails. Built in 1904 and restored twice, in 1976 and 2005, she hauled stone and sand between far-flung construction sites until 1968. ⊠ *Off Quai Gustave-Ador, Eaux-Vives* ☎ 022/7322944.

QUICK BITES

Gelateria Arlecchino. The ice-cream maestros at Gelateria Arlecchino, across the street from the Jet d'Eau, crank out some 50 homemade flavors, including ginger-lime, tiramisu, pineapple mint, green tea, licorice, and several sugar-free options. There's a second location in the city center at 13 rue de Berne. ⊠ *1 rue du 31-Décembre, Eaux-Vives* ☎ *022/7367060* ⊕ *www.larlecchino.ch.*

Parc La Grange. The remnants of a 1st-century Roman villa crown the hillside in this gracious, sun-dappled park, once the private grounds of an 18th-century villa overlooking the lake. William Favre's bequest of his family's domain to the city in 1917 stipulated that the park be made available to the public during the day and closed at night. It is still the only green space in Geneva to be locked when the sun goes down. More than 240 different types of roses share the exceptional rose garden, where new varieties of roses compete for prizes each June. The Orangerie and the Théâtre de Verdure stage performances and open-air concerts through the summer months. ⊠ *Quai Gustave-Ador, Eaux-Vives.*

VIEILLE VILLE

Geneva's Old Town (Vieille Ville), a tight cluster of museums, boutiques, historical sites, and sidewalk cafés capped by the cathedral, represents the city's core. The cantonal government's executive, legislative, and judicial branches operate within its walls; the Left Bank radiates out from its slopes.

13

TOP ATTRACTIONS

Auditoire de Calvin (*Calvin's Lecture Hall*). Reformed services in English, Italian, Spanish, Dutch, and German made this simple Gothic structure, built in the 15th century on the site of two prior churches, a potent international gathering place for 16th-century Protestant refugees. The Scots reformer John Knox preached here from 1556 to 1559 while he translated the Bible into English, initiating the Presbyterian church; Calvin and his successors used the space to teach theology and train missionaries into the 18th century. Today the auditoire hosts the Church of Scotland, the Dutch Reformed Community, and the Waldensian Church of Italy. ⊠ *1 pl. de la Taconnerie, Vieille Ville* 🖼 *Free.*

★ **Cathédrale St-Pierre** (*St. Peter's Cathedral*). A stylistic hybrid scarred by centuries of religious upheaval and political turmoil, this imposing cathedral somehow survived the ages with its dignity intact. The massive Neoclassical facade was an 18th-century addition meant to shore up 12th-century Romanesque-Gothic walls; stained-glass windows, the Duke of Rohan's tomb, a few choir stalls, and the 15th-century **Chapel of the Maccabees** hint at lavish alternatives to Calvin's plain chair. Fifteenth-century bells and bird's-eye city views reward those who climb the **North Tower.** ⊠ *Cour St-Pierre, Vieille Ville* 🕾 *022/3117575* ⊕ *www.saintpierre-geneve.ch* 🖼 *North tower 4 SF* ☉ *June–Sept., Mon.– Sat. 9:30–6:30, Sun. noon–6:30; Oct.–May, Mon.–Sat. 10–5:30, Sun. noon–5:30.*

Fondation Baur (*Baur Foundation*). Alfred Baur's lovingly preserved collection of Far Eastern art packs more than 10 centuries of Chinese ceramics and jade, Japanese smoking paraphernalia, prints, lacquerware, and sword fittings—some 9,000 objects in all—into a tranquil 19th-century town house on the edge of the Vieille Ville. Thematic temporary exhibits occupy the basement. English texts introduce each room. ⊠ *8 rue Munier-Romilly, Vieille Ville* 🕾 *022/7043282* ⊕ *www. fondation-baur.ch* 🖼 *10 SF* ☉ *Tues.–Sun. 2–6.*

Hôtel de Ville (*City Hall*). Fourteen of sixteen countries present signed the first Geneva Convention in the ground-floor **Alabama Hall** on August 22, 1864, making it the birthplace of the International Red Cross, and the League of Nations convened its first assembly here on November 15, 1920. The canton's executive and legislative bodies meet here; until 1958 government functionaries lived here. But the history of this elegant vaulted compound begins in 1455, when the city built a large fortified tower, the **Tour Baudet,** to house the State Council Chamber. Its ramp, an architectural anomaly added during the Reformation, was used by the councilors to reach the third-floor meeting hall without dismounting from their donkeys, a practice which gave name to the tower, as *baudet* means donkey in French. ✉ *2 rue de l'Hôtel-de-Ville, Vieille Ville* 🕿 *022/3272118* ⊕ *www.geneve.ch* ✆ *Free* ⊙ *Daily; information booth weekdays 9– noon and 2–5.*

Fodor's Choice **Monument de la Réformation** (*Wall of the Reformers*). Conceived on a grand scale and erected between 1909 and 1917, this solemn 325- by 30-foot swath of granite pays homage to the 16th-century religious movement spearheaded by Guillaume Farel, Jean Calvin, Théodore de Bèze, and John Knox. Smaller statues of major Protestant figures, bas-reliefs, and inscriptions connected with the Reformation flank the lifelike giants as they hover over Bern, Geneva, and Edinburgh's coats of arms; Oliver Cromwell is surrounded by Pilgrims praying on the deck of the *Mayflower* and the 1689 presentation of the Bill of Rights to King William and Queen Mary by the English Houses of Parliament. The Reformation's—and Geneva's—motto, *Post Tenebras Lux* (After Darkness, Light), spreads over the whole. The location lies just below the Vieille Ville. ✉ *Parc des Bastions, Vieille Ville.*

★ **Musée Barbier-Mueller.** Josef Mueller began acquiring fine primitive art from Africa, Southeast Asia, and the Americas in 1907. Today his family's vast, inspired collection of sculpture, masks, shields, textiles, and ornaments spans six continents and seven millennia. A small selection is on view at any given time, displayed like jewels in warm, spotlighted vaults of scrubbed stone. ✉ *10 rue Jean-Calvin, Vieille Ville* 🕿 *022/3120270* ⊕ *www.barbier-mueller.ch* ✆ *8 SF* ⊙ *Daily 11–5.*

Fodor's Choice **Musée International de la Réforme** (*International Museum of the Reformation*). Period artifacts, carefully preserved documents, and engaging audiovisuals explain the logic behind the Protestant Reformation. This sophisticated, modern, and remarkably friendly museum explores its impact as a religious, cultural, and philosophical phenomenon and traces its roots from the early 16th century through today. The sparkling 18th-century premises, on the site where Geneva voted to adopt the Reform, connect by underground passage to the Site Archéologique. All signage and audio-guide material are in English. ✉ *4 rue du Cloître, Vieille Ville* 🕿 *022/3102431* ⊕ *www.musee-reforme.ch* ✆ *13 SF, 16 SF with Site Archéologique* ⊙ *Tues.–Sun. 10–5.*

★ **Place du Bourg-de-Four.** Ancient roads met in this layered Vieille Ville square before heading south to Annecy and Lyon, east to Italy and the

---

MONEY-SAVING TIP

The **Passeport Musées** is a little booklet that, when stamped at the door like a passport, allows one free entrance each to the Fondation Baur, Fondation Martin Bodmer, Musée des Suisses dans le Monde, Musée Barbier-Mueller, Musée International de la Croix-Rouge et du Croissant-Rouge, Musée International de la Réforme, and Patek Philippe Museum. Tourist information booths, many hotels, and the museums themselves sell the booklets. They are valid for three months, cost 20 SF, and can be handed off to a friend.

The Wall of the Reformers commemorates major figures in the 16th-century Protestant Reformation.

Chablais, north to the Rues Basses, and west through the center of town to the bridge. Once a Roman cattle market, later flooded with refugees, it's still the quintessential Genevois crossroads where shoppers, lawyers, workers, and students all meet for drinks around an 18th-century fountain. ⊠ *Meeting point of Rue Etienne-Dumont, Rue Saint-Léger, and Rue de l'Hôtel-de-Ville, Vieille Ville.*

Site Archéologique. Archaeologists found multiple layers of history underneath the Cathédrale St-Pierre when its foundations began to falter in 1976. Excavations have so far yielded remnants of two 4th-century Christian sanctuaries, mosaic floors from the late Roman Empire, three early churches, and an 11th-century crypt. The first Romanesque cathedral on the site was built in 1000. Audio guides in English and careful lighting help navigate the (reinforced) underground maze that remains. ⊠ *6 cour St-Pierre, Vieille Ville* ☎ *022/3117574* ⊕ *www. site-archeologique.ch* 🖾 *8 SF, 16SF with Musée International* ☉ *Daily 10–4:30.*

Fodor's Choice
★

WORTH NOTING

Eglise Saint-Germain (*Saint-Germain Church*). This pristine 15th-century sanctuary served as a Protestant temple, a butcher's warehouse, a foundry, and a government meeting hall before Napoléon's troops returned it to Catholicism in 1803. The second chapel on the left maps a structural lineage that began in AD 400, and the steeple dates from the 14th century. Today's whitewashed walls, strategic lighting, and stained glass frame weekly classical music concerts in summer. Attending a concert or a service (the latter occurs at 10 on Sunday) is usually

A GOOD WALK: VIEILLE VILLE

Stroll through Parc des Bastions from its Place Neuve entrance. Geneva's university (on your right) is descended from Calvin's ground-breaking academy; the **Monument de la Réformation** spreads along the park wall to your left. Access Rue de la Croix-Rouge, then Promenade de la Treille, from steps to the Monument's right.

Past the *Marronnier Officiel* (Official Chestnut Tree) is the **Hôtel de Ville**, seat of Geneva's cantonal government. By the statue of statesman Charles Pictet de Rochemont, head right through the 18th-century portico, then right again at No. 2 rue de l'Hôtel-de-Ville into the government complex courtyard.

Across the street, **Maison Tavel** is worth a stop. Turn right after leaving Maison Tavel, then right again into Grand-Rue. Espace Jean-Jacques Rousseau (No. 40), the philosopher's birthplace, features an audiovisual overview of his life. By No. 28, turn left into Ruelle du Sautier, which empties out by the **Eglise Saint-Germain**. Follow Rue des Granges; the 18th-century rooms of Fondation Zoubov (No. 2) can be visited on weekday afternoons.

Continue through Place du Grand-Mézel, Geneva's 15th-century Jewish ghetto. To the left, Rue de la Cité connects the Old Town with its ancient river crossing. Head back up Grand-Rue and turn left down Rue de la Pélisserie, which becomes Rue Jean-Calvin; the **Musée Barbier-Mueller** is here. Calvin and his family lived across from No. 11 from 1543 until his death in 1564.

Proceed via Rue Otto-Barblan to Cour Saint-Pierre, home to the **Musée International de la Réforme, Cathédrale St-Pierre,** and the **Site Archéologique.** This has been Geneva's spiritual center since the time of Celtic goddesses. Take Rue du Cloître to the Reformation museum. Upon leaving the museum, turn left then right into Rue de l'Evêché behind the cathedral. The chapel straight ahead is the **Auditoire de Calvin.** Back at Cour Saint-Pierre, you'll see the entrance to the Site Archéologique to your right. Finish with the view from the cathedral towers.

Via Rue de l'Evêché, go to Rue des Barrières; ascend the stairs leading to Terrasse Agrippa-d'Aubigné for a terrific view of the cathedral and 15th-century Madeleine church below.

Then head down the ramp to the right into Rue de la Fontaine. Walk up past the Lutheran Church to **Place du Bourg-de-Four** and into Rue Etienne-Dumont.

Continue straight to Place Franz-Liszt—after the composer, who lived here—and turn left onto Promenade de Saint-Antoine. Descend the steps marked **Site Archéologique** to stroll through the massive remains of Geneva's defense walls, then ride the elevator up and cross the bridge to the **Musée d'Art et d'Histoire.**

You can't miss the cupolas crowning the 19th-century Eglise Russe, which may be visited. Follow Rue François Le Fort to Rue Munier-Romilly where the **Fondation Baur** museum is the last building on the right.

your only chance to see the inside. ✉ *9 rue des Granges, Vieille Ville* ⊕ *www.concerts-st-germain.ch.*

Maison Tavel (*Tavel House*). Vaulted cellars and ground-floor kitchens display medieval graffiti, 15th-century tiles, and a guillotine in Geneva's oldest house, now a museum focused on life in the city from 1334 to the 1800s. Seventeenth-century ironwork, doors, and other fragments of long-demolished houses fill the first floor; a bourgeois home complete with 18th-century wallpaper is re-created on the second. The enormous Magnin Model (which depicts Geneva as it looked before its elaborate defense walls came down in 1850) is housed in the attic. ✉ *6 rue du Puits-St-Pierre, Vieille Ville* ☎ *022/4183700* ⊕ *www.ville-ge.ch/mah* ☞ *Free* ◷ *Tues.–Sun. 11–6.*

Musée d'Art et d'Histoire (*Museum of Art and History*). The 15th-century *Miracle of the Fishes*, in which Jesus paces the waters of Lac Léman, keeps things focused locally at this museum built in 1910. The collection includes Switzerland's largest concentration of Egyptian art, Escalade-era weapons, Alpine landscapes from both ends of the 19th century, and substantial modern art. There is often a fee for temporary exhibits. ✉ *2 rue Charles-Galland, Vieille Ville* ☎ *022/4182600* ⊕ *www.ville-ge. ch/mah* ☞ *Free* ◷ *Tues.–Sun. 11–6.*

Muséum d'Histoire Naturelle (*Museum of Natural History*). Large, evocative wildlife dioramas complete with sound effects cover most major animal types at this spacious museum. Large quantities of fossils, gigantic crystals, precious stones, and a case full of polyhedrons ensure that the place is always swarming with local school groups. Swiss geology, the history of the solar system, and thematic temporary exhibits round out the collection; most labels are in French. The museum is a short walk away on the outskirts of the Vieille Ville. ✉ *1 rte. de Malagnou, Malagnou* ☎ *022/4186300* ⊕ *www.ville-ge.ch/mhng* ☞ *Free* ◷ *Tues.–Sun. 10–5.*

PLAINPALAIS

Reclaimed from the swamps that formed the confluence of the Rhône and Arve rivers as recently as 1850, the area centered on the diamond-shaped Plaine de Plainpalais is now home to contemporary art galleries, traveling circuses, weekly markets, local and regional media, the sprawling Université de Genève, and remnants of a late-19th-century industrial past.

TOP ATTRACTIONS

Centre d'Art Contemporain (*Center for Contemporary Art*). Andy Warhol, Cindy Sherman, Nan Goldin, Pippilotti Rist, Thomas Scheibitz, and Shirana Shabhaz are some of the pioneering Swiss and international artists who have presented work here since 1974. The center's four annual exhibits tend to be transdisciplinary and shocking in their quest to examine the practice of art in a cultural context. ✉ *10 rue des Vieux-Grenadiers, Plainpalais* ☎ *022/3291842* ⊕ *www.centre.ch* ☞ *5 SF* ◷ *Tues.–Sun. 11–6.*

Fodor'sChoice
★ **Patek Philippe Museum.** In this breathtaking private collection you'll discover delicate gold watch cases, complicated watch innards, lifelike portrait miniatures, and softly lighted enameled fans, pens, pocket knives,

The Patek Philippe Museum underscores Geneva's watchmaking reputation with a beautiful collection of timekeeping pieces and other artifacts.

snuffboxes, telescopes, and vanity pistols that shoot singing birds. Most of the objects displayed in this former watchmaking workshop are hundreds of years old; many were created in Geneva by Patek Philippe, one of the city's most venerable watchmaking companies. Meticulously restored workbenches, audiovisual displays, classical music, and a horological library complete the picture; the 2½-hour guided tour (in English at 2:30 on Saturday) puts it all in context. All signage is in English. ✉ *7 rue des Vieux-Grenadiers, Plainpalais* ☎ *022/8070910* ⊕ *www. patekmuseum.com* ✆ *10 SF, tour 15 SF* ⊙ *Tues.–Fri. 2–6, Sat. 10–6.*

Place Neuve. Aristocratic town houses now overlook Geneva's opera house, the Musée Rath, the Conservatoire de Musique, and the gilded wrought-iron entrance to the Parc des Bastions, but until 1850 this wide-open space was the city's heavily fortified main southern gate. The equestrian statue at the center of the square honors Guillaume-Henri Dufour, the first general of Switzerland's federal army and the first person to map the country. The large bust of Henry Dunant, founder of the International Red Cross, marks the spot where public executions once took place. ✉ *Intersection of Bd. du Théâtre, Rue de la Corraterie, Rue de la Croix-Rouge, and Rue Bartholoni, Plainpalais.*

WORTH NOTING

Musée d'Art Moderne et Contemporain (*Museum of Modern and Contemporary Art*). Concrete floors and fluorescent lighting set the tone for this gritty collection of stark, mind-stretching, post-1960 art. Better known as MAMCO, the museum shares its former factory compound with separate centers for contemporary photography and publishing. The industrial surroundings help juxtapose aesthetic approaches; temporary exhibits add current artists to the mix. ⊠ *10 rue des Vieux-Grenadiers, Plainpalais* ☎ *022/3206122* ⊕ *www.mamco.ch* 💷 *8 SF* ⊙ *Tues.–Fri. noon–6, weekends 11–6.*

Musée Rath. Switzerland's original fine arts museum, inaugurated in 1826 and named for its late benefactor, Simon Rath, housed Geneva's growing collections of art and archaeology until they overflowed to the Musée d'Art et d'Histoire in 1910. Now the Rath hosts two major temporary exhibitions each year; they range in focus from archaeology to contemporary art. ⊠ *Pl. Neuve, Plainpalais* ☎ *022/4183340* ⊕ *www. ville-ge.ch/mah* 💷 *10 SF* ⊙ *Tues.–Sun. 11–6.*

13

WHERE TO EAT

Relatively few restaurants focus on a see-and-be-seen angle; what unites diners at the best ones, whether simple cafés or gastronomic havens, is an appreciation for good food (read "slow food"—the noted food movement which puts emphasis on locally sourced ingredients, regional tastes, and authentic preparations).

Increasingly, there's a "non-French" spin to Geneva's dining scene: note the rise of tapas-style "grazing" menus, places that offer both light menus and five-course meals, and signature restaurants run by well-known chefs. At the other end of the scale, fast food usually runs to fresh sandwiches, interesting salads, and warm quiche to go; lunchtime plats du jour and bakeries with tearooms are delicious budget options.

While dress-code days are gone, casual elegant is rule of thumb. Hours for meals generally remain noon to 2 pm and 7 to 9:30 or 10 pm; pubs, bars, and clubs satisfy hungry night owls. And yes, after the stores close on Saturday afternoon Geneva's city center is virtually dormant—and most, but by no means all, restaurants close. That's because the Genevois spend their weekends eating at country inns and village cafés.

Geneva restaurants (and bars and clubs) are all nonsmoking. Some are now charging for the *carafe d'eau* (tap water). Since it is not local custom to take small children to better restaurants, amenities (and welcome) may be poor if you arrive with babies in tow. Tipping? Local diners may leave the change as a gesture when they leave, but tipping for exceptional service is up to the customer and is still the exception, not the rule.

Prices in the reviews are the average cost of a main course at dinner or, if dinner is not served, at lunch. Use the coordinate (✛ B2) at the end of each listing to locate a site on the Where to Stay and Eat in Geneva map.

RIVE DROITE (RIGHT BANK)

INTERNATIONAL AREA

$$ ✕ **La Perle du Lac.** Built in 1827, this sprawling lakeside chalet set amid
FRENCH magnificently manicured public parks comes dramatically into its own in summer. Pink tablecloths and hanging geraniums frame an unobstructed view of Mont Blanc and the glassed-in Orangerie is a rainy-day alternative to the covered terrace. While the wine list is good and the

BEST BETS FOR GENEVA DINING

Fodor'sChoice★

Bistrot du Boeuf Rouge, p. 542
Cafe des Banques, p. 549
Café des Bains, p. 548
Le Chat Botté, p. 542
Les Trois Verres, p. 550

Best By Price

$

Chez Ma Cousine, p. 545
Taverne de la Madeleine, p. 548

$$

Au Pied-de-Cochon, p. 545
Bistrot du Boucher, p. 544
Café des Bains, p. 548
Cafe des Banques, p. 549
La Favola, p. 545
Les Trois Verres, p. 550
L'Hôtel-de-Ville, p. 548
L'Opéra Bouffe, p. 544

$$$

Bistrot du Boeuf Rouge, p. 542
Brasserie Lipp, p. 543
Roberto, p. 544
Vertig'O, p. 543

$$$$

Le Chat Botté, p. 542
Il Lago, p. 543
Le Lion d'Or, p. 544

Best By Experience

GREAT VIEW

Le Chat Botté, p. 542
Le Lion d'Or, p. 544
La Perle du Lac, p. 541

ROMANTIC

La Favola, p. 545

French-accented seasonal cuisine competent, if it's haute gastronomy you're after, don't come here. This place is about location, location, location. An excellent compromise on a nice day is to come for a coffee or a plat du jour at lunch on what they call the "brasserie terrace." The Mouettes Genevoises water taxis dock directly out front. [$] *Average main: 45 SF* ✉ *126 rue de Lausanne, International Area* ☎ *022/9091020* 🌐 *www.laperledulac.ch* ⏲ *Closed Mon. and Jan.* ✣ *G1*

LES PÂQUIS

$$$ FRENCH Fodor'sChoice ★ ✕ **Bistrot du Boeuf Rouge.** The true-blue menu draws hordes of local and visiting cognoscenti to this cozy downtown bistro mere blocks from the major hotels. The gently cluttered dining room is filled with Art Nouveau posters, wood paneling with a soft patina, and glass panels that provide a sense of privacy. Waiters soften absolute correctness with a local sense of humor. Many of the house specialties—boudin noir, rillettes, foie gras, andouillettes, pistachio-filled sausage—are made onsite, and the tender *filet de boeuf* barely requires a knife. And save space for dessert—the silky *crème caramel* may be the best in town. [$] *Average main: 46 SF* ✉ *17 rue Alfred-Vincent, Les Pâquis* ☎ *022/7327537* 🌐 *www.boeufrouge.ch* ⏲ *Closed weekends* ✣ *F1.*

$$$$ FRENCH Fodor'sChoice ★ ✕ **Le Chat Botté.** The elegant dining room of the Beau-Rivage is dressed in rich upholstery and tapestries, but is generally used only when the weather's cold. Between May and September, service is moved to the flower-filled terrace upstairs with its majestic harbor views. The menu also evolves with the seasons: chef Dominique Gauthier tweaks the details of his lineup every few months, and dishes may include such

delights as zucchini blossom stuffed with mushrooms and topped with Parmesan foam, duckling lacquered with spices and a caramelized peach with ginger, or the local lake perch. The vast wine cellar features 40,000 handpicked and often rare bottles. $ *Average main: 70 SF* ⊠ *Beau-Rivage Hotel, 13 quai du Mont-Blanc, Les Pâquis* ☎ *022/7166920* ⊕ *www.beau-rivage.ch* ⌂ *Reservations essential* ⊘ *Closed Sun.* ✛ *F1*

$$$
ITALIAN
✕ **Le Jardin.** The dining room of Le Richemond is adorned in crimson and crystal, but it's the terrace with views of the lake that steals the show at this see-and-be-seen destination. The menu features seasonal dishes and Italian classics like spaghetti with clams and panfried veal Milanese. One of the restaurant's more unique offerings is the weekday business lunch of two or three courses, which includes low-calorie, healthy options like gazpacho, a seafood casserole, and fresh fruit. $ *Average main: 55 SF* ⊠ *Le Richemond, Jardin Brunswick, Les Pâquis* ☎ *022/7157100* ⊕ *www.lerichemond.com* ✛ *E1.*

CENTRE VILLE RIVE DROITE

$$$$
ITALIAN
★
✕ **Il Lago.** Decorated with rich brocades, glittering chandeliers, and bright frescoes, this robin's egg–blue dining room has plenty of light streaming through a wall of windows. Diners enjoy classic dishes from northern Italy and a menu of Italian, French, and Swiss wines. If risotto with Swiss chard and cuttlefish, wild sea bass with roasted artichokes, or seared scallops in a chestnut reduction were served at Versailles (instead of the Four Seasons, where Il Lago is located), this is what it might be like. In season, there's a gorgeous sidewalk terrace complete with olive trees and aromatic herbs. $ *Average main: 75 SF* ⊠ *Four Seasons, 33 quai des Bergues, Centre Ville Rive Droite* ☎ *022/9087110* ⊕ *www.fourseasons.com/geneva* ⌂ *Reservations essential* ✛ *E2.*

$$$
FRENCH
✕ **Vertig'O.** In a contemporary setting with a warm and friendly feel, executive chef Jérôme Manifacier's seasonal French fare is available à la carte under headings like "Creative Thinking About Fish" and "Delights Around Dessert" or as one of several tasting menus. Options include a five-course menu at 125 SF and a seven-course option at 170 SF, as well as a unique four-course vegetarian menu. Swiss wine is a focus here. The bar adjoining the restaurant serves snacks and a few hot dishes. $ *Average main: 65 SF* ⊠ *Hôtel de la Paix, 11 quai du Mont-Blanc, Centre Ville Rive Droite* ☎ *022/9096066* ⊕ *www.hoteldelapaix.ch* ⌂ *Reservations essential* ⊘ *Closed Sun and Mon. No lunch Sat.* ✛ *E2*

RIVE GAUCHE (LEFT BANK)

CENTRE VILLE RIVE GAUCHE

$$$
FRENCH
✕ **Brasserie Lipp.** The "Années Folles" decor—green-and-white tiles, mustard-yellow ceilings, warm wood—and busy waiters in ankle-length aprons channel Paris as Genevois diners of all stripes tuck into hearty portions of *choucroute* (sauerkraut) with pork and potatoes, vegetable couscous, tartares of beef or fish, and heaping platters of seafood. Also on the menu is a pound of steak—at 99.50 SF it's by far the most expensive thing on the menu, and it's for two. The dining room expands onto a delightful summer terrace at the foot of the Vieille Ville, and, unusually for Geneva, this place serves late: the kitchen stays open until

12:45 am. $ *Average main: 50 SF* ✉ *Confédération-Centre, 8 rue de la Confédération, Centre Ville Rive Gauche* ☎ *022/3111011* ⊕ *www. brasserie-lipp.com* ✛ *D4.*

$$$

STEAKHOUSE

✕ **Le Relais de l'Entrecôte.** It is rare to find a line of people waiting for a table anywhere in Geneva, so the fact that it's commonplace outside this bustling wood-paneled Parisian import means the tender strips of grilled steak drenched in herb-based *sauce maison* (house sauce) are a true cut above. A crisp green salad sprinkled with walnuts, robust house wine, and thin, golden fries complete the only option on the menu; but don't worry, there's a second portion on the way, and the desserts—like the flower bouquets adorning the restaurant—are fabulous. One caveat: the staff can sometimes be less than helpful. $ *Average main: 55 SF* ✉ *49 rue du Rhône, Centre Ville Rive Gauche* ☎ *022/3106004* ⊕ *www.relaisentrecote.fr* ✛ *F4.*

$$$

ITALIAN

✕ **Roberto.** Roberto Carugati, who celebrated his 100th birthday in 2012, turned the family restaurant over to his daughter, Marietta. She oversees the red-gold dining room he opened in 1945, but don't be surprised to see him drop in. The easy formality he perfected continues to lure lawyers, bankers, politicians, and fashionable Italians for melt-in-the-mouth gnocchi with butter and sage, grilled sole, *vitello tonnato* (chilled veal in a tuna sauce), and risotto with saffron served from shining copper and silver pots. Unusual and rare Italian wines keep conversation flowing into the night. $ *Average main: 50 SF* ✉ *10 rue Pierre-Fatio, Centre Ville Rive Gauche* ☎ *022/3118033* ⌖ *Reservations essential* ⊙ *Closed Sun. No dinner Sat.* ✛ *G5*

EAUX-VIVES

$$

STEAKHOUSE

✕ **Bistrot du Boucher.** Aperitifs are on the house, steak tartare is mixed to your taste, and waiters wear long aprons and solemn expressions as they bring out the *cote de boeuf* (rib steak) to be viewed before it's carved. Cheeky cow posters, figurines, and paintings add a sly hilarity to the Art Nouveau woodwork and stained-glass ceiling; the homemade chocolate-pear tart is decadently serious. $ *Average main: 44 SF* ✉ *15 av. Pictet-de-Rochemont, Eaux-Vives* ☎ *022/7365636* ⊙ *Closed Sun. No lunch Wed. and Sat.* ✛ *H5*

$$$$

FRENCH

✕ **Le Lion d'Or.** The hilltop village of Cologny is Geneva's Beverly Hills with a view, and this sleek sophisticated spot takes full advantage of its real estate. Burnished-silk walls and picture windows frame the sun setting over the lake and Jura Mountains in the main dining room, and the second-floor lounge-bar looks south toward the city. Strategically placed orchids soften the enormous portrait in the lobby and the shaded outdoor patio-terrace floats under a blue sky and above the herb garden. Seasonal cuisine by local celebrity chefs Gilles Dupont and Tommy Byrne is modern, light, full of Asian accents, and artfully presented. The bistro next door shares the restaurant's kitchen, but not its prices. $ *Average main: 70 SF* ✉ *5 pl. Pierre-Gautier, Cologny* ☎ *022/7364432* ⊕ *www.liondor.ch* ⌖ *Reservations essential* ⊙ *Closed weekends* ✛ *H3.*

$$

FRENCH

✕ **L'Opéra Bouffe.** The mood at L'Opéra Bouffe is casual-chic and friendly, with rows of wine bottles on floor-to-ceiling shelving, large framed mirrors, opera posters on the walls, and classical music in the background. For a menu that changes monthly, the chef rolls out subtle updates of traditional French and Mediterranean fare imbued with world accents. How about dessert? Hot apple pie with a scoop of ice cream is the perennial favorite. $ *Average main: 35 SF* ⊠ *5 av. de Frontenex, Eaux-Vives* ☎ *022/7366300* ⊕ *www.operabouffe.ch* ⊗ *Closed Sun. No lunch Sat.* ✛ *H5*

VIEILLE VILLE

$$ ╳ **Au Pied-de-Cochon.** Low ceilings, whitewashed beams, and a worn zinc
FRENCH bar give context to simple regional dishes like cassoulet, *émincé de veau* (veal strips in a cream sauce), *filets de perches* (perch fillets), and the namesake pigs' feet (served grilled or stuffed)—the selection varies. The crowd can be noisy, and table service can occasionally be a tad gruff, but locals and tourists keep streaming in, not least because it's one of the few places in town that serves meals straight through from noon to 10 pm. The terrace is great for people-watching. $ *Average main: 35 SF* ⊠ *4 pl. du Bourg-de-Four, Vieille Ville* ☎ *022/3104797* ⊕ *www. pied-de-cochon.ch* ✛ *E5*.

$ ╳ **Chez Ma Cousine.** There are three of these appealingly decorated
FRENCH restaurants around town: this one in Vieille Ville, as well as one on Rue Lissignol in Centre Ville Rive Droite and one in the International Area. The idea is basic: lunch and dinner, you get half a roast chicken, Provençal-style potatoes, and green salad for 14.90 SF. Sauce for the chicken is optional (and a bit extra), and they serve a few salads as mains in the same price area. But otherwise that's it, except for desserts. Chez Ma Cousine is understandably popular, not only because the food's cheap and good, but also because sitting outside in the Vielle Ville and International Area is great for people-watching. $ *Average main: 15 SF* ⊠ *6 pl. du Bourg-de-Four, Vieille Ville* ☎ *022/3109696* ⊕ *www. chezmacousine.ch* ✛ *E5*.

$$ ╳ **La Favola.** Lace curtains, embroidered tablecloths, antique silver, col-
ITALIAN lections of teapots and Murano glass, and a vertiginous spiral staircase strike a delicate balance between rustic and fussy in this wood-paneled dollhouse located on the street where Jean Calvin, the Protestant reformer, used to live. The food echoes the decor: part country simple, part city chic. The carpaccio is paper-thin, the pasta homemade, the risotto seasonal, and the tiramisu divine. Regional Swiss and Italian wines reflect the chef's roots in Turin. $ *Average main: 40 SF* ⊠ *15 rue Jean-Calvin, Vieille Ville* ☎ *022/3117437* ⌂ *Reservations essential* ⊗ *Closed Sun. No lunch Sat.* ✛ *E5*

$$ ╳ **Les Armures.** A robust Swiss menu has made this Vieille Ville insti-
SWISS tution a magnet for local street sweepers, foreign heads of state, and everyone in between. Before tucking into a fondue or *raclette* (melted cheese served with small potatoes in their skins, pickled pearl onions, and gherkins), order a starter of air-dried meat cut paper thin—a specialty of the canton of Grisons. Other choices include *Schübling* (sausage) or veal strips in cream sauce: both come with sinfully delicious *Rösti*, a buttery cake of grated potatoes. The kitchen serves until 11:30 pm (11 on Sunday) and in season you can sit outdoors and soak up the Old Town's historic vibe. $ *Average main: 40 SF* ⊠ *1 rue du Puits-St-Pierre, Vieille Ville* ☎ *022/3103442* ⊕ *www.hotel-les-armures.ch* ✛ *E5*.

13

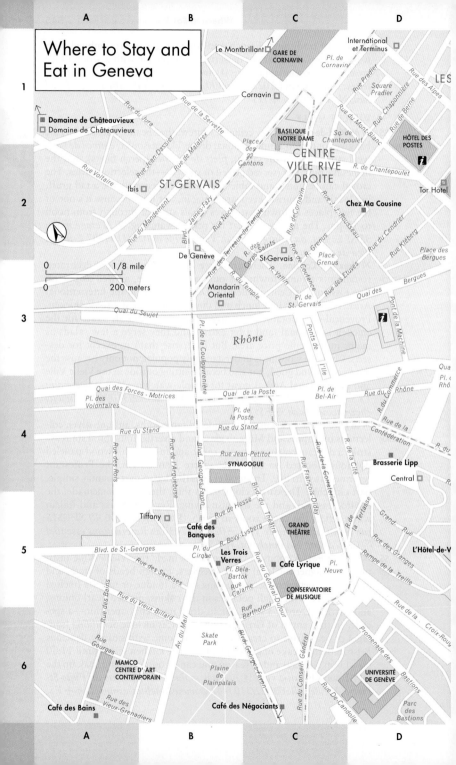

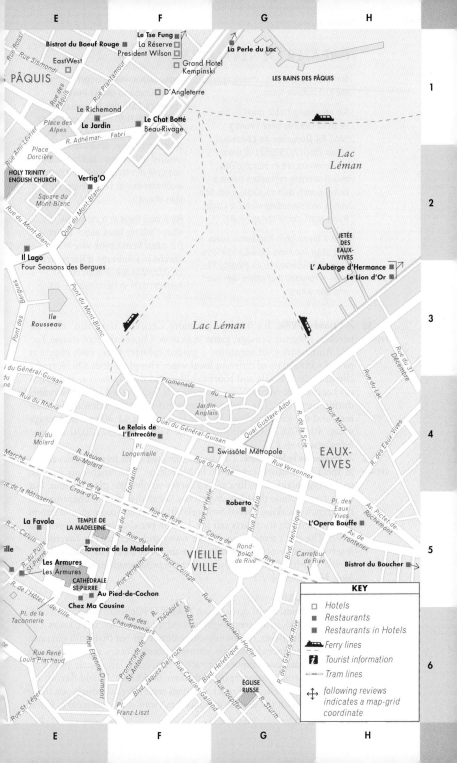

GREATER GENEVA EATS

Some of Geneva's top dining options are just outside town.

For an unforgettable meal in the heart of Geneva wine country, head for **Domaine de Château-vieux** (☎ 022/7531511 ⊕ www.chateauvieux.ch) in Satigny. This award-winning restaurant packs a heavy punch with exquisite food, fine wines, and sweeping views, though these don't come cheap. ✛ A1.

Take a break from traditional Swiss fare at Le Tse Fung (☎ 022/9595959 ⊕ www.lareserve.ch), an elegant Chinese restaurant that offers dim sum and fine wines.

Those with smaller budgets might opt for Domaine owner Philippe Chevrier's **Café des Négociants** (☎ 022/3003130 ⊕ www.negociants.ch) in Carouge, which boasts a good selection of wine. Reservations are required at Domaine de Chateuvieux and Café des Negociants and highly recommended at Le Tse Fung, so plan ahead.

For a cozy meal in a storybook-village setting, head about 16 km (10 miles) from Centre Ville Rive Gauche to **L'Auberge d'Hermance** (☎ 022/7511368 ⊕ www.hotel-hermance.ch) in Hermance. ✛ H3.

$$
FRENCH
✕ **L'Hôtel-de-Ville.** It's hard to get more Genevois than this: filets de perches, *longeole* sausage, game in season. Choose the five-course Terroir Ambassador set menu for a guided culinary tour; each course is paired with a glass of different local wine. This place does a brisk trade, clients include locals and tourists alike, and the location at the political heart of the Vieille Ville guarantees a loyal crowd of civil servants during the week. The dining room transfers to the sidewalk in summer, and the kitchen closes late for Geneva—at 11:30 pm. $ *Average main: 40 SF* ✉ *39 Grand-Rue, Vieille Ville* ☎ *022/3117030* ⊕ *www.hdvglozu.ch* ✛ *E5.*

$
FRENCH
✕ **Taverne de la Madeleine.** This sunny, elevated stone terrace looks across at the 15th-century Temple de la Madeleine. The lunch-only kitchen in this big, plain, friendly canteen serves wholesome plats du jour, but must-tries include the filets de perches (a fish dish that is ubiquitous in the French-speaking part of Switzerland), chocolate mousse, and lemon pie. Homemade fruit tarts sell for 3.50 SF per slice between 3 pm and 6 pm. The city's temperance league owns and operates the Taverne, so it serves no wine or beer. $ *Average main: 24 SF* ✉ *20 rue Toutes-Âmes, Vieille Ville* ☎ *022/3106070* ⊕ *www.tavernedelamadeleine.ch* ☻ *Closed Sun. No dinner* ✛ *E5.*

PLAINPALAIS

$$
ECLECTIC
Fodor'sChoice
★
✕ **Café des Bains.** Right across from MAMCO (Geneva's museum of contemporary art), in an arty neighborhood that has come to be known as QuARTier des Bains, this trendy-chic eatery-cum-bar that spills out onto a sidewalk terrace during the summer months mixes a classic French café look with contemporary touches (featuring large-scale prints by star Swiss artist-photographer Balthasar Burkhard). World flavors are injected into a basically French seasonal repertoire, although one thing that's always on the dessert menu is American-style cheesecake. Good

Geneva's Vieille Ville has many delightful outdoor cafés.

wines are on offer, many sold by the glass. [$] *Average main: 40 SF* ✉ *26 rue des Bains, Plainpalais* ☎ *022/3215798* 🌐 *www.cafedesbains.com* ✍ *Reservations essential* 🕓 *Closed Sun. and Mon.* ⊕ *A6*

$$ MODERN EUROPEAN Fodor's Choice ★ 🍴 **Cafe des Banques.** This sleek, contemporary restaurant illuminated by sculptural chandeliers and dressed in white, chocolate, and taupe serves a mix of traditional and modern seasonal dishes to a chic crowd. While the menu is updated seasonally, specialties like the sesame-crusted tuna with bok choy and airy stracciatella with pillowy house-made blinis are always on offer. The focus on the seasons extends to the wine list, which focuses on Swiss, French, and Italian wines and changes regularly. The entire experience ends on a sweet—and nostalgic note—with large candy jars filled with M&Ms, gummy bears, and other childhood favorites. [$] *Average main: 38 SF* ✉ *6 Rue de Hesse, Plainpalais* ☎ *022/3114498* 🌐 *www.cafedesbanques.com* 🕓 *Closed weekends* ⊕ *B5.*

$$ FRENCH 🍴 **Café Lyrique.** At this relaxed corner brasserie opposite the Grand Théâtre, black-and-white floor tiles offset warm yellow walls, wedding-cake ceilings, and portraits of Beethoven, Verdi, Strauss, and Liszt. The menu focuses on the Swiss version of comfort food, starting with soups and salads, moving on to pasta, fish, and sirloin with the special house butter, and ending with desserts that taste as good as they look. Time your arrival carefully, as it's bursting with business folk at lunch, and pre- and post-opera crowds sweep through at night; an alternative is afternoon tea. Try and sit in the brasserie or on the terrace; it's livelier than the dining room. [$] *Average main: 35 SF* ✉ *12 bd. du Theatre, Plainpalais* ☎ *022/3280095* 🌐 *www.cafe-lyrique.ch* 🕓 *Closed weekends* ⊕ *C5.*

$$ ITALIAN Fodor's Choice ★

🍴 **Les Trois Verres.** Sunlight streaming through large windows, impeccable service, and seasonal Italian fare make this corner bistro a bright addition to the Genevois dining scene. Diners of all stripes choose between dark maroon banquettes and cherry-colored chairs for plates of homemade pastas, including the pillowy ravioli stuffed with eggplant and topped an airy burrata. Among the hearty favorites are veal picatta and tender *filet de boeuf* in a three-pepper sauce. The Italian-heavy cellar includes nearly 30 wines by the glass every season. There's a wraparound sidewalk terrace surrounded by large shrubs for added privacy on the busy street. [$] *Average main: 40 SF* ✉ *Place du Cirque, Plainpalais* ☎ *022/3208462* 🌐 *www.lestroisverres.ch* 🕒 *Closed Sun. No lunch Sat.* ✥ *B5*

GREATER GENEVA

$$$$ CHINESE

🍴 **Le Tse Fung.** Plush red velvet chairs and golden accents encourage guests to linger at Le Tse Fung, an elegant Chinese restaurant tucked into the lower level of this resort overlooking the lake. The menu offers several prix-fixe meals that range from the 90 SF "Opal," which includes spring rolls, steamed dumplings, and Mongolian-style beef, to the 160 SF "Diamond," a satisfying combination of Peking duck with pancakes, sole fillets with ginger; and sliced beef with basil. For those who would prefer a dim sum approach, the restaurant includes extensive à la carte choices, including 20 types of steamed or grilled dumplings and two styles of Peking duck served over two courses. Reserve ahead, as the place often fills up. [$] *Average main: 90 SF* ✉ *La Reserve, 301 rte. de Lausanne, Bellevue* ☎ *022/9595959* 🌐 *www.lareserve.ch* ✥ *F1* .

WHERE TO STAY

The palace-style hotel continues to be the defining image of the city's hospitality. There is something quintessentially Geneva about the wealth these places ooze, and the waterfront ones on the Right Bank give you sweeping views of the city's other iconic features: the Jet d'Eau, Old Town, La Rade (the waterfront), river, lake, and mountains. They're also near parks—another of the city's points of pride—for that early-morning jog as the sun rises across the water.

Overall, the hospitality sector has seen an overhaul in Geneva these past years, as owners recognize that decor matters and that updates (and upkeep) are essential. Genuinely gracious, go-the-extra-mile-with-a-smile service remains vexingly confined to the professionally trained top and family-run bottom of the rate structure, but the good news is that the concept of gracious service is making across-the-board inroads.

Geneva hotels do err on the expensive side, and the practice of massively hiking up rates during events like the annual car show in March persists. Speaking of which, large events can suddenly fill entire hotels, so book as early as you can. And, because this is a conference-and-convention driven town, leisure visitors will find lower prices on weekend stays.

As for breakfast (if not included), you won't readily find places outside the big hotels that do bacon and eggs, but if you're happy with croissants and coffee, head for the nearest café. As for practicalities, many

BEST BETS FOR GENEVA LODGING

Fodor's Choice★	$$	Best By Experience
Domaine de Château-vieux, p. 556	**Domaine de Château-vieux**, p. 556	
Four Seasons des Bergues, p. 554	**Le Montbrillant**, p. 554	BEST SERVICE
		Four Seasons des Bergues, p. 554
Best By Price	$$$	**De Genève**, p. 554
	Eastwest, p. 552	**Mandarin Oriental**, p. 555
$	**Swissôtel Métropole**, p. 555	**Tiffany**, p. 556
D'Angleterre, p. 551	**Tiffany**, p. 556	
Ibis, p. 555		MOST ROMANTIC
International et Terminus, p. 552	$$$$	**D'Angleterre**, p. 551
St-Gervais, p. 555	**D'Angleterre**, p. 551	**Domaine de Château-vieux**, p. 556
Tor Hôtel, p. 554	**Les Armures**, p. 555	
	Grand Hotel Kempinski, p. 552	**Eastwest**, p. 552
	La Reserve, p. 556	**Tiffany**, p. 556

13

places accept children up to a certain age for free, or another bed can be put in your room for a low extra. Wi-Fi is now common (often at an added cost). Depending on the category of hotel, there is a "taxe de séjour" between 1.50 and 6 SF per person and per night. Check when you are booking if they are including this in the quoted rate or not.

Prices in the reviews are the lowest cost of a standard double room in high season. Use the coordinate (⊕ B2) at the end of each listing to locate a site on the Where to Stay and Eat in Geneva map.

RIVE DROITE (RIGHT BANK)

LES PÂQUIS

$$$$
HOTEL
Beau-Rivage. This gracious, history-rich landmark hotel is awash with tasseled drapes and Louis Something furniture; standard rooms may be less *époque* but still bask in the vibe, and all rooms (and public spaces) feed from a grand five-story atrium. **Pros:** family-owned; history buffs will want to see the enclosed artifacts of Austrian Empress Sissi, who was killed outside the hotel. **Cons:** even with a recent refurbishment, the hotel shows its age in spots. $ *Rooms from: 850 SF* ⊠ *13 quai du Mont-Blanc, Les Pâquis* ☎ *022/7166666* ⊕ *www.beau-rivage.ch* ⤣ *90 rooms, 11 suites* ⓘ*No meals* ⊕ *F1.*

$$$$
HOTEL
Fodor's Choice
★
D'Angleterre. Impeccable taste, total discretion, and a passion for detail mark this stylish boutique hotel where thematic decorations stretch from African to Baroque. **Pros:** one of the best examples of a luxurious boutique hotel you'll find anywhere; beautifully maintained; smiling, friendly service. **Cons:** cramped elevator. $ *Rooms from: 720*

SF ✉ *17 quai du Mont-Blanc, Les Pâquis* ☎ *022/9065555* 🌐 *www.dangleterrehotel.com* 🛏 *39 rooms, 6 suites* 🍴 *No meals* ✥ *F1.*

$$$ HOTEL 🏨 **EastWest.** This small hotel has sleek interiors that blend East and West design elements. **Pros:** aesthetics; sophistication; luxurious sensuality. **Cons:** space (closets et al) can be a little tight for some; the sensibilities may be a tad too refined. [$] *Rooms from: 480 SF* ✉ *6 rue des Pâquis, Les Pâquis* ☎ *022/7081717* 🌐 *www.eastwesthotel.ch* 🛏 *37 rooms, 4 suites* 🍴 *No meals* ✥ *E1.*

$$$$ HOTEL 🏨 **Grand Hotel Kempinski.** This palatial hotel is a one-stop shop for travelers, with contemporary guest rooms, more than a dozen chic boutiques, an impressive fitness center with an indoor pool, an expanded spa, several excellent restaurants, and one of Geneva's trendiest nightclubs, the Java. **Pros:** big-city buzz; fabulous views; striking dinner atmosphere (torches aflame outside picture windows). **Cons:** a certain anonymity. [$] *Rooms from: 550 SF* ✉ *19 quai du Mont-Blanc, Les Pâquis* ☎ *022/9089081* 🌐 *www.kempinski-geneva.com* 🛏 *412 rooms* 🍴 *No meals* ✥ *F1.*

$ HOTEL 🏨 **International et Terminus.** The leafy outdoor terrace, soft yellow facade, and peach-paneled lobby impose civility on this modest hotel's central but chaotic location on a busy street opposite the Gare Cornavin. **Pros:** a more-than-correct deal for the money; restaurant terrace is an oasis in a noisy area. **Cons:** car access is awkward, and parking fees add to costs. [$] *Rooms from: 155 SF* ✉ *20 rue des Alpes, Les Pâquis* ☎ *022/9069777* 🌐 *www.international-terminus.ch* 🛏 *60 rooms, 3 suites* ✥ *D1.*

$$$$ HOTEL 🏨 **Le Richemond.** Dressed up in crimson and crystal grandeur, this stately hotel wins over guests with its pied-à-terre vibe and impeccable service. **Pros:** retains a luxe home-away-from-home-feel; chill-out zone; his-and-hers massage therapy room. **Cons:** corporate-style decor in many rooms; floral arrangements in the public spaces can seem incongruous. [$] *Rooms from: 800 SF* ✉ *Jardin Brunswick, Les Pâquis* ☎ *022/7157000* 🌐 *www.roccofortecollection.com* 🛏 *83 rooms, 26 suites* 🍴 *No meals* ✥ *E1.*

$$$$ HOTEL 🏨 **President Wilson.** It has a no-thrills modern exterior, but one step inside and you'll be seduced by wafting scents from perfumed candles and the high-glitter-cum-slice-of-nature lobby and public salons. **Pros:** loads of polished eat-and-drink options; you can reserve the spa's hot tub, sauna, and chill-out room for yourself. **Cons:** unequivocal opulence may seem a bit flashy to some; the rooms, while fully up to snuff, a bit same-y. [$] *Rooms from: 850 SF* ✉ *47 quai Wilson, Les Pâquis* ☎ *022/9066666* 🌐 *www.hotelpwilson.com* 🛏 *180 rooms, 48 suites* 🍴 *No meals* ✥ *F1.*

CENTRE VILLE RIVE DROITE

$$$ HOTEL 🏨 **Cornavin.** The comic-book character Tintin made this hotel famous with *L'Affaire Tournesol* (*The Calculus Affair*) in 1956. **Pros:** those views; that neat ride in the glass-walled elevator past Geneva's tallest clock. **Cons:** occasionally feels bland and impersonal. [$] *Rooms from: 428 SF* ✉ *Gare de Cornavin, Centre Ville Rive Droite* ☎ *022/7161212* 🌐 *www.fhotels.ch* 🛏 *176 rooms, 4 suites* 🍴 *No meals* ✥ *C1.*

WHERE SHOULD I STAY?

	NEIGHBORHOOD VIBE	PROS	CONS
Les Pâquis	You'll pay a lot for a room overlooking the lake, but the water, Rade (waterfront), and Alps views from the waterfront are the city's best.	Easy access to everywhere else; very lively; no shortage of 24/7 entertainment options, from seedy to deluxe.	Some dislike the extreme contrasts—neighborhood ranges from the Red Light District to shabby-poor to shabby-chic to very, very chic (or at least expensive); can get noisy.
Centre Ville Rive Droite	Along the axis linking the main train station to the Old Town, this is a mixed and busy area with all types of accommodation, from superbudget to grandest of the grand.	It's all about location: you're near the train station (therefore six minutes from the airport) and public transportation hubs, yet within walking distance of all of downtown—Right or Left Bank.	Lacks personality, although things do perk up as you approach the waterfront; traffic congestion and noise can be a problem.
St-Gervais	Except for the quay along the Rhône, this is not one of the prettier parts of town. There are fewer hotels here, but those there are include some of the best budget spots in town.	Just a short walk across Coulouvrenière Bridge away from Plainpalais; some good shopping, like Manor department store.	Dies down completely at night and on Sunday, when the abundance of unaesthetic-at-the-best-of-times buildings behind the riverfront can start to seem more than a little glum.
Centre Ville Rive Gauche	Pullulating with activity during the business (and shopping) day, it is relatively deserted here at night and especially on Sunday. The handful of hotels in the area range from budget to five-star.	A stone's throw from the Rade, Old Town, and Eaux-Vives; walking distance from Plainpalais and the Right Bank neighborhoods; great shopping on Rue du Rhône.	Although a few very attractive eateries remain open on Sunday, many find the way this part of town empties out when the businesses and shops close to be disconcerting.
Vieille Ville	There's a cobblestoned, historic vibe here, with antiques shops and lifestyle boutiques, many museums, and a fair share of restaurants and bars, though fewer hotels.	Everything's open on weekends, but weekday crowds are absent—many find the resulting gentle yet animated Old Town vibe particularly appealing then.	Some peoples' pros are others' cons, and some deem the Old Town stilted, overpriced and too quiet by half.
Plainpalais	Populated by bankers, students, and musicians, there's a lot going on here, and it's within easy walking distance of attractions. There are few hotels here, but most of them are budget.	Many art galleries and some museums; the site of weekly farmers' and flea markets; neighboring Carouge is a short tram ride away.	If you like your neighborhoods cohesive, this is not for you; there's everything from shabby poor, student, bleakly middle-class, to high culture and banking, and it fails to come together.

13

Geneva's opulent Four Seasons des Bergues hotel dates back to 1834.

$$$$ HOTEL Fodor's Choice ★ 🏨 **Four Seasons des Bergues.** Unpretentious service, lavish decor, luxurious details, and a first-rate location gives this palace an inner glow. **Pros:** what can you say about perfection? **Cons:** all this perfection comes at a price. [$] *Rooms from: 775 SF* ✉ *33 quai des Bergues, Centre Ville Rive Droite* ☎ *022/9087000* 🌐 *www.fourseasons.com/geneva* 🛏 *70 rooms, 45 suites* 🍴 *No meals* ⊕ *E2.*

$$ HOTEL 🏨 **Le Montbrillant.** Exposed stone walls and massive wooden beams channel mountain lodges in the lobby of this busy family-run hotel behind the Gare Cornavin. **Pros:** friendly desk staff; good value. **Cons:** hard to access by car; for some it's a bit too close to the train station. [$] *Rooms from: 250 SF* ✉ *2 rue de Montbrillant, Centre Ville Rive Droite* ☎ *022/7337784* 🌐 *www.montbrillant.ch* 🛏 *58 rooms, 24 studios* 🍴 *Breakfast* ⊕ *C1.*

$ HOTEL 🏨 **Tor Hôtel.** Within easy walking distance of both the main train station and the lake, this nicely remodeled hotel occupies three upper floors of a building across from the English Church. **Pros:** super-central location; staff gets kudos for friendliness. **Cons:** space can be tight; noise may be a problem; during hot weather the lack of air-conditioning is felt. [$] *Rooms from: 140 SF* ✉ *3 rue Ami-Lévrier, Centre Ville Rive Droite* ☎ *022/9098820* 🌐 *www.torhotel.com* 🛏 *22 rooms, 6 studios and apartments* 🍴 *Breakfast* ⊕ *D2.*

ST-GERVAIS

$ HOTEL 🏨 **De Genève.** This family-run place has its own brand of charm and an exceptionally caring staff. **Pros:** very personal, original decor; they take pride in good service. **Cons:** chalet lobby-cum-breakfast area can get very crowded. [$] *Rooms from: 180 SF* ✉ *1 pl. Isaac-Mercier,*

St-Gervais ☎ 022/7323264 🌐 www.hotel-de-geneve.ch 🛏 39 rooms 🍴 Breakfast ✥ B2.

$ HOTEL 🏨 **Ibis.** This cheerful chain hotel is extremely convenient if you're arriving late or departing early: breakfast starts as early as 4 am, the reception desk is staffed around the clock, and the train station is a 10-minute walk away. **Pros:** nicely conceived hotel; great value. **Cons:** not in a pretty location; space is at a premium; breakfast adds to the tab. [$] *Rooms from: 175 SF ✉ 10 rue Voltaire, St-Gervais ☎ 022/3382020 🌐 www.ibishotel.com 🛏 64 rooms ✥ B2.*

13

$$$$ HOTEL 🏨 **Mandarin Oriental.** Elegant interiors, attentive service, and fabulous Rhône views add to the appeal of this Asian-influenced hotel. **Pros:** a natural, easy vibe; the luxury of spaciousness. **Cons:** at these prices, there shouldn't be a charge for Wi-Fi. [$] *Rooms from: 980 SF ✉ 1 quai Turrettini, St-Gervais ☎ 022/9090000 🌐 www.mandarinoriental.com/geneva 🛏 166 rooms, 31 suites 🍴 No meals ✥ B3.*

$ HOTEL 🏨 **St-Gervais.** Most of the rooms at this old Right Bank inn have been spruced up, with a lick of paint to the walls and the floors stripped of carpeting to reveal parquet. **Pros:** easy train-station access; friendly vibe; good value for money. **Cons:** some find the bar and lobby a bit dark; mostly shared bathroom facilities; not ideal for drivers. [$] *Rooms from: 119 SF ✉ 20 rue des Corps-Saints, St-Gervais ☎ 022/7324572 🌐 www.stgervais-geneva.ch 🛏 26 rooms, 2 with bath 🍴 Breakfast ✥ C2.*

RIVE GAUCHE (LEFT BANK)

CENTRE VILLE RIVE GAUCHE

$ HOTEL 🏨 **Central.** Indonesian wood, warm terra-cotta, intense pastel greens and blues, and exotic flowers reflect the Gangsted family's ties to Bali in this friendly, low-cost hotel. **Pros:** friendly reception area; more expensive rooms are exceptionally spacious. **Cons:** tiny elevator; cheaper rooms have tight bathrooms; if you're driving, pay parking will add a tidy slice to costs. [$] *Rooms from: 155 SF ✉ 2 rue de la Rôtisserie, Centre Ville Rive Gauche ☎ 022/8188100 🌐 www.hotelcentral.ch 🛏 26 rooms, 1 suite, 8 apartments 🍴 Breakfast ✥ D4.*

$$$ HOTEL 🏨 **Swissôtel Métropole.** Massive scrubbed-stone arches, swirled wrought-iron sconces, lush carpeting, and the immediate proximity of high-voltage Rue du Rhône shopping give this 1854 Left Bank palace an air of urban gentility and center-city bustle. **Pros:** central location; bar has a cozy feel. **Cons:** limited space for cars, so arrivals and departures can be stressful; some complain that rooms, although renovated, don't reflect the absolute latest in five-star decor. [$] *Rooms from: 480 SF ✉ 34 quai du Général-Guisan, Centre Ville Rive Gauche ☎ 022/3183200 🌐 www.geneva.swissotel.com 🛏 111 rooms, 16 suites 🍴 No meals ✥ F4.*

VIEILLE VILLE

$$$$ HOTEL 🏨 **Les Armures.** Original 17th-century stonework, colorful frescoes, painted beams, and tapestries adorn the lobby and some rooms in this low-key luxury hotel near the cathedral; others have clean modern lines and restful deep-brown accents. **Pros:** at the heart of Geneva's historic quarter; buffet breakfast is included in the room rate. **Cons:** not a lot of amenities; too quiet for some. [$] *Rooms from: 520 SF ✉ 1 rue du*

Puits-St-Pierre, Vieille Ville ☎ *022/3109172* 🌐 *www.hotel-les-armures.ch* 🛏 *27 rooms, 5 suites* 🍴 *Breakfast* ✣ *E5.*

PLAINPALAIS

$$$ HOTEL ★ 🏨 **Tiffany.** This pretty Art Nouveau–style hotel has undergone a renovation and expansion that embraces its 19th-century originality but gives it a contemporary edge. **Pros:** new rooms feature traveler-friendly technology like built-in adapters. **Cons:** standard bathrooms in the original wing have been spiffed up but not replaced. [$] *Rooms from: 480 SF* ✉ *20 rue de l'Arquebuse, Plainpalais* ☎ *022/7081616* 🌐 *www.hotel-tiffany.ch* 🛏 *57 rooms, 8 suites* 🍴 *No meals* ✣ *B5.*

GREATER GENEVA

$$ B&B/INN Fodor's Choice ★ 🏨 **Domaine de Châteauvieux.** A whole different Geneva experience can be yours once you take a Rhône meander out here and wind up in the heart of the Geneva wine country. **Pros:** lovely wine-country setting; fabulous restaurant. **Cons:** restaurant books up fast, so reserve ahead; no elevator; a cab to or from the airport or city center can run up to 80 SF. [$] *Rooms from: 250 SF* ✉ *16 chemin de Châteauvieux, Peney-Dessus, Satigny* ☎ *022/7531511* 🌐 *www.chateauvieux.ch* 🛏 *12 rooms, 1 suite* ✣ *A1.*

$$$$ RESORT 👶 ★ 🏨 **La Réserve.** Nestled on the shores of Lake Geneva, this contemporary resort in a residential suburb resembles a grand African lodge. **Pros:** luxurious atmosphere; impeccable service; complete and utter pampering. **Cons:** outside the center of the city. [$] *Rooms from: 560 SF* ✉ *301 rte. de Lausanne, Bellevue* ☎ *022/9595959* 🌐 *www.lareserve.ch* 🛏 *85 rooms, 17 suites* 🍴 *No meals* ✣ *F1.*

NIGHTLIFE AND THE ARTS

Genève Agenda. *Genève Agenda* publishes monthly English and French listings of concerts, performances, temporary exhibits, restaurants, and clubs. A popular guide, it is also called the *Monthly Guide of Geneva*—free copies are available from tourist information booths and hotels, and the publication can also be downloaded from the website. 🌐 *www.le-guide.ch.*

NIGHTLIFE

A successful night out in Geneva—whether exclusive, trendy, or pub-based—can hinge on understanding that you are not in a major metropolis. Though bars and clubs have lots of life, much of it English-speaking, it may not always be possible to party till dawn.

RIVE DROITE (RIGHT BANK)

BARS

Mr. Pickwick Pub. Popular with English speakers is Mr. Pickwick Pub. ✉ *80 rue de Lausanne, Les Pâquis* ☎ *022/7316797* 🌐 *www.mrpickwick.ch.*

Mulligan's. Guinness is on tap and soccer matches are on the telly at Mulligan's, which is proudly Irish-owned and -operated. ⊠ *14 rue Grenus, St-Gervais* ☎ *022/7328576* ⊕ *www.ireland.ch.*

CLUBS

Javaclub. A crowd of local fashionistas and a big-city vibe make Javaclub a place to see and be seen. ⊠ *Grand Hôtel Kempinski, 19 quai du Mont-Blanc, Les Pâquis* ☎ *022/9089098* ⊕ *www.javaclub.ch.*

Shakers. The cocktails are potent and the dance hits are current at Shakers. ⊠ *4 rue Arnold-Winkelried, Centre Ville Rive Droite* ☎ *022/3105598* ⊕ *www.shakers.ch.*

RIVE GAUCHE (LEFT BANK)

BARS

Arthur's Rive Gauche. For a sophisticated vibe, try Arthur's Rive Gauche. ⊠ *7–9 rue du Rhône, Centre Ville Rive Gauche* ☎ *022/8103260* ⊕ *www. arthurs.ch.*

Boulevard du Vin. When it comes to wine bars, Boulevard du Vin tops a lot of lists. ⊠ *3 bd. Georges-Favon, Plainpalais* ☎ *022/3109190* ⊕ *www. boulevard-du-vin.ch.*

La Clémence. In the warmer months you can sit outside at quintessentially Genevese La Clémence. ⊠ *20 pl. du Bourg-de-Four, Vieille Ville* ☎ *022/3122498* ⊕ *www.laclemence.ch.*

Little Buddha. Little Buddha has a chill-out vibe in an opulent setting. If you're feeling peckish, there's always something to nibble. ⊠ *10 rue Jean-François Bartholoni, Plainpalais* ☎ *022/3071000* ⊕ *www. littlebuddhageneva.com.*

Senso Le Lobby. Senso Le Lobby is a sleek and soigné bar. Tasty dishes are also available. ⊠ *56 bis rue du Rhône, Centre Ville Rive Gauche* ☎ *022/3103990* ⊕ *www.senso-living.ch.*

CLUBS

Griffin's Club. The softly textured walls seem to ripple at Geneva's poshest nightspot, where you'll find glam illuminated columns and plenty of low-slung leather banquettes. Look at a menu before you order, as the prices are not for the faint of wallet. ⊠ *36 bd. Helvétique, Eaux-Vives* ☎ *022/7352829* ⊕ *www.griffinsclub.com.*

GREATER GENEVA

CLUBS

Bypass. This trendy place lures cosmopolitan twenty- and thirtysomethings to the outer edge of Carouge. ⊠ *1 carrefour de l'Etoile, Acacias* ☎ *022/3006565* ⊕ *www.bypass-geneve.ch.*

Chat Noir. Up-and-coming musicians from around the world perform live at the small, relaxed, and affordable Chat Noir. ⊠ *13 rue Vautier, Carouge* ☎ *022/3071040* ⊕ *www.chatnoir.ch.*

THE ARTS

Geneva's legacy as a cultural crossroads has produced an unusually rich arts scene for a city of its size: most performance spaces in town are roadhouses, through which flow a steady stream of foreign as well as

Swiss artists. Tickets remain on sale from theater box offices up to the day of performance, but it's wise to book ahead.

TICKETS

FNAC Rive. The ticket service at FNAC Rive manages sales for an ever-changing list of events. ✉ *16 rue de Rive, Centre Ville Rive Gauche* ☎ *022/8161256* ⊕ *www.ch.fnacspectacles.com.*

RIVE DROITE (RIGHT BANK)

MUSIC AND DANCE

Sud des Alpes. Nervy improvisation and contemporary jazz is on the bill at Sud des Alpes. ✉ *10 rue des Alpes, Les Pâquis* ☎ *022/7165630* ⊕ *www.amr-geneve.ch.*

RIVE GAUCHE (LEFT BANK)

FILM

English-language films are always screened somewhere in town—check local newspaper listings for the initials *v.o.*, short for *version originale* (original version).

CAC Voltaire. The CAC Voltaire organizes ongoing festivals of classic films in the basement of the Grütli Arts Center. ✉ *16 rue du Général-Dufour, Plainpalais* ☎ *022/3207878* ⊕ *www.ville-ge.ch/culture/grutli.*

MUSIC AND DANCE

Bâtiment des Forces Motrices. Classical music, opera, contemporary dance, and the occasional film festival cycle through the Bâtiment des Forces Motrices. ✉ *2 pl. des Volontaires, Plainpalais* ☎ *022/3221220* ⊕ *www.bfm.ch.*

Grand Théâtre. Between June and September, the Grand Théâtre stages more than a dozen operas, ballets, and recitals. ✉ *Pl. Neuve, Plainpalais* ☎ *022/4183130* ⊕ *www.geneveopera.ch.*

Victoria Hall. Geneva's classical concert venue is the 19th-century Victoria Hall, with an imposing stone facade and an interior that uses liberal amounts of gold leaf. ✉ *14 rue du Général-Dufour, Plainpalais* ☎ *022/4183500* ⊕ *www.ville-ge.ch/vh.*

Orchestre de la Suisse Romande. The opulent Victoria Hall is home to the venerable Orchestre de la Suisse Romande. ✉ *Rue du Général-Dufour 14, Plainpalais* ☎ *022/8070000* ⊕ *www.osr.ch*

THEATER

Am Stram Gram. The creative, colorful French children's theater Am Stram Gram draws inspiration from myths, traditional tales, lyric poetry, and contemporary writing. ✉ *56 rte. de Frontenex, Eaux-Vives* ☎ *022/7357924* ⊕ *www.amstramgram.ch.*

Comédie de Genève. Anne Bisang's Comédie de Genève stages modern dramas and international classics in French. ✉ *6 bd. des Philosophes, Plainpalais* ☎ *022/3205001* ⊕ *www.comedie.ch.*

Théâtre du Grütli. The experimental Théâtre du Grütli fills its spare, flexible space with contemporary Swiss and foreign plays in French. ✉ *16 rue du Général-Dufour, Plainpalais* ☎ *022/8884488* ⊕ *www.grutli.ch.*

SPORTS AND THE OUTDOORS

SWIMMING

The Genevois love their beaches, which open in May and stay crowded through September.

Bains des Pâquis. A laid-back and popular concrete sunbathing area surrounds a protected swimming zone and casual restaurant at Bains des Pâquis. ⊠ *30 quai du Mont-Blanc, Les Pâquis* ☎ *022/7322974* ⊕ *www.bains-des-paquis.ch.*

13

Genève-Plage. A huge outdoor pool, multilevel diving boards, and a waterslide are among the amenities at Genève-Plage. Although technically in Cologny, this beach is just over the Eaux-Vives line. ⊠ *Port Noir, Cologny* ☎ *022/7362482* ⊕ *www.geneve-plage.ch.*

SHOPPING

Most shops are open Monday through Wednesday from 9 to 7, Thursday and Friday until 7:30, and Saturday until 6. Many stores close on Sunday. A word to the wise: myriad variations on this basic picture will continue, including closing over lunch, so if you want to be sure call ahead.

RIVE DROITE (RIGHT BANK)

AUCTIONS

As a jewelry capital rivaled only by New York, and an international center for Swiss watchmakers, Geneva regularly hosts high-profile auctions by the major houses.

Antiquorum. Collector timepieces are the specialty at Antiquorum. ⊠ *3 rue du Mont-Blanc, Centre Ville Rive Droite* ☎ *022/9092850* ⊕ *www. antiquorum.com.*

Sotheby's. Sotheby's displays exquisite lots of jewelry and watches in May and November. ⊠ *13 quai du Mont-Blanc, Les Pâquis* ☎ *022/9084800* ⊕ *www.sothebys.com.*

SPECIALTY STORES
BOOKS

Payot. The popular chain Payot helps you keep abreast of current trends. ⊠ *5 rue de Chantepoulet, Centre Ville Rive Droite* ☎ *022/7318950* ⊕ *www.payot.ch.*

RIVE GAUCHE (LEFT BANK)

AUCTIONS

Christie's. This world-famous auction house offers wine as well as exclusive jewelry and watches twice a year. ⊠ *8 pl. de la Taconnerie, Vieille Ville* ☎ *022/3191766* ⊕ *www.christies.com.*

There are many antiques shops to browse in Vieille Ville.

DEPARTMENT STORES

Bongénie. This boutique has floor after floor filled with designer clothing and high-end cosmetics. ✉ *34 rue du Marché, Centre Ville Rive Gauche* ☎ *022/8181111.*

Globus. This department store excels at home accessories, kitchen utensils, men's and women's clothing, and gourmet food. ✉ *48 rue du Rhône, Centre Ville Rive Gauche* ☎ *022/3195050.*

MARKETS

Halle de Rive. Flavorful cheeses, fresh flowers, local wines, and fine Swiss chocolate are among the items on offer all day Monday through Saturday at Halle de Rive. A vibrant seasonal fruit-and-vegetable market fills Boulevard Helvétique on Wednesday and Saturday mornings. ✉ *17 rue Pierre-Fatio/29 bd. Helvétique, Centre Ville Rive Gauche* ⊕ *www.halle-de-rive.com.*

Place de la Fusterie. Arts-and-crafts vendors crowd Place de la Fusterie every Thursday. ✉ *Off rue du Marché, Centre Ville Rive Gauche.*

Plaine de Plainpalais. Flea market stalls move into position around the Plaine de Plainpalais on Wednesday and Saturday, replacing the Tuesday, Friday, and Sunday morning fruit-and-vegetable stands. ✉ *Plainpalais.*

SPECIALTY STORES
ANTIQUES

Antiquités Scientifiques. This shop buys, sells, and assesses telescopes, barometers, microscopes, binoculars, sundials, and cameras. ✉ *19 rue du Perron, Vieille Ville* ☎ *022/3100706.*

Galerie Grand-Rue. Galerie Grand-Rue deals in largely 19th-century oils and works on paper, including original prints of Geneva and elsewhere. ✉ *25 Grand-Rue, Vieille Ville* ☎ *022/3117685* ⊕ *www.galerie-grand-rue.ch.*

Librairie Ancienne. Head to Librairie Ancienne for leather-bound and gilt first editions. Most are not in English. ✉ *20 Grand-Rue, Vieille Ville* ☎ *022/3102050* ⊕ *www.librairie-ancienne.ch.*

Regency House. Well-polished English furniture fills the Regency House. ✉ *3 rue de l'Hôtel-de-Ville, Vieille Ville* ☎ *022/3103540* ⊕ *www.regencyhouse.ch.*

13

BOOKS

Librairie Archigraphy. This shop sells art, design, and architecture books in a setting worthy of its subjects. ✉ *1 pl. de l'Ile, Centre Ville Rive Gauche* ☎ *022/3116008* ⊕ *www.archigraphy.ch.*

Librairie Bernard Letu. An inspired range of multilingual art and photography titles fills Librairie Bernard Letu. ✉ *2 rue Jean-Calvin, Vieille Ville* ☎ *022/3104757* ⊕ *www.letubooks.com.*

Off the Shelf. This shop lures English-speaking browsers with a sunny space and a handpicked selection. ✉ *15 bd. Georges-Favon, Plainpalais* ☎ *022/3111090* ⊕ *www.offtheshelf.ch.*

CHOCOLATE

Arn. Silky, handmade white-chocolate truffles top the selection at Arn. ✉ *12 pl. du Bourg-de-Four, Vieille Ville* ☎ *022/3104094.*

Auer. Local cobblestones inspired Henri Auer's *pavés glacés,* creamy bite-size delicacies that have become Genevois classics. His descendants at Auer maintain the tradition. ✉ *4 rue de Rive, Centre Ville Rive Gauche* ☎ *022/3114286.*

Du Rhône. This shop has sold chocolate since 1875 when (it's said) even passing coach horses stopped and wouldn't budge until someone gave them a praline. ✉ *3 rue de la Confédération, Centre Ville Rive Gauche* ☎ *022/3115614.*

Merkur. Merkur stocks Swiss-theme gift boxes, individual bars, and huge Champagne truffles. There's also a branch at 4 rue de la Tour-de-l'Ile in Centre Ville Rive Gauche. ✉ *40 rue du Rhône, Centre Ville Rive Gauche* ☎ *022/3107633.*

Rohr. This kitchen models its smooth, rich signature truffles after old Geneva garbage cans. Don't be fooled; Rohr stocks the best chocolate in town. Another location is at 4 rue de l'Enfer in Centre Ville Rive Gauche. ✉ *3 pl. du Molard, Centre Ville Rive Gauche* ☎ *022/3116303.*

GIFTS AND SOUVENIRS

Mercerie Catherine B. This boutique sells Swiss-themed samplers—hearts, flowers, chalets, cows—already framed or ready for you to embroider yourself. ✉ *17 rue de la Cité, Vieille Ville* ☎ *022/3107779* ⊕ *www.merceriecatherineb.com.*

Zwilling J.A. Henckels. You'll find everything from well-designed manicure sets to kitchen gadgets at Zwilling J.A. Henckels. ✉ *19 pl. Longemalle, Centre Ville Rive Gauche* ☎ *022/3124052* ⊕ *www.j-a-henckels.com.*

Watches are one of the most popular (and expensive) Geneva souvenirs.

JEWELRY

Bucherer. Bucherer sells luminous pearls and diamonds of all sizes. It's also the place for prestigious, indestructible Rolex models. Look for another branch at 22 rue du Mont-Blanc in Centre Ville Rive Droite. ✉ *45 rue du Rhône, Centre Ville Rive Gauche* ☎ *022/3196266* ⊕ *www. bucherer.com.*

Bulgari. This world-famous chain favors heavy gold necklaces and rings crusted with jewels. ✉ *30 rue du Rhône, Centre Ville Rive Gauche* ☎ *022/3177070* ⊕ *www.bulgari.com.*

Cartier. This luxury brand famously renders feline grace in diamonds, rubies, and emeralds. ✉ *35 rue du Rhône, Centre Ville Rive Gauche* ☎ *022/8185454* ⊕ *www.cartier.com.*

Chopard. Chopard creates icelike necklaces out of inlaid diamonds. Another location can be found at 27 rue du Rhône, Centre Ville Rive Gauche. ✉ *8 rue de la Confédération, Centre Ville Rive Gauche* ☎ *022/ 3113728* ⊕ *www.chopard.com.*

Gilbert Albert. The shop in Centre Ville Rive Gauche lets nature inspire interchangeable stones wrapped in curvaceous, coral-like gold. ✉ *24 rue de la Corraterie, Centre Ville Rive Gauche* ☎ *022/3114833.*

PAPER GOODS

Bookbinders. Clean lines and vibrant color define the writing paper and fabric-bound photo albums at Bookbinders. ✉ *15 rue de la Fontaine, Vieille Ville* ☎ *022/3016450* ⊕ *www.bookbindersdesign.com.*

Brachard. This shop has wonderful papers, cards, pens, exquisite notebooks—and don't miss Brachard Contemporary across the street to the right, up the stairs at No. 7, then upstairs again in the passageway. ✉ *10 rue de la Corraterie, Centre Ville Rive Gauche* ☎ *022/8170555* ⊕ *www.brachard.ch.*

Ordning & Reda. Spiral and perfect-bound notebooks, photo albums, and monochromatic cards form tall swaths of color at Ordning & Reda. ✉ *20 rue de Rive, Centre Ville Rive Gauche* ☎ *022/8101020* ⊕ *www. ordning-reda.com.*

WATCHES

Franck Muller. This shop creates complicated modern timepieces. ✉ *1 rue de la Tour-de-l'Ile, Centre Ville Rive Gauche* ☎ *022/8180030* ⊕ *www. franckmuller.com.*

Patek Philippe. A bit of history: Patek Philippe occupies the 1839 building where Antoine Norbert de Patek invented the winding mechanism inside all watches. ✉ *41 rue du Rhône, Centre Ville Rive Gauche* ☎ *022/8095050* ⊕ *www.patek.com.*

Piaget. This retailer wraps its ultraflat tourbillions in sleek white gold. ✉ *40 rue du Rhône, Centre Ville Rive Gauche* ☎ *022/8170200* ⊕ *www. piaget.com.*

Vacheron Constantin. The oldest watch company in Geneva, Vacheron Constantin sold its first design in 1755. ✉ *1 pl. Longemalle, Centre Ville Rive Gauche* ☎ *022/3161740* ⊕ *www.vacheron-constantin.com.*

GREATER GENEVA

GIFTS AND SOUVENIRS

Epsetera. Crafts, including carved wooden toys, make Epsetera fun for all ages. ✉ *29 rue Saint-Joseph, Carouge* ☎ *022/9490263* ⊕ *www. epsetera.ch.*

SPAS

After the Rain. Opened in 2002, this urban day spa was one of the region's first places for head-to-toe pampering. This four-level oasis nods to the natural elements through decor and treatments: on the water-themed floor, for example, the walls are painted soothing blues and sculptural lights hint at water droplets. Treatments include facials, massages, and body wraps, as well as more unique offerings like the signature After the Rain massage, which takes place partially under a shower of deliciously warm water. ✉ *4 passage des Lions, Centre Ville Rive Droite* ☎ *022/8190150* ⊕ *www.aftertherain.ch* ⌁ *140 SF–280 SF for massage; 270 SF–990 SF for spa packages. Sauna, steam room. Services: Ayuerveda, facials, massage, nails, scrubs, waxing.*

La Réserve Spa. On the shores of Lake Geneva, this spa includes more than 21,000 square feet of creamy white fabrics and dark, rich wood. Inside are 17 treatment rooms, sauna and steam rooms, a health-conscious café, and large fitness center with an indoor pool. Guests are pampered by therapists who offer a mix of traditional offerings like body wraps to innovative options that include lympho-draining techniques. The spa also offers a full menu of fitness classes. ✉ *La Réserve,*

301 rte. de Lausanne, Bellevue ⊕ www.lareserve.ch ☞ 180 SF 50-min massage. 3,200 SF–9,500 SF treatment packages. Hair salon, sauna, steam room. Gym with: cardiovascular machines, free weights, weight-training equipment. Services: acupuncture, anti-aging, facial, body scrubs, massage, nail care, tanning. Classes and programs: aerobics, body sculpting, fitness analysis, flexibility training, nutritional analysis, nutritional counseling, personal training, Pilates, strength training, stretching, weight management, weight training, yoga.

Le Spa at Le Richemond. Tucked away on the lower level of this grande dame, this cozy spa radiates calm with soft lighting, soothing music, and golden-hued mosaics. In just over 4,000 square feet, the spa includes a sauna, fitness center, five treatment rooms, and a Turkish-style hammam. The individually tailored treatments—which include massages, facials, and beauty treatments—include Eastern rituals. ✉ *Le Richemond, Jardin Brunswick, Les Pâquis ☎ 022/7157000 ⊕ www. lerichemond.ch ☞ 90SF–240 SF for massage. Sauna. Gym with: cardiovascular machines, free weights, weight-training. Services: facials, massages, nail treatment, waxing.*

Le Spa Grand Hotel Kempinski. Caramel-colored walls, pale gold lighting, and natural materials like bamboo and stone set a soothing tone in this 15,000-square-foot spa inside the Grand Hotel Kempinski. Here you'll find a dozen treatment rooms, a fitness center, indoor swimming pool, yoga room, and Turkish-style hammam. Treatments include body scrubs and wraps, facials, and massage, as well as ceremonial treatments that incorporate traditions from Siam, Bali, and Polynesia. For a real splurge, book the spa suite with a tub, private steam bath, and terrace. ✉ *Grand Hotel Kempinski, 19 Quai du Mont Blanc, Les Pâquis ☎ 022/9089081 ⊕ www.kempinski.com ☞ 175 SF 50-min massage, 251 SF–414 SF ceremonial treatments. Sauna, steam room. Gym with: cardiovascular machines, free weights, weight-training equipment. Services: Ayurveda, body, facial, hands and feet, massage, slimming. Classes and programs: body sculpting, fitness analysis, personal training, yoga.*

UNDERSTANDING
SWITZERLAND

Vocabulary

VOCABULARY

ENGLISH	FRENCH	FRENCH PRONUNCIATION

BASICS

ENGLISH	FRENCH	FRENCH PRONUNCIATION
Yes/no	Oui/non	wee/no
Please	S'il vous plaît	seel voo **play**
Thank you	Merci	mare-**see**
De rien	You're welcome	deh ree-**enh**
Excuse me	Pardon	pahr-**doan**
Hello	Bonjour	bohn-**zhoor**
Goodbye	Au revoir	o ruh-**vwahr**

NUMBERS

ENGLISH	FRENCH	FRENCH PRONUNCIATION
One	Un	un
Two	Deux	deuh
Three	Trois	twa
Four	Quatre	**cat**-ruh
Five	Cinq	sank
Six	Six	seess
Seven	Sept	set
Eight	Huit	weat
Nine	Neuf	nuf
Ten	Dix	deess

DAYS

ENGLISH	FRENCH	FRENCH PRONUNCIATION
Today	Aujourd'hui	o-zhoor-**dwee**
Tomorrow	Demain	deh-**menh**
Yesterday	Hier	yair
Morning	Matin	ma-**tenh**
Afternoon	Après-midi	ah-pray-mee-**dee**
Night	Nuit	nwee
Monday	Lundi	**lahn**-dee
Tuesday	Mardi	**mahr**-dee
Wednesday	Mercredi	**mare**-kruh-dee
Thursday	Jeudi	**juh**-dee
Friday	Vendredi	**vawn**-dra-dee
Saturday	Samedi	**sam**-dee
Sunday	Dimanche	**dee**-mawnsh

*Prevalent Swiss-German dialect

GERMAN	GERMAN PRONUNCIATION	ITALIAN	ITALIAN PRONUNCIATION
BASICS			
Ja/nein	yah/nine	Sí/No	see/no
Bitte	**bit**-uh	Per favore	pear fa-**voh**-reh
Danke	**dahn**-kuh	Grazie	**grah**-tsee-ay
Bitte schön	**bit**-uh **shern**	Prego	**pray**-go
Entschuldigen Sie *Äxgüsi	ent-**shool**-de-gen-zee	Scusi	**skoo**-zee **ax**-scu-see
Guten Tag *Grüezi *Grüss Gott	**goot**-en **tahk** **grit**-zee groos got	Buon giorno	bwohn **jyohr**-noh
Auf Widersehen *Ufwiederluege *Tschüss (*familiar*)	Auf **vee-der**-zane oof-**vee-der**-lawgah choohs	Arrivederci	a-ree-vah-**dare**-chee
NUMBERS			
Eins	eints	Uno	**oo**-no
Zwei	tsvai	Due	**doo**-ay
Drei	dry	Tre	tray
Vier	fear	Quattro	**kwah**-troh
Fünf	fumph	Cinque	**cheen**-kway
Sechs	zex	Sei	say
Sieben	**zee**-ben	Sette	**set**-ay
Acht	ahkt	Otto	**oh**-to
Neun	noyn	Nove	**no**-vay
Zehn	tsane	Dieci	dee-**eh**-chee
DAYS			
Huete	**hoi**-tah	Oggi	**oh**-jee
Morgen	**more**-gehn	Domani	do-**mah**-nee
Gestern	geh-**shtairn**	Ieri	ee-veh-ree
Morgen	**more**-gehn	Mattina	ma-**tee**-na
Nachmittag	nahkt-**mit**-ahk	Pomeriggio	po-mer-**ee**-jo
Nacht	nahkt	Notte	Noh-teh
Montag	**mohn**-tahk	Lunedì	**loo**-neh-dee
Dienstag	**deens**-tahk	Martedì	**mahr**-teh-dee
Mittwoch	**mit**-vohk	Mercoledì	**mare**-co-leh-dee
Donnerstag	**doe**-ners-tahk	Giovedì	**jo**-veh-dee
Freitag	**fry**-tahk	Venerdì	**ven**-air-dee
Samstag	**zahm**-stahk	Sabato	**sah**-ba-toe
Sonntag	**zon**-tahk	La Domenica	lah doe-**men**-ee-ca

ENGLISH	FRENCH	FRENCH PRONUNCIATION

USEFUL PHRASES

Do you speak English?	Parlez-vous anglais?	par-lay-vooz awng-**gleh**
I don't speak French/ German/ Italian.	Je ne parle pas français.	juh nuh parl pah fraun-**seh**
I don't understand.	Je ne comprends pas.	juh nuh kohm-prawhn **pah**
I don't know.	Je ne sais pas.	juh nuh say **pah**
I am American/ British.	Je suis américain/	jhu anglais sweez a-may-ree-**can**/awn-**glay**
I am sick.	Je suis malade.	juh swee ma-**lahd**
Please call a doctor.	Appelez un docteur s'il vous plâit.	a-pe-lay uhn dohk-**tore** seel voo **play**
Have you any rooms?	Est-ce que vous avez une chambre?	Ehskuh vooz- ah-vay-oon **shahm**-br
How much does it cost?	C'est combien?	say comb-bee-**enh**
Do you accept . . . (credit card)	Est-ce que vous acceptez . . .	Ehskuh voo zahksehptay . . .
Too expensive	Trop cher	troh **shehr**
It's beautiful.	C'est très beau.	say tray boh
Help!	Au secours!	o say-**koor**
Stop!	Arrêtez!	a-ruh-**tay**

GETTING AROUND

Where is . . .	C'est où . . .	say oo
The train station?	la gare?	la gahr
The post office?	la poste?	la pohst
The hospital?	l'hôpital?	lo-pee-**tahl**
Where are the rest rooms?	Où sont les toilettes?	oo sohn lay **twah**-let
Left	A gauche	a **gohsh**
Right	À droite	a **drwat**
Straight ahead	Tout droit	**too drwat**

*Prevalent Swiss-German dialect

GERMAN	GERMAN PRONUNCIATION	ITALIAN	ITALIAN PRONUNCIATION
USEFUL PHRASES			
Sprechen Sie Englisch?	Shprek-hun zee **eng**-glish	Parla inglese?	**par**-la een **glay**-zay
Ich sprech kein Deutsch.	ihkh **shprek**-uh kine doych	Non parlo italiano.	non **par**-lo ee-tal-**yah**-no
Ich verstehe nicht.	ihkh fehr-**stay**-eh nikht	Non capisco.	non ka-**peess**-ko
Ich habe keine Ahnung.	ihkh hah-beh kine-eh **ah**-nung	Non lo so.	non lo **so**
Ich bin Amerikaner(in). Engländer(in).	ihkh bin a-mer-i **kah**-ner(in)/ **eng**- glan-der(in)	Sono americano(a)/ Sono inglese.	**so**-no a-may-ree-**kah**-no(a)/**so**-no een-**glay**-zay
Ich bin krank.	ihkh bin **krahnk**	Sto male.	sto **ma**-lay
Bitte rufen einen Arzt.	**bit**-uh **roof**-en ine-en **ahrtst**	Chiami un dottore per favore.	kee-**ah**-mee oon doe-**toe**-ray pear fah-**voh**-reh
Haben sie ein Zimmer?	**Ha**-ben zee ine **tsimmer**	C'e una camera libera?	chay **oo**-nah **cam**-er-ah **lee**-ber-eh
Wieviel kostet das?	**vee**-feel **cost**-et dahs	Quanto costa?	**kwahn**-toe-**coast**-a
Nehmen Sie . . .	**nay**-men zee . . .	Posso pagare . . .	**pohs**-soh pah-**gah**-reh . . .
Es kostet zu viel.	es **cost**-et tsu feel	Troppo caro	**troh**-poh **cah**-roh
Das ist schön.	dahs is **shern**	É bello(a).	eh **bell**-oh
Hilfe!	**hilf**-uh	Aiuto!	a-**yoo**-toe
Halt!	hahlt	Alt!	ahlt
GETTING AROUND			
Wo ist . . .	**vo** ist	Dov'è . . .	doe-**veh**
Der Bahnhof?	dare **bahn**-hof	la stazione?	la sta-tsee-**oh**-nay
Die Post?	dee **post**	l'ufficio postale?	loo-**fee**-cho po-**sta**-lay
Das Krankenhaus? *Das Spital?	dahs **krahnk**-en-house dahs shpee-**tahl**	l'ospedale?	lo-spay-**dah**-lay
Wo ist die Toilette?	vo ist dee twah-**let**-uh	Dov'è il bagno?	doe-**vay** eelbahn-yo
Links	links	a sinistra	a see-**neess**-tra
Rechts	rechts	a destra	a-**des**-tra
geradeaus	geh-**rod**-uh ouse	Avanti dritto	a-**vahn**-tee **dree**-to

ENGLISH	FRENCH	FRENCH PRONUNCIATION

DINING OUT

ENGLISH	FRENCH	FRENCH PRONUNCIATION
Waiter/Waitress	Monsieur/ Mademoiselle	muh-**syuh**/ mad-mwa-**zel**
Please give me . . .	S'il vous plait, donnez-moi . . .	see voo **play** doh nay **mwah**
The menu	La carte	la cart
The bill/check	L'addition	la-dee-see-**ohn**
A fork	Une fourchette	ewn four-**shet**
A knife	Un couteau	uhn koo-**toe**
A spoon	Une cuillère	ewn kwee-**air**
A napkin	Une serviette	ewn sair-vee-**et**
Bread	Du pain	due penh
Butter	Du beurre	due bur
Milk	Du lait	due lay
Pepper	Du poivre	due **pwah**-vruh
Salt	Du sel	due sell
Sugar	Du sucre	due **sook**-ruh
Coffee	Un café	uhn kahfay
Tea	Un thé	uhn tay
Mineral water *carbonated*/still	De l'eau minéral *gazeuse/non gazeuse*	duh loh meenehrahl gahzuhz/noh(n) gahzuhz
Wine	Vin	venh
Cheers!	A votre santé!	ah vo-truh sahn-**tay**

GERMAN	GERMAN PRONUNCIATION	ITALIAN	ITALIAN PRONUNCIATION
DINING OUT			
Herr Ober/ Fraülein	hehr **oh**-ber **froy**-line	Cameriere(a)	kah-meh-**ryeh**-reh(rah)
Bitte geben sie mir . . .	**bit**-uh gay behn zee-**meer**	Mi dia por favore	mee **dee**-a pear-fah-**voh**-reh . . .
Die speisekarte	dee **shpie**-zeh-car-tuh	Il menù	eel may-**noo**
Die Rechnung	dee **rekh**-nung	Il conto	eel **cone**-toe
Eine Gabel	**ine**-eh-**gah**-buhl	Una forchetta	oona for-**ket**-a
Ein messer	I-nuh-**mess**-ehr	Un coltello	oon kol-**tel**-o
Einen Löffel	I-nen **ler**-fuhl	Un cucchiaio	oon koo-kee-**ah**-yo
Die Serviette	dee zair-vee-**eh**-tuh	Il tovagliolo	eel toe-va-lee-**oh-lo**
Brot	broht	Il pane	eel **pa**-nay
Butter	**boo**-tehr	Il burro	eel **boo**-roh
Milch	meelch	Il latte	eel **lot**-ay
Pfeffer	**fef**-fehr	Il pepe	eel **pay**-pay
Salz	zahlts	Il sale	eel **sah**-lay
Zucker	**tsoo**-kher	Lo zucchero	loh **tsoo**-ker-o
eine Kaffee	**ine**-eh **kah**-feh	un caffè	oon kahf-**feh**
einen Tee	**ine**-en tay	un tè	oon teh
Mineral wasser *mit gas/ohne gas*	mi-neh-**raal**-**vahs**-sehr mit gahz/**oh**-nuh gahz	L'acqua minerale *gassata/naturale*	l'ah kwa mee-neh-**rah**-leh gahs-**sah**-tah/ nah-too-**rah**-leh
Wein	vine	Il vino	eel **vee**-noh
Zum Wohl! *Proscht	zoom vole prosht	Salute!	sah-**loo**-teh

Travel Smart
Switzerland

WORD OF MOUTH

"I've . . . always felt the Swiss Pass was a great deal. I always end up using it more than I expected: like in the Berner Oberland, on a whim just hopping a boat from Interlaken on Lake Thun in late afternoon just for a relaxing float with spectacular scenery all around."

—PalenQ

GETTING HERE AND AROUND

Switzerland offers perhaps the best transit network in Europe: impeccable express-ways studded with emergency phones; trams and buses winding through city streets; steamers crisscrossing blue lakes; and the famous trains, whose wheels roll to a stop under the station clock just as the second hand sweeps to 12.

Once at the station, a web of transportation options gets you even closer to those spectacular views: cogwheel trains grind up 45-degree slopes, lifts and gondolas sail silently to vantage points, tiny Alpine Metros bore through granite up to green tundra above 8,000 feet.

Traveling by car is the surest way to penetrate every nook and cranny of the Swiss landscape, but if you invest in a rail pass, you will not feel cut off. Most Swiss trains intersect with private excursion networks and allow for comfortable sightseeing itineraries without huge layovers. And there's always a sturdy yellow postbus, following its appointed rounds at minimal cost; connections to obscure villages and trails are free to holders of the Swiss Pass, and accessible by public transport.

▌ AIR TRAVEL

The entire country of Switzerland is smaller in area than the state of West Virginia, so flying from one region to another is a luxury that, considering how efficient the trains are, few travelers require— unless there's a convenient connection from your intercontinental arrival point (Geneva, Zürich) to a smaller airport (Basel, Bern, Lugano, and Sion).

In Switzerland you will not usually need to check in more than an hour before boarding. Be sure to check your airline's limit on checked and carry-on luggage; most airlines accept one carry-on item, while Swiss and other national carriers will turn a blind eye to two.

For 22 SF per bag round-trip, passengers on Swiss and partner airlines with tickets on Swiss Federal Railways can forward their luggage to their final destination, allowing them to travel unencumbered. Baggage check-in and airline boarding passes can be arranged at more than 50 train stations around Switzerland, but can only be done less than 24 hours in advance. An English-language "Fly-Rail Baggage" brochure is available free of charge from the Swiss Federal Railways.

Note that many budget airlines such as easyJet charge for food and drink during flights.

Swiss even stocks Nicorette gum. Flying time to Geneva or Zürich is about 1 hour from London, 8 hours from New York, 9 hours from Chicago, 11 hours from Los Angeles, 11 hours from San Francisco, and 23 to 25 hours from Sydney.

In Switzerland there is no longer a need to reconfirm your flight, though it won't hurt to do so. Swiss and other airlines now send electronic delay messages to passengers who provide cell phone numbers.

Airline Security Issues Transportation Security Administration ⊕ www.tsa.gov.

AIRPORTS

The major gateways are the Zürich Airport (ZRH) and Geneva's Cointrin Airport (GVA). Most Swiss flights will fly via Zürich Airport, the airline's hub. Be sure to allow yourself at least an hour to transfer to your connecting flight. The EuroAirport on the outskirts of Basel is used by many airlines as a stopover and has low-cost flights to numerous destinations across Europe. Its proximity to Zürich makes it very convenient.

International Airports Cointrin Airport (GVA) ☏ 022/7177105 ⊕ www.gva.ch. **EuroAirport Freiburg-Basel-Mulhouse** (MLH) Basel: EuroAirport Freiburg-Basel-Mulhouse. ☏ 061/3253111 ⊕ www.euroairport.com.

Zürich Airport (ZRH) ☎ 043/8162211 ⊕ www.
zurich-airport.com.

FLIGHTS

Swiss International Air Lines, the national carrier more commonly known simply as Swiss, flies from Boston, Chicago, Los Angeles, San Francisco, Miami, and New York to Zürich, as well as from New York and San Francisco to Geneva. United flies from Newark and Washington to Geneva and from Washington, Miami, Chicago, Newark, and Los Angeles to Zürich. American Airlines connects New York with Zürich, while Delta flies from New York and Atlanta to Zürich.

Low-cost airlines flying into Geneva include easyJet (from London and other European cities), Darwin Airline (from Lugano, Florence, Venice, and other European cities), and flybe (from Exeter, the Isle of Man, and Southampton). If you're headed to Zürich, then easyJet (from London and Manchester), bmibaby (from Edinburgh), Helvetic Airways (from Cardiff, Bristol or Inverness), and Air Berlin (from London, Ibiza, and other European destinations) are among the low-cost carriers.

Airline Contacts American Airlines
☎ 800/433–7300 in the U.S., 0848/000730 in Switzerland ⊕ www.aa.com. **British Airways** ☎ 0844/493–0787 in U.K., 0848/845845 in Switzerland ⊕ www.britishairways.com.**Delta Airlines** ☎ 800/221–1212 for U.S. reservations, 800/241–4141 for international reservations, 0848/000872 in Switzerland ⊕ www.delta.com. **Swiss** ☎ 877/359–7947, 0848/700700 in Switzerland ⊕ www.swiss.com. **United Airlines** ☎ 800/864–8331 for reservations, 044/2124717 in Switzerland ⊕ www.united.com.

Low-Cost Carriers Air Berlin
☎ 0848/737800 in Switzerland. **bmibaby** ☎ 0905/8282828 in the UK ⊕ www.bmibaby.com. **Darwin Airline** ☎ 0848/177177 in Switzerland ⊕ www.darwinairline.com. **easyJet** ☎ 0843/104–5000 in U.K. ⊕ www.easyjet.com. **flybe** ☎ 0871/700–2000 in U.K. ⊕ www.flybe.

com. **Helvetic Airways** ☎ 044/2708500 in Switzerland ⊕ www.helvetic.com.

▌ BOAT TRAVEL

All of Switzerland's larger lakes are crisscrossed by elegant steamers, some of them restored paddle steamers. Their café-restaurants serve drinks, snacks, and hot food at standard mealtimes; toilet facilities are provided. Service continues year-round but is greatly reduced in winter. Unlimited travel is free to holders of the Swiss Pass. The Swiss Card and the Flexipass may also be used for boat travel. For some travel such as night cruises, you may have to pay a fee. The Swiss Card doesn't give you any discount on Lake Maggiore.

Tickets can be purchased at ticket booths near the docks before departure; for some shorter boat rides tickets are also sold at a counter on board before departure. Tourism offices usually have the latest schedules, though it may be better to check with the boat companies. Credit cards are generally accepted, as are Swiss francs and euros.

The Compagnie Générale de Navigation offers excursion boat rides on Lake Geneva from around 20 to 100 SF, depending on the distance covered and the type of excursion. Numerous options are available on Lake Luzern, including with Schifffahrtsgesellschaft des Vierwaldstättersees. In the Ticino, the Navigazione Lago di Lugano and Navigazione Lago Maggiore-Bacino Svizzero run frequent daily boat trips. In Zürich, boat rides of 1½ to 8 hours are available in summer with Zürichsee Schifffahrtsgesellschaft. In winter, the number of boat rides dwindles.

Information Compagnie Générale de Navigation ✉ Rhodanie 17, Lausanne ☎ 0848/811848 ⊕ www.cgn.ch. **Navigazione Lago di Lugano** ✉ Viale Castagnola 12, Lugano ☎ 091/9715223 ⊕ www.lakelugano.ch. **Navigazione Lago Maggiore-Bacino Svizzero** ✉ Via di Motta 1, Locarno ☎ 0848/811122 ⊕ www.navigazionelaghi.it. **Schifffahrtsgesellschaft**

des Vierwaldstättersees ⊠ *Werftestr. 5,*
Luzern ☎ *041/3676767* ⊕ *www.lakelucerne.*
ch .*Zürichsee Schifffahrtsgesellschaft*
⊠ *Mythenquai 333, Zürich* ☎ *044/4871333*
⊕ *www.zsg.ch.*

▌ BUS TRAVEL

Switzerland's famous yellow postbuses
(called *Postautos, cars postaux, auto-*
postali), with their loud tritone horns,
link main cities with villages off the
beaten track and even crawl over the
highest mountain passes. Both postbuses
and city buses follow posted schedules to
the minute: you can set your watch by
them. You can pick up a free schedule for
a particular route in most postbuses; full
schedules are included in train schedule
books. You can also check the Swiss Post
website. Watch for the yellow sign with
the picture of a bus. Postbuses are handy
for hikers: walking itineraries are available at some postbus stops.

There's also a special scenic postbus route,
the Palm Express. This route goes from
St. Moritz to Lugano via the Maloja
Pass. The buses run daily from mid-
June through mid-October and from late
December through the first week of January. From the second week of January to
the first week of June and from late October to mid-December, the Palm Express
scheduled is curtailed and the buses run
only from Friday to Sunday. Reservations
are obligatory and can be made online,
as well as at any train station or tourist office. The Swiss Pass gives unlimited
travel on postbuses. You may have to pay
a supplement of 5 SF to 20 SF on some
of the Alpine routes; check the timetables
or ask the staff.

Be sure to ask whether reservations are
required, as is the case for some Alpine
pass routes.

Note that information about prices and
schedules on the Swiss Post bus system
are at least as readily available on the
main Swiss train website, ⊕ *www.sbb.*
ch (which covers both national train and

bus routes), as on the less-comprehensive
Swiss Post website.

Bus Information Swiss Post ☎ *0848/888888*
⊕ *www.postbus.ch.*

▌ CAR TRAVEL

GASOLINE

If there's one thing that's generally cheaper
in Switzerland than elsewhere in western
Europe, it's gasoline. If you are crossing
borders, try to fill the tank in Switzerland, as both regular and diesel gasoline
are cheaper than in neighboring countries.
Regular unleaded gas costs just over 1.90
SF per liter (about $8.70 a gallon). Prices
are slightly higher in mountain areas. Be
sure to have some 10 SF and 20 SF notes
available, as many gas stations (especially
in the mountains) have vending-machine
pumps that operate even when they're
closed. Simply slide in a bill and fill your
tank. Many of these machines also accept
major credit cards with precoded PINs.
You can request a receipt (*Quittung* in
German, *quittance* in French, *ricevuta* in
Italian) from the machine.

PARKING

Parking areas are clearly marked. In blue
or red zones a *Parkenscheibe, disque de*
stationnement, or *disco orario* (provided
in rental cars or available free from banks,
tourist offices, or police stations) must be
placed clearly in the front window noting
the time of arrival. These zones are slowly
being replaced by metered-parking white
zones. Each city sets its own time allot-
ments for parking; the limits are posted.
Metered parking is often paid for at communal machines that vary from city to
city. Some machines simply accept coins
and dispense tickets. At others you'll need
to punch in your parking space or license
plate number, then add coins. The ticket
for parking may or may not have to be
placed in your car window; this information is noted on the machine or ticket.
Parking in public lots normally costs 2 SF
for the first hour, increasing by 1 SF every
half hour thereafter, although prices vary

by location, with cities charging more than small towns.

ROAD CONDITIONS

Road signs throughout the country use a color-coded system, with the official route numbers in white against a colored background. Expressway signs are green, while other major roads have signs in blue (unlike in the rest of Europe, where the colors are reversed). Signs for smaller roads are white with black lettering. All signage indicates the names of upcoming towns as well, and it is generally easiest to use these names for navigating.

Swiss roads are well surfaced, but when you are dealing with mountains they do wind a lot, so don't plan on achieving high average speeds. When estimating likely travel times, look carefully at the map: there may be only 32 km (20 miles) between one point and another—but the road may cross an Alpine pass. There is a well-developed expressway network, though some notable gaps still exist in the south along an east–west line, roughly between Lugano and Sion. In addition, tunnels—notably the St. Gotthard—are closed at times for repairs or weather conditions, or they become bottlenecks in heavy traffic. A combination of steep or winding routes and hazardous weather means some roads will be closed in winter. Signs are posted at the beginning of the climb.

To find out about road conditions, traffic jams, itineraries, and so forth, you can turn to two places: the Swiss Automobile Club has operators standing by on weekdays from 8 to 5 to provide information in many languages. Dues-paying members of the Touring Club of Switzerland may contact the organization for similar information. Note that neither of these numbers gets you breakdown service. For frequent and precise information in Swiss languages, you can dial 163, or tune in to local radio stations.

Automobile Associations American Automobile Association (*AAA*) ☎ *800/765–0766*

⊕ *www.aaa.com.* **Swiss Automobile Club** ☎ *031/3283111* ⊕ *www.acs.ch.* **Touring Club of Switzerland** ☎ *090/0571234 0.86 SF per min* ⊕ *www.tcs.ch.*

ROADSIDE EMERGENCIES

All road breakdowns should be called in to the countrywide emergency numbers, 117 (for the police) or 140 (for roadside assistance). If you are on an expressway, pull over to the shoulder and look for arrows pointing you to the nearest orange radio-telephone, called bornes SOS; use these phones instead of a mobile phone because they allow police to find you instantly and send help. There are SOS phones every kilometer (roughly every ½ mile), on alternating sides of the expressway.

Emergency Services Police ☎ *117.*

RULES OF THE ROAD

As in most of the rest of Europe, driving is on the right. Vehicles on main roads have priority over those on smaller roads. At intersections, priority is given to the driver on the right except when driving on a road with right of way and when merging into traffic circles, where priority is given to the drivers coming from the left. In residential areas in some places—notably Geneva—traffic coming from the right has the right of way.

In urban areas the speed limit is 50 kph (30 mph); on major roads it's 80 kph (50 mph), and on expressways, the limit ranges from 100 kph (60 mph) to 120 kph (75 mph). On expressways the left lane is only for passing other cars; you must merge right as soon as possible. It is illegal to make a right-hand turn on a red light. The blood-alcohol limit is 0.05.

In spite of its laid-back image, Switzerland suffers from aggressive driving. Tailgating, though illegal, is a common problem, as is speeding. If you are being tailgated on the expressway, just move into the right lane and ignore any high-beam flashing and visible signs of road rage behind you. If you are driving extra slowly, let the people behind you pass.

Children under age seven are not permitted to sit in the front seat. Use headlights in heavy rain, in poor visibility, or in tunnels—they are compulsory. Always carry your valid license and car-registration papers; there are occasional roadblocks to check them. Wear seat belts in the front- and backseats—they are mandatory.

To use the expressways, you must display a sticker, or *vignette*, on the top-center or lower corner of the windshield. You can buy one at the border or in post offices, gas stations, and garages. A vignette costs 40 SF or €33 and is valid for a year. Driving without a vignette puts you at risk for getting a 200 SF fine. Cars rented within Switzerland already have these stickers; if you rent a car elsewhere in Europe, ask if the rental company will provide the vignette for you.

Traffic going up a mountain has priority, except for postbuses coming down, in which case the ascending traffic must make way for the buses. A sign with a yellow post horn on a blue background means that postbuses have priority. On winding mountain roads, a brief honk as you approach a curve is a good way of warning any oncoming traffic. In winter be sure your car has snow tires and snow chains. They are mandatory in some areas and advisable in most. Snow-chain service stations have signs marked *service de chaînes à neige* or *schneekettendienst*, meaning that snow chains are available for rent.

CAR RENTAL

If booked from overseas, rates in Zürich and Geneva begin at around $50 a day and $200 a week for an economy car with air-conditioning, a manual transmission, and unlimited mileage (instead of $130 a day and $590 a week when booked in the country). These prices do not include the 7.6% tax on car rentals. Significant savings can be made by booking in advance through a third-party wholesale website. European companies like Europcar and Sixt often have better deals.

Your own driver's license is acceptable in Switzerland, but an International Driving Permit (IDP)—available from the American and Canadian automobile associations and, in the United Kingdom, from the Automobile Association and Royal Automobile Club—is a good idea. An official translation of your license done in 10 languages, it can help local law enforcement understand the terms of your license (IDPs are only valid in conjunction with a valid license). If you intend to expand your trip beyond Switzerland, you may need an IDP to rent a car. The minimum age is generally 18. Note that some agencies do not allow you to drive cars into Italy. In Switzerland some rental agencies charge daily fees of about 25 SF for drivers under 25. If you wish to pay cash, agencies will request a deposit.

▓**TIP**➜ Since 2010, all children under the age of 12 who are less than 59 inches tall must be fastened in an infant car seat, child seat, or booster seat while riding in a motor vehicle. If you are traveling with children and renting a car, be sure to ask the rental car company for the appropriate seats in advance, or plan on taking trains and buses instead. (There are no exemptions to this rule for taxis, and finding a taxi willing to provide the seats is nearly impossible.)

CAR RENTAL RESOURCES

Local Agencies Europcar ☎ 044/8044646 ⊕ www.europcar.ch. **Sixt** ☎ 0848/884444 ⊕ www.sixt.ch.

Major Agencies Alamo ☎ 877/222–9075 ⊕ www.alamo.com. **Avis** ☎ 800/230–4898 ⊕ www.avis.com. **Budget** ☎ 800/472–3325 ⊕ www.budget.com. **Hertz** ☎ 800/654–3001 ⊕ www.hertz.com. **National Car Rental** ☎ 877/222–9058 ⊕ www.nationalcar.com.

Wholesalers Auto Europe ☎ 888/223–5555 ⊕ www.autoeurope.com. **Europe by Car** ☎ 212/581–3040, 800/223–1516 ⊕ www.europebycar.com. **Eurovacations** ☎ 877/471–3876 ⊕ www.eurovacations.com. **Kemwel** ☎ 877/820–0668 ⊕ www.kemwel.com.

▌ TRAIN TRAVEL

The Swiss Federal Railways, or SBB/CFF/FFS, boasts one of the world's densest transportation networks. Trains and stations are clean and, as you'd expect, service is extremely prompt. Trains described as Inter-City or Express are the fastest, stopping only in principal towns. *Regionalzug, train régional,* and *treno regionale* mean "local train."

In addition to the federal rail lines there are some private rail lines, such as the Montreux-Oberland-Bernois line and the Rhätische Bahn. Most private lines are integrated into the main network and generally accept discount rail passes or offer a reduction on the price.

If you're planning to use the trains extensively, get the official timetable (Kursbuch, horaire or orario) for 16 SF. The excellent Swiss Federal Railways website allows you to work out itineraries, including suburban trains, trams, and buses.

▌**TIP**➜ Since January 2012, tickets aren't available onboard Express trains, so make sure to buy them in advance. Fines for riding without a valid ticket are a painful 100 SF.

TRAIN TIPS

If you are eager to read or get some work done on the train, try the quiet zone compartments, available on a number of routes in Switzerland. Travelers are asked not to use cell phones, listen to music, or engage in loud conversation. Most Inter-City and Express trains feature power outlets in both first- and second-class cars. If you need Internet access, keep an eye out for the laptop icon.

If you happen to suffer from motion sickness, note that the Swiss ICN trains—and the German ICE, the French TGV, and the Italian Cisalpino—all use "tilt technology" for a less jerky ride. One side effect, however, is that some passengers might get "seasick," especially if the track is curvy (as it is between Biel/Bienne and Geneva). An over-the-counter drug for motion sickness should help. Also close the shades and avoid looking out the window.

Consider a first-class ticket only if the extra comfort is worth the price. The principal difference between first and second class, the only two options, is space: first-class cars are less crowded. Seat size is also larger, upholstery fancier, and you usually will be delivered to the track position closest to the station.

RAIL PASSES

If Switzerland is your only destination in Europe, there are numerous passes available for visitors. The **Swiss Pass** is the best value, offering unlimited travel on Swiss Federal Railways, postbuses, Swiss lake steamers, and the local bus and tram services of 41 cities. It also gives reductions on many privately owned railways, cable cars, and funiculars. And it gives you access to more than 400 museums in the country.

The card is available from Switzerland Tourism and from travel agents outside Switzerland, including Rail Europe and Europe On Rail. You can get a card valid for 4 days (266 SF second class; 425 SF first class); 8 days (384 SF second class; 614 SF first class); 15 days (465 SF second class; 744 SF first class), 22 days (536 SF second class; 857 SF first class); or one month (590 SF second class; 944 SF first class). There's also the **Flexipass,** offering the same for 3 to 6 days in a 30-day period at the user's convenience (254 SF–405 SF second class; 406 SF–648 SF first class). There's an approximately 15% discount on the Swiss Pass and the Flexipass for two or more people. With both passes, reservation fees may be applicable on certain routes.

The **STS Family Card** is available at no cost to nonresidents of Switzerland and Liechtenstein. With this card, children under 16 accompanied by a parent travel for free.

Within some tourist areas, regional holiday passes are available. Their discount offers vary; prices vary widely, too, depending on the region and period of validity. Passes are available from Switzerland Tourism and local tourist boards, as well as the train stations, but to be on the safe side inquire well in advance.

The **Swiss Card,** which can be purchased in the United States through Rail Europe, as well as at train stations at the Zürich and Geneva airports and in Basel, is valid for 30 days and grants full round-trip travel from your arrival point to any destination in the country, plus a half-price reduction on any further excursions during your stay (186 SF second class; 275 SF first class). For more information about train travel, get the free "Swiss Travel System" or "Discover Switzerland" brochures from Switzerland Tourism.

Switzerland is one of 23 countries in which you can use a **Eurail Global Pass,** which provides unlimited first-class rail travel in all the participating countries. If you plan to rack up the miles, get a standard pass. These are available for 15 days ($673), 21 days ($868), one month ($1,069), two months ($1,508), and three months ($1,859).

If your plans call for limited train travel, look into a less-expensive **Eurail Select Pass.** You get a set number of travel days during a specified time period. For example, a two-month pass allows between 5 and 15 days of rail travel; costs range between $524 and $938. Keep in mind that the Eurail Select Pass is good only for five countries that border each other.

In addition to standard Eurail Passes, ask about special rail-pass plans. Among these are the Eurail Youth Pass (for those under age 26) and the Eurail Saver Passes (which give a discount for two or more people traveling together).

Many travelers assume that rail passes guarantee them a seat. Not so. You should book seats ahead even if you are using a rail pass. Seat reservations are required on some European trains, particularly high-speed trains, and are a good idea during busy seasons and on popular routes. You also will need a reservation if you purchase sleeping accommodations. Whichever pass you choose, remember that you must make your purchase before you leave for Europe. The Swiss Federal Railways has a user-friendly site that lets you check fares and schedules. You can also call its hotline, which has information in English.

Train Contacts Eurail ⊕ *www.eurail. com.* **Jungfraubahnen** ☎ *033/828–7233* ⊕ *www.jungfrau.ch.* **Matterhorn Gotthard Bahn** ☎ *027/927–7000* ⊕ *www. matterhorngotthardbahn.ch.* **Montreux Oberland Bernois** ☎ *021/989–8190* ⊕ *www.mob. ch.* **Rail Europe** ☎ *800/622-8600 in the U.S., 800/361–7245 in Canada* ⊕ *www.raileurope. com.* **Rhätische Bahn** ☎ *081/288–6565* ⊕ *www.rhb.ch.* **Swiss Federal Railways** ☎ *0900/300300 1.19 SF per min* ⊕ *www. sbb.ch.*

CHANNEL TUNNEL

With the Channel Tunnel completing a seamless route, you can leave London around noon on the Eurostar and (thanks to connections via Paris–Lyon on the French *train à grande vitesse,* or TGV) have a late supper in Geneva. Note that the TGV tracks connecting Geneva and Paris are a bit bumpy, which can be unsettling for sensitive passengers.

SCENIC ROUTES

Switzerland makes the most of its Alpine rail engineering, which cuts through the icy granite landscape above 6,560 feet, by offering special trains that cross over spectacular passes with panoramic cars. The most popular sightseeing itineraries take 4–11 hours' travel time. For information on these and other scenic routes, contact Swiss Federal Railways or Railtour Suisse, Switzerland's largest train-tour company.

⇨ *For more information on scenic routes, see the Scenic Journeys feature in Chapter 1.*

Scenic Tour Information Railtour Suisse ✉ *Bernstrasse 164, Zollikofen* ☎ *031/378– 0101* ⊕ *www.railtour.ch.* **Swiss Federal Railways** ☎ *0900/300300 1.19 SF per min* ⊕ *www.sbb.ch.*

ESSENTIALS

■ ACCOMMODATIONS

Switzerland is almost as famous for its hotels as it is for its mountains, watches, and chocolates; its standards in hospitality are extremely high. Rooms are impeccably clean and well maintained, but prices are accordingly steep. Americans accustomed to spacious motels with two double beds, a big TV, and a bath-shower combination may be disappointed in their first venture into the legendary Swiss hotel's small spaces and limited facilities.

■**TIP→** Where no address is provided in the hotel listings, none is necessary: in smaller towns and villages, a postal code is all you need. To find the hotel on arrival, watch for the official street signs pointing the way to every hotel that belongs to the local tourist association.

Air-conditioning is not as prevalent as in the United States; evenings are generally cool, so Alpine air often stands in for air-conditioning. Unfortunately, global warming has had a real impact in Europe and you may discover that even early October can prove hot and sticky in Switzerland; if this poses a major problem for you, spend the extra money to book at a hotel that offers air-conditioning (and also be sure it will be functioning during the time you are at the hotel).

Most hotels in Switzerland allow children under a certain age to stay in their parents' room at no extra charge, but others charge for them as extra adults; be sure to find out the cutoff age for children's discounts. The Swiss Hotel Association has listings of family-friendly hotels throughout the country. Supervised playrooms are available in some of the better hotels, and many winter resorts provide lists of reliable babysitters. For recommended local sitters, check with your hotel.

Particularly in ski resorts or in hotels where you'll be staying for three days or more, you may be quoted a room price per person including *demipension* (half board). This means you've opted to have breakfast included and to eat either lunch or dinner in the hotel, selecting from a limited, fixed menu. Unless you're holding out for a gastronomic adventure, your best bet is to take half board. Most hotels will be flexible if you come in from the slopes craving a steaming pot of fondue, and they will then subtract the day's pension supplement from your room price, charging you à la carte instead.

Prices in the reviews are the lowest cost of a standard double room in high season, including tax, service, and breakfast only. Note that a hotel's prices may vary widely during the rest of the year and that the half board available at many hotels, which may be only slightly more than our listed room cost, significantly increases the value of these hotel stays. When comparing lodging options, check the hotels' low season rates and meal plans.

Our local writers vet every hotel to recommend the best overnights in each price category, from budget to expensive. Unless otherwise specified, you can expect private bath, phone, and TV in your room. For expanded reviews, facilities, and current deals, visit Fodors.com.

BED-AND-BREAKFASTS

You can order brochures and get information about bed-and-breakfasts from the user-friendly website of Bed and Breakfast Switzerland, ⊕ *www.bnb.ch*. You can also make reservations through the site.

FARM STAYS

Participating farm families register with the Schweizerischer Bauernverband (Swiss Farmers Association), listing the birth dates of their children, rooms and facilities, and types of animals your children can see. Prices are often considerably lower than those of hotels and vacation flats. You should be reasonably fluent in French or German, depending on the

LOCAL DO'S AND TABOOS

GREETINGS
In Switzerland it's polite to say hello and good-bye (*bonjour, au revoir; grüezi, auf Wiedersehen; buongiorno, arrivederci*) to everyone you speak to, from police officers to cashiers. The standard gesture for each is a simple handshake. In the German-, French-, and Italian-speaking cantons, it is standard for friends to greet each other with three kisses on the cheek. Hugging is much less common.

LANGUAGE
One of the best ways to avoid being an Ugly American is to learn a little of the local language. You need not strive for fluency; even just mastering a few basic words and terms is bound to make chatting with the locals more rewarding.

Nearly 70% of the population of Switzerland speaks one dialect or another of German; Swiss German can be a far cry from High German, although standard German is generally understood. French is spoken in the southwest, around Lake Geneva, and in the cantons of Fribourg, Neuchâtel, Jura, Vaud, in parts of Bern, and in most of Valais. Italian is spoken in Ticino and parts of Graubünden. In the Upper and Lower Engadine, in the canton of Graubünden, the last gasp of a Romance language called Romansh is still in daily use. In the areas most frequented by English-speaking tourists—Zermatt, the Berner Oberland, the Engadine, Luzern—people in the tourist industry all speak English. See the vocabulary section in this book for helpful words and phrases.

region of your stay—although these days, at least one family member will probably speak some English. More information is available through Switzerland Tourism.

Contacts Schweizerischer Bauernverband (*Swiss Farmers Association*) ✉ *Laurstrasse 10, Brugg* ☏ *056/4625111* ⊕ *www.sbv-usp. ch.* **Verein Ferien auf dem Bauernhof** (*Swiss Holiday Farms Association*) ✉ *Neuengasse 15, Bern* ☏ *031/329–6699* ⊕ *www. bauernhof-ferien.ch.*

HOTELS
When selecting a place to stay, an important resource can be the Swiss Hotel Association (SHA), a rigorous and demanding organization that maintains a specific rating system for lodging standards. Four out of five Swiss hotels belong to this group and take their stars seriously.

In contrast to more casual European countries, stars in Switzerland have precise meaning: a five-star hotel is required to have a specific staff–guest ratio, a daily change of bed linens, and extended hours for room service. In contrast, a two-star hotel must have telephones in the rooms, soap in the bathrooms, and fabric tablecloths in the restaurant. But the SHA standards have nothing to say about the quality of the decor and the grace of service. Thus you may find a five-star hotel that meets the technical requirements but has shabby appointments, leaky plumbing, or a rude concierge, or a good, family-run two-star pension that makes you feel like royalty.

Some rules of thumb: if you are looking for American-style comfort—a big bed and TV, minibar, safe—you will probably be happiest in four-star business-class hotels. A number of four-star hotels in Switzerland are part of the Best Western chain. If you are looking for moderate prices, regional atmosphere, family ownership (and the pride and care for details that implies), but don't care about a TV or minibar, look for three stars: just about every such room (but not all) has at least a shower and toilet. Two stars will get you

Language Regions of Switzerland

GERMANY

FRANCE

Basel

Zürich

GERMAN

AUSTRIA

LIECHTEN-STEIN

Bern

Fribourg

FRENCH

ROMANSH

St. Moritz

ITALIAN

Sierre

Bellinzona

Geneva

ITALY

| 0 | | 60 miles |
| 0 | | 90 km |

tidy, minimal comfort, with about a third of the rooms having private toilet and bathing facilities. One-star properties are rare: they have only shared facilities and no phone available in-house and generally fall below the demanding Swiss national standard.

Several hotels in the SHA are given the designation of *Landgasthof* or *relais de campagne* ("country inn"). These generally are rustic-style lodgings typical of the region. Not all are off the beaten path; some are in the middle of small market towns or resorts. The SHA distinguishes them as offering especially high-quality service, personal attention, and parking.

Many hotels close for a short period during their region's off-season. Closing dates often vary from year to year, so be sure to call ahead and check.

A few useful phrases in French, German, and Italian: a room with a bath (*une chambre avec salle de bain, ein Zimmer mit Bad, una camera con bagno)*; a room with a view (*une chambre avec vue, ein Zimmer mit Aussicht, una camera con vista)*; a quiet room (*une chambre calme, ein ruhiges Zimmer, una camera tranquilla)*.

Contacts Swiss Hotel Association ✉ Monbijoustr. 130, Bern ☎ 031/3704111 ⊕ www. swisshotels.com.

INNS

Travelers on a budget can find help from the *Check-in E & G Hotels* guide (E & G stands for *einfach und gemütlich*: roughly, "simple and cozy"), available through Switzerland Tourism. These comfortable little hotels have banded together to dispel Switzerland's intimidating image as an elite, overpriced vacation spot and offer simple two-star standards in memorable, atmospheric inns.

Other organizations can help you find unusual properties. The Relais & Châteaux group seeks out manor houses, historic buildings, and other places that offer a luxurious atmosphere, with most of its properties having prices to match. A similar group, Romantik Hotels and Restaurants, combines architectural interest, historic atmosphere, and fine regional food. Relais du Silence hotels are usually isolated in a peaceful, natural setting, with first-class comforts.

Contacts Relais & Châteaux ☎ *800/735–2478* ⊕ *www.relaischateaux.com.* **Relais du Silence** ☎ *02/2567–5501* ⊕ *www.silencehotel. com.* **Romantik Hotels and Restaurants** ☎ *800/650–8018 in the U.S.* ⊕ *www. romantikhotels.com.*

⇨ *For more information on accommodations in Switzerland, see the Lodging Primer in Chapter 1.*

▌ COMMUNICATIONS

INTERNET

Many hotels and public places have been turned into Wi-Fi (in Europe: WLAN) hot spots. Usually you must pay a fee to log on, though some hotels provide the service for free. The cost is generally high, at 5 SF for a half hour or 25 SF for one full day's access. Some cities provide Wi-Fi service for free. If you didn't bring your laptop, you'll often find Internet terminals in airports and train stations.

PHONES

The good news is that you can now make a direct-dial telephone call from virtually any point on earth. The bad news? You can't always do so cheaply. Calling from a hotel is almost always the most expensive option; hotels usually add huge surcharges to all calls, particularly international ones. In some countries you can phone from call centers or even the post office. Calling cards usually keep costs to a minimum, but only if you purchase them locally. And then there are mobile phones, which are sometimes more prevalent—particularly in the developing world—than landlines; as expensive as mobile-phone calls can be, they are still usually a slightly cheaper option than calling from your hotel.

The country code for Switzerland is 41. When dialing a Swiss number from abroad, drop the initial 0 from the local area code.

CALLING WITHIN SWITZERLAND

Dial 1811 or 1818 for information within Switzerland (1.70 SF for the initial connection, 1.40 SF the first minute and around 0.22 SF thereafter) 24 hours a day. All telephone operators speak English, and instructions are printed in English in all telephone booths.

Dial the local area code (including the 0) when calling any local number.

There's direct dialing to everywhere in Switzerland. For local area codes, consult the pink pages, and for international country and city codes, consult the green-banded pages at the front of the telephone book. Include the area code preceded by 0 when dialing anywhere within Switzerland.

To make a local call on a pay phone, pick up the receiver, insert a phone card, and dial the number. A local call costs 0.50 SF plus 0.10 SF for each additional unit. Toll-free numbers begin with 0800. Swisscom phone cards are available in 5 SF, 10 SF, or 20 SF units; they're sold at post offices, train stations, airports, and kiosks. Slip a card into an adapted public phone, and a continual readout will tell you how much money is left on the card. The cost of the call will be counted against the card, with any remaining value still good for the next time you use it. If you drain the card and still need to talk, the readout will warn you: you can either pop in a new card or make up the difference with coins. Many phone booths now also accept Visa, MasterCard, and American Express cards.

CALLING OUTSIDE SWITZERLAND

The country code is 1 for the United States and Canada, 61 for Australia, 64 for New Zealand, and 44 for the United Kingdom.

You can dial most international numbers direct from Switzerland, adding 00 before the country code. If you want a number that cannot be reached directly, or if you need an international phone number, dial 1811 or 1818 for a connection. It's cheapest to use the booths in train stations and post offices: calls made from your hotel cost a great deal more. Current rates for calls to the United States, United Kingdom, and Canada, Australia and New Zealand are 0.12 SF per minute weekdays and 0.10 SF per minute on weekends and Swiss holidays.

CALLING CARDS

A variety of international phone cards in denominations of 10 to 50 SF are available in newspaper shops. They often offer the cheapest rates. You can use the code on the card until you run out of units.

MOBILE PHONES

If you have a multiband phone (some countries use different frequencies than what are used in the United States) and your service provider uses the world-standard GSM network (as do T-Mobile, AT&T, and Verizon), you can probably use your phone abroad. Roaming fees can be steep, however: 99¢ a minute is considered reasonable. And overseas you normally pay the toll charges for incoming calls. It's almost always cheaper to send a text message than to make a call, since text messages have a very low set fee (often less than 5¢).

If you just want to make local calls, consider buying a new SIM card (note that your provider may have to unlock your phone for you to use a different SIM card) and a prepaid service plan in the destination. You'll then have a local number and can make local calls at local rates. If your trip is extensive, you could also simply buy a new cell phone in your destination, as the initial cost will be offset over time.

■ **TIP →** If you travel internationally frequently, save one of your old mobile phones or buy a cheap one on the Internet; ask your cell phone company to unlock it for you, and take it with you as a travel phone, buying a new SIM card with pay-as-you-go service in each destination.

Cellular phones (*natels*) for use in Switzerland can be rented before you leave on your trip or at the airports. You can arrange for a rental on a daily, weekly, or monthly basis.

Contacts Cellular Abroad ☎ 800/287–5072 ⊕ www.cellularabroad.com. **Mobal** ☎ 888/888–9162 ⊕ www.mobal.com. **Planet Fone** ☎ 888/988–4777 ⊕ www.planetfone. com. **Rentaphone** ☎ 044/5050130 ⊕ www. rentaphone.ch.

■ CUSTOMS AND DUTIES

When entering Switzerland, a visitor who is 17 years or older may bring in 200 cigarettes or 50 cigars or 250 grams of tobacco; 2 liters of alcohol up to 15 proof and 1 liter over 15 proof. Visitors over 17 may bring gifts valued at up to 300 SF duty-free. Medicine, such as insulin, is allowed for personal use only.

Switzerland Information Federal Customs Administration ⊕ www.ezv.admin.ch/index. html.

U.S. Information U.S. Customs and Border Protection ⊕ www.cbp.gov.

■ EATING OUT

Breakfast in Switzerland tends to be little more than coffee with bread, butter, and marmalade. If you prefer a lot of milk in your coffee, ask for a *renversé* in French (literally, *upside-down*) or a *Milchkaffee* in German. Increasingly popular in German-speaking Switzerland is the *latte macchiato*, steamed milk with espresso but very little foam, or the cappuccino, lots of steamed and foamy milk with espresso. The signature Bircher muesli—invented by Dr. Maximilian Oskar

Bircher-Benner at his diet clinic at the end of the 19th century—is available in most supermarkets (such as Migros and Coop) and can make a hearty lunch, especially when served with plain or fruit yogurt instead of milk.

Many restaurants close after lunch (as of 3 pm) and reopen for dinner (about 6 pm). In remote regions it may prove difficult to find kitchens open past 9 or 10 pm, so plan ahead. Many restaurants are closed on Sunday and many close for the entire month of August or even longer. Bars often close at 1 or 2 am, although clubs continue serving into the wee hours.

For lunch or dinner, most regions offer cheese specialties. Remember when eating these tasty dishes that you tend to be full before your brain registers the fact, and the fatty cheeses can result in difficult digestion. Fondue (literally, "melted" in French) originated in the western part of Switzerland and comes in regional varieties, of which the fondue *moitié-moitié* is the most famous (combining equal portions of Gruyère and Vacherin). Bits of white bread are skewered on long, thin forks and twirled in the melted cheese. Anyone losing his or her piece of bread has to perform some small activity as "penance," like singing a song, or paying for the next round. The grilled cheese remaining in the bottom of the *caquelon* is known as the *religieuse* ("the nun") and is a favorite.

The other big cheese specialty is *raclette* from the canton of Valais. Traditionally, the cut surface of half a cheese wheel is exposed to a fire and the melted cheese is consistently scraped off (*racler* means "to scrape") and eaten with baked potatoes, pickled white onions, and other condiments. Another cheesy dish is a *Malakoff*, a chunk of Gruyère that is pressed onto a piece of toast and then deep-fried. You may order only one Malakoff at a time (which may be a blessing in disguise to those who tend to bite off more than they can chew).

A crisp wine as you dine or a shot of kirsch after a meal can help soothe your overtaxed stomach. Some fondue experts recommend washing these heavy cheese dishes down with hot black tea and not drinking too much while eating.

There are other fondues that are not so "cheesy." *Fondue bourguignonne* involves dipping bits of meat (veal, beef, chicken, or even horse) in hot oil. The lighter "Chinese" variation (*fondue chinoise*) features meat, fish, and vegetables cooked in bouillon. The boiled or fried tidbits are dipped in condiments. There is also a sweet fondue, with fruits dipped in hot chocolate sauce.

On a lighter note, the French-speaking cantons pride themselves on *filets de perche* (fried perch fillets), possibly the most popular dish in the region. A few variations on the theme exist—some with herbs or cognac sauce—but the traditional version is served with lemon and french fries on the side. German-speaking Switzerland made its mark in culinary history with the ubiquitous *Rösti*, a grated potato pancake—often spruced up with herbs, bacon, or cheese—that is served with nearly any meat or sausage. Competing with Rösti for most popular side dish, *Spaetzle* (egg-flour dumplings) continue to be fashioned according to age-old local traditions (though toss-in-boiling-water-and-serve packets have a strong following). Ticino, to the south, has preserved its penchant for Italian cuisine with a simple touch that reflects the former poverty of the region: risotto, gnocchi, polenta, and pasta dishes appear on most menus. Graubünden has its own set of specialties, also harking back to its regional history as a canton cut off from the world during the winter months. *In Capuns, Maluns, and Pizzokels,* you are likely to encounter a variety of stews and sausages. Classics such as *truite meunière* (trout rolled in flour, fried in butter, and served with lemon and parsley) are also standard fare.

Children's menus are available in many restaurants around Switzerland;

otherwise, you can usually request a child-size portion and the prices will be adjusted accordingly.

Unless otherwise noted, the restaurants listed in this guide are open daily for lunch and dinner. Prices in the reviews are the average cost of a main course at dinner or, if dinner is not served, at lunch.

PAYING

Credit cards are widely accepted. Euros are also often accepted, though change will come in Swiss francs. Note that service is included unless indicated on the menu. It is customary to leave a small tip in cash (up to 10% depending on how pleased you are with the service).

⇨ *For guidelines on tipping, see Tipping below.*

RESERVATIONS AND DRESS

Regardless of where you are, it's a good idea to make a reservation if you can. We only mention them specifically when reservations are essential (there's no other way you'll ever get a table) or when they are not accepted. For famed restaurants, book as far ahead as you can (often 30 days), and reconfirm as soon as you arrive. (Large parties should always call ahead to check the reservations policy.) We mention dress only when men are required to wear a jacket or a jacket and tie.

WINES, BEER, AND SPIRITS

Quality and diversity are the hallmarks of Swiss wine, celebrated in annual festivals where everyone samples the year's harvest. They may not be widely exported, but Swiss wines are generally available in restaurants, and you can also get to know them in wine cellars (often with delicious local cheese). All of Switzerland's 23 cantons produce wines, but six areas outdo the rest: Valais, Vaud, Geneva, the Three Lakes region in western Switzerland, the German-speaking region of eastern Switzerland, and Ticino. Chasselas is by far the most successful among white grapes, and Pinot Noir among the reds. Other top white-grape varieties include Müller-Thurgau and Sylvaner; reds feature Gamay and Merlot.

Switzerland counts more than 120 official active breweries that regularly produce lager, *Spezialbier* (slightly stronger and a touch more bitter than lager), and *Festbier* (strong, dark holiday beer produced at Easter and Christmas and sometimes sold as *Bockbier* or *Märzenbier*). Specialty beers includes the amber *Altbier*, the corn-infused *Maisbier*, and *Weizenbier* (wheat beer).

Switzerland is brimming with spirits—most notably, *kirsch* (cherry spirit) from Zug and the Lake Luzern region has gained worldwide recognition. Plums are used to make *Zwetschgenwasser*. The tiny damassine plum, supposedly brought back from Damascus by a crusading knight, is distilled into the delightfully fragrant *Damassine*, available in Saignelégier. The many apple spirits include *Träsch* and *Gravensteiner*; pears and apricots from the Valais give their spirit to the redolent *Williamine and Abricotine*. A unique variety of grappa is up for grabs in the grottoes of Ticino; this potent firewater gets its name and taste from the skins of the grape. Prohibited for 90 years until 2005, absinthe is a specialty of the Val de Travers in western Switzerland, the spirit's birthplace.

▌ELECTRICITY

The electrical current in Switzerland is 220 volts, 50 cycles alternating current (AC); wall outlets take plugs that have two or three round prongs. The two-pronged Continental-type plugs can be used throughout the country.

Consider making a small investment in a universal adapter, which has several types of plugs in one lightweight, compact unit. Most laptops and mobile-phone chargers are dual voltage (i.e., they operate equally well on 110 and 220 volts) so require only an adapter. These days the same is true of small appliances such as hair dryers. Always check labels and manufacturer instructions to be sure. Don't use 110-volt outlets marked "for shavers only" for high-wattage appliances such as hair dryers.

▌ EMERGENCIES

Foreign Embassies American Embassy ✉ *Sulgeneckstr. 19, Bern* ☏ *031/357–7011, 031/357–7777 24-hr emergency hotline* ⊕ *bern.usembassy.gov.* **Consular Agency Geneva** ✉ *Rue Versonnex 7, Geneva* ☏ *022/8405160.* **Consular Agency Zürich** ✉ *Dufourstr. 101, Zürich* ☏ *043/4992960.*

General Emergency Contacts Ambulance ☏ *144.* **Fire** ☏ *118.* **Police** ☏ *117.*

▌ HEALTH

When hiking or skiing in the mountains, be aware of the dangers of altitude sickness: numbness, tingling, nausea, drowsiness, headaches, and vision problems. If you experience discomfort, return to a lower altitude as soon as possible. It's a good idea to limit strenuous activity on the first day at extra-high-altitude resorts. Adults with heart problems may want to avoid all excursions above 6,500 feet. If you're traveling with a child under two years old, you may be advised by locals not to carry him or her on excursions above 6,500 feet; check with your pediatrician before leaving home.

Travelers should also be mindful of other afflictions such as heat stroke, dehydration, sunstroke, frostbite, and snow blindness. To avoid snow blindness, wear sunglasses with side shields or goggles, especially if you have light-colored eyes. You should wear sunscreen all through the year; many different brands are available at ski shops near the slopes. In rural areas, take precautions against ticks, especially in spring and summer. Wear long sleeves, long pants, and boots, and apply insect repellent containing the powerful repellent DEET. Two vaccines against tick-borne infections are available in Europe: TicoVac (also known as FSME

Immun) and Encepur, but neither has been approved in the United States. Remove ticks with tweezers, grasping the insect by the head.

OVER-THE-COUNTER REMEDIES
Basic over-the-counter medicines are available from pharmacies (*pharmacie, Apotheke, farmacia*), which are recognizable thanks to signs with green crosses.

▌ HOURS OF OPERATION

Most businesses still close for lunch in Switzerland, generally from noon or 12:30 to 1:30 or 2, but this is changing, especially in larger cities and in the German-speaking part of the country. All remain closed on Sunday. Banks are open weekdays from 8:30 to 4:30 or 5, and always close during lunch. Post offices generally are open limited hours on Saturday.

Gas station kiosks are usually open daily from 6:30 am until 9 pm. Automatic pumps, which accept major credit cards and Swiss bank notes, are in service 24 hours a day.

Museums generally close on Monday. There is, however, an increasing trend toward staying open late one night a week, usually on Thursday or Friday evening.

Pharmacies generally are open weekdays from 9 to 1 and 2 to 6, and Saturday 9 to 1. In cities, they tend to stay open through the lunch hour. To find out which pharmacy is covering the late-night shift, check listings posted near or on the window of any pharmacy.

Shops are generally open every day except Sunday. They usually close early (4 or 5 pm) on Saturday except in larger cities, where they stay open until 6 on Saturday and often stay open until 8 or 9 one day a week. Smaller stores close for an hour or two for lunch. Stores in train stations in larger cities often open on Sunday (until 9 pm); in the Geneva and Zürich airports, shops are open on Sunday.

HOLIDAYS

National holidays include New Year's Day, Good Friday (March or April), Easter Sunday and Monday (March or April), Ascension Day (May), Whitsunday and Whitmonday (May), Swiss National Holiday (August 1), and Christmas and Boxing Day (December 25–26). Labor Day (May 1) is also celebrated in some regions.

▌ MAIL

Mail rates are divided into first-class "A" (airmail) and second-class "B" (surface). Letters and postcards to North America weighing up to 20 grams (about .70 ounce) cost 1.90 SF and 1.60 SF. It generally takes 3 to 7 business days to reach the United States when mailed first class and 7 to 15 in second class.

If you're uncertain where you'll be staying, you can have your mail, marked *poste restante* or *postlagernd,* sent to any post office in Switzerland. It needs the sender's name and address on the back, and you'll need proof of identity to collect it. You can also have your mail sent to American Express for a small fee; if you are a cardholder or have American Express traveler's checks, the service is free. Postal codes precede the names of cities and towns in Swiss addresses.

SHIPPING PACKAGES

FedEx and UPS operate out of Basel, Bern, Geneva, Lugano, and Zürich, although overnight service is guaranteed only to selected European destinations. An envelope weighing up to 1.1 pounds will cost about 105 SF to the United States and Canada.

▌ MONEY

The Swiss franc's value has risen against many currencies over the past several years and the franc has benefited from the European financial crisis, rising nearly 25% against the euro. Switzerland remains one of the most expensive countries on the continent for travelers, and you may find yourself shocked by the price of a light lunch or a generic hotel room. A cup of coffee or a small beer costs about 3.50 SF in a simple restaurant; ordinary wines, sold by the deciliter ("déci"), a small pour of roughly 3.5 ounces, start at about 3.80 SF. These prices almost double in resorts, city hotels, and fine restaurants. A plain, one-plate daily lunch special averages 15–20 SF. A city bus ride costs between 2 SF and 3 SF, a short cab ride 18 SF.

If you are traveling on a tight budget, avoid staying in the most-well-known resorts and cities; Geneva, Zürich, Zermatt, Gstaad, and St. Moritz are especially expensive. If you are traveling by car, you have the luxury of seeking out small family hotels in villages, where costs are relatively low. You can find inexpensive meals at the cafeterias of Migros or Coop supermarkets and at Manor department stores.

Prices throughout this guide are given for adults. Substantially reduced fees are almost always available for children, students, and senior citizens.

ATMS AND BANKS

Your own bank will probably charge a fee for using ATMs abroad; the foreign bank you use may also charge a fee. Nevertheless, you'll usually get a better rate of exchange at an ATM than you will at a currency-exchange office or even when changing money in a bank. And extracting funds as you need them is a safer option than carrying around a large amount of cash.

CREDIT CARDS

Although it's usually cheaper (and safer) to use a credit card abroad for large purchases (so you can cancel payments or be reimbursed if there's a problem), note that some credit card companies *and* the banks that issue them add substantial percentages to all foreign transactions, whether they're in a foreign currency or not. Check on these fees before leaving home, so there won't be any surprises when you get the bill. (If you plan to use your credit card for cash advances, you'll need to apply for a PIN at least two weeks before your trip.)

■ TIP➔ Before you charge something, ask the merchant whether or not he or she plans to do a dynamic currency conversion (DCC). In such a transaction the credit-card processor (shop, restaurant, or hotel, not Visa or MasterCard) converts the currency and charges you in dollars. In most cases you'll pay the merchant a 3% fee for this service in addition to any credit-card company and issuing-bank foreign-transaction surcharges.

Dynamic currency conversion (DCC) programs are becoming increasingly widespread. Merchants who participate in them are supposed to ask whether you want to be charged in dollars or the local currency, but they don't always do so. And even if they do offer you a choice, they may well avoid mentioning the additional surcharges. The good news is that you *do* have a choice. And if this practice really gets your goat, you can avoid it entirely thanks to American Express; with its cards, DCC simply isn't an option.

Reporting Lost Cards American Express ☎ 800/528-2122 in the U.S., 623/492-3932 collect from abroad ⊕ www.americanexpress. com. **Diners Club** ☎ 800/234-6377 in the U.S., 303/799-1504 collect from abroad ⊕ www.dinersclub.com. **MasterCard** ☎ 800/627-8372 in the U.S., 636/722-7111 collect from abroad ⊕ www.mastercard. com. **Visa** ☎ 800/847-2911 in the U.S.,

410/581-9994 collect from abroad ⊕ www. visa.com.

CURRENCY AND EXCHANGE

The unit of currency in Switzerland is the Swiss franc (SF), available in notes of 10, 20, 50, 100, 200, and 1,000 (the currency symbol for the franc is CHF). Francs are divided into centimes (in Suisse Romande) or Rappen (in German Switzerland). There are coins for 5, 10, 20, and 50 centimes. Larger coins are the 1-, 2-, and 5-franc pieces.

At this writing (fall 2012), 1 Swiss franc equals 1.03 U.S. dollars, 1.03 Canadian dollars, and 0.66 pounds sterling. Keep in mind that more than 300 train stations have currency exchange offices that are open daily, including lunch hours, when many banks are closed. These booths swap currency, buy and sell traveler's checks in various currencies, and cash Eurocheques.

■ TIP➔ Even if a currency-exchange booth has a sign promising no commission, rest assured that there's some kind of huge, hidden fee. (Oh, that's right. The sign didn't say no fee). And as for rates, you're almost always better off getting foreign currency at an ATM or exchanging money at a bank.

Currency Conversion Google ⊕ www. google.com. **XE.com** ⊕ www.xe.com.

▮ PACKING

In most of Switzerland, dress is casual. City dress is more formal. Men would be wise to pack a jacket and tie if dining in any of the expensive restaurants reviewed in this book, even in mountain resorts; otherwise, a button-up shirt or elegant sweater are standard at night. Also keep in mind that sneakers or jeans won't cut it for most upscale restaurants or clubs, even when paired with a good shirt. Women wear skirts more frequently here than in the United States, though anything fashionable is fine. Except at the chicest hotels in international resorts, you won't need formal evening dress.

⇨ *For more information on packing, see Gear in the Chapter 1 Planner.*

PASSPORTS

Australian, British, Canadian, New Zealand, and U.S. citizens need only a valid passport to enter Switzerland for stays of up to 90 days.

RESTROOMS

Restroom standards are high even for public toilets. In Switzerland's large city stations, look for "McClean" restrooms. They have nothing to do with the red-and-yellow hamburger chain; instead, they're immaculate, sleekly designed spaces, with bathrooms, changing stations, showers, and a toiletries kiosk. Entrance is 1 SF or 2 SF (showers 12 SF) depending on the extent of your use. If you use the facilities at a bar, it's appropriate to buy a drink. Basel has made waves with its public toilets with one-way glass—no one can see you when you're inside, but you have a view of the entire street.

SPORTS AND THE OUTDOORS

BIKING

Switzerland has developed an extensive network of bike trails that crisscross the country, following mountain passes or rivers or set up with a specific theme in mind. The nine national bike routes include the popular (and easy) Mitteland route number 5, the scenic Alpine Panorama route number 4, and the steep Graubünden route number 6. Switzerland also claims 53 regional bike roads. Detailed maps can be bought at kiosks and post offices. A user-friendly website provides information about difficulty, route length, and road conditions. If you want to enjoy the ride without worrying about luggage, several companies offer guided tours. These range from an easy day's ride to a two-week Alpine excursion, with sightseeing side trips and stays at deluxe hotels along the way.

Contacts Bike Switzerland ✉ *22 rue des Grottes, Geneva* ☎ *078/6016957* ⊕ *www.bikeswitzerland.com.* **DuVine Adventures** ✉ *667 Somerville Ave., Somerville, Massachusetts, USA* ☎ *888/396–5383* ⊕ *www.duvine.com.* **SwitzerlandMobility Foundation** ✉ *Spitalgasse 34, Bern* ☎ *031/3180128* ⊕ *www.switzerlandmobility.org.*

HIKING

The Swiss Alps are crisscrossed with hiking trails; yellow trail indicators are standard all over the country. Hiking is an especially popular pastime in the German-speaking areas, such as the Berner Oberland. For suggested hiking itineraries, including lists of huts for overnight stays, contact regional tourist offices or the Fédération Suisse de Tourisme Pédestre (Swiss Hiking Federation); many newspaper stands, train stations, and bookstores also carry detailed topographical maps with marked trails.

Contacts Fédération Suisse de Tourisme Pédestre (*Swiss Hiking Federation*). ✉ *Monbijoustrasse 61, Bern* ☎ *031/37010 20* ⊕ *www.swisshiking.ch.*

SKIING

Switzerland's legendary phenomenal ski slopes are bolstered by excellent transportation networks, plentiful vacation packages, and impressive visitor facilities.

Slope difficulty levels are indicated with color codes. A black slope is the most difficult; red indicates intermediate levels; blue is for beginners. A daily bulletin of weather conditions is available by calling ☎ *0900/162333* (3 SF connection then 1.5 SF per minute); reports are in the local language.

Serious skiers may want to join the Swiss Alpine Club. It's not necessary to be fluent in a local language to enjoy the club's excursions, which often involve a lot of climbing. A colorful booklet of mountain-club refuges called "Hütten der Schweizer

Alpen" can be ordered for 46 SF from the club's comprehensive website.

▌ TAXES

What you see is what you pay in Switzerland: restaurant checks and hotel bills include all taxes.

If your purchases in a single shop total 300 SF and the goods are exported within 30 days of the purchase date, you may reclaim the VAT (8% in Switzerland). This tax is included in the sales price of most items.

When making a purchase, ask for a VAT refund form and find out whether the merchant gives refunds—not all stores do. Have the form stamped like any customs form by customs officials when you leave the country or, if you're visiting several European Union countries, when you leave the EU. After you're through passport control, take the form to a refund-service counter for an on-the-spot refund (which is usually the quickest and easiest option), or mail it to the address on the form after you arrive home. You receive the total refund stated on the form, but the processing time can be long, especially if you request a credit card adjustment.

Global Blue is a Europe-wide service with 225,000 affiliated stores and more than 700 refund counters at major airports and border crossings. Its refund form, called a Tax Free Form, is the most common across the European continent. The service issues refunds in the form of cash or credit card adjustment.

V.A.T. Refunds Global Blue ☎ 646/808–3766 ⊕ www.global-blue.com.

▌ TIME

Situated in the same time zone as Paris (GMT+1), Switzerland is one hour ahead of London, six hours ahead of New York, nine hours ahead of Los Angeles, and nine hours behind Sydney. Since 2007, daylight saving time starts a month earlier in the United States, so during that period the time difference is one hour less.

Time Zones Timeanddate.com ⊕ www.timeanddate.com/worldclock.

▌ TIPPING

Despite all protests to the contrary and menus marked *service compris*, the Swiss *do* tip at restaurants, but it's not done as a percentage. Instead, they give quantities anywhere from the change from the nearest franc to 10 SF or more for a world-class meal that has been exquisitely served.

If, in a café, the waitress settles the bill at the table, fishing the change from her leather purse, give her the change on the spot—or calculate the total, including tip, and tell her the full sum before she counts it onto the tabletop. If you need to take more time to calculate, leave it on the table, though this isn't common practice in outdoor cafés. If you're paying for a meal with a credit card, try to tip with cash instead of filling in the tip slot on the slip: not all managers are good about doling out the waiters' tips in cash. Bartenders are also tipped along these lines.

Tipping porters and doormen is easier: 2 SF per bag is adequate in good hotels, 1 SF per trip in humbler lodgings (unless you travel heavy). To tip other hotel personnel, you can leave an appropriate amount with the concierge or, for cleaning staff, with a note of thanks in your room. Porter service fees at Geneva and Zürich airports depend on the distance covered and number of bags, but average out at around 5 SF per bag. Tip taxi drivers the change or an extra couple of francs, depending on the length of the drive and whether they've helped with your bags.

▌ TRIP INSURANCE

Comprehensive trip insurance is valuable if you're booking a very expensive or complicated trip (particularly to an isolated region), or if you're booking far in advance. Comprehensive policies typically cover trip cancellation and interruption, letting you cancel or cut your trip short because of illness, or, in some cases, acts of terrorism in your destination. Such policies might also cover evacuation and medical care. (For trips abroad you should have at least medical-only coverage.) Some policies also cover you for trip delays because of bad weather or mechanical problems, as well as for lost or delayed luggage.

Another type of coverage to consider is financial default—that is, when your trip is disrupted because a tour operator, airline, or cruise line goes out of business. Generally you must buy this when you book your trip or shortly thereafter, and it's available to you only if your operator isn't on a list of excluded companies.

Always read the fine print of your policy to make sure that you're covered for the risks that most concern you. Compare several policies to be sure you're getting the best price and range of coverage available.

Insurance Comparison Info Insure My Trip
☎ 800/487-4722 ⊕ www.insuremytrip.com.
Square Mouth ☎ 800/240-0369 ⊕ www.squaremouth.com.

Comprehensive Insurers Allianz ☎ 800/284-8300 ⊕ www.allianztravelinsurance.com.
CSA Travel Protection ☎ 800/711-1197 ⊕ www.csatravelprotection.com. **Travelex Insurance** ☎ 800/228-9792 ⊕ www.travelex-insurance.com.**Travel Guard Chartis** ☎ 800/826-4919 ⊕ www.travelguard.com.
Travel Insured International ☎ 800/243-3174 ⊕ www.travelinsured.com.

▌ VISITOR INFORMATION

The Switzerland Tourism website (⊕ *www.myswitzerland.com*) allows you to customize a vacation and then book it through an interactive travel planner. When you're in Switzerland, AngloPhone is an English-language information service giving details on hotels, restaurants, museums, nightlife, skiing, what to do in an emergency, and more. Lines are open weekdays 9–noon and 2–7. Calls cost 2.15 SF per minute.

All About Switzerland AngloPhone
☎ 0900/576444. **Great Outdoor Recreation Pages** (*GORP*) ⊕ www.gorp.com. **Pro Helvetia** ⊕ www.pro-helvetia.ch. **Swiss Broadcasting Corporation** ⊕ www.swissinfo.ch. **Swissart Network** ⊕ www.swissart.ch. **Swissworld** ⊕ www.swissworld.org. **Switzerland Tourism** ☎ 800/10020029 ⊕ www.myswitzerland.com.

INDEX

PHOTO CREDITS

1, Busse Yankushev / age fotostock. 3, Switzerland Tourism/swiss-image.ch/Max Schmid. Chapter 1: Experience Switzerland: 6-7, B van Dierendonck / age fotostock. 8, Basel Tourismus Byline: swiss-image.ch/Andreas Gerth. 9 (left), Ticino Turismo Byline: swiss-image.ch. 9 (right), Switzerland Tourism By-Line: swiss-image.ch/Roland Gerth. 10, Bern Tourismus By-Line: swiss-image.ch/Terence du Fresne. 11 (left), swiss-image.ch/Photo by Andy Mettler. 11 (right), Grindelwald Tourismus By-Line: swissimage. ch. 14, Switzerland Tourism By-Line: swiss-image.ch/Christof Schuerpf. 16 (top left), Switzerland Tourism By-line: swiss-image.ch//Max Schmid. 16 (bottom left), Sasha Buzko/Shutterstock. 16 (top right), D.H.Snover/Shutterstock. 16 (bottom right), Jungfrau Railways By-Line swiss-image.ch. 17 (top left), Switzerland Tourism By-line: swiss-image.ch/Stephan Engler. 17 (bottom left), Dan Breckwoldt/Shutterstock. 17 (top right), ENGADIN St. Moritz By-line: swiss-image.ch/Andrea Badrutt 17 (bottom right), Schweiz Tourismus By-Line: swiss-image.ch/Franziska Pfenniger. 18 (left), Rhaetische Bahn By-line: swissimage. ch/Peter Donatsch. 18 (top right), Switzerland Tourism By-line: swiss-image.ch/Stephan Engler. 18 (bottom center), Grindelwald Tourismus By-Line: swiss-image.ch. 18 (bottom right), Schweiz Tourismus By-Line: swiss-image.ch/Philipp Giegel. 19 (top left), UFT By-line: wiss-image.ch/Atelier Mamco. 19 (bottom left), giulio andreini / age footstock. 19 (right), Saas-Fee Tourism By-line: swiss-image.ch. 20, swiss-image.ch/Photo by Remy Steinegger. 21, Switzerland Tourism By-line: swiss-image.ch/Stephan Engler. 22, Switzerland Tourism Byline: swiss-image.ch/Christoph Schuerpf Fotomontage. 23 (left), Switzerland Tourism By-Line: swiss-image.ch/Christof Sonderegger. 23 (right), Jungfraubahnen Byline: swiss-image.ch. 24, Ticino Turismo Byline: swiss-image.ch/Remy Steinegger. 25, ELLEN GILHUYS/The Leading Hotels of the World. 27 (left), Rhaetische Bahn By-line: swiss-image.ch. 27 (right), Fotograf Marc Eggimann/MCH Messe Schweiz (Basel) AG. 28, Switzerland Tourism By-Line: swiss-image.ch/Christof Sonderegger. 29, Switzerland Tourism By-line: swiss-image.ch/Christoph Schuerpf. 34-35 (top), Jungfrau Railways/swiss-image.ch. 34 (bottom left), Switzerland Tourism/swiss-image.ch/Robert Boesch. 34 (bottom right), Switzerland Tourism/swiss-image.ch/Christof Sonderegger. 36, Switzerland Tourism/swiss-image.ch/Max Schmid. 37 (left), Valais Tourism/swiss-image/Thomas Andenmatten. 37 (right), Switzerland Tourism/swiss-image.ch/Christof Schuerpf. 38, Rhaetische Bahn/swiss-image.ch/Andrea Badrutt. 39, Rhaetische Bahn/swiss-image.ch/Peter Donatsch. 40, Sonderegger Christof / age fotostock. Chapter 2: Zürich: 41, Switzerland Tourism By-Line: swiss-image.ch/Christof Schuerpf. 42, Roland Fischer/wikipedia.org. 43, Switzerland Tourism By-Line: swiss-image.ch/Christof Sonderegger. 44, Switzerland Tourism By-line: swiss-image.ch/Samuel Mizrachi. 45, robanhk/Roban Kramer/Flickr. 46, Switzerland Tourism By-Line: swiss-image.ch/Christof Schuerpf. 52-53, Jürgen Held / age fotostock. 59, Quadriga Images / age fotostock. 60, Switzerland Tourism By-Line: swiss-image.ch/Christof Schuerpf. 62, Switzerland Tourism By-line: swiss-image.ch/Christoph Schuerpf. 67, Switzerland Tourism By-line: swiss-image.ch/Samuel Mizrachi. 70, travelstock44 / Alamy. 79, WIDDER HOTEL. 80, Summit Hotels & Resorts. 82, Switzerland Tourism By-Line: swiss-image.ch/Christof Sonderegger. 84, Stefan Schmidlin/The Dolder Grand. 86, Jürgen Held / age fotostock. Chapter 3: Eastern Switzerland and Liechtenstein 89, Schweiz Tourismus By-line: swiss-image.ch/Lucia Degonda. 90, Switzerland Tourism By-line: swiss-image.ch/Christof Sonderegger. 91 (top), Switzerland Tourism By-Line: swissimage. ch/Roland Gerth. 91 (bottom), Switzerland Tourism By-line: swiss-image.ch/Christof Sonderegger. 92, Stephen French/clubfoto/iStockphoto. 93 (top), Stefan-Xp/Wikimedia Commons. 93 (bottom), Encoded /Wikimedia Commons. 94, Switzerland Tourism By-line: swiss-image.ch/Christof Sonderegger. 101, Switzerland Tourism By-line: swiss-image.ch/Christof Sonderegger. 104, Switzerland Tourism By-Line: swiss-image.ch/Christof Sonderegger. 111, Switzerland Tourism By-line: swiss-image.ch/Stephan Engler. 115, Switzerland Tourism By-line: swiss-image.ch//Max Schmid. 119, Switzerland Tourism By-Line: swiss-image.ch/Roland Gerth. 123, McPHOTO / age fotostock. Chapter 4: Graubünden: 127, Destination Davos Klosters Byline: swiss-image.ch. 128, ENGADIN St. Moritz By-line: swissimage.ch/Andrea Badrutt. 129, Schweiz Tourismus By-Line: swiss-image.ch. 130, Switzerland Tourism By-line: swiss-image.ch/Christof Sonderegger. 136, Switzerland Tourism By-Line: swiss-image.ch/Christof Sonderegger. 139, Ferienregion Heidiland By-line: swiss-image.ch/Daniel Kalberer. 145, Tschuggen Hotel Group. 148, Destination Davos Klosters By-line: swiss-image.ch/Cedric Kienscherff. 150, Romantik Hotel Chesa Grischuna Klosters. 153, Destination Davos Klosters Byline: swiss-image.ch. 156, Schweiz Tourismus By-Line: swiss-image.ch/Franziska Pfenniger. 160, Sonderegger Christof / age fotostock. 164, Switzerland Tourism By-line: swiss-image.ch/Stephan Engler. 168-69, Switzerland Tourism By-line: ST/swiss-image.ch/Robert Boesch. 170, Pontresina Tourismus Byline: swiss-image.ch/Torsten Krueger. 172, Grand Hotel Kronenhof. 174-175, ENGADIN St. Moritz/swiss-image.ch/Andrea Badrutt. 176 (left), ENGADIN St. Moritz/swiss-image.ch/Daniel Martinek. 176 (top right), Destination Davos Klosters/swiss-image.ch. 176 (bottom right), Schweiz Tourismus/swiss-image.ch/Christof Sonderegger. 177 (top left), Destination Davos

Klosters/swiss-image.ch. 177 (bottom left), Schweiz Tourismus/swiss-image.ch/Christian Perret. 177 (right), ENGADIN St. Moritz. 178 and 179, ENGADIN St. Moritz/swiss-image.ch/Andrea Badrutt. 180, ENGADIN St. Moritz By-line: swiss-image.ch/Christian Perret. 183, ENGADIN St. Moritz By-line: swiss-image.ch/Daniel Martinek. Chapter 5:Ticino: 189, Ticino Turismo Byline: swiss-image.ch. 190, Ticino Turismo Byline: swiss-image.ch/RemySteinegger. 191 (top), Switzerland Tourism By-Line: swiss-image.ch/Christof Schuerpf. 191 (bottom), Switzerland Tourism By-line: swiss-image.ch/Walter Storto. 192, Switzerland Tourism By-line: swissimage.ch/Christof Schuerpf. 193 (top), Ticino Turismo Byline: swiss-image.ch/Remy Steinegger. 193 (bottom), Ticino Turismo Byline: swiss-image.ch/Christoph Sonderegger. 194, Ticino Turismo Byline:swiss-image.ch/Remy Steinegger. 195 (top), Ticino Turismo Byline: swiss-image.ch/Remy Steinegger. 195 (bottom) and 196, Ticino Turismo Byline: swiss-image.ch/Christoph Sonderegger. 202, Bellinzona Turismo By-line: swiss-image.ch. 206 and 212, Ticino Turismo Byline: swiss-image.ch/Remy Steinegger. 218, Switzerland Tourism By-Line: swiss-image.ch/Roland Gerth. 220, Ticino Turismo Byline: swissimage.ch/Remy Steinegger. 225, Courtesy of Hotel Dellago. Chapter 6: Luzern and Central Switzerland:227, Switzerland Tourism By-Line: swiss-image.ch/Christof Sonderegger. 228 (top), SGV Luzern By-line: swiss-image.ch. 228 (bottom), Schweiz Tourismus By-Line: swiss-image.ch/Franziska Pfenniger. 230, Luzern Tourismus Byline: swiss-image.ch. 231 (top), Chin tin tin/Wikimedia Commons. 231 (bottom), SGV Luzern By-line: swiss-image.ch. 232, Switzerland Tourism By-line: ST/swiss-image.ch. 237, wcpmedia/Shutterstock 240, Lazar Mihai-Bogdan/Shutterstock. 243, Luzern Tourismus AG By-line:swiss-image.ch. 246, Switzerland Tourism By-line: swiss-image.ch/Christof Sonderegger. 252, Switzerland Tourism By-line: swiss-image.ch/Franziska Pfenniger. 254-55, Switzerland Tourism By-Line:swiss- image.ch/Christof Sonderegger. 258, Schweiz Tourismus By-Line: swiss-image.ch/Christof Sonderegger. 261, MatthiasKabel/Wikimedia Commons. 264, Switzerland Tourism By-line: swiss-image.ch/Max Schmid. Chapter 7: Basel: 267, Switzerland Tourism By-line: swiss-image.ch/Christoph Schuerpf. 268, Lazar Mihai-Bogdan/Shutterstock. 269 (top), MCH Messe Schweiz (Basel) AG. 269 (bottom), Switzerland Tourism By-line: swiss-image.ch/Christof Sonderegger. 270 and 273, Basel Tourismus/Byline: swiss-image.ch. 280, Ingolf Pompe / age fotostock. 282, Basel Tourismus/Byline: swissimage.ch. 284, Switzerland Tourism By-line: swiss-image.ch/Stephan Engler. 287, Basel Tourismus/Byline: swiss-image.ch. 289, Switzerland Tourism By-Line: swiss-image.ch/Christoph Schuerpf. 295, Basel Tourismus/Byline: swiss-image.ch. 296, Schweiz Tourismus By-Line: swiss-image.ch/Christof Sonderegger. Chapter 8: Fribourg and Neuchâtel: 301, UFT By-line: swiss-image.ch/OT Moleson. 302, Ronald Sumners/Shutterstock. 303 (top), Lazar Mihai-Bogdan/Shutterstock. 303 (bottom), Switzerland Tourism By-line: ST/swiss-image.ch. 304, Olivier Savoy/La Maison du Gruyère. 305 (top), swiss-image.ch/Photo by Andy Mettler. 305 (bottom), edseloh/Wikimedia Commons. 306, Switzerland Tourism By-line: swiss-image.ch/Stephan Engler. 312, Switzerland Tourism By-line: swiss-image.ch/Stephan Engler. 318-19, José Fuste Raga / age fotostock. 320, Switzerland Tourism By-line: swiss-image.ch/Roland Gerth. 324, UFT By-line: Swiss-image.ch/Franck Auberson. 331, Switzerland Tourism By-line:swiss-image.ch/Stephan Engler. 332, Switzerland Tourism By-Line: swiss-image.ch/Christof Sonderegger. Chapter 9: Bern: 335 and 336 (top), Bern Tourismus By-Line: swiss-image.ch/Terence du Fresne. 336 (bottom), Andreas Praefcke/Wikimedia Commons. 337 (top), Norbert Derec/Shutterstock. 337 (bottom), Switzerland Tourism By-line: ST/swiss-image.ch/Christof Sonderegger. 338, Bern Tourism By-line: ST/swiss-image.ch. 341, WYSOCKI Pawel / age fotostock. 345, Alan Smithers/iStockphoto. 347, URF / age fotostock. 352, Etienne / age fotostock. 354, itibits, Nora del Ceroî. 359, Ingolf Pompe/age foto stock. 365, Switzerland Tourism By-line: swiss-image.ch/Stephan Engler. Chapter 10:Berner Oberland: 367, Switzerland Tourism By-Line: swiss-image.ch/Christof Sonderegger. 368, Jungfrau Railways By-Line swiss-image.ch. 369 (top), Switzerland Tourism By-line: swiss-image.ch/Stephan Engler. 369 (bottom), Switzerland Tourism By-line: swiss-image.ch/Lucia Degonda. 370, Switzerland Tourism By-Line: swiss-image.ch/Christof Sonderegger. 376, David Tomlinson / age fotostock. 381, Switzerland Tourism By-line: swiss-image.ch/Roland Gerth. 385, BrendanDias/Shutterstock. 386, Grindelwald Tourismus By-Line: swiss-image.ch. 388, Schweiz Tourismus By-Line: swiss-image.ch/Christof Sonderegger. 390-91, Switzerland Tourism By-Line: swiss-image.ch/Roland Gerth. 392 (bottom left), Wengen-Muerren- Lauterbrunnental Tourismus AG By-line: swiss-image.ch. 392-93 (map), berann.com. 393 (top), Switzerland Tourism By-Line: swiss-image.ch/Christof Sonderegger. 393 (bottom), Schweiz Tourismus By-line: swiss-image.ch/Christof Sonderegger. 394 and 395, Jungfrau Railways By-Line swiss-image.ch. 396 (top), Ingolf Pompe / age fotostock. 396 (bottom), Wengen-Muerren-Lauterbrunnental Tourismus AG By-line: swiss-image.ch. 397, Glenn van der Knijff / age fotostock. 398, Doug Pearson/age fotostock. 399, Schilthornbahn AG By-line: swiss-image.ch/Jost von Allmen. 402-03, Ingolf Pompe / age fotostock. 406, Alberto Paredes / age fotostock. 408, Switzerland Tourism By-line:swiss-image.ch/Marcus Gyger. 410, Switzerland Tourism By-line: swiss-image.ch/Max Schmid. 416, Ingolf Pompe / age fotostock. Chapter 11: Valais: 419, Bettmeralp

ABOUT OUR WRITERS

Kati Clinton Robson followed the Von Trapp family's example and journeyed across the Alps in search of a new life. After a period of extensive travel, Kati has spent the past eight years writing and editing for various travel and corporate clients. When she's not hiking in remote valleys, BBQing by Lake Zürich, or indulging in Swiss cheese, she can be found introducing her husband to the pantheon of classic Hollywood cinema. For this edition, she updated our Graubünden and Travel Smart chapters.

Kelly DiNardo keeps waiting to be told to get a real job. Until then, she'll drink cocktails, drive racecars, sweat through Bikram yoga classes, learn the secrets of a burlesque dancer, and travel the world all in the name of work. After graduating from Cornell University, she spent 14 years in Washington, D.C., before moving to Lausanne, Switzerland, where she is learning to appreciate raclette, yodeling, and the Alpine horn. She is the author of *Gilded Lili: Lili St. Cyr and the Striptease Mystique,* and her writing has appeared in *Glamour, O, Redbook, USA Today,* and the *Washington Post.* For this edition, she updated the chapter on Geneva.

Adam Graham is an American journalist who moved from Brooklyn to Zürich in 2011. He writes for the *New York Times, National Geographic Traveler,* the *Wall Street Journal, Travel + Leisure,* and several other travel publications. For this edition, he updated the Valais and Eastern Switzerland and Liechtenstein chapters.

Katrin Gygax was born in Zürich. Her family moved to California when she was four and to Vancouver when she was six, and then she didn't stop traveling for the next 28 years. Now based in Zürich with her own translating business, she writes movie reviews, mystery novels, and sings whenever possible. For this edition, she updated the chapter on Zürich.

Rachel Marusak Hermann is an independent journalist reporting on subjects that range from public health issues and innovation trends to urban renewal and climate change for publications including *Intellectual Property Watch,* a nonprofit Geneva-based news service, and swissinfo.ch, a division of the Swiss Broadcasting Corporation. Originally from the United States, she studied broadcast journalism in Strasbourg, France, and worked for France 24, a Paris-based international news channel. Today she calls Basel home, where she lives with her husband and dog. They love to go on adventures in the surrounding countryside or in the nearby Vosges Mountains. For this edition updated the Basel chapter.

Alexis Munier sold everything she owned and relocated to Europe a decade ago. In addition to her position as Editorial Manager for a large NGO, Munier is the author of nine books, including the infamous *Talk Dirty Series* and *The Big Black Book of Very Dirty Words.* This opera singer-turned-wordsmith lived and worked in Russia, Slovenia, and Italy before settling down in Lausanne with her two small children and badly behaved poodle. For this edition, she updated our Experience, Vaud, Ticino, and Fribourg and Neuchatel chapters.

Susan Vogel-Misicka was born in Boston but has a few drops of Helvetian blood. She has lived in Switzerland since 2001, mainly in canton Lucerne and more recently in the city of Bern. During that time, the journalist/editor has contributed to a variety of media, including *Zürich Dining Out Guide, Living and Working in Switzerland, Swiss News* magazine, World Radio Switzerland, and swissinfo.ch, a division of the Swiss Broadcasting Corporation. Like her two Swiss cats, Susan agrees that taking the train is more relaxing than driving. For this edition, she updated the chapters on Luzern and central Switzerland, Bern, and the Berner Oberland.